Dear Reader

With the aim of giving a maximum amount of information in a limited number of pages Michelin has adopted a system of symbols which is today known the world over.

Failing this system the present publication would run to six volumes.

Judge for yourselves by comparing the descriptive text below with the equivalent extract from the Guide in symbol form.

> 🏨 ❀❀ **Cheval Blanc** (Durand) Ⓜ 🍴, 🕿 28 31 42, ≤ lake, 🏡 « garden » — 🚾 🛁 🐾 🚗. AE
> *closed December and Wednesday* — **M** 80/145 st — 🍽 22 — **32 rm** 145/210
> **Spec.** Ris de veau à la crème, Poularde bressanne, tarte flambée. **Wines.** Viré, Morgon.

A comfortable hotel where you will enjoy a pleasant stay and be tempted to prolong your visit.

The excellence of the cuisine, which is personally supervised by the proprietor Mr Durand, is worth a detour.

The hotel in its quiet secluded setting away from the built-up-area offers every modern amenity.

To reserve phone 28 31 42.

The hotel affords a fine view of the lake ; in good weather it is possible to eat out of doors. The hotel is enhanced by an attractive garden.

Bedrooms with private bathroom with toilet or private shower without toilet. Telephone in room.

Parking facilities, under cover, are available to all guests with this Guide.

The hotel accepts payment by American Express credit cards.

The establishment is closed throughout December and every Wednesday.

Prices : st = service is included in all prices. There should be no supplementary charge for service, taxes or VAT on your bill.

The set meal prices range from 80 F for the lowest to 145 F for the highest.

The cost of continental breakfast served in the bedroom is 22 F.

32 bedroomed hotel. The charges vary from 145 F for a single to 210 F for the best twin bedded room.

Included for the gourmet are some culinary specialities, recommended by the hotelier : Ris de veau à la crème, Poularde bressanne, tarte flambée. In addition to the best quality wines you will find many of the local wines worth sampling : Viré, Morgon.

This demonstration clearly shows that each entry contains a great deal of information. The symbols are easily learnt and to know them will enable you to understand the Guide and to choose those establishments that you require.

CONTENTS

In addition to those situated in the main cities, restaurants renowned for their exceptional cuisine will be found in the towns printed in italics.

NEW YORK

GMT − 5

DIRECT DAILY FLIGHTS
Total time of journey
(in hours)

Amsterdam	9 1/4
Barcelona	9 1/4
Berlin	12 3/4
Bruxelles	10 3/4
Dublin	10
Düsseldorf	9 1/4
Frankfurt	9 3/4
Genève	9 1/2
Glasgow	10
Hamburg	11
København	9 3/4
Lisboa	8 3/4
London	9 1/2
Luxembourg	11 1/2
Madrid	9 1/4
Milano	9 3/4
München	11 3/4
Oslo	9 1/2
Paris	9 3/4
Roma	10 1/2
Stockholm	11 1/2
Zürich	9 3/4

J.F. KENNEDY

AIRPORT

IRL

DUBLIN

GMT   GMT + 1

Glasgow

Edinburgh

GB

Liverpool   Leeds

Manchester

Birmingham

London

Amsterdam   NL

Den Haag

Rotterdam   Düssel

Brugge   Antwerpen

Bruxelles/   B   K

Brussel

L

Luxembourg

Paris

Strasbour

*Vallée
de la Loire*

F

Genève

Lyon

Torir

Bordeaux   Mòr

Nice

Cannes

Marseille

Barcelona

Madrid

P

E

Lisboa

Valencia

Sevilla

Málaga

6

MA   DZ

AIRPORTS

Amsterdam Schiphol
Antwerpen Deurne
Barcelona
Basel Bâle/Mulhouse
Berlin Tegel
Birmingham International
Bordeaux Mérignac
Bruxelles-Brussel National
Dublin
Düsseldorf Lohausen
Edinburgh Turnhouse
Firenze
Frankfurt Rhein-Main
Genève Cointrin
Glasgow
Hamburg Fuhlsbüttel
Hannover Langenhagen
København Kastrup
Köln Köln/Bonn
Leeds Leeds/Bradford
Lisboa
Liverpool
London Heathrow, Gatwick
Luxembourg Findel
Lyon Satolas
Madrid Barajas
Málaga
Manchester
Marseille Marignane
Milano Forlanini di Linate
München Riem
Napoli Capodichino
Nice Nice Côte-d'Azur
Oslo Fornebu
Palermo Punta-Raisi
Paris Charles-de-Gaulle, Orly
Roma Leonardo da Vinci
Rotterdam Zestienhoven
Salzburg
Sevilla San Pablo
Stockholm Arlanda
Strasbourg Entzheim
Stuttgart Echterdingen
Torino Citta di Torino
Valencia Manises
Venezia Marco Polo
Wien Schwechat
Zürich Kloten

DISTANCES BY ROAD

(in kilometres)

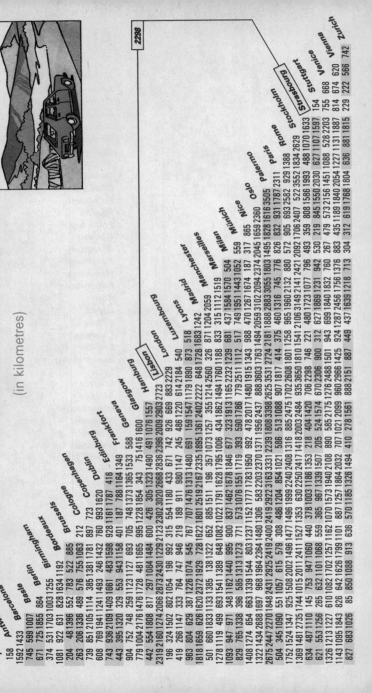

The chart is a lower-triangular road-distance matrix. Reading each row left-to-right gives the distances from the row's city to the preceding cities (Amsterdam, Antwerp, Barcelona, Basle, Berlin, Birmingham, Bordeaux, Brussels, Cologne, Copenhagen, Dublin, Edinburg, Frankfort, Geneva, Glasgow, Hamburg, Lisbon, London, Luxembourg, Lyons, Madrid, Manchester, Marseilles, Milan, Munich, Nice, Oslo, Palermo, Paris, Rome, Stockholm, Strasbourg, Stuttgart, Venice, Vienna).

From city	Distances (km) to preceding cities
Antwerp	158
Barcelona	1592 1433
Basle	745 599 1007
Berlin	671 725 1855 864
Birmingham	374 531 1703 1003 1255
Bordeaux	1081 922 631 828 1634 1192
Brussels	204 48 1396 552 783 522 885
Cologne	263 206 1336 489 576 755 1063 212
Copenhagen	739 851 2105 1114 385 1381 1781 897 723
Dublin	608 769 1941 1241 1493 246 1432 760 993 1620
Edinburg	743 936 2109 1409 1661 483 1598 928 1161 1787 416
Frankfort	443 395 1320 329 553 943 1158 401 187 788 1164 1349
Geneva	904 752 748 259 1123 1127 693 705 748 1373 1365 1533 588
Glasgow	779 1004 2176 1476 1728 481 1665 995 1228 1854 343 75 1416 1600
Hamburg	442 554 1808 817 297 1084 1484 600 426 305 1323 1490 491 1076 1557
Lisbon	2319 2160 1274 2066 2873 2430 1229 2123 2302 2836 2396 2009 2903 2723
London	196 324 1502 802 1054 196 992 315 554 1180 433 671 742 926 669 883 2229
Luxembourg	419 266 1147 333 764 747 946 219 189 911 980 1147 245 486 1220 614 2184 540
Lyons	963 804 629 387 1226 1074 545 767 707 1476 1313 1480 691 159 1547 1179 1890 873 518
Madrid	1818 1659 626 1620 2372 1929 728 1622 1801 2519 2167 2335 1895 1361 2402 2222 648 1728 1683 1242
Manchester	501 660 1833 1133 1385 138 1322 652 885 1511 196 357 1073 1257 355 1214 2560 326 711 1204 2059
Marseilles	1278 1119 499 693 1541 1389 648 1082 1022 1791 1628 1795 1006 434 1862 1494 1760 1188 833 315 1112 1519
Milan	1093 947 971 348 1162 1440 995 900 837 1462 1678 1846 677 323 1913 1165 2232 1239 681 437 1584 1570 504
Munich	829 765 1338 386 585 1313 1273 771 517 1083 1313 1385 652 885 1511 196 357 779 2511 1112 517 749 951 1443 1052
Nice	1408 1274 654 663 1339 1544 803 1237 1152 1777 1783 1950 992 478 2017 1480 1915 1343 988 470 1267 1674 187 317 865
Oslo	1322 2434 2688 1697 968 1964 2364 1480 1306 563 2203 2370 1371 1956 2437 1494 3603 1763 1494 2059 3102 2094 2374 2045 1659 2360
Palermo	2675 2447 2270 1848 2431 2925 2419 2400 2419 2922 3163 3331 2239 1808 3398 2625 3531 2724 2181 1888 2683 3055 1803 1495 1828 1616 3505
Paris	504 345 1090 551 1057 615 579 308 486 1204 854 1021 586 513 1088 907 1817 414 375 465 1316 745 776 826 832 931 2311
Rome	1752 1524 1347 925 1508 2002 1496 1477 1496 1999 2240 2408 1316 885 2475 1702 2608 1801 1258 965 1960 2132 880 572 905 693 2582 929 1388
Stockholm	1369 1481 2735 1744 1015 2011 2411 1527 1353 630 2250 2417 1418 2003 2484 935 3650 1810 1541 2106 3149 2141 2421 2092 1706 2407 522 3552 1834 2629
Strasbourg	634 487 1110 145 753 947 1060 440 378 1003 1186 1353 218 404 1420 706 2298 746 221 480 1723 1077 796 493 359 808 1586 1993 488 1070 1633
Stuttgart	621 553 1256 265 632 1101 1088 559 365 967 1339 1507 205 524 1574 670 2306 900 312 627 1869 1231 942 530 219 845 1550 2030 627 1107 1597 154
Venice	1326 1213 1227 610 1082 1702 1257 1162 1070 1573 1940 2108 890 585 2175 1276 2488 1501 943 699 1840 1832 760 267 479 573 2156 1451 1088 528 2203 755 668
Vienna	1143 1095 1843 826 642 1626 1799 1101 887 1257 1864 2032 707 1021 2099 960 2966 1425 924 1287 2456 1756 1376 883 435 1189 1840 2054 1287 1131 1887 814 674 620
Zurich	827 683 1026 85 850 1088 913 636 570 1185 1326 1494 410 278 1561 882 2151 887 449 437 1639 1218 713 304 312 619 1768 1804 636 881 1815 229 222 566 742

AIR LINKS (in hours)

3 1/2   not daily

HAMBURG — FUHLSBÜTTEL → FORNEBU — OSLO

23/4

Hamburg   Lisbon   Oslo

Cities (diagonal chart labels): Amsterdam, Antwerp, Barcelona, Basle, Berlin, Birmingham, Bordeaux, Brussels, Cologne, Copenhagen, Dublin, Edinburgh, Frankfort, Geneva, Glasgow, Hamburg, Lisbon, London, Luxembourg, Lyons, Madrid, Manchester, Marseilles, Milan, Munich, Nice, Oslo, Palermo, Paris, Rome, Stockholm, Strasbourg, Stuttgart, Venice, Vienna, Zurich

9

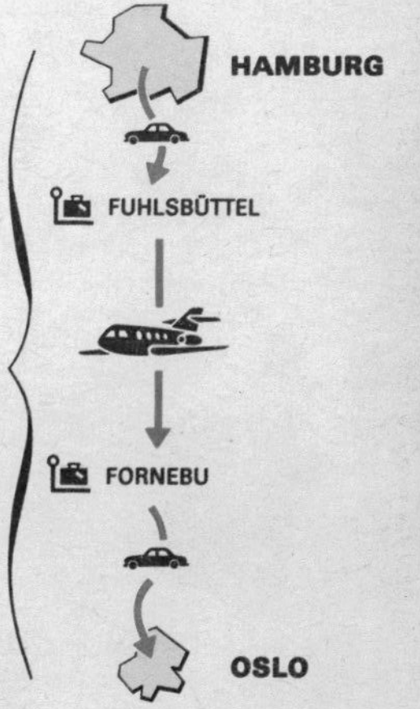

This revised edition from
Michelin Tyre Company's Tourism Department
offers you a selection of
hotels and restaurants in the main European cities.
The latter have been chosen for
their business or tourist interest.

In addition the guide indicates establishments,
located in other towns,
renowned for the excellence of their cuisine.

We hope that the guide will help you
with your choice of a hotel or restaurant
and prove useful for your sightseeing.
Have an enjoyable stay.

Signs and symbols

HOTELS AND RESTAURANTS

CLASS, STANDARD OF COMFORT

Luxury in the traditional style	🏨 XXXXX
Top class comfort	🏨 XXXX
Very comfortable	🏨 XXX
Good average	🏨 XX
Quite comfortable	🏠 X
In its class, hotel with modern amenities	M

AMENITY

Pleasant hotels	🏨 ... 🏠
Pleasant restaurants	XXXXX ... X
Particularly attractive feature	« Park »
Very quiet or quiet secluded hotel	🐦
Quiet hotel	🐦
Exceptional view — Panoramic view	⩽ sea, ❄
Interesting or extensive view	⩽

CUISINE

Exceptional cuisine in the country, worth a special journey	✿✿✿
Excellent cooking : worth a detour	✿✿
An especially good restaurant in its class	✿
Other recommended carefully prepared meals	M

HOTEL FACILITIES

🛗 TV	Lift (elevator) — Television in room
▭	Air conditioning
⇔wc ⇔	Private bathroom with toilet, private bathroom without toilet
🚿wc 🚿	Private shower with toilet, private shower without toilet
☎	Telephone in room : direct dialling for outside calls
⊘	Telephone in room : outside calls connected by operator
⚲ ⌇ ▨	Hotel tennis court(s) — Outdoor or indoor swimming pool
⇔s 🚲 ⛰s	Sauna — Garden — Beach with bathing facilities
🎪	Meals served in garden or on terrace
🚗 🚗 Ⓟ	Free garage — Charge made for garage — Car park
⛐	Bedrooms accessible to the physically handicapped
🛋	Equipped conference hall
🐕̸	Dogs are not allowed
without rest.	The hotel has no restaurant

PRICES

These prices are given in the currency of the country in question. Valid for 1985 the rates shown should only vary if the cost of living changes to any great extent.

Meals

M 65/110	Set meal prices
M a la carte 80/160	" a la carte " meals

Hotels

30 rm 110/240	Lowest price for a comfortable single and highest price for the best double room

Breakfast

� 22 🍵 17	Price of breakfast
Bb	Breakfast with choice from buffet

Service and taxes

s. t.	Service only included. V.A.T. only included.

In Austria, Denmark, Germany, Italy, Norway, Sweden, Switzerland, Spain and Portugal, prices shown are inclusive, that is to say service and V.A.T. included.

SIGHTS

Worth a journey
Worth a detour
Interesting

TOWN PLANS

Main conventional signs

Tourist Information Centre..

Hotel, restaurant — Reference letter on the town plan ....

Place of interest and its main entrance ⎫
Interesting church or chapel .... ⎬ Reference letter on the town plan ..

Shopping street — Public car park ....

Tram ....

Underground station ....

One-way street ....

Church or chapel — Poste restante, telegraph — Telephone ....

Public buildings located by letters :

Police (in large towns police headquarters) — Theatre — Museum ....

Coach station — Airport — Hospital — Covered market ....

Ruins — Monument, statue — Fountain ....

Garden, park, wood — Cemetery, Jewish cemetery ....

Outdoor or indoor swimming pool — Racecourse — Golf course ....

Cable-car — Funicular ....

Sports ground, stadium — View — Panorama.........................

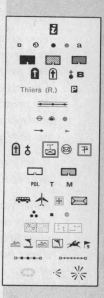

Names shown on the street plans are in the language of the country to conform to local signposting.

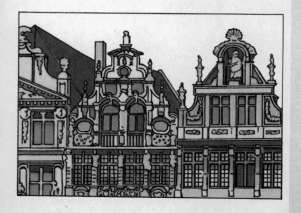

13

Avec cette nouvelle édition,
les Services de Tourisme du Pneu Michelin
vous proposent une sélection
d'hôtels et restaurants
des principales villes d'Europe,
choisies en raison de leur vocation internationale
sur le plan des affaires et du tourisme.

Vous y trouverez également les grandes tables
situées hors de ces grandes villes.

Nous vous souhaitons d'agréables séjours
et espérons que ce guide vous aidera utilement
pour le choix d'un hôtel,
d'une bonne table
et pour la visite des principales curiosités.

HOTELS ET RESTAURANTS

CLASSE ET CONFORT

Grand luxe et tradition
Grand confort
Très confortable
Bon confort
Assez confortable
Dans sa catégorie, hôtel d'équipement moderne

L'AGRÉMENT

Hôtels agréables
Restaurants agréables
Élément particulièrement agréable
Hôtel très tranquille, ou isolé et tranquille
Hôtel tranquille
Vue exceptionnelle, panorama
Vue intéressante ou étendue

« Park »

≼ sea, ☀

≼

LA TABLE

Une des meilleures tables du pays, vaut le voyage
Table excellente, mérite un détour
Une très bonne table dans sa catégorie
Autre table soignée

L'INSTALLATION

🛗 📺	Ascenseur, Télévision dans la chambre
▤	Air conditionné
🛁wc 🛁	Bain et wc privés, bain sans wc
🚿wc 🚿	Douche et wc privés, douche privée sans wc
☎	Téléphone dans la chambre direct avec l'extérieur
✆	Téléphone dans la chambre relié par standard
✕ ⚲ ▨	Tennis — Piscine : de plein air ou couverte
🛋s ⚘ 🏖s	Sauna — Jardin — Plage aménagée
☂	Repas servis au jardin ou en terrasse
🚗 🚗 ⓟ	Garage gratuit — Garage payant — Parc à voitures
♿	Chambres accessibles aux handicapés physiques
♨	L'hôtel reçoit les séminaires
🐕	Accès interdit aux chiens
without rest.	L'hôtel n'a pas de restaurant

LES PRIX

Les prix sont indiqués dans la monnaie du pays. Établis pour l'année 1985, ils ne doivent être modifiés que si le coût de la vie subit des variations importantes.

Au restaurant

M 65/110 — Prix des repas à prix fixes

M a la carte 80/160 — Prix des repas à la carte

A l'hôtel

30 rm 110/240 — Prix minimum pour une chambre d'une personne et maximum pour la plus belle chambre occupée par deux personnes

Petit déjeuner

🍵 22 ☕ 17 — Prix du petit déjeuner.

Bb — Petit déjeuner buffet

Service et taxes

s.   t. — Service compris   T.V.A. comprise

En Allemagne, Autriche, Danemark, Italie, Norvège, Suède, Suisse, Espagne et Portugal, les prix indiqués sont nets.

LES CURIOSITÉS

Vaut le voyage
Mérite un détour
Intéressante

LES PLANS

Principaux signes conventionnels

Information touristique . . . .

Hôtel, restaurant – Lettre les repérant sur le plan . . . .

Monument intéressant et entrée principale ⎫
Église ou chapelle intéressante . . . . ⎬ Lettre les repérant sur le plan . . . . . .

Rue commerçante – Parc de stationnement public. . . . .

Tramway . . . .

Station de métro . . . .

Sens unique . . . .

Église ou chapelle – Poste restante, télégraphe – Téléphone . . . .

Édifices publics repérés par des lettres :

Police (dans les grandes villes commissariat central) – Théâtre – Musée . . . .

Gare routière – Aéroport – Hôpital – Marché couvert . . . .

Ruines – Monument, statue – Fontaine. . . . .

Jardin, parc, bois – Cimetière, cimetière israélite. . . . .

Piscine de plein air, couverte – Hippodrome – Golf . . . .

Téléphérique – Funiculaire . . . .

Stade – Vue – Panorama . . . .

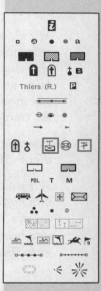

Les indications portées sur les plans sont dans la langue du pays, en conformité avec la dénomination locale.

*Mit dieser Neuauflage
präsentieren Ihnen die Michelin-Touristikabteilungen
eine Auswahl von Hotels und Restaurants
in europäischen Hauptstädten
von internationaler Bedeutung
für Geschäftsreisende und Touristen.*

*Besonders gute Restaurants in der näheren Umgebung
dieser Städte wurden ebenfalls aufgenommen.*

*Wir wünschen einen angenehmen Aufenthalt
und hoffen, daß Ihnen dieser Führer
bei der Wahl eines Hotels, eines Restaurants
und beim Besuch der Hauptsehenswürdigkeiten
gute Dienste leisten wird.*

Zeichen und Symbole

HOTELS UND RESTAURANTS

KLASSENEINTEILUNG UND KOMFORT

Großer Luxus und Tradition	
Großer Komfort	
Sehr komfortabel	
Mit gutem Komfort	
Mit ausreichendem Komfort	
Moderne Einrichtung	

ANNEHMLICHKEITEN

Angenehme Hotels
Angenehme Restaurants
Besondere Annehmlichkeit
Sehr ruhiges oder abgelegenes und ruhiges Hotel
Ruhiges Hotel
Reizvolle Aussicht, Rundblick
Interessante oder weite Sicht

« Park »

≤ sea, ⁂
≤

KÜCHE

Eine der besten Küchen des Landes : eine Reise wert
Eine hervorragende Küche : verdient einen Umweg
Eine sehr gute Küche : verdient Ihre besondere Beachtung
Andere sorgfältig zubereitete Mahlzeiten

19

EINRICHTUNG

🛗 📺	Fahrstuhl — Fernsehen im Zimmer
▭	Klimaanlage
🛏wc 🛏	Privatbad mit wc, Privatbad ohne wc
🛁wc 🛁	Privatdusche mit wc, Privatdusche ohne wc
☎	Zimmertelefon mit direkter Außenverbindung
☏	Zimmertelefon mit Außenverbindung über Telefonzentrale
✕ ⌁ ▨	Tennis — Freibad — Hallenbad
⬄s ⬅ ▲s	Sauna — Garten — Strandbad
♨	Garten-, Terrassenrestaurant
🚗 🚗 Ⓟ	Garage kostenlos — Garage wird berechnet — Parkplatz
♿	Für Körperbehinderte leicht zugängliche Zimmer
🏛	Konferenzraum
🐕	Das Mitführen von Hunden ist unerwünscht
without rest	Hotel ohne Restaurant

DIE PREISE

Die Preise sind in der jeweiligen Landeswährung angegeben. Sie gelten für das Jahr 1985 und können nur geändert werden, wenn die Lebenshaltungskosten starke Veränderungen erfahren.

Im Restaurant

M 65/110 — Feste Menupreise

M a la carte 80/160 — Mahlzeiten "a la carte"

Im Hotel

30 rm 110/240 — Mindestpreis für ein Einzelzimmer und Höchstpreis für das schönste Doppelzimmer für zwei Personen

Frühstück

☕ 22 ☕ 17 — Preis des Frühstücks

Bb — Frühstücksbuffet

Bedienungsgeld und Gebühren

s.   t. — Bedienung inbegriffen — MWSt inbegriffen.

In Dänemark, Deutschland, Italien, Norwegen, Österreich, Schweden, Schweiz, Spanien und Portugal sind die angegebenen Preise Inklusivpreise.

SEHENSWÜRDIGKEITEN

Eine Reise wert
Verdient einen Umweg
Sehenswert

STADTPLÄNE

Erklärung der wichtigsten Zeichen

Informationsstelle . . . .

Hotel, Restaurant — Referenzbuchstabe auf dem Plan . . . .

Sehenswertes Gebäude mit Haupteingang ⎫
Sehenswerte Kirche oder Kapelle . . . . ⎭ Referenzbuchstabe auf dem Plan . . .

Einkaufsstraße — Öffentlicher Parkplatz, Parkhaus

Straßenbahn . . . .

U-Bahnstation . . . .

Einbahnstraße . . . .

Kirche oder Kapelle — Postlagernde Sendungen, Telegraph — Telefon . . . .

Öffentliche Gebäude, durch Buchstaben gekennzeichnet :

Polizei (in größeren Städten Polizeipräsidium) — Theater — Museum . . . .

Autobusbahnhof — Flughafen — Krankenhaus — Markthalle . . . .

Ruine — Denkmal, Statue — Brunnen . . . .

Garten, Park, Wald — Friedhof, Jüd. Friedhof . . . .

Freibad — Hallenbad — Pferderennbahn — Golfplatz und Lochzahl . . . .

Seilschwebebahn — Standseilbahn . . . .

Sportplatz — Aussicht — Rundblick . . . .

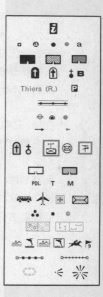

*Die Angaben auf den Stadtplänen erfolgen, überein-
stimmend mit der örtlichen Beschilderung, in der Landes-
sprache.*

3

21

この新しいガイドブックの中で、ミシュランタイヤ観光部は、ビジネスと観光の両面において、国際的に重要な位置を占めることを条件に選択されたヨーロッパ主要都市のホテル、レストランをご紹介しています。

勿論、これらの都市以外でも、良いホテル、レストランを見つけられることもあるでしょう。

私たちは、皆様の快適な滞在を願うと共に、このガイドブックが、ホテル、レストランの選択、主な見所の訪問にお役に立つことを希望致します。

記号
と
シンボルマーク

ホテルとレストラン

等級と快適さ

超高級、伝統的
トップクラス
たいへん快適
快適
かなり快適
等級内での近代的設備のホテル

居心地

居心地よいホテル
居心地よいレストラン
心地よさを生む特別な理由（例：花咲く庭園）
大変静かなホテル又は人里離れた静かなホテル
静かなホテル
素晴しい景色（例：海）、パノラマ
興味深い景色・展望

« Park »

≤ sea,

≤

料理

極上の料理（これを味わうための）旅行の値うちあり
寄り道するに価する素晴しい料理
該当する等級内での大変おいしい料理
その他の心のこもった料理

M

設備

⑤ TV 📺	エレベーター、室内にテレビ付き
	空調設備
🛏wc🛏	専用の浴室とトイレ付。浴室は専用、トイレ無し。
🚿wc🚿	専用シャワーとトイレ付。シャワーは専用、トイレ無し。
☎	室内に電話あり、外線直通
☎	室内に電話あり、交換台を通す
✂ ⊐ ⊠	テニスコート。屋外プール。屋内プール。
🏖 🏌 ⛰	サウナ。くつろげる庭。整備された海水浴場。
🍴	食事は庭またはテラスでできる
🚗 🚙 Ⓟ	車庫無料。車庫有料。駐車場
♿	身体障害者用の部屋あり
🔔	会議又は研修会の出来るホテル
🐕	犬の連れ込みおことわり
without rest.	レストランの無いホテル

料金

料金は1985年のその国の貨幣単位で示してありますが、物価の変動などで変わる場合もあります。

レストラン

M 65/110
M a la carte
80/160

定食、ア・ラ・カルトそれぞれの最低料金と最高料金。

ホテル

30 rm 110/240

一人部屋の最低料金110と二人部屋の最高料金240。

朝食

🍵 22　☕ 17
Bb

朝食料金。
ビュッフェでの朝食。

サービス料と税金

s.　t.

サービス料込み。付加価値税込み。

ドイツ、オーストリア、デンマーク、イタリア、ノルウェー、スウェーデン、スイス、スペイン、ポルトガルに関しては正価料金。

名　所

旅行する価値がある…………………………	★★★
行程変更する価値がある……………………	★★
興味深い…………………………………………	★

地　図

主な記号

ツーリストインフォメーション………………………………	ⓘ
ホテル・レストラン──地図上での目印番号……………	▫ ⓐ ● a
興味深い歴史的建造物と、その中央入口　地図の上での	
興味深い教会または聖堂　　　　　　目印番号 …………	
商店街──公共用駐車場……………………………………	Thiers (R.)　🅿
路面電車………………………………………………………	
地下鉄駅………………………………………………………	
一方通行路……………………………………………………	
教会または聖堂──留置郵便、電報、電話………………	
公共建造物、記号は下記の通り……………………………	
警察(大都市では、中央警察署)──劇場──美術館、博物館……	POL.　T　M
長距離バス発着所──空港──病院──屋内市場…………	
遺跡──歴史的建造物、像──泉…………………………	
庭園、公園、森林──墓地──イスラエル人の墓地……	
屋外プール、屋内プール──競馬場──ゴルフ場………	
ロープウェイ──ケーブルカー……………………………	
スタジアム──景色──パノラマ…………………………	

道路地図上の名称は、地方の標識に合わせて、その国の言葉で表記
されています。

25

Austria

Österreich

Vienna
Salzburg

PRACTICAL INFORMATION

LOCAL CURRENCY

Austrian Schilling ; 100 S = 4.483 US $ (Jan. 85)

TOURIST INFORMATION

In Vienna : Österreich-Information, Margaretenstr. 1, ✆ (0222) 57 57 14
Niederösterreich-Information, Paulanergasse 11, ✆ (0222) 56 61 07
In Salzburg : Landesverkehrsamt, Mozartplatz 5, ✆ (0662) 4 15 61

BREAKDOWN SERVICE

ÖAMTC : See addresses in the text of Vienna and Salzburg

ARBÖ : in Vienna : Mariahilfer Str. 180, ✆ (0222) 85 35 35
in Salzburg : Münchner Bundesstr. 9, ✆ (0662) 3 36 01

In Austria the ÖAMTC and the ARBÖ make a special point of assisting foreign motorists. They have motor patrols covering main roads.

SHOPPING and BANK HOURS

Shops are open from 9am to 6pm, but often close for a lunch break. They are closed Saturday afternoon, Sunday and Bank Holidays (except the shops in railway stations).

Branch offices of banks are open from Monday to Friday between 8am and 12.30pm (in Salzburg 12am) and from 1.30pm to 3pm (in Salzburg 2pm to 4.30pm), Thursday to 5.30pm (only in Vienna).

In the index of street names those printed in red are where the principal shops are found.

TIPPING

Service is generally included in hotel and restaurant bills. But in Austria, it is usual to give more than the expected tip in hotels, restaurants and cafés. Taxi-drivers, porters, barbers and theatre attendants also expect tips.

SPEED LIMITS

The speed limit in built up areas (indicated by place name signs at the beginning and end of such areas) is 50 km/h - 31 mph ; on motorways 130 km/h - 80 mph and on all other roads 100 km/h - 62 mph.

SEAT BELTS

The wearing of seat belts in Austria is compulsory for drivers and front seat passengers.

FOREIGN EXCHANGE

Hotels, restaurants and shops de not always accept foreign currencies and it is wise, therefore, to change money and cheques at the banks and exchange offices which are found in the larger stations, airports and at the frontier.

VIENNA

SIGHTS

HOFBURG★★★ BV

Imperial Palace of the Habsburgs (Kaiserpalast der Habsburger) : Swiss Court – Castle Chapel – Amalienhof – Stallburg – Leopold Wing – Ballhausplatz – Imperial Chancellery – Spanish Riding School – Neue Burg – Josefsplatz – Michaelerplatz – In der Burg – Capuchins Crypt – Church of the Augustinians. Art Collections : Imperial Treasury★★★ – Imperial Apartments★★ – Austrian National Library (Great Hall★) – Collection of Court Porcelain and Silver★★ – Collection of Arms and Armour★★ – Collection of Old Musical Instruments★ – Albertina (Dürer Collection★) – Museum of Ephesian Sculpture (Reliefs of Ephesus★★).

BUILDINGS AND MONUMENTS

St Stephen's Cathedral★★ (Stephansdom) CV – Schönbrunn★★ (Apartments★★★, Park★★, Coach Room★) S – Upper and Lower Belvedere★★ (Oberes und Unteres Belvedere) (Terraced Gardens and Art Collections★) DX and S – Opera★ (Staatsoper)★ CV – Church of St Charles★ (Karlskirche) CX – Church of St Michael (Michaeler Kirche) BCV – Church of the Monorities (Minoritenkirche) BV – Church of the Teutonic Order (Deutschordenskirche) (Altarpiece★, Treasure★) CV – Church of the Jesuits (Jesuitenkirche) CV B – Church of Our Lady of the River Bank (Maria am Gestade) CU – Church of the Faithful Virgin (Maria Treu) S F – Mozart Memorial (Mozart-Gedenkstätte) CV D – Dreimäderlhaus BU K.

STREETS, PLACES, PARKS

Kärntner Straße CVX – Graben (Colum of the Pest) CV – Am Hof (Colum to the Virgin) BV – Herrengasse★ BV – Maria-Theresien-Platz BV – Prater★ (Giant Whell, ≤★) S – Oberlaapark★ S – Heldenplatz BV – Burggarten BV – Volksgarten BV – Rathausplatz BV.

IMPORTANT MUSEUMS (Hofburg and Belvedere see above)

Museum of Fine Arts★★★ (Kunsthistorisches Museum) BV – Historical Museum of the City of Vienna★★ (Historisches Museum der Stadt Wien) CX M1 – Austrian Folklore Museum★★ (Österreichisches Museum für Volkskunde) S M2 – Gallery of Painting and Fine Arts★ (Gemäldegalerie der Akademie der Bildenden Künste) BX M3 – Natural History Museum★ (Naturhistorisches Museum) BV M4 – Birthplace of Schubert (Schubert-Museum) R M5 – Austrian Museum of Applied Arts★ (Österreichisches Museum für angewandte Kunst) DV M6.

EXCURSIONS

Danube Tower★★ (Donauturm) R – Leopoldsberg ≤★★ R – Kahlenberg ≤★ R – Klosterneuburg Abbey (Stift Klosterneuburg) (Altarpiece by Nicolas of Verdun★) R – Grinzing R – Baden★ S – Vienna Woods★ (Wienerwald) S.

VIENNA (WIEN) Austria 987 ⑩, 426 ⑫ – pop. 1 527 000 – alt. 156 m. – ✆ 0222.
✈ Wien-Schwechat by ②, ✆ 7 77 00 – ☎ ✆ 56 50 29 89.
Exhibition Centre, Messeplatz 1, ✆ 9 31 52 40.
🛈 Tourist-Information, Opernpassage (Basement). ✆ 43 16 08 – ÖAMTC, Schubertring. ✆ 72 99
Budapest 208 ③ – München 435 ⑥ – Praha 292 ① – Salzburg 292 ⑥ – Zagreb 362 ⑤.

City districts (Stadtbezirke) 1-9 :

🏨🏨🏨 **Imperial** (converted 19 C palace), Kärntner Ring 16, ⊠ A-1015, 𝒫 65 17 65, Telex 112630 — 🛗 🗐 🏋. 🅰🅴 ⓪ 🔳 VISA. ⚘ rest   CX **a**
M a la carte 270/570 (booking essential) — **Imperial Café M** a la carte 195/340 — **162 rm** 1390/3580.

🏨🏨🏨 **Sacher**, Philharmonikerstr. 4, ⊠ A-1015, 𝒫 52 55 75/5 14 56, Telex 112520, « Antique furniture, restaurant Sacherstöckl » — 🛗 🗐 🔲. ⚘ rest   CV **x**
M a la carte 265/620 — **124 rm** 1050/3000.

🏨🏨🏨 **Bristol**, Kärntner Ring 1, ⊠ A-1015, 𝒫 52 95 52, Telex 112474 — 🛗 🗐 rest 🔲 🏋. 🅰🅴 ⓪ 🔳 VISA. ⚘ rest   CX **m**
M 275/500 a la carte 220/410 (see also Korso rest. below) — **128 rm** 2200/3320.

🏨🏨 ❀ **Hotel im Palais Schwarzenberg** 🐾, Schwarzenbergplatz 9, ⊠ A-1030, 𝒫 78 45 15, Telex 136124, « Converted 1727 baroque palace, park », ⚘ — 🛗 🅿 🏋. 🅰🅴 ⓪ 🔳 VISA
M a la carte 275/625 (booking essential) — **40 rm** 1850/4250   CX
Spec. Zwiebeltörtchen "Vulgaris", Zanderstrudel mit Krebsmousse in Rotweinsauce, Masthuhn und Kalbshirn im Netz mit Entenlebersauce.

🏨🏨 ❀ **Hilton International-Rôtisserie Prinz Eugen**, Landstraßer Hauptstr. 2 (near Stadtpark), ⊠ A-1030, 𝒫 75 26 52, Telex 136799, 🛗 — 🛗 🗐 🔲 🕭 🏋. 🅰🅴 ⓪ 🔳 VISA. ⚘ rest   DV **k**
M a la carte 330/650 (booking essential, closed Saturday lunch) — **Café am Park M** a la carte 165/390 — **620 rm** 1760/2770
Spec. Feine Nudeln mit Flußkrebsen in Basilikum, Das Beste vom Kalb mit Kräutermousseline, Tafelspitz mit Apfelkren und Schnittlauchsauce.

🏨🏨 **Intercontinental**, Johannesgasse 28, ⊠ A-1030, 𝒫 75 05, Telex 131235, 🛗 — 🛗 🗐 🔲 🕭 🏋. 🅰🅴 ⓪ 🔳 VISA. ⚘ rest   DX **p**
Restaurants : — **Rôtisserie M** a la carte 240/560 — **Brasserie M** a la carte 125/340 — **500 rm** 1840/4810.

🏨🏨 **Hotel de France**, Schottenring 3, ⊠ A-1010, 𝒫 34 35 40, Telex 114360, 🛗 — 🛗 🗐 rest 🔲 🏋. 🅰🅴 ⓪ 🔳 VISA   BU **b**
M a la carte 255/530 — **186 rm** 1070/2450 Bb.

🏨🏨 **König von Ungarn**, Schulerstr. 10, ⊠ A-1010, 𝒫 52 65 20, Telex 116240 — 🛗 🔲 🏋.
⚘ rest   CV **n**
32 rm.

🏨🏨 **Biedermeier**, Landstraßer Hauptstr. 28 (at Sünnhof), ⊠ A-1030, 𝒫 75 55 75, Telex 11 10 39 — 🛗 🔲 ⇔ 🏋. 🅰🅴 ⓪ 🔳 VISA   S **w**
M a la carte 240/465 — **200 rm** 1500/1700.

🏨🏨 **Ambassador**, Neuer Markt 5, ⊠ A-1010, 𝒫 52 75 11, Telex 111906 — 🛗. 🅰🅴 ⓪ 🔳 VISA
M a la carte 220/520 — **107 rm** 1170/2200.   CV **s**

🏨🏨 **Europa**, Neuer Markt 3, ⊠ A-1015, 𝒫 52 15 94, Telex 112292 — 🛗 🗐 🔲 🕭 🏋. 🅰🅴 ⓪ 🔳 VISA. ⚘ rest   CV **a**
M a la carte 220/440 — **102 rm** 1020/1670 Bb.

🏨 **Stefanie**, Taborstr. 12, ⊠ A-1020, 𝒫 24 24 12, Telex 134589 — 🛗 🔲 ⇔wc 🛏wc 🕿 ⇔ 🏋. 🅰🅴 ⓪ 🔳 VISA   DU **d**
M a la carte 195/400 — **140 rm** 1080/1460 Bb.

🏨 **Amadeus** without rest, Wildpretmarkt 5, ⊠ A-1010, 𝒫 63 87 38 — 🛗 🔲 ⇔wc 🛏wc 🕿. 🅰🅴 ⓪   CV **y**
closed 24 December - 7 January — **30 rm** 815/1480.

🏨 **Capricorno** without rest, Schwedenplatz 3, ⊠ A-1010, 𝒫 63 31 04, Telex 115266 — 🛗 🔲 ⇔wc 🛏wc 🕿 ⇔ 🅿. 🅰🅴   DV **f**
46 rm 820/1320.

🏨 **K u. K Palais Hotel** without rest (modern hotel in a former palace), Rudolfsplatz 11, ⊠ A-1010, 𝒫 63 13 53, Telex 134049 — 🛗 🔲 ⇔wc 🛏wc 🕿   CU **h**
66 rm Bb.

🏨 **Hungaria**, Rennweg 51, ⊠ A-1030, 𝒫 73 25 21, Telex 13 17 97 — 🛗 ⇔wc 🛏wc 🕿 ⇔. 🅰🅴 ⓪ 🔳 VISA. ⚘ rest   S **h**
M a la carte 180/330 🍴 — **168 rm** 850/1400.

🏨 **ETAP Hotel Belvedere**, Am Heumarkt 35, ⊠ A-1030 — 🛗 🔲 ⇔wc 🕿 ⇔ 🏋. 🅰🅴 ⓪ 🔳 E   CX **e**
M a la carte 150/350 🍴 — **211 rm** 850/1280 Bb.

🏨 **Dorkahof** without rest, Breite Gasse 9, ⊠ A-1070, 𝒫 9 31 34 50, Telex 136614 — 🛗 ⇔wc 🛏wc 🕿. 🅰🅴 ⓪ 🔳 VISA   S **u**
55 rm 680/1300 Bb.

🏨 **Astoria**, Führichgasse 1, ⊠ A-1015, 𝒫 52 65 85, Telex 112856 — 🛗 ⇔wc 🕿. 🅰🅴 ⓪ 🔳 VISA   CV **r**
M 215 — **108 rm** 1070/1650 Bb.

🏨 **Prinz Eugen**, Wiedner Gürtel 14, ⊠ A-1040, 𝒫 65 17 41, Telex 132483 — 🛗 ⇔wc 🛏wc 🅰🅴 ⓪ 🔳 VISA   S **a**
M a la carte 182/365 — **106 rm** 1000/1870.

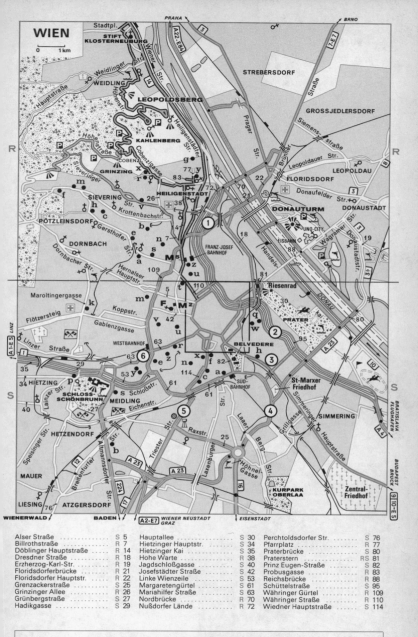

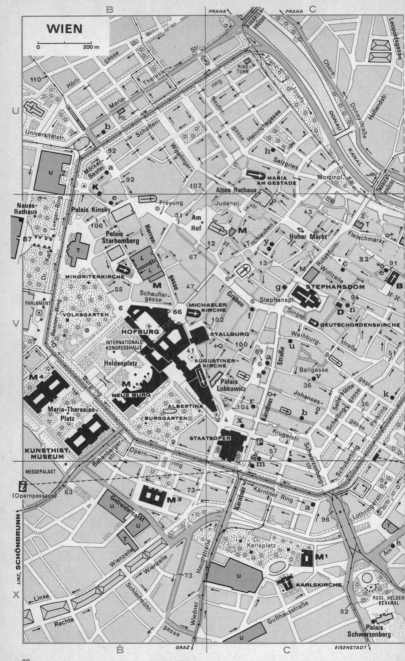

STREET INDEX TO WIEN TOWN PLANS

🏨 **Strudlhof** ⏳ without rest, Pasteurgasse 1, ✉ A-1090, ℰ 31 25 22, Telex 135256 — 🔊
🖭wc ☎ ⇔ R u
48 rm.

🏨 **President**, Wallgasse 23, ✉ A-1060, ℰ 57 36 36/5 99 90, Telex 112523 — 🔊 🗏 📺 🖭wc
☎ ⇔ 🛁. 🖭 ⓓ 🅔 *VISA* S e
M a la carte 135/310 — **77 rm** 990/1490.

🏨 **Kummer**, Mariahilfer Str. 71 A, ✉ A-1061, ℰ 57 36 95, Telex 111417 — 🔊 🖭wc 🖭wc ☎.
🛠 rest S r
110 rm.

🏨 **Erzherzog Rainer**, Wiedner Hauptstr. 27, ✉ A-1041, ℰ 65 46 46, Telex 132329 — 🔊
🗏 rest 📺 🖭wc 🖭wc ☎ 🛁. 🖭 ⓓ 🅔 *VISA* S f
M a la carte 175/390 (closed Saturday and Sunday November - March) 🍷 — **84 rm** 825/1550.

🏨 **Attaché** without rest, Wiedner Hauptstr. 71, ✉ A-1040, ℰ 65 18 18, Telex 111146 — 🔊 📺
🖭wc 🖭wc ☎ S c
23 rm.

🏨 **Graben**, Dorotheergasse 3, ✉ A-1010, ℰ 52 15 31 — 🔊 🖭wc 🖭wc ☎. 🖭 ⓓ 🅔 *VISA*
Restaurants : — **Altenberg M** a la carte 140/220 — **Trattoria Santo Stefano M** a la carte
147/330 — **46 rm** 710/1450 Bb. CV f

🏨 **Mailberger Hof** ⏳ without rest, Annagasse 7, ✉ A-1010, ℰ 52 06 41, Telex 133828 — 🔊
📺 🖭wc ☎ CV b
40 rm.

🏨 **Am Parkring**, Parkring 12, ✉ A-1015, ℰ 52 65 24, Telex 113420, ← — 🔊 🗏 📺 🖭wc ☎
⇔. 🖭 ⓓ 🅔 *VISA*. 🛠 CV k
M a la carte 140/340 — **64 rm** 950/1460 Bb.

🏨 **Am Stephansplatz**, Stephansplatz 9, ✉ A-1010, ℰ 63 56 05, Telex 114334 — 🔊 📺
🖭wc 🖭wc ☎. 🖭 ⓓ 🅔 *VISA* CV g
M a la carte 145/320 — **62 rm** 940/1450 Bb.

🏨 **Alpha** without rest, Boltzmanngasse 8, ✉ A-1090, ℰ 31 16 46, Telex 115749 — 🔊 🖭wc
🖭wc ☎ ⇔. 🖭 ⓓ 🅔 *VISA* R u
70 rm 880/1295.

🏨 **Alba**, Margaretenstr. 53, ✉ A-1050, ℰ 57 55 85, Telex 113264 — 🔊 🗏 rm 📺 🖭wc ☎
⇔. 🖭 ⓓ 🅔 *VISA* S n
M a la carte 155/290 — **46 rm** 980/1390 Bb.

🏨 **Atlanta** without rest, Währinger Str. 33, ✉ A-1090, ℰ 42 12 39, Telex 115002 — 🔊 🖭wc
🖭wc ☎ RS t
69 rm.

🏨 **Albatros**, Liechtensteinstr. 89, ✉ A-1090, ℰ 34 35 08, Telex 114300, ⇌, 🔲 — 🔊 🗏 📺
🖭wc ☎ ⇔ 🛁 R z
70 rm Bb.

🏵🏵🏵🏵 **Korso**, Mahlerstr. 2 (at Bristol-H.), ✉ A-1015, ℰ 52 16 42 — 🗏. 🖭 ⓓ 🅔 *VISA*. 🛠 CV m
Saturday lunch only — **M** a la carte 300/530 (booking essential).

🏵🏵🏵 ❀ **Steirereck**, Rasumofskygasse 2 / Ecke Weißgerberlände, ✉ A-1030, ℰ 73 31 68 —
🖭 S q
closed Saturday, Sunday, Bank Holidays and 22 December - 1 January — **M** a la carte
230/470 (booking essential) (wine list with more than 440 wines)
Spec. Pasteten und Terrinen vom Wagen, Lammtörtchen in Essigsauce, Calvados-Apfelsuppe mit
Zimtsoufflé.

🏵🏵🏵 ❀ **Hauswirth**, Otto-Bauer-Gasse 20, ✉ A-1060, ℰ 57 12 61 — 🖭 ⓓ 🅔 *VISA* S z
closed Sunday and Bank Holidays — **M** a la carte 225/450 (booking essential)
Spec. Nudeln mit Steinpilzen in Kerbelschaum (July to October), Bachforellenfilet auf Wurzeljulienne mit
Krensauce, Kalbsbries mit Gänseleber in Blätterteig.

🏵🏵🏵 **Zu den drei Husaren**, Weihburggasse 4, ✉ A-1010, ℰ 52 11 92/5 13 17 88 — 🖭 ⓓ 🅔
VISA CV u
dinner only, closed 15 July - 15 August and Sunday from mid November to March — **M** a
la carte 275/650 (booking essential).

🏵🏵🏵 **Kervansaray** (Turkish rest.), Mahlerstr. 9, ✉ A-1010, ℰ 52 88 43 — 🗏. 🖭 ⓓ 🅔 *VISA*. 🛠
closed Sunday — **M** a la carte 250/540 (booking essential) — **Hummer Bar** *(dinner only,
mainly Seafood)* **M** 300/625. CVX t

🏵🏵🏵 **Belvedere Stöckl**, Prinz-Eugen-Str. 25, ✉ A-1030, ℰ 78 41 98, « Garden » — 🅔 *VISA*
M a la carte 255/510.

🏵🏵 ❀ **Mattes**, Schönlaterngasse 8, ✉ A-1010, ℰ 52 62 75 — 🖭 ⓓ 🅔 *VISA*. 🛠 CV e
dinner only, closed Sunday, Bank Holidays and August — **M** a la carte 330/540 (booking
essential)
Spec. Gänsestopfleber im Kohlblatt, Nudeln mit Flußkrebsen und Basilikum, Gratinierte Kutteln mit Thymian.

🏵🏵 **Kupferdachl**, Schottengasse 7, ✉ A-1010, ℰ 63 93 81 — 🖭 ⓓ 🅔 *VISA* BU a
closed Saturday lunch, Sunday and 27 July - 18 August — **M** a la carte 215/405 (booking
essential).

🏵🏵 **Schubertstüberln**, Schreyvogelgasse 4, ✉ A-1010, ℰ 63 71 87 — 🖭 ⓓ 🅔 *VISA* BV e
closed Sunday and 24 to 30 December — **M** a la carte 200/380 🍷.

XX **Steinerne Eule**, Halbgasse 30, ⊠ A-1070, 𝒫 93 22 50, 🌳 – ⓓ Ε 𝚅𝙸𝚂𝙰   S v
     M a la carte 195/400.

XX **Steirer Stüberl**, Wiedner Hauptstr. 111, ⊠ A-1050, 𝒫 55 43 49 – ⓓ Ε 𝚅𝙸𝚂𝙰   S c
     closed Sunday – **M** a la carte 160/340 ♣.

XX **Zum Kuckuck**, Himmelpfortgasse 15, ⊠ A-1010, 𝒫 52 84 70/5 12 84 70   CV v
     closed Saturday, Sunday and 1 to 21 July – **M** a la carte 200/430 (booking essential).

XX **Salut** (French rest.), Wildpretmarkt 3, ⊠ A-1010, 𝒫 63 13 22 – 𝙰𝙴 ⓓ 𝚅𝙸𝚂𝙰   CV y
     closed Sunday and Bank Holidays – **M** a la carte 290/430.

XX **Wiener Rathauskeller** (vaults with murals turn of the century), Rathausplatz 1,
     ⊠ A-1010, 𝒫 42 12 19   BV
     closed Sunday – **M** a la carte 170/350 ♣.

X **Do und Co** (Bistro in a delicatessen store), Akademiestr. 3, ⊠ A-1010, 𝒫 52 64 74 – �_
     closed from 6.30 p.m. and Sunday – **M** a la carte 190/325 (booking essential).   CV t

X **Wein-Comptoir**, Bäckerstr. 6, ⊠ A-1010, 𝒫 52 17 60 – 𝙰𝙴 ⓓ Ε 𝚅𝙸𝚂𝙰   CV c
     closed Saturday, Sunday, Bank Holidays and 22 December - 1 January – **M** a la carte
     140/400 (booking essential).

X **Goldener Hecht**, Waaggasse 5, ⊠ A-1040, 𝒫 57 06 95, 🌳   S x
     M a la carte 126/370.

City districts (Stadtbezirke) 12-15 :

🏨 **Parkhotel Schönbrunn** (former imperial guest-house), Hietzinger Hauptstr. 10, ⊠ A-1131,
     𝒫 82 26 76, Telex 132513, Massage, 🌳, 🏊, 🌱 – 🛗 📺 ⌂wc 🛎wc ☎ 🏛 🌳 rest
     487 rm.   S p

🏨 **Novotel Wien-West**, Wientalstraße (Auhof motorway station), ⊠ A-1140, 𝒫 97 25 42,
     Telex 135584, 🏊, 🌱 – 🛗 📺 ⌂wc ☎ 🕭 🅿 🏛 𝙰𝙴 ⓓ Ε 𝚅𝙸𝚂𝙰   by A 1
     M a la carte 155/328 – **115 rm** 900/1280 Bb.

🏨 **Garten Hotel Altmannsdorf**, Hoffingergasse 26, ⊠ A-1120, 𝒫 84 63 17, Telex 135327,
     🌳, Park, 🌳 – 🛗 📺 ⌂wc 🛎wc ☎ ⟺ 🅿 🏛 𝙰𝙴 ⓓ Ε 𝚅𝙸𝚂𝙰   S b
     closed 23 to 29 December – **M** a la carte 167/430 – **41 rm** 820/1450 Bb.

🏨 **Reither**, Graumanngasse 16, ⊠ A-1150, 𝒫 85 61 65, Telex 136430, 🌳, 🏊 – 🛗 📺 ⌂wc
     ☎ ⟺ 𝙰𝙴 ⓓ Ε 𝚅𝙸𝚂𝙰 🌳 rest   S y
     closed 24 to 28 December – **M** a la carte 150/280 (dinner only) – **50 rm** 790/1100 Bb.

🏛 **Jagdschloß** without rest, Jagdschloßgasse 79, ⊠ A-1130, 𝒫 84 35 08, 🏊, 🌱 – 🛗
     ⌂wc 🛎wc ☎   by Jagdschloßgasse   S
     40 rm 600/930.

🏛 **Kaiserpark-Schönbrunn**, Grünbergstr. 9, ⊠ A-1120, 𝒫 83 86 10, Telex 134754 – 🛗 📺
     ⌂wc 🛎wc ☎   S s
     M (dinner only) – **46 rm** Bb.

🏛 **Ekazent** without rest, Hietzinger Hauptstr. 22, ⊠ A-1130, 𝒫 82 74 01, Telex 134352 –
     🛗 ⌂wc ☎ 𝙰𝙴 ⓓ Ε 𝚅𝙸𝚂𝙰   S p
     45 rm 750/1040.

XX **Altwienerhof** with rm (wine list with 400 wines), Herklotzgasse 6, ⊠ A-1150,
     𝒫 83 71 45, 🌳, « Winter garden » – 🛗 🛎wc ☎ 𝙰𝙴   S y
     closed 26 January - 11 February – **M** a la carte 202/420 (booking essential, closed Saturday)
     – **24 rm** 480/820 Bb.

X **Schenke Steinmetz** (Heurigen rest.), Firmiangasse 23, ⊠ A-1130, 𝒫 82 22 16
     (booking essential).   by Hietzinger Hauptstraße   S

City districts (Stadtbezirke) 16-19 :

🏨 **Modul** Ⓜ, Peter-Jordan-Str. 78, ⊠ A-1190, 𝒫 47 15 84, Telex 76736 – 🛗 🍽 📺 🕭 ⟺ 🅿
     🏛 – **42 rm** Bb.   R b

🏨 **Maté**, Ottakringer Str. 34, ⊠ A-1170, 𝒫 43 61 33, Telex 115485, 🌳, 🏊 – 🛗 🍽 rest 🛗
     ⌂wc ☎ 🅿 𝙰𝙴 ⓓ Ε 𝚅𝙸𝚂𝙰   S m
     M a la carte 120/320 – **125 rm** 700/1380 Bb.

🏨 **Clima Villenhotel** 🌸, Nussberggasse 2c, ⊠ A-1190, 𝒫 37 15 16, Telex 115670, « Rest.
     Bockkeller, vaulted cellar with Tyrolian farmhouse furniture », 🌳, 🏊, 🏊, 🌱 – 🛗 📺
     ⌂wc ☎ ⟺ 🅿 🏛 𝙰𝙴 ⓓ Ε 𝚅𝙸𝚂𝙰   R g
     M a la carte 175/300 (dinner only, closed Sunday) ♣ – **33 rm** 970/1520 Bb – 8 apartment
     2880.

🏨 **Cottage** without rest, Hasenauerstr. 12, ⊠ A-1190, 𝒫 31 25 71, Telex 134146 – 🛗 📺
     ⌂wc 🛎wc ☎ 🏛 𝙰𝙴 ⓓ Ε 𝚅𝙸𝚂𝙰   R n
     23 rm 900/1400 Bb.

🏛 **Hadrigan**, Maroltinger Gasse 68, ⊠ A-1160, 𝒫 92 54 26, Telex 135951 – 🛗 ⌂wc 🛎wc
     ☎   S k
     47 rm.

🏛 **Gartenhotel Glanzing** 🌸 without rest, Glanzinggasse 23, ⊠ A-1190, 𝒫 47 42 72 – 🛗
     📺 ⌂wc ☎ ⟺   R c
     21 rm 450/1100.

🏛 **Schild** without rest, Neustift am Walde 97, ⊠ A-1190, 𝒫 44 21 91, 🌱 – 🛗 ⌂wc 🛎wc
     ☎ 🅿   R f
     34 rm 510/830.

XX **Sailer**, Gersthofer Str. 14, ✉ A-1180, ☏ 47 21 21, 🌣, « Kellerstuben » – 🜄 ⑩ E 𝘝𝘐𝘚𝘈 R e
closed Sunday, Bank Holidays and 28 July - 18 August – **M** a la carte 155/390 (booking essential).

XX **Bürgerhof**, Gentzgasse 127, ✉ A-1180, ☏ 47 34 41 – 🜄 ⑩ E 𝘝𝘐𝘚𝘈 R a
M a la carte 123/360.

XX **Zauberlehrling**, Lazaristengasse 2, ✉ A-1180, ☏ 34 51 35 – 🜄 ⑩ 𝘝𝘐𝘚𝘈 R s
dinner only, closed Sunday, Bank Holidays, 22 July - 18 August and 23 December - 1 January – **M** a la carte 205/380.

X **Römischer Kaiser**, Neustift am Walde 2, ✉ A-1190, ☏ 44 11 04, Terraced garden with ⩽ Vienna R h
closed Tuesday, Wednesday and 7 January - 6 February – **M** a la carte 110/260 ⌀.

X **Eckel**, Sieveringer Str. 46, ✉ A-1190, ☏ 32 32 18, 🌣 – 🜄 ⑩ R v
closed Sunday, Monday and 11 to 19 August – **M** a la carte 166/380 ⌀.

Heurigen and Buschen-Schänken (wine gardens) – (mostly self-service, hot and cold dishes from buffet, prices according to weight of chosen meals, Buschen-Schänken sell their own wines only) :

X Oppolzer, Himmelstr. 22, ✉ A-1190, ☏ 32 24 16, « Garden » R r
closed until 5 p.m., Sunday, Bank Holidays and 22 December - 6 January – **M** a la carte : buffet (booking essential) ⌀.

X **Altes Preßhaus**, Cobenzlgasse 15, ✉ A-1190, ☏ 32 23 93, 🌣, « Old vaulted wine cellar » – 🜄 ⑩ E 𝘝𝘐𝘚𝘈 R x
closed until 4 p.m. and 7 January - 19 February – **M** a la carte 125/215 (and buffet) ⌀.

X Fuhrgassl Huber (Wine-garden with Viennese Schrammelmusik), Neustift am Walde 68, ✉ A-1190, ☏ 44 14 05, « Court-terrace » R m

X **Grinzinger Hauermandl**, Cobenzlgasse 20, ✉ A-1190, ☏ 32 30 27, 🌣 – 🜄 ⑩ E 𝘝𝘐𝘚𝘈 R x
closed until 5.30 p.m. and Sunday – **M** a la carte 129/275 ⌀.

X Wolff (Buschenschank), Rathstr. 44, ✉ A-1190, ☏ 44 23 35, « Terraced Garden » R m
closed Monday to Saturday until 2.30 p.m., Sunday until 11.30 a.m. – **M** a la carte : buffet ⌀.

X **Grinzinger Weinbottich**, Cobenzlgasse 28, ✉ A-1190, ☏ 32 42 37, « Shady garden » – 🜄 ⑩ E 𝘝𝘐𝘚𝘈 R x
closed until 5.30 p.m. and Monday – **M** a la carte 129/260 ⌀.

X Mayer (Buschenschank with Viennese Schrammelmusik), Pfarrplatz 2, ✉ A-1190, ☏ 37 12 87, « Shady garden » – 🜄 E R y
closed until 4 p.m. and 22 December - 12 January – **M** a la carte : buffet ⌀.

at Perchtoldsdorf ⑤ : 10 km :

X **Killermann** (Heurigen-Lokal), Sonnbergstr. 22, ✉ A-2380 Perchtoldsdorf, ☏ (0222) 86 81 81, 🌣 – ⋙
closed until 6 p.m., Sunday, Monday and August – **M** a la carte: buffet, self-service (booking essential).

at Vösendorf S : 11 km by A 2 or B 17 S :

🏨 **Park-Hotel**, Parkallee 2 (recreation centre El Dorado), ✉ A-2334 Vösendorf, ☏ (0222)13 48 55, 🌣, Massage, ⟳, ⌱, 🟦, ⟿, ⚒ (indoor) – 🛗 ▤ 📺 ⟐ ⓟ ⚴. 🜄 ⑩ E 𝘝𝘐𝘚𝘈. ⋙ rest
M a la carte 145/350 – **Park Royal** *(closed Sunday)* **M** a la carte 250/600 – **195 rm** 1280/3040 Bb.

🏨 **Novotel Wien-Süd**, Shopping City Süd, ✉ A-2334 Vösendorf, ☏ (0222) 67 65 06, Telex 134793, ⌱ – 🛗 ▤ rest 📺 ⟿wc ☎ ⟐ ⓟ ⚴. 🜄 ⑩ E 𝘝𝘐𝘚𝘈
M a la carte 138/280 – **102 rm** 950/1280 Bb.

at Schwechat ③ : 13 km by B 9 :

🏨 **Jesuitenmühle**, Werkbachgasse 30, ✉ A-2320 Schwechat, ☏ (0222) 77 71 23, Telex 135020, ⟳ – 🛗 📺 ⟿wc 🝢wc ☎ ⓟ ⚴. 🜄
M a la carte 150/220 (dinner only) ⌀ – **62 rm** 595/840 Bb.

🏨 **Reinisch**, Mannswörther Str. 76 (Mannswörth), ✉ A-2323 Schwechat, ☏ 77 72 90/77 82 18, 🌣 – 🝢wc ☎ ⓟ. 𝘝𝘐𝘚𝘈
closed 24 December - 6 January – **M** a la carte 100/210 – **36 rm** 430/700.

at Vienna-Schwechat airport ② : 20 km :

🏨 **Novotel Wien Airport** ⬧, ✉ A-1300 Schwechat, ☏ (0222) 77 66 66, Telex 111566, 🌣, ⌱ – 🛗 ▤ rest 📺 ⟿wc ☎ ⟐ ⚴ (with ▤). 🜄 ⑩ E 𝘝𝘐𝘚𝘈
M 125/270 – **127 rm** 900/1160 Bb.

at Groß-Enzersdorf E : 16 km, by Erzherzog-Karl-Str. R :

🏨 **Am Sachsengang**, Schloßhofer Str. 60 (B 3), ✉ A-2301 Groß-Enzersdorf, ☏ (02249) 29 01, Telex 13 62 36, « Terrace », Massage, ⟳, 🟦, ⟿ – ⟿wc ☎ ⟐ ⓟ ⚴. 🜄 E 𝘝𝘐𝘚𝘈
M a la carte 195/340 – **54 rm** 690/950 Bb.

at Baden ⑤ : 28 km by B 17 or A 2 — Spa — ❀ 02252 :

🏨 **Sauerhof zu Rauhenstein**, Weilburgstr. 11, ⊠ A-2500 Baden, ✆ 4 12 51, Telex 14334, ☆, Massage, ⚓, ≦s, ☒, ⚓, ✇ — 🛗 �📺 ❻ 🄿 ⚐. ⒶⒺ ⓄⒹ E
M a la carte 108/445 — **87 rm** 1000/1400 Bb.

🏨 **Parkhotel**, Kaiser-Franz-Ring 5, ⊠ A-2500 Baden, ✆ 4 43 86, Telex 14461, ☆, Massage, ⚓, ≦s, ☒, 🌸 — 🛗 ⌖wc ☎ ⟸ 🄿. ⒶⒺ ⓄⒹ E 𝖵𝖨𝖲𝖠 ✻ rest
M a la carte 150/310 — **90 rm** 830/1290 Bb.

🏨 Gutenbrunn ⤢, Pelzgasse 22, ✆ A-2500 Baden, ✆ 4 81 71, Telex 14304, ☆, direct entrance to the spa-centre — 🛗 ⌖wc ☎ 🄿 ⚐. ✻ rest
90 rm Bb.

🏨 **Krainerhütte**, Helenental (W : 6 km), ⊠ A-2500 Baden, ✆ 4 45 11, Telex 14303, ☆, ≦s, ☒, 🌸, ✇ — 🛗 ⌖wc �🌀wc ☎ 🄿 ⚐. ⒶⒺ ⓄⒹ E
M a la carte 170/460 — **67 rm** 800/1320 Bb.

at motorway A 1 W : 30 km :

🏨 **Motor-Hotel Grossram**, ⊠ A-3033 Großram, ✆ (02773) 66 51, Telex 15692 — 🛗 📺 ⌖wc ☎ ❻ 🄿 ⚐. ⒶⒺ ⓄⒹ E 𝖵𝖨𝖲𝖠
M a la carte 143/275 — **42 rm** 560/740.

SALZBURG 5020. Austria 𝟿𝟾𝟽 ㉝. 𝟺𝟸𝟼 ⑲ ⑳ — pop. 140 000 — alt. 425 m — ❀ 0662.

See : Site (Stadtbild)★★ EY **K** — Hohensalzburg★★ : ≤★★ (from the Künberg Bastion) FZ — St. Peter's Churchyard (Petersfriedhof)★★ EFZ — St. Peter's Church (Stiftskirche St. Peter)★★ EZ — Residenz★★ EFZ — Natural History Museum (Haus der Natur)★★ EY **M2** — Franciscan's Church (Franziskanerkirche)★ EZ **A** — Getreidegasse★ EY — Mirabell Gardens (Mirabellgarten)★ CV — Hettwer Bastei★ : ≤★ FY — Castle and the Museum (Burg und Museum)★ : ☀★★ (from the Reck watch-tower) FZ **M3** — Mozart's Birthplace (Mozarts Geburtshaus) EY **D**.

Envir. : Road to the Gaisberg (Gaisbergstraße)★★ (≤★) by ① — Untersberg★ by ② : 10 km (with ⛷).

🛬 ✆ 71 54 14 22.

Exhibition Centre (Messegelände), Linke Glanzeile 65, ✆ 3 45 66.

🛈 Tourist Information (Stadtverkehrsbüro), Auerspergstr. 7, ✆ 7 15 11.

ÖAMTC, Alpenstr. 102, ✆ 2 05 01.

Wien 292 ① — Innsbruck 177 ③ — München 140 ③.

Plans on following pages

🏨 **Österreichischer Hof**, Schwarzstr. 5, ✆ 7 25 41, Telex 633590, « Salzach-side setting, terrace with ≤ old town and castle » — 🛗 📺 ⌖wc ⚐ (with ⌖) ⒶⒺ ⓄⒹ E   EY **b**
Restaurants : — **Roter Salon M** a la carte 200/460 — **Salzach Grill M** a la carte 110/350 — **125 rm** 980/2300.

🏨 **Salzburg Sheraton Hotel** Ⓜ, Auerspergstr. 4, ✆ 79 32 10, Telex 632518, entrance to the spa facilities — 🛗 ≡ 📺 ⚐. ⒶⒺ ⓄⒹ E 𝖵𝖨𝖲𝖠 ✻ rest   CV **s**
Restaurants : — **Mirabell M** a la carte 220/480 — **Bistro M** a la carte 75/200 — **165 rm** 1350/2150 Bb.

🏨 **Bristol**, Makartplatz 3, ✆ 7 35 57, Telex 633337 — 🛗 📺 ⒶⒺ ⓄⒹ. ✻ rest   EY **a**
March - 5 November — **M** a la carte 235/600 — **90 rm** 1520/3040 (half-board only).

🏨 **Goldener Hirsch**, Getreidegasse 37, ✆ 4 15 11/84 15 11, Telex 632967, « 15 C Patrician house, tastefully furnished » — 🛗 ≡ rest. ⒶⒺ ⓄⒹ E 𝖵𝖨𝖲𝖠   EY **e**
M a la carte 230/520 — **57 rm** 1300/3500.

🏨 **Winkler**, Franz-Josef-Str. 7, ✆ 7 35 13, Telex 633961 — 🛗 ⌖wc ☎. ⒶⒺ ⓄⒹ E 𝖵𝖨𝖲𝖠 CDV **f**
M a la carte 150/400 — **103 rm** 810/1800 Bb.

🏨 Europa, Rainerstr. 31, ✆ 7 33 91, Telex 633424, rest. on the 14th floor with ≤ Salzburg and environs — 🛗 ⌖wc �🌀wc ☎ 🄿 ⚐ (with ≡)   DV **s**
104 rm Bb.

🏨 **Pitter**, Rainerstr. 6, ✆ 7 85 71, Telex 633532, ☆ — 🛗 ⌖wc �🌀wc ☎ ⚐. ⒶⒺ ⓄⒹ E 𝖵𝖨𝖲𝖠. ✻ rest   CV **n**
M a la carte 100/310 — **220 rm** 500/1400.

🏨 **Kasererhof**, Alpenstr. 6, ✆ 2 12 65, Telex 633477, 🌸 — 🛗 📺 ⌖wc �🌀wc ☎ ❻ 🄿. ⒶⒺ E 𝖵𝖨𝖲𝖠   by ②
M *(closed Saturday and Sunday)* a la carte 160/380 — **51 rm** 700/2100 Bb.

🏨 **Hohenstauffen** without rest, Elisabethstr. 19, ✆ 7 21 93 — 🛗 ⌖wc �🌀wc ☎ ⟸. ⒶⒺ ⓄⒹ E 𝖵𝖨𝖲𝖠   CV **e**
28 rm 540/1190.

🏨 **Fuggerhof** without rest, Eberhard-Fugger-Str. 9, ✆ 2 04 79, ≤, ☒, 🌸 — ⌖wc �🌀wc ☎ ⟸ 🄿   by Bürglsteinstr. DX
closed December - 8 January — **13 rm** 490/1150.

🏠 **Schaffenrath**, Alpenstr. 115, ℰ 2 31 53, Telex 633207 – 🛗 🛏wc ▥wc ☎ 🅿 🏌. ÆE ⑩
E ▥. ❀ rm   by ②
M a la carte 90/240 – **50 rm** 550/980.

🏠 **Stieglbräu**, Rainerstr. 14, ℰ 7 76 92, Telex 633671, Garden – 🛗 🛏wc ▥wc ☎ 🅿 🏌.
ÆE ⑩ E ▥   CV **y**
M a la carte 100/280 – **50 rm** 490/1300.

🏠 **Wolf-Dietrich**, Wolf-Dietrich-Str. 7, ℰ 7 12 75, Telex 633877, ⇋, 🏊 – 🛗 🛏wc ▥wc
☎. ÆE ⑩ E ▥   DV **g**
M *(closed Sunday, January to March and November)* a la carte 140/340 – **32 rm** 390/1300.

XXX Café Winkler, Mönchsberg 32 (access by 🛗, 15 A.S.), ℰ 41 21 50, ≤ Salzburg, « Modern
café-rest. on the Mönchsberg, terraces » – 🏌   EY

XX **K u. K Restaurant am Waagplatz**, Waagplatz 2, ℰ 4 21 56, 😶, « Medieval dinner
with period performance in the Freysauff-Keller (by arrangement) » – ÆE ⑩ E ▥
M a la carte 125/365 (booking essential) 🍴.   FZ **h**

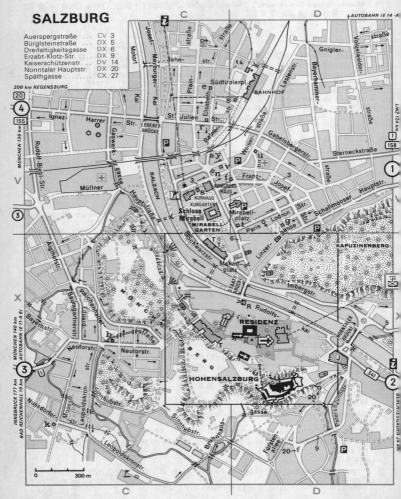

SALZBURG

Auerspergstraße . . . CV 3
Bürglsteinstraße . . . DX 5
Dreifaltigkeitsgasse . . DX 6
Erzabt-Klotz-Str. . . . DX 9
Kaiserschützenstr. . . DV 14
Nonntaler Hauptstr. . . DX 20
Späthgasse . . . . CX 27

XX   Das Beisl, Neutorstr. 28, ℰ 4 27 41   CX **b**
(booking essential).

XX   **Zum Mohren**, Judengasse 9, ℰ 4 23 87/84 23 87   FY **g**
closed Sunday, Bank Holidays and November — **M** a la carte 170/300 (booking essential).

at Salzburg-Flughafen 5035 by ③ :

🏨 **Flughafen-H.**, Innsbrucker Bundesstr. 105, ℰ 4 01 22, Telex 633671 — 🛗 🚿wc ☎ 🅿 🎿 AE ① E VISA
M a la carte 120/380 — **15 rm** 300/1000.

at Salzburg-Parsch by Bürglsteinstr. DX :

🏨🏨 **Fondachhof** ⌖, Gaisbergstr. 46, ℰ 2 09 06, Telex 632519, ≤, « 18 C Manor house in a park », ≘s, 🏊, 🦅 — 🛗 TV ☎ 🅿 AE ① E VISA
15 March - October — (Rest. for residents only) — **30 rm** 800/2250.

🏨🏨 **Cottage**, Joseph-Messner-Str. 12, ℰ 2 45 71, Telex 632011, Massage, ≘s, 🏊 — 🛗 TV 🚿wc ☎ 🅿 🎿 AE ① E VISA
M a la carte 170/340 — **104 rm** 750/1840 Bb.

🏨🏨 **Haus Ingeborg** ⌖ without rest, Sonnleitenweg 9, ℰ 2 17 49, Telex 631141, ≤ town and Hohensalzburg, ≘s, 🏊, 🦅 — TV 🚿wc ☎ 🅿 AE ①
March-October — **11 rm** 1200/3200.

on the Heuberg NE : 3 km by ① — alt. 565 m :

🏨 **Schöne Aussicht**, ⊠ 5023 Salzburg, ℰ (0662) 7 82 26, « Garden with ≤ Salzburg and Alps », ≘s, 🏊, 🦅, 🍴 — 🚿wc 🚿wc ☎ 🅿 🎿 AE ①
March-October — **M** a la carte 100/350 — **30 rm** 460/840 Bb.

on the Gaisberg by ① :

🏨 **Kobenzl** 🍽, Judenbergalpe (E : 9 km alt. 750 m), ✉ 5020 Salzburg, ☎ (0662) 2 17 76, Telex 633833, 🍴, « Beautiful panoramic-location with ≤ Salzburg and Alps », 🛁, 🔳 – 📺 🚗 🅿 🅰 🅰🅴 🎿 rest
end March - mid November — **M** a la carte 210/475 — **38 rm** 1200/2800 Bb.

🏨 **Berghotel Zistel-Alm** 🍽, (E : 12 km alt. 1 001 m), ✉ 5025 Salzburg-Aigen, ☎ (0662) 2 01 04, ≤ Alps, 🍴, 🔳, 🚗 – 🚾 🛁wc ☎ 🚗 🅿 🅰🅴 ⑩
closed November - 22 December — **M** a la carte 95/280 — **24 rm** 210/790.

at Anif 5081 by ② : 7 km :

🏨 **Romantik-H. Schloßwirt** (17 C inn with Biedermeier furniture), ☎ (06246) 21 75, Telex 631169, « Garden », 🚗 – 🛗 🚾wc 🛁wc ☎ 🚗 🅿 🅰🅴 ⑩ 🅴 𝗩𝗜𝗦𝗔
closed February — **M** a la carte 180/350 — **35 rm** 490/1050 Bb.

🏨 **Friesacher**, ☎ (06246) 20 75, Telex 632943, « Garden », 🚗, 🍴 – 🛗 🚾wc 🛁wc ☎ 🅿 🛁 ⑩
M *(closed Wednesday September - May)* a la carte 95/280 — **70 rm** 420/910.

Benelux

Belgium

Brussels
Antwerp
Bruges

Luxembourg

Netherlands

Amsterdam
The Hague
Rotterdam

PRACTICAL INFORMATION

LOCAL CURRENCY
Belgian Franc : 100 F = 1.574 US $ (Jan. 85) can also be used in Luxembourg
Dutch Florin : 100 Fl. = 27.914 US $ (Jan. 85)

TOURIST INFORMATION
In Belgium : The B.B.B. Tourist House, rue du Marché-aux-Herbes 61, Brussels, open from 9am to 6pm (Sundays 1 to 5pm) in winter, and 9am to 8pm (weekends 9am to 7pm) in Summer.
In the Netherlands : Offices in Amsterdam open daily from 9am to 11.30pm ; in Den Haag (Scheveningen) weekdays from 9am to 9pm, Sundays 9am to 6pm, and in Rotterdam weekdays 9am to 6pm, Sundays 10am to 6pm.

FOREIGN EXCHANGE
In Belgium, banks close at 3.30pm and weekends ; **in the Netherlands,** banks close at 5.00pm and weekends, Schiphol Airport exchange offices open daily from 6.30am to 11.30pm.

TRANSPORT
Taxis : may be hailed in the street, found day and night at taxi ranks or called by telephone.
Bus, tramway : practical for long and short distances and good for sightseeing.

POSTAL SERVICES
Post offices open Monday to Friday from 9am to 5pm in Benelux.

SHOPPING
Shops and boutiques are generally open from 8am to 7pm in Belgium and Luxembourg, and from 9am to 6pm in the Netherlands. The main shopping areas are :
in Brussels : Rue Neuve, Porte de Namur, Avenue Louise - Second-hand goods and antiques : Brussels antique market on Saturday from 9am to 3pm, and Sunday from 9am to 1pm (around place du Grand-Sablon) - Flower market (Grand-Place) on Sunday morning.
in Antwerp : Bird Market : Sunday 8.30am to 1pm - Antwerp diamond quarter.
in Bruges : Calashes on the Market Place for shopping and town sightseeing.
in Amsterdam : Kalverstraat, Leidsestraat, Nieuwendijk, P.C. Hoofstraat and Utrechtsestraat. Second-hand goods and antiques. Amsterdam Flea Market (near Waterlooplein).
in Den Haag : Hoogstraat, Karte Poten, Paleispromenade, De Passage and Spuistraat.
in Rotterdam : Binnenweg, Hoogstraat, Karel Doormonstraat, Lijnbaan and Stadthuisplein.

BREAKDOWN SERVICE
RACB : rue d'Arlon 53, Brussels ✆ (02) 230 08 68 and **TCB :** rue de la Loi 44, Brussels ✆ (02) 233 22 11 operate a 24 hour breakdown service. In the Netherlands, **ANWB**-Wegenwacht also offer 24 hour assistance.

TIPPING
In Benelux, prices include service and taxes. You may choose to leave a tip if you wish but there is no obligation to do so.

SPEED LIMITS
In Belgium and Luxembourg, the maximum speed limits are 120 km/h-74 mph on motorways and dual carriageways, 90 km/h-56 mph on all other roads and 60 km/h-37 mph in built-up areas. In the Netherlands, 100 km/h-62 mph on motorways and "autowegen", 80 km/h-50 mph on other roads and 50 km/h-31 mph in built-up areas.

SEAT BELTS
In each country, the wearing of seat belts is compulsory.

BRUSSELS

SIGHTS

See : Market Square★★★ (Grand-Place) LZ – Manneken Pis★★ KZ – Rue des Bouchers LZ – St. Michael's Cathedral★★ FU – Place du Grand Sablon★ and the Church
of Notre-Dame du Sablon★ FVD – Anderlecht : Erasmus's House★.

Museums : Old Masters Gallery★★★ (Musée d'Art ancien : Brueghel) FV – Royal
museum of Art and History★★★ (antiques, Belgian decorative art) – Musical Instru-
ments★★ FV M18.

Env. Forest of Soignes★★ – Tervuren : Royal Museum of Central Africa★ ⑥ : 13 km
– Beersel : Castle★ S : 11 km – Gaasbeek : estate and castle★ SW : 12 km by rue
de Lennick – Meise : Bouchout Estate★(Domaine de Bouchout) : Plant Palace★★ by
① : 13 km – Grimbergen : Confessional★ in the church of St. Servais (St. Servaas-
kerk) by ① : 18 km – Vilvoorde : Choir stalls★ of Our Lady's Church (O.L. Vrouwkerk).

BRUSSELS **(Bruxelles - Brussel) 1000** Brabant **213** ⑱ and **409** ⑬ – Pop. 982 434
agglomeration – ✆ 02.

🛢 🛢 Château de Ravenstein at Tervuren by ⑥ : 13 km ✆ 7675801.

✈ National NE : 12 km ✆ 7518080 – **Air Terminal :** Air Terminus, r. du Cardinal-Mercier 35 LZ
✆ 5119060.

🚗 ✆ 2186050 ext. 4106.

🛈 r. du Marché-aux-Herbes 61 ✆ 5138940 – Tourist Association of the Province, r. Marché-aux-Herbes 61 ✆ 5130750.
Paris 308 ⑨ – Amsterdam 204 ① – Düsseldorf 222 ⑤ – Lille 116 ⑫ – Luxembourg 219 ⑦.

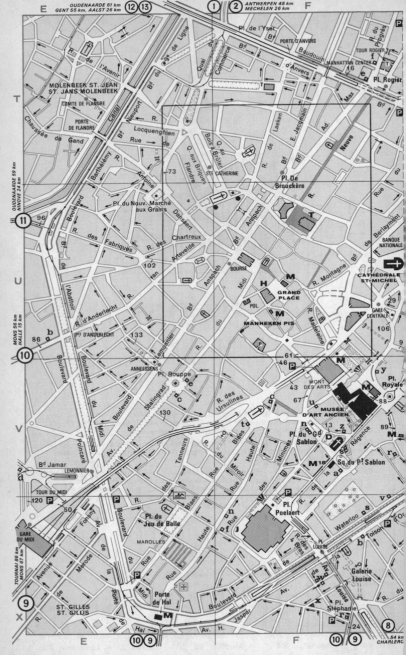

BRUXELLES
BRUSSEL
CENTRE

Room prices are subject to the addition of a local tax of 6%

Centre

North (Porte d'Anvers, Place Rogier) FT :

🏨🏨 **Brussels-Sheraton** Ⓜ, pl. Rogier 3, ⊠ 1000, ℰ 2193400, Telex 26887, ⬜ – |≣| ▤ 📺 ☎
  🔥 ⟨◯⟩ – 🔼. 🄰🄴 ⓪ 💳 *VISA*
FT e
M a la carte 600/1200 – ☲ 390 – **483 rm** and **43** apartments 3900/5800.

🏨 **New Hotel Siru and Rest. Le Couvert,** pl. Rogier 1, ⊠ 1000, ℰ 2177580 and
2178308 (rest.), Telex 21722 – |≣| 📺 ⟨◯⟩wc 🗋wc 🄰🄴 ⓪. ⁒
FT f
M *(closed Saturday dinner and Sunday)* 995 – **100 rm** ⬤ 1895/2670 – P 2715/3275.

North (Botanique, Porte de Schaerbeek) GHT :

🏨🏨 **Hyatt Regency Brussels** Ⓜ, r. Royale 250, ⊠ 1030, ℰ 2194640, Telex 61871 – |≣| ▤
📺 ☎ 🔥 ⟨◯⟩ – 🔼. 🄰🄴 ⓪ 💳 *VISA*. ⁒ rest
GT r
M 790/1190 – ☲ 375 – **315 rm** 4025/5195.

XX **Den Botaniek,** r. Royale 328, ⊠ 1030, ℰ 2184838, 🌤, « Garden-terrace » – 🄰🄴 ⓪ 💳
VISA
GT n
closed Saturday, Sunday and 21 December-1 January – **M** a la carte 1270/1750.

Town Centre (Bourse, Grand'Place, Pl. de Brouckère, Ste-Catherine)

🏨🏨🏨 **Amigo,** r. Amigo 1, ⊠ 1000, ℰ 5115910, Telex 21618, « Tasteful decor » – |≣| ▤ rest 📺
☎ ⟨◯⟩ – 🔼. 🄰🄴 ⓪ 💳 *VISA*. ⁒ rest
KZ h
M a la carte 650/1120 – **183 rm** ☲ 3300/4750.

🏨🏨 **Royal Windsor H.** Ⓜ, r. Duquesnoy 5, ⊠ 1000, ℰ 5114215, Telex 62905 – |≣| ▤ 📺 ☎
⟨◯⟩ – 🔼. 🄰🄴 ⓪ 💳 *VISA*. ⁒
LZ k
M a la carte 1230/1930 – **300 rm** ☲ 5100/5980.

🏨🏨 **Jolly H. Atlanta** without rest., bd A.-Max 7, ⊠ 1000, ℰ 2170120, Telex 21475 – |≣| 📺
☎ ⟨◯⟩ – 🔼. 🄰🄴 ⓪ 💳 *VISA*
LY a
242 rm ☲ 3300/4875.

🏨🏨 **Président Nord** without rest., bd A.-Max 107, ⊠ 1000, ℰ 2190060, Telex 61417 – |≣| 📺
🄰🄴 ⓪ 💳 *VISA*
LY b
63 rm ☲ 2330/2760.

🏨🏨 **Bedford,** r. Midi 135, ⊠ 1000, ℰ 5127840, Telex 24059 – |≣| ▤ rest 📺 ☎ ⟨◯⟩ – 🔼. 🄰🄴
LY – *VISA*. ⁒
KZ r
M 650 – **250 rm** ☲ 2525/3410.

🏨 **Arenberg** Ⓜ without rest., r. d'Assaut 15, ⊠ 1000, ℰ 5110770, Telex 25660 – |≣| 📺
⟨◯⟩wc 🗋wc ☎. 🄰🄴 ⓪ 💳 *VISA*. ⁒
LZ p
155 rm ☲ 2500/3200.

🏠 **Sainte-Catherine** Ⓜ without rest., r. Joseph Plateau 2 (Pl. Ste-Catherine), ⊠ 1000, ℰ
5137620, Telex 22476 – |≣| 🗋wc ☎ 🔥. *VISA*
KY s
⬤ 150 – **234 rm** 1530/1780.

🏠 **Queen Anne** without rest., bd Émile-Jacqmain 110, ⊠ 1000, ℰ 2171600 – |≣| ⟨◯⟩wc ☎.
🄰🄴 ⓪ 💳 *VISA*
LY y
60 rm ☲ 1325/1765.

🏠 **La Légende,** r. Etuve 33, ⊠ 1000, ℰ 5128290 – |≣| ⟨◯⟩wc ☎
KZ p
closed 13 December-January – **M** *(closed Wednesday)* a la carte 510/700 – **31 rm** ⬤
880/1180.

XXXX ❀❀ **Maison du Cygne,** Grand'Place 9, ⊠ 1000, ℰ 5118244, « Ancient mansion, elegant
decor » – |≣| 🄰🄴 ⓪ 💳 *VISA*
LZ q
closed 13 to 18 August, Christmas-New Year, Saturday lunch and Sunday – **M** a la carte
1450/2300
Spec. Potée de crustacés, Salade de solettes au jus de truffes, Dos d'agneau façon du Cygne.

XXX **Huîtrière,** quai aux Briques 20, ⊠ 1000, ℰ 5120866, Seafood – 🄰🄴 ⓪ 💳 *VISA*
KY v
M a la carte 1400/1850.

XXX **Cheval Marin,** Marché-aux-Porcs 25, ⊠ 1000, ℰ 5130287, Ancient decor – 🄰🄴 ⓪ 💳
VISA
KY u
closed Sunday dinner – **M** a la carte 880/1600.

XXX **Café de Paris,** r. Vierge Noire 12, ⊠ 1000, ℰ 5123940 – 🄰🄴 ⓪ 💳 *VISA*
KY x
closed Saturday lunch, Sunday and 15 July-14 August – **M** 1075/1675.

XXX **Ravenstein,** r. Ravenstein 1, ⊠ 1000, ℰ 5127768, 🌤, « 15C manor house » – 🄰🄴 ⓪ 💳
VISA
FV y
closed Saturday lunch, Sunday and August – **M** a la carte 1030/1330.

XXX **Filet de Boeuf,** r. Harengs 8, ⊠ 1000, ℰ 5119559, « Old Brussels decor » – 🄰🄴 ⓪ 💳
VISA
LZ s
closed Saturday lunch, Sunday and August – **M** a la carte 1500/1820.

XX ❀ **Sirène d'Or** (Van Duuren), pl. Ste-Catherine 1 a, ⊠ 1000, ℰ 5135198 – 🄰🄴 ⓪ 💳 *VISA*
KY n
closed Sunday, Monday, July and 23 to 27 December – **M** a la carte 1200/1780
Spec. Fricassée de sole et ris de veau aux jets de houblon (March-April), Bouillabaisse, Escalopes de
homard sautées au gingembre.

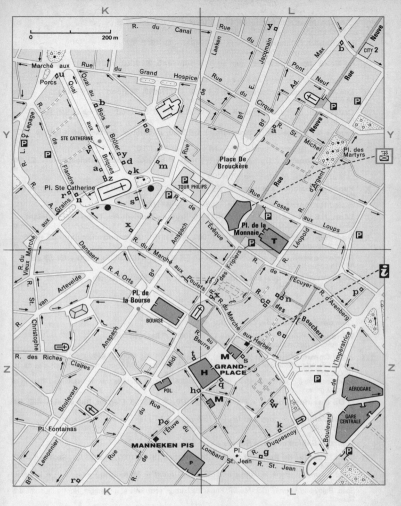

XX **Bon Vieux Temps,** 1st floor, r. Marché-aux-Herbes 12, ⊠ 1000, ☎ 2181546, « Ancient Brussels residence » – AE ⓪ E
closed Saturday lunch, Sunday and July – **M** 595/995.
LZ **x**

XX **Tête d'Or,** r. Tête d'Or 9, ⊠ 1000, ☎ 5110201, « Old Brussels decor » – AE ⓪ E *VISA*
closed Saturday, Sunday and 20 July-8 August – **M** a la carte 1230/1930.
KZ **t**

XX **Éperon d'Or,** r. Éperonniers 8, ⊠ 1000, ☎ 5125239 – AE ⓪ E *VISA*
closed Saturday, Sunday and 21 July-14 August – **M** 500/1000.
LZ **w**

XX **Perraudin,** r. St-Jean 49, ⊠ 1000, ☎ 5111388 – AE ⓪ E
closed Sunday dinner, Monday and August – **M** 900.
LZ **g**

XX **Serge et Anne,** r. Peuplier 23, ⊠ 1000, ☎ 2181662 – AE ⓪
closed Wednesday and August – **M** a la carte 760/1200.
KY **e**

XX **Chez François,** quai aux Briques 2, ⊠ 1000, ☎ 5116089, Seafood – AE ⓪ E *VISA*
closed Monday and June – **M** a la carte 830/1460.
KY **z**

XX **Rôtiss. Au Cochon d'Or,** quai au Bois-à-Brûler 15, ⊠ 1000, ☎ 2180771 – AE ⓪ E
closed Sunday dinner, Monday and September – **M** 600/1100.
KY **y**

XX **L'Ami Michel,** pl. du Samedi 17, ⊠ 1000, ℰ 2175377 – 🖭 **E**   KY **m**
closed Sunday and Monday – **M** a la carte 1300/1620.

XX **Le Chablis,** r.Flandre 6, ⊠ 1000, ℰ 5124631 – 🖭 ⓪ **E** 𝐕𝐈𝐒𝐀   KY **r**
closed Saturday lunch and Sunday – **M** 650/1460.

XX **Le Saint Jean des Prés,** quai au Bois-à-Brûler 5, ⊠ 1000, ℰ 2185901 – 🖭 ⓪ **E** 𝐕𝐈𝐒𝐀
🦐   KY **d**
closed Sunday dinner – **M** a la carte 750/1120.

XX **Les Algues,** pl. Ste-Catherine 15, ⊠ 1000, ℰ 2179012, Seafood – 🖭 ⓪ **E** 𝐕𝐈𝐒𝐀   KY **k**
M 675.

XX **Crustacés,** quai aux Briques 8, ⊠ 1000, ℰ 5131493, Seafood – 🖭 ⓪ **E** 𝐕𝐈𝐒𝐀. 🦐
M a la carte 770/1400.   KY **a**

X **Armes de Bruxelles,** r. Bouchers 13, ⊠ 1000, ℰ 5115598, Brussels atmosphere – 🖭
⓪ **E** 𝐕𝐈𝐒𝐀   LZ **c**
closed Monday and 5 June-4 July – **M** a la carte 740/1280.

X **Rôtiss. Vincent,** r. Dominicains 8, ⊠ 1000, ℰ 5112302, Brussels atmosphere – 🖭 ⓪
E 𝐕𝐈𝐒𝐀   LZ **n**
closed August – **M** a la carte 570/1100.

X **Passage,** Galerie de la Reine 30, ⊠ 1000, ℰ 5123731, Pub rest., Brussels atmosphere –
🖭 ⓪ **E** 𝐕𝐈𝐒𝐀   LZ **e**
closed Wednesday and Thursday in June-July – **M** 500/950.

X **Léon,** r. Bouchers 18, ⊠ 1000, ℰ 5111415, Brussels atmosphere, Open until midnight
M a la carte 540/930.   LZ **c**

X **Ogenblik,** Galerie des Princes 1, ⊠ 1000, ℰ 5116151, Open until midnight – 🖭 ⓪ **E**
closed Sunday – **M** a la carte 1040/1530.   LZ **n**

X **Marie-Joseph,** quai au Bois-à-Brûler 47, ⊠ 1000, ℰ 2180596, Seafood – 🖭 ⓪ 𝐕𝐈𝐒𝐀
M a la carte 1050/1200.   KY **b**

X **Rugbyman Nr 1,** quai aux Briques 4, ⊠ 1000, ℰ 5125640, Shellfish – 🖃   KY **z**
M a la carte 980/1940.

Centre South

Quartier Place Rouppe, Lemonnier EV :

🏠 **Windsor** without rest., pl. Rouppe 13, ⊠ 1000, ℰ 5112014 – 🛗   EV **e**
closed Christmas-New Year – **24 rm** 🖙 1020/1625.

XXX ❀❀❀ **Comme Chez Soi** (Wynants), pl. Rouppe 23, ⊠ 1000, ℰ 5122921 – 🖃. 🖭 ⓪
closed Sunday, Monday, July and Christmas-New Year – **M** (booking essential) a la carte   EV **c**
1650/2200
Spec. Consommé glacé d'écrevisses à la citronnelle (July-August), Filets de sole, mousseline au Riesling et
crevettes grises.

XXX ❀ **Da Gesuino** (Todde), r. Fiennes 3, ⊠ 1070, ℰ 5215163, Elegant, Italian rest. – 🖭 ⓪
E   EV **d**
closed Saturday, Sunday and 19 July-18 August – **M** a la carte 980/1690
Spec. Raviolis de homard, Sole florentine, Foie de veau.

Quartier Sablon et Place Royale FV :

XXX ❀❀ **L'Écailler du Palais Royal,** r. Bodenbroek 18, ⊠ 1000, ℰ 5128751, Seafood – 🖭
⓪ **E** 𝐕𝐈𝐒𝐀   FV **z**
closed Sunday, Bank Holidays and 29 July-August – **M** (booking essential) a la carte
1350/2400
Spec. Huîtres au Vouvray (Oct.-March), Étuvée de barbue, écrevisses et gingembre, Rizotto de homard à
l'absinthe.

XXX ❀ **Chez Christopher,** pl. Chapelle 5, ⊠ 1000, ℰ 5126891, early 20C – 🖭 ⓪ **E** 𝐕𝐈𝐒𝐀
closed Saturday, Sunday, Bank Holidays, Christmas-New Year and 5 to 26 August – **M** a   FV **t**
la carte 1400/2100
Spec. Langoustines à notre façon, Escalope de saumon poêlée au miel et au limon, Magret de canard à la
Kriek et aux cerises du nord.

XXX **Les Gourmands,** pl. Grand Sablon 39a (village gourmand), ⊠ 1000, ℰ 5136749, In a
luxury shopping centre – 🖃. 🖭 ⓪ **E** 𝐕𝐈𝐒𝐀   FV **n**
closed Saturday lunch, Sunday and mid July-mid August – **M** a la carte 1840/2320.

XXX **Debussy,** pl. Petit Sablon 2, ⊠ 1000, ℰ 5128041 – 🖭 ⓪ **E** 𝐕𝐈𝐒𝐀   FV **s**
closed Saturday lunch, Sunday, Bank Holidays and 6 July-6 August – **M** a la carte
1270/2000.

XXX **En Provence,** pl. Petit-Sablon 1, ⊠ 1000, ℰ 5111208, Rustic – 🖃. 🖭 ⓪   FV **s**
closed Sunday – **M** a la carte 1350/2000.

XX **Au Duc d'Arenberg,** pl. Petit-Sablon 9, ⊠ 1000, ℰ 5111475, Rustic Pub-rest. – 🖭 ⓪
𝐕𝐈𝐒𝐀   FV **a**
M a la carte 1350/1800.

✗ ❀ **Trente rue de la Paille,** r. Paille 30, ✉ 1000, ☎ 5120715 – 🆎 ⓘ **E** 𝗩𝗜𝗦𝗔 FV **u**
closed Saturday lunch, Sunday, Bank Holidays and July – **M** a la carte 1130/1560.

✗ **Les Années Folles,** r. Haute 17, ✉ 1000, ☎ 5135858 – 🆎 ⓘ **E** FV **c**
closed Saturday lunch and Sunday – **M** 800/1050.

✗ **Au Vieux Saint-Martin,** Grand Sablon 38, ✉ 1000, ☎ 5126476, Pub-rest., Open until
midnight FV **n**
M a la carte 730/1000.

✗ **J. et B.,** r. Baudet 5, ✉ 1000, ☎ 5120484, Open until 11 p.m. – 🆎 ⓘ **E** 𝗩𝗜𝗦𝗔 FV **r**
closed Saturday lunch, Sunday, 21 to 28 July and 11 to 18 August – **M** 625/950.

Quartier Porte Louise, Palais Justice, Place Stéphanie FX :

🏨 **Hilton International Brussels** Ⓜ, bd Waterloo 38, ✉ 1000, ☎ 5138877, Telex 22744,
« Rest. of 27th floor with ≤ on town » – 🛗 ▤ 📺 🅿 🕭 ⇔ – 🔬. 🆎 ⓘ **E** 𝗩𝗜𝗦𝗔. ⁒ rest
M a la carte 1340/1960 – ⊻ 410 – **369 rm** 4100/5550. FX **s**

🏨 **Ramada-Brussels** Ⓜ, chaussée de Charleroi 38, ✉ 1060, ☎ 5393000, Telex 25539 – 🛗
▤ 📺 ☎ – 🔬. 🆎 ⓘ **E** 𝗩𝗜𝗦𝗔
M *(closed Sunday)* a la carte 1240/1700 – ⊻ 365 – **201 rm** 3150/3850.

🏨 **Ascot** without rest., pl. Loix 1, ✉ 1060, ☎ 5388835, Telex 25010 – 🛗 ☎. 🆎 ⓘ **E**. ⁒
58 rm ⊻ 1600/2000.

🏨 **Delta** Ⓜ without rest., chaussée de Charleroi 17, ✉ 1060, ☎ 5390160, Telex 63225 – 🛗
📺 ⇌wc ☎ ⇔ – 🔬. 🆎 ⓘ **E** 𝗩𝗜𝗦𝗔 FX **r**
254 rm ⊻ 2250/2850.

🏨 **Diplomat** Ⓜ without rest., r. Jean-Stas 32, ✉ 1060, ☎ 5374250, Telex 61012 – 🛗 📺
⇌wc ☎. 🆎 ⓘ **E** 𝗩𝗜𝗦𝗔. ⁒ FX **x**
68 rm ⊻ 2250/2850.

🏨 **La Cascade** without rest., r. Source 14, ✉ 1060, ☎ 5388830, Telex 26637 – 🛗 📺 ⇌wc
☎ ⇔ 🅿 – 🔬. 🆎 ⓘ **E** 𝗩𝗜𝗦𝗔. ⁒
42 rm ⊻ 2025/2515.

✗✗✗✗✗ ❀ **Carlton** bd Waterloo 28, ✉ 1000, ☎ 5137831, « Luxurious decor, fountain visible
wine cellar » – ▤. 🆎 ⓘ **E** 𝗩𝗜𝗦𝗔 FX **v**
closed Saturday lunch, Sunday and mid July-mid August – **M** a la carte 2040/3140.

✗✗ **La Closerie,** r. Jourdan 15, ✉ 1060, ☎ 5381448 FX **w**
closed 21 July-14 August – **M** a la carte 1100/1400.

✗✗ **Cheval Blanc,** r. Haute 204, ✉ 1000, ☎ 5123771 – 🆎 ⓘ **E** 𝗩𝗜𝗦𝗔. ⁒ FX **n**
closed Sunday dinner – **M** a la carte 830/1140.

✗✗ **Al Piccolo Mondo,** r. Jourdan 19, ✉ 1060, ☎ 5388794, Italian rest. – 🆎 ⓘ **E** 𝗩𝗜𝗦𝗔
M a la carte 750/1260. FX **w**

✗✗ **Meo Patacca,** r. Jourdan 20, ✉ 1060, ☎ 5381546, Italian rest., Open until 1 a.m. – 🆎
ⓘ **E** 𝗩𝗜𝗦𝗔 FX **w**
closed Sunday – **M** a la carte 820/1400.

✗ **Au Beurre Blanc,** r.Faucon 2a, ✉ 1000, ☎ 5130111 – 🆎 ⓘ **E** FX **f**
closed Saturday lunch, Sunday, Easter, last two weeks August and Christmas-New Year –
M a la carte 770/1480.

Quartier Porte de Namur, Luxembourg, Palais des Académies GV :

✗✗✗ **Bernard,** 1st floor, r. Namur 93, ✉ 1000, ☎ 5128821, Seafood – 🆎 ⓘ GV **c**
closed Saturday, Monday dinner, Bank Holidays and July – **M** a la carte 1050/1750.

✗✗ **Marie-José ''Chez Callens''** with rm, r. Commerce 73, ✉ 1040, ☎ 5120843 – 🛗
⇌wc 🛁wc ⇔. 🆎 ⓘ **E** 𝗩𝗜𝗦𝗔 GV **x**
M *(closed Saturday dinner and Sunday)* a la carte 690/1090 – **17 rm** ⊻ 850/1600.

Quartier Porte de Namur (côté Tour), Quartier St. Boniface GX :

✗✗ **Charles-Joseph,** r. E. Solvay 9, ✉ 1050, ☎ 5134390 – 🆎 ⓘ **E** 𝗩𝗜𝗦𝗔 GX **r**
closed Saturday lunch, Sunday and August – **M** 850/1450.

✗✗ **Old Mario,** r. Alsace Lorraine 44, ✉ 1050, ☎ 5116161, Italian rest. – 🅿. 🆎 ⓘ **E** 𝗩𝗜𝗦𝗔
closed Saturday and Sunday – **M** a la carte approx. 1400. GX **e**

Centre East

Quartier St.Josse, Square Marie-Louise, Square Ambiorix, Cité Eu HU :

🏨 **Charlemagne** without rest., bd Charlemagne 25, ✉ 1040, ☎ 2302135, Telex 22772 – 🛗
⇌wc ☎ – 🔬 HU **a**
62 rm.

✗✗ **Gigotin,** r. Stevin 102, ✉ 1040, ☎ 2303091, ⌖ – 🆎 ⓘ **E** HU **n**
closed Saturday, Sunday, Bank Holidays and 15 July-15 August – **M** a la carte 750/1080.

Rue de la Loi, Quartier Schuman, Quartier Léopold HV :

🏨 **Brussels Europa H.** Ⓜ, r. de la Loi 107, ✉ 1040, ☎ 2301333, Telex 25121 – 🛗 ▤ 📺 ☎
🅿 – 🔬. 🆎 ⓘ **E** 𝗩𝗜𝗦𝗔. ⁒ rest HV **s**
M *(closed Saturday, Sunday and August)* a la carte 1000/1500 – ⊻ 315 – **240 rm**
3065/4035.

Quartier Cité Administrative, Madou, Parc de Bruxelles GU :

🏨🏨 **Astoria and Rest. Palais Royal,** r. Royale 103, ✉ 1000, 𝒫 2176290, Telex 25040 – 🛗
📺 ☎ – 🚇 . 🖭 ⓸ Ɛ 𝓥𝓘𝓢𝓐 . 🍽 rest
GTU **b**
M *(closed Saturday, Sunday and Bank Holidays)* 880/1150 – ⌑ 300 – **125 rm** 2750/3555
– P 4250.

🏨🏨 **Président Centre** 🅼 without rest., r. Royale 160, ✉ 1000, 𝒫 2190065, Telex 26784 – 🛗
🖿 📺 ☎ . 🖭 ⓸ Ɛ 𝓥𝓘𝓢𝓐
GU **a**
73 rm ⌑ 2550/2760.

🏨🏨 **City Garden** 🅼 without rest., with suites, r. Joseph II 59, ✉ 1040, 𝒫 2300945, Telex
63570 – 🛗 📺 ☎ ⟵ . 🖭 𝓥𝓘𝓢𝓐 . 🍽
GU **r**
🛏 150 – **96 rm** 1920/2475.

🏢 **Congrès and Rest. Le Carrousel,** r. Congrès 42, ✉ 1000, 𝒫 2171890 – 🛗 📥wc 🛗
. 🖭 ⓸ Ɛ 𝓥𝓘𝓢𝓐
GU **c**
M a la carte 1000/1300 – **38 rm** ⌑ 690/1190 – P 1740.

🏢 **Résidence Sabina** without rest., r. Nord 78, ✉ 1000, 𝒫 2182637 – 🛗 ☎
GU **e**
16 rm ⌑ 680/1050.

XXX **Astrid ''Chez Pierrot'',** r. de la Presse 21, ✉ 1000, 𝒫 2173831, Classic – 🖭 ⓸ Ɛ 𝓥𝓘𝓢𝓐
closed Sunday, Easter and 15 July-14 August – **M** a la carte 750/1400.
GU **d**

Suburbs

North

Quartier Basilique (Koekelberg, Ganshoren, Jette) :

XXX ✿✿ **Dupont,** av. Vital-Riethuisen 46, ✉ 1080, 𝒫 4275450, Classic-elegant – 🖭 ⓸ Ɛ
closed Monday, Tuesday and mid July-mid August – **M** a la carte 1230/1950
Spec. Beurrée d'huîtres sur chiffonade de witloof (September-April), Aiguillettes de pigeonneau aux baies
de genévrier, Râble de lièvre au thym frais (15 October-10 January).

XXX ✿✿ **Bruneau,** av. Broustin 73, ✉ 1080, 𝒫 4276978, Classic-elegant – 🖭 ⓸ Ɛ 𝓥𝓘𝓢𝓐
*closed holiday Thursdays, Tuesday dinner, Wednesday, mid June-mid July and Christmas-
New Year* – **M** a la carte 1770/2600
Spec. Saumon au gros sel, Viennoise de turbot, Dos de lapereau en croûte.

XXX **Park Side,** av. Panthéon 4, ✉ 1080, 𝒫 4242482, Classic-elegant – 🖭 ⓸ Ɛ 𝓥𝓘𝓢𝓐
closed Sunday dinner, Monday and 15 August-1 September – **M** a la carte 1040/1330.

XXX **Au Chaudron d'Or,** Drève du Château 71, ✉ 1080, 𝒫 4283737, « Converted farm-
house » – ℗ . 🖭 ⓸ Ɛ 𝓥𝓘𝓢𝓐 . 🍽
closed Sunday dinner and Monday – **M** a la carte 1390/1920.

XX ✿ **Le Sermon** (Kobs), av. Jacques-Sermon 91, ✉ 1090, 𝒫 4268935 – 🖭 Ɛ
closed Sunday, Monday and 25 June-29 July – **M** carte 1280/1800
Spec. Moules au champagne (September-March), Sole Sermon.

XX **Pannenhuis,** r. Léopold-1er 317, ✉ 1090, 𝒫 4258373, « Converted 17C inn » – 🖭 ⓸ Ɛ
𝓥𝓘𝓢𝓐
M a la carte 1020/1750.

XX **Cambrils,** av. Charles-Quint 365, ✉ 1080, 𝒫 4669582, �ある – 🖿
closed Sunday and 2 July-2 August – **M** 425/1070.

Quartier Centenaire and Atomium (Laeken, Wemmel, Strombeek-Bever) :

XXX **De Kam,** chaussée de Bruxelles 7, ✉ 1810, 𝒫 4600374, Rustic – ℗ . 🖭 ⓸ 𝓥𝓘𝓢𝓐
*closed Sunday dinner, Monday, Tuesday dinner, Wednesday dinner and 5 August-1 Sep-
tember* – **M** 1050/1650.

XXX ✿✿ **Eddie Van Maele,** chaussée Romaine 964, ✉ 1810, 𝒫 4785445, « Flower terrace
and garden » – 🖭 ⓸ . 🍽
closed Sunday, Monday, Thursday dinner, July and 23 December-January – **M** (booking
essential) a la carte 1800/2300
Spec. Biscuit de truite et saumon fumé aux épinards glacés, Mille-feuille de fruits et sorbets.

XXX **Centenaire,** av. J.-Sobieski 84, ✉ 1020, 𝒫 4786623 – 🖭 ⓸ Ɛ 𝓥𝓘𝓢𝓐
closed Sunday dinner, Monday, July and 24 to 31 December – **M** 975/1475.

XX **Val Joli,** r. Leestbeek 16, ✉ 1820, 𝒫 4783443, �?, « Garden-terrace » – ℗ . 𝓥𝓘𝓢𝓐
closed Monday, Tuesday and 14 to 29 October – **M** 690/1090.

XX **Aub. Arbre Ballon,** chaussée de Bruxelles 416, ✉ 1810, 𝒫 4789759 – ℗ . 🖭 ⓸ Ɛ
closed Monday and last 3 weeks July – **M** 595/995.

XX **Castel,** av. Houba-de-Strooper 96, ✉ 1020, 𝒫 4784392 – 🖭 ⓸ Ɛ 𝓥𝓘𝓢𝓐
closed Tuesday dinner and 16 to 31 August – **M** 650/1000.

XX ✿ **Les Baguettes Impériales,** av. J. Sobieski 70, ✉ 1020, 𝒫 4796732, Vietnamese rest.
– 🖭 . 🍽
closed Sunday dinner, Tuesday and August – **M** a la carte 800/1100.

XX **Figaro,** r. Émile-Wauters 137, ✉ 1020, 𝒫 4786529
closed Sunday dinner, Monday and July – **M** a la carte 870/1240.

X **Adrienne Atomium,** Parc Expositions, ✉ 1020, 𝒫 4783000, ≤, Hors d'œuvre – 🖭 ⓸
Ɛ 𝓥𝓘𝓢𝓐
closed Sunday, Bank Holidays and July – **M** (lunch only except Friday and Saturday)
500/590.

West

Anderlecht :

XX **La Réserve,** chaussée de Ninove 675, ⊠ 1080, ℰ 5222653 – 🖭 ⓞ ☲ ⋘
closed Saturday lunch, Tuesday and 15 July-5 August – **M** a la carte 1070/1650.

X **Sporting,** r. Veeweyde 22, ⊠ 1070, ℰ 5236003 – 🖭 ⓞ ☲ ⋘
closed Sunday dinner, Monday and 15 July-12 August – **M** a la carte 630/1270.

Molenbeek St-Jean (Sint-Jans Molenbeek) :

XXX ❀ **Béarnais** (Dela Rue), bd Mettewie 318, ⊠ 1080, ℰ 5231151, Classic – ▣. 🖭 ⓞ ☲
VISA
closed Sunday and Monday dinner – **M** a la carte 1540/2270
Spec. Râble de lièvre à la betterave (15 October-10 January), Bécasse et ris de veau au champagne (15 October-10 January), Filet de Saint-Pierre à la graine de moutarde.

XX ❀ **Michel Haquin,** chaussée de Gand 395, ⊠ 1080, ℰ 4283961 – 🖭 ⓞ ☲ *VISA*
closed Tuesday, Wednesday and July – **M** 1400/1800.

Berchem Ste Agathe (Sint-Agatha Berchem) :

XX **Saule,** chaussée de Gand 1110, ⊠ 1080, ℰ 4656682 – 🖭 ⓞ ☲ *VISA*
closed Sunday dinner, Monday and July – **M** a la carte 850/1380.

South

Bois de la Cambre :

🏠 **Lloyd George** without rest., av. Lloyd George 12, ⊠ 1050, ℰ 6483072 – ▮ ⌷wc ⋔ ☏.
🖭 ⓞ ☲ *VISA*
14 rm ⌷ 885/1970.

XXXX ❀❀ **Villa Lorraine,** av. Vivier-d'Oie 75, ⊠ 1180, ℰ 3743163, Classic-elegant – ℗. 🖭
ⓞ ☲ *VISA*
closed Sunday and 2 to 24 July – **M** (booking essential) a la carte 1700/3450.
Spec. Ecrevisses Villa Lorraine, Caneton au miel et vinaigre de Xérès, Soufflé au chocolat et jus de noix vertes.

Quartier "Ma Campagne" (Ixelles, St-Gilles) :

🏠 **Forum** 🅜 without rest., av. Haut-Pont 2, ⊠ 1060, ℰ 3430100, Telex 62311 – ▮ 🆀 ⌷wc
☏ – 🔺
78 rm ⌷ 2050/2560.

XXX ❀ **Chouan** (Fleuvy), av. Brugmann 100, ⊠ 1060, ℰ 3440999, Seafood – ▣. 🖭 ⓞ ☲ *VISA*
closed Sunday in May-June, Saturday lunch and July-25 August – **M** a la carte 1300/2050
Spec. Bouquet de raie sur salade de chêne, Loup de mer grillé au fenouil, Huîtres et coquillages (15 September-April).

XX **France,** chaussée de Charleroi 132, ⊠ 1060, ℰ 5385975
closed Saturday, Sunday and August – **M** (lunch only) 760.

XX **L'Auvergne,** r. Aqueduc 61, ⊠ 1050, ℰ 5373125, Classic interior – 🖭 ⓞ ☲
closed Sunday in July-August, Sunday dinner, Monday and 21 July-20 August – **M** 425/645.

Quartier Avenue Louise et Bascule (Ixelles) :

🏠 **Mayfair** without rest., quick-lunch, av. Louise 381, ⊠ 1050, ℰ 6499800, Telex 24821 – ▮
🆀 ☏ ↩ – 🔺 🖭 ⓞ ☲
100 rm ⌷ 3590/4510.

🏠 **Arcade Stephanie** 🅜, av. Louise 91, ⊠ 1050, ℰ 5390240, Telex 25558 – ▮ 🆀 ☏. 🖭
ⓞ ☲ *VISA* ⋘
M a la carte 550/1160 – **142 rm** ⌷ 2700/3350.

🏠 **Brussels,** av. Louise 315, ⊠ 1050, ℰ 6402415, Telex 25075 – ▮ 🆀 ☏. 🖭 ⓞ ☲ *VISA* ⋘
40 rm ⌷ 1910/3130.

🏠 **L'Agenda** 🅜 without rest., r. Florence 6, ⊠ 1050, ℰ 5390031, Telex 63947 – ▮ 🆀 ☏
↩. 🖭 ⓞ ☲ *VISA*
⌷ 220 – **38 rm** 1830/2120.

🏠 **Alfa Louise** without rest., r. Blanche 4, ⊠ 1050, ℰ 5379210, Telex 62434 – ▮ 🆀 ⌷wc
☏ ↩. 🖭 ⓞ ☲ *VISA*
65 rm ⌷ 2160/2500.

XXXX **Parc Savoy,** r. Emile Claus 3, ⊠ 1050, ℰ 6401522 – 🖭 ⓞ ☲ *VISA*
closed Saturday, Sunday and July – **M** a la carte 1170/1670.

XXX ❀❀ **Cravache d'Or,** pl. A.-Leemans 10, ⊠ 1050, ℰ 5383746 – ▣. 🖭 ⓞ ☲ *VISA*
closed Saturday lunch – **M** a la carte 1850/2600
Spec. Huîtres au champagne (15 September-April), Truffe à la croque au sel et grillettes au beurre truffé, Coquilles St-Jacques aux oursins (October-April).

XXX **Fontaine de Perles,** av. Louise 124, ⊠ 1050, ℰ 6480770, ☆, Chinese rest. – 🖭 ⓞ ☲
VISA
closed Saturday lunch – **M** a la carte 580/1080.

XX **Tagawa,** av. Louise 279, ✉ 1050, ℰ 6405095, Japanese rest. – ▤. AE D E. ⊠
closed Sunday, Bank Holidays and after 20.30 h. – **M** 520/2050.

XX **Comme Ça,** r. Châtelain 61, ✉ 1050, ℰ 6496290, ⛱ – AE D E VISA
closed Sunday, Monday dinner and 3 weeks July – **M** 595/1350.

XX **Armagnac,** chaussée de Waterloo 591, ✉ 1060, ℰ 3457373 – AE D E VISA
closed Sunday, Monday dinner and 21 July-14 August – **M** 700/825.

X **Arche de Noé,** r. Beau-Site 27, ✉ 1050, ℰ 6475383 – AE D E VISA
closed Sunday and August – **M** a la carte 760/1320.

X **La Thailande,** av. Legrand 29, ✉ 1050, ℰ 6402462, Thaï rest.
closed Sunday – **M** a la carte 780/1270.

X **Anlo II,** chaussée de Waterloo 678, ✉ 1180, ℰ 6498899, Chinese rest. – ▤. AE E VISA
M a la carte 740/980.

Forest (Vorst) :

XX ✿ **De Reu,** chaussée de Bruxelles 226, ✉ 1190, ℰ 3435460 – AE E
closed Tuesday, February and August – **M** (booking essential) a la carte 1100/1900
Spec. Foie d'oie frais au naturel, Agneau sarladaise aux truffes du Périgord, Mousse glacée au marc de Gewürztraminer.

Quartier Boondael (Ixelles) :

XXXX ✿✿ **L'Oasis** (Beyls), Place Marie-José 9, ✉ 1050, ℰ 6484545, « Elegant » – ▤ P. AE D E VISA. ⊠
closed Sunday dinner, Monday and 1 to 21 August – **M** a la carte 1690/2390
Spec. Epinards farcis aux huîtres et au caviar, Jardinière de jambonette de Bresse truffée, Nougat glacé aux amandes.

XXX **La Pomme Cannelle,** av. F.-Roosevelt 6, ✉ 1050, ℰ 6407788 – AE D E VISA. ⊠
closed Saturday lunch and Sunday – **M** a la carte 1400/2150.

XXX **Aub. de Boendael,** square du Vieux-Tilleul 12, ✉ 1050, ℰ 6727055, Grill, « Rustic » – AE D E VISA
closed Saturday, Sunday, Bank Holidays, 1 to 8 January, 5 to 27 August and 23 to 31 December – **M** a la carte 950/1840.

XX **Le Chalet Rose,** av. Bois de la Cambre 49, ✉ 1050, ℰ 6727864, ⛱, « Ancient interior, terrace » – P. AE D E VISA
closed Saturday lunch, Sunday and Bank Holidays – **M** a la carte 1620/2150.

Uccle (Ukkel) :

🏨 **County House,** Square des Héros 2, ✉ 1180, ℰ 3754420, Telex 22392 – ⇕ TV ⊡wc ℡ 🚗 P – ⛴. AE D E VISA
M 575/1250 – **96 rm** ⊐ 1150/1850.

XXX ✿ **Kolmer,** Drève de Carloo 18, ✉ 1180, ℰ 3755653, ⛱, « Elegant, Garden-terrace » – P. AE D E VISA
closed Sunday, Monday, 5 to 26 February and 3 to 24 September – **M** a la carte 1420/1970
Spec. Emincé de volaille à l'alsacienne, Feuilleté de langoustines au cresson, Foie d'oie frais maison.

XXX **Prince d'Orange,** av. Prince-d'Orange 1, ✉ 1180, ℰ 3744871, ⛱, Classic – P. AE D E VISA
closed Monday except Bank Holidays – **M** 775/1175.

XXX **Le Taillis,** av. Floréal 47, ✉ 1180, ℰ 3455731, ⛱ – AE D E VISA
closed Sunday dinner, Monday, September and 1 week February – **M** 1290/1590.

XXX **Arcades,** chaussée de Waterloo 1441, ✉ 1180, ℰ 3743516 – AE D E VISA
closed Sunday dinner and Monday – **M** a la carte 1020/1550.

XX **Villa d'Este,** r. Etoile 142, ✉ 1180, ℰ 3778646, ⛱ – P. D VISA
closed Sunday dinner, Monday, August and 23 December-6 January – **M** a la carte 1100/1750.

XX **Les Délices de la Mer,** chaussée de Waterloo 1020, ✉ 1180, ℰ 3755467, ⛱, Seafood – P. AE D E VISA
closed Sunday – **M** 1250/1750.

XX **L'Éléphant Bleu,** chaussée de Waterloo 1120, ✉ 1180, ℰ 3744962, Thaï rest. – ▤. AE D E VISA
closed Wednesday and 2 weeks August – **M** a la carte 790/1130.

XX **Dikenek,** chaussée de Waterloo 830, ✉ 1180, ℰ 3748346, ⛱, Rustic tavern – ▤. AE D E VISA
closed Easter, last week August, Wednesday dinner from September to July and Saturday lunch – **M** a la carte 1120/1580.

XX **Les Pélerins,** av. de Fré 190, ✉ 1180, ℰ 3742046 – P. AE D E
closed Saturday and Sunday – **M** a la carte approx. 900.

XX **Le Calvados,** av. de Fré 182, ✉ 1180, ℰ 3747098 – AE D E VISA
closed Sunday and July – **M** a la carte 1160/2040.

XX **Ventre-Saint-Gris,** r. Basse 10, ✉ 1180, ℰ 3752755 – AE D E VISA
M 750/1175.

XX **L'Ascoli,** chaussée de Waterloo 940, ⊠ 1180, ℰ 3755775, 佘 , Italian rest. – **℗** **AE** **⑩** **E** **VISA**
closed Sunday and August – **M** a la carte approx. 1200.

XX **Pavillon Impérial,** chaussée de Waterloo 1296, ⊠ 1180, ℰ 3746751, Chinese rest. – ▤. **⑩**. ※
closed Wednesday and July-August – **M** 595/1400.

XX **Pierrot au Surcouf,** r. Doyenné 89, ⊠ 1180, ℰ 3457538 – **AE** **⑩** **E** **VISA**
closed Sunday dinner, Monday, August and early February – **M** a la carte 800/1600.

X **Bouquet d'Asie,** chaussée de Waterloo 1116, ⊠ 1180, ℰ 3743196, South East Asian rest. – **AE** **⑩** **E** **VISA**
closed Sunday and 15 to 31 July – **M** a la carte 750/960.

X **Willy et Marianne,** chaussée d'Alsemberg 705, ⊠ 1180, ℰ 3436009 – **AE** **⑩** **E** **VISA**
closed Tuesday dinner, Wednesday and 1 to 15 August – **M** a la carte 720/1040.

X **De Hoef,** r. Edith-Cavell 218, ⊠ 1180, ℰ 3743417, 佘 , 17C inn – **AE** **⑩** **E** **VISA**
closed 10 to 31 July, 24 and 31 December – **M** 565.

East

Quartier Cinquantenaire (Etterbeek) :

🏨 **Chelton Concorde** Ⓜ 🦢 without rest., r. Véronèse 48, ⊠ 1040, ℰ 7364095, Telex 64253 – |電| **TV** – 🔬. **AE** **E** **VISA**
⊊ 200 – **41 rm** 2600/2800.

XX **Fontaine de Jade,** av. Tervuren 5, ⊠ 1040, ℰ 7363210, Chinese rest. – ▤. **AE** **⑩** **E**
closed Tuesday – **M** 950.

XX **Le Montgomery,** av. Tervuren 105, ⊠ 1040, ℰ 7336792 – **AE** **⑩** **E** **VISA**
closed Saturday, Sunday dinner and mid July-mid August – **M** a la carte 900/1680.

XX **Casse-Dalle,** av. Celtes 37, ⊠ 1040, ℰ 7336625 – **AE**
closed Saturday lunch, Sunday, 12 to 27 May and 22 to 31 December – **M** a la carte 630/1250.

Quartier Place Eugène-Flagey (Ixelles) :

XX **Piano à Bretelles,** r. A.-Dewitte 40, ⊠ 1050, ℰ 6476105 – **AE**
closed Saturday lunch, Sunday and August – **M** a la carte 760/1210.

Quartier Place Meiser (Schaerbeek) :

🏨 **Lambermont** Ⓜ without rest., bd Lambermont 322, ⊠ 1030, ℰ 2425595, Telex 62220 – |電| **TV** ☎. **AE** **E** **VISA**
42 rm ⊊ 1750/2250.

🏠 **Plasky** without rest., av. Eugène-Plasky 212, ⊠ 1040, ℰ 7337518 – |電| ☐wc 🔔 ☏. **AE** **⑩** **E** **VISA**
⊊ 110 – **30 rm** 880/1495.

XXX **Le Meiser,** bd Gén.-Wahis 55, ⊠ 1030, ℰ 7353769, Classic – **AE** **⑩** **E** **VISA**
closed Saturday and Sunday – **M** a la carte 880/1800.

XX **L'Armor,** av. Milcamps 126, ⊠ 1040, ℰ 7331981 – **AE** **⑩** **E** **VISA**. ※
closed Saturday lunch, Sunday and 15 July-8 August – **M** a la carte 1120/1580.

XX **Victor Hugo,** r. Victor Hugo 167, ⊠ 1040, ℰ 7354225, 佘 – **AE** **⑩** **E** **VISA**
closed Wednesday – **M** 550/980.

X **La Sole,** bd Aug. Reyers 165, ⊠ 1040, ℰ 7364138 – **AE** **⑩** **E** **VISA**
closed Sunday – **M** a la carte 1070/1450.

X **Au Cadre Noir,** av. Milcamps 158, ⊠ 1040, ℰ 7341445 – **AE** **⑩** **E** **VISA**
closed Saturday lunch, Sunday dinner, Monday and 1 to 21 July – **M** a la carte 740/1070.

X **Anak Timoer,** av. Rogier 357, ⊠ 1030, ℰ 7338987, Indonesian and Chinese rest. – **AE** **⑩** **E** **VISA**
closed Sunday dinner, Wednesday, Easter, mid July-mid August and Christmas-New Year – **M** a la carte 620/940.

Auderghem (Oudergem) :

XX **L'Abbaye de Rouge Cloître,** Rouge Cloître 8, ⊠ 1160, ℰ 6724525, ≼, 佘 , « Garden setting » – **℗**. **AE** **⑩** **E** **VISA**
closed Sunday dinner, Monday, Christmas-New-Year and February – **M** 1175.

X ❀ **La Grignotière,** chaussée de Wavre 2045, ⊠ 1160, ℰ 6728185 – **AE** **⑩** **VISA**
closed Sunday, Monday and 1 to 20 August – **M** 790.

Evere :

🏨 **Belson** Ⓜ without rest., chaussée de Louvain 805, ⊠ 1140, ℰ 7350000, Telex 64921 – |電| **TV** ☎. **AE** **⑩** **E** **VISA**
90 rm ⊊ 2860/4150.

Woluwé-St-Lambert (Sint-Lambrechts-Woluwé) :

🏠 **Armorial** without rest., bd Brand-Whitlock 101, ⊠ 1200, ℰ 7345636 – 📺 🛏wc 🏠 ☜.
🖭 ⓪ 🖪 𝑉𝐼𝑆𝐴
15 rm 🍽 700/1750.

🏠 **Léopold III** without rest., square Jos.-Charlotte 11, ⊠ 1200, ℰ 7628288 – 🛏 ☎
15 rm 🍽 750/1400.

🏠 **Résidence Lambeau** without rest., av. Lambeau 150, ⊠ 1200, ℰ 7338414 – 📺 🛏 ☜
12 rm 🍽 980/1580.

XXX ❀ **Mon Manège à Toi,** r. Neerveld 1, ⊠ 1200, ℰ 7700238, « Villa with flower garden »
– 🅿. 🖭 ⓪ 🖪 𝑉𝐼𝑆𝐴
closed Saturday, Sunday, 7 to 31 July and 24 to 31 December – **M** a la carte 1550/2280
Spec. Foie de canard poêlé aux mangues et fruits de la passion, Poêlée de langoustines au basilic, Filets de
St.Pierre aux girolles.

XXX **Coq en Pâte,** r. Tomberg 259, ⊠ 1200, ℰ 7621971 – 🖭 ⓪ 🖪
closed Monday and 15 July-19 August – **M** a la carte 860/1170.

XX **Sugito,** 1st floor, bd Brand-Whitlock 107, ⊠ 1200, ℰ 7335045, Indonesian rest. – 🖭 ⓪
🖪 𝑉𝐼𝑆𝐴
closed Monday – **M** a la carte 510/940.

XX **Le Relais de la Woluwe,** pl. Verheyleweghen 2, ⊠ 1200, ℰ 7626636 – 🖭 ⓪ 🖪 𝑉𝐼𝑆𝐴
closed Saturday lunch and Sunday – **M** a la carte 970/1250.

XX **Le Grand Veneur,** r. Tomberg 253, ⊠ 1200, ℰ 7706122, Rustic – 🖭 ⓪ 🖪
closed Tuesday and July – **M** 1080/1380.

XX **Le Chaplin,** av. Prince Héritier 22, ⊠ 1200, ℰ 7713415, 😤 – 🖭 ⓪ 🖪 𝑉𝐼𝑆𝐴
closed Sunday dinner, Monday and September – **M** a la carte 880/1270.

Woluwé-St-Pierre (Sint-Pieters Woluwé) :

XXX **Des 3 Couleurs,** av. Tervuren 453, ⊠ 1150, ℰ 7703321
closed Saturday lunch, Sunday dinner, Monday and 2 weeks April – **M** a la carte 1500/2000.

XX **La Salade Folle,** av. Jules Dujardin 9, ⊠ 1150, ℰ 7701961, Grill – 🖭 ⓪ 🖪 𝑉𝐼𝑆𝐴
closed Sunday dinner, Monday, 17 February-2 March and 1 to 17 September – **M** a la
carte 850/1420.

Watermael-Boitsfort (Watermael-Bosvoorde) :

🏠 **Aub. du Souverain** without rest., av. Fauconnerie 1, ⊠ 1170, ℰ 6721601 – 📺 🏠. 🖭
closed 15 July-14 August – **12 rm** 🍽 1000/1300.

XXX **Trois Tilleuls** 🦢 with rm, Berensheide 8, ⊠ 1170, ℰ 6723014 – 📺 🛏wc ☜. 🖭 ⓪ 🖪
𝑉𝐼𝑆𝐴. 🦋 rm
M *(closed Sunday)* a la carte 820/1640 – **8 rm** 🖙 1005/2585.

XX **Samambaia,** r. Philippe Dewolfs 7, ⊠ 1170, ℰ 6728720, 😤, Brazilian rest., « Tasteful
decor » – 🖭 ⓪ 🖪
closed Sunday, Monday and 21 July-21 August – **M** a la carte 850/1110.

XX **Le Canard Sauvage,** chaussée de la Hulpe 194, ⊠ 1170, ℰ 6730975 – 🖭 ⓪ 🖪 𝑉𝐼𝑆𝐴
closed Saturday and 15 July-17 August – **M** a la carte 1080/1490.

Brussels environs

at Diegem : 🅒 Machelen – pop. 11 300 – ⊠ 1920 Diegem – ✪ 02 :

🏨 **Holiday Inn** 🅜, Holidaystraat 7, near Brussels-Zaventem motorway, ℰ 7205865, Telex
24285, 🏊, 🦋 – 🗐 📺 ☎ 🕭 🅿 – 🔬. 🖭 ⓪ 🖪 𝑉𝐼𝑆𝐴. 🦋 rest
M 795 ,dinner a la carte – **288 rm** 🖙 4065/5440.

🏨 **Sofitel** 🅜, Bessenveldstraat 15, Brussels-Zaventem motorway Diegem exit, ℰ 7206050,
Telex 26595, 🏊 – 🗐 📺 ☎ 🅿 – 🔬. 🖭 ⓪ 🖪 𝑉𝐼𝑆𝐴. 🦋 rest
M *(closed Saturday and Sunday)* a la carte 950/1800 – 🖙 350 – **125 rm** 3520/3850.

🏨 **Novotel** 🅜, Olmenstraat (near Brussels-Zaventem motorway), ℰ 7205830, Telex 26751,
🏊 heated, 🦅 – 🗐 📺 🛏wc ☎ 🅿 – 🔬. 🖭 ⓪ 🖪 𝑉𝐼𝑆𝐴
M a la carte 720/1190 – 🖙 250 – **158 rm** 2650/2900.

at Essene 🅒 Hekelgem, by ⑫ : 18 km, by E 5 outway Ternat – pop. 11 165 – ⊠ 1705
Essene – ✪ 053 :

XXXX ❀ **Host. Bellemolen** 🦢 with rm, Stationstraat 11, SW : 1,5 km, ℰ 666238, ≼, « Tastefully converted 12C mill », 🦅 – 🛏wc 🅿 – 🔬. 🖭 ⓪ 🖪 𝑉𝐼𝑆𝐴.
closed Sunday dinner, Monday, 8 July-1 August and 23 December-1 January – **M** a la
carte 1120/1930 – 6 rm 🖙 1850/2500
Spec. Trois délices en salade au jus de truffes, Coquilles St-Jacques meunière chiconettes, Ris de veau aux
écrevisses et champignons de Paris.

at Groenendaal : – ⊠ 1990 Hoeilaart – ✪ 02 :

XXXX ❀❀❀ **Romeyer,** chaussée de Groenendaal 109, ℰ 6570581, « Stately home, ≼ garden
and private lake » – 🅿. 🖭 ⓪ 🖪 𝑉𝐼𝑆𝐴
closed Sunday dinner, Monday except Bank Holidays, February and August – **M** a la carte
2000/2500
Spec. Homard sauté aux bigorneaux, Blanc de faisan aux clous de girofles (15 October-January), Agneau
persillé, poêlé de champignons des bois (September-December).

XXX ❀ **Aloyse Kloos,** chaussée de la Hulpe 2, ℰ 6573737, 龠, Classic-elegant – **P**. AE ⓞ
E VISA
closed Sunday dinner, Monday, 19 August-11 September and 11 to 29 March – **M** a la
carte 1060/1550
Spec. Jambon de nos fumoirs, Ecrevisses à la Luxembourgeoise (June-February), Dos de lapin au coulis de
cèpes et basilic.

at Groot-Bijgaarden (Grand-Bigard) Ⓒ Dilbeek, by ⑫ : 7 km – pop. 36 003 – ⊠ 1720
Groot-Bijgaarden – ✿ 02 :

XXXX ❀❀ **De Bijgaarden,** I. Van Beverenstraat 20 (near castle), ℰ 4664485, ≼ – AE ⓞ E VISA
closed Sunday – **M** a la carte 1630/1950
Spec. Saumon mariné à l'aneth, Selle d'agneau cloutée aux truffes, Homard rôti beurre au caviar d'Iran.

XXX ❀ **Michel** (Coppens), Schepen Gossetlaan 31, ℰ 4666591 – AE ⓞ
closed Sunday, Monday and August – **M** 1150/1750
Spec. Foie d'oie grillé au poivre vert, Blanc de turbot à la marinière, Crêpe normande.

at Jezus-Eik by ⑦ : 12 km – ⊠ 1900 Overijse – ✿ 02 :

XXXX ❀❀ **Barbizon** (Deluc), Welriekendedreef 95, ℰ 6570462 – **P**. AE E
closed Tuesday, Wednesday, 16 July-6 August and 29 January-February – **M** (booking
essential) a la carte 1500/2200
Spec. Homard en chemise beurre Barbizon, Salade de jeunes épinards au foie d'oie chaud (March-September), Chariot de gourmandises.

ANTWERP (ANTWERPEN) 2000 ②①② ⑮ and ④⓪⑨ ④ – pop. 183 025 – ✿ 03.

See : Old Antwerp★★★ : Cathedral★★★ and Market Square★ (Grote Markt) FY – Rubens'
House★★ (Rubenshuis) GZ – Butchers' House★ (Vleeshuis) : museum FY **D** – Rubens' burial
chapel★ in the St. James' church (St-Jacobskerk) GY – The port★★ (Haven) ⚓ FY – Zoo★★
(Dierentuin) EU.

Museums : Royal Art Gallery★★★ (Koninklijk Museum voor Schone Kunsten) CV – Plantin-
Moretus★★★ (ancient printing-office) FZ – Mayer Van den Bergh★★ (Brueghel) GZ – Maritime
Steen★ (Nationaal Scheepvaartmuseum Steen) FY **M¹**.

ns ns Kapellenbos by ② : 22 km, Georges Capiaulei 2 ℰ 6668456 and 6666190 – ns Uilenbaan 15
at Wommelgem by ⑥ ℰ3530292.

🛈 Suikerrui 19 ℰ 2320103 and 2322284 – Inquiry Office, Koningin Astridplein ℰ 2330570 – Tourist
association of the province, Karel Oomsstraat 11 ℰ 2162810.

Brussels 48 ⑩ – Amsterdam 158 ④ – Luxembourg 266 ⑨ – Rotterdam 103 ④.

Plans on following pages

Room prices are subject to the addition of a local tax of 6%

Town Centre

🏨 **Plaza** M without rest., Charlottalei 43, ⊠ 2018, ℰ 2395970, Telex 31531 – 🛗 TV ☎. AE
ⓞ E VISA
EV **v**
⚏ 230 – **79 rm** 1940/3590.

🏨 **De Keyser** M, De Keyserlei 66, ⊠ 2018, ℰ 2340135, Telex 34219 – 🛗 ≡ rest TV ☎ –
🔬 AE ⓞ E VISA. ≉ rm
EU **b**
M (closed Saturday lunch and Sunday) a la carte 1090/1790 – **117 rm** ⚏ 2790/4050.

🏨 **Switel Eurotel** M, Copernicuslaan 2, ⊠ 2018, ℰ 2316780, Telex 33965, ⬚, ≉ – 🛗
≡ rest TV ☎ ⟚ – 🔬 AE ⓞ E VISA
EV **k**
M a la carte approx. 900 – ⚏ 250 – **348 rm** 2150/3000.

🏨 **Empire** M without rest., Appelmansstraat 31, ⊠ 2018, ℰ 2314755, Telex 33909 – 🛗 TV.
AE ⓞ E VISA
DU **s**
70 rm ⚏ 2050/3110.

🏨 **Alfa Congress** M, Plantin en Moretuslei 136, ⊠ 2018, ℰ 2353000, Telex 31959 – 🛗 TV
⟚wc ☎ ⟚ **P** – 🔬. ≉
EV **s**
M (closed Saturday and Sunday) a la carte 750/1240 – **61 rm** ⚏ 1360/2070.

🏨 **Antwerp Tower Hotel** M without rest, with 11 apartments in annex, Van Ertbornstraat
10, ⊠ 2018, ℰ 2340120, Telex 34478 – 🛗 TV ⟚wc ⟚ – 🔬. AE ⓞ E VISA. ≉
DU **b**
40 rm ⚏ 2150/2600.

🏨 **Terminus** without rest., F. Rooseveltplaats 9, ⊠ 2008, ℰ 2314795 – 🛗 ⟚wc 🔔 ⟚. AE
ⓞ
DU **y**
42 rm ⚏ 925/1850.

Park Warwick M ≶ (open Spring 1985), Desguinlei 94, ⊠ 2018, ℰ 2164800, Telex 33368
– 🛗 ≡ TV ⟚wc ☎ ⟚ **P** – 🔬 – 222 rm.

XXX ❀ **Vateli,** Kipdorpvest 50, ℰ 2331781, Classic – ≡ **P**. AE ⓞ E VISA
DU **g**
closed Sunday, Monday, Bank Holidays and 1 to 30 July – **M** a la carte 1400/2150
Spec. Caneton à la rouennaise, Turbot grillé, Escalope de ris de veau au céleri.

XXX **De Lepeleer,** Lange St-Annastr. 8, ℰ 2342225, « Rustic interior » – **P**. AE ⓞ VISA
closed Sunday and Bank Holidays – **M** a la carte 1750/1950.
DU **n**

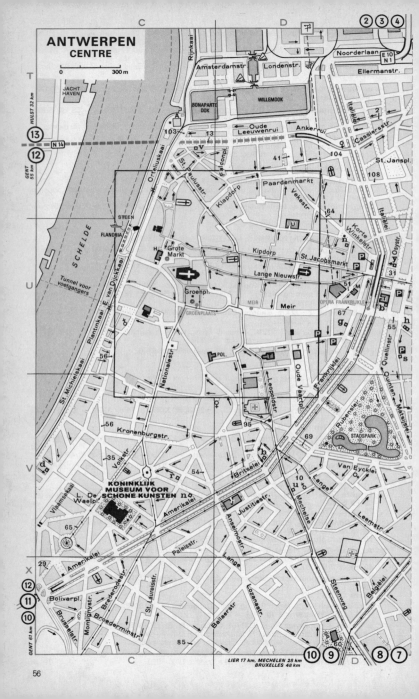

STREET INDEX TO ANTWERPEN TOWN PLANS

Continued on next page

57

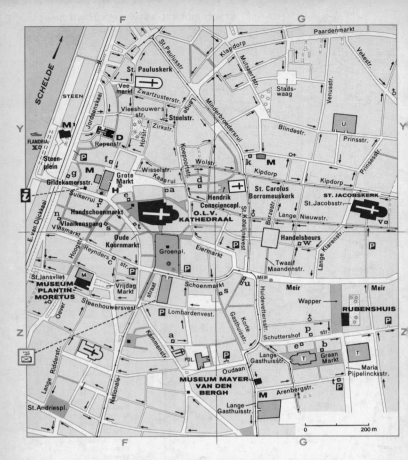

STREET INDEX TO ANTWERPEN TOWN PLANS (Concluded)

XXX **Liang's Garden,** Markgravelei 141, ⌧ 2018, ☎ 2372222, Chinese rest. –
closed Wednesday and 5 to 22 August – **M** a la carte 1100/1530.

XXX **Romantica,** Mechelsesteenweg 41, ☎ 2315435 – 🍽. ※   DV **u**
closed Sunday, Bank Holidays and August – **M** a la carte 1350/2000.

XXX **Relais Estérel,** Tolstraat 70, ☎ 2373261, Open until 1 a.m. – 🍽. ⃟ **E** 𝘝𝘐𝘚𝘈. ※   CV **n**
closed Thursday, July-5 August and 18 to 28 February – **M** (dinner only) a la carte 1510/
1780.

XX **De Poterne,** Desguinlei 186, ⌧ 2018, ☎ 2382824 – ⃟
closed Saturday lunch, Sunday and 12 August-1 September – **M** a la carte 1180/1700.

XX **Sawadee,** 1st floor, Britselei 16, ☎ 2330859, Thaï rest., « Ancient mansion » – ⃟ ⊙ **E**   DV **b**
closed Tuesday and 2 to 30 August – **M** a la carte approx. 1000.

XX **Epicurus,** Verbondstraat 44, ☎ 2373699 – ※   CV **r**
closed Sunday lunch, Sunday, Monday and 4 to 26 August – **M** 1150/1600.

XX **Panaché,** Statiestr. 17, ⌧ 2018, ☎ 2326905, Open until 1 a.m. – 🍽. ⃟ ⊙ 𝘝𝘐𝘚𝘈   EU **q**
closed 1 to 28 August – **M** a la carte 680/1120.

XX **La Moule Parquée,** Wapenstraat 18, ☎ 2384908, Seafood – 🍽. ⊙ **E** 𝘝𝘐𝘚𝘈   CV **d**
closed Saturday lunch, Monday and 1 to 15 May – **M** a la carte 1000/1300.

XX **Gourmet sans Chiqué,** Vestingstraat 3, ⌧ 2018, ☎ 2329002, Alsacian atmosphere –
⊙ **E** 𝘝𝘐𝘚𝘈   DU **h**
closed Friday, Saturday lunch, 19 January-2 February and 2 to 26 August – **M** 1050.

X **Solmar,** Breidelstraat 23, ⌧ 2018, ☎ 2325053, Portugese rest., Open until midnight –
🍽. ⃟ ⊙ **E**. ※   EU **r**
closed Tuesday and February – **M** a la carte 730/1190.

X **Rimini,** Vestingstraat 5, ⌧ 2018, ☎ 2314290, Italian rest.   DU **h**
closed Wednesday and 30 July-29 August – **M** a la carte 710/1130.

Old Antwerp

🏯 **Alfa Theater** Ⓜ without rest., Arenbergstraat 30, ☎ 2311720, Telex 33910 – 🔌 📺 ☎ –
🔥. ⃟ ⊙ **E** 𝘝𝘐𝘚𝘈   GZ **t**
83 rm ⇆ 1960/2600.

XXXX ❀❀ **La Pérouse,** Steenplein (pontoon), ☎ 2323528, ≤, « Anchored vessel » – 🍽 ℗. ⃟
⊙ **E**. ※   FY **x**
*15 September-end May except Sunday, Monday, Bank Holidays, 25 December-7 January
and Good Friday* – **M** (booking essential) a la carte 1470/1970
Spec. Hure de crustacés, Galettes et raviolis de langoustines aux liserons, Mille-feuille de sandre aux choux
verts.

XXX ❀❀ **Sir Anthony Van Dijck** (Paesbrugghe), 1st floor, Oude Koornmarkt 16 (Vlaey-
kensgang), ☎ 2316170, « Situated in a 16C lane, rustic interior » – ⃟ ⊙ **E**. ※   FY **s**
*closed 6 to 13 April, 27 May, 1 to 24 August, 11 November, 21 to 31 December, Saturday
lunch and Sunday* – **M** a la carte 1280/1940
Spec. Salade d'huîtres au saumon et au witloof (Oct.-March), Filet de selle d'agneau en croûte, Rognon de
veau à la bière de Rodenbach.

XXX **La Rade,** 1st floor, Van Dijckkaai 8, ☎ 2334963, « 18C mansion » – ⃟ **E** 𝘝𝘐𝘚𝘈   FY **g**
closed Saturday lunch, Sunday, Bank Holidays and end July-end August – **M** 995.

XXX **'t Fornuis,** Reyndersstraat 24, ☎ 2336270, « Rustic » – ⃟ ⊙. ※   FZ **c**
closed Saturday, Sunday, last 3 weeks August and 24 December-2 January – **M** a la carte
1250/1800.

XX **Criterium,** Schuttershofstraat 39, ☎ 2328346, Elegant interior – ⃟ ⊙ **E** 𝘝𝘐𝘚𝘈. ※
closed Saturday lunch, Sunday, Bank Holidays, 29 July-17 August and 23 to 31 December
– **M** a la carte 1170/2080.   GZ **p**

XX **Laurent,** Korte Klarenstraat 5, ☎ 2329547 – ⃟ **E**. ※   GZ **w**
closed 27 February-5 March and 20 August-4 September – **M** a la carte 1150/2050.

XX **Cigogne d'Alsace,** Wiegstraat 9, ☎ 2339716 – ⃟ ⊙ **E** 𝘝𝘐𝘚𝘈. ※   GZ **u**
closed Sunday, Bank Holidays and 22 December-1 January – **M** a la carte 1450/2000.

XX **De Kerselaar,** Grote Pieter Potstraat 22, ☎ 2335969 – ⃟ ⊙ 𝘝𝘐𝘚𝘈   FY **n**
closed 1 to 7 April, 1 to 21 July, Saturday lunch, Sunday and Monday lunch – **M** a la carte
1100/1370.

XX **V.I.P. Diners,** Lange Nieuwstraat 95, ☎ 2331317 – ⃟ ⊙ **E** 𝘝𝘐𝘚𝘈   GY **v**
closed Saturday lunch, Sunday, Bank Holidays, Easter and 28 July-18 August – **M**
1000/1150.

XX **Manoir,** Everdijstraat 13, ☎ 2327697, « Old panelling » – ⃟ ⊙ **E** 𝘝𝘐𝘚𝘈   FZ **a**
closed Wednesday dinner and July – **M** a la carte 1100/1780.

XX **Koperen Ketel,** Wiegstraat 5, ☎ 2311014 – ⃟ ⊙   GZ **u**
closed Saturday lunch, Sunday, Bank Holidays and end June-end July – **M** a la carte
670/1360.

XX **De Zeven Schaken,** Braderijstraat 24 (Grote Markt), ☎ 2337003, « Rustic » – ⃟ ⊙ **E**
𝘝𝘐𝘚𝘈   FY **f**
closed Saturday lunch, Sunday and 1 to 21 August – **M** 875/1450.

XX **Preud'homme,** Suikerrui 28, ☎ 2334200 – ⃟ ⊙ 𝘝𝘐𝘚𝘈. ※   FY **r**
closed Tuesday and February – **M** a la carte 1140/1730.

XX **Zagreb,** Brouwersvliet 30, 𝒫 2310173, Yugoslavian rest. – AE ⓘ E VISA. ⅍   CT **v**
closed Sunday, Sunday and 15 July-9 August – **M** a la carte 910/1390.

XX **Meirbrug,** 1st floor, Wiegstraat 1, 𝒫 2336700 – AE ⓘ E VISA   GZ **u**
closed Sunday and 1 to 28 July – **M** a la carte 900/1380.

XX **De Twee Atheners,** Keizerstraat 2, 𝒫 2320851, Greek rest., Open until 2 a.m. – ▤. ⓘ
E   GY **k**
closed Wednesday except Bank Holidays and August – **M** a la carte 590/900.

X **Henri,** Graanmarkt 3, 𝒫 2329258 – AE ⓘ E VISA. ⅍   GZ **b**
closed Saturday lunch, Sunday and September – **M** a la carte 700/1250.

X **Fourchette,** Schuttershofstraat 28, 𝒫 2313335 – AE ⓘ   GZ **e**
*closed Saturday lunch, Sunday, Monday, Bank Holidays, 14 July-6 August and 22
December-6 January* – **M** a la carte 980/1100.

X **Bistro 15,** Schrijnwerkerstraat 15, 𝒫 2337826 – AE ⓘ VISA. ⅍   GZ **s**
closed Sunday and 15 August-6 September – **M** (lunch only Monday to Thursday, dinner
only Friday and Saturday) a la carte 900/1070.

X **Rooden-Hoed,** Oude Koornmarkt 25, 𝒫 2332844, Mussels in season – ▤. AE. ⅍
closed Wednesday, 18 to 24 February and 12 June-10 July – **M** a la carte 890/1210.   FY **t**

X **A l'Ombre de la Cathédrale,** Handschoenmarkt 17, 𝒫 2324014 – AE ⓘ E VISA. ⅍
closed Monday from October to April and Tuesday – **M** a la carte 660/1150.   FY **e**

X **Peerdestal,** Wijngaardstraat 8, 𝒫 2319503, Open until midnight – AE ⓘ E VISA   FY **d**
closed Sunday – **M** a la carte 560/1440.

X **'t Boerenbrood,** Torfbrug 3, 𝒫 2326798   FY **a**
closed Saturday lunch, Monday, Thursday and July-5 August – **M** a la carte approx. 750.

Left Bank (Linker Oever)

XX **Lido,** Hanegraefstraat 8, ✉ 2050, 𝒫 2193590, Chinese rest. – ▤. AE ⓘ E
closed Tuesday and Wednesday – **M** a la carte approx. 1000.

Environs

North – ✉ 2030 :

🏨 **Novotel** Ⓜ, Luithagen-Haven 6, 𝒫 5420320, Telex 32488, ⤢ heated, ⅍ – ≣ ▤ rest ▣
⌷wc ☎ ᕫ Ⓟ – 🏛. AE ⓘ VISA
M a la carte 600/990 – ⌸ 240 – **119 rm** 1720/2350.

XXX **Terminal,** Leopolddok 214, 𝒫 5412680, ≤ harbour – Ⓟ
closed Saturday, Sunday and August – **M** (lunch only) a la carte 720/1540.

South – ✉ 2020 :

🏨 Crest H. Ⓜ, G. Legrellelaan 10, 𝒫 2372900, Telex 33843 – ≣ ▤ ▣ ☎ ᕫ Ⓟ – 🏛 –
306 rm.

at Berchem – pop. 45 128 – ✉ 2600 Berchem – ☻ 03 :

X Ten Carvery, Rooiplein 6, 𝒫 2304733, Grill, « Converted ancient farm »

X **Euterpia,** Generaal Capiaumontstraat 2, 𝒫 2368356, 🍴
closed Monday and Tuesday – **M** (dinner only) a la carte 1050/1350.

at Borgerhout – pop. 43 556 – ✉ 2200 Borgerhout – ☻ 03 :

🏨 **Holiday Inn** Ⓜ, Luitenant Lippenslaan 66, 𝒫 2359191, Telex 34479, ⤢ – ≣ ▤ ▣ ☎ ᕫ
Ⓟ – 🏛. AE ⓘ E VISA
M a la carte approx. 1200 – **176 rm** ⌸ 2400/3050.

at Deurne – pop. 76 744 – ✉ 2100 Deurne – ☻ 03 :

XXX **Den Uyl,** Bosuil 1, 𝒫 3243404, « Converted farm » – Ⓟ. AE ⓘ E VISA
closed Saturday lunch, Sunday and July – **M** a la carte 1210/1520.

XX **Périgord,** Turnhoutsebaan 273, 𝒫 3255200 – AE ⓘ E VISA. ⅍
closed Tuesday dinner, Wednesday, Saturday lunch and July – **M** 1025/1425.

at Mortsel – pop. 26 534 – ✉ 2510 Mortsel – ☻ 03 :

🏠 **Bristol International** without rest., Edegemstraat 1, 𝒫 4498049 – ≣ 🛁wc 🕾. AE ⓘ E
VISA
closed 20 December-5 January – **26 rm** ⬛ 790/1190.

at Wilrijk – pop. 42 349 – ✉ 2610 Wilrijk – ☻ 03 :

XXX **Kasteel Steytelinck,** St. Bavostraat 20, 𝒫 8287875, « Converted castle, parkside setting » – AE ⓘ E. ⅍
closed Saturday lunch, Monday, 1 week February and 4 to 8 July – **M** a la carte 1200/1650.

at Aartselaar : by ⑩ : 10 km – pop. 12 749 – ✉ 2630 Aartselaar – ☻ 03 :

XXX ❀ **Lindenbos,** Boomsesteenweg 139, 𝒫 8880965, « Converted castle with park » – Ⓟ.
AE ⓘ ⅍
closed Monday and August – **M** 1500/1750.

at Brasschaat : by ④ : 11 km – pop. 32 845 – ✉ 2130 Brasschaat – ☎ 03 :

Kasteel van Brasschaat, Miksebaan 40, ✆ 6518537, ←, « Converted castle in an extensive park » – wc Ⓟ. AE ⓓ
M a la carte approx. 1200 – **16 rm** 770/1540.

XXX **Halewijn,** Donksesteenweg 212 (Ekeren-Donk), ✆ 6450490, – ▤. AE ⓓ E
closed Monday – **M** a la carte 1050/1690.

at Ekeren : by ② : 11 km – pop. 30 271 – ✉ 2070 Ekeren – ☎ 03 :

XX **Hof de Bist,** Veltwijcklaan 258, ✆ 6646130 – Ⓟ. AE ⓓ E
closed Sunday – **M** a la carte approx. 1400.

at Kapellen : by ② : 15,5 km – pop. 22 477 – ✉ 2080 Kapellen – ☎ 03 :

XXX ✿ **De Bellefleur** (Buytaert), Antwerpsesteenweg 253, ✆ 6646719 – Ⓟ. AE ⓓ
closed Saturday, Sunday and July – **M** (booking essential) a la carte 1590/2000
Spec. Langoustines à la citronelle, Chevreuil aux cèpes (Oct.-March), Pâtisserie.

XX **De Graal,** Kapellenboslei 11 (N : 5 km by N 222 direction Kalmthout), ✆ 6665510, « Terrace and garden » – AE ⓓ E
closed Saturday lunch and Tuesday – **M** a la carte 1300/1500.

XX **De Pauw,** Antwerpsesteenweg 48, ✆ 6642282 – AE ⓓ E VISA
closed Tuesday dinner and Wednesday dinner – **M** a la carte 1020/1630.

X **Cappelleke,** Dorpstraat 70, ✆ 6646728 – AE
closed Tuesday, Wednesday and 16 August-4 September – **M** 850.

at Kontich : by ⑨ : 12 km – pop. 18 003 – ✉ 2550 Kontich – ☎ 03 :

XXX **Alexander's,** Mechelsesteenweg 318, ✆ 4572631 – Ⓟ. AE ⓓ E VISA.
closed Sunday dinner, Monday and July – **M** 1195.

at Schelle : by ⑩ : 10 km – pop. 7 079 – ✉ 2621 Schelle – ☎ 03 :

XXX **Tolhuis-Veer,** Tolhuisstraat 325 - W : 2 km near river Rupel, ✆ 8876578, « Country house atmosphere » – Ⓟ. AE ⓓ E VISA
closed Saturday lunch and Monday – **M** 1250.

at Schoten : 10 km – pop. 30 774 – ✉ 2120 Schoten – ☎ 03 :

XXX **Kleine Barreel,** Bredabaan 1147, ✆ 6458584 – ▤ Ⓟ. ⓓ
M a la carte 1000/1650.

XXX **Uilenspiegel,** Brechtsebaan 277, ✆ 6516145, « Terrace and garden » – Ⓟ. AE ⓓ E VISA
closed Saturday lunch and Monday – **M** 975/1625.

XX **Witte Raaf,** Horstebaan 97, ✆ 6588664, – Ⓟ. AE ⓓ E VISA
closed Wednesday dinner, Saturday lunch, Sunday and 19 August-7 September – **M** a la carte 1180/1840.

XX **Peerdsbos,** Bredabaan 1293, ✆ 6457469 – Ⓟ. ⓓ.
closed 25 January-8 February, 6 to 20 June, 8 to 20 September and Monday, Tuesday except Bank Holidays – **M** a la carte 730/1280.

XX **Ten Weyngaert,** Winkelstapstraat 151, ✆ 6455516, Grill, « Converted 17C farm » – ▤ Ⓟ. AE ⓓ E VISA.
M a la carte 910/1330.

at Wijnegem : 10 km – pop. 8 186 – ✉ 2110 Wijnegem – ☎ 03 :

XXX **Ter Vennen,** Merksemsebaan 278, ✆ 3538140, « Converted farm, elegant interior » – ▤ Ⓟ. ⓓ
closed Monday – **M** 875/1575.

BRUGES (BRUGGE) 8000 West-Vlaanderen 213 ③ and 409 ② – pop. 118 146 agglomeration – ☎ 050.

See : Trips on the canals★★★ CY – Procession of the Holy Blood★★★ – Belfry and Halles★★★ CY – Market square★★ (Markt) CY – Market-town★★ (Burg) CY – Beguinage★★ (Begijnhof) CZ – Basilica of the Holy Blood★ – Church of Our Lady★ : tower★★, statue of the Madonna★★, tombstone of Mary of Burgundy★★ CZ **S** – Rosery quay (Rozenhoedkaai) ←★★ CY – Dyver ←★★ CZ – St. Boniface bridge : site★★ CZ – Chimney of the "Brugse Vrijë" in the Court of Justice (Gerechtshof) CY **J.**

Museums : Groeninge★★★ CZ – Memling (St. John's Hospital)★★★ CZ – Gruuthuse★ CZ **M**[1] – Arents House★ (Arentshuis) CZ **M**[4].

Envir. : Zedelgem : baptismal font★ in the St.Lawrence's church by ⑥ : 10,5 km.

ℹ Markt 7 ✆ 330711 – Tourist association of the province, Vlamingstraat 55 ✆ 337344.

Brussels 96 ③ – Ghent 44 ③ – Lille 72 ⑪ – Ostend 28 ⑤.

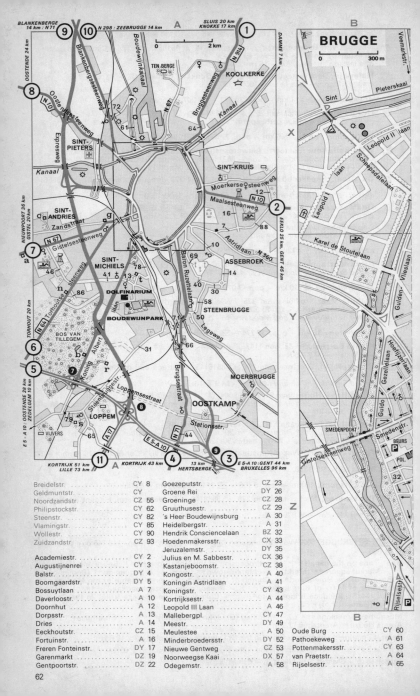

BRUGGE

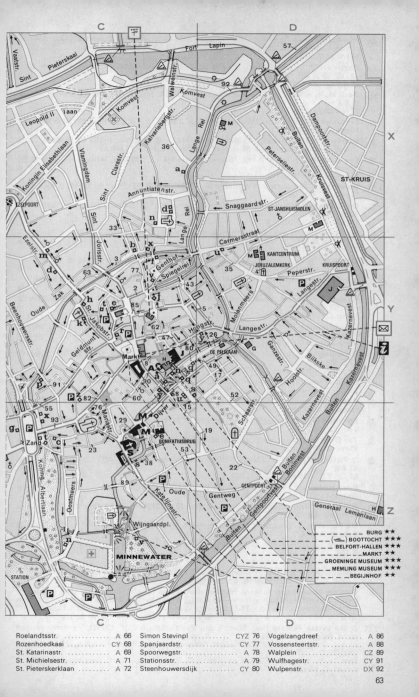

Orangerie ⑤ without rest., Karthuizerinnestraat 10, ℰ 341649, Telex 82443, « Ancient mansion with tasteful decor » – |▒| 🖵 ☎ – 🛦. 🕮 ⓞ 🖅 *VISA* CY **y**
18 rm ⊑ 2050/4600.

Portinari Ⓜ ⑤ without rest., 't Zand 15, ℰ 341034, Telex 82400 – |▒| 🖵 ☎ ⅙ 🚗 ⑫ –
🛦. 🕮 ⓞ 🖅 *VISA*. ⅙ CZ **x**
32 rm ⊑ 1900/3100.

Park H. Ⓜ without rest., Vrijdagmarkt 5, ℰ 333364, Telex 81686 – |▒| 🖵 ☎ – 🛦. 🕮 ⓞ
🖅 *VISA* CZ **g**
62 rm ⊑ 2160/3120.

Erasmus Ⓜ without rest., Wollestraat 35, ℰ 335781, ≼ – |▒| 🖵 ⌷wc ☎. 🕮 🖅 *VISA*. ⅙ CY **a**
10 rm ⊑ 2350/4700.

Boudewijn I, 't Zand 21, ℰ 336999, Telex 81163 – |▒| 🖵 ⌷wc ☎. 🕮 ⓞ 🖅 *VISA* CZ **t**
closed 14 to 30 November – **M** *(closed Tuesday)* 500/950 – **11 rm** ⊑ 1470/2600.

Die Swaene ⑤ without rest., Steenhouwersdijk 1, ℰ 339629, Telex 82446, ≼ – |▒| 🖵
⌷wc 🏢 ☎. 🕮 🖅 *VISA* CY **g**
17 rm ⊑ 1400/3100.

Pand H. ⑤ without rest., Pandreitje 16, ℰ 334434 – |▒| 🖵 ⌷wc ☎. 🕮 🖅 *VISA* CY **u**
17 rm ⊑ 1900/2400.

De Biskajer Ⓜ ⑤ without rest., Biskajersplein 4, ℰ 341506 – |▒| 🖵 ⌷wc 🏢wc ☎. 🕮
ⓞ 🖅 *VISA*. ⅙ CY **j**
17 rm ⊑ 2700/3300.

Navarra without rest., St-Jacobsstraat 41, ℰ 340561, Telex 81035 – |▒| ⌷wc 🏢wc ☎ –
🛦. 🕮 ⓞ 🖅 *VISA* CY **k**
64 rm ☎ 1000/2800.

Europ H. ⑤ without rest., Augustijnenrei 18, ℰ 337975 – |▒| ⌷wc 🏢wc ☎. 🖅. ⅙
March-11 November – **28 rm** ⊑ 1825/2700. CY **b**

Ter Brughe ⑤ without rest., Oost-Gisthelhof 2, ℰ 340324 – ⌷wc ☎. 🕮 ⓞ 🖅 *VISA* CY **x**
closed January – **20 rm** ⊑ 1850/2300.

Azalea without rest., Wulfhagestraat 43, ℰ 331478, Telex 81282, 🐎 – 🖵 ⌷wc 🏢wc ☎
🛦. 🕮 ⓞ 🖅 *VISA* CY **p**
15 rm ⊑ 1960/2420.

Bourgoensch Hof ⑤ without rest., Wollestraat 39, ℰ 331645, ≼ canals and ancient
Flemish houses – |▒| ⌷wc 🏢wc ☎ 🚗. ⅙ CY **a**
week-ends only mid November-December – **12 rm** ⊑ 1700/3700.

Groeninghe ⑤ without rest., Korte Vuldersstraat 29, ℰ 336495, Telex 82446 – 🏢wc ☎.
🕮 🖅 *VISA* CZ **c**
closed January – **8 rm** ⊑ 1475/1800.

Bryghia without rest., Oosterlingenplein 4, ℰ 338059 – |▒| ⌷wc 🏢wc ☎. 🕮 🖅 *VISA*. ⅙ CY **f**
closed 10 January-14 February – **18 rm** ⊑ 1450/1970.

Aragon without rest., Naaldenstraat 24, ℰ 333533 – |▒| ⌷wc 🏢wc ☎. 🖅 *VISA* CY **t**
16 rm ⊑ 1600/2600.

Egmond ⑤ without rest., Minnewater 15, ℰ 341445 – 🏢wc ☎ ⑫. 🕮 ⓞ *VISA* CZ **v**
8 rm ⊑ 1450/2700.

Ter Duinen without rest., Langerei 52, ℰ 330437 – |▒| 🏢wc ☎ 🚗. 🕮 ⓞ 🖅 *VISA* CX **a**
10 rm ⊑ 1075/1600.

't Putje, 't Zand 31, ℰ 332847, Buffet lunch, open until 1 a.m. – 🖵 ⌷wc ☎ 🚗 – 🛦.
🕮 *VISA* CZ **t**
M 395/625 – **10 rm** ☎ 2100/2750.

Post Hotel without rest., Hoogstraat 18, ℰ 337889 – |▒| 🏢wc. *VISA* DY **y**
closed 3 to 31 January – **22 rm** ☎ 1600/1800.

Hans Memling without rest., Kuipersstraat 18, ℰ 332096 – |▒| 🖵 🏢wc ☎ CY **e**
17 rm ⊑ 1550/2000.

De Pauw ⑤ without rest., St-Gilliskerkhof 8, ℰ 337118 – 🏢wc ☎ CX **d**
8 rm ☎ 830/1470.

Fevery ⑤ without rest., Collaert Mansionstraat 3, ℰ 331269 – |▒| ⌷wc 🏢wc ☎. 🕮 ⓞ
🖅 *VISA* CX **d**
11 rm ⊑ 1080/1410.

Jacobs ⑤ without rest., Baliestraat 1, ℰ 339831 – |▒| ⌷wc 🏢wc ☎. ⅙ CX **n**
closed 7 to 31 January – **28 rm** ⊑ 880/1685.

XXX **Duc de Bourgogne** with rm, Huidenvettersplaats 12, ℰ 332038, « old style interior, ≼
canals and old Flemish houses » – 🍽 rest 🖵 ⌷wc ☎. 🕮 ⓞ 🖅 *VISA*. ⅙ rm CY **n**
*closed Sunday dinner from 15 October to 15 March, Tuesday lunch from 15 March to 15
October, Monday, July and January* – **M** a la carte approx. 1700 – **9 rm** ⊑ 1850/3700.

XXX ❀ **De Witte Poorte** (Van Boven), Jan Van Eyckplein 6, ℰ 330883, « Former vaulted
store, garden » – ⓞ *VISA* CY **v**
closed Sunday, Monday, last 2 weeks February and last 2 weeks August – **M** a la carte
1600/2000
Spec. Terrine de foie d'oie, Queues de langoustines aux petits légumes et beurre blanc, Médaillon de
homard aux filets de sole.

XXX **De Zilveren Pauw,** Zilverstraat 41, ℰ 335566, ⛲, « Belle-époque interior, patio » – CY z
AE ① E VISA
closed Wednesday, 14 to 27 February and 18 to 31 July – **M** 980/2000.

XXX **Den Braamberg,** Pandreitje 11, ℰ 337370, Classic-elegant – AE ① VISA CY u
closed Sunday dinner, Thursday and 15 to 30 August – **M** a la carte 1350/2000.

XXX ❀ **De Karmeliet,** Jeruzalemstraat 1, ℰ 338259 – AE ① E. ⊗ DY u
closed Sunday dinner, Monday and 20 August-5 September – **M** 1750.

XX **'t Pandreitje,** Pandreitje 6, ℰ 331190, « Elegant interior » – AE ① E VISA ⊗ CDY s
closed 2 to 17 June, 15 to 30 December, Sunday and Monday – **M** 1450/1750.

XX ❀ **De Snippe** (Huysentruyt), Ezelstraat 52, ℰ 337070, AE ① E VISA CY m
closed Sunday, Monday lunch, 3 to 22 February and 7 to 15 July – **M** (booking essential) a
la carte 1360/1750
Spec. Laitue soufflée aux queues de langoustines, Foie d'oie frais aux écrevisses, Queues de langoustines à
la ciboulette.

XX **Den Gouden Harynck,** Groeninge 25, ℰ 337637 – AE ① E VISA CZ e
closed Sunday, Monday, 22 July-4 August and 16 to 30 December – **M** a la carte approx.
1600.

XX **'t Bourgoensche Cruyce** ⌚ with rm, Wollestraat 41, ℰ 337926, ≼ canals and old CY a
Flemish houses – TV ⌂wc ⋔. AE ① VISA
*closed February, Tuesday from May to October and Sunday, Monday lunch from October
to May* – **M** a la carte 1250/1650 – **6 rm** ⊡ 1300/1700.

XX **Criterium,** 't Zand 12, ℰ 331984, ⛲ – AE ① E VISA CZ x
closed 2 to 18 July, 22 to 31 October, Tuesday dinner except July-August and Wednesday
– **M** 650/1150.

XX **'t Lammetje,** Braambergstraat 3, ℰ 332495 – AE ① E VISA CY q
closed Monday, 28 August-5 September and 11 February-1 March – **M** a la carte 1090/1330.

X **'t Presidentje,** Ezelstraat 21, ℰ 339521 – AE ① E VISA CY d
closed Wednesday dinner, Sunday and 17 June-6 July – **M** a la carte 780/1250.

X **'t Kluizeke,** Sint Jacobstraat 58, ℰ 341224 – AE ①. ⊗ CY h
closed Wednesday – **M** 980.

X **De Watermolen,** Oostmeers 130, ℰ 332448, ⛲, « Terrace » – E VISA CZ n
*closed Monday dinner, Thursday dinner from October to end March, Tuesday dinner,
Wednesday, first 3 weeks October and first 2 weeks March* – **M** 460/725.

X **Postiljon,** Katelijnestraat 3, ℰ 335616 – AE ① E VISA CZ s
closed Sunday dinner, Tuesday and 20 November-7 December – **M** a la carte 750/940.

X **Malpertuus,** Eiermarkt 9, ℰ 333038 – AE VISA CY r
closed Wednesday and July – **M** 400/750.

South – ✉ 8200 – ✆ 050 :

🏨 **Novotel** M, Chartreuseweg 20, ℰ 382851, Telex 81507, ⛲, ⊥, ⋈ – ⧫ ≡ rest TV
⌂wc ☎ ᴊ ❷ – ⚐. AE ① E VISA A r
M a la carte 640/1150 – ⊡ 265 – **101 rm** 1725/2375.

XXXX ❀❀ **Weinebrugge** (Galens), Koning Albertlaan 242, ℰ 384440 – ❷ A b
closed Wednesday, Thursday and 2 September-2 October – **M** (week-end booking essential) a la carte 1700/2400
Spec. Fricassée de homard et turbot au Sauternes, Escalope de saumon aux chicons et fromage de chèvre,
Foie d'oie frais en gelée au vieux Porto.

XXX **Casserole** (Hotel. school), Groene Poortdreef 17, ℰ 383888, « Country atmosphere » –
❷. AE A t
closed 29 June-16 August – **M** (lunch only except Friday and Saturday) a la carte 1170/1480.

South-West – ✉ 8200 – ✆ 050 :

🏨 **Pannenhuis** M, Zandstraat 2, ℰ 311907, ≼, ⛲, « Garden-terrace » – TV ☎ ᴊ ❷ –
⚐. AE ① E VISA. ⊗ rest A g
M (*closed 15 to 31 January, Tuesday dinner from October to 15 July and Wednesday*) a la
carte 770/1320 – **21 rm** ⊡ 1250/2600 – ½ p 1750/2000.

XXX ❀ **Ter Heyde** ⌚ with rm, Torhoutsesteenweg 620 (by ⑥ : 8 km on N 64), ℰ 383858, ≼,
« Stately home in extensive grounds » – TV ⌂wc ☜ ⇆ ❷. ① E. ⊗ rm
closed Wednesday dinner, Thursday and 15 December-18 January – **M** 1650 – 5 rm ⊡
1750/2500.

XX **Vossenburg** ⌚ with rm, Zandstraat 272 (Coude Ceuken), ℰ 317026, « Converted castle
in a park » – ⋔wc ❷. ⊗ A c
closed 15 to 30 November – **M** (*closed Tuesday and Sunday dinner*) 575/795 – 8 rm ⊡
955/1360.

X **De Boekeneute,** Torhoutsesteenweg 380, ℰ 382632, ⛲ – ❷. AE ① E VISA A n
closed Sunday dinner, Monday and 16 to 31 August – **M** a la carte 850/1200.

at Loppem Ⓒ Zedelgem, South : 5 km – pop. 19 494 – ✉ 8021 Loppem – ✆ 050 :

XX **Bakkershof,** Parklaan 16, ℰ 824987 – ❷. ① A s
closed Tuesday dinner from 15 October to 15 April and Wednesday – **M** a la carte
940/1520.

65

at Oostkamp by ④ bridge E5 then 2nd street on the left – pop. 20 081 – ⊠ 8020 Oostkamp – 🕙 050 :

XX **De Kampveldhoeve**, Kampveldstraat 16, ℰ 824258, ≤, « Country atmosphere » – ❷
closed Tuesday – **M** 850/1350.

at Ruddervoorde Ⓒ Oostkamp, by ④ : 12 km – pop. 20 081 – ⊠ 8040 Ruddervoorde – 🕙 050 :

🏠 **Leegendael** 🦐, Kortrijkstraat 486, ℰ 277699, ≤, « Country atmosphere », 🚗 – 🛏️wc
🚗 ❷. 🝙 ⑩ 🝙 *VISA*, 🦐 rest
closed Monday, Sunday dinner and 5 to 26 February – **M** 1150/1950 – 🖭 300 – **9 rm** 1450/1950.

at Sint-Kruis by ② : 6 km – ⊠ 8310 Sint-Kruis – 🕙 050 :

🏠 **Lodewijk van Male**, Maalsesteenweg 488, ℰ 355763, « Extensive park with lake » – 🛏️wc 🝙wc ❷. 🦐
M *(closed Sunday dinner and Monday)* a la carte 670/1120 – **14 rm** 🖭 875/1310 – P 1460/1775.

XX **Jonkman**, Maalsesteenweg 438, ℰ 360767, ≤, 🍽️ – 🝙 ⑩
closed Sunday, Monday lunch and 1 to 15 October – **M** a la carte 1450/2030.

at Varsenare by ⑦ : 6,5 km – ⊠ 8202 Varsenare – 🕙 050 :

XX **Stuivenberg**, Gistelsteenweg 27, ℰ 318402, 🍽️ – ❷   A a
closed Sunday dinner and Monday – **M** a la carte 1130/1370.

at Waardamme Ⓒ Oostkamp, by ④ : 11 km – pop. 20 081 – ⊠ 8041 Waardamme – 🕙 050 :

XXX **Ter Talinge**, Rooiveldstraat 46, ℰ 279061, « Country atmosphere, terrace » – ❷. 🝙 ⑩ *VISA*
closed Wednesday dinner and Thursday – **M** a la carte 920/1230.

at Zedelgem by ⑥ : 10,5 km – pop. 19 494 – ⊠ 8210 Zedelgem – 🕙 050 :

🏨 **Zuidwege** Ⓜ without rest., Torhoutsesteenweg 126, ℰ 201339 – 🛏️wc 🝙wc ☎ ❷. 🝙 🝙 *VISA*
closed Tuesday dinner and 21 to 31 December – **17 rm** 🖭 700/2200.

🏨 **Bonne Auberge**, Torhoutsesteenweg 201, ℰ 209525, Telex 81227 – 📶 🛏️wc 🝙 🚗 ❷ – 🝙. 🝙 ⑩ 🝙 *VISA*. 🦐 rest
closed December-January – **M** *(closed Sunday)* a la carte 850/1330 – **27 rm** 🖭 1200/2000.

XX **Ter Leepe**, Torhoutsesteenweg 168, ℰ 200197 – ❷. 🝙 ⑩ *VISA*
closed Wednesday dinner, Sunday and 15 July-4 August – **M** 675/1250.

Mariakerke 8400 West-Vlaanderen 🔢 ② and 🔢 ① – pop. 69 039 – 🕙 059 – 27 km.

XX ✿✿ **Au Vigneron** (Daue), Aartshertogstraat 80, ℰ 704816 – 🝙 ⑩ 🝙 *VISA*
closed 10 to 29 September, 20 February-9 March, Sunday dinner except July-August and Monday – **M** (Saturday and Sunday booking essential) a la carte 1500/2250
Spec. Trois services de homard, Turbot Edouard Nignon, Crêpe abricotine.

Knokke 8300 West-Vlaanderen 🔢 ⑪ and 🔢 ② – pop. 29 730 – 🕙 050 – 17 km.

XXX ✿✿ **Aquilon** (De Spae), 1st floor, Lippenslaan 306, ℰ 601274, « Elegant decoration » – 🝙 🝙. 🦐
closed December-14 February, Sunday dinner, Monday and Tuesday from 15 September to Easter, Tuesday dinner from Easter to 15 September and Wednesday – **M** (Saturday and Sunday booking essential) a la carte 1500/2350
Spec. Feuilleté aux asperges et écrevisses, Foie d'oie au naturel, Ris de veau aux champignons des bois sauce truffée.

Oostkerke 8350 West-Vlaanderen 🔢 ③ and 🔢 ② – pop. 9 971 – 🕙 050 – 7 km.

XX ✿✿ **Bruegel** (Fonteyne), Damse Vaart Zuid 26, ℰ 500346, ≤, « Rustic interior » – ❷. 🝙 ⑩ 🝙
closed Tuesday, Wednesday and January-February – **M** (Saturday and Sunday booking essential) a la carte 1700/2450
Spec. Terrine d'anguilles, Sole de Zeebrugge aux crevettes grises, Soufflé chaud aux pralins et pistaches.

Waregem 8790 West-Vlaanderen 🔢 ⑮ and 🔢 ⑪ – pop. 33 575 – 🕙 056 – 47 km.

South : 2 km, near motorway :

XXX ✿✿ **'t Oud Konijntje** (Desmedt), Bosstraat 53, ℰ 601937, « Elegant inn - garden setting » – ❷. 🝙 ⑩ 🝙 *VISA*
closed Thursday dinner, Friday, Sunday dinner, 22 July-12 August and 23 December-2 January – **M** a la carte 1250/1850
Spec. Langouste Alexandre, Turbot à la moutarde, Cul de lapin.

LUXEMBOURG

SIGHTS

See : Site★★ – Old Luxembourg★★ – "Promenade de la Corniche" ≤★★ and the rocks of the city ≤★★ DY – The Bock cliff ≤★★, Bock Casemates★★ DY – Place de la Constitution ≤★★ DY – Grand-Ducal Palace★ DY K – Our Lady's Cathedral (Notre Dame)★ DY L – Grand-Duchess Charlotte Bridge★ DY – State Museum★★ DY

LUXEMBOURG 8 ⑧ and 409 ㉘ – pop. 78 724.

 Höhenhof, near Airport ✆ 34090.

✈ Findel by ③ : 6 km ✆ 47981 and 47983 – **Air terminal :** pl. de la Gare ✆ 481820.

🛈 pl. d'Armes. ✉ 2011. ✆ 22809.

Amsterdam 419 ⑧ – Bonn 190 ③ – Brussels 219 ⑧.

Plan on next page

Luxembourg-Centre :

🏨 **Le Royal** M, bd Royal 12, ✉ 2449, ✆ 41616, Telex 2979, 🏊 – 🛗 🖭 📺 ☎ ♿ 🚗 – 🏛 AE ⓄD E VISA
CY **e**
M a la carte 1200/1840 – **180 rm** ⟷ 4800/5800.

🏨 **Cravat,** bd Roosevelt 29, ✉ 2450, ✆ 21975, Telex 2846, ≤ – 🛗 📺 ☎ – 🏛 AE ⓄD E VISA. ⌇ rest
DY **a**
M 900 – **59 rm** ⟷ 2100/3700.

🏨 **Rix H.** without rest., bd Royal 20, ✉ 2449, ✆ 27545, Telex 1234 – 🛗 📺 ⇌wc 🛁wc ☎ Ⓟ – 🏛. ⌇
CY **b**
closed 21 December-2 January – **22 rm** ⟷ 1290/2790.

🏨 **Français and Rest. Kiosque,** pl. d'Armes 14, ✉ 1136, ✆ 23009 – 🛗 🛁wc ☎. AE ⓄD E VISA
DY **p**
M a la carte 560/1030 – **26 rm** ⟷ 1835/2270 – P 2700.

XXX ✿✿ **St-Michel** (Guillou), 1st floor, r. Eau 32, ✉ 1449, ✆ 23215, Seafood, « Rustic interior » – AE E VISA
DY **e**
closed 1 to 30 August, 25 December-4 January, Saturday and Sunday – **M** (booking essential) a la carte 1530/2100
Spec. Raviolis de langoustines ou de foie d'oie chaud, Nage de rougets et de langoustines aux huîtres, Filet de bœuf à la ficelle. **Wines** Pinot gris, Auxerrois.

XXX **Gourmet,** r. Chimay 8, ✉ 1333, ✆ 25561, Classic – AE
DY **h**
closed Sunday dinner, Monday, 22 January-14 February and 22 July-14 August – **M** a la carte 930/1260.

XXX **Alsacien,** r. du Curé 24, ✉ 1368, ✆ 28250 – VISA. ⌇
DY **r**
closed Saturday, Sunday, Bank Holidays and August – **M** a la carte 1130/1590.

67

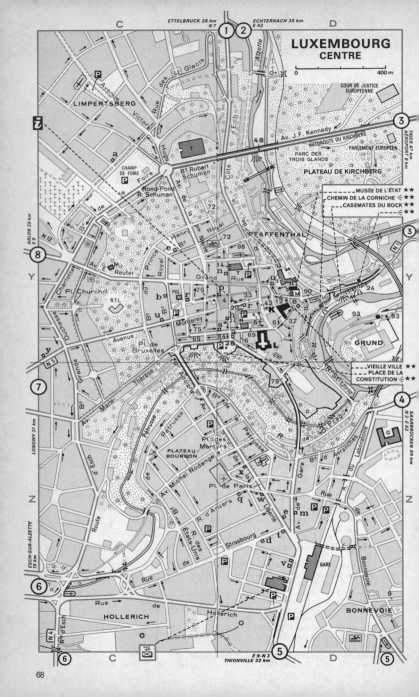

LUXEMBOURG
CENTRE

0   400 m

ETTELBRUCK 28 km
N 7
ECHTERNACH 35 km
E 42

LIMPERTSBERG

COUR DE JUSTICE
EUROPÉENNE

Av. J.F. Kennedy
AUTOROUTE DU KIRCHBERG
PARLEMENT EUROPÉEN

TRIER 47 km
AÉROPORT 8 km

PARC DES
TROIS GLANDS

PLATEAU DE KIRCHBERG

CHAMP
DE FOIRE

Rond-Point
R. Schuman

MUSÉE DE L'ÉTAT ★★
CHEMIN DE LA CORNICHE ★★
CASEMATES DU BOCK ★★

ARLON 29 km
N 12
E 9

PFAFFENTHAL

Me
Reuter

Pl. Churchill

R.T.L.

GRUND

Pl. de
Bruxelles

VIEILLE VILLE ★★
PLACE DE LA
CONSTITUTION ★★

LONGWY 31 km

SAARBRÜCKEN 99 km
N 2 E 42

Pl. des
Martyrs

PLATEAU
BOURBON

Pl. de Paris

ESCH-SUR-ALZETTE
19 km

GARE

Strasbourg

HOLLERICH

BONNEVOIE

E 9-N 3
THIONVILLE 32 km

68

STREET INDEX TO LUXEMBOURG TOWN PLAN

XXX Astoria, av. du X-Septembre 14, ✉ 2550, ℰ 446223 – AE ◑ E VISA — DY **s**
closed Saturday, August and 23 December-1 January – **M** (lunch only) a la carte 1200/1690.

XXX Le Vert Galant, 1st floor, r. Aldringen 23 (r. Poste), ✉ 1118, ℰ 470822 – AE ◑ E VISA — CY **r**
closed Saturday and Sunday – **M** a la carte 1250/1730.

XX Caesar, av. Monterey 18, ✉ 2163, ℰ 470925, « Tasteful decor » – AE VISA — CY **u**
M 595/795.

XX Theatre, r. Beaumont 3, ✉ 1219, ℰ 40534 – AE VISA ⅜ — DY **n**
closed Sunday dinner, Monday and 20 August-9 September – **M** a la carte 940/1550.

XX L'Obernai, r. Palais de Justice 1, ✉ 1841, ℰ 22212 – AE VISA — DY **u**
closed Saturday lunch, Sunday, 15 July-5 August and 22 to 31 December – **M** a la carte 960/1450.

X Gëlle Fra, r. Notre-Dame 10, ✉ 2240, ℰ 471794 – AE E VISA ⅜ — CY **y**
closed Wednesday dinner, Thursday, August and 23 December-5 January – **M** 500/800.

Luxembourg-Station :

🏨 Kons, pl. Gare 24, ✉ 1616, ℰ 486021, Telex 2306 – ⟦⟧ ☎ – 🔒 AE ◑ E VISA ⅜ rest — DZ **v**
M (closed Sunday) 550/1800 – **141 rm** 2300/3180.

🏨 Nobilis and Rest. Calao M, av. Gare 47, ✉ 1611, ℰ 494971, Telex 3212 – ⟦⟧ 🖭 TV ☎ — DZ **m**
🚗 AE ◑ E VISA
M 500/795 — 🖙 240 – **43 rm** 2350/2600.

🏨 Central-Molitor, av. Liberté 28, ✉ 1930, ℰ 489911, Telex 2613 – ⟦⟧ TV AE ◑ E VISA — DZ **x**
⅜ rest
M (closed Friday and mid December-mid January) 585/820 – **36 rm** 🖙 1900/2500.

🏨 President, pl. Gare 32, ✉ 1024, ℰ 486161, Telex 1510 – ⟦⟧ TV 🛏 ▥wc ☎ AE ◑ E VISA — DZ **v**
closed July – **M** (closed Saturday, Sunday and Bank Holidays) 500 – **40 rm** 🖙 2500/3000.

🏨 Ardennes M without rest., av. Liberté 59, ✉ 1931, ℰ 488141 – ⟦⟧ TV ▥wc ▥wc ☎ ⅜ — DZ **e**
21 rm

🏨 Bristol without rest., r. Strasbourg 11, ✉ 2561, ℰ 485829 – ⟦⟧ TV ▥wc ☎ ⓟ AE ◑ E — DZ **d**
VISA ⅜
29 rm 🖙 1100/2300.

🏨 City without rest., r. Strasbourg 1, ✉ 2561, ℰ 484608 – ⟦⟧ 🛏wc ▥wc ☎ AE ◑ E VISA — DZ **t**
closed 7 December-3 January – 🖙 180 – **20 rm** 800/2145.

XXX Cordial, 1st floor, pl. Paris 1, ✉ 2314, ℰ 488538, « Elegant interior » – ⅜ — DZ **w**
closed Friday, Saturday lunch and July – **M** a la carte 1170/1800.

XX Italia with rm, r. Anvers 15, ✉ 1130, ℰ 486626, 🛋, Italian rest. – ▥wc ☜. AE ◑ E VISA — DZ **q**
M a la carte 730/1130 – **22 rm** 🖙 1600/2200.

Upland of Kirchberg – ✉ Luxembourg :

🏨 Holiday Inn M, Kirchberg, ✉ 2015, ℰ 437761, Telex 2751, 🔲 – ⟦⟧ 🖭 TV ☎ 👍 ⓟ – 🔒
AE ◑ E VISA ⅜ rest
M (closed Saturday lunch) a la carte 620/1120 – **260 rm** 🖙 3200/4300.

North, at Limpertsberg – ✉ Luxembourg :

XX Osteria del Teatro, Allée Scheffer 21, ✉ 2520, ℰ 28811, Italian rest. – AE ◑ E VISA — CY **a**
closed Monday and 25 July-14 August – **M** a la carte 620/1050.

North-East – ✉ Luxembourg :

XXX Le Grimpereau, r. Cents 140, ✉ 1319, ℰ 436787, « Converted villa, garden setting » –
ⓟ AE ◑ E VISA
closed Saturday lunch, Sunday, Bank Holidays, 2 weeks August, Christmas-New Year and Easter – **M** a la carte 1520/1830.

at Dommeldange – ⊠ Dommeldange :

🏨 **Novotel** Ⓜ, rte d'Echternach E 42, ⊠ 1453, 🖉 435643, Telex 1418, ⬛, ✗ – 🛗 🍽 rest
🔲 ☎ 🅿 – 🔬 ⒶⒺ Ⓞ ᴇ 𝘝𝘐𝘚𝘈
M a la carte 630/1000 – **253 rm** ⊑ 2400/3000 – P 3200.

🍴🍴 ❀ **Host. Grünewald** with rm, rte d'Echternach 10, ⊠ 1453, 🖉 431882 – 🍽 rest 🛏wc
🍴wc ☜ 🅿 ⒶⒺ ⓄⒺ 𝘝𝘐𝘚𝘈
closed 7 to 23 January – **M** *(closed Saturday lunch and Sunday)* (booking essential
Saturday) a la carte 1150/1640 – **28 rm** ⊑ 1900/2800
Spec. Mousse de jambon, Quenelles de brochet, Chevreuil au Chablis (September-April). **Wines** Pinot gris,
Koepfchen.

Inter-Continental Ⓜ ⣿ (open Spring 1985), r. Jean Engling, ⊠ 1466, 🖉 43781, Telex
3754, ≤, ⬛, ✗ – 🛗 🔲 🛏wc ☜ 🅔 🅿 – 🔬 – 346 rm.

at Hesperange – pop. 9 090 – ⊠ Hespérange :

🍴🍴🍴 ❀ **L'Agath** (Steichen) with rm, rte de Thionville 274, ⊠ 5884, 🖉 488687, 🌤, « Classic-
elegant », 🌤 – 🔲 🛏wc 🍴wc ☎ 🅿 ⒶⒺ ⓄⒺ 𝘝𝘐𝘚𝘈
closed Sunday, Easter, mid July-mid August and 1 November – **M** *(closed Saturday
lunch, Sunday and Monday lunch)* a la carte 1450/1850 – 7 rm ⊑ 1350/2900
Spec. Soupe froide de homard, Turbot truffé de St-Jacques, Pigeon des Landes à la crème d'ail. **Wines** Pinot
gris.

at the skating-rink of Kockelscheuer – ⊠ Luxembourg :

🍴🍴🍴 ❀ **Patin d'Or**, Patinoire de Kochelscheuer, ⊠ 1899, 🖉 26499, ≤ – 🍽 🅿. ⒶⒺ ᴇ 𝘝𝘐𝘚𝘈
closed Saturday lunch, Monday, last 2 weeks August and last 2 weeks December – **M** a la
carte 1310/1860.

Airport by ③ : 8 km – ⊠ Luxembourg :

🏨🏨 **Aérogolf-Sheraton** Ⓜ ⣿, rte de Trèves, ⊠ 1019, 🖉 34571, Telex 2662, ≤ – 🛗 🍽 🔲
☎ 🅿 – 🔬 ⒶⒺ ⓄⒺ 𝘝𝘐𝘚𝘈. 🍽 rest
M a la carte 790/1430 – ⊑ 275 – **148 rm** 2550/4200 – P 2935/3485.

▮**Diekirch** ⑧ ③ and ⓵⓪⑨ ㉘ – pop. 5 585 – 35 km :

🍴🍴🍴 ❀❀ **Hiertz** with rm, r. Clairefontaine 1, ⊠ 9201, 🖉 803562, « Tasteful decoration, terrace
and flower garden » – 🅿. ᴇ
*closed Monday dinner, Tuesday, end August-beginning September and 20 December-14
January* – **M** (booking essential) a la carte 900/1370 – **7 rm** ⊑ 1300/1800
Spec. Foie gras frais, Homard aux frisons de concombres et tomates. **Wines** Riesling.

▮**Echternach** ⑧ ④ and ⓵⓪⑨ ㉗ – pop. 4 159 – 35 km :

at Geyershof SW : 7 km by E 42 ⒸConsthum – pop. 278 – ⊠ Echternach :

🍴🍴🍴 ❀❀ **La Bergerie** (Phal), ⊠ 6251, 🖉 79464, ≤, 🌤, « Converted farm, country atmosphere » – 🅿. ⒶⒺ ᴇ 𝘝𝘐𝘚𝘈
closed Sunday dinner, Monday, last 2 weeks November and February – **M** a la carte
1330/1880
Spec. Filets de sole fumés, Sandre au Pinot noir, Agneau et son salpicon truffé. **Wines** Riesling.

AMSTERDAM

SIGHTS

See : Old Amsterdam★★★ : the canals★★★ (Grachten) : Singel, Herengracht, Reguliersgracht, Keizersgracht, boattrip★ (Rondvaart) – Beguine Convent★★ (Begijnhof) LY – Dam : New Church★ (Nieuwe Kerk) LXY – Flower market★ (Bloemenmarkt) LY – Rembrandt Square (Rembrandtsplein) MY – Small Bridge (Magere Brug) MZ.

Museums : Rijksmuseum★★★ KZ – Rijksmuseum Vincent van Gogh★★★ – Municipal★★ (Stedelijk Museum) : Modern Art – History of Amsterdam★★ (Amsterdams Historisch Museum) LY – Madame Tussaud★ : wax museum LY M¹ – Museum Amstelkring Ons'Lieve Heer op Solder : ancient secret chapel★ MX M⁴ – Rembrandt's House★ (Rembrandthuis) : (graphic arts of the master) MY M⁵ – Maritime Museum of the Netherlands★ (Nederlands Scheepvaart Museum) – The Tropics Museum★ (Tropenmuseum) – Allard Pierson★ : archaeological collections.

AMSTERDAM Noord-Holland 🔲🔲 ③ and 🔲🔲🔲 ⑩ ㉗ ㉘ – Pop. 687 397 – ✆ 0 20.

🏨 Zwarte Laantje 4 at Duivendrecht ✆ (0 20) 943650.
🏌 Sportpark Overamstel, Jan Vroegopsingel ✆ (0 20) 651863.

✈ at Schiphol SW : 9,5 km ✆ (0 20) 5110432 (information) and (0 20) 434242 (reservations) – Air Terminal : Central Station ✆ (0 20) 495575.

🚗 (Departure from 's-Hertogenbosch) ✆ (0 20) 238383 and (0 20) 141959 (Schiphol).

🛈 Stationsplein (Koffiehuis), ✉ 1012 AB ✆ 266444 – Tourist Association of the Province, Rokin 9-15, ✉ 1012 KK, ✆ 221016, Telex 12324.

Bruxelles 204 ③ – Düsseldorf 227 ③ – Den Haag 60 ④ – Luxembourg 419 ③ – Rotterdam 76 ④.

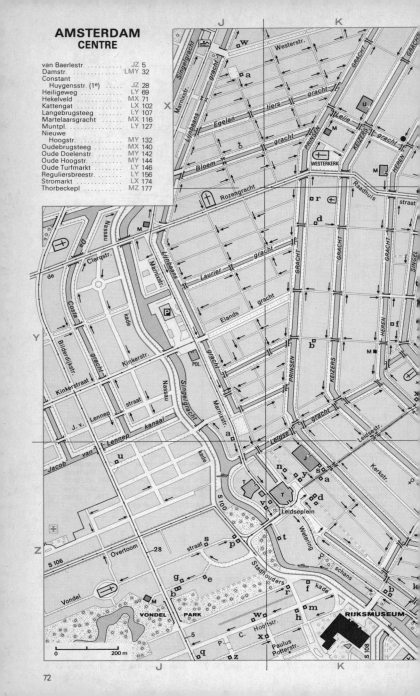

AMSTERDAM
CENTRE

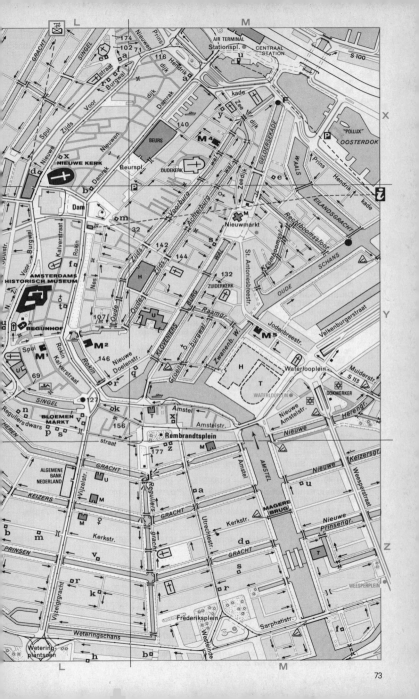

Centre

🏨🏨 **Amstel and Rest. La Rive,** Professor Tulpplein 1, ✉ 1018 GX, ☎ 226060, Telex 11004, « Shaded terrace ≼ Amstel » – 🛗 📺 ☎ ❼ – 🔥 🝙 ⓐ E 𝖵𝖨𝖲𝖠 🎱 MZ **f**
M *(closed Saturday lunch and Sunday lunch)* 53/110 – ⌑ 26 – **111 rm** 275/500.

🏨🏨 **Sonesta and Rest. Rib Room** Ⓜ, Kattengat 1, ✉ 1012 SZ, ☎ 212223, Telex 17149 – 🛗 🝙 rest 📺 ☎ & ⟷ – 🔥 🝙 ⓐ E. 🎱 rest LX **a**
M 75/122 – ⌑ 23 – **425 rm** 325/375.

🏨🏨 **Amsterdam Marriott and Rest. Port O'Amsterdam** Ⓜ, Stadhouderskade 21, ✉ 1054 ES, ☎ 835151, Telex 15087 – 🛗 🝙 📺 ☎ & ⟷ – 🔥 🝙 ⓐ E 𝖵𝖨𝖲𝖠. 🎱 rest JZ **p**
M 65 – ⌑ 23 – **395 rm** 360/455.

🏨🏨 **Europe and Rest. Excelsior,** Nieuwe Doelenstraat 2, ✉ 1012 CP, ☎ 234836, Telex 12081, ≼ – 🛗 🝙 rest 📺 – 🔥 🝙 ⓐ E 𝖵𝖨𝖲𝖠 LY **r**
M 55/150 – ⌑ 23 – **79 rm** 400/450.

🏨🏨 **Victoria,** Damrak 1, ✉ 1012 LG, ☎ 234255, Telex 16625 – 🛗 🝙 rest ☎ – 🔥 🝙 ⓐ E 𝖵𝖨𝖲𝖠. 🎱 rest MX **a**
M *(closed Sunday)* a la carte 47/80 – **160 rm** ⌑ 188/277.

🏨 **Pulitzer and Rest. Goudsbloem,** Prinsengracht 323, ✉ 1016 GZ, ☎ 228333, Telex 16508 – 🛗 🝙 rest 📺 ☎ – 🔥 🝙 ⓐ. 🎱 rest KY **y**
M *(closed Saturday lunch and Sunday lunch)* a la carte 71/100 – ⌑ 19 – **194 rm** 225/275.

🏨 **Doelen and Rest. Café Savarin,** Nieuwe Doelenstraat 24, ✉ 1012 CP, ☎ 220722, Telex 14399 – 🛗 📺. 🝙 ⓐ E. 🎱 rest MY **q**
M 30/45 – ⌑ 17 – **85 rm** 193/262.

🏨 **American,** Leidsekade 97, ✉ 1017 PN, ☎ 245322, Telex 12545 – 🛗 📺 ☎ – 🔥 🝙 ⓐ E 𝖵𝖨𝖲𝖠. 🎱 rest JKZ **v**
M *(Café Américain)* a la carte 39/71 – ⌑ 21 – **185 rm** 165/295.

🏨 **Carlton** without rest., Vijzelstraat 2, ✉ 1017 HK, ☎ 222266, Telex 11670 – 🛗 📺 ☎ – 🔥 🝙 ⓐ E 𝖵𝖨𝖲𝖠 LY **v**
⌑ 17 – **156 rm** 193/262.

🏨 **Caransa and Rest. Four Seasons,** Rembrandtsplein 19, ✉ 1017 CT, ☎ 229455, Telex 13342 – 🛗 🝙 📺 ☎ – 🔥 🝙 ⓐ E 𝖵𝖨𝖲𝖠 MY **x**
M a la carte 56/90 – ⌑ 17 – **66 rm** 193/262 – P 350.

🏨 **Gd H. Krasnapolsky and Rest.Le Reflet d'Or,** Dam 9, ✉ 1012 JS, ☎ 5549111, Telex 12262 – 🛗 📺 ☎ & ⟷ – 🔥 🝙 ⓐ E 𝖵𝖨𝖲𝖠. 🎱 rest LY **m**
M 27/70 – **356 rm** ⌑ 220/360.

🏨 **Port van Cleve,** Nieuwe Zijds Voorburgwal 178, ✉ 1012 SJ, ☎ 244860, Telex 13129 – 🛗 📺 – 🔥 🝙 ⓐ E 𝖵𝖨𝖲𝖠 LX **d**
M a la carte 44/65 – **110 rm** ⌑ 134/248 – P 169/187.

🏨 **Arthur Frommer and Rest. Oranjehof,** Noorderstraat 46, ✉ 1017 TV, ☎ 220328, Telex 14047 – 🛗 ❼. 🝙 ⓐ E 𝖵𝖨𝖲𝖠 🎱 LZ **k**
M *(dinner only)* 30 – **90 rm** ⊑ 138/180 – ½ p 167/184.

🏨 **Centraal,** Stadhouderskade 7, ✉ 1054 ES, ☎ 185765, Telex 12601 – 🛗 📺 ☎ – 🔥 🝙 ⓐ E 𝖵𝖨𝖲𝖠. 🎱 rm JZ **p**
M *(Travellers Grill)* *(open until midnight)* a la carte 46/61 – **116 rm** ⌑ 141/219.

🏨 **Ambassade** without rest., Herengracht 341, ✉ 1016 AZ, ☎ 262333, Telex 10158 – 🛏wc 🝙. 🝙 E 𝖵𝖨𝖲𝖠 KY **f**
39 rm ⌑ 74/155.

🏨 **Parkhotel,** Stadhouderskade 25, ✉ 1071 ZD, ☎ 717474, Telex 11412 – 🛗 🝙 rest 🛏wc ☎ ⟷ – 🔥 🝙 ⓐ E 𝖵𝖨𝖲𝖠. 🎱 KZ **f**
M 31/49 – **184 rm** ⌑ 174/247 – P 182/232.

🏨 **Schiller,** Rembrandtsplein 26, ✉ 1017 CV, ☎ 231660, Telex 14058 – 🛗 🛏wc 🝙wc 🝙 MZ **z**
M a la carte 41/74 – ⌑ 20 – **97 rm** 193/262.

🏨 **Owl Hotel** without rest., Roemer Visscherstraat 1, ✉ 1054 EV, ☎ 189484, Telex 13360 – 🛗 🛏wc 🝙wc 🝙. 🝙 E 𝖵𝖨𝖲𝖠 JZ **e**
34 rm ⌑ 93/135.

🏨 **Choura** without rest., Marnixstraat 372, ✉ 1016 XX, ☎ 237524, Telex 15362 – 🛗 📺 🛏wc 🝙wc. 🝙 E JY **a**
22 rm ⌑ 89/188.

🏨 **Asterisk** without rest., Den Texstraat 16, ✉ 1017 ZA, ☎ 262396 – 🛏wc 🝙wc. E 𝖵𝖨𝖲𝖠 LZ **h**
19 rm ⌑ 55/135.

🏨 **Parklane** without rest., Plantage Parklaan 16, ✉ 1018 ST, ☎ 224804 – 🝙wc. 🎱
9 rm ⌑ 85/105.

🏨 **Nicolaas Witsen** without rest., Nicolaas Witsenstraat 6, ✉ 1017 ZH, ☎ 266546 – 🛗 🛏wc 🝙wc 🝙 MZ **b**
32 rm ⊒ 50/110.

🏨 **Linda** without rest., Stadhouderskade 131, ✉ 1074 AW, ☎ 625668 – 🝙wc. 🎱
closed November – **17 rm** ⊒ 65/135.

🏨 **Roode Leeuw,** Damrak 93, ✉ 1012 LP, ☎ 240396 – 🛗 🛏wc ☎ – 🔥 🝙 𝖵𝖨𝖲𝖠 LXY **b**
M a la carte 32/43 – **85 rm** ⌑ 75/152 – P 100/132.

XXXX **Dikker en Thijs and Alexander H.** with rm, Prinsengracht 444, angle Leidsestraat, ✉ 1017 KE, ☎ 267721, Telex 13161 – |$| TV ⌂wc ⌂wc ☎. AE ⓓ E VISA. ✂ KZ **s**
M *(closed Sunday)* (dinner only, open until midnight) 65/85 – ☕ 15 – **25 rm** 140/190.

XXX ✿ **Boerderij** (Wunneberg), Korte Leidsedwarsstraat 69, ✉ 1017 PW, ☎ 236929, Rustic atmosphere – ▤. AE ⓓ E VISA. ✂ KZ **d**
closed Saturday lunch, Sunday and 15 July-3 August – **M** a la carte 85/114
Spec. Assiette du pêcheur, Ris de veau aux morilles.

XXX **Martinn,** 12th floor, De Ruyterkade 7, ✉ 1013 AA, ☎ 256277, ≼ – ▤. AE ⓓ E
closed Saturday and Sunday – **M** 50/80.

XXX **Swarte Schaep,** 1st floor, Korte Leidsedwarsstraat 24, ✉ 1017 RC, ☎ 223021, « 17C interior » – ▤. AE ⓓ E VISA KZ **d**
closed 5, 25, 26, 31 December and 1 January – **M** 75/88.

XXX **Lido,** Leidsekade 105, ✉ 1017 PP, ☎ 263300 – ▤. AE ⓓ E VISA KZ **t**
closed Sunday and Monday – **M** (dinner only) a la carte 38/70.

XXX **Bali,** 1st floor, Leidsestraat 89, ✉ 1017 NZ, ☎ 227878, Indonesian rest. – ▤. AE E VISA KZ **a**
closed Sunday and 5, 24, 31 December – **M** 42/50.

XX **Prinsenkelder,** Prinsengracht 438, ✉ 1017 KE, ☎ 267721 – AE ⓓ E VISA. ✂ KZ **s**
closed Saturday and Sunday lunch – **M** 55/65.

XX **Les Quatre Canetons,** Prinsengracht 1111, ✉ 1017 JJ, ☎ 246307 – AE ⓓ E VISA. ✂
closed Saturday lunch, Sunday, Easter, Whitsuntide and New Year – **M** 58/75. MZ **d**

XX **Treasure,** Nieuwe Zijds Voorburgwal 115, ✉ 1012 RH, ☎ 234061, Chinese rest. – AE ⓓ E. ✂ LX **x**
M a la carte 50/90.

XX **L'Entrée,** 1st floor, Reguliersdwarsstraat 42, ✉ 1017 BM, ☎ 258788 – AE ⓓ E. ✂
closed Sunday – **M** a la carte 45/88. LY **s**

XX **Dynasty,** Reguliersdwarsstraat 30, ✉ 1017 BM, ☎ 268400, ☂, Oriental rest. – ▤. AE ⓓ E VISA. ✂ LY **p**
M (dinner only) a la carte 38/68.

XX **Oesterbar,** Leidseplein 10, ✉ 1017 PT, ☎ 232988, Seafood – ▤. AE. ✂ KZ **y**
M a la carte 42/84.

XX **Pêcheur,** Reguliersdwarsstraat 32, ✉ 1017 BM, ☎ 243121, Seafood. – AE ⓓ E VISA
closed Saturday lunch, Sunday lunch, 5, 24 and 31 December – **M** a la carte 40/77. LY **s**

XX **Indonesia,** 1st floor, Singel 550, ✉ 1017 AZ, ☎ 232035, Indonesian rest. – ▤. AE ⓓ E VISA LY **v**
M 27/40.

XX **Le Rêve,** Kerkstraat 148, ✉ 1017 GR, ☎ 241394, Painting collection – AE ⓓ E VISA
closed Tuesday, 30 April, 5 to 22 August, 5 December and 23 December-15 January – **M** (dinner only) a la carte 40/60. LZ **b**

XX **Da Canova,** Warmoesstraat 9, ✉ 1012 HT, ☎ 266725, Italian rest. – AE ⓓ E MX **y**
closed Sunday and Monday – **M** (dinner only) a la carte 53/67.

XX **Camargue,** Reguliersdwarsstraat 7, ✉ 1017 BJ, ☎ 239352 – ▤. AE ⓓ E VISA. ✂
closed Saturday lunch and Sunday lunch – **M** a la carte 51/80. LY **n**

XX **Tai-Pan,** Marnixstraat 406, ✉ 1017 PL, ☎ 254389, Chinese rest. – ▤. AE ⓓ E VISA. ✂
closed Monday – **M** (dinner only) 38/48. JKZ **v**

XX **Lotus,** Binnen Bantammerstraat 5, ✉ 1011 CH, ☎ 242614, Chinese rest. – ▤. AE ⓓ E VISA MX **e**
M *(dinner only)* a la carte 35/55.

XX **Sancerre,** Reestraat 28, ✉ 1016 DN, ☎ 278794 – AE E KY **d**
closed Easter, Whitsuntide, Christmas and New Year – **M** (dinner only) 45/80.

XX **Vijff Vlieghen,** Spuistraat 294, ✉ 1012 VX, ☎ 248369, « Old Dutch atmosphere » – AE ⓓ E VISA KY **h**
closed 5, 25, 26 and 31 December – **M** (dinner only) 58/78.

XX **Kopenhagen,** Rokin 84, ✉ 1012 KX, ☎ 249376, Danish rest. – ▤. AE ⓓ E LY **t**
closed Sunday – **M** 25/55.

XX **Bacchus,** Spuistraat 3 e, ✉ 1012 SP, ☎ 230051 – ▤. AE ⓓ E VISA LX **r**
M a la carte 54/88.

XX **Les Trois Neufs,** Prinsengracht 999, ✉ 1017 KM, ☎ 229044 – AE ⓓ E VISA LZ **v**
closed Monday and mid July-mid August – **M** a la carte 37/55.

XX **Adrian,** Reguliersdwarsstraat 21, ✉ 1017 BJ, ☎ 239582, Open until midnight – ▤. AE ⓓ E VISA LY **n**
closed Saturday lunch and Sunday lunch – **M** 38/85.

XX **Dorrius,** Nieuwe Zijds Voorburgwal 336, ✉ 1012 RX, ☎ 235245, Dutch rest. – AE ⓓ E VISA LY **u**
closed Sunday lunch, 25, 26 and 31 December – **M** a la carte 54/64.

XX **Opatija,** Weteringschans 93, ✉ 1017 RZ, ☎ 225184, Balkan rest. KZ **b**
M (dinner only) 27/43.

XX **Djawa,** 1st floor, Korte Leidsedwarsstraat 18, ✉ 1017 RC, ☎ 246016, Indonesian rest. – ▤. AE ⓓ E VISA. ✂ KZ **n**
closed 31 December – **M** (dinner only) 25/37.

※ **Provençal,** Weteringschans 91, ⊠ 1017 RZ, ℰ 239619 – 🆎 ⓪ E. 🏖   KZ **b**
closed Sunday – **M** (dinner only) a la carte 53/61.

※ **Cartouche,** Anjeliersstraat 177, ⊠ 1015 NG, ℰ 227438 – 🆎 ⓪ E 𝒱𝒾𝒮𝒜 🏖   JX **a**
closed Monday – **M** (dinner only) a la carte 66/85.

※ **Valentijn,** Kloveniersburgwal 6, ⊠ 1012 CT, ℰ 242028 – 🍴. 🆎 ⓪ E 🏖   MY **s**
closed 1 to 6 January – **M** (dinner only) 50/90.

※ **Ardjuna,** 1st floor, Reguliersbreestraat 21, ⊠ 1017 CL, ℰ 220204, Indonesian rest. – 🆎
⓪ E 𝒱𝒾𝒮𝒜. 🏖   LY **k**
M 25/29.

South and West Quarters

🏨 **Amsterdam Hilton** Ⓜ with Japanese rest. **Kei**, Apollolaan 138, ⊠ 1077 BG, ℰ 780780,
Telex 11025 – 📶 🍽 rest 📺 ☎ Ⓟ – 🏛. 🆎 ⓪ E 𝒱𝒾𝒮𝒜. 🏖
M a la carte 41/68 – ⊊ 24 – **274 rm** 220/425.

🏨 ❀ **Dikker en Thijs Garden Hotel and Rest. De Kersentuin** Ⓜ, Dijsselhofplantsoen
7, ⊠ 1077 BJ, ℰ 642121, Telex 15453 – 📶 🍽 📺 ☎ Ⓟ – 🏛. 🆎 ⓪ E 𝒱𝒾𝒮𝒜
M *(closed Saturday lunch and Sunday)* 68/100 – **97 rm** ⊊ 194/267.

🏨 **Okura and Rest. Ciel Bleu** Ⓜ with Japanese rest. **Yamazato**, Ferdinand Bolstraat 175,
⊠ 1072 LH, ℰ 787111, Telex 16182, « Rest. on the 23rd floor with ≤ town », ☛ – 📶 🍽
📺 ☎ ⇌ Ⓟ – 🏛. 🆎 ⓪ E 𝒱𝒾𝒮𝒜 🏖 rest
M **(Ciel Bleu)** (dinner only, open until midnight) a la carte 68/109 – ⊊ 23 – **402 rm**
300/340.

🏨 **Apollohotel,** Apollolaan 2, ⊠ 1077 BA, ℰ 735922, Telex 14084, « Terrace with ≤ canal »
– 📶 📺 ☎ ♿ Ⓟ – 🏛. 🆎 ⓪ E
M *(closed Saturday lunch)* a la carte 64/91 – ⊊ 23 – **217 rm** 275/330.

🏨 **Crest H. Amsterdam** Ⓜ, De Boelelaan 2, ⊠ 1083 HJ, ℰ 429855, Telex 13647 – 📶 🍽
📺 Ⓟ – 🏛. 🆎 ⓪ E 𝒱𝒾𝒮𝒜. 🏖 rest
M 38 – ⊊ 17 – **260 rm** 207/325.

🏨 **Novotel Amsterdam** Ⓜ, Europaboulevard 10, ⊠ 1083 AD, ℰ 5411123, Telex 13375 –
📶 🍽 rest 📺 ☎ Ⓟ – 🏛. 🆎 ⓪ E 𝒱𝒾𝒮𝒜. 🏖
M a la carte 34/79 – **600 rm** ⊊ 185/225 – P 243.

🏨 **Jan Luyken** without rest., Jan Luykenstraat 58, ⊠ 1071 CS, ℰ 764111, Telex 16254 – 📶
📺 ☎. 🆎 ⓪ E   JZ **x**
63 rm ⊊ 153/195.

🏨 **Memphis,** De Lairessestraat 87, ⊠ 1071 NX, ℰ 733141, Telex 12450 – 📶. 🆎 ⓪ E 𝒱𝒾𝒮𝒜.
🏖
M 31/75 – **81 rm** ⊊ 179/257 – P 187/237.

🏨 **Delphi** without rest., Apollolaan 105, ⊠ 1077 AN, ℰ 795152, Telex 16659 – 📶 📺 ⌂wc
☞. 🆎 ⓪ E 𝒱𝒾𝒮𝒜
48 rm ⊊ 115/180.

🏨 **Apollofirst,** Apollolaan 123, ⊠ 1077 AP, ℰ 730333, Telex 13446 – 📶 📺 ⌂wc ☞. 🆎
⓪ E 𝒱𝒾𝒮𝒜
M (dinner only) a la carte 38/85 – **35 rm** ⊊ 130/170 – P 146/198.

🏨 **Atlas H.,** Van Eeghenstraat 64, ⊠ 1071 GK, ℰ 766336, Telex 17081 – 📶 📺 ⌂wc ☞.
🆎 ⓪ E 𝒱𝒾𝒮𝒜
M a la carte 38/59 – **24 rm** ⊊ 105/155.

🏨 **Casa 400,** James Wattstraat 75, ⊠ 1097 DL, ℰ 651171, Telex 14677 – 📶 🛗wc ☞ – 🏛.
🆎
June-September – **M** 27/31 – **400 rm** 🍴 96/168.

🏨 **Zandbergen** without rest., Willemsparkweg 205, ⊠ 1071 HB, ℰ 769321 – 📺 ⌂wc
🛗wc ☞. 🆎 ⓪ E 𝒱𝒾𝒮𝒜
17 rm ⊊ 58/140.

🏨 **Borgmann** 🦢 without rest., Koningslaan 48, ⊠ 1075 AE, ℰ 735252 – 📶 ⌂wc 🛗wc ☞.
🆎 ⓪ E
15 rm ⊊ 55/120.

🏨 **Toro** 🦢 without rest., Koningslaan 64, ⊠ 1075 AG, ℰ 737223 – ⌂wc 🛗 ☞. 🆎 ⓪ E
12 rm ⊊ 55/120.

🏨 **Fita** without rest., Jan Luykenstraat 37, ⊠ 1071 CL, ℰ 790976 – 🛗wc. 🏖   JZ **z**
20 rm 🍴 75/100.

✕✕✕ **Parkrest. Rosarium,** Europa boulevard, Amstelpark 1, ⊠ 1083 HZ, ℰ 444085, 🌇,
« Flowered park » – 🏛. 🆎 ⓪ E 𝒱𝒾𝒮𝒜
closed Sunday – **M** 50/105.

✕✕ **Fong Lie,** P.C. Hooftstraat 80, ⊠ 1071 CB, ℰ 716404, Chinese rest. – 🍴. 🆎 ⓪   JZ **w**
closed Monday, Bank Holidays, 2nd week July-1 August and 3rd week December – **M** a la
carte 50/78.

✕✕ **Henri Smits,** 1st floor, Beethovenstraat 55, ⊠ 1077 HN, ℰ 791715 – 🍴. 🆎 ⓪ E 𝒱𝒾𝒮𝒜
closed 25 and 26 December – **M** 48.

✕✕ **Bistro Lapin,** 1st floor, Scheldeplein 3, ⊠ 1078 GR, ℰ 642211 – 🍴. 🏖
M (dinner only) a la carte 27/65.

XX **Keijzer,** Van Baerlestraat 96, ⌷ 1071 BB, ℰ 711441 – ⒜⒠ ⒪ E. ⛛
closed Sunday, Easter, Whitsuntide and 1 January – **M** a la carte 50/65.

XX **Miranda Paviljoen,** Amsteldijk 223, ⌷ 1079 LK, ℰ 445768 – ⒫
closed Christmas and New Year – **M** 44/82.

XX **Hamilcar,** Overtoom 306, ⌷ 1054 JC, ℰ 837981, Tunisian rest. – ⒜⒠ ⒪ E
M (dinner only) a la carte 30/50.

X **L'Entrecôte,** P.C. Hooftstraat 70, ⌷ 1071 CB, ℰ 737776, 1920 Style, Grill rest.   JZ **w**
closed Sunday, Monday, Bank Holidays and July – **M** a la carte approx. 40.

X **Rembrandt,** P.C. Hooftstraat 31, ⌷ 1071 BM, ℰ 629011 – ▤. ⒜⒠ ⒪ E *VISA*   KZ **h**
closed Monday – **M** a la carte 40/74.

X ⊛ **Trechter,** Hobbemakade 63, ⌷ 1071 XL, ℰ 711263 – ⒜⒠ ⒪ E *VISA*. ⛛
closed Sunday, Monday, Bank Holidays and 16 July-5 August – **M** (dinner only) a la carte 50/80.

X **Les Frères,** Bosboom Toussaintstraat 70, ⌷ 1054 AV, ℰ 187905   JZ **u**
closed Sunday, Bank Holidays and 15 July-3 August – **M** (dinner only) a la carte 39/46.

X **Sama Sebo,** P.C. Hooftstraat 27, ⌷ 1071 BL, ℰ 628146, Indonesian rest. – ▤. ⒜⒠ E
closed Sunday, last 2 weeks July and last 2 weeks December – **M** 25/38.   KZ **m**

Environs

at Schiphol – ⊛ 0 20 :
🛈 Airport, arrival ℰ 175657.

🏨 **Hilton International Schiphol and Rest. Dutch Oven** Ⓜ, Herbergierstraat 1, ⌷ 1118 ZK (near airport), ℰ 5115911, Telex 15186, ◪ – 🛗 ▤ 📺 ☎ ⅋ ⒫ – ⛐. ⒜⒠ ⒪ E. ⛛ rest
M a la carte 57/95 – 🍽 19 – **204 rm** 300/360.

XXX **Aviorama** with Indonesian rest. **Ken Dedes,** 3rd Floor, Schipholweg 1, airport, ⌷ 1118 AA, ℰ 152150, ⇐ – ▤. ⒜⒠ ⒪ E *VISA*
closed 24 and 25 December – **M** a la carte 43/73.

near The Hague motorway A 4 :

🏨 **Euromotel Amsterdam** Ⓜ, Oude Haagseweg 20, ⌷ 1066 BW, ℰ 179005, Telex 15524 – 🛗 📺 ⅋ ⒫ – ⛐. ⒜⒠ ⒪ E *VISA*
M a la carte 33/53 – **157 rm** 🚗 105/138 – P 143.

XX **De Boekanier,** Oude Haagseweg 49, ⌷ 1066 BV, ℰ 173525 – ⒫. ⒜⒠ ⒪ E
closed Saturday, Sunday and 27 July-18 August – **M** 65/110.

on The Hague motorway A 4 by ④ : 15 km – ⊛ 0 2503 :

🏨 **Schiphol** Ⓜ, Kruisweg 495, ⌷ 2132 NA, ℰ 15851, Telex 74546 – 🛗 ▤ rest 📺 ☎ ⅋ ⒫ – ⛐. ⒜⒠ ⒪ E
M *(closed Saturday and Sunday lunch)* a la carte 66/88 – 🍽 19 – **166 rm** 215/280.

Amstelveen Noord-Holland ⅋⅋⅋ ③ and ⅋⅋⅋ ⑩⑳ – pop. 68 894 – ⊛ 0 20 – 11 km.

XXXX ⊛ **Molen De Dikkert,** Amsterdamseweg 104a, ⌷ 1182 HG, ℰ 411378, « 17C converted mill » – ⒫. ⒜⒠ ⒪ E *VISA*
closed Saturday lunch, Sunday lunch, 27 July-18 August and 31 December-6 January – 80/135
Spec. Mariage de canard et foie gras, Pintade marbrée aux truffes, Ecrevisses aux petits légumes.

XXX ⊛ **Rôtiss. Ile de France,** Pieter Lastmanweg 9, ⌷ 1181 XG, ℰ 453509 – ▤. ⛛
closed Sunday, Monday and 22 December-13 January – **M** a la carte 75/88
Spec. Huîtres au champagne (15 October-15 April), Rognon d'agneau aux trois moutardes, Magret de canard en croûte.

Bosch en Duin Utrecht ⅋⅋⅋ ⑭ – pop. 61 329 – ⊛ 0 30 – 50 km.

XXX ⊛⊛ **Hoefslag,** Vossenlaan 28, ⌷ 3735 KN, ℰ (0 30) 784395, ⇐ – ⒫. ⒜⒠ ⒪ E
closed Sunday and Monday – **M** a la carte 88/115
Spec. Bouillabaisse à notre façon, Agneau de lait aux aromates (January-August), Raviolis de homard.

Pleasant hotels and restaurants
are shown in the Guide by a red sign.
Please send us the names
of any where you have enjoyed your stay.
Your Michelin Guide will be even better.
🏨 … 🏠   XXXXX … X

The HAGUE (Den HAAG or 's-GRAVENHAGE) Zuid-Holland **211** ⑩ and **408** ⑨ – pop. 449 338 – ✪ 0 70.

See : Scheveningen★★ – Binnenhof★ : The Knights' Room★ (Ridderzaal) JV **A** – Hofvijver (Court pool) ✦★ JV – Lange Voorhout★ JV – Panorama Mesdag★ HV **B** – Madurodam★.

Museums : Mauritshuis★★★ JV – Municipal★★ (Gemeentemuseum) – Bredius★ HX **M¹** – Mesdag★ HU **M²**.

🛏 Gr. Haesebroekseweg 22 at Wassenaar N : 4 km ✆ (0 1751) 79607.

✈ Amsterdam-Schiphol NE : 37 km ✆ (0 70) 648030, (0 20) 5110432 (information) and (0 20) 434242 (reservations) – Rotterdam-Zestienhoven SE : 17 km ✆ (0 10) 157633 (information) and (0 10) 378211, 155430 (reservations).

🚆 (departs from 's-Hertogenbosch) ✆ (0 70) 824141.

🛈 Zwolsestraat 30 (Scheveningen). ✉ 2587 VJ. ✆ 546200.

Amsterdam 60 – Brussels 177 – Rotterdam 26 – Delft 13

Plan opposite

🏨 **Promenade and Rest. Cigogne** Ⓜ, van Stolkweg 1, ✉ 2585 JL, ✆ 525161, Telex 31162, « Elegant decoration, collection of modern paintings » – 🛗 🍽 rest 📺 ☎ Ⓟ – 🅰. 🆎 ⑩ Ε VISA
Ⓜ 60/88 – ☞ 20 – **101 rm** 190/250.

🏨 **Sofitel** Ⓜ, Koningin Julianaplein 35, ✉ 2595 AA, ✆ 814901, Telex 34001 – 🛗 🍽 📺 ☎ 👤 ⇌ – 🅰. 🆎 ⑩ Ε VISA. ✵ rest
Ⓜ a la carte 55/105 – ☞ 18 – **143 rm** 205/255.

🏨 **Des Indes and Le Restaurant,** Lange Voorhout 54, ✉ 2514 EG, ✆ 469553, Telex 31196 – 🛗 🍽 rest 📺 ☎ 👤 – 🅰. 🆎 ⑩ Ε VISA   JV **s**
Ⓜ a la carte 57/88 – ☞ 25 – **77 rm** 250/300.

🏨 **Central and Rest. Sir Edward,** Lange Poten 6, ✉ 2511 CL, ✆ 469414, Telex 32000 – 🛗 🍽 rest 📺 – 🅰. 🆎 ⑩ Ε VISA   JV **g**
Ⓜ *(closed Friday and Saturday)* 25/49 – **137 rm** 110/190.

🏨 **Bel Air,** Johan de Wittlaan 30, ✉ 2517 JR, ✆ 502021, Telex 31444, 🔲 – 🛗 🍽 ☎ 👤 Ⓟ – 🅰. 🆎 ⑩ Ε. ✵ rest
Ⓜ a la carte 60/93 – ☞ 14 – **350 rm** 125/168 – P 149/190.

🏨 **Parkhotel-De Zalm** without rest. (annex 🏨), Molenstraat 53, ✉ 2513 BJ, ✆ 624371, Telex 33005 – 🛗 ⇌ – 🅰. 🆎 ⑩ Ε VISA   HV **a**
130 rm ☞ 59/188.

🔺🔺🔺🔺 **Royal,** Lange Voorhout 44, ✉ 2514 EG, ✆ 600772 – ✵   JV **t**
closed Sunday – Ⓜ 43/50.

🔺🔺🔺 ⊛ **Saur,** 1st floor, Lange Voorhout 51, ✉ 2514 EC, ✆ 463344, Seafood – 🍽. 🆎 ⑩ Ε VISA. ✵   JV **h**
closed Saturday lunch, Sunday and Bank Holidays – Ⓜ a la carte 98/123
Spec. Turbot en papillote, Homard nonante-huit, Sole Lafayette.

🔺🔺🔺 **House of Lords,** Hofstraat 4, ✉ 2511 CN, ✆ 644771 – 🆎 ⑩ Ε VISA. ✵   JV **g**
closed Sunday and Monday – Ⓜ a la carte 71/104.

🔺🔺🔺 **Raden Ajoe,** Lange Poten 31, ✉ 2511 CM, ✆ 644592, Indonesian rest. – 🍽. 🆎 ⑩ Ε VISA   JV **a**
Ⓜ a la carte approx. 54.

🔺🔺 **Gemeste Schaap,** Raamstraat 9, ✉ 2512 BX, ✆ 639572, Old Dutch interior – 🆎 ⑩ Ε VISA   HX **y**
closed 15 July-2 August and Thursday from April to September – Ⓜ (dinner only) a la carte 48/75.

🔺🔺 **Aubergetie,** Nieuwe Schoolstraat 19, ✉ 2514 HT, ✆ 648070 – 🆎 ⑩   JV **b**
closed Tuesday – Ⓜ (dinner only) 53/73.

🔺🔺 **Frederik Hendrik,** Frederik Hendrikplein 1, ✉ 2582 AT, ✆ 541044 – 🆎 ⑩ Ε VISA. ✵
closed 31 December – Ⓜ (dinner only) a la carte 43/78.

🔺🔺 **Hof van Brederode,** Grote Halstraat 3, ✉ 2513 AX, ✆ 646455, « Converted cellar of a 16C townhall » – 🆎 ⑩ Ε VISA   HV **s**
closed Saturday lunch and Sunday – Ⓜ a la carte 53/75.

🔺🔺 **Roberto,** Noordeinde 196, ✉ 2514 GS, ✆ 464977, Italian rest. – 🆎 ⑩ Ε   HV **k**
closed Saturday lunch, Sunday lunch and Tuesday – Ⓜ a la carte 65/78.

🔺🔺 **La Grande Bouffe,** Maziestraat 10, ✉ 2514 GT, ✆ 654274 – 🆎 ⑩ Ε   HV **k**
closed Saturday lunch, Sunday lunch, 22 July-19 August and 26 December-5 January – Ⓜ 57/83.

🔺🔺 **Table du Roi,** Prinsestraat 130, ✉ 2513 CH, ✆ 461908 – 🍽. 🆎 ⑩. ✵   HV **g**
closed Monday, Tuesday and 29 July-20 August – Ⓜ a la carte 54/72.

🔺🔺 **Garoeda,** Kneuterdijk 18a, ✉ 2514 EN, ✆ 465319, Indonesian rest. – 🆎 ⑩ Ε VISA. ✵   HV **e**
closed Sunday lunch – Ⓜ a la carte 30/49.

🔺🔺 **Mata Hari,** Koningin Julianaplein 35 (in the drugstore Babylon), ✉ 2595 AA, ✆ 851268, Indonesian cuisine – 🍽. 🆎 ⑩ Ε VISA. ✵
closed Sunday – Ⓜ (with Chinese cuisine) 25/45.

The Hague-West :

XXX Le Coq d'Or, Leyweg 533, ✉ 2545 GG, ✆ 664407 – ▤.

at Scheveningen – ☎ 0 70 :

⛴ Shipping connections with Great Yarmouth : Norfolk Line, Kranenburgweg 211 ✆ (0 70) 514601.

ℹ Zwolsestraat 30, ✉ 2587 VJ, ✆ 546200.

Kurhaus and Rest. La Coquille, Gevers Deijnootplein 30, ✉ 2586 CK, ✆ 520052, Telex 33295, ≤, Casino on ground-floor – |‡| ▤ rest TV ☎ ♿ – 🏊. AE ⓓ E. ✂ rest
M a la carte 78/97 – **254 rm** ☕ 209/302.

Europa Crest H., Zwolsestraat 2, ✉ 2587 VJ, ✆ 512651, Telex 33138, 🏊 – |‡| TV ☎ – 🏊. AE ⓓ E VISA
M a la carte 48/102 – ☕ 21 – **174 rm** 149/218.

Eurotel, Gevers Deijnootweg 63, ✉ 2586 BJ, ✆ 512821, Telex 32799 – |‡| ▤ rest TV 🛁wc 🚿wc ☎ P – 🏊. AE ⓓ E VISA
April-September – **M** (dinner only) 35/80 – **77 rm** ☕ 110/210.

XXX ✿ **Seinpost,** Zeekant 60, ✉ 2586 AD, ✆ 555250, ≤ – AE ⓓ E
closed Saturday lunch, Sunday, Monday and end July-mid August – **M** 85/115.

XXX **Raden Mas,** Gevers Deijnootplein 125, ✉ 2586 CR, ✆ 545432, Indonesian rest. – ▤. AE ⓓ E VISA
M a la carte approx. 55.

XXX **Paddock,** Strandweg 155, ✉ 2586 JM, ✆ 541154, ≤ – ▤ P. AE ⓓ VISA
M a la carte 64/97.

XX **Bali** with rm, Badhuisweg 1, ✉ 2587 CA, ✆ 502434, Indonesian rest. – 🛁wc ☎. AE ⓓ. ✂ rm
M 25/45 – **34 rm** ☕ 40/90.

XX **Dionysos,** Gevers Deijnootplein 223, ✉ 2586 CT, ✆ 501419, 🍽, Greek rest. – AE ⓓ. ✂
M a la carte 49/83.

XX **Les Pieds dans l'Eau,** Dr. Lelykade 33, ✉ 2583 CL, ✆ 550040 – AE ⓓ
closed Thursday – **M** (dinner only) a la carte 61/79.

on the way to Wassenaar : 3 km :

XXX **Boerderij De Hoogwerf,** Zijdelaan 20, ✉ 2594 BV, ✆ 475514, 🍽, « 17C Farm » – P. AE ⓓ VISA. ✂
closed Sunday and Bank Holidays – **M** a la carte 64/89.

at Kijkduin : 4 km – ☎ 0 70 :

Atlantic, Deltaplein 200, ✉ 2554 EJ, ✆ 254025, Telex 33399, ≤, 🏊 – |‡| P – 🏊. AE ⓓ E VISA
M 25/80 – ☕ 15 – **60 rm** and **58** apartments 140/160.

Zeehaghe M without rest., Deltaplein 675, ✉ 2554 GK, ✆ 256262, Telex 31407, ≤ – |‡| TV P – 🏊. AE ⓓ E VISA
☕ 20 – **42 rm** and 28 apartments 140/200.

XX **Turpin,** Deltaplein 616, ✉ 2554 GJ, ✆ 687881 – AE ⓓ E
M 38/53.

XX **Bretagne,** Deltaplein 510, ✉ 2554 GH, ✆ 233801 – ▤. AE ⓓ
closed Monday – **M** (dinner only) 39/87.

Leidschendam Zuid-Holland **211** ⑫ and **408** ⑩ – pop. 30 239 – ☎ 0 70 – 50 km.

XXX ✿ **Chagall,** Weigelia 20, ✉ 2262 AB, ✆ 276910, « Lake side setting » – ▤. AE ⓓ E VISA
closed Sunday dinner and Monday – **M** 69/84
Spec. Terrine de foie gras de canard aux raisins, Grillade de coquilles St-Jacques, Gigot d'agneau à l'ail doux.

XXX ✿ **Villa Rozenrust,** Veursestraatweg 104, ✉ 2265 CG, ✆ 277460, 🍽 – P. AE ⓓ E VISA
closed Saturday, Sunday lunch and 2 weeks August – **M** a la carte 55/95
Spec. Salade de homard à la crème de truffes, Escalope de saumon Maître Pierre, Entrecôte au moka.

In addition to establishments indicated by
XXXXX ... X ,
many hotels possess
good class restaurants.

ROTTERDAM Zuid-Holland **211** ⑫ and **408** ㉔㉕ – pop. 558 832 – ✪ 0 10.

See : The harbour★★★ KZ – Lijnbaan★ (Shopping center) JKY – St. Laurence Church (Grote-of St. Laurenskerk) : interior★ KY **D** – Euromast★ (tower) (⚘★★, ◄★) JZ.

Museums : Boymans van Beuningen★★★ JZ – History Museum★ "De Dubbele Palmboom".

🎦 Kralingseweg 200 ℘ (0 10) 527646.

✈ Zestienhoven ℘ (0 10) 157633 (information) and (0 10) 155430, 322745 (reservations).

🚄 (departs from 's-Hertogenbosch) ℘ (0 10) 117100.

🚢 Europoort to Kingston-upon-Hull : Shipping connections North Sea Ferries (Cie Noordzee Veerdiensten) ℘ (0 1819) 62077.

🛈 Stadhuisplein 19, ✉ 3012 AR, ℘ 136000, Telex 21228 and Central Station ℘ 136006.

Amsterdam 76 – The Hague 23 – Antwerp 103 – Brussels 152 – Utrecht 57.

Plan on next page

🏨 **Hilton International Rotterdam,** Weena 10, ✉ 3012 CM, ℘ 144044, Telex 22666 – ‖‖
▤ rest ⊤⊽ ☎ ♨ – 🛗. 🆀 ⓞ Ⓔ ⓋⓈⒶ
M a la carte 33/76 – �æ 23 – **259 rm** 215/355.   JKY **a**

🏨 **Parkhotel,** Westersingel 70, ✉ 3015 LB, ℘ 363611, Telex 22020 – ‖‖ ▤ rest ⊤⊽ ☎ ♨ –
🛗. 🆀 Ⓔ. ⚘
M a la carte 54/88 – **157 rm** �æ 115/231.   JZ **a**

🏨 **Atlanta,** Aert van Nesstraat 4, ✉ 3012 CA, ℘ 110420, Telex 21595 – ‖‖ ☎ – 🛗. 🆀 ⓞ
Ⓔ
M a la carte 60/93 – �æ 16 – **167 rm** 125/180 – P 155/190.   KY **e**

🏨 **Central and Rest. Alexander,** Kruiskade 12, ✉ 3012 EH, ℘ 140744, Telex 24040 – ‖‖
▤ rest ⊤⊽ – 🛗. 🆀 ⓞ Ⓔ ⓋⓈⒶ. ⚘ rest
M 28/35 – **64 rm** �æ 112/193 – P 140/195.   KY **u**

🏨 **Rijnhotel and Rest. Falstaff,** Schouwburgplein 1, ✉ 3012 CK, ℘ 333800, Telex
21640 – ‖‖ ☎ – 🛗. 🆀 ⓞ Ⓔ ⓋⓈⒶ   JY **e**
M 35 – **140 rm** � 108/220 – P 160.

🏨 **Scandia,** Willemsplein 1, ✉ 3016 DN, ℘ 134790, Telex 21662, ◄ – ‖‖ ⇌wc ⓙwc ☎. 🆀
ⓞ Ⓔ ⓋⓈⒶ. ⚘
M a la carte 43/70 – �æ 15 – **57 rm** 68/175.

🏨 **Pax** without rest., Schiekade 658, ✉ 3032 AK, ℘ 663344 – ‖‖ ⇌wc ⓙwc. 🆀 ⓞ Ⓔ ⓋⓈⒶ
45 rm �æ 51/111.   JY **m**

🏨 **Emma** without rest., Nieuwe Binnenweg 6, ✉ 3015 BA, ℘ 365533, Telex 25320 – ‖‖ ⊤⊽
ⓙwc ☎ ♨. 🆀 Ⓔ ⓋⓈⒶ   JZ **w**
26 rm ⊟byte 120/150.

🏨 **Savoy,** Hoogstraat 81, ✉ 3011 PJ, ℘ 139280, Telex 21525 – ‖‖ ⊤⊽ ⇌wc ⓙwc ☎. 🆀 ⓞ
Ⓔ ⓋⓈⒶ. ⚘   KY **n**
M (closed Saturday and Sunday) (dinner only) a la carte 44/57 – �æ 16 – **94 rm** 106/148.

🏨 **Van Walsum,** Mathenesserlaan 199, ✉ 3014 HC, ℘ 363275 – ⇌wc ⓙwc ☎. 🆀 Ⓔ ⓋⓈⒶ.
⚘ rest   JZ **e**
M (closed after 8 p.m.) 25 – **29 rm** ⊟byte 50/120 – P 90.

🏨 **Baan** without rest., Rochussenstraat 345, ✉ 3023 DH, ℘ 770555 – ⊤⊽ ⓙwc. ⚘
closed 15 December-4 January – **14 rm** ⊟byte 45/90.

🏨 **Bienvenue** without rest., Spoorsingel 24, ✉ 3033 GL, ℘ 669394 – ⓙwc. 🆀 ⓞ Ⓔ ⓋⓈⒶ
10 rm �æ 45/85.   JY **d**

🏨 **Breitner** without rest., Breitnerstraat 23, ✉ 3015 XA, ℘ 360262 – ⇌wc ☎. 🆀 ⓞ Ⓔ
ⓋⓈⒶ   JZ **d**
22 rm ⊟byte 40/95.

🏨 **Geervliet** without rest., 's-Gravendijkwal 14, ✉ 3014 EA, ℘ 366109 – ⓙwc   JZ **b**
closed 10 December-1 January – **15 rm** ⊟byte 68/88.

🏨 **Heemraad** without rest., Heemraadssingel 90, ✉ 3021 DE, ℘ 775461 – ⓙwc. Ⓔ ⓋⓈⒶ. ⚘
⊆ 5 – **10 rm** ⊟byte 40/80.

🏨 **Holland** without rest., Provenierssingel 7, ✉ 3033 ED, ℘ 653100 – 🆀 Ⓔ ⓋⓈⒶ   JY **n**
24 rm ⊟byte 48/80.

XXX ✿ **Coq d'Or,** 1st floor, Van Vollenhovenstraat 25, ✉ 3016 BG, ℘ 366405, ⏚, (quick bar
lunch) – ▤. 🆀 ⓞ Ⓔ ⓋⓈⒶ   KZ **a**
closed Saturday, Sunday, Bank Holidays and 21 December-1 January – **M** a la carte 64/98
Spec. Mousse de canard et foie d'oie, Coquilles St-Jacques au champagne, Gratin de homard Thermidor.

XXX **La Vilette,** Westblaak 160, ✉ 3012 KM, ℘ 148692 – ▤. 🆀 ⓞ Ⓔ   JZ **t**
closed Saturday lunch, Sunday, Bank Holidays and 15 July-4 August – **M** a la carte
80/112.

XXX **Old Dutch,** Rochussenstraat 20, ✉ 3015 EK, ℘ 360242, « Old Dutch interior » – ▤. 🆀
ⓞ Ⓔ ⓋⓈⒶ   JZ **r**
closed Saturday, Sunday, Easter and Whitsuntide – **M** 65/88.

XXX **Euromast** (Rest. The Balloon mid-height of a tower of 180 m - Entrance : 7,5 Fl),
Parkhaven 20, ✉ 3016 AM, ℘ 364811, ⚘ city and port – ▤. 🆀 ⓞ Ⓔ ⓋⓈⒶ. ⚘   JZ
closed Monday from 15 October to 15 March – **M** a la carte 60/90.

XXX **Archipel,** Westblaak 82, ✉ 3012 KM, ℘ 116533, Indonesian rest. – ▤. 🆀 ⓞ Ⓔ ⓋⓈⒶ. ⚘
M 25/40.   JKZ **v**

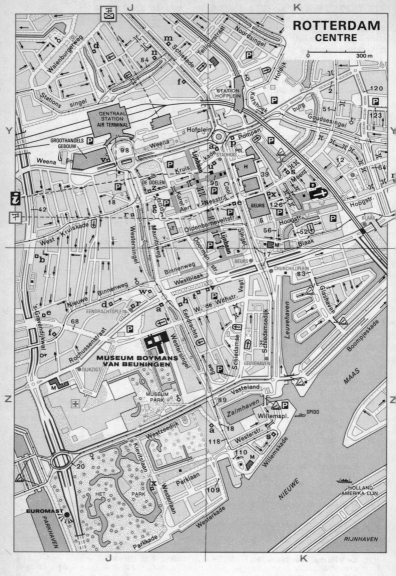

ROTTERDAM
CENTRE

0   300 m

XX **Beef Eater,** Stationsplein 45, ⊠ 3013 AK, 𝒫 119551, English Pub rest. – ▤. 𝗔𝗘 ⓞ 𝗘
VISA   JY v
M a la carte 35/78.

XX **Chez François,** Stationsplein 45, ⊠ 3013 AK, 𝒫 119551, Pub rest. – ▤. 𝗔𝗘 ⓞ 𝗘 *VISA*
M a la carte 35/78.   JY v

XX **Don Quijote,** Stationsplein 45, ⊠ 3013 AK, 𝒫 119551, Spanish rest. – ▤. 𝗔𝗘 ⓞ 𝗘 *VISA*
M a la carte 35/78.   JY v

XX **New Yorker,** Stationsplein 45, ⊠ 3013 AK, 𝒫 119551, Counter rest. – ▤. 𝗔𝗘 ⓞ 𝗘 *VISA*
M a la carte 35/78.   JY v

XX **Tokaj,** Stationsplein 45, ⊠ 3013 AK, 𝒫 119551, Hungarian rest. – ▤. 𝗔𝗘 ⓞ 𝗘 *VISA*
M a la carte 35/78.   JY v

XX **Viking,** Stationsplein 45, ⊠ 3013 AK, 𝒫 119551, Scandinavian rest. – ▤. 𝗔𝗘 ⓞ 𝗘 *VISA*
M a la carte 35/78.   JY v

XX **Festival,** Schouwburgplein 53, ⊠ 3012 CL, 𝒫 333888 – 𝗔𝗘 ⓞ 𝗘   JY z
closed Sunday – **M** a la carte 56/88.

XX **Indonesia,** 1st floor, Rodezand 34, ⊠ 3011 AN, 𝒫 148588, Indonesian rest. – ▤. 𝗔𝗘 ⓞ
𝗘 *VISA*   KY x
M 25/40.

XX **Marie Antoinette,** Pompenburg 652 (Hofplein), ⊠ 3011 AX, 𝒫 333595 – 𝗔𝗘 ⓞ 𝗘 *VISA*
closed Sunday lunch – **M** a la carte 47/80.   KY p

XX **Aub. Marie Louise,** Bergweg 64, ⊠ 3036 BC, 𝒫 671919 – ℗. 𝗔𝗘 ⓞ 𝗘 *VISA*
closed Monday – **M** a la carte 59/96.

XX **Statenhof,** Bentinckplein 1, ⊠ 3039 KL, 𝒫 661508 – 𝗘
M 40/85.

XX **Bistrocôte,** Havenstraat 9, ⊠ 3024 SE, 𝒫 778083 – 𝗔𝗘 ⓞ 𝗘 *VISA*
closed Wednesday – **M** a la carte 39/74.

XX Chalet Suisse, Kievitslaan 31, ⊠ 3016 CG, 𝒫 365062, « Parkside cottage » – ▤   JZ x

at Rotterdam-East :

XXX **In den Rustwat,** Honingerdijk 96, ⊠ 3062 NX, 𝒫 134110, « 16C converted house » –
▤ ℗. 𝗔𝗘 ⓞ 𝗘
closed Sunday, Bank Holidays and 15 to 29 July – **M** a la carte 59/85.

at Rotterdam-South :

🏨 Zuiderparkhotel, Dordtsestraatweg 285, ⊠ 3083 AJ, 𝒫 850055, Telex 28755 – |≸| 𝗧𝗩 ☎ ℗
– 🔬
75 rm.

at Ommoord NE : 7 km – ✪ 0 10 :

XXX **Keizershof,** Martin Luther Kingweg 7, ⊠ 3069 EW, 𝒫 551333, « Renovated Saxon
farm » – ℗. 𝗔𝗘 ⓞ 𝗘
M 38/90.

Denmark

Danmark

Copenhagen

PRACTICAL INFORMATION

LOCAL CURRENCY

Danish Kroner : 100 D.Kr = 8.821 US $ (Jan. 85)

SHOPPING IN COPENHAGEN

Strøget (Department stores, exclusive shops, boutiques).
Kompagnistraede (Antiques).
See also in the index of street names, those printed in red are where the principal shops are found.

TIPPING

In Denmark, all hotels and restaurants include a service charge. As for the taxis, there is no extra charge to the amount shown on the meter.

FOREIGN EXCHANGE

Banks are open between 9.30am and 4.00pm (6.00pm on Thursdays) on weekdays except Saturdays. The main banks in the centre of Copenhagen, the Central Station and the Airport have exchange facilities outside these hours.

TOURIST INFORMATION

The telephone number and address of the Tourist Information office is given in the text under **i**.

CAR HIRE

The international car hire companies have branches in Copenhagen - Your hotel porter will be able to give details and help you with your arrangements.

SPEED LIMITS

The maximum permitted speed in cities is 60 km/h - 37mph, outside cities 80 km/h - 50mph and 100 km/h - 62mph on motorways.

SEAT BELTS

The wearing of seat belts is compulsory for drivers and front seat passengers.

COPENHAGEN

SIGHTS

See : Tivoli★★★ : May 1 to September 15 BZ – Harbour and Canal Tour★★★ (Kanal-tur) : May to September 15 (Gammel Strand and Nyhavn) – Little Mermaid★★★ (Den Lille Havfrue) DX – Strøget★★ BCYZ – Nyhavn★★ DY – Amalienborg★★ : Changing of the Guard at noon DY – Rosenborg Castle★★ (Rosenborg Slot) CX Christiansborg Palace★★ (Christiansborg Slot) CZ – Old Stock Exchange★★ (Børsen) CZ – Round Tower★★ (Rundetårn) CY **D** Gråbrødretorv★ CY **28** – Gammel Strand★ CZ **26** – Marble Church★ (Marmorkirke) DY **E** – Royal Chapel and Naval Church★ (Holmen's Kirke) CZ **B** – King's Square★ (Kongens Nytorv) DY – Charlottenborg Palace★ (Charlottenborg Slot) DY **F** – Citadel★ (Kastellet) DX – Christianshavn★ DZ – Botanical Garden★ (Botanisk Have) BX – Frederiksberg Garden★ (Frederiks-berg Have) AZ – Town Hall (Radhus) : World Clock★ (Jen Olsen's Verdensur) BZ **H**. Breweries – Porcelain Factories – Danish Design Centre ('' Den Permanente '') AZ.

Museums : Ny Carlsberg Glyptotek★★★ (Glyptoteket) BZ – National Museum★★ (Nationalmuseet) CZ – Royal Museum of Fine Arts★★ (Statens Museum for Kunst) CX – Thorvaldsen Museum★ CZ **M1** – Royal Arsenal Museum★ (Tøjhusmuseet) CZ **M2** – Royal Theatre Museum★ (Teaterhistoriskmuseum) CZ **M3** – Copenhagen City Museum★ (By Museum) AZ **M4**.

Outskirts : Open Air Museum★★ (Frilandsmuseet) NW : 12 km BX – Ordrupgaard Museum★ (Ordrupgaardsamlingen) N : 10 km CX – Dragør★ SW : 13 km DZ.

COPENHAGEN (KØBENHAVN) Danmark 920 L 3 – pop. 622 000 – ✆ 01.

🏌 Dansk Golf Union 56 ✆ (01) 13.12.21.

✈ Copenhagen/Kastrup SW : 10 km ✆ (01) 54.17.01 – Air Terminal : main railway station.

🚗 Motorail for Southern Europe : ✆ (01) 14.17.01.

🚢 Further information from the D S B, main railway station or tourist information centre (see below).

🛈 Danmarks Turistråd, H.C. Andersens Bould. 22 ✆ (01) 11.13.25

Berlin 385 – Hamburg 305 – Oslo 583 – Stockholm 630.

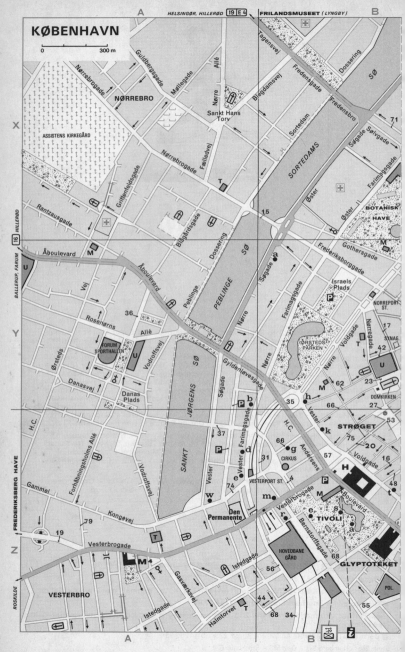

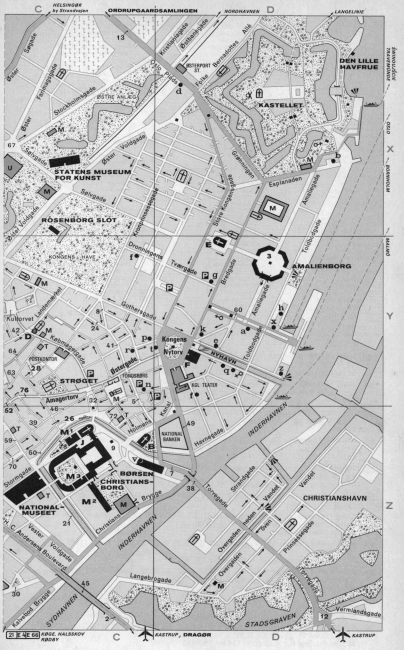

STREET INDEX TO KØBENHAVN TOWN PLAN

Angleterre, Kongens Nytorv 34, ⊠ 1050 K, ℰ 12 00 95, Telex 15877 – ⊟ ⊡ ☎ ♨ ▣
ℰ ▦ ⚶.
 CDY t
M (buffet lunch) 75 a la carte 250/300 – ⊂⊃ 75 – **139 rm** 825/1650.

SAS Scandinavia ▥, Amager Boulevard 70, ⊠ 2300 S, ℰ 11 23 24, Telex 31330, ≤
city, ⇔, « Panoramic restaurant on 25th floor », ⬚ – ⊟ ⊡ ☎ ☻. ♨ ▣ ▣ ① ℰ ▦
M 3 Crowns a la carte 255/335 – ⊂⊃ 66 – **543 rm** 1025/1210. by Amager Boulevard CZ

Sheraton - Copenhagen ▥, 6 Vester Søgade, ⊠ 1601 V, ℰ 14 35 35, Telex 27450, ⇔ –
⊟ ⊡ ☎ ⇄. ♨
 AZ w
474 rm.

Plaza - Sheraton ▥, Bernstorffsgade 4, ⊠ 1577 V, ℰ 14 92 62, Telex 15330, « Antiques
and paintings, Library bar » – ⊟ ⊟ ⊡ ☎. ♨ ▣ ① ℰ ▦
 BZ r
M a la carte 195/410 – ⊂⊃ 75 – **98 rm** 760/1250.

Impérial ▥, Vester Farimagsgade 9, ⊠ 1606 V, ℰ 12 80 00, Telex 15556 – ⊟ ⊡ ☎ ♿.
♨ ▣ ① ℰ ▦ ⚶
 AZ e
M a la carte 250/318 – **163 rm** ⊂⊃ 700/1250.

Royal ▥, Hammerichsgade 1, ⊠ 1611 V, ℰ 14 14 12, Telex 27155, ≤, ⇔ – ⊟ ⊡ ☎ ⇄
☻. ♨ – **275 rm.**
 BZ m

Kong Frederick, Vester Voldgade 25-27, ⊠ 1552 V, ℰ 12 59 02, Telex 19702, « Victorian
pub and restaurant, antiques » – ⊟ ⊡ ☎. ♨
 BZ k
M Queen's – **127 rm.**

Richmond, Vester Farimagsgade 33, ⊠ 1625 V, ℰ 12 33 66, Telex 19767 – ⊟. ♨. ▣
① ℰ ▦
 AY b
M (see **La Cocotte** below) – **132 rm** ⊂⊃ 670/960.

Admiral, Toldbodgade 24-28, ⊠ 1253 K, ℰ 11 82 82, Telex 15941, ≤, « Former 18C
warehouse » – ⊟ ☎ ☻. ♨ ▣ ① ℰ ▦
 DY h
M (buffet lunch) 99 a la carte 149/275 – ⊂⊃ 55 – **366 rm** 420/900.

Mercur, Vester Farimagsgade 17, ⊠ 1625 V, ℰ 12 57 11, Telex 19767, ⚶ – ⊟ ⇄wc
⇄. ▣ ① ℰ ▦
 AZ d
M (closed Bank Holiday lunch and Sunday) a la carte 107/230 – **113 rm** ⊂⊃ 620/950.

Codan ▥ without rest., Sankt Annae Plads 21, ⊠ 1250 K, ℰ 13 34 00, Telex 15815, ⇔ –
⊟ ⊡ ⇄wc ♨. ▣ ① ℰ ▦
 DY x
M (see **Admiral H.**) – ⊂⊃ 55 – **134 rm** 380/830.

🏛 **71 Nyhavn** 🦞, Nyhavn 71, ✉ 1051 K, ⌀ 11 85 85, Telex 27558, ⪡, « Former warehouse »
– ▮ 📺 ⇱wc ▥wc ☎, 🔥, 🖭 ⓞ **E** *VISA*   DY **z**
M *(closed 24 to 26 December)* (buffet lunch) 142 a la carte 180/317 – **82 rm** ⌑ 703/868.

🏛 **Opera,** Tordenskjoldsgade 15, 1055 K, ⌀ 12 15 19, Telex 15812 – ▮ ⇱wc ▥wc ☎
66 rm   DY **f**

🏛 **Ascot** without rest., Studiestraede 57, ✉ 1554 V, ⌀ 12 60 00, Telex 15730 – ▮ 📺 ⇱wc
▥wc ☎, 🖭 ⓞ **E** *VISA*   BZ **g**
58 rm ⌑ 430/695.

🏛 **Neptun** without rest., Sankt Annae Plads 18, ✉ 1250 K, ⌀ 13 89 00, Telex 19554 – ▮ 📺
⇱wc ☎, 🖭 ⓞ **E** *VISA*   DY **a**
60 rm ⌑ 410/620.

🏛 **Kong Arthur** without rest., Nørre Søgade 11, ✉ 1370 K, ⌀ 11 12 12, Telex 16512, ⇚ –
▮ 📺 ⇱wc ▥wc ☎, 🖭 ⓞ **E** *VISA*   BY **a**
53 rm ⌑ 460/735.

🏛 **Park** without rest., Jarmers Plads 3, ✉ 1551 V, ⌀ 13 30 00, Telex 15692 – ▮ 📺 ⇱wc
▥wc ☎, 🖭 ⓞ **E** *VISA* 🦌   BY **h**
⌑ 45 – **66 rm** 240/770.

🏛 **Danmark** without rest., Vester Voldgade 89, 1552 V, ⌀ 11 48 06 – ▮ 📺 ⇱wc ▥wc ☎
⇨, 🦌   BZ **t**
closed 20 December-3 January – **49 rm** ⌑ 375/595.

XXX ⬩ **Kong Hans,** Vingardsstraede 6, ✉ 1070 K, ⌀ 11 68 68, « Ancient vaulted cellar » –
🖭 ⓞ **E** *VISA*   CY **n**
closed 15 July-15 August and Bank Holidays – **M** (dinner only) a la carte 455/550
Spec. Veau de Lait aux Morilles, Gibiers (Season), Desserts du Roi Jean.

XXX **Bourgogne,** Dronningens Tvaergade 2, ✉ 1302 K, ⌀ 14 80 66   DY **g**

XXX **La Cocotte,** (at Richmond H.), Vester Farimagsgade 33, ✉ 1606 V, ⌀ 14 04 07 – 🖭 ⓞ
E *VISA*   AZ **d**
closed Sunday, 1 week at Christmas and Bank Holidays – **M** a la carte 152/289.

XX ⬩ **Les Etoiles,** Dronningens Tvaergade 43, ✉ 1302 K, ⌀ 15 05 54 – 🖭 ⓞ **E** *VISA*   CY **f**
closed Sunday, July and Bank Holidays – **M** (dinner only) a la carte 255/295
Spec. Menu poisson de la Baltique.

XX ⬩ **Saison,** (at østerport H.), Oslo Plads 5, ✉ 2100 ø, ⌀ 11 22 66, Telex 15888 – 🖭 ⓞ **E**
VISA   DX **d**
closed Saturday lunch, Sunday, Monday, July, 23 December-2 January and Bank Holidays
– **M** a la carte 140/290
Spec. Menu aux poissons, Menu végétarien, Gibier pendant la saison de chasse.

XX **Leonore Christine,** Nyhavn 9, ✉ 1051 K, ⌀ 13 50 40 – ⓞ **E** *VISA*   DY **e**
closed Saturday lunch, Sunday, last 2 weeks July and Bank Holidays – **M** a la carte
220/292.

XX **Den Sorte Ravn,** Nyhavn 14, ✉ 1051 K, ⌀ 13 12 33 – 🖭 ⓞ **E** *VISA*   DY **q**
M a la carte 72/308.

XX **Els,** Store Strandstraede 3, ✉ 1255 K, ⌀ 14 13 41, « 19C wall paintings » – ▦   DY **k**
M 148/196.

X **L'Alsace,** Ny Ostergade 9, ✉ 1101 K, ⌀ 14 57 43 – 🖭 ⓞ **E** *VISA*   CY **r**
closed Sunday – **M** a la carte 118/275.

X **Egoisten,** Hovedvagtsgade 2, ✉ 1103 K, ⌀ 12 79 71 – 🖭 ⓞ **E** *VISA*   CY **p**
closed Saturday and Sunday – **M** a la carte 157/260.

X **Lumskebugten,** Esplanaden 21, ✉ 1263 K, ⌀ 15 60 29   DX **b**

X **Børskaelderen,** Børsen, Børsgade 2, ✉ 1217 K, ⌀ 12 14 40   CZ **v**

X **Gilleleje,** Nyhavn 10, ✉ 1051 K, ⌀ 12 58 58, « Old sailors inn » – ⓞ **E** *VISA*   DY **q**
closed Sunday, Christmas Day and July – **M** (buffet lunch) 178 a la carte 197/298.

in Tivoli :

XXX **Divan 2,** Tivoli Gardens, Vesterbrogade 3, ✉ 1620 V, ⌀ 12 51 51, « Floral decoration
and terrace » – 🖭 ⓞ **E** *VISA*   BZ **a**
May-mid September – **M** a la carte 265/395.

XXX **Belle Terrasse,** Tivoli Gardens, Vesterbrogade 3, ✉ 1620 V, ⌀ 12 11 36, « Floral decoration and terrace » – 🖭 ⓞ **E** *VISA*   BZ **s**
May-mid September – **M** a la carte 195/362.

XXX **La Crevette,** Tivoli Gardens, Vesterbrogade 3, 1620 V, ⌀ 14 68 47, Seafood, « Floral
decoration and terrace » – 🖭 ⓞ **E** *VISA*   BZ **e**
May-mid September – **M** a la carte 195/375.

at Søllerød N : 19 km by exit Tagensvej – BX – and A 43 – ✉ 2840 Holte – ⓼ 02
Holte :

XXX **Søllerød Kro,** Søllerødvej 35, ⌀ 80 25 05, « 17C thatched inn » – ⓟ, 🖭 ⓞ *VISA*
closed 24 December – **M** a la carte 185/330.

France

PRACTICAL INFORMATION

LOCAL CURRENCY

French Franc : 100 F = 10.282 US $ (Jan. 85)

TOURIST INFORMATION IN PARIS

Paris "Welcome" Office (Office de Tourisme de Paris - Accueil de France), closed Sundays : 127 Champs-Élysées, 8th, ℰ 723 61 72, Telex 61 19 84
American Express 11 Rue Scribe, 9th, ℰ 266 09 99

FOREIGN EXCHANGE OFFICES

Banks : close at 5pm and at weekends
Orly Airport : daily 6.30am to 11.30pm
Charles de Gaulle Airport : daily 6am to 11.30pm

TRANSPORT IN PARIS

Taxis : may be hailed in the street when showing the illuminated sign-available day and night at taxi ranks or called by telephone
Bus-Métro (subway) : for full details see the Michelin Plan de Paris no 11. The metro is quickest but the bus is good for sightseeing and practical for short distances.

POSTAL SERVICES

Local post offices : open Mondays to Fridays 8am to 7pm ; Saturdays 8am to noon
General Post Office, 52 rue du Louvre, 1st : open 24 hours

SHOPPING IN PARIS

Department stores : Boulevard Haussmann, Rue de Rivoli and Rue de Sèvres
Exclusive shops and boutiques : Faubourg St-Honoré, Rue de la Paix and Rue Royale
Second-hand goods and antiques : Flea Market (Porte Clignancourt) ; Swiss Village (Avenue de la Motte Picquet), Louvre des Antiquaires (Place du Palais Royal), Flea Market - type shops around the "Halles" (the old Paris Central Market)

AIRLINES

T.W.A. : 101 Champs Élysées, 8th, ℰ 720 62 11
PAN AM : 1 Rue Scribe, 9th, ℰ 266 45 45
BRITISH AIRWAYS : 91 Champs Elysées, 8th, ℰ 778 14 14
AIR FRANCE : 119 Champs Élysées, 8th, ℰ 535 61 61
AIR INTER : 12 Rue de Castiglione, 1st, ℰ 539 25 25
U.T.A. : 3 Boulevard Malesherbes, 8th, ℰ 838 80 80

BREAKDOWN SERVICE

Certain garages in central and outer Paris operate a 24 hour breakdown service. If you breakdown the police are usually able to help by indicating the nearest one.

TIPPING

Service is generally included in hotel and restaurants bills. But you may choose to leave more than the expected tip to the staff. Taxi-drivers, porters, barbers and theatre or cinema attendants also expect a small gratuity.

SPEED LIMITS

The maximum permitted speed in built up areas is 60 km/h - 37 mph ; on motorways the speed limit is 130 km/h - 80 mph and 110 km/h - 68 mph on dual carriageways. On all other roads 90 km/h - 56 mph.

SEAT BELTS

The wearing of seat belts is compulsory for drivers and front seat passengers.

PARIS
and environs

PARIS 75 Maps : **10**, **11**, **12** and **14** G. Paris.

Population : Paris 2 166 449 ; Ile-de-France region : 10 034 108.

Altitude : Observatory : 60 m ; Place Concorde : 34 m

Air Terminals : Esplanade des Invalides, 7th, ℰ 323 96.53 — Palais des Congrès, Porte Maillot, 17th, ℰ 299 20 18

Airports : see Orly and Charles de Gaulle (Roissy)

Railways, motorail, sleepers : apply to the appropriate railway station (S.N.C.F.)

ARRONDISSEMENTS

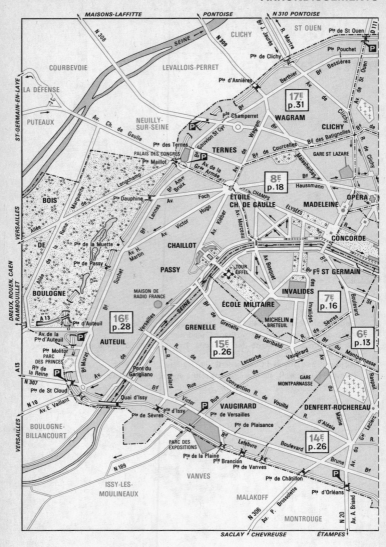

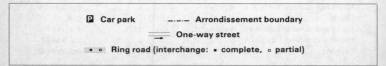

P Car park ‒‒‐‒‐ Arrondissement boundary

═══ One-way street

═●═ Ring road (interchange: ■ complete, ◻ partial)

AND DISTRICTS

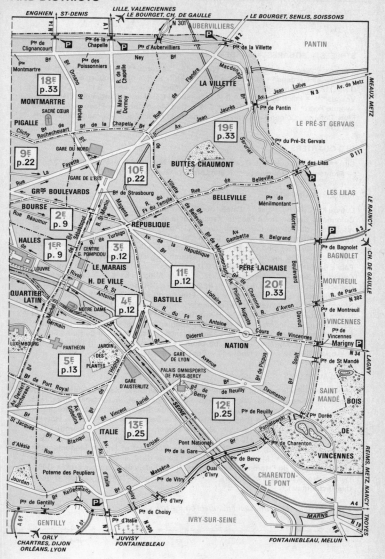

SIGHTS

STREETS — SQUARES — GARDENS

Champs-Élysées★★★ F 8, F 9, G 10 — Place de la Concorde★★★ G 11 (Obelisk of Luxor) — Tuileries Gardens★★ (Jardin des Tuileries) H 12 — Rue du Faubourg St-Honoré★★ G 11, G 12 — Avenue de l'Opéra★★ G 13 — Place Vendôme★★ G 12 — Place des Vosges★★ — Place du Tertre★★ D 14 — Botanical Gardens★★ (Jardin des Plantes) — Avenue Foch★ F 7 — Rue de Rivoli★ G 12 — Rue Mouffetard★ — Place de la Bastille (July Column : Colonne de Juillet) — Place de la République — Grands Boulevards F 13, F 14.

OLD QUARTERS

Cité★★★ (Ile St-Louis, The Quays) J 14, J 15 — Le Marais★★★ — Montmartre★★★ D 14 — Montagne Ste Geneviève★★ (Latin Quarter : Quartier Latin) K 14.

MAIN MONUMENTS

Louvre★★★ (Royal Palace : Palais des Rois de France ; Cour Carrée, Perrault's Colonnade, Embankment Façade : façade sur le quai, the "two arms" of the Louvre : les "bras" du Louvre, Carrousel Triumphal Arch : Arc de Triomphe du Carrousel, and The Parterres.) H 13 — Notre Dame Cathedral★★★ K 15 — Sainte Chapelle★★★ J 14 — Arc de Triomphe★★★ F 8 (Place Charles de Gaulle) — Eiffel Tower★★★ (Tour Eiffel) J 7 — The Invalides★★★ (Dôme Church : église, Napoléon's tomb) J 10 — Palais Royal★★ H 13 — Madeleine★★ G 11 — Opera★★ F 12 — St. Germain l'Auxerrois Church★★ H 14 — Conciergerie★★ J 14 — Ecole Militaire★★ K 9 — Luxembourg★★ (Palace, gardens : palais, jardins) — Panthéon★★ — St. Séverin Church★★ K 14 — St. Germain des Prés Church★★ J 13 — St. Etienne du Mont Church★★ — St. Sulpice Church★★ K 13 — Hôtel de Lamoignon★★, Hôtel Guénégaud★★ (museum of the Chase : musée de la chasse) — Hôtel de Rohan★★ — Soubise Palace★★ — The Sacré Cœur Basilica★★ D 14 — Maine Montparnasse Tower★★ (Tour) — Institute of France★ (Institut de France) J 13 — Radio France House★ (Maison de Radio France) — Palais des Congrès★ — St. Roch Church★ G 13 — Alexandre III Bridge★ (Pont Alexandre III) H 10 — Pont Neuf J 14 — Pont des Arts J 13.

MAIN MUSEUMS

Louvre★★★ (Stele of the Vultures : stèle des Vautours, Seated Scribe : Scribe accroupi, Vénus de Milo, Winged Victory of Samothrace : Victoire de Samothrace, Nymphs of Jean Goujon, Mona Lisa : La Joconde, Regent diamond : le Régent...) H 13 — Jeu de Paume★★★ (Impressionists) G 11 — Decorative Arts★★ H 13 — Hôtel de Cluny and its museum (The Lady and the Unicorn : la Dame à la Licorne) K 14 — Rodin★★ (hôtel de Biron) J 10 — Hôtel Carnavalet★★ — Georges Pompidou Centre★★ (Modern Art Museum) H 15 — Chaillot Palace (Museum of French Monuments★★, Museum of Man★★, Maritime Museum★★ : Palais de Chaillot, musées des Monuments Français, de l'Homme, de la Marine) H 7 — Palais de la Découverte★★ G 10 — Conservatoire des Arts et Métiers★★ (National Technical Museum : musée National des Techniques).

K 14, G 10 : *Reference letters and numbers on the town plan.*

■ ALPHABETICAL LIST OF HOTELS AND RESTAURANTS

■ HOTELS, RESTAURANTS

Listed by districts and arrondissements

(List of Hotels and Restaurants in alphabetical order, see pp 5 to 8)

G 12 : These reference letters and numbers correspond to the squares on the Michelin **Map of Paris** n° ⬛⬛. **Paris Atlas** n° ⬛⬛. **Map of Paris** n° ⬛⬛ and **Map with street index** n° ⬛⬛.

Consult any of the above publications when looking for a car park nearest to a listed establishment.

Opéra, Palais-Royal, Halles, Bourse.

1st and 2nd arrondissements.
1st : ⊠ 75001
2nd : ⊠ 75002

Ritz 🦢, 15 pl. Vendôme (1st) 𝒫 260.38.30, Telex 220262, 🍴, « Indoor garden » – 📳 ▤ 📺 🕿 👶 🅿. 🆎 ① 🄴 *VISA*
M Rest see Ritz-Espadon below – ⊊ 70 – **163 rm** 1 500/1 900, 53 apartments.
G 12

Inter-Continental, 3 r. Castiglione (1st) 𝒫 260.37.80, Telex 220114, 🍴 – 📳 ▤ 📺 🕿 👶 – 🔏 1000. 🆎 ① 🄴 *VISA*. 🎇 rest
st. : **Rôtiss. Rivoli M** 190/290 - **café Tuileries M** 80/130 – ⊊ 80 – **500 rm** 1 310/1 831, 27 apartments.
G 12

Meurice, 228 r. Rivoli (1st) 𝒫 260.38.60, Telex 230673 – 📳 ▤ 📺 🕿 👶 – 🔏 40. 🆎 ① 🄴 *VISA*
st. : **M** a la carte 235/340 – ⊊ 85 – **151 rm** 1 360/1 937, 32 apartments.
G 12

Lotti, 7 r. Castiglione (1st) 𝒫 260.37.34, Telex 240066 – 📳 ▤ rest 📺 🕿 👶 – 🔏 25. 🆎 ① 🄴 *VISA*
M a la carte 150/240 - **Grill M** a la carte approx. 170 – ⊊ 65 – **126 rm** 830/1 370.
G 12

Westminster and rest. Le Céladon, 13 r. Paix (2nd) 𝒫 261.57.46, Telex 680035 – 📳 ▤ rm 📺 🕿 ⇔ – 🔏 80. 🆎 ① 🄴 *VISA*
closed August – st. : **M** (closed Saturday and Sunday out of season) a la carte 190/350 – ⊊ 60 – **84 rm** 900/1 350, 18 apartments.
G 12

Résidence St-James et Albany Ⓜ, 202 r. Rivoli (1st) 𝒫 260.31.60, Telex 213031 – 📳 📺 🕿 🅿 – 🔏 50-150. 🆎 ① 🄴 *VISA*. 🎇
rest. **Le Noailles** (closed Saturday and Sunday) **M** a la carte approx. 190 – ⊊ 40 – **145 rm** 600/850, 3 apartments.
H 12

Louvre-Concorde, pl. A.-Malraux (1st) 𝒫 261.56.01, Telex 220412 – 📳 📺 🕿 👶. 🆎 ① 🄴 *VISA*
st. : **M** a la carte approx. 140 👶 – ⊊ 45 – **223** 690/920, 7 apartments.
H 13

Édouard VII, 39 av. Opéra (2nd) 𝒫 261.56.90, Telex 680217 – 📳 📺 🕿. 🆎 ① *VISA*   G 13
M Rest see Delmonico below – **96 rm** ⊊ 609/759, 4 apartments.

Mayfair Ⓜ without rest., 3 r. Rouget-de-Lisle (1st) 𝒫 260.38.14, Telex 240037 – 📳 📺 🕿 👶. 🆎 ① 🄴 *VISA*
st. : ⊊ 50 – **53 rm** 570/750.
G 12

France et Choiseul, 239 r. St-Honoré (1st) 𝒫 261.54.60, Telex 680959, 🍴 – 📳 📺 🕿 – 🔏 30-200. 🆎 ① *VISA*. 🎇
st. : **M** a la carte 115/155 👶 – **128 rm** ⊊ 520/660, 7 apartments.
G 12

Cusset Ⓜ, 95 r. Richelieu (2nd) 𝒫 297.48.90, Telex 670245 – 📳 ▤ rest 📺 🕿. 🄴 *VISA*   F 13
les Deux Ducs (closed Sunday) **M** a la carte approx. 110 👶 – **115 rm** ⊊ 236/420 – P 260/450.

Cambon Ⓜ without rest., 3 r. Cambon (1st) 𝒫 260.38.09, Telex 240814 – 📳 📺 🕿. 🆎 ① 🄴 *VISA*
st. : **44 rm** ⊊ 550/750.
G 12

François without rest., 3 bd Montmartre (2nd) 𝒫 233.51.53, Telex 211097 – 📳 📺 🕿. 🆎 *VISA*. 🎇
st. : **64 rm** ⊊ 380/483, 11 apartments.
F 14

Normandy, 7 r. Échelle (1st) 𝒫 260.30.21, Telex 670250 – 📳 📺 🕿 – 🔏 50. 🆎 ① 🄴 *VISA*
st. : **M** (closed Saturday and Sunday) 140 – ⊊ 33 – **120 rm** 470/780, 8 apartments.
H 13

7

🏨 **Favart** without rest., 5 r. Marivaux (2nd) ℰ 297.59.83, Telex 213126 – 🛗 📺 🛁wc 🚿wc
☎
st. : **37 rm** ⌑ 241/267.
F 13

🏨 **Richepanse** without rest., 14 r. Richepanse (1st) ℰ 260.36.00, Telex 210811 – 🛗 📺
🛁wc 🚿wc ☎. 🅰🅴. 🏖
st. : **43 rm** ⌑ 346/381.
G 12

🏨 **Montana H. Tuileries** Ⓜ without rest., 12 r. St-Roch (1st) ℰ 260.35.10, Telex 204401 –
🛗 📺 🛁wc 🚿wc ☎. 𝖵𝖨𝖲𝖠
st. : ⌑ 22 – **25 rm** 280/438.
G 12

🏨 **Du Piémont** Ⓜ without rest, 22 r. Richelieu (1st) ℰ 296.44.50 – 🛗 📺 🛁wc 🚿wc ☎. 🅰🅴
Ⓞ 🅴 𝖵𝖨𝖲𝖠
st. : ⌑ 20 – **28 rm** 239/379.
G 13

🏨 **Gd H. de Champagne** without rest., 17 r. J.-Lantier (1st) ℰ 261.50.05, Telex 215955 – 🛗
📺 🛁wc 🚿wc ☎. 🏖
45 rm.
J 14

🏨 **Gaillon Opéra** without rest, 9 r. Gaillon (2nd) ℰ 742.47.74, Telex 215716 – 🛗 📺 🛁wc
☎. 🅰🅴 Ⓞ 𝖵𝖨𝖲𝖠
st. : ⌑ 21 – **26 rm** 386/417.
G 13

🏨 **Louvre-Forum** Ⓜ without rest, 25 r. du Bouloi (1st) ℰ 236.54.19, Telex 240288 – 🛗 📺
🛁wc 🚿wc ☎. 🅰🅴 Ⓞ 𝖵𝖨𝖲𝖠. 🏖
st. : ⌑ 18 – **28 rm** 224/295.
H 14

🏨 **Ducs de Bourgogne** without rest., 19 r. Pont-Neuf (1st) ℰ 233.95.64 – 🛗 🛁wc 🚿wc
☎. 𝖵𝖨𝖲𝖠. 🏖
st. : ⌑ 19 – **49 rm** 210/221.
H 14

🏨 **Ducs d'Anjou** without rest., 1 r. Ste-Opportune (1st) ℰ 236.92.24 – 🛗 🛁wc 🚿wc ☎.
𝖵𝖨𝖲𝖠
st. : **38 rm** ⌑ 143/247.
H 14

🏨 **St-Romain** without rest., 7 r. St-Roch (1st) ℰ 260.31.70 – 🛗 🛁wc 🚿wc ☎
st. : ⌑ 20 – **33 rm** 350/350.
G 13

🏨 **Family** without rest., 35 r. Cambon (1st) ℰ 261.54.84 – 🛗 🛁wc 🚿wc ☎ 🕭
st. : ⌑ 16 – **25 rm** 139/227.
G 12

🍽🍽🍽🍽🍽 ❀❀ **Ritz-Espadon,** 15 pl. Vendôme (1st) ℰ 260.38.30, 🌤 – 🅿. 🅰🅴 Ⓞ 🅴 𝖵𝖨𝖲𝖠. 🏖
M a la carte 290/380.
Spec. Omble chevalier (November-31 December), Canard, Crêpes flambées.
G 12

🍽🍽🍽🍽 ❀❀ **Grand Vefour,** 17 r. Beaujolais (1st) ℰ 296.56.27, Pre-Revolutionary (late 18C) Café
Style – 🍴. 🅰🅴 Ⓞ 🅴 𝖵𝖨𝖲𝖠. 🏖
closed August, Saturday and Sunday – **M** a la carte 240/330.
Spec. Salade de homard et ris de veau, Filet de barbue, Suprême de pigeonneau.
G 13

🍽🍽🍽🍽 **Drouant,** pl. Gaillon (2nd) ℰ 742.56.61 – 🍴. 🅰🅴 Ⓞ 🅴 𝖵𝖨𝖲𝖠
at the rest. M a la carte 210/310 - **at the Grill** (closed August, Saturday and Sunday) **M** a la
carte approx. 220 🍷.
G 13

🍽🍽🍽 ❀ **Mercure Galant,** 15 r. Petits-Champs (1st) ℰ 297.53.85
closed Saturday lunch, Sunday and Bank Holidays – **M** a la carte 180/240.
Spec. Filets tièdes de pageot à l'huile d'olive, Escalopes de foie gras frais poêlées, Mille et une feuilles.
G 13

🍽🍽🍽 ❀❀ **Gérard Besson,** 5 r. Coq Héron (1st) ℰ 233.14.74 – Ⓞ 𝖵𝖨𝖲𝖠
closed 6 to 28 July, 21 December-5 January, Saturday, Sunday and Bank Holidays – **M** 160
(lunch) a la carte 170/270
Spec. Gibier (season), Biscuit glacé à la framboise.
H 14

🍽🍽🍽 **Delmonico,** 39 av. Opéra (2nd) ℰ 261.44.26, Telex 680217 – 🍴. 🅰🅴 Ⓞ 𝖵𝖨𝖲𝖠
closed Sunday – **M** a la carte 190/270.
G 13

🍽🍽🍽 **Chez Vong,** 10 r. Grande-Truanderie (1st) ℰ 296.29.89 – 🅰🅴 Ⓞ 𝖵𝖨𝖲𝖠
closed Sunday – **M** a la carte 120/160.
H 15

🍽🍽🍽 **Pierre ''A la Fontaine Gaillon'',** pl. Gaillon (2nd) ℰ 265.87.04 – 🅰🅴 Ⓞ 🅴 𝖵𝖨𝖲𝖠
closed 4 August-2 September, Saturday lunch and Sunday – **M** 120/195.
G 13

🍽🍽🍽 ❀ **Goumard,** 17 r. Duphot (1st) ℰ 260.36.07 – 🅰🅴 Ⓞ 🅴 𝖵𝖨𝖲𝖠
closed Sunday – **M** a la carte 180/240
Spec. Fond d'artichaut aux petits crustacés, Filets de rouget au confit de légumes, Marquise au café sauce
pralin.
G 12

🍽🍽 **La Table de Jeannette,** 12 r. Duphot (1st) ℰ 260.05.64 – 🅰🅴 Ⓞ 🅴 𝖵𝖨𝖲𝖠
closed 2 to 26 August, 24 December-2 January, Saturday and Sunday – **st. : M** a la carte
150/220.
G 12

XX ⊛ **Chez Pauline** (Génin), 5 r. Villedo (1st) ☎ 296.20.70 — 🍴 **VISA**   G 13
closed July, 22 December-2 January, Saturday dinner and Sunday — **M** (🍴 1st floor) a la
carte 140/220
Spec. Ris de veau en croûte, Foie gras frais, Mariage de champignons sauvages et gibier (October-January).

XX ⊛ **Bistro d'Hubert,** 36 pl. Marché St-Honoré (1st) ☎ 260.03.00 — **AE VISA**   G 12
closed Sunday and Monday — **M** 140 (lunch) and a la carte 200/280
Spec. Ragoût de soles et d'écrevisses (June-September), Filet de selle d'agneau au whisky et safran,
Feuillantine de poires caramélisées (September-June).

XX **Aux Trois Turbigo,** 3 r. Turbigo (1st) ☎ 508.18.05 — **AE ① VISA**   H 14
closed Saturday lunch and Sunday — **M** a la carte 125/180.

XX **La Tour Hassan,** 27 r. Turbigo (2nd) ☎ 233.79.34, Moorish decor — 🍴 **AE ① E VISA**
closed Monday — **M** a la carte 110/145.   G 15

XX ⊛ **Pierre Traiteur,** 10 r. Richelieu (1st) ☎ 296.09.17 — **AE ① VISA**   H 13
closed August, Saturday and Sunday — **M** a la carte 145/235
Spec. Foie gras en terrine, Cêpes farcis à la rouergate, Rognon de veau rôti à l'échalote.

XX **Velloni,** 22 r. des Halles (1st) ☎ 260.12.50 — **AE ① VISA**   H 14
closed 15 to 31 August and Sunday — **st. : M** a la carte 130/170.

XX **Baumann Baltard,** 9 r. Coquillière (1st) ☎ 236.22.00 — 🍴 **AE ① E VISA**   H 14
st. : **M** a la carte 120/170.

XX **La Main à la Pâte,** 35 r. St-Honoré (1st) ☎ 508.85.73 — **AE ① VISA**   H 14
closed Sunday — **st. : M** a la carte 155/210 ♨.

XX **Le Petit Coin de la Bourse,** 16 r. Feydeau (2nd) ☎ 508.00.08 — **AE VISA**   F 14
closed Saturday and Sunday — **M** a la carte 125/175.

XX **La Corbeille,** 154 r. Montmartre (2nd) ☎ 261.30.87 — **VISA**   G 14
closed Saturday, Sunday and Bank Holidays — **st. : M** a la carte 190/270.

XX **La Barrière Poquelin,** 17 r. Molière (1st) ☎ 296.22.19 — **AE VISA**   G 13
closed 1 to 21 August, Saturday lunch and Sunday — **M** a la carte 150/215.

XX **La Maison des Foies Gras,** 7 r. Gomboust (1st) ☎ 261.02.93 — **AE ① VISA** . ✂   G 13
closed Saturday (except dinner from September to 30 June) and Sunday — **st. : M** (booking
essential) a la carte 160/230.

XX **Pile ou Face,** 52 bis r. N.-D. des Victoires (2nd) ☎ 233.64.33   G 14
closed August, Saturday, Sunday and Bank Holidays — **M** a la carte 120/170.

XX **Le Soufflé,** 36 r. Mt-Thabor (1st) ☎ 260.27.19 — 🍴 **AE ① E VISA**   G 12
closed Sunday and Bank Holidays — **M** a la carte 105/160.

XX **Saudade,** 34 r. Bourdonnais (1st) ☎ 236.30.71 — **AE ① VISA**   H 14
closed 1 August-5 September and Sunday — **st. : M** a la carte 105/150.

XX **Vaudeville,** 29 r. Vivienne (2nd) ☎ 233.39.31 — **AE ① VISA**   FG 14
M a la carte 90/125 ♨.

XX **La Ferme Irlandaise,** 30 pl. Marché St.-Honoré (1st) ☎ 296.02.99 — **AE VISA**   G 12
closed 23 December-2 January, Sunday dinner and Monday — **st. : M** 150/200.

XX ⊛ **Pharamond,** 24 r. Grande-Truanderie (1st) ☎ 233.06.72 — **AE ① VISA**   H 15
closed July, Monday lunch and Sunday — **M** a la carte 120/165
Spec. Tripes à la mode de Caen, St-Jacques au cidre (season), Grillades.

XX **Pied de Cochon** (24hr service), 6 r. Coquillière (1st) ☎ 236.11.75 — **AE ① VISA**   H 14
M a la carte 100/190.

XX **Caveau du Palais,** 19 pl. Dauphine (1st) ☎ 326.04.28 — **AE VISA**   J 14
closed Saturday and Sunday. — **M** a la carte 125/180.

XX **Chez Gabriel,** 123 r. St-Honoré (1st) ☎ 233.02.99 — **AE ① VISA**   H 14
closed August, Sunday dinner and Monday dinner — **M** a la carte 95/150.

XX **Pasadena,** 7 r. du 29-Juillet (1st) ☎ 260.68.96 — **AE VISA**   G 12
closed August, Saturday dinner and Sunday — **M** a la carte 90 à 140 ♨.

X ⊛ **Aux Petits Pères** (Chez Yvonne), 8 r. N.-D.-des-Victoires (2nd) ☎ 260.91.73 — **AE VISA**
closed August, February Holidays, Saturday and Sunday — **M** (booking essential) a la
carte 90/170   G 14
Spec. St-Jacques à la provençale (October-April), Ris de veau toulousaine, Faisan (hunting season) or
pintade aux choux.

X **Jéroboam,** 8 r. Monsigny (2nd) ☎ 261.21.71   G 13

X **Chez Georges,** 1 r. Mail (2nd) ☎ 260.07.11 — **AE ① VISA**   G 14
closed Sunday and Bank Holidays — **M** a la carte 100/170.

X **Cochon Doré,** 16 r. Thorel (2nd) ☎ 233.29.70 — 🍴   G 15
closed Wednesday — **M** 62 b.i./128 b.i..

X **Louis XIV,** 1bis pl. Victoires (1st) ☎ 261.39.44   G 14
closed August, Saturday and Sunday — **M** a la carte 120/180.

X **Paul,** 15 pl. Dauphine (1st) ☎ 354.21.48 — ✂   J 14
closed August, Monday and Tuesday — **M** a la carte 90/120 ♨.

Bastille, République, Hôtel de Ville.

3rd, 4th and 11th arrondissements.
  3rd : ✉ 75003
  4th : ✉ 75004
  11th : ✉ 75011

Holiday Inn Ⓜ, 10 pl. République (11th) ℰ 355.44.34, Telex 210651, ☂ − ⌷ kitchenette
🍴 📺 ☎ ♿ Ⓟ − 🏧 150. 🅰🅴 ⑩ 🄴 𝗩𝗜𝗦𝗔 — **G 17**
st. : Belle Époque (Classic) **M** à la carte 150/240 ♨ − **Le Jardin d'hiver** (Coffee-Shop) **M** à
la carte approx. 110 ♨ − **316 rm** ⛴ 740/1 070, 16 apartments.

Deux Iles Ⓜ without rest., 59 r. St.-Louis-en-l'Ile (4th) ℰ 326.13.35 − ⌷ ⌷wc ⋔wc ☎ — **K 16**
st. : ⌷ 25 − **17 rm** 315/370.

Lutèce Ⓜ without rest., 65 r. St-Louis-en-l'Ile (4th) ℰ 326.23.52 − ⌷ ⌷wc ⋔wc ☎ — **K 16**
st. : ⌷ 24 − **23 rm** 352/375.

Bretonnerie without rest., 22 r. Ste-Croix-de-la-Bretonnerie (4th) ℰ 887.77.63 − ⌷ — **J 16**
⌷wc ⋔wc ☎. 🄴. 🛁
st. : ⌷ 20 − **31 rm** 195/380.

Marais without rest., 2 bis r. Commines (3rd) ℰ 887.78.27 − ⌷ ⌷wc ⋔wc ☎. 🅰🅴 𝗩𝗜𝗦𝗔 — **H 17**
st. : ⌷ 18 − **38 rm** 150/255.

Place des Vosges without rest., 12 r. Birague (4th) ℰ 272.60.46 − ⌷ ⌷wc ⋔wc ☎. 🅰🅴 — **J 17**
⑩ 🄴 𝗩𝗜𝗦𝗔. 🛁
st. : ⌷ 20 − **16 rm** 168/278.

Vieux Marais without rest., 2 r. Plâtre (4th) ℰ 278.47.22 − ⌷ ⌷wc ⋔wc ☎. 🛁 — **H 16**
st. : **30 rm** ⌷ 180/300.

Nord et Est without rest., 49 r. Malte (11th) ℰ 700.71.70 − ⌷ ⌷wc ⋔wc ☎. 🛁 — **G 17**
closed 26 July-2 September and 23 December-2 January − st. : ⌷ 17 − **44 rm** 150/200.

Notre-Dame without rest., 51 r. Malte (11th) ℰ 700.78.76 − ⌷ ⌷wc ⋔wc ☎. 🛁 — **G 17**
closed August − st. : ⌷ 16 − **54 rm** 98/200.

XXX **Ambassade d'Auvergne,** 22 r. Grenier St-Lazare (3rd) ℰ 272.31.22 − 🍴. 🅰🅴 ⑩ 🄴 𝗩𝗜𝗦𝗔
closed Sunday − st. : **M** a la carte 120/185. — **H 15**

XX ✿ **Quai des Ormes** (Masraff), 72 quai Hôtel de Ville (4th) ℰ 274.72.22 − 🍴. 𝗩𝗜𝗦𝗔
closed August-2 September, Saturday and Sunday − **M** 135 (lunch) and a la carte 180/260
Spec. Ravioli de champignons (except July-September), Râble de lapereau aux morilles, Chaud froid de
poires à la pistache..

XX **Bofinger,** 5 r. Bastille (4th) ℰ 272.87.82 − 🅰🅴 ⑩ 🄴 𝗩𝗜𝗦𝗔 — **J 17**
M a la carte 120/180 ♨.

XX **L'Acadien,** 35 bd Temple (3rd) ℰ 272.27.94 − 🅰🅴 ⑩ 🄴 𝗩𝗜𝗦𝗔 — **G 17**
closed 3 to 25 August and Sunday − st. : **M** 100/165.

XX ✿ **Chardenoux,** 1 r. J.-Vallès (11th) ℰ 371.49.52 − 🅰🅴 𝗩𝗜𝗦𝗔 — **· K 20**
closed Saturday, Sunday and Bank Holidays − st. : **M** a la carte 175/225.

XX ✿ **A Sousceyrac** (Asfaux), 35 r. Faidherbe (11th) ℰ 371.65.30 − Ⓟ. 🅰🅴 𝗩𝗜𝗦𝗔 — **J 19**
closed 30 March-8 April, August, Saturday and Sunday − **M** a la carte 135/170
Spec. Foie gras frais, Ris de veau aux champignons, Cassoulet (Monday, Wednesday and Friday).

XX **Repaire de Cartouche,** 8 bd Filles-du-Calvaire (11th) ℰ 700.25.86 − Ⓟ. 𝗩𝗜𝗦𝗔 — **H 17**
closed 20 July-18 August, February Holidays, Saturday and Sunday − **M** a la carte 125/180.

XX **Coconnas,** 2 bis pl. Vosges (4th) ℰ 278.58.16 − 🅰🅴 ⑩ 𝗩𝗜𝗦𝗔 — **J 17**
closed 15 December-15 January, Monday and Tuesday − **M** a la carte 200/285.

XX **Guirlande de Julie,** 25 pl. des Vosges (3rd) ℰ 887.94.07 − 🅰🅴 — **J 17**
closed February, Monday and Tuesday − **M** 156 b.i. (lunch) and a la carte approx. 180.

XX **Wally,** 16 r. Le Regrattier (4th) ℰ 325.01.39 − 🅰🅴 ⑩ 𝗩𝗜𝗦𝗔. 🛁 — **K 15**
closed Sunday and lunch : Saturday and Monday − **M** 185 b.i.

XX **Pyrénées Cévennes,** 106 r. Folie-Méricourt (11th) ℰ 357.33.78 — **G 17**
closed August, 24 December-2 January, Saturday, Sunday and Bank Holidays − **M** a la
carte 130/200.

XX **Taverne des Templiers,** 106 r. Vieille-du-Temple (3rd) ℰ 278.74.67 − 𝗩𝗜𝗦𝗔 — **H 17**
closed August, Saturday and Sunday − **M** a la carte 120/175.

XX **Au Gourmet de l'Isle**, 42 r. St-Louis-en-l'Ile (4th) ℘ 326.79.27 — ▦
closed 25 July-1 September, Monday and Thursday – **M** 85. K 16

XX **Péché Mignon**, 5 r. Guillaume-Bertrand (11th) ℘ 357.02.51 – *VISA*
closed August, Monday dinner and Sunday – **st. : M** a la carte 130/180. H 19

X ✿ **Benoît**, 20 r. St-Martin (4th) ℘ 272.25.76 — ℗
closed 3 to 26 August, 21 December-1 January, Saturday and Sunday – **st. : M** a la carte 190/240 J 15
Spec. Soupe de moules, Compotiers de boeuf en salade et museau, Boeuf mode braisé bourgeoise.

X **Tuboeuf**, 26 r. de Montmorency (4th) ℘ 272.31.04 – *VISA*. ❀
closed August, Saturday and Sunday – **st. : M** 125/175. H 16

**Quartier Latin, Luxembourg,
Jardin des Plantes.**

5th and 6th arrondissements.

5th : ✉ 75005
6th : ✉ 75006

🏨 **Lutétia Concorde**, 45 bd Raspail (6th) ℘ 544.38.10, Telex 270424 — ▯ ▤ ▣ ☎ – ⚙
25-600. ▦ ⓞ Ɛ *VISA* K 12
st. : M 65/95 ▯ – ☳ 45 – **286 rm** 580/1 100, 17 apartments.

🏨 **Victoria Palace** ঌ, 6 r. Blaise-Desgoffe (6th) ℘ 544.38.16, Telex 270557 – ▯ ▣ ☎
⬤➡. ▦ *VISA*. ❀
st. : M 120 – **110 rm** ☳ 490/655. L 11

🏨 **Littré** ঌ, 9 r. Littré (6th) ℘ 544.38.68, Telex 203852 – ▯ ▣ ☎ ℗ – ⚙ 25. ▦ Ɛ *VISA*. ❀
st. : M *(closed Sunday)* 120 – **95 rm** ☳ 490/610, 4 apartments. L 11

🏨 **Relais Christine** Ⓜ ঌ without rest, 3 r. Christine (6th) ℘ 326.71.80, Telex 202606 – ▯
▤ ▣ ⬤ – ⚙ 25. ▦ ⓞ *VISA*. ❀
st. : ☳ 45 – **33 rm** 770/810, 17 apartments. J 14

🏨 **Abbaye St-Germain** Ⓜ ঌ without rest, 10 r. Cassette (6th) ℘ 544.38.11, ⤬ – ▯ ☎.
st. : 45 rm ☳ 420/525. K 12

🏨 **Odéon H.,** Ⓜ without rest, 3 r. Odéon (6th) ℘ 325.90.67, Telex 202943 – ▯ ☎. ▦ ⓞ
VISA. ❀
st. : ☳ 420/450. K 13

🏨 **Madison H.** without rest, 143 bd St-Germain (6th) ℘ 329.72.50 – ▯ ☎. ❀
st. : ☳ 16 – **57 rm** 191/295. J 13

🏨 **Angleterre** without rest, 44 r. Jacob (6th) ℘ 260.34.72 – ▯ ☎. ▦ ⓞ *VISA*. ❀
st. : ☳ 22 – **30 rm** 300/450. J 13

🏨 **Scandinavia** without rest, 27 r. Tournon (6th) ℘ 329.67.20 – ⌂wc ☏. ❀
closed August – **st. :** ☳ 20 – **22 rm** 279. K 13

🏨 **Panthéon** Ⓜ without rest, 19 pl. Panthéon (5th) ℘ 354.32.95 – ▯ ▣ ⌂wc ☎. ▦ ⓞ
VISA. ❀
st. : ☳ 22 – **34 rm** 390/460. L 14

🏨 **Grands Hommes** Ⓜ without rest 17 pl. Panthéon (5th) ℘ 634.19.60, Telex 200185 – ▯
▣ ⌂wc ☎. ▦ *VISA*. ❀
st. : ☳ 22 – **32 rm** 390/460. L 14

🏨 **des Saints-Pères** without rest, 65 r. des Sts-Pères (6th) ℘ 544.50.00, Telex 205424 – ▯
⌂wc ☎ ὦ. ❀
st. : ☳ 24 – **40 rm** 350/500, 3 apartments 800. J 12

🏨 **Delavigne** without rest, 1 r. C.-Delavigne (6th) ℘ 329.31.50, Telex 201579 – ▯ ⌂wc
🛁wc ☎. ❀
st. : ☳ 20 – **34 rm** 250/340. K 13

🏨 **Pas-de-Calais** without rest, 59 r. Sts-Pères (6th) ℘ 548.78.74 – ▯ ⌂wc 🛁wc ☎ J 12
st. : ☳ 23 – **41 rm** 287/324.

🏨 **Marronniers** Ⓜ ঌ without rest, 21 r. Jacob (6th) ℘ 325.30.60, ⤬ – ▯ ⌂wc 🛁wc ☎.
st. : ☳ 23 – **37 rm** 299/322. J 13

🏨 **Ferrandi** without rest, 92 r. Cherche-Midi (6th) ℘ 222.97.40, Telex 205201 – ▯ ⌂wc
🛁wc ☎
st. : ☳ 25 – **41 rm** 320/360. L 11

🏨 **St-Germain-des-Prés** without rest, 36 r. Bonaparte (6th) ℘ 326.00.19 – ▯ ▣ ⌂wc
🛁wc ☎. ▦. ❀
st. : 30 rm ☳ 400/650. J 13

🏦 **Terminus Montparnasse** without rest, 59 bd Montparnasse (6th) ℰ 548.99.10, Telex 202636 — 🕼 📺 🛁wc 🏮wc ☎. **E** 𝑽𝑰𝑺𝑨 L 11
closed August – st. : ⏢ 27 – **63 rm** 276/405.

🏦 **Collège de France** Ⓜ without rest, 7 r. Thénard (5th) ℰ 326.78.36 — 🕼 📺 🛁wc 🏮wc ☎. 🖭. ⚶ K 14
st. : ⏢ 18 – **29 rm** 249/270.

🏦 **Gd H. des Principautés Unies** Ⓜ without rest, 42 r. Vaugirard (6th) ℰ 634.44.90 — 🕼 📺 🛁wc 🏮wc ☎. ⚶ K 13
closed August – st. : **25 rm** ⏢ 110/320.

🏦 **Louis II** without rest, 2 r. St.-sulpice (6th) ℰ 633.13.80 — 🕼 🛁wc 🏮wc ☎. 𝑽𝑰𝑺𝑨 K 13
st. : ⏢ 24 – **22 rm** 315/375.

🏦 **d'Isly** without rest, 29 r. Jacob (6th) ℰ 326.32.39 — 🕼 🛁wc 🏮wc ☎. ⚶ J 13
st. : **36 rm** ⏢ 156/325.

🏦 **Seine** without rest, 52 r. Seine (6th) ℰ 634.22.80 — 🕼 📺 🛁wc 🏮wc ☎. 🖭 ⓪ 𝑽𝑰𝑺𝑨. ⚶ J 13
st. : **30 rm** ⏢ 165/320.

🏦 **Rennes Montparnasse** without rest, 151 bis r. Rennes (6th) ℰ 548.97.38, Telex 250048 — 🕼 🛁wc 🏮wc ⚛. 🖭 𝑽𝑰𝑺𝑨 L 12
closed 1 to 29 August – st. : ⏢ 26 – **38 rm** 220/395.

🏦 **Aviatic** without rest, 105 r. Vaugirard (6th) ℰ 544.38.21, Telex 200372 — 🕼 📺 🛁wc ☎. 🖭 ⓪ 𝑽𝑰𝑺𝑨 L 11
st. : **43 rm** ⏢ 320/440.

🏤 **Nations** without rest, 54 r. Monge (5th) ℰ 326.45.24 — 🕼 🛁wc 🏮wc ☎. 𝑽𝑰𝑺𝑨. ⚶ L 15
st. : ⏢ 22 – **38 rm** 185/254.

🏤 **Welcome** Ⓜ without rest, 66 r. Seine (6th) ℰ 634.24.80 — 🕼 🛁wc 🏮wc ⚛. ⚶ J 13
st. : ⏢ 21 – **30 rm** 180/264.

🏤 **Gd H. Suez** without rest, 31 bd St-Michel (5th) ℰ 634.08.02, Telex 202019 — 🕼 📺 🛁wc 🏮wc ☎. 🖭 ⓪ **E** 𝑽𝑰𝑺𝑨. ⚶ K 14
st. : ⏢ 16 – **49 rm** 160/276.

🏤 **Albe** without rest, 1 r. Harpe (5th) ℰ 634.09.70 — 🕼 🛁wc 🏮wc ☎. ⚶ K 14
st. : **41 rm** ⏢ 165/282.

🏤 **Odéon** without rest, 13 r. St-Sulpice (6th) ℰ 325.70.11 — 🕼 📺 🛁wc 🏮wc ☎. 🖭 ⓪. ⚶ K 13
st. : **26 rm** ⏢ 300/450.

🏤 **Muséum** without rest, 9 r. Buffon (5th) ℰ 331.51.90 — 🕼 📺 🛁wc 🏮wc ☎ L 16
st. : ⏢ 22 – **24 rm** 196/221.

🏤 **St-Sulpice** without rest, 7 r. C.-Delavigne (6th) ℰ 634.23.90 — 🕼 🛁wc 🏮wc ☎. 𝑽𝑰𝑺𝑨 K 13
st. : ⏢ 18 – **41 rm** 185/223.

XXXXX ❀❀❀ **Tour d'Argent** (Terrail), 15 quai Tournelle (5th) ℰ 354.23.31, « Little museum showing the development of eating utensils, ≼ Notre-Dame, in the cellar : an illustrated history of wine » — 🖭 ⓪ 𝑽𝑰𝑺𝑨 K 16
closed Monday – **M** 195 (lunch) and a la carte 390/525
Spec. Canard au sang Tour d'Argent.

XXX ❀❀ **Jacques Cagna**, 14 r. Gds-Augustins (6th) ℰ 326.49.39, « Old Parisian house » — 🖃 🖭 𝑽𝑰𝑺𝑨 J 14
closed August, 24 December-2 January, Saturday and Sunday – **M** 185 (lunch) and a la carte 230/310
Spec. Pétoncles sauce cressonnette, Fricassée de homard aux cèpes, Canard au vin.

XXX ❀❀ **Relais Louis XIII**, 1 r. Pont de Lodi (6th) ℰ 326.75.96, « 16C cellar, fine furniture » — 🖃 🖭 ⓪ **E** 𝑽𝑰𝑺𝑨 J 14
closed 29 July-26 August, 1 to 7 January, Monday lunch and Sunday – **M** a la carte 215/270
Spec. Dégustation de poissons de petite pêche, Feuilleté de foie gras et ris de veau, Terrine aux deux chocolats.

XXX ❀ **Villars Palace**, 8 r. Descartes (5th) ℰ 326.39.08 — 🖭 ⓪ **E** 𝑽𝑰𝑺𝑨 L 15
closed Saturday lunch – **M** (rest.) a la carte 225/315 – **La Saumoneraie**
Spec. Panaché de poissons fumés, Feuilleté de langoustines, Ragoût de St-Jacques et écrevisses.

XXX ❀ **Duquesnoy**, 30 r. Bernardins (5th) ℰ 354.21.13 — 🖭 𝑽𝑰𝑺𝑨 K 15
closed August, Saturday lunch, Sunday and Bank Holidays – **M** 140 (lunch) and a la carte 195/275
Spec. Mousse de cèpes au beurre de truffe (season), Chou vert farci aux langoustines, Canette aux citrons et poivre verts.

XXX **Chat Grippé**, 87 r. d'Assas (6th) ℰ 354.70.00 — 🖃 🖭 𝑽𝑰𝑺𝑨 LM 13
closed August, Saturday lunch and Monday – **M** a la carte 155/210.

XX **Aub. des Deux Signes,** 46 r. Galande (5th) ℰ 325.46.56, « Medieval decor » — AE ⊙
 E VISA
  closed Sunday and Bank Holidays — **M** a la carte 185/275.
K 14

XX ❀ **Dodin-Bouffant,** 25 r. F.-Sauton (5th) ℰ 325.25.14 — ▤. ⊙ VISA
  closed August, Christmas Holidays, Saturday and Sunday — **M** a la carte 155/220
  Spec. Râgout de moules, Ragoût de canard et ris de veau, Soufflé aux fruits.
K 15

XX ❀❀ **Ambroisie** (Pacaud), 65 quai de la Tournelle (5th) ℰ 633.18.65 — AE VISA
  closed 10 to 31 August, February Holidays, Sunday and Monday — **st. : M** 180 (lunch) and
  a la carte 230/300
  Spec. Mousse de poivrons, Langoustines grillées au beurre d'estragon, Millefeuille aux fruits.
K 15

XX **Le Pactole,** 44 bd St-Germain (5th) ℰ 633.31.31 — VISA
  closed Saturday lunch and Sunday — **st. : M** a la carte 180/240.
K 15

XX **Coupe-Chou,** 11 r. Lanneau (5th) ℰ 633.68.69 — AE VISA
  closed Sunday lunch — **M** a la carte 115/200.
K 14

XX **Sud Ouest,** 40 r. Montagne Ste Geneviève (5th) ℰ 633.30.46, « 13C Crypt » — AE ⊙ E
  VISA
  closed August and Sunday — **M** a la carte 120/150.
K 15

XX **Atelier Maître Albert,** 1 r. Maître-Albert (5th) ℰ 633.13.78 — ▤
  closed August and Bank Holidays — **M** (dinner only) 135 b.i..
K 15

XX ❀ **Miravile** (Keller), 25 quai de la Tournelle (5th) ℰ 634.07.78 — AE ⊙ VISA
  closed Sunday — **st. : M** a la carte 180/245
  Spec. Terrine de brochet, Filet d'agneau sous croûte de sel, Crêpes soufflées à la liqueur.
K 15

XX **La Truffière,** 4 r. Blainville (5th) ℰ 633.29.82 — ▤. AE ⊙ E VISA. ⚞
  M a la carte 160/235.
L 15

XX **Taverne Basque,** 45 r. Cherche-Midi (6th) ℰ 222.51.07 — AE VISA
  closed 11 to 19 August, Sunday dinner and Monday — **M** a la carte 105/180.
K 12

XX **La Foux,** 2 r. Clément (6th) ℰ 354.09.53 — ▤. AE
  closed Sunday and Bank Holidays — **st. : M** a la carte 145/235.
K 13

XX **Les Arêtes,** 165 bd Montparnasse (6th) ℰ 326.23.98 — AE VISA
  closed Saturday lunch and Monday — **st. : M** a la carte 160 à 255.
M 13

XX **Chez Tante Madée,** 11 r. Dupin (6th) ℰ 222.64.56 — AE ⊙
  closed Saturday lunch and Sunday — **st. : M** a la carte 180/225.
K 12

XX **L'Apollinaire,** 168 bd St.-Germain (6th) ℰ 326.50.30 — ▤. AE ⊙ E VISA
  closed 20 December-5 January — **M** a la carte 125/190.
J 12

XX **Le Sybarite,** 6 r. Sabot (6th) ℰ 222.21.56 — ▤. AE ⊙ VISA. ⚞
  closed 22 December-2 January, Saturday lunch and Sunday — **M** 130.
K 12

XX **Au Grilladin,** 13 r. Mézières (6th) ℰ 548.30.38 — VISA
  closed 1 to 7 April, August, 24 December-2 January, Monday lunch and Sunday — **st. : M**
  a la carte 120/185.
K 12

XX **Joséphine** (Chez Dumonet), 117 r. Cherche-Midi (6th) ℰ 548.52.40 — VISA
  closed July, 21 to 30 December, Saturday and Sunday — **M** a la carte 140/215.
L 11

XX **Dominique,** 19 r. Bréa (6th) ℰ 327.08.80 — AE ⊙ E VISA
  closed July — **M** a la carte 100/200.
L 12

X ❀ **Allard** (Mme Allard), 41 r. St-André-des-Arts (6th) ℰ 326.48.23 — ▤. ⊙ VISA
  closed August, 21 December-2 January, Saturday, Sunday and Bank Holidays — **st. : M**
  (booking essential) a la carte 140/230
  Spec. Poissons au beurre blanc, Gibier (season).
K 14

X **Balzar,** 49 r. Écoles (5th) ℰ 354.13.67 — ⚞
  closed August and Tuesday — **M** a la carte 105/155.
K 14

X **Moissonnier,** 28 r. Fossés-St-Bernard (5th) ℰ 329.87.65
  closed August, Sunday dinner and Monday — **M** a la carte 100/150.
K 15

X **Au Charbon de Bois,** 16 r. Dragon (6th) ℰ 548.57.04 — ▤. ⊙ VISA
  closed Monday lunch and Sunday — **M** a la carte 90/130.
J 12

X **Étienne de Bigorre,** 14 r. Dauphine (6th) ℰ 326.49.81 — AE ⊙
  closed 7 to 16 April, August, 22 December-2 January, Sunday and Monday — **M** a la carte
  90/145 ⚘.
J 14

X **Chez Maître Paul,** 12 r. Monsieur-le-Prince (6th) ℰ 354.74.59 — AE VISA
  closed August, 24 December-2 January, Sunday and Monday — **M** a la carte 100/145.
K 13

X **Moulin à Vent,** 20 r. Fossés-St-Bernard (5th) ℰ 354.99.37 — AE VISA
  closed August and Sunday — **M** a la carte 120/165.
K 15

X **Le Mange Tout,** 30 r. Lacépède (5th) ℰ 535.53.93 — ⊙ VISA
  closed August, 24 February-4 March, Monday lunch and Sunday — **st. : M** a la carte
  95/145.
L 15

Don't get lost, use **Michelin Maps** *which are kept up to date.*

**Faubourg-St-Germain,
Invalides,
École Militaire.**

7th arrondissement.
7th : ⊠ 75007

🏛 **Pont Royal and rest. Les Antiquaires,** 7 r. Montalembert 🏛 544.38.27, Telex 270113
– 🛗 🍽 rm 📺 ☎ – ♨ 50. 🌐 ⓪ 🃏 *VISA*　　　　　　　　　　　　　　　　J 12
st. : **M** *(closed August and Sunday)* 180 b.i. – **75 rm** ☑ 790/1 020, 5 apartments.

🏛 **Sofitel Bourbon** Ⓜ, 32 r. St-Dominique 🏛 555.91.80, Telex 250019 – 🛗 🍽 📺 ☎ ♿
↔ – ♨ 50. 🌐 ⓪ 🃏 *VISA*　　　　　　　　　　　　　　　　　　　　H 10
st. : **M** Rest. see **Le Dauphin** below – ☑ 65 – **112 rm** 940/1 150.

🏛 **Cayré-Copatel** Ⓜ without rest, 4 bd Raspail 🏛 544.38.88, Telex 270577 – 🛗 📺 ☎ –
♨ 50. 🌐 ⓪ 🃏 *VISA*　　　　　　　　　　　　　　　　　　　　　J 12
st. : **130 rm** ☑ 530/560.

🏛 **St-Simon** without rest, 14 r. St-Simon 🏛 548.35.66, « Antique furniture » – 🛗 ☎. 🚫
st. : ☑ 50 – **29 rm** 500/550, 5 apartments 800.　　　　　　　　　　J 11

🏛 **Université** without rest, 22 r. Université 🏛 261.09.39 – 🛗 ☎. 🚫　　　　J 12
st. : ☑ 28 – **27 rm** 325/550.

🏛 **Montalembert** without rest, 3 r. Montalembert 🏛 548.68.11, Telex 200132 – 🛗. 🃏　J 12
st. : **61 rm** ☑ 460/640.

🏛 **La Bourdonnais,** 111 av. La Bourdonnais 🏛 705.45.42, Telex 201416 – 🛗 📺 🪑 ☎. ⓪
VISA　　　　　　　　　　　　　　　　　　　　　　　　　　　　　　J 9
st. : **M** Rest. see **La Cantine des Gourmets** below – **56 rm** ☑ 280/340.

🏛 **Suède** Ⓜ without rest, 31 r. Vaneau 🏛 705.00.08, Telex 200596 – 🛗 🚾 🛁wc ☎. 🌐
🚫　　　　　　　　　　　　　　　　　　　　　　　　　　　　　　K 11
st. : **40 rm** ☑ 313/405.

🏛 **De Varenne** Ⓜ 🌳 without rest, 44 r. Bourgogne 🏛 551.45.55 – 🛗 📺 🚾 🛁wc ☎.
🌐　　　　　　　　　　　　　　　　　　　　　　　　　　　　　　　J 10
st. : ☑ 21 – **24 rm** 240/360.

🏛 **Résidence Elysées Maubourg** Ⓜ without rest, 35 bd Latour-Maubourg 🏛 556.10.78,
Telex 206227 – 🛗 📺 🚾 🛁wc ☎. 🌐 ⓪ *VISA*. 🚫　　　　　　　　H 10
st. : **30 rm** ☑ 430/540.

🏛 **Bourgogne et Montana,** 3 r. Bourgogne 🏛 551.20.22, Telex 270854 – 🛗 🚾 🛁wc
🍽. 🌐 *VISA*　　　　　　　　　　　　　　　　　　　　　　　　　　H 11
st. : **M** *(closed August, Saturday and Sunday)* 120 – **30 rm** ☑ 260/400, 5 apartments.

🏛 **Lenox** Ⓜ without rest, 9 r. Université 🏛 296.10.95 – 🛗 📺 🚾 🛁wc ☎. *VISA*　J 12
st. : ☑ 20 – **32 rm** 240/378.

🏛 **Académie** without rest, 32 r. des Sts-Pères 🏛 548.36.22, Telex 205650 – 🛗 📺 🚾
🛁wc ☎. 🌐 ⓪ 🃏 *VISA*　　　　　　　　　　　　　　　　　　　　J 12
st. : ☑ 22 – **34 rm** 360/440.

🏛 **Beaugency** Ⓜ without rest, 21 r. Duvivier 🏛 705.01.63, Telex 201494 – 🛗 📺 🚾
🛁wc ☎. 🌐 ⓪ *VISA*. 🚫　　　　　　　　　　　　　　　　　　　　J 9
st. : ☑ 19 – **30 rm** 395/405.

🏛 **St-Germain** without rest, 88 r. Bac 🏛 548.62.92 – 🛗 🚾wc 🛁wc ☎. 🌐　　J 11
st. : ☑ 21 – **29 rm** 223/330.

🏛 **Tourville** Ⓜ without rest, 16 av. Tourville 🏛 705.52.15, Telex 250786 – 🛗 📺 🚾 🛁wc
☎. 🌐 *VISA*. 🚫　　　　　　　　　　　　　　　　　　　　　　　　J 9
st. : ☑ 18,50 – **31 rm** 210/295.

🏛 **Derby H.** without rest, 5 av. Duquesne 🏛 705.12.05, Telex 206236 – 🛗 🚾wc 🛁wc ☎.
🌐 ⓪ 🃏 *VISA*　　　　　　　　　　　　　　　　　　　　　　　　　J 9
st. : ☑ 19 – **44 rm** 260/295.

🏛 **Solférino** without rest, 91 r. Lille 🏛 705.85.54 – 🛗 🚾wc 🛁wc ☎. 🚫　　H 11
closed 23 December-4 January – st. : ☑ 21 – **34 rm** 130/269.

🏛 **Lindbergh** without rest, 5 r. Chomel 🏛 548.35.53, Telex 201777 – 🛗 🚾wc 🛁wc ☎. 🌐
⓪ 🃏 *VISA*　　　　　　　　　　　　　　　　　　　　　　　　　　K 12
st. : ☑ 20 – **26 rm** 224/271.

🏛 **Verneuil-St-Germain** without rest, 8 r. Verneuil 🏛 260.24.16 – 🛗 📺 🚾wc 🛁wc ☎.
　　　　　　　　　　　　　　　　　　　　　　　　　　　　　　　J 12
st. : ☑ 22 – **26 rm** 330/385.

🏠 **Mars H.** without rest, 117 av. La Bourdonnais ✆ 705.42.30 – 🛗 ⇄wc ⋔wc ☎. 🛠 J 9
st. : ⊠ 18 – **24 rm** 104/235.

🏠 **Turenne** without rest, 20 av. Tourville ✆ 705.99.92, Telex 203407 – 🛗 ⇄wc ⋔wc ☎. 𝔸𝔼
𝕍𝕀𝕊𝔸 J 9
st. : ⊠ 18 – **34 rm** 157/262.

🏠 **Kensington** without rest, 79 av. La Bourdonnais ✆ 705.74.00 – 🛗 ⇄wc ⋔wc ☎. 𝔸𝔼 ⓞ
𝕍𝕀𝕊𝔸 J 9
st. : ⊠ 18 – **26 rm** 197/258.

🏠 **Champ de Mars** without rest, 7 r. champ de Mars ✆ 551.52.30 – 🛗 ⇄wc ⋔wc ☎. 𝕍𝕀𝕊𝔸
closed 15 to 31 August – st. : ⊠ 18 – **25 rm** 250/265. J 9

🏠 **Résidence d'Orsay** without rest, 93 r. Lille ✆ 705.05.27 – 🛗 ⇄wc ⋔wc ☎. 🛠 H 11
closed August – st. : ⊠ 20 – **32 rm** 130/260.

🏠 **Muguet** without rest, 11 r. Chevert ✆ 705.05.93 – 🛗 ⇄wc ⋔wc ☎ J 9
closed 28 July-1 September – st. : ⊠ 18 – **43 rm** 110/220.

🏠 **L'Empereur** without rest, 2 r. Chevert ✆ 555.88.02 – 🛗 ⇄wc ⋔wc ☎ J 9
st. : ⊠ 18 – **35 rm** 190/255.

XXXX ❀❀❀ **L'Archestrate** (Senderens), 84 r. Varenne (Mr Senderens is expected to leave in
spring 1985) ✆ 551.47.33 – 𝔸𝔼 ⓞ 𝕍𝕀𝕊𝔸 J 10
closed 3 to 27 August, 21 December-2 January, Saturday and Sunday – **M** a la carte
365/455
Spec. Foie gras grillé, Ravioli de pétoncles, Canard Apicius.

XXXX ❀❀ **Le Divellec**, 107 r. Université ✆ 551.91.96 – 𝔸𝔼 ⓞ E 𝕍𝕀𝕊𝔸 🛠 H 10
closed 3 August-3 September, 23 December-3 January, Sunday and Monday – **M** a la
carte 220/350
Spec. Huîtres frémies à la laitue de mer, Filet de St-Pierre en forestière, Poêlée de langoustines au foie de
canard.

XXXX ❀ **Jules Verne**, Eiffel Tower : 2nd platform, lift in south leg ✆ 555.61.44, Telex 205789,
⩽ Paris – 🍽 🅿 𝔸𝔼 𝕍𝕀𝕊𝔸 🛠 J 7
M a la carte 230/300
Spec. Salade tiède de ris de veau et queues d'écrevisses, Turbot et palourdes au beurre de ciboulette, Grand
dessert "Jules Verne".

XXX ❀ **Chez les Anges**, 54 bd Latour-Maubourg ✆ 705.89.86 – 🍽. 𝔸𝔼 ⓞ E 𝕍𝕀𝕊𝔸 J 9
closed Sunday dinner and Monday – **M** a la carte 185/265
Spec. Oeufs en meurette, Blanc de turbot Albert Benoist, Foie de veau.

XXX ❀ **Le Dauphin** (Sofitel Bourbon), 32 r. St-Dominique ✆ 555.91.80 – 🍽. 𝔸𝔼 ⓞ E 𝕍𝕀𝕊𝔸
st. : **M** a la carte 220/290 H 10
Spec. Crème de coques et de palourdes au safran, Rosettes d'agneau rôties au basilic, Gratin de fruits au
coulis de fraises.

XXX ❀ **La Bourgogne** (Julien), 6 av. Bosquet ✆ 705.96.78 – 𝔸𝔼 ⓞ 𝕍𝕀𝕊𝔸 H 9
closed August, Saturday lunch and Sunday – **M** a la carte 145/210
Spec. Gibier, Ris de veau aux morilles, Bouribout.

XXX ❀ **La Flamberge** (Albistur), 12 av. Rapp ✆ 705.91.37 – 🍽. 𝔸𝔼 ⓞ E 𝕍𝕀𝕊𝔸 H 8
closed 4 August-4 September, Saturday lunch and Sunday – st. : **M** a la carte 195/265
Spec. Foie gras de canard, Gibier (season), Tarte chaude aux fruits.

XXX **Chez Françoise**, Aérogare des Invalides ✆ 705.49.03 – 𝔸𝔼 ⓞ 𝕍𝕀𝕊𝔸 H 10
closed August, Sunday dinner and Monday – **M** a la carte 120/180.

XX ❀ **La Cantine des Gourmets**, 113 av. de La Bourdonnais ✆ 705.47.96 – 𝔸𝔼 ⓞ 𝕍𝕀𝕊𝔸 J 9
closed August, Saturday and Sunday – st. : **M** a la carte 190/280
Spec. Marinière de sole et d'écrevisses, Pigeonneau en navarin, Crème de potiron aux St-Jacques.

XX ❀ **Récamier** (Cantegrit), 4 r. Récamier ✆ 548.86.58 – ⓞ E 𝕍𝕀𝕊𝔸 K 12
closed Sunday – **M** a la carte 180/265
Spec. Oeufs en meurette, Mousse de brochet, Boeuf bourguignon.

XX ❀ **Ferme St-Simon** (Vandenhende), 6 r. St-Simon ✆ 548.35.74 – 𝕍𝕀𝕊𝔸 J 11
closed 1 to 20 August, Saturday lunch and Sunday – **M** 140 b.i (lunch) and a la carte
150/230
Spec. Duo d'oursins en demi-glace (December-March), Grillandine "Denise Fabre", Ballotine de lièvre (end
September-mid December).

XX ❀ **Conticini**, 4 r. Pierre-Leroux ✆ 306.99.39 – 🍽. 𝔸𝔼 ⓞ 𝕍𝕀𝕊𝔸 K 11
closed August, Saturday lunch and Sunday – **M** a la carte 150/200
Spec. Pâtes fraîches aux huîtres et foie gras, Ragoût de homard à l'aneth, Confit de canard.

XX **le Florence**, 22 r. Champ de Mars ✆ 551.52.69 – 𝔸𝔼 𝕍𝕀𝕊𝔸 J 9
closed July, Sunday and Monday – **M** 100/160.

XX **Le Galant Verre**, 12 r. Verneuil ✆ 260.84.56 – 𝔸𝔼 ⓞ E 𝕍𝕀𝕊𝔸 J 12
closed Sunday – **M** a la carte 160/270.

XX ❀ **Bistrot de Paris**, 33 r. Lille ✆ 261.16.83, bistro style – 𝕍𝕀𝕊𝔸 J 12
closed 27 July-20 August, Saturday and Sunday – **M** a la carte 165/215.

XX ❀ **Vert Bocage**, 96 bd Latour-Maubourg ✆ 551.48.64 – 𝔸𝔼 ⓞ 𝕍𝕀𝕊𝔸 J 9
closed August, Saturday and Sunday – **M** a la carte 155/235
Spec. Tarte à la tomate, Turbot beurre blanc, Ris de veau.

XX **Antoine et Antoinette**, 16 av. Rapp ✆ 551.75.61 – 𝔸𝔼 ⓞ 𝕍𝕀𝕊𝔸 H 8
closed 15 April-15 May, Saturday and Sunday – **M** a la carte 130/215.

XX **Aux Délices de Szechuen,** 40 av. Duquesne ✆ 306.22.55 – ▤. AE VISA K 10
closed 5 to 19 August, 21 to 25 December and Monday – **st. : M** a la carte 105/170 🌡.

XX ✿ **La Boule d'Or,** 13 bd Latour-Maubourg ✆ 705.50.18 – AE ◑ VISA H 10
closed August, Saturday lunch and Monday – **M** a la carte 150/215
Spec. Foie gras de canard, Millefeuille de sole et langoustines, Soufflé au citron.

XX **Chez Ribe,** 15 av. Suffren ✆ 566.53.79 – AE ◑ E VISA J 7
closed August, Saturday and Sunday – **M** a la carte 140/210.

XX ✿ **Gildo** (Bellini), 153 r. Grenelle ✆ 551.54.12 J 9
closed Easter, Whitsun, 14 July-1 September, Christmas Holidays, Sunday and Monday – **M** a la carte 115/160
Spec. Agneau de lait à la romaine (January-April), Tortelloni au Gorgonzola, Scampi au thym.

XX **Le Champ de Mars,** 17 av. Motte-Picquet ✆ 705.57.99 – ◑ VISA J 9
closed 14 July-16 August, Tuesday dinner and Monday – **M** a la carte 100/160.

XX **Quai d'Orsay,** 49 quai d'Orsay ✆ 551.58.58 – AE ◑ E VISA H 9
closed Sunday – **M** a la carte 190/260.

X ✿ **Pantagruel** (Israël), 20 r. Exposition ✆ 551.79.96 – ◑ VISA J 9
closed August, Saturday lunch and Sunday – **st. : M** a la carte 130/200
Spec. Cassolette d'escargots, Soufflé à la mousse de St-Jacques (October-April), Gibier (October-April).

X ✿ **Tan Dinh,** 60 r. Verneuil ✆ 544.04.84 J 12
closed 15 August-1 September and Sunday – **M** a la carte 110/165.

X **La Calèche,** 8 r. Lille ✆ 260.24.76 – AE ◑ E VISA J 12
closed 5 to 27 August, 23 December-2 January, Saturday and Sunday – **st. : M** a la carte 120/180.

X **Aub. Champ de Mars,** 18 r. Exposition ✆ 551.78.08 – AE ◑ VISA J 9
closed 5 to 25 August, Saturday lunch and Sunday – **M** a la carte 105/155 🌡.

X **Vin sur Vin,** 20 r. Monttessuy ✆ 705.14.20 – ▤ H 8
closed 11 to 18 August and Sunday – **st. : M** a la carte approx 110.

Champs-Élysées, St-Lazare, Madeleine.

8th arrondissement.
8th : ✉ 75008

Plaza-Athénée, 25 av. Montaigne ✆ 723.78.33, Telex 650092 – 🛗 ▤ TV ☎ – 🚶 30-100. AE ◑ E VISA. ✻ rest G 9
M Rest. see **Régence and Relais Plaza** below – ☕ 60 – **174 rm** 1 400/1 530, 44 apartments.

Crillon, 10 pl. Concorde ✆ 265.24.24, Telex 290204 – 🛗 TV ☎ ♿ – 🚶 30-150. AE ◑ E VISA. ✻ rest G 11
st. : L'Obelisque M a la carte approx. 140 - Rest. see **Les Ambassadeurs** below – ☕ 73 – **152 rm** 1 485/1 950, 48 apartments.

Bristol, 112 fg St-Honoré ✆ 266.91.45, Telex 280961, 🏊, 🌳 – 🛗 ▤ TV ☎ Ⓟ – 🚶 40-150. AE ◑ E VISA. ✻ F 10
st. : M Rest. see **Bristol** below – ☕ 75 – **155 rm** 1 060/2 360, 40 apartments.

George V, 31 av. George-V ✆ 723.54.00, Telex 650082 – 🛗 ▤ TV ☎ ♿ – 🚶 800. AE ◑ E VISA G 8
Rest. **Les Princes M** a la carte 240/400 – ☕ 50 – **289 rm** 1 740/2 490, 59 apartments.

Prince de Galles, 33 av. George-V ✆ 723.55.11, Telex 280627, 🌂 – 🛗 TV ☎ – 🚶 40-200. AE ◑ E VISA. ✻ rest G 8
closed March and April – **st. : M** 180/315 – ☕ 85 – **150 rm** 1 325/1 820, 26 apartments.

Warwick and rest. La Couronne Ⓜ, 5 r. Berri ✆ 563.14.11, Telex 642295 – 🛗 ▤ TV ☎ 🚗 – 🚶 120. AE ◑ E VISA F 9
st. : M *(closed August, Sunday and Bank Holidays)* 175 b.i./195 – ☕ 70 – **142 rm** 1 100/1 400, 5 apartments.

La Trémoille, 14 r. La Trémoille ✆ 723.34.20, Telex 640344 – 🛗 TV ☎. AE ◑ E VISA G 9
M a la carte 130/180 🌡 – ☕ 46 – **99 rm** 880/1 450, 13 apartments.

Claridge Bellman Ⓜ, 37 r. François 1er ✆ 723.90.03, Telex 641150, « Fine old furniture » – 🛗 ▤ rest TV ☎. AE ◑. ✻ G 9
st. : M *(closed Saturday and Sunday)* a la carte 160/235 – ☕ 43 – **42 rm** 575/795.

Royal Monceau, 35 av. Hoche ✆ 561.98.00, Telex 650361, 🌂, 🏊 – 🛗 ▤ TV ☎ ♿ – 🚶 600. AE ◑ E VISA. ✻ rest E 8
st. : Le Jardin M a la carte 270/380 **Le Carpaccio M** a la carte 240/350 – ☕ 70 – **209 rm** 1 000/1 600, 25 apartments.

🏨 **Frantel-Windsor** Ⓜ, 14 r. Beaujon ℰ 563.04.04, Telex 650902 — 🛗 🖃 rest 📺 ☎ – 🛗
120. 🅰🅴 Ⓞ 🅴 𝘝𝘐𝘚𝘈
   F 8
st. : M Rest. see **Le Clovis** below – 😊 42 – **135 rm** 740/920.

🏨 **Lancaster,** 7 r. Berri ℰ 359.90.43, Telex 640991, 🍴 – 🛗 🖃 📺 ☎ – 🛗
   F 9
M (closed Saturday and Sunday) a la carte 190/270 – 😊 60 – **57 rm** 850/1 330, 10 apartments.

🏨 **Napoléon,** 40 av. Friedland ℰ 766.02.02, Telex 640609 – 🛗 📺 ☎ – 🛗 30-100. 🅰🅴 Ⓞ 🅴
𝘝𝘐𝘚𝘈
   F 8
st. : Rest. see **Napoléon Baumann** below – 😊 35 – **108 rm** 600/950, 32 apartments.

🏨 **Château Frontenac,** 54 r. P.-Charron ℰ 723.55.85, Telex 660994 – 🛗 📺 ☎ – 🛗 25. 🅰🅴
Ⓞ 🅴 𝘝𝘐𝘚𝘈. 🍴
   G 9
st. : Pavillon Russe M a la carte 160/280 – 😊 45 – **101 rm** 590/820.

🏨 **California** without rest, 16 r. Berri ℰ 359.93.00, Telex 660634 – 🛗 📺 ☎ – 🛗 70-150. 🅰🅴
Ⓞ 🅴 𝘝𝘐𝘚𝘈
   F 9
st. : 😊 33 – **188 rm** 790/970, 3 apartments.

🏨 **Concorde-St-Lazare,** 108 r. St-Lazare ℰ 294.22.22, Telex 650442 – 🛗 📺 ☎ – 🛗 100.
🅰🅴 🅴 𝘝𝘐𝘚𝘈
   E 12
st. : Café Terminus M a la carte approx. 150 🍷 – 😊 45 – **324 rm** 720/960.

🏨 **Bedford,** 17 r. Arcade ℰ 266.22.32, Telex 290506 – 🛗 📺 ☎ – 🛗 80. 🅴 𝘝𝘐𝘚𝘈. 🍴 rest F 11
st. : M (closed August, Saturday and Sunday) (lunch only) 115 b.i. – **137 rm** 😊 420/590, 10 apartments.

🏨 **Queen Elizabeth,** 41 av. Pierre-1er-de-Serbie ℰ 720.80.56, Telex 641179 – 🛗 📺 ☎ –
🛗 25. 🅰🅴 Ⓞ 🅴 𝘝𝘐𝘚𝘈
   G 8
st. : M (closed Sunday and dinner Monday to Friday) 120 b.i./160 b.i. – 😊 55 – **60 rm** 600/950, 7 apartments.

🏨 **Etap St-Honoré** Ⓜ without rest, 15 r. Boissy d'Anglas ℰ 266.93.62, Telex 240366 – 🛗
📺 ☎ – 🛗 40. 🅰🅴 Ⓞ 🅴 𝘝𝘐𝘚𝘈
   G 11
st. : 😊 24 – **104 rm** 340/404, 8 apartments.

🏨 **Castiglione,** 40 r. Fg-St-Honoré ℰ 265.07.50, Telex 240362 – 🛗 📺 ☎ – 🛗 30. 🅰🅴 Ⓞ 🅴
𝘝𝘐𝘚𝘈
   G 11
M a la carte approx. 200 – 😊 55 – **98 rm** 735/975, 15 apartments.

🏨 **Royal Malesherbes** Ⓜ, 24 bd Malesherbes ℰ 265.53.30, Telex 660190 – 🛗 📺 ☎ – 🛗
30. 🅰🅴 Ⓞ 🅴 𝘝𝘐𝘚𝘈
   F 11
st. : a la carte approx. 130 🍷 – **102 rm** 😊 600/700.

🏨 **Royal-Madeleine** without rest, 29 r. Arcade ℰ 266.13.81, Telex 641458 – 🛗 📺 ☎. 🅰🅴
Ⓞ 𝘝𝘐𝘚𝘈. 🍴
   F 11
st. : 😊 44 – **67 rm** 645/830.

🏨 **Résidence Champs-Elysées** Ⓜ without rest, 92 r. La Boëtie ℰ 359.96.15, Telex 650695
– 🛗 📺 ☎. 🅰🅴 Ⓞ 🅴 𝘝𝘐𝘚𝘈
   F 9
st. : 😊 39 – **85 rm** 577/760.

🏨 **Roblin and rest. Le Mazagran,** 6 r. Chauveau-Lagarde ℰ 265.57.00, Telex 640154 –
🛗 📺 ☎. 𝘝𝘐𝘚𝘈
   F 11
M (closed August, Saturday and Sunday) a la carte 150/205 - **Grill M** a la carte approx. 120
🍷 – **70 rm** 😊 410/530.

🏨 **Printemps and rest. Chez Martin,** 1 r. Isly ℰ 294.12.12, Telex 290744 – 🛗 📺 ☎ –
🛗 25. 🅴
   F 12
st. : M (closed Sunday) 85 b.i. – **69 rm** 😊 250/515.

🏨 **Vernet,** 25 r. Vernet ℰ 723.43.10, Telex 290347 – 🛗 ☎. 🅰🅴 Ⓞ 🅴 𝘝𝘐𝘚𝘈
   F 8
st. : M (closed August, Saturday and Sunday) 185 – 😊 40 – **63 rm** 620/910.

🏨 **Elysées-Marignan** without rest, 12 r. Marignan ℰ 359.58.61, Telex 660018 – 🛗 📺 ☎.
🅰🅴 Ⓞ 🅴 𝘝𝘐𝘚𝘈
   G 9
st. : 71 rm 😊 785/980.

🏨 **Royal H.** without rest, 33 av. Friedland ℰ 359.08.14, Telex 280965 – 🛗 📺 ☎. 🅰🅴 Ⓞ 🅴
𝘝𝘐𝘚𝘈. 🍴
   F 8
st. : 😊 30 – **57 rm** 475/595.

🏨 **Powers** without rest, 52 r. François-1er ℰ 723.91.05, Telex 642051 – 🛗 📺 ☎. 🅰🅴 𝘝𝘐𝘚𝘈. 🍴
st. : 😊 24 – **54 rm** 210/510, 3 apartments.
   G 9

🏨 **Alison** Ⓜ without rest, 21 r. Surène ℰ 265.54.00, Telex 640435 – 🛗 📺 🛁wc 🚿wc
🅰🅴 Ⓞ 🅴 𝘝𝘐𝘚𝘈. 🍴
   F 11
st. : 😊 21 – **35 rm** 233/356.

🏨 **Concortel** without rest, 19 r. Pasquier ℰ 265.45.44, Telex 660228 – 🛗 📺 🛁wc 🚿wc
☎. 🅰🅴 Ⓞ
   F 11
st. : 😊 21 – **38 rm** 315/360, 8 apartments.

🏨 **L'Arcade** without rest, 7 r. Arcade ℰ 265.43.85 – 🛗 📺 🛁wc ☎
   F 11
st. : 47 rm 😊 270/350.

🏨 **Bradford** without rest, 10 r. St-Philippe-du-Roule ℰ 359.24.20, Telex 648530 – 🛗 🛁wc
🚿wc 🅰🅿. 🍴
   F 9
st. : 48 rm 😊 287/325.

🏨 **Colisée** Ⓜ without rest, 6 r. Colisée ℰ 359.95.25, Telex 643101 – 🛗 📺 🛁wc ☎. 🅰🅴 Ⓞ
🅴 𝘝𝘐𝘚𝘈
   F 9
st. : 44 rm 😊 370/485.

🏨 **St Augustin** without rest, 9 r. Roy 𝒸 293.32.17, Telex 641919 — 📶 TV ⌂wc ⋔wc ☎. 🆎 ⓞ Ε 𝘝𝘐𝘚𝘈
F 11
st. : ⌷ 15 − **62 rm** 330/408.

🏨 **Elysées Ponthieu** Ⓜ without rest, 24 r. Ponthieu 𝒸 225.68.70, Telex 640053 — 📶 TV ⌂wc ⋔wc ☎. 🆎 ⓞ 𝘝𝘐𝘚𝘈
F 9
st. : **62 rm** ⌷ 525/550.

🏨 **Angleterre-Champs-Élysées** Ⓜ without rest, 91 r. La Boétie 𝒸 359.35.45, Telex 640317 — 📶 TV ⌂wc ☎. 🆎 ⓞ 𝘝𝘐𝘚𝘈
F 9
st. : ⌷ 21 − **40 rm** 211/320.

🏨 **Résidence Saint-Philippe** without rest, 123 r. Fg-St-Honoré 𝒸 359.86.99 — 📶 ⌂wc ⋔wc ☎. ⅏
F 9-10
st. : **38 rm** ⌷ 291/410.

🏨 **Royal Alma** without rest, 35 r. Jean-Goujon 𝒸 225.83.30, Telex 641428 — 📶 ⌂wc ⋔wc ☎. 🆎 𝘝𝘐𝘚𝘈
G 9
st. : **83 rm** ⌷ 750.

🏨 **Franklin Roosevelt** without rest, 18 r. Clément-Marot 𝒸 723.61.66, Telex 614797 — 📶 ⌂wc ⋔wc ☎. 🆎 𝘝𝘐𝘚𝘈. ⅏
G 9
st. : **45 rm** ⌷ 350/380.

🏨 **Rond-Point des Champs-Elysées** without rest, 10 r. Ponthieu 𝒸 359.55.58, Telex 642386 — 📶 TV ⌂wc ⋔wc ☎. 🆎 ⓞ Ε 𝘝𝘐𝘚𝘈. ⅏
F 10
st. : ⌷ 19 − **46 rm** 324/385.

🏨 **Brescia** Ⓜ without rest, 16 r. Edimbourg 𝒸 522.14.31, Telex 660714 — 📶 TV ⌂wc ⋔wc ☎. 🆎 ⓞ Ε 𝘝𝘐𝘚𝘈. ⅏
E 11
st. : ⌷ 19 − **38 rm** 190/275.

🏨 **Washington** without rest, 43 r. Washington 𝒸 561.10.76 — 📶 TV ⌂wc ⋔wc ☎. 🆎 𝘝𝘐𝘚𝘈. ⅏
F 9
st. : ⌷ 21 − **23 rm** 175/300.

🏨 **West End** without rest, 7 r. Clément-Marot 𝒸 720.30.78, Telex 611972 — 📶 TV ⌂wc ☎. 🆎 ⓞ 𝘝𝘐𝘚𝘈
G 9
st. : **60 rm** ⌷ 380/840.

🏨 **Queen Mary** without rest, 9 r. Greffulhe 𝒸 266.40.50, Telex 640419 — 📶 ⌂wc ⋔wc ☎.
F 12
st. : ⌷ 25 − **36 rm** 269/392.

🏨 **Atlantic** without rest, 44 r. Londres 𝒸 387.45.40, Telex 650477 — 📶 ⌂wc ⋔wc ☎. 🆎 𝘝𝘐𝘚𝘈. ⅏
E 12
st. : ⌷ 21 − **93 rm** 205/320.

🏨 **Lido** without rest, 4 passage Madeleine 𝒸 266.27.37 — 📶 ⌂wc ⋔wc ☜. 🆎 𝘝𝘐𝘚𝘈. ⅏ F 11
st. : **29 rm** ⌷ 155/340.

🏨 **Opal** without rest, 19 r. Tronchet 𝒸 265.77.97, Telex 217152 — 📶 TV ⌂wc ⋔wc ☎. 🆎 𝘝𝘐𝘚𝘈
F 12
st. : ⌷ 22 − **36 rm** 280/350.

🏨 **Élysées** without rest, 100 r. La Boétie 𝒸 359.23.46 — 📶 TV ⌂wc ⋔wc ☜. 🆎 ⓞ Ε 𝘝𝘐𝘚𝘈. ⅏
F 9
st. : **30 rm** ⌷ 288/327.

🏨 **Lord Byron** without rest, 5 r. Chateaubriand 𝒸 359.89.98, 🚗 — 📶 TV ⌂wc ⋔wc ☎. ⅏
F 9
st. : ⌷ 22 − **30 rm** 310/445, 7 apartments.

🏠 **Ministère** without rest, 31 r. Surène 𝒸 266.21.43 — 📶 TV ⌂wc ⋔wc ☎ F 11
st. : **32 rm** ⌷ 150/350.

🏠 **Lavoisier-Malesherbes** without rest, 21 r. Lavoisier 𝒸 265.10.97 — 📶 ⌂wc ⋔wc ☜. ⅏
F 11
st. : **32 rm** ⌷ 240/275.

XXXXX ✿✿ **Lasserre,** 17 av. Franklin-D.-Roosevelt 𝒸 359.53.43, Roof open in fine weather — ▣. ⅏
G 10
closed 4 August-2 September, Sunday and Monday − **M** a la carte 310/380.
Spec. Filet de sandre dans sa cuisson beurrée, Ris de veau saisi en chiffonnade, Rocher meringué.

XXXXX ✿✿ **Laurent,** 41 av. Gabriel 𝒸 723.79.18 − 🆎 ⓞ. ⅏
G 11
closed Saturday lunch, Sunday and Bank Holidays − **M** lunch 300 b.i. and a la carte 310/475.
Spec. Salade de homard, Médaillon de veau aux morilles, Deux soufflés "Laurent".

XXXXX ✿✿ **Ledoyen,** carré Champs-Élysées 𝒸 266.54.77 − 🅿
G 10
closed 2 August-3 September and Sunday − **M** a la carte 260/370.
Spec. Terrine de lapereau, Filet de turbot aux écailles de courgettes, Les trois filets poêlés.

XXXXX ❀❀❀ **Taillevent,** 15 r. Lamennais 🕿 561.12.90 — 🍽. 🛇
F 9
   closed 27 July-26 August, February Holidays, Saturday, Sunday and Bank Holidays – **M**
(booking essential) a la carte 255/350
Spec. Langoustines aux pâtes fraîches, Foie de canard chaud au gingembre, Ballotine aux cinq parfums.

XXXXX ❀ **Régence,** 25 av. Montaigne 🕿 723.78.33, 🍴 — 🖭 ⓞ Ε 𝗩𝗜𝗦𝗔. 🛇
G 9
   closed 20 December-2 January – **M** a la carte 285/415
Spec. Soufflé de homard, Filet d'agneau à la sauge Margherita, Ananas San Miguel.

XXXXX ❀❀ **Les Ambassadeurs,** 10 pl. Concorde 🕿 265.24.24, 🍴, « 18C decor » — 🖭 ⓞ Ε
𝗩𝗜𝗦𝗔. 🛇
G 11
   st. : **M** a la carte 285/415
Spec. Rouelles d'artichauts frais aux truffes, Filet de boeuf à la ficelle, Velours aux épices des quatre voleurs.

XXXXX ❀❀ **Bristol,** 112 r. Fg St-Honoré 🕿 266.91.45 — 🅿. 🖭 ⓞ Ε 𝗩𝗜𝗦𝗔. 🛇
F 10
   st. : **M** a la carte 310/380
Spec. Salade landaise, Escalope de turbot au Sauternes, Mignon de veau à la graine de moutarde.

XXXXX **Lucas-Carton,** 9 pl. Madeleine (Planned to be taken over by Mr Senderens in spring
1985) 🕿 265.22.90, « Fine 1900's decor » — 🅿. 🖭 ⓞ Ε 𝗩𝗜𝗦𝗔
G 11
   closed Saturday lunch and Friday – **M** a la carte 250/345.

XXXX ❀ **Lamazère,** 23 r. Ponthieu 🕿 359.66.66 — 🍽. 🖭 ⓞ 𝗩𝗜𝗦𝗔. 🛇
F 9
   closed August and Sunday – **M** a la carte 210/335
Spec. Truffe Lamazère, Sole aux truffes, Cassoulet aux trois confits.

XXXX ❀❀ **La Marée,** 1 r. Daru 🕿 763.52.42 — 🍽. 🖭 ⓞ
E 8
   closed August, Saturday and Sunday – **M** a la carte 230/320
Spec. Belons au champagne, Loup au citron vert et gingembre, Farandole des pâtisseries.

XXXX ❀ **Pavillon Elysée,** 10 av. Champs-Elysées (1st floor) 🕿 265.85.10 — 🅿. 🖭 ⓞ 𝗩𝗜𝗦𝗔 G 10
   closed 1 to 31 August, Saturday and Bank Holidays – **M** a la carte 310/450
Spec. Langoustines en robe verte, Paletot de pigeonneau et son chou farci, Pâtisseries.

XXXX ❀ **Fouquet's Élysées,** 99 av. Champs-Élysées 🕿 723.70.60 — 🖭 ⓞ 𝗩𝗜𝗦𝗔
F 8
   M (1st floor) *(closed 15 July-1 September, Saturday and Sunday)* a la carte 205/295
Spec. Salade Louis Delluc, St.-Jacques au miel d'acacia (season), Ris de veau braisé aux langoustines.

XXXX ❀❀ **Chiberta,** 3 r. Arsène-Houssaye 🕿 563.77.90 — 🖭 ⓞ 𝗩𝗜𝗦𝗔
F 8
   closed August, Saturday, Sunday and Bank Holidays – **M** a la carte 215/305
Spec. Sabayon d'huîtres, Marbré de rouget, Fricassée de homard.

XXX **Napoléon Baumann,** 38 av. Friedland 🕿 227.99.50 — 🍽. 🖭 ⓞ Ε 𝗩𝗜𝗦𝗔
F 8
M 168.

XXX ❀ **Copenhague,** 142 av. Champs-Élysées 🕿 359.20.41, 🍴 — 🍽. 🖭 ⓞ Ε 𝗩𝗜𝗦𝗔
F 8
   M *(closed 28 July-25 August, 1 to 8 January, Sunday and Bank Holidays)* a la carte 160/250
🛇 - **Flora Danica M** a la carte 155/225
Spec. Saumon mariné à l'aneth, Canard salé à la danoise, Filets de renne aux navets.

XXX **Au Vieux Berlin,** 32 av. George-V 🕿 720.88.96 — 🍽. 🖭 ⓞ Ε 𝗩𝗜𝗦𝗔
G 8
   closed Saturday and Sunday – **M** a la carte 155/215.

XXX ❀ **Clovis,** 4 r. B.-Albrecht 🕿 561.15.32 — 🖭 ⓞ Ε 𝗩𝗜𝗦𝗔
F 8
   closed August, 20 December-1 January, Saturday, Sunday and Bank Holidays – st. : **M** a
la carte 190/300
Spec. Dos de daurade poelé aux oursins, Ris de veau et langoustines à l'oseille, Soufflé froid au chocolat.

XXX **Chez Vong,** 27 r. Colisée 🕿 359.77.12 — 🖭 ⓞ 𝗩𝗜𝗦𝗔
F 10
   closed Sunday – **M** a la carte 120/165.

XXX **Relais-Plaza,** 21 av. Montaigne 🕿 723.46.36 — 🍽. 🖭 ⓞ Ε 𝗩𝗜𝗦𝗔. 🛇
G 9
   closed August – **M** a la carte 235/320.

XXX **Indra,** 10 r. Cdt-Rivière 🕿 359.46.40 — 🖭 ⓞ Ε 𝗩𝗜𝗦𝗔
F 9
   closed Saturday lunch and Sunday – st. : **M** a la carte 110/160.

XX **Le Petit Montmorency,** 5 r. Rabelais 🕿 225.11.19 — 🍽
F 10

XX **La Dariole,** 49 r. Colisée 🕿 225.66.76 — 🖭 ⓞ 𝗩𝗜𝗦𝗔
F 10
   closed Saturday, Sunday and Bank Holidays – st. : **M** a la carte 165/230.

XX **Ruc,** 2 r. Pépinière 🕿 522.66.70 — 🍽. 🖭 ⓞ Ε 𝗩𝗜𝗦𝗔
F 11
   closed August – **M** (1st floor) a la carte 165/215.

XX **Les Trois Moutons,** 63 av. F.-D.-Roosevelt 🕿 225.26.95 — 🍽. 🖭 ⓞ 𝗩𝗜𝗦𝗔
F 10
   st. : **M** 150 b.i./225 b.i..

XX **St Germain,** 74 av. Champs-Elysées 🕿 563.55.45 — 🖭 ⓞ Ε 𝗩𝗜𝗦𝗔
G 9
   closed Saturday, Sunday and Bank Holidays – **M** a la carte 140/180.

XX **Chez Max,** 19 r. Castellane 🕿 265.33.81 — 𝗩𝗜𝗦𝗔
F 11
   closed 29 July-2 September, Thursday dinner, Saturday, Sunday and Bank Holidays – **M** a
la carte 150/250.

XX **Androuët,** 41 r. Amsterdam 🕿 874.26.93 — 🖭 ⓞ 𝗩𝗜𝗦𝗔
E 12
   closed Sunday and Bank Holidays – **M** a la carte 130/190.

XX **Artois,** 13 r. Artois 🕿 225.01.10
F 9
   closed 14 July-1 September, Saturday and Sunday – **M** (booking essential) a la carte
105/170.

XX **Le Grenadin,** 46 r. Naples 🕿 563.28.92 — 🖭 𝗩𝗜𝗦𝗔
E 11
   closed Saturday and Sunday – **M** a la carte 180/230.

XX **Tong Yen,** 1 bis r. Jean-Mermoz ✆ 225.04.23 — 🍽. 🄰🄴 ⓞ ☰ 𝘝𝘐𝘚𝘈   F 10
closed 1 to 21 August – **M** a la carte 130/180.

XX **Rose des Sables,** 9 r. Washington ✆ 563.36.73   F 9
closed Sunday – **M** a la carte approx 110.

XX **Chez Modeste,** 8 r. Miromesnil ✆ 265.20.39 — 🍽. 𝘝𝘐𝘚𝘈   F 10
closed 10 to 20 August, Saturday and Sunday – **M** a la carte 130/175.

XX **Annapurna,** 32 r. Berri ✆ 563.91.56 — 🄰🄴 ⓞ   F 9
closed Saturday lunch and Sunday – **M** a la carte 110/145.

XX **Stresa,** 7 r. Chambiges ✆ 723.51.62 — 🄰🄴 ⓞ   G 9
closed August, 18 December-4 January, Saturday dinner, Sunday and Bank Holidays – **M**
a la carte 155/215.

XX **Le Sarladais,** 2 r. Vienne ✆ 522.23.62 — 🍽. 🄰🄴 ☰ 𝘝𝘐𝘚𝘈   E 11
closed August, 23 December-2 January, Saturday lunch, Sunday and Bank Holidays – **M**
a la carte 110/160.

XX **Chez Bosc,** 7 r. Richepanse ✆ 260.10.27   G 12
closed August, Saturday, Sunday and Bank Holidays – **M** a la carte 135/195.

XX **Le Bonaventure,** 35 r. J. Goujon ✆ 225.02.58, 🌭, 🌳 — 🄰🄴 𝘝𝘐𝘚𝘈. ✻   G 9
closed Saturday lunch and Sunday – **M** a la carte 135/205.

XX **Le Manoir Normand,** 77 bd Courcelles ✆ 227.38.97 — 🄰🄴 ⓞ 𝘝𝘐𝘚𝘈   E 8
closed 10 August-5 September and Sunday – **M** a la carte 125/175.

XX **Bistro des Champs,** 18 av. F. Roosevelt ✆ 562.08.37 — 𝘝𝘐𝘚𝘈   F 10
M a la carte 120/170.

X **Le Capricorne,** 81 r. Rocher ✆ 522.64.99 — 𝘝𝘐𝘚𝘈   E 10-11
closed 6 to 14 April, 27 July-4 September, Saturday and Sunday – **M** a la carte 85/130 ♨.

Opéra, Gare du Nord,
Gare de l'Est,
Grands Boulevards.

9th and 10th arrondissements.
    9th : ✉ 75009
    10th · ✉ 75010

🏨 **Le Gd Hôtel,** 2 r. Scribe (9th) ✆ 268.12.13, Telex 220875 — 🛗 📺 ☎ — 🔬 25-500. 🄰🄴 ⓞ
☰ 𝘝𝘐𝘚𝘈. ✻ rest   F 12
st. : Le Patio *(closed August)* **M** (lunch only) 170 b.i./185 b.i. and see **Café de la Paix** below
— � 70 — **564 rm** 1 040/1 170, 19 apartments.

🏨 **Scribe** Ⓜ, 1 r. Scribe (9th) ✆ 742.03.40, Telex 214653 — 🛗 🍽 📺 ☎ ♿ — 🔬 150. 🄰🄴 ⓞ
☰ 𝘝𝘐𝘚𝘈. ✻ rest   F 12
st. : **M** a la carte 170/240 — ⊑ 70 — **206 rm** 950/1 500, 11 apartments.

🏨 **Ambassador-Concorde,** 16 bd Haussmann (9th) ✆ 246.92.63, Telex 650912 — 🛗 📺
☎ ♿ — 🔬 30. 🄰🄴 ⓞ ☰ 𝘝𝘐𝘚𝘈. ✻   F 13
st. : **M** *(closed July and 6 to 27 December)* a la carte approx. 180 — **300 rm** ⊑ 820/1 040, 4
apartments.

🏨 **Commodore,** 12 bd Haussmann (9th) ✆ 246.72.82, Telex 280601 — 🛗 📺 ☎ ♿. 🄰🄴 ⓞ ☰
𝘝𝘐𝘚𝘈   F 13
st. : **M** 155 ♨ — ⊑ 38 — **149 rm** 715/800, 11 apartments.

🏨 **Brébant** Ⓜ, 32 bd Poissonnière (9th) ✆ 770.25.55, Telex 280127 — 🛗 🍽 rest 📺 ☎. 🄰🄴
ⓞ ☰ 𝘝𝘐𝘚𝘈   F 14
st. : **M** 88/160 — **129 rm** ⊑ 430/490.

🏨 **Terminus Nord** without rest, 12 bd Denain (10th) ✆ 280.20.00, Telex 660615 — 🛗 📺 ☎
♿ — 🔬 40. 🄰🄴 ⓞ ☰ 𝘝𝘐𝘚𝘈. ✻   E 15-16
st. : **225 rm** ⊑ 310/495.

🏨 **Astra** without rest, 29 r. Caumartin (9th) ✆ 266.15.15, Telex 210408 — 🛗 📺 ☎. 🄰🄴 ⓞ ☰
𝘝𝘐𝘚𝘈   F 12
st. : **85 rm** ⊑ 494/505.

🏨 **Blanche Fontaine** ⌇ without rest, 34 r. Fontaine (9th) ✆ 526.72.32, Telex 660311 — 🛗
📺 ☎ ⬌. 🄰🄴 𝘝𝘐𝘚𝘈. ✻   D 13
st. : **49 rm** ⊑ 250/380.

🏨 **St-Pétersbourg** without rest, 33 r. Caumartin (9th) ✆ 266.60.38, Telex 680001 — 🛗 📺
☎. 🄰🄴 𝘝𝘐𝘚𝘈   F 12
st. : ⊑ 19 — **120 rm** 426/433.

🏨 **Franklin et du Brésil,** 19 r. Buffault (9th) ✆ 280.27.27, Telex 640988 — 🛗 📺 ☎. 🄰🄴 ⓞ
☰ 𝘝𝘐𝘚𝘈. ✻ rest   E 14
Les Années Folles *(closed July, Saturday and Sunday)* **M** a la carte 110/160 — ⊑ 22 —
64 rm 374/459.

🏨 **Carlton's H.** without rest, 55 bd Rochechouart (9th) ✆ 281.91.00, Telex 640649 — 🛗
🚻wc ☎. ₳ℇ ⓪ ℇ 𝘝𝘐𝘚𝘈. ⋙
D 14
st. : **95 rm** 🖙 320/350, 6 apartments.

🏨 **Paris Est** Ⓜ without rest, cour d'Honneur (10th) ✆ 241.00.33, Telex 217916 — 🛗 📺
🚻wc 🚻wc ☎ — 🔬 50-450.
E 16
st. : 🖙 18,50 — **31 rm** 196/405.

🏨 **Gisendre** Ⓜ without rest, 6 r. Fromentin (9th) ✆ 280.36.86, Telex 641797 — 🛗 📺 🚻wc
🚻wc ☜. ₳ℇ ⓪ ℇ 𝘝𝘐𝘚𝘈. ⋙
D 13
st. : 🖙 21 — **32 rm** 270.

🏨 **Gare Est** Ⓜ without rest, 27 r. Caumartin (9th) ✆ 742.95.95, Telex 680702 — 🛗 📺
🚻wc 🚻wc ☎. ₳ℇ ⓪ ℇ 𝘝𝘐𝘚𝘈
F 12
st. : **40 rm** 🖙 525/550.

🏨 **Athènes** Ⓜ without rest, 21 r. d'Athènes (9th) ✆ 874.00.55, Telex 640715 — 🛗 📺
🚻wc ☎. ₳ℇ ⓪ 𝘝𝘐𝘚𝘈. ⋙
E 12
st. : 🖙 22 — **36 rm** 287/367.

🏨 **Chamonix** Ⓜ without rest, 8 r. d'Hauteville (10th) ✆ 770.19.49, Telex 641177 — 🛗 📺
🚻wc ☜. ₳ℇ ⓪ ℇ. ⋙
F 15
st. : 🖙 25 — **35 rm** 420/600.

🏨 **Moris** Ⓜ without rest, 13 r. R.-Boulanger (10th) ✆ 607.92.08, Telex 212024 — 🛗 📺
🚻wc 🚻wc ☎. ₳ℇ ⓪ ℇ 𝘝𝘐𝘚𝘈. ⋙
G 16
st. : 🖙 21 — **48 rm** 340/380.

🏨 **Florida** without rest, 7 r. Parme (9th) ✆ 874.47.09, Telex 640410 — 🛗 📺 🚻wc 🚻wc ☎.
₳ℇ ⓪ 𝘝𝘐𝘚𝘈
D 12
st. : **31 rm** 🖙 274/495.

🏨 **Modern' Est** without rest, 91 bd Strasbourg (10th) ✆ 607.24.72 — 🛗 🚻wc 🚻wc ☎. ⋙
E 16
st. : 🖙 22 — **30 rm** 240/280.

🏨 **Capucines** without rest, 6 r. Godot-de-Mauroy (9th) ✆ 742.06.37 — 🛗 🚻wc 🚻wc ☎
F 12
st. : **45 rm** 🖙 243/316.

🏨 **Morny** without rest, 4 r. Liège (9th) ✆ 285.47.92, Telex 660822 — 🛗 📺 🚻wc ☎. ₳ℇ ⓪
ℇ 𝘝𝘐𝘚𝘈
E 12
st. : **43 rm** 🖙 370/454.

🏨 **London Palace** without rest, 32 bd Italiens (9th) ✆ 824.54.64, Telex 642360 — 🛗 🚻wc
🚻wc ☎. ₳ℇ ℇ 𝘝𝘐𝘚𝘈. ⋙
F 13
st. : 🖙 21 — **48 rm** 244/365.

🏨 **Gare du Nord** without rest, 33 r. St-Quentin (10th) ✆ 878.02.92, Telex 642415 — 🛗
🚻wc 🚻wc ☜. 𝘝𝘐𝘚𝘈
E 16
st. : 🖙 21 — **48 rm** 168/346.

🏨 **Hélios** without rest, 75 r. Victoire (9th) ✆ 874.28.64, Telex 641255 — 🛗 🚻wc 🚻wc ☎. ₳ℇ
⓪ ℇ 𝘝𝘐𝘚𝘈
F 13
st. : 🖙 25 — **50 rm** 276/438.

🏨 **Résidence Mauroy** Ⓜ without rest, 11 bis r. Godot-de-Mauroy (9th) ✆ 742.50.78 — 🛗
📺 🚻wc 🚻wc ☎. ₳ℇ ⓪ ℇ 𝘝𝘐𝘚𝘈
F 12
closed August — st. : 🖙 21 — **26 rm** 191/326.

🏨 **Florence** without rest, 26 r. Mathurins (9th) ✆ 742.63.47 — 🛗 🚻wc 🚻wc ☜. ₳ℇ ⓪ F 12
🖙 24 — **20 rm** 247/327.

🏨 **Montholon-Lafayette** without rest, 4 r. Riboutté (9th) ✆ 246.83.44 — 🛗 🚻wc 🚻wc
☎
E 14
st. : **38 rm** 🖙 246/262.

🏨 **Montréal** without rest, 23 r. Godot-de-Mauroy (9th) ✆ 265.99.54 — 🛗 🚻wc 🚻wc ☜.
₳ℇ ⓪ ℇ 𝘝𝘐𝘚𝘈
F 12
st. : 🖙 22 — **14 rm** 166/312, 5 apartments.

🏨 **Français** without rest, 13 r. 8 Mai 1945 (10th) ✆ 607.42.02, Telex 230431 — 🛗 🚻wc 🚻wc
☎. 𝘝𝘐𝘚𝘈
E 16
st. : 🖙 17 — **71 rm** 190/220.

🏨 **Peyris** without rest, 10 r. Conservatoire (9th) ✆ 770.50.83, Telex 650197 — 🛗 🚻wc 🚻wc
☜. 𝘝𝘐𝘚𝘈
F 14
st. : **50 rm** 🖙 190/295.

🏨 **Gd H. Haussmann** without rest, 6 r. Helder (9th) ✆ 824.76.10, Telex 650018 — 🛗 📺
🚻wc 🚻wc ☎. ₳ℇ. ⋙
F 13
st. : **58 rm** 🖙 251/352.

🏨 **Pax H.** without rest, 47 r. Trévise (9th) ✆ 770.84.75, Telex 650197 — 🛗 🚻wc 🚻wc ☜.
𝘝𝘐𝘚𝘈
E 14
st. : **52 rm** 🖙 225/275.

🏠 **Gd H. Lafayette Buffault** without rest, 6 r. Buffault (9th) ✆ 770.70.96, Telex 642180 —
🛗 🚻wc 🚻wc ☎
E 14
st. : 🖙 17,50 — **47 rm** 150/257.

🏠 **Campaville Montmartre** Ⓜ without rest, 21 bd Clichy (9th) ✆ 874.01.12, Telex 643572
— 🛗 📺 🚻wc 🚻wc ☎. 𝘝𝘐𝘚𝘈
D 13
st. : 🖙 22 — **84 rm** 233/280.

🏠 **Victor Massé** without rest, 32 bis r. Victor-Massé (9th) 🕿 874.37.53 — 🛗 🛏wc ⛔ 🐾.
🔘. 🎄
fermé 1 to 25 August – **st. :** 🛏 18 – **40 rm** 132/227.
E 13

🏠 **Campanile** without rest, 11 r. P.-Sémard (9th) 🕿 878.28.94, Telex 643861 — 🛗 📺 🛏wc
🛏wc 🕿. 🏧
st. : 🛏 24 – **45 rm** 225/280.
E 15

🏠 **Résidence Magenta** without rest, 35 r. Y.-Toudic (10th) 🕿 607.63.13 — 🛗 🛏wc 🐾. 🏧
st. : 29 rm 🛏 179/215.
F 17

🏠 **Laffon** without rest, 25 r. Buffault (9th) 🕿 878.49.91 — 🛗 🛏wc 🛏wc 🐾. 🇪 🏧
closed 25 July-26 August – **st. :** 🛏 15,50 – **46 rm** 88/214.
E 14

🏠 **Nord** without rest, 47 r. Albert-Thomas (10th) 🕿 201.66.00 — 🛗 🛏wc 🐾. 🎄
st. : 🛏 17 – **22 rm** 130/195.
F 16

🏠 **Fénelon** without rest, 23 r. Buffault (9th) 🕿 878.32.18 — 🛗 🛏wc 🛏wc 🐾. 🎄
st. : 🛏 16,50 – **36 rm** 125/230.
E 14

🏠 **Blanche H.** without rest, 69 r. Blanche (9th) 🕿 874.16.94 — 🛗 🛏wc 🛏 🐾. 🎄
st. : 🛏 14,50 – **53 rm** 60/190.
D 12

XXXX **Café de la Paix,** pl. Opéra (9th) 🕿 742.97.02 — 🍽. 🏧 🔘 🇪 🏧
st. : Rest. Opéra *(closed August)* **M** a la carte 225/295 - **Relais Capucines M** snack a la
carte approx. 135 🍷.
F 12

XXX ✿ **Nicolas,** 12 r. Fidélité (10th) 🕿 246.84.74 — 🏧 🔘 🏧
closed August, Monday dinner and Saturday – **M** a la carte 140/205
Spec. Foie gras frais, Poissons, Canard aux fruits.
F 16

XX ✿ **Au Chateaubriant,** 23 r. Chabrol (10th) 🕿 824.58.94, Collection of paintings — 🍽.
🏧. 🎄
closed August, Sunday and Monday – **M** a la carte 140/210
Spec. Scampi fritti, Paglia e fieno alla Contadina, Millefeuille aux framboises.
E 15

XX ✿✿ **Chez Michel** (Tounissoux), 10 r. Belzunce (10th) 🕿 878.44.14 — 🍽. 🏧 🔘 🏧
closed 1 to 26 August, February Holidays, Friday and Saturday – **M** (booking essential) a
la carte 195/285
Spec. Salade de langoustines aux kiwis, Ris de veau, Coktails de glace miel et pruneaux confits.
E 15

XX **Mövenpick,** 12 bd Madeleine (9th) 🕿 742.47.93 — 🍽. 🏧 🔘 🇪 🏧
M a la carte approx. 110 🍷 **Café des Artistes M** a la carte 140/190
G 12

XX **Atlantique,** 51 bd Magenta (10th) 🕿 208.27.20 — 🍽. 🏧 🔘 🇪 🏧
closed 1 August-6 September, Sunday and Monday – **M** a la carte 180/255.
F 16

XX **Le Quercy,** 36 r. Condorcet (9th) 🕿 878.30.61 — 🏧 🔘 🏧
closed August and Sunday – **st. : M** a la carte 130/190.
E 15

XX **Rest. du Casino,** 41 r. Clichy (9th) 🕿 280.34.62 — 🏧 🔘 🇪 🏧
closed Saturday, Sunday and Bank Holidays – **M** 135 b.i./160.
E 12

XX **Chez Casimir,** 6 r. Belzunce (10th) 🕿 878.32.53 — 🏧 🔘 🏧
closed Saturday lunch and Sunday – **st. : M** a la carte 180/235.
E 15

XX **Ty Coz,** 35 r. St-Georges (9th) 🕿 878.42.95, sea-food only. 🏧 🔘
closed Sunday and Monday – **st. : M** a la carte approx. 190.
F 13

XX **Le Saintongeais,** 62 r. Fg Montmartre (9th) 🕿 280.39.92 — 🏧 🏧
closed 5 to 25 August, Saturday lunch and Sunday – **st. : M** a la carte 125/160.
E 14

XX **Julien,** 16 r. Fg St-Denis (10th) 🕿 770.12.06, Early 20C decor — 🏧 🔘 🏧
closed July – **M** a la carte 90/145 🍷.
F 15

XX **Petit Riche,** 25 r. Le Peletier (9th) 🕿 770.68.68, late 19C decor — 🏧 🏧
closed 10 August-1 September and Sunday – **st. : M** a la carte 120/175.
F 13

XX **Brasserie Flo,** 7 cour Petites-Écuries (10th) 🕿 770.13.59, 1900 Setting — 🍽. 🏧 🔘 🏧
closed August – **M** a la carte 90/125 🍷.
F 15

XX **Terminus Nord,** 23 r. Dunkerque (10th) 🕿 285.05.15 — 🏧 🔘 🏧
M 97 🍷.
E 16

XX **Aux Deux Canards,** 58 r. Fg Poissonnière (10th) 🕿 770.03.23 — 🏧 🔘 🏧
closed August and Sunday – **M** 75.
F 15

XX **Pagoda,** 50 r. Provence (9th) 🕿 874.81.48 — 🏧
closed Sunday in August – **M** a la carte 80/120.
F 13

XX **La P'tite Tonkinoise,** 56 Fg Poissonnière (10th) 🕿 246.85.98
closed 1 August-15 September, Sunday and Monday – **M** a la carte 105/155.
F 15

X **Relais Beaujolais,** 3 r. Milton (9th) 🕿 878.77.91
closed August, Saturday, Sunday and Bank Holidays – **M** 120 b.i./180 b.i.
E 14

X **La Grille,** 80 Fg Poissonnière (10th) 🕿 770.89.73 — 🔘
closed August, February Holidays, Saturday and Sunday – **st. : M** a la carte 95/140.
E 15

Bastille, Gare de Lyon,
Place d'Italie,
Bois de Vincennes.

12th and 13th arrondissements.
   12th : ✉ 75012
   13th : ✉ 75013

🏨🏨 **Équinoxe** Ⓜ without rest, 40 r. Le Brun (13th) 𝒫 337.56.56, Telex 201476 — ▮ 📺 ☎ 🚗
49 rm.
N 15

🏨🏨 **Paris-Lyon-Palace and Rest. Relais de la Méditerranée,** 11 r. Lyon (12th) 𝒫
307.29.49, Telex 213310 — ▮ 📺 ☎ – 🔬 150. 🆎 ⓞ Ⅰ 🆅🆂🆄. ⅍ rest
L 18
M a la carte 125/195 – ☞ 20 – **128 rm** 294/325.

🏨🏨 **Modern H. Lyon** without rest, 3 r. Parrot (12th) 𝒫 343.41.52, Telex 230369 — ▮ 📺 ☎.
🆎
L 18
st. : ☞ 20 – **53 rm** 212/314.

🏨🏨 **Relais de Lyon** Ⓜ without rest, 64 r. Crozatier (12th) 𝒫 344.22.50, Telex 216690 — ▮ 📺
☎ – 🔬 25. 🆎 ⓞ Ⅰ 🆅🆂🆄
K 19
st. : ☞ 20 – **34 rm** 380.

🏨 **Terminus-Lyon** without rest, 19 bd Diderot (12th) 𝒫 343.24.03, Telex 230702 — ▮ 📺
🖃wc 🏚wc ☎. 🆎 Ⅰ 🆅🆂🆄. ⅍
L 18
st. : ☞ 20 – **61 rm** 295/331.

🏨 **Terrasses** without rest, 74 r. Glacière (13th) 𝒫 707.73.70 — ▮ 🖃wc 🏚wc ☎. 🆅🆂🆄. ⅍
st. : ☞ 17,50 – **52 rm** 120/245.
N 14

🏨 **Gd H. Gobelins** without rest, 57 bd St-Marcel (13th) 𝒫 331.79.89 — ▮ 📺 🖃wc 🏚wc
🖃 st. : **45 rm** ☞ 189/265.
M 16

🏨 **Slavia** without rest, 51 bd St-Marcel (13th) 𝒫 337.81.25, Telex 205542 — ▮ 📺 🖃wc
🏚wc ☎. ⅍
M 16
st. : ☞ 17 – **37 rm** 210/225, 6 apartments.

🏨 **Marceau** without rest, 13 r. Jules-César (12th) 𝒫 343.11.65 — ▮ 🖃wc 🏚wc ☎. ⅍ K 17
closed August – **st. :** ☞ 19 – **51 rm** 98/212.

🏨 **Timhôtel** without rest, 22 r. Barrault (13th) 𝒫 580.67.67, Telex 205461 — ▮ 🖃wc
🏚wc 🖃. 🆎 ⓞ Ⅰ 🆅🆂🆄
P 15
st. : ☞ 23 – **73 rm** 253/277.

🏨 **Viator** without rest, 1 r. Parrot (12th) 𝒫 343.11.00 — ▮ 🖃wc 🏚wc 🖃. ⅍
st. : ☞ 15 – **45 rm** 144/195.
L 18

🏨 **Jules César** without rest, 52 av. Ledru-Rollin (12th) 𝒫 343.15.88, Telex 670945 — ▮
🖃wc 🏚wc 🖃. ⅍
K 18
st. : ☞ 17,50 – **48 rm** 160/185.

🏨 **Rubens** without rest, 35 r. Banquier (13th) 𝒫 331.73.30 — ▮ 🖃wc 🏚wc 🖃
st. : ☞ 16 – **50 rm** 120/220.
N 16

🏨 **Arts** without rest, 8 r. Coypel (13th) 𝒫 707.76.32 — ▮ 🖃wc 🏚wc 🖃
st. : ☞ 15,50 – **40 rm** 80/190.
N 16

🏨 **Résidence des Gobelins** without rest, 9 r. Gobelins (13th) 𝒫 707.26.90 — ▮ 📺 🖃wc
🏚wc 🖃. 🆎 🆅🆂🆄. ⅍
N 15
st. : ☞ 19 – **32 rm** 199/288.

🏨 **Terminus et Sports** without rest, 96 cours Vincennes (12th) 𝒫 343.97.93 — ▮ 📺
🖃wc 🏚wc 🖃. ⅍
L 23
st. : ☞ 18 – **43 rm** 140/250.

🏨 **Palym H.** without rest, 4 r. E.-Gilbert (12th) 𝒫 343.24.48 — ▮ 🖃wc 🏚wc 🖃
L 18
st. : **51 rm** ☞ 128/212.

🏨 **Nouvel H.** without rest, 24 av. Bel Air (12th) 𝒫 343.01.81, Telex 240139, 🚗 – 🖃wc
🏚wc ☎. 🆎 ⓞ 🆅🆂🆄
L 21
st. : ☞ 30 – **28 rm** 132/320.

XXX ❀ **Au Pressoir** (Seguin), 257 av. Daumesnil (12th) 𝒫 344.38.21 — ▤. 🆅🆂🆄
M 22
closed August, February Holidays, Saturday and Sunday – **st. : M** a la carte 185/290
Spec. Assiette de fruits de mer (november-April), Rouget en bécasse, Pigeonneau rôti au vin rouge.

XXX **Train Bleu,** Gare de Lyon (12th) 𝒫 343.09.06, « Fine murals recalling the journey from
Paris to the Mediterranean » — 🆎 ⓞ Ⅰ 🆅🆂🆄
L 18
M (1st floor) a la carte 140/195.

XX ❀❀ **Au Trou Gascon** (Dutournier), 40 r. Taine (12th) 𝒫 344.34.26 — ▤. 🆅🆂🆄
M 21
closed 14 July-15 August, Christmas Day to 1 January, Saturday and Sunday – **st. : M**
(booking essential) a la carte 190/255
Spec. Ravioli de homard au basilic, Filet de biche Rossini, Croustade frangipane.

XX **Sologne,** 164 av. Daumesnil (12th) 𝒫 307.68.97 — ▤. 🆅🆂🆄
M 21
closed Sunday and Monday.

XX **La Frégate,** 30 av. Ledru-Rollin (12th) ℰ 343.90.32 – 𝖵𝖨𝖲𝖠. ✷   L 18
closed August, February Holidays, Saturday and Sunday – **M** a la carte 145/180.

XX **Le Traversière,** 40 r. Traversière (12th) ℰ 344.02.10 – 𝖠𝖤 ⓞ 𝐄 𝖵𝖨𝖲𝖠   L 18
closed 12 July-30 August and dinner Sunday and Bank Holidays – **M** a la carte 130/175.

XX **Potinière du Lac,** 4 pl. E.-Renard (12th) ℰ 343.39.98 – ⓞ 𝖵𝖨𝖲𝖠   N 23
closed 10 to 25 September, 10 to 31 December and Monday – **M** a la carte 120/180.

X **Petit Marguery,** 9 bd. Port-Royal (13th) ℰ 331.58.59 – 𝖠𝖤 ⓞ 𝐄 𝖵𝖨𝖲𝖠   M 15
closed August, 23 December-2 January, Sunday and Monday – **st. : M** a la carte 140/190.

X **Etchegorry,** 41 r. Croulebarbe (13th) ℰ 331.63.05 – 𝖠𝖤 ⓞ 𝖵𝖨𝖲𝖠   N 15
closed Sunday – **M** 110 b.i/160 b.i.

X **Relais du Périgord,** 15 r. Tolbiac (13th) ℰ 583.07.48 – 𝖠𝖤 ⓞ 𝖵𝖨𝖲𝖠   P 18
closed 15 August-15 September, Christmas Day to 1 January, Saturday, Sunday and Bank Holidays – **M** a la carte 125/195.

X **Quincy,** 28 av. Ledru-Rollin (12th) ℰ 628.46.76 – 𝖠𝖤 ⓞ   L 17
closed 15 August-15 September, Saturday, Sunday and Monday – **M** a la carte 115/170.

X **Les Algues,** 66 av. Gobelins (13th) ℰ 331.58.22 – 𝖠𝖤 𝖵𝖨𝖲𝖠   N 15
closed 4-26 August, 22 December-6 January, Sunday and Monday – **M** a la carte 135/180.

X **Le Rhône,** 40 bd Arago (13th) ℰ 707.33.57 – ⓞ 𝖵𝖨𝖲𝖠   N 14
closed August, Saturday, Sunday and Bank Holidays – **M** (booking essential) a la carte 80/130 ♨.

X **Michèle,** 39 r. Daviel (13th) ℰ 580.09.13 – 𝖵𝖨𝖲𝖠   P 14
closed Tuesday dinner and Sunday – **st. : M** a la carte 125/155.

**Vaugirard,
Gare Montparnasse, Grenelle,
Denfert-Rochereau.**

14th and 15th arrondissements.
14th : ⊠ 75014
15th : ⊠ 75015

🏨 **Hilton** Ⓜ, 18 av. Suffren (15th) ℰ 273.92.00, Telex 200955, 🏦 – 🛗 ▤ 📺 ☎ ♿ 🅿 – 🔬 40 - 1 200. 𝖠𝖤 ⓞ 𝐄 𝖵𝖨𝖲𝖠   J 7
st. : Rest : Le Toit de Paris ≤ Paris, *(closed August and Sunday)* **M** a la carte 250/320 ✷ - **Western M** 191 b.i.– **la Terrasse M** 103/179 – ☲ 65 – **456 rm** 1 043/1 323, 10 apartments.

🏨 **Sofitel Paris** Ⓜ, 8 r. L.-Armand (15th) ℰ 554.95.00, Telex 200432, indoor pool overlooking Paris – 🛗 ▤ 📺 ☎ ♿ ⟷ – 🔬 30 - 1 200. 𝖠𝖤 ⓞ 𝐄 𝖵𝖨𝖲𝖠. ✷ rest   N 5
st. : Rest. see Le Relais de Sèvres below - **La Tonnelle** (Brasserie) **M** a la carte approx. 120 ♨ – ☲ 50 – **620 rm** 620/890, 15 apartments.

🏨 **Nikko** Ⓜ, 61 quai Grenelle (15th) ℰ 575.62.62, Telex 260012, ≤, 🔲 – 🛗 ▤ 📺 ☎ 🅿 – 🔬 40 - 800. 𝖠𝖤 ⓞ 𝐄 𝖵𝖨𝖲𝖠   K 6
st. : M Rest. see **Les Célébrités** below - **Brasserie Pont Mirabeau M** a la carte approx. 155 - **Japanese rest. Benkay M** a la carte 220/330 – ☲ 55 – **755 rm** 800/1 400, 9 apartments.

🏨 **Montparnasse Park H.** Ⓜ, 19 r. Cdt-Mouchotte (14th) ℰ 320.15.51, Telex 200135, ≤, 🏦 – 🛗 ▤ 📺 ☎ ♿ 🅿 – 🔬 25 - 1 400. 𝖠𝖤 ⓞ 𝐄 𝖵𝖨𝖲𝖠. ✷ rest   M 11
st. : Montparnasse 25 M 230/245 - **La Ruche M** 125 ♨ – ☲ 46 – **906 rm** 755/995, 44 apartments.

🏨 **P.L.M. St-Jacques** Ⓜ, 17 bd St-Jacques (14th) ℰ 589.89.80, Telex 270740 – 🛗 ▤ 📺 ☎ ⟷ – 🔬 40 - 1 000. 𝖠𝖤 ⓞ 𝐄 𝖵𝖨𝖲𝖠   N 13-14
st. : Café Français (1st floor) **M** 145 b.i./200 b.i.- **Le Patio** (3rd floor) **M** a la carte approx. 110 ♨ – ☲ 40 – **783 rm** 737/824, 14 apartments 1 021/1 075.

🏨 **Mercure Paris Porte de Versailles** Ⓜ, at Vanves r. Moulin ⊠ 92170 Vanves ℰ 642.93.22, Telex 202195 – 🛗 ▤ 📺 ☎ ♿ 🅿 – 🔬 350. 𝖠𝖤 ⓞ 𝐄 𝖵𝖨𝖲𝖠   P 7
M (brasserie) a la carte approx. 110 ♨ – ☲ 35 – **387 rm** 474/527.

🏨 **L'Aiglon** without rest., 232 bd Raspail (14th) ℰ 320.82.42 – 🛗 📺 ☎ ⟷. 𝖠𝖤 𝖵𝖨𝖲𝖠. ✷
st. : ☲ 22 – 42 rm 260/340, 8 apartments.   M 12

🏨 **Holiday Inn** Ⓜ, porte Versailles (15th) ℰ 533.74.63, Telex 260844 – 🛗 ▤ 📺 ☎ ♿ ⟷ – 🔬 130. 𝖠𝖤 ⓞ 𝐄 𝖵𝖨𝖲𝖠   N 7
st. : M 85/150 ♨ – ☲ 41 – **90 rm** 530/680.

🏨 **Montcalm** Ⓜ without rest., 50 av. F.-Faure (15th) ℰ 554.97.27, Telex 203174, 🌺 – 🛗 📺 ☎. 𝖠𝖤 ⓞ 𝐄 𝖵𝖨𝖲𝖠   M 6
st. : 41 rm ☲ 370/430.

🏨 **Lenox** Ⓜ without rest, 15 r. Delambre (14th) ℰ 335.34.50, Telex 260745 – 🛗 📺 ☎. 𝖠𝖤   M 12
st. : ☲ 20 – 52 rm 350/420.

🏨 **Orléans Palace H.** without rest, 185 bd Brune (14th) ℰ 539.68.50, Telex 260725 – 🛗 📺 ☎ – 🔬 35. 𝖠𝖤 ⓞ 𝐄 𝖵𝖨𝖲𝖠   R 11
st. : ☲ 20 – 92 rm 240/320.

🏨 **Waldorf** Ⓜ without rest, 17 r. Départ (14th) ℰ 320.64.79, Telex 201677 — 🛗 📺 🛏wc
🚿wc ☎. 🅰🅔 ⓪ 💳. ⚶
st. : ⬛ 23 – **30 rm** 340/424. L 11

🏨 **Messidor** Ⓜ without rest, 330 r. Vaugirard (15th) ℰ 828.03.74, Telex 204606, 🚗 — 🛗
🛏wc 🚿wc ☎ ⇄. 💳
st. : **74 rm** ⬛ 197/400. M 8

🏨 **Résidence Champs de Mars** without rest., 7 r. Gén. de Larminat (15th) ℰ 734.74.04 —
🛗 📺 🛏wc 🚿wc ☎. 💳. ⚶
st. : ⬛ 20 – **43 rm** 200/280. K 8

🏨 **Châtillon H.** 🐾 without rest, 11 square Châtillon (14th) ℰ 542.31.17 — 🛗 🛏wc 🚿wc
☎. ⚶
closed August – st. : ⬛ 15 – **31 rm** 150/185. P 11

🏨 **France** without rest, 46 r. Croix-Nivert (15th) ℰ 783.67.02 — 🛗 🛏wc 🚿wc 📞
st. : ⬛ 19 – **30 rm** 198/260. L 8

🏨 **Midi** without rest, 4 av. René-Coty (14th) ℰ 327.23.25 — 🛗 🛏wc 🚿wc 📞
st. : ⬛ 10 – **50 rm** 130/205. N 13

🏨 **Joigny** without rest, 8 r. St-Charles (15th) ℰ 579.33.35, Telex 204057 — 🛗 📺 🛏wc
🚿wc ☎. 🅰🅔 ⓪ 🅔 💳. ⚶
st. : ⬛ 30 – **39 rm** 245/320. K 7

🏨 **Tourisme** without rest, 66 av. La-Motte-Picquet (15th) ℰ 734.28.01 — 🛗 🛏wc 🚿wc 📞.
⚶
st. : ⬛ 13 – **60 rm** 130/210. K 8

🏩 **Campaville Paris Tour Eiffel** Ⓜ without rest, 64 r. Sextius Michel (15th) ℰ 578.61.33 — 🛗
📺 🛏wc 🚿wc ☎
75 rm. K 7

🏩 **Pasteur** Ⓜ without rest, 33 r. Dr.-Roux (15th) ℰ 783.53.17 — 🛗 📺 🛏wc 🚿wc ☎. 🅔 💳
closed 25 July-30 August – st. : ⬛ 17,50 – **19 rm** 180/240. M 10

🏩 **Virginia** without rest, 66 r. Père Corentin (14th) ℰ 540.70.90 — 🛗 🛏wc 🚿wc 📞. ⚶ R 12
st. : ⬛ 16 – **54 rm** 87/204.

🏩 **Pacific H.** without rest, 11 r. Fondary (15th) ℰ 575.20.49 — 🛗 🛏wc 🚿wc 📞. 🅔. ⚶ K 7
st. : **66 rm** ⬛ 114/228.

🏩 **Baldi** without rest, 42 bd Garibaldi (15th) ℰ 783.20.10 — 🛗 🛏wc 🚿wc 📞 L 9
st. : ⬛ 18 – **28 rm** 184/215.

🏩 **Fondary** without rest, 30 r. Fondary (15th) ℰ 575.14.75 — 🛗 🛏wc 📞. ⚶ L 8
st. : ⬛ 16 – **23 rm** 83/152.

🗙🗙🗙🗙 ❀ **Les Célébrités,** 61 quai Grenelle (15th) ℰ 575.62.62, ≼ — 🔲 🅟. 🅰🅔 ⓪ 🅔 💳 K 6
st. : **M** 220 (lunch) and a la carte 285/385.
Spec. Salade de langoustines rôties, Blanc de turbot au basilic, Aiguillette de canette de Bresse rôtie.

🗙🗙🗙 ❀ **Morot Gaudry,** 6 r. Cavalerie (15th) (8th floor) ℰ 567.06.85, ≼, open-air terrace — 🔲
🅟. 💳 K 8
closed Saturday and Sunday – st. : **M** a la carte 190/250
Spec. Foie de canard au Ste-Croix-du-Mont, Ragoût de crêtes et rognons de coq au jus de truffes, Grouse
rôtie (1 September-28 February).

🗙🗙🗙 ❀ **Olympe,** 8 r. N. Charlet (15th) ℰ 734.86.08 — 🅰🅔 ⓪ 💳 L 10
closed 1 to 24 August, 22 December-4 January, Monday and lunch except Thursday – st. :
M a la carte 270/385
Spec. St-Pierre aux oignons et épinards, Agneau au romarin, Pigeon rôti sauce aux cèpes.

🗙🗙🗙 **Armes de Bretagne,** 108 av. du Maine (14th) ℰ 320.29.50 — ▦. 🅰🅔 ⓪ 🅔 💳 N 11
closed 29 April-6 May, 4 to 25 August, Sunday dinner and Monday except Bank Holidays
– **M** a la carte 155/260.

🗙🗙🗙 ❀ **Relais de Sèvres,** 8 r. L.-Armand (15th) ℰ 554.95.00 — 🅟. 🅰🅔 ⓪ 🅔 💳. ⚶ N 5
closed August, Saturday and Sunday – st. : **M** a la carte 200/280
Spec. Ravioli de petits gris, Rognonade de lapin, Nougat glacé au gingembre confit.

🗙🗙🗙 ❀ **Le Duc** (Minchelli), 243 bd Raspail (14th) ℰ 322.59.59 M 12

🗙🗙🗙 **Moniage Guillaume** with rm, 88 r. Tombe Issoire (14th) ℰ 322.96.15 — 📺 🛏 🚿 ☎. 🅰🅔
⓪ 🅔 💳 P 12
M a la carte 195/295 – ⬛ 19 – **7 rm** 195/235.

🗙🗙 ❀ **Aquitaine** (Mme Massia), 54 r. Dantzig (15th) ℰ 828.67.38, 🌹 — 🅰🅔 ⓪ 🅔 💳 N 8
closed Sunday and Monday – st. : **M** a la carte 205/255
Spec. Poissons au beurre blanc, Confit de canard (15 September-15 July), Grillade de boeuf.

🗙🗙 ❀ **Bistro 121,** 121 r. Convention (15th) ℰ 557.52.90 — 🅰🅔 ⓪ 🅔 💳 M 7
closed 14 July-20 August, 22-30 December, Sunday dinner and Monday – **M** a la carte
165/250
Spec. Foie de canard, Poissons à la nage de homard, Poule au pot farcie.

XX **Le Pfister,** 1 r. Dr.-Jacquemaire-Clemenceau (15th) ℰ 828.51.38 — *VISA*   L 8
closed August, Saturday lunch, Sunday and Bank Holidays — **st. : M** a la carte 185/250.

XX **Chez Albert,** 122 av. Maine (14th) ℰ 320.21.69 — AE ⓞ E *VISA*   N 11
closed 12 to 26 August and Monday — **st. : M** a la carte 175/245.

XX ⊛ **Gérard et Nicole,** 6 av. J.-Moulin (14th) ℰ 542.39.56 — AE *VISA*   P 12
closed mid-July-mid-August, Saturday and Sunday — **st. : M** a la carte 190/255
Spec. St-Jacques au beurre d'oursins (October-March), Rougets à l'huile d'olive, Magret de mulard au gros sel.

XX ⊛ **Le Dôme,** 108 bd du Montparnasse (14th) ℰ 335.25.81 — AE ⓞ *VISA*   LM 12
closed Monday — **M** a la carte 170/250
Spec. Fricassée de langoustines à l'estragon, Ragoût de sole et foie gras, Rougets poêlés au basilic.

XX **Vallon de Vérone,** 53 r. Didot (14th) ℰ 543.18.87 — *VISA*
closed August, Saturday lunch and Sunday — **st. : M** a la carte 130/200.

XX **Napoléon et Chaix,** 46 r. Balard (15th) ℰ 554.09.00 — AE E *VISA*   M 5
closed August — **M** a la carte 150/220.

XX **La Chaumière des Gourmets,** 22 pl. Denfert-Rochereau (14th) ℰ 321.22.59 — AE ⓞ
VISA   N 12
closed August, 1 to 7 March, Saturday, Sunday and Bank Holidays — **M** a la carte 160/225.

XX ⊛ **Pierre Vedel,** 19 r. Duranton (15th) ℰ 558.43.17 — ⌖   M 6
closed Saturday and Sunday — **st. : M** (booking essential) a la carte 145/180
Spec. Moussette de saumon, Fricassée de pétoncles et goujonnette de sole au safran, Tête de veau en pot-au-feu.

XX **Le Clos Morillons,** 50 r. Morillons (15th) ℰ 828.04.37 — *VISA*   N 8
closed July, Saturday lunch and Sunday — **st. : M** a la carte 160/200.

XX **Chaumière Paysanne,** 7 r. L.-Robert (14th) ℰ 320.76.55 — AE ⓞ E *VISA*   M 12
closed August, Monday lunch and Sunday — **st. : M** a la carte 130/210.

XX **Petite Bretonnière,** 2 r. Cadix (15th) ℰ 828.34.39 — AE *VISA*   N 7
closed 5 to 25 August, Saturday and Sunday — **st. : M** a la carte 130/165.

XX **La Giberne,** 42 bis av. Suffren (15th) ℰ 734.82.18 — AE ⓞ *VISA*   J 8
closed 11 August-2 September, Saturday and Sunday — **M** a la carte 125/190.

XX **Pinocchio,** 124 av. Maine (14th) ℰ 321.26.10 — AE ⓞ *VISA*   N 11
closed Saturday lunch and Sunday — **st. : M** a la carte 115/170.

XX **Le Copreaux,** 15 r. Copreaux (15th) ℰ 306.83.35 — AE ⓞ E *VISA*   M 9
closed August, 24 December-3 January, Saturday and Sunday — **M** a la carte 135/205.

XX **La Chaumière,** 54 av. F.-Faure (15th) ℰ 554.13.91 — ⓞ *VISA*   M 7
closed August, Monday dinner and Tuesday — **M** a la carte 130/160.

XX **Le Caroubier,** 8 av. Maine (15th) ℰ 548.14.38   M 11
closed August and Sunday — **M** 120 b.i./150 b.i..

X ⊛ **La Cagouille,** 89 rue Daguerre (14th) ℰ 322.09.01   N 11
closed 27 July-10 September, Sunday and Monday — **st. : M** a la carte 135/180
Spec. Cuisine charentaise.

X **Trois Horloges,** 73 r. Brancion (15th) ℰ 828.24.08 — AE ⓞ E *VISA*   N 9
st. : M 120 b.i./150 b.i..

X **La Bonne Table,** 42 r. Friant (14th) ℰ 539.74.91 — *VISA*   R 11
closed July, 23 December-4 January, Saturday, Sunday and Bank Holidays — **st. : M** a la carte 115/180.

X **La Rabolière,** 13 r. Mademoiselle (15th) ℰ 250.35.29   L 7
closed August, Sunday and Monday — **M** a la carte 110/170.

X **Chaumière du Petit Poucet,** 10 r. Desnouettes (15th) ℰ 828.60.91 — *VISA*   N 7
closed July, Saturday dinner and Sunday — **M** a la carte 85/115.

X **Bonne Auberge,** 33 r. Volontaires (15th) ℰ 734.65.49 — AE ⓞ E *VISA*   M 9
closed August, Saturday and Sunday — **st. : M** a la carte 120/160.

X **Senteurs de Provence,** 295 r. Lecourbe (15th) ℰ 557.11.98 — *VISA*   M 6
closed 27 July-19 August, Sunday and Monday — **M** a la carte approx. 140.

X **La Cour,** 12 r. Cepré (15th) ℰ 566.66.17 — AE ⓞ *VISA*   L 9
closed Sunday — **M** a la carte 105/150 ⌂.

Do not mix up :

Comfort of hotels	: 🏨🏨🏨 ... 🏠, 🏡
Comfort of restaurants	: XXXXX ... X
Quality of the cuisine	: ⊛⊛⊛, ⊛⊛, ⊛

**Passy, Auteuil,
Bois de Boulogne,
Chaillot, Porte Maillot.**

16th arrondissement.

🏰 **La Pérouse and rest. l'Astrolabe** Ⓜ, 40 r. La Pérouse ✉ 75116, ℰ 500.83.47, Telex
613420 – 📶 🎦 📺 ☎. 🆎 ⓪ Ⅎ 𝑉𝐼𝑆𝐴
F 7
st. : **M** *(closed Saturday, Sunday and Bank Holidays)* a la carte 210/300 – 🖙 46 – **9 rm**
990, 27 apartments.

🏰 **Baltimore** Ⓜ, 88 bis av. Kléber, ✉ 75116, ℰ 553.83.33, Telex 611591 – 📶 📺 ☎ – ⚔
100. 🆎 ⓪ 𝑉𝐼𝑆𝐴
G 7
118 rm 🖙 785/980.

🏯 **Résidence du Bois** ⬲ without rest, 16 r. Chalgrin, ✉ 75116, ℰ 500.50.59, « Refined
decor, garden » – 📺 ☎
F 7
st. : **17 rm** 🖙 580/975, 3 apartments.

🏯 **Alexander** Ⓜ without rest, 102 av. Victor-Hugo, ✉ 75116, ℰ 553.64.65, Telex 610373 –
📶 📺 ☎. 🕸
G 6
st. : **60 rm** 🖙 430/660.

🏯 **Union H. Étoile** Ⓜ without rest, 44 r. Hamelin, ✉ 75116, ℰ 553.14.95, Telex 611394 –
📶 kitchenette 📺 ☎. 🆎
G 7
st. : 🖙 27 – **29 rm** 320/445, 13 apartments.

🏯 **Victor Hugo** without rest, 19 r. Copernic, ✉ 75116, ℰ 553.76.01, Telex 630939 – 📶 📺
☎. 🆎 ⓪ Ⅎ 𝑉𝐼𝑆𝐴. 🕸
G 7
st. : 🖙 29 – **75 rm** 305/450.

🏯 **Rond-Point de Longchamp and rest Belles Feuilles** Ⓜ, 86 r. Longchamp, ✉
75116, ℰ 505.13.63, Telex 620653 – 📶 🎦 rest 📺 ☎. 🆎 ⓪
G 6
st. : **M** *(closed August, Saturday and Sunday)* a la carte 150/230 🍴 – 🖙 28 – **59 rm**
380/400.

🏯 **Régina de Passy** without rest, 6 r. Tour, ✉ 75016, ℰ 524.43.64, Telex 630004 – 📶
kitchenette 📺 ☎. 🆎 ⓪ 𝑉𝐼𝑆𝐴 🕸
H6-J6
st. : 🖙 23 – **54 rm** 102/311.

🏯 **Majestic** without rest, 29 r. Dumont-d'Urville, ✉ 75116, ℰ 500.83.70 – 📶 📺 ☎. 🆎 ⓪
Ⅎ 𝑉𝐼𝑆𝐴
F 7
st. : **27 rm** 🖙 550/700, 3 apartments.

🏯 **Fremiet** ⬲ without rest, 6 av. Fremiet, ✉ 75016, ℰ 524.52.06, Telex 630329 – 📶 📺 ☎.
🆎 ⓪ Ⅎ 𝑉𝐼𝑆𝐴
J 6
st. : 🖙 15 – **34 rm** 375/485.

🏯 **Massenet** without rest, 5 bis r. Massenet, ✉ 75016, ℰ 524.43.03, Telex 620682 – 📶
☎. 🆎 ⓪ Ⅎ 𝑉𝐼𝑆𝐴. 🕸
J 6
st. : **41 rm** 🖙 230/485.

🏯 **Elysées Bassano** Ⓜ without rest, 24 r. Bassano ✉ 75116 ℰ 720.49.03, Telex 611559 –
📶 📺 ☎. 🆎 ⓪ Ⅎ 𝑉𝐼𝑆𝐴
G 8
st. : **40 rm** 🖙 525/550.

🏯 **Floride Etoile** Ⓜ without rest, 14 r. St-Didier ✉ 75116 ℰ 727.23.36, Telex 615087 – 📶
📺 ☎ – ⚔ 40. 🆎 ⓪ Ⅎ 𝑉𝐼𝑆𝐴. 🕸
G 7
st. : 🖙 25 – **60 rm** 440.

🏯 **Residence Foch** without rest, 10 r. Marbeau ✉ 75116 ℰ 500.46.50, Telex 630886 – 📶
📺 ☎
F 6
21 rm 🖙 385/450, 4 apartments 600.

🏯 **Kléber** without rest, 7 r. Belloy, ✉ 75116, ℰ 723.80.22, Telex 612830 – 📶 📺 ☎. 🆎 ⓪ Ⅎ
st. : **21 rm** 🖙 410/495.
G 7

🏯 **Sévigné** without rest 6 r. Belloy ✉ 75116, ℰ 720.88.90, Telex 610219 – 📶 📺 ☎. 🆎 ⓪
Ⅎ st. : **30 rm** 🖙 345/453.
G 7

🏨 **Longchamp** without rest, 68 r. Longchamp ✉ 75116 ℰ 727.13.48, Telex 610342 – 📶 📺
🛁wc 🚿wc ☎. 🆎 ⓪
G 6
st. : 🖙 25 – **23 rm** 320/400.

🏨 **Ambassade** Ⓜ without rest, 79 r. Lauriston ✉ 75116 ℰ 553.41.15, Telex 613643 – 📶 📺
🛁wc 🚿wc ☎. 🆎 ⓪ Ⅎ 𝑉𝐼𝑆𝐴. 🕸
G 7
closed 15 July-31 August and Christmas Holidays – st. : 🖙 25 – **38 rm** 250/370.

🏨 **Sylva** without rest, 3 r. Pergolèse, ✉ 75116, ℰ 500.38.12, Telex 612245 – 📶 🛁wc ☎.
🆎 ⓪ Ⅎ st. : 🖙 19 – **37 rm** 285/312.
E 6

🏠 **Eiffel Kennedy** without rest, 12 r. Boulainvilliers ✉ 75016 ℰ 524.45.75, Telex 614895 –
📶 📺 🛁wc 🚿wc ☎. 🆎 ⓪ 𝑉𝐼𝑆𝐴. 🕸
J 5
st. : 🖙 20 – **30 rm** 347.

🏠 **Queen's H.** Ⓜ without rest, 4 r. Bastien Lepage ✉ 75016 ℰ 288.89.85 – 📶 📺 🛁wc
🚿wc ☎
K 4
st. : 🖙 16 – **22 rm** 173/295.

XXXX ✿✿ **Faugeron,** 52 r. Longchamp, ⊠ 75116, ℰ 704.24.53 – 🗐, ❀   G 7
closed August, 24 December-2 January, Saturday, Sunday and Bank Holidays – **M** a la carte 200/280
Spec. Bavarois aux pointes d'asperges (May-July), Grenouilles et mousse tiède estragonnette, Parfaits ''Époux'' chocolat et menthe.

XXXX ✿✿ **Vivarois** (Peyrot), 192 av. V.-Hugo, ⊠ 75116, ℰ 504.04.31 – 🗐, 🖭 ⓞ 𝘝𝘐𝘚𝘈   G 5
closed August, Saturday, Sunday and Bank Holidays – **M** a la carte 220/330
Spec. Relais des quatre saisons, Poissons, Queue de boeuf au Cornas.

XXXX ✿✿✿ **Jamin** (Robuchon), 32 r. Longchamp, ⊠ 75116, ℰ 727.12.27 – 🗐, 🖭 ⓞ 𝘝𝘐𝘚𝘈   G 7
closed 1-28 July, Saturday and Sunday – **M** (booking essential) a la carte 200/395
Spec. Ravioli de langoustines au chou, Galette de noix de St.-Jacques aux truffes (end December-end March), Morue fraîche poêlée aux fins aromates.

XXX ✿ **Toit de Passy** (6th floor), 94 av. P.-Doumer ⊠ 75016, ℰ 524.55.37, 🌣 – 🗐 🅿. 𝘝𝘐𝘚𝘈
closed Saturday, Sunday and Bank Holidays – **M** 155 (lunch) and a la carte 250/320   H J 5
Spec. Soupe d'huîtres (1 October-15 April), Assortiment de poissons à l'oseille, Millefeuille aux fruits rouges (15 May-30 September).

XXX Tsé-Yang, 25 av. Pierre 1er de Serbie ⊠ 75016 ℰ 720.68.02 – 🗐   G 8

XXX ✿ **Pavillon des Princes,** 69 av. Porte d'Auteuil ⊠ 75016 ℰ 605.65.50, 🌣. 🖭 ⓞ 𝘝𝘐𝘚𝘈
st. : **M** 194   K 1
Spec. Matelote de lotte à la tapenade, Daurade à la crème d'ail, Gigot de pintade farci ''Paysanne''.

XXX ✿ **Ferrero,** 38 r. Vital ⊠ 75016 ℰ 504.42.42 – 🖭 ⓞ 𝘝𝘐𝘚𝘈   H 5
closed 10 August-3 September, 22 December-5 January, Saturday, Sunday and Bank Holidays – **M** a la carte 220/280
Spec. Verrine de foie gras d'oie, Champignons (season), Bar en croûte.

XXX **Sully d'Auteuil,** 78 r. d'Auteuil ⊠ 75016 ℰ 651.71.18. 🖭 𝘝𝘐𝘚𝘈   K 3
closed July, Christmas Day, Saturday lunch and Sunday – **M** 200 b.i./300 b.i..

XXX **Ramponneau,** 21 av. Marceau ⊠ 75116 ℰ 720.59.51 – 🖭 ⓞ 𝘝𝘐𝘚𝘈   G 8
closed August – **M** a la carte 150/245.

XXX ✿ **Michel Pasquet,** 59 r. La-Fontaine, ⊠ 75016, ℰ 288.50.01 – 🖭 ⓞ 𝘝𝘐𝘚𝘈   K 4
closed August, Saturday except dinner from 1 September to 30 April and Sunday – **st. : M** a la carte 205/275
Spec. Cassolette de grenouilles et escargots au fenouil, Embeurrade de homard et langoustines à l'estragon, Pigeonneau en bécasse aux pleurotes.

XXX **Morens,** 10 av. New-York, ⊠ 75116, ℰ 723.75.11 – 🖭 ⓞ 𝘝𝘐𝘚𝘈   H 8
closed August, 24 December-2 January, Saturday and Sunday – **M** a la carte 145/225.

XXX ✿✿ **Guy Savoy,** 28 r. Duret ⊠ 75116 ℰ 500.17.67 – 🗐, 𝘝𝘐𝘚𝘈, ❀   F 6
closed Saturday and Sunday – **M** a la carte 180/285
Spec. Huîtres en nage glacées, Lotte aux échalotes confites, Ragoût de Champignons (August-November).

XXX ✿✿ **Le Petit Bedon** (Ignace), 38 r. Pergolèse ⊠ 75116 ℰ 500.23.66 – 🗐, 🖭 ⓞ 𝘝𝘐𝘚𝘈   F 6
closed August, Saturday and Sunday – **M** a la carte 150/215
Spec. Foie gras frais de canard, Tourteau frais Tante Louise, Ris de veau aux morilles.

XX ✿ **Al Mounia,** 16 r. Magdebourg, ⊠ 75116, ℰ 727.57.28, moroccan specialities – 🖭.   G 7
closed August and Sunday – **M** a la carte approx. 125.

XX ✿ **Paul Chêne,** 123 r. Lauriston, ⊠ 75116, ℰ 727.63.17 – 🗐, 🖭 ⓞ 𝘝𝘐𝘚𝘈   G 6
closed August, 24 December-2 January, Saturday and Sunday – **M** a la carte 155/235.
Spec. Soupe d'écrevisses et de filets de sole, Rognon de veau aux trois moutardes, Beignets de pommes.

XX ✿ **Conti,** 72 r. Lauriston ⊠ 75116 ℰ 727.74.67 – 🗐, 𝘝𝘐𝘚𝘈   G 7
closed August, Saturday, Sunday and Bank Holidays – **M** a la carte 165/205
Spec. Ravioles de chou aux grillons de ris de veau (1 November-31 January), Natte de sole au beurre rouge (1 October-28 February), Sabayon au Porto.

XX ✿ **Jenny Jacquet,** 136 r. Pompe ⊠ 75116 ℰ 727.50.26 – 𝘝𝘐𝘚𝘈, ❀   G 6
closed August, Saturday and Sunday – **M** a la carte approx. 140/180
Spec. Assiette de brochet et d'écrevisses, Fricassée de volaille à l'angevine, Beuchelle tourangelle (September-December).

XX **Relais d'Auteuil,** 31 bd Murat ⊠ 75016 ℰ 651.09.54 – 🖭 𝘝𝘐𝘚𝘈   M 3
closed 15 to 31 August, Saturday lunch and Sunday – **st. : M** 140.

XX **Le Gd Chinois,** 6 av. New York, ⊠ 75116, ℰ 723.98.21 – 🖭 ⓞ   H 8
closed 12 to 27 August and Monday – **M** a la carte 100/160.

X **Au Clocher du Village,** 8 bis r. Verderet, ⊠ 75016, ℰ 288.35.87 – 𝘝𝘐𝘚𝘈   L 4
closed August, Saturday and Sunday – **M** a la carte 90/150.

X **Le Valéry,** 55 r. Lauriston, ⊠ 75016, ℰ 553.55.48 – 𝘝𝘐𝘚𝘈   F 7
closed August, Saturday and Sunday – **st. : M** a la carte 135/200.

X **Le Moï,** 7 r. G. Courbet ⊠ 75016 ℰ 704.95.10   G 6
st. : M a la carte 95/135.

in the Bois de Boulogne :

XXXX ✿✿ **Pré Catelan** (Lenôtre), ✉ 75016, ✆ 524.55.58, ☂, ⛱ – ℗. AE ◑ VISA H 2
closed February Holidays, Sunday dinner and Monday – **M** a la carte 280/400
Spec. Langoustines à la coriandre et au citron, Canard à la rouennaise, Farandole de desserts.

XXXX ✿ **Grande Cascade,** ✉ 75016, ✆ 506.33.51, ≤ – ℗. AE ◑ E VISA
closed 20 December-21 January – **M** *(lunch only from 15 October to 15 May)* 190 (lunch) and a la carte 220/290
Spec. Huîtres chaudes au beurre de citron vert (September-May), Minute de rougets aux pâtes fraîches (May-October), Panaché de filets mignons et abats.

Clichy, Ternes, Wagram.

17th arrondissement.

17th : ✉ 75017

Concorde Lafayette Ⓜ, 3 pl. Gén.-Koenig ✆ 758.12.84, Telex 650892, « Bar with ✳ on 34th floor » – ⇕ kitchenette ▤ TV ☎. AE ◑ E VISA E 6
st. : Rest. see **L'Étoile d'Or** below – **L'Arc-en-Ciel M** 155 ♁ - Coffee Shop **Les Saisons M** a la carte approx. 135 ♁ – ☕ 47 – **975 rm** 990/1 250, 24 apartments.

Méridien Ⓜ, 81 bd Gouvion-St-Cyr (pte Maillot) ✆ 758.12.30, Telex 290952 – ⇕ kitchenette ▤ TV ☎ ℗ – 🪑 150 - 1 000. AE ◑ E VISA. ✂ rest E 6
st. : Rest. see **Le Clos de Longchamp** below - **Café l'Arlequin M** a la carte approx. 130 ♁ – **Le Yamato** (Japanese rest) **M** a la carte approx. 110 – **La Maison Beaujolaise M** 112 b.i./148 b.i. – ☕ 56 – **990 rm** 980/1 250, 16 apartments.

Splendid Etoile Ⓜ without rest, **1 bis av. Carnot** ✆ **766.41.41, Telex 280773** – ⇕ TV ☎ ♿. AE ◑ E VISA. ✂ F 7
st. : ☕ 45 – **57 rm** 500/730, 3 apartments.

Regent's Garden ⛰ without rest, **6 r. P.-Demours** ✆ **574.07.30, Telex 640127,** « Garden » – ⇕ TV ☎. AE ◑ E VISA E 7
st. : ☕ 24 – **41 rm** 410/600.

Magellan Ⓜ ⛰ without rest, **17 r. J.B.-Dumas** ✆ **572.44.51, Telex 660728,** ⛱ – ⇕ ☎. AE ◑ E VISA D 7
st. : **75 rm** ☕ 285/325.

Mercure Ⓜ without rest, **27 av. Ternes** ✆ **766.49.18, Telex 650679** – ⇕ ▤ TV ☎ ℗. AE ◑ E VISA E 8
st. : ☕ 30 – **56 rm** 370/391.

Balmoral without rest, **6 r. Gén.-Lanrezac** ✆ **380.30.50, Telex 642435** – ⇕ TV ☎. AE ◑
st. : **57 rm** ☕ 350/420. E 7

Banville without rest, **166 bd Berthier** ✆ **267.70.16, Telex 643025** – ⇕ ⛀wc ⛆wc ☎. VISA D 8
st. : **40 rm** ☕ 322/342.

Courcelles Ⓜ without rest, **184 r. Courcelles** ✆ **763.65.30, Telex 642252** – ⇕ TV ⛀wc ⛆wc ☎. AE ◑ E VISA D 8
st. : ☕ 29 – **42 rm** 356/405.

Stella without rest, **20 av. Carnot** ✆ **380.84.50, Telex 660845** – ⇕ TV ⛀wc ⛆wc ☎. AE ◑ VISA. ✂ E 7
st. : ☕ 19 – **36 rm** 212/326.

Royal Magda without rest, **7 r. Troyon** ✆ **764.10.19, Telex 641068** – ⇕ TV ⛀wc ☎. AE ◑ VISA E 8
st. : ☕ 20 – **28 rm** 355/477, 10 apartments.

Empire H. Ⓜ without rest, **3 r. Montenotte** ✆ **380.14.55, Telex 643232** – ⇕ TV ⛀wc ⛆wc ☎. AE ◑ E VISA. ✂ E 8
st. : ☕ 22 – **47 rm** 218/387.

Tivoli Étoile Ⓜ without rest, **7 r. Brey** ✆ **380.31.22, Telex 643107** – ⇕ TV ⛀wc ☎. AE ◑ E VISA E 8
st. : **30 rm** ☕ 350/420.

Mercédès without rest, **128 av. Wagram** ✆ **227.77.82, Telex 660751** – ⇕ TV ⛀wc ⛆wc ☎. AE ◑ VISA D 9
st. : ☕ 20 – **37 rm** 310.

Régence-Étoile without rest, **24 av. Carnot** ✆ **380.75.60, Telex 641914** – ⇕ TV ⛀wc ⛆wc ☎. AE VISA. ✂ E 7
st. : ☕ 22 – **38 rm** 225/360.

Belfast without rest, **10 av. Carnot** ✆ **380.12.10, Telex 642777** – ⇕ TV ⛀wc ⛆wc ☎. AE ◑ VISA. ✂ E 7
st. : ☕ 19 – **54 rm** 320/500.

🏨 **Astrid** without rest, 27 av. Carnot ℰ 380.56.20, Telex 642065 — 🕸 🖚wc 🛏wc ☎. 🐾 E 7
closed 5 to 25 August – **st. : 40 rm** ⌐ 230/295.

🏨 **Palma** without rest, 46 r. Brunel ℰ 574.29.93, Telex 660183 — 🕸 📺 🖚wc 🛏wc ☎. 🐾
st. : ⌐ 17 – **37 rm** 218/255. E 7

🏨 **Astor** without rest, 36 r. P.-Demours ℰ 227.44.93, Telex 650078 — 🕸 📺 🖚wc 🛏wc ☎
48 rm. D 8

🏨 **Trois Couronnes** Ⓜ without rest, 30 r. Arc de Triomphe ℰ 380.46.81, Telex 660182 —
📺 🖚wc 🛏wc ☎. 🆎 ⓞ Ε 𝑽𝑰𝑺𝑨 E 7
closed 24 December-1 January – **st. :** ⌐ 20 – **20 rm** 330/350.

🏨 **Prima H.,** 167 r. Rome ℰ 622.21.09, Telex 642186 — 🕸 📺 🖚wc 🛏wc ☎
st. : **M** (coffee shop only) a la carte approx. 90 ⚱ – ⌐ 20 – **30 rm** 185/240. C 10

🏩 **Néva** without rest, 14 r. Brey ℰ 380.28.26 — 🕸 🖚wc 🛏wc ☎. 𝑽𝑰𝑺𝑨. 🐾 E 8
⌐ 20 – **35 rm** 250/320.

🏩 **Bel'Hôtel** without rest, 20 r. Pouchet ℰ 627.34.77, Telex 642396 — 🕸 🖚wc 🛏 ☎. 𝑽𝑰𝑺𝑨
closed August – **st. :** ⌐ 18 – **30 rm** 85/220. B 11

XXXX 🕸🕸 **Michel Rostang,** 20 r. Rennequin ℰ 763.40.77 — 🔲. 𝑽𝑰𝑺𝑨 D 8
closed 22 July-20 August, February Holidays, Saturday (except dinner from October to
March), Sunday and Bank Holidays – **M** 155 (lunch) and a la carte 195/270
Spec. Oeufs de caille en coque d'oursins (October-March), Fricassée de soles, Canette de Bresse au sang
(May-December).

XXX 🕸🕸 **Le Bernardin** (Le Coze), 18 r. Troyon ℰ 380.40.61 — 🆎 𝑽𝑰𝑺𝑨 E 8
closed August, Sunday and Monday – **M** a la carte 200/315
Spec. Oursins chauds au beurre d'oursins (November-April), Escalope de saumon à la crème d'ail
(February-August), Rôti de lotte aux choux (October-April).

XXX 🕸 **Clos de Longchamp,** 81 bd. Gouvion-St-Cyr (Pte Maillot) ℰ 758.12.30 — 🆎 ⓞ Ε
𝑽𝑰𝑺𝑨 E 6
closed week-end and Bank Holidays in July-August – **st. : M** a la carte 225/300
Spec. Ballotin de sole aux girolles, Crépinette de volaille aux écrevisses, Mignardises.

XXX 🕸 **Étoile d'Or,** 3 pl. Gén.-Koenig ℰ 758.12.84, Telex 650905 — 🔲. 🆎 ⓞ Ε E 6
st. : **M** a la carte 205/260
Spec. Crépinettes vertes aux huîtres (September-April), Duo de bar et saumon mimosa, Filet d'agneau à la
crème d'estragon.

XXX 🕸 **Timgad** (Laasri), 21 r. Brunel ℰ 574.23.70, « Moorish decor » — 🔲. 🆎 ⓞ 𝑽𝑰𝑺𝑨. 🐾 E 7
closed August and Sunday – **M** a la carte 135/180
Spec. Tagine, Couscous, Méchoui.

XXX 🕸 **Manoir de Paris,** 6 r. Pierre-Demours ℰ 572.25.25 — 🆎 ⓞ 𝑽𝑰𝑺𝑨 E 7
closed 8 to 30 July, Saturday and Sunday – **M** a la carte 185/265
Spec. Aillade de cuisses de grenouilles et escargots en cassolette, Suprême de canard sauvage au foie gras,
Desserts.

XXX 🕸 **Apicius** (Vigato), 122 av. Villiers ℰ 380.19.66 — 🆎 𝑽𝑰𝑺𝑨 D 8
closed 8 to 30 August, Saturday (except dinner from end September-mid May) and Sunday
– **st. : M** a la carte 200/260
Spec. Croquette de moelle de boeuf, Escalope de saumon frais aux huîtres, Grand dessert au chocolat amer.

XXX **Chez Laudrin,** 154 bd Péreire ℰ 380.87.40 🅿. 🆎 𝑽𝑰𝑺𝑨 D 7
closed 1 to 7 april, Saturday and Sunday – **st. : M** a la carte 160/250.

XX 🕸 **La Coquille,** 6 r. Débarcadère ℰ 574.25.95 — 🔲. 𝑽𝑰𝑺𝑨 E 7
closed 30 July-1 September, 24 to 30 December, Sunday, Monday and Bank Holidays – **M**
a la carte 150/230
Spec. St-Jacques au naturel (1 October-15 May), Ris de veau à la crème et morilles, Soufflé au praslin de
noisettes.

XX **Baumann,** 64 av. Ternes ℰ 574.16.66 — 🔲. 🆎 ⓞ Ε 𝑽𝑰𝑺𝑨 E 7
st. : **M** a la carte 125/200 ⚱.

XX **L'Écrevisse,** 212 bis bd Péreire ℰ 572.17.60 — 🔲. 🆎 ⓞ 𝑽𝑰𝑺𝑨 E 6
closed August, Saturday and Sunday – **M** a la carte 160/235.

XX 🕸 **Paul et France,** 27 av. Niel ℰ 763.04.24 — 🆎 ⓞ 𝑽𝑰𝑺𝑨 D 8
closed 14 July-15 August, Saturday and Sunday – **M** a la carte 140/220
Spec. Terrine de la marée, Barbue au beurre de poivron rouge, Rognon de veau Paul et France.

XX **La Truite Vagabonde,** 17 r. Batignolles ℰ 387.77.80 — 🆎 ⓞ 𝑽𝑰𝑺𝑨 D 11
closed Sunday – **M** 200.

XX **La Braisière,** 54 r. Cardinet ℰ 763.40.37 — 𝑽𝑰𝑺𝑨 D 9
closed August, Saturday lunch from 30 September to 30 April and Sunday – **st. : M** a la
carte 140/210.

XX 🕸 **Chez Guyvonne** (Cros), 14 r. Thann ℰ 227.25.43 D 9-10
closed 8 to 29 July, 23 December-5 January, Saturday, Sunday and Bank Holidays – **M** a
la carte 155/240
Spec. Pain d'écrevisses (August-March), Oreille et ris de veau aux truffes, Crêpes soufflées aux poires.

XX **Lajarrige,** 16 av. Villiers ℰ 763.25.61 – 🆎 VISA
closed Sunday – **M** a la carte 135/210.   D 10

XX ✿ **Le Petit Colombier** (Fournier), 42 r. Acacias ℰ 380.28.54 – VISA
closed 27 July-19 August, 24 December-2 January, Sunday lunch and Saturday – **M** a la
carte 140/225   E 7
   Spec. Escargots en croquemitoufle, Rognon de veau Palais Royal, Farandole de pâtisseries maison.

XX ✿ **Chez Augusta** (Bareste), 98 r. Tocqueville ℰ 763.39.97 – ⓞ VISA
closed August, Sunday and Bank Holidays – **M** a la carte 175/235   C 9
   Spec. Salade Augusta, Bouillabaisse, Nage de St-Pierre.

XX **Epicure 108,** 108 r. Cardinet ℰ 763.50.91 – VISA
closed Sunday and Monday – **M** a la carte 135/190.   D 10

XX **Chez Georges,** 273 bd Pereire ℰ 574.31.00 – VISA
closed August – **M** a la carte 135/180.   E 6

XX **La Toque,** 16 r. Tocqueville ℰ 227.97.75 – VISA
closed 14 July-15 August, Saturday and Sunday – **st. : M** a la carte 115/180.   D 10

XX **Chez Léon,** 32 r. Legendre ℰ 227.06.82 – ⓞ VISA
closed 31 July-31 August, Saturday, Sunday and Bank Holidays – **st. : M** a la carte
120/190.   D 10

X ✿ **La Petite Auberge** (Harbonnier), 38 r. Laugier ℰ 763.85.51 – ⓞ VISA   D 7-8
closed August, Sunday, Monday and Bank Holidays – **M** (booking essential) a la carte
155/225
   Spec. Turbot Camille Renault, Carré d'agneau Emile Compard, Tarte aux pommes.

X **Le Beudant,** 97 r. des Dames ℰ 387.11.20 – 🆎 ⓞ VISA
closed Saturday lunch and Sunday – **M** a la carte 160/220.   D 11

X **La Soupière,** 154 av. Wagram ℰ 227.00.73 – 🆎 VISA   D 9
closed 10 to 18 August, 21 to 31 December, Saturday and Sunday – **st. : M** a la carte
150/205.

X ✿ **Mère Michel** (Gaillard), 5 r. Rennequin ℰ 763.59.80 – VISA   E 8
closed August, Saturday, Sunday and Bank Holidays – **st. : M** (booking essential) a la
carte 140/200
   Spec. Cressonnette de foies de volaille au Xérès, Poissons beurre blanc, Omelette soufflée.

X **Le Pain et le Vin,** 1 r. d'Armaillé ℰ 763.88.29 – VISA   E 7
closed 26 July-19 August, 24 December-2 January, Saturday and Sunday – **st. : M** a la
carte approx. 110.

Montmartre, La Villette, Belleville.

18th, 19th and 20th arrondissements.

   18th : ✉ 75018
   19th : ✉ 75019
   20th : ✉ 75020

🏨 **Terrass'H.** Ⓜ, 12 r. J.-de-Maistre (18th) ℰ 606.72.85, Telex 280830 – 🛗 ▤ rest 📺 ☎ ᴆ
– 🔥 30. 🆎 ⓞ ᴇ VISA   C 13
st. : Coffee Shop **L'Albaron M** a la carte approx. 100 ᴊ – **95 rm** ⊆ 410/650, 13 apartments
640/750.

🏨 **Mercure Paris Montmartre** Ⓜ without rest, 1 r. Caulaincourt (18th) ℰ 294.17.17,
Telex 640605 – 🛗 📺 ☎ ᴆ, 🆎 ⓞ ᴇ VISA   D 12
st. : ⊆ 36 – **308 rm** 479/509.

🏨 **H. Le Laumière** without rest, 4 r. Petit (19th) ℰ 206.10.77 – 🛗 ➡️wc ⋔wc ☜. ⊱
st. : ⊆ 16 – **54 rm** 90/225.   D 19

🏨 **Super H.,** 208 r. Pyrénées (20th) ℰ 636.97.48 – 🛗 ▤ rest ➡️wc ⋔wc ☜. VISA   G 21
closed August – **st. : M** (closed Sunday) 74/150 ᴊ – **28 rm** ⊆ 141/283.

🏨 **Regyn's Montmartre** without rest, 18 pl. Abbesses (18th) ℰ 254.45.21 – 🛗 📺 ➡️wc
⋔wc ☎. 🆎 ⓞ VISA   D 13
st. : ⊆ 17 – **22 rm** 284/315.

🏨 **Pyrénées Gambetta** without rest, 12 av. Père Lachaise (20th) ℰ 797.76.57 – 🛗 ➡️wc
⋔wc ☎   H 21
st. : 30 rm ⊆ 115/270.

🏨 **Prima-Lepic** without rest, 29 r. Lepic (18th) ℰ 606.44.64 – 🛗 ➡️wc ⋔wc ☜. 🆎 ⓞ. ⊱
st. : ⊆ 18 – **38 rm** 140/204.   D 13

🏨 **Capucines Montmartre** without rest, 5 r. A.-Bruand (18th) ℰ 252.89.80 – 🛗 📺 ➡️wc
⋔wc ☎. 🆎 ⓞ   D 13
☜ 17 – **30 rm** 205/300.

🏨 **Luxia** without rest, 8 r. Seveste (18th) ℰ 606.84.24 – 🛗 ➡️ ⋔wc ☜. 🆎 ⓞ
st. : ⊆ 15 – **48 rm** 135/265.   D 14

🏨 **Eden H.** without rest, 90 r. Ordener (18th) ℰ 264.61.63 – 🛗 ➡️wc ⋔wc ☎. 🆎. ⊱   B 14
st. : ⊆ 15 – **35 rm** 140/230.

XXX ⊛ **Beauvilliers** (Carlier), 52 r. Lamarck (18th) ☎ 254.19.50, « 1900's decor, terrace » – _VISA_ . ⅜   C 14
closed September, Monday lunch and Sunday – **M** a la carte 215/275
Spec. Filets de rouget grillés, Boudin de faisan aux cêpes (1 October-20 March), Canette au vin de figues.

XXX ⊛ **Cochon d'Or**, 192 av. Jean-Jaurès (19th) ☎ 607.23.13 – ▤ . 🄰🄴 ⓓ 🄴 _VISA_   C 20
M a la carte 155/215
Spec. Salade de tête de veau, Salade de St-Jacques (October-April), Grillades.

XXX **Charlot 1ᵉʳ "Merveilles des Mers"**, 128 bis bd Clichy (18th) ☎ 522.47.08 – 🄰🄴 ⓓ 🄴   D 12
closed 8 July-28 August – **M** a la carte 160/225

XXX ⊛ **Relais Pyrénées** (Marty), 1 r. Jourdain (20th) ☎ 636.65.81 – 🄰🄴 ⓓ 🄴 _VISA_   F 20
closed August and Saturday – **M** a la carte 170/225
Spec. Foie gras frais de canard, Saumon frais au Champagne, Confit d'oie.

XXX **Dagorno**, 190 av. J.-Jaurès (19th) ☎ 607.02.29. 🄰🄴 ⓓ 🄴 _VISA_   C 20
closed Saturday – **M** a la carte 150/260.

XX ⊛ **Petit Pré** (Verges), 1 r. Bellevue (19th) ☎ 208.92.62   E 21
closed Saturday, Sunday and Bank Holidays – **st. : M** a la carte 160/225
Spec. Calamars farcis, Fricassée de lapereau au citron, Soupe de fraises poêlées.

XX **Chez le Baron**, 65 r. Manin (19th) ☎ 205.72.72 – 🄰🄴 _VISA_   D 19
closed August, Saturday lunch and Sunday – **M** a la carte 165/250.

XX **Le Clodenis**, 57 r. Caulaincourt (18th) ☎ 606.20.26. 🄰🄴 ⓑ _VISA_ . ⅜   C 13
closed Sunday and Monday – **M** 110 (lunch) and a la carte 185/250.

XX **Sanglier Bleu**, 102 bd Clichy (18th) ☎ 606.07.61 – ▤ . 🄰🄴 ⓓ 🄴 _VISA_   D 12
closed 15 July-15 August and Saturday lunch – **M** a la carte 110/200.

XX **Grandgousier**, 17 av. Rachel (18th) ☎ 387.66.12 – 🄰🄴 ⓓ _VISA_   D 12
closed Saturday lunch and Sunday – **M** a la carte 130/190.

XX **Au Clair de la Lune**, 9 r. Poulbot (18th) ☎ 258.97.03 – 🄰🄴 ⓓ _VISA_   D 14
closed February Holidays, Monday lunch and Sunday – **M** a la carte 140/200.

XX **Deux Taureaux**, 206 av. J.-Jaurès (19th) ☎ 607.39.31 – 🄰🄴 ⓓ _VISA_   C 21
closed Saturday and Sunday – **st. : M** a la carte 130/180.

XX **Boeuf Couronné**, 188 av. Jean-Jaurès (19th) ☎ 607.89.52 – 🄰🄴 ⓓ 🄴 _VISA_   C 20
closed Sunday – **M** a la carte 115/195.

XX **La Chaumière**, 46 av. Secrétan (19th) ☎ 607.98.62 – 🄰🄴 ⓓ 🄴 _VISA_   E 18
closed August and Sunday – **st. : M** a la carte 105/190.

XX **Chez Frézet**, 181 r. Ordener (18th) ☎ 606.64.20 – _VISA_   B 13
closed August, February Holidays, Saturday, Sunday and Bank Holidays – **M** a la carte 115/180.

X **Le Pichet**, 174 r. Ordener (18th) ☎ 627.85.28 – ⓓ _VISA_   B 13
closed August and Sunday – **M** a la carte 85/140 🍷.

X **Relais Normand**, 32 bis r. d'Orsel (18th) ☎ 606.92.57 – 🄰🄴 🄴 _VISA_   D 14
closed 5 to 26 August, 15 to 31 January, Friday dinner and Saturday – **st. : M** 56/99.

X **Marie-Louise**, 52 r. Championnet (18th) ☎ 606.86.55 – ⓓ _VISA_   B 15
closed end July to early September, Sunday, Monday and Bank Holidays – **M** a la carte 80/130.

X **Le Sancerre**, 13 av. Corentin Cariou (19th) ☎ 607.80.44   B 19 B
closed Easter, August, Saturday, Sunday and Bank Holidays – **M** a la carte 110/165.

Environs

Bagnolet 93170 Seine-St-Denis 101 ⑯ – pop. 32 557 – alt. 86 – ✿ 1.
Paris 6 – Bobigny 10 – Lagny 27 – Meaux 40.

🏨 **Novotel Paris Bagnolet** M, av. République, Porte de Bagnolet interchange ℘ 360.
02.10, Telex 670216, ⌁ – 🖩🖩 📺 ☎ 🅿 – 🔬 25 - 800. 🖭 ⓸ E 𝓥𝓘𝓢𝓐
L'Oeuf et la Poule M 145 b.i. – **coffee shop** M a la carte approx. 95 ⅄ – ⌁ 33 – **611 rm**
429/458.

Bougival 78380 Yvelines 101 ⑱ – pop. 8 487 – alt. 40 – ✿ 3.
Paris 18 – Rueil-Malmaison 3,5 – St-Germain-en-Laye 7 – Versailles 7 – Le Vésinet 4.

XXXX ✿ **Coq Hardy,** 16 quai Rennequin-Sualem (N 13) ℘ 969.01.43, « Terraced flower gardens,
elegant setting » – 🅿. 🖭 ⓸ 𝓥𝓘𝓢𝓐
closed Wednesday – **M** (Sunday booking essential) 200 (lunch) and a la carte 290/370
Spec. Foie gras de canard, Blanc de volaille des gourmets, Nougat glacé.

XXXX **Château de la Jonchère** M ⅏ with rm, ℘ 918.57.03, 🍴, parc, ⌁, ⅗ – 📺 ⌂wc ☎
🅿 – 🔬 30. 🖭 ⓸ E 𝓥𝓘𝓢𝓐, ⅗ rm
st. : **M** 150/250 – ⌁ 40 – **6 rm** 700/800.

XXX ✿✿ **Le Camelia** (Delaveyne), 7 quai G.-Clemenceau ℘ 969.03.02 – 🖭 ⓸ 𝓥𝓘𝓢𝓐
closed Sunday dinner and Monday – **M** a la carte 230/320
Spec. Champignons (October-January), Turbot en terrine, Tendron de veau.

XX **Cheval Noir,** 14 quai G.-Clemenceau ℘ 969.00.96, 🍴 – 𝓥𝓘𝓢𝓐
closed August, Wednesday dinner and Thursday – **M** a la carte 100/160 ⅄.

Boulogne-Billancourt ◁⑤▷ 92100 Hauts-de-Seine 101 ⑳ – pop. 102 595 – alt. 35 – ✿ 1.
See : Bois de Boulogne★★ : Municipal Floral Garden★ (Fleuriste municipal) – Albert
Kahn Gardens★ – Paul Landowski Museum★.
Paris (by Porte de St-Cloud) 10 – Nanterre 7 – Versailles 11.

🏨 **Sélect H.** M without rest, 66 av. Gén.-Leclerc ℘ 604.70.47, Telex 206029 – 🖩 ⌂wc
🖩wc ☎ 🅿. 𝓥𝓘𝓢𝓐
st. : ⌁ 18 – **64 rm** 211/261.

🏨 **Excelsior** without rest, 12 r. Ferme ℘ 621.08.08 – 🖩 🖩wc ☎. 🖭
st. : ⌁ 15,50 – **52 rm** 177/200.

XXX ✿ **Au Comte de Gascogne,** 89 av. J.-B.-Clément ℘ 603.47.27, « Winter garden » –
🖩. 🖭 ⓸ 𝓥𝓘𝓢𝓐
closed August, Saturday and Sunday – **M** a la carte 190/260
Spec. Foie frais de canard (October-March), Homard entier rôti au fenouil (April-October), Aiguillettes de
canard aux figues fraîches (October-March).

XX ✿ **La Bretonnière,** 120 av. J.-B.-Clément ℘ 605.73.56 – 🖭 ⓸ 𝓥𝓘𝓢𝓐
closed Saturday lunch and Sunday – **M** a la carte 170/250.

XX **La Bergerie,** 87 av. J.-B.-Clément ℘ 605.39.07 – 🖭 ⓸ 𝓥𝓘𝓢𝓐
closed 10 to 25 August, Monday dinner and Sunday – **M** a la carte 165/215.

XX **La Petite Auberge Franc Comtoise,** 86 av. J.-B.-Clément ℘ 605.67.19 – 🖭 ⓸ 𝓥𝓘𝓢𝓐
closed 1 to 29 August and Sunday – **M** a la carte 145/210.

XX **Laux... à la Bouche,** 117 av. J.-B.-Clément ℘ 825.43.88 – 𝓥𝓘𝓢𝓐
closed 11 to 19 August, Saturday and Sunday in July and August – **M** a la carte 110/180.

X **La Galère,** 112 r. Gén.-Gallieni ℘ 605.64.51 – 𝓥𝓘𝓢𝓐, ⅗
closed August, Saturday and Sunday – **M** a la carte 90/140.

Le Bourget 93350 Seine-St-Denis 101 ⑰ – pop. 11 021 – alt. 66.
See : Aviation Museum★.
Paris 15 – Bobigny 5 – Chantilly 34 – Meaux 38 – St-Denis 6,5 – Senlis 36.

🏨 **Novotel** M, at Blanc-Mesnil ZA pont Yblon ⊠ 93150 Le Blanc-Mesnil ℘ 867.48.88,
Telex 230115, ⌁ – 🖩 🖩 rest 📺 ☎ 🅿 – 🔬 250. 🖭 ⓸ E 𝓥𝓘𝓢𝓐
M a la carte approx. 110 ⅄ – ⌁ 29 – **141 rm** 248/290.

Châteaufort 78117 Yvelines 101 ㉒ – pop. 780 – alt. 153 – ✿ 3.
Paris 27 – Arpajon 28 – Rambouillet 25 – Versailles 10.

XXX ✿ **La Belle Epoque** (Peignaud), 10 pl. Mairie ℘ 956.21.66, 🍴, « Country inn overlooking
a small valley » – 🖭 ⓸ 𝓥𝓘𝓢𝓐
closed 12 August-4 September, 23 December-7 January and Sunday dinner – **M** 250
b.i./400 b.i.
Spec. Petits gris à la nage, Morue fraîche aux germes de soja, Fondant d'agneau à l'essence de truffes.

Clichy 92110 Hauts-de-Seine 101 ⑮ – pop. 47 000 – alt. 30 – ۞ 1.

Paris 6,5 – Argenteuil 7 – Nanterre 10 – Pontoise 27 – St-Germain-en-Laye 17.

XXX ۞ **Barrière de Clichy**, 1 r. de Paris ℰ 737.05.18 – ▤. 〽 ⓘ 𝒱𝒮𝒜
closed Saturday lunch and Sunday – **M** a la carte 200/260
Spec. Terrine de foie gras frais, Coquilles St-Jacques (October-April), Ris de veau braisé au jus de truffes.

Courbevoie 92400 Hauts-de-Seine 101 ⑭ – pop. 59 931 – alt. 34 – ۞ 1.

See : La Défense★★ : Exhibition (National Centre for Industry and Technology), Manhattan Tower★★★, Fiat Tower★, GAN Tower★, – Perspective★ from the parvis.

Paris (by Porte Champerret) 11 – Asnières 3 – Levallois-Perret 3,5 – Nanterre 4 – St-Germain-en-Laye 14.

🏨 **Novotel Paris La Défense**, 2 bd Neuilly ℰ 778.16.68, Telex 630288 – ▯ ▤ 📺 ☎ ♿
🚗 – 🔏 25-150. 〽 ⓘ ⴹ 𝒱𝒮𝒜
M a la carte approx. 110 ⅊ – 🕮 40 – **276 rm** 490.

🏨 **Penta** ⓜ, 18 r. Baudin ℰ 788.50.51, Telex 610470 – ▯ ▤ rest 📺 ☎ ⓟ – 🔏 25 - 300. 〽
ⓘ ⴹ 𝒱𝒮𝒜, ❦ rest
st. : l'**Atelier M** a la carte 100/140 ⅊ – 🕮 8 – **494 rm** 405/435.

Créteil ⓟ 94000 Val-de-Marne 101 ㉗ – pop. 71 705 – alt. 49 – ۞ 1.

See : Town Hall★ : parvis★..
🛈 1 r. F.-Mauriac ℰ 899.88.47.
Paris 12 – Bobigny 17 – Évry 22 – Lagny 26 – Melun 36.

🏨 **Novotel** ⓜ ॐ, ℰ 207.91.02, Telex 670396, ⌇ – ▯ ▤ 📺 ☎ ⓟ – 🔏 25 - 200. 〽 ⓘ ⴹ
𝒱𝒮𝒜
M (coffee shop only) a la carte approx. 110 ⅊ – 🕮 29 – **110 rm** 278/292.

Écouen 95440 Val d'Oise 101 ⑥ – pop. 4 386 – alt. 150.

See : Château★★ : Renaissance Museum★★ (tapestry of David and Bathsheba★★★).

Enghien-les-Bains 95880 Val d'Oise 101 ⑤ – pop. 9 739 – alt. 50 – Spa – Casino – ۞ 3.

See : Lake★ – 🎋 of Domont ℰ 991.07.50, N : 8 km.
🛈 2 bd Cotte ℰ 412.41.15.
Paris 18 – Argenteuil 6 – Chantilly 32 – Pontoise 20 – St-Denis 6 – St-Germain-en-Laye 23.

🏨 **Grand Hôtel**, 85 r. Gén.-de-Gaulle ℰ 412.80.00, Telex 697842, ≼, �, « Attractive flower garden » – ▯ 📺 ☎ ⓟ – 🔏 35. 〽 ⓘ 𝒱𝒮𝒜, ❦ rest
closed 2 to 29 January – **st. : M** 125/200 – 🕮 36 – **50 rm** 345/445, 3 apartments 715 – P 631/731.

🏠 **Villa Marie Louise** ॐ without rest., 49 r. Malleville ℰ 964.82.21, 🌳 – ▯ 🚿wc 🛁wc
🕮
st. : 🕮 14,50 – **22 rm** 128/190.

XXXX ۞۞ **Duc d'Enghien**, at the Casino ℰ 412.90.00, ≼ lake – ▤. 〽 ⓘ 𝒱𝒮𝒜. ❦
closed 2 to 30 January, Sunday dinner and Monday – **M** a la carte 115/310
Spec. Salade de homard aux fines herbes (May-October), Bar en écailles de concombre, Pigeon au foie gras en paupiette de chou.

XX **Aub. Landaise**, 32 bd d'Ormesson ℰ 412.78.36 – 〽 𝒱𝒮𝒜
closed August, February Holidays, Sunday dinner and Wednesday – **st. : M** a la carte 120/160.

XX **A la Carpe d'Or**, 91 r. Gén.-de-Gaulle ℰ 412.79.53, ≼ – 〽 ⓘ 𝒱𝒮𝒜
closed Sunday dinner and Monday – **M** a la carte 130/180 ⅊.

Gennevilliers 92230 Hauts-de-Seine 101 ⑮ – pop. 45 445 – alt. 29 – ۞ 1.

🛈 177 av. Gabriel Péri (closed morning) ℰ 799.33.92.
Paris 11 – Nanterre 12 – Pontoise 23 – St-Denis 4 – St-Germain-en-Laye 20.

XX ۞ **Julius**, 6 bd Camélinat ℰ 798.79.37 – ▤. 𝒱𝒮𝒜
closed Saturday lunch and Sunday – **M** a la carte 150/210
Spec. Terrine tiède d'escargots de mer (September-March), Canette de Barbarie, Navarin au citron vert.

Grigny 91350 Essonne 101 ㉟ – pop. 26 181 – ۞ 6 – Paris 26 – Evry 7 – Versailles 32.

XXX **Château du Clotay** ॐ with rm, 8 r. du Port ℰ 906.89.70, park, �, ⌇ – 📺 🚿wc ☎
ⓟ. 〽 ⓘ 𝒱𝒮𝒜
closed February Holidays, Sunday dinner and Monday – **M** 140/205 – 🕮 32 – **10 rm** 350/620.

Houilles 78800 Yvelines 101 ⑬ – pop. 29 854 – alt. 31 – ۞ 3.

Paris 17 – Argenteuil 6 – Maisons-Laffitte 5 – St-Germain-en-Laye 8.

XX ۞ **Gambetta** (Poirier), 41 r. Gambetta ℰ 968.52.12 – 〽 𝒱𝒮𝒜
closed 23 March-10 April, August, Sunday dinner and Monday – **st. : M** a la carte 170/230
Spec. Feuilleté de rouget aux huîtres chaudes, Fricassée de homard au sauternes, Millefeuille aux fruits.

Livry-Gargan 93190 Seine-St-Denis 101 ⑱ – pop. 32 806 – alt. 63 – ⚙ 1.

ℹ pl. H. de Ville (closed morning) ✆ 330.61.60.

Paris 19 – Aubervilliers 13 – Aulnay-sous-Bois 5,5 – Bobigny 7,5 – Meaux 28 – Senlis 42.

XXX **Aub. St-Quentinoise,** 23 av. République ✆ 381.13.08, 🏕 – AE VISA. ✂
closed Sunday dinner and Monday – **st. : M** (booking essential for dinner) 130 (lunch) and a la carte 170/240.

Longjumeau 91160 Essonne 101 ㉟ – pop. 18 395 – alt. 72 – ⚙ 6.

Paris 21 – Chartres 70 – Dreux 82 – Évry 16 – Melun 39 – Orléans 96 – Versailles 21.

🏨 **Relais St-Georges** Ⓜ ⛰, at Saulx-les-Chartreux SW : 3 km ✉ 91160 Longjumeau ✆ 448.36.40, ≤, park – 🛗 TV ☎ 🚗 P – 🎪 60-100. AE ⓓ E VISA
closed August – **st. : M** 80/150 – ☕ 30 – **38 rm** 210/300 – P 340/410.

🏨 **Relais des Chartreux** Ⓜ, at Saulxier SW : 2 km ✉ 91160 Longjumeau ✆ 909.34.31, Telex 691245, ≤, 🏊, 🎾 – 🛗 TV ☎ P – 🎪 250. AE E VISA
st. : M 100/135 – ☕ 24 – **100 rm** 218/240 – P 410.

Maisons-Laffitte 78600 Yvelines 101 ⑬ – pop. 22 892 – alt. 40 – ⚙ 3.

See : Château★.

Paris 21 – Argenteuil 8,5 – Mantes-la-Jolie 37 – Poissy 8 – Pontoise 18 – St-Germain 8 – Versailles 24.

XXX ✿✿ **Le Tastevin** (Blanchet), 9 av. Eglé ✆ 962.11.67, 🏕, 🌳 – AE ⓓ VISA
closed 19 August-11 September, 1 to 15 February, Monday dinner and Tuesday – **st. : M** a la carte 175/220.

XXX ✿✿ **Vieille Fontaine** (Clerc), 8 av. Gretry ✆ 962.01.78, « Garden » – AE ⓓ VISA
closed August, Sunday and Monday – **M** a la carte 230/295
Spec. Huîtres chaudes aux trois saveurs, Marmite de poissons "en Macaroni", Cassoulet.

XX **Le Laffitte,** 5 av. St-Germain ✆ 962.01.53 – AE VISA. ✂
closed August, Tuesday dinner and Wednesday – **st. : M** 170 b.i./220 b.i..

Marne-la-Vallée 77206 S.-et-M. 101 ⑲ – ⚙ 6.

Paris 26 – Meaux 28 – Melun 35.

S.E : **6 km by Lagny traffic interchange A 4 :**

🏨 **Novotel** Ⓜ, ✆ 005.91.15, Telex 691990, 🏕, 🏊 – 🛗 ▤ TV 🛁wc ☎ ♿ P – 🎪 150. AE ⓓ E VISA
M a la carte approx. 95 🌡 – ☕ 30 – **92 rm** 301/322.

Meudon 92190 Hauts-de-Seine 101 ㉔ – pop. 49 004 – alt. 100 – ⚙ 1.

See : Terrace★ : ⁂★ – Meudon Forest★.

Paris 12 – Boulogne-Billancourt 3 – Clamart 3,5 – Nanterre 11 – Versailles 10.

XXX ✿ **Relais des Gardes,** at Bellevue, 42 av. Gallieni ✆ 534.11.79 – AE ⓓ VISA
closed August, Sunday dinner and Saturday – **st. : M** a la carte 170/225
Spec. Civet de sole, Pot-au-feu de canard (except in summer), Feuilleté tiède aux pommes.

Montrouge 92120 Hauts-de-Seine 101 ㉕ – pop. 38 632 – alt. 74 – ⚙ 1.

Paris (by Porte d'Orléans) 6 – Boulogne-Billancourt 6,5 – Longjumeau 14 – Nanterre 15 – Versailles 16.

🏨 **Mercure** Ⓜ, 13 r. F.-Ory ✆ 657.11.26, Telex 202528 – 🛗 ▤ rest TV ☎ ♿ P. AE ⓓ E VISA
st. : M a la carte approx. 130 🌡 – ☕ 34 – **185 rm** 427/459.

Morangis 91420 Essonne 101 ㉟ – pop. 9 464 – alt. 76 – ⚙ 6.

Paris 22 – Évry 16 – Longjumeau 4,5 – Versailles 23.

XX ✿ **Rêve d'Alsace,** Pl. P. Brossolette ✆ 909.14.78, 🏕 – AE ⓓ VISA
closed Monday dinner, Sunday and Bank Holidays – **M** a la carte 130/225
Spec. Tarte à la confiture d'oignons, Gigot de poulette farci au fumet de gingembre, Marbré de mousses aux deux chocolats.

Neuilly-sur-Seine 92200 Hauts-de-Seine 101 ⑮ – pop. 64 450 – alt. 36 – ⚙ 1.

See : Bois de Boulogne★★ : Jardin d'acclimatation★, (Children's Amusement Park, Miniature Railway and Zoo in the Bois de Boulogne), Bagatelle★ (Park and Garden) National Museum of Popular Art and traditions★★ – Palais des Congrès★ : main conference hall★★, ≤★ from hotel Concorde-La Fayette.

Paris (by Porte Neuilly) 8 – Argenteuil 12 – Nanterre 5,5 – Pontoise 37 – St-Germain 14 – Versailles 18.

🏨 H.Club Méditerranée Ⓜ, 58 bd. V.-Hugo ✆ 758.11.00, Telex 610971, 🏕, Club atmosphere, 🌳 – 🛗 ▤ rm TV ☎ – 🎪 150
335 rm.

🏨 **Parc Neuilly** without rest, 4 bd Parc ✆ 624.32.62, Telex 613689 – 🛗 TV 🛁wc 🚿wc ☎
st. : ☕ 16 – **71 rm** 174/225.

🏨 **Roule** without rest, 37 bis av. du Roule ✆ 624.60.09 – 🛗 🛁wc 🚿wc ☎
st. : ☕ 17,50 – **35 rm** 159/220.

XXX ☘ **Jacqueline Fénix,** 42 av. Ch.-de-Gaulle ℇ 624.42.61 – ■. VISA
closed August, Christmas Day to 1 January, Saturday and Sunday – **st. : M** a la carte 200/
280
Spec. Millefeuille de rable de lapereau, Fricassée d'artichaut et de sole aux herbes, Noisettes d'agneau et rognon de veau au beurre de persil.

XX **Jarrasse,** 4 av. Madrid ℇ 624.07.56 – AE O VISA
closed 16 July-3 September, Sunday (except lunch from 3 September to 31 March) and Monday – **M** a la carte 175/270.

XX **Tonnelle Saintongeaise,** 32 bd Vital Bouhot ℇ 624.43.15, ⏳
closed 15 August-8 September, 22 December-6 January, Saturday and Sunday – **M** a la carte 110/140.

XX ☘ **Bourrier,** 1 pl. Parmentier ℇ 624.11.19
closed 1 to 20 August, Saturday (except dinner from 1 October to Easter) Sunday and Bank Holidays – **st. : M** 180/250
Spec. Salade de canard, Anguille rôtie, Navet fourré au foie gras (season).

XX **Chau'veau,** 59 r. Chauveau ℇ 624.46.22 – O VISA
closed August, Saturday and Sunday – **M** a la carte 90/145.

XX **Truffe Noire,** 2 pl. Parmentier ℇ 624.94.14 – AE VISA
closed August, February Holidays, Friday dinner and Saturday – **M** a la carte 140/180.

XX **Focly,** 10 r. P.-Chatrousse ℇ 624.43.36 – AE VISA
closed 12 to 27 July – **M** a la carte 70/100.

X **Chez Livio,** 6 r. longchamp ℇ 624.81.32
closed 1 to 29 August and 24 December-2 January – **M** a la carte 85/105 ♭.

▪ **Nogent-sur-Marne** ┬┬┬ 94130 Val-de-Marne 101 ⑧ – pop. 24 696 – alt. 56 – ⚇ 1.
≢ 5 av. Joinville (closed morning) ℇ 873.75.90.
Paris 14 – Créteil 6,5 – Montreuil 5 – Vincennes 4.

⛩ **Nogentel** M, 8 r. Port ℇ 872.70.00, Telex 210116, < – ▌▌ TV ☏ – ✄ 250. AE O E VISA
rest. **Le Panoramic** *(closed August)* **M** a la carte 175/220 - Grill **Le Canotier M** a la carte approx. 95 – **61 rm**.

▪ **Orly (Paris Airport)** 94396 Val-de-Marne 101 ⑨ – pop. 23 886 – alt. 89 – ⚇ 1.
✈ Information : ℇ 884.32.10.
Paris 16 – Corbeil-Essonnes 17 – Longjumeau 9 – Villeneuve-St-Georges 12.

⛩ **Hilton Orly** M, near air terminal ℇ 687.33.88, Telex 250621, < – ▌▌ ■ TV ☏ ♻ Ⓜ – ✄
300. AE O E VISA, ✄ rest
st. : Le Café du Marché M a la carte approx. 120 ♭ - **La Louisiane** *(closed August, Saturday and Sunday)* **M** a la carte 140/200 – ⏳ 41 – **379 rm** 420/810.

Orly Airport South :

XX **Le Grillardin,** ℇ 687.24.25, Telex 204233, < – ■. AE O E VISA
st. : M (lunch only) 150 b.i..

Orly Airport West :

XXX **Maxim's,** ℇ 687.16.16, < – ■. AE VISA
st. : M 190 and a la carte.

XX **Jardin d'Orly,** ℇ 687.16.16, < – ■. AE VISA
closed August, Saturday and Sunday – **st. : M** a la carte 130/170.

X **La Galerie,** ℇ 687.16.16, < – VISA
st. : M a la carte approx. 110 ♭.

▪ **Pontoise** ┬┬┬ 95300 Val-d'Oise 196 ④⑤ – pop. 29 411 – alt. 27 – ⚇ 3.
≢ 6 pl. Petit Martroy ℇ 038.24.45.
Paris 34 – Beauvais 55 – Dieppe 135 – Mantes-la-Jolie 39 – Rouen 91.

at Cormeilles-en-Vexin NW by D 915 – ✉ 95830 Cormeilles-en-Vexin :

XXX ☘☘ **Relais Ste-Jeanne** (Cagna), on D 915 ℇ 466.61.56, « Garden » – Ⓜ. AE O VISA
closed 4 to 24 August, Christmas Day, February Holidays, Sunday dinner, Tuesday dinner and Monday – **st. : M** (booking essential) 280 and a la carte
Spec. Soufflé de foie de canard, Escalope de ris de veau aux morilles, Huîtres chaudes au Champagne (September-June).

▪ **Le Pré St-Gervais** 93310 Seine-St-Denis 101 ⑦ – pop. 13 313 – alt. 71 – ⚇ 1.
Paris (by Porte de Pantin) 7 – Bobigny 5 – Lagny 27 – Meaux 38 – Senlis 44.

X ☘ **Au Pouilly Reuilly** (Thibault), 68 r. A.-Joineau ℇ 845.14.59 – AE O VISA
closed 1 August-5 September, Sunday and Bank Holidays – **M** a la carte 90/165
Spec. Pâté de grenouilles, Foie de veau aux girolles, Rognon de veau dijonnaise.

Puteaux 92800 Hauts-de-Seine 101 ⑭ – pop. 36 143 – alt. 36 – ✪ 1.

See : La Défense★★ : C.N.I.T.★ Exhibition Hall (National Centre for Industry and Technology), Manhattan Tower★★★, Fiat tower★, GAN Tower★ – Perspective★ of the parvis, G. Paris.

Paris 10 – Nanterre 3 – Pontoise 35 – St-Germain-en-Laye 11 – Versailles 14.

XX ✿ **Gasnier,** 7 bd Richard-Wallace ✆ 506.33.63 – AE ⓓ VISA
closed 27 June-31 July, February Holidays, Saturday lunch, Sunday and Bank Holidays – **st. : M** (booking essential) a la carte 190/270
Spec. Foie gras frais de canard, Cassoulet, Confit de canard aux cèpes.

Roissy-en-France 95 Val-d'Oise 101 ⑧ – pop. 1 411 – ✉ 95500 Gonesse – ✪ 1.

✈ **Charles de Gaulle ✆ 862.22.80.**

Paris 26 – Chantilly 28 – Meaux 36 – Pontoise 44 – Senlis 28.

in the airport area :

Sofitel Ⓜ, ✆ 862.23.23, Telex 230166, ⛆, ✗ – |‡| TV ☎ ♿ Ⓟ – 🛆 25 - 500. AE ⓓ E VISA. ✗ rest
Panoramic rest. **Les Valois** *(closed Saturday lunch and Sunday)* **M** 190 b.i. - **Le Jardin** (brasserie) (ground floor) **M** a la carte approx. 100 ♁ - **Pizzeria** (ground floor) *(closed Saturday, Sunday and Bank Holidays)* **M** a la carte approx. 75 ♁ – ☐ 39 – **352 rm** 418/579, 8 apartments 690.

in the airport nr. 1 :

XXXX ✿ **Maxim's,** ✆ 862.16.16 – ▤. AE VISA
st. : M (lunch only) a la carte 285/375
Spec. Papillote de saumon à la julienne de légumes, Blanc de daurade aux endives et citron vert (season), Poulet de Bresse à la marjolaine.

XX **Grill Maxim's,** ✆ 862.24.16 – ▤. AE VISA
st. : M 175.

at the railway station :

Arcade, ✆ 862.49.49, Telex 212989 – ⛆wc ☎ Ⓟ – **354 rm.**

Rueil-Malmaison 92500 Hauts-de-Seine 101 ⑬ – pop. 64 545 – alt. 15 – ✪ 1.

See : Château de Bois-Préau★ – Church (organ-corse★) – Malmaison (château : museum★★).

Paris 15 – Argenteuil 12 – Nanterre 1,5 – St-Germain-en-Laye 7,5 – Versailles 11.

XXX ✿ **El Chiquito,** 126 av. Paul-Doumer ✆ 751.00.53, ☂, « Garden » – Ⓟ. VISA
closed August, Saturday, Sunday and Bank Holidays – **M** a la carte 185/235
Spec. Médaillon de lotte au vinaigre et miel, Filet de bar au beurre rouge, Filets de sole aux morilles.

XXX **Pavillon Joséphine,** 191 av. N. Bonaparte ✆ 751.01.62, ☂ – AE ⓓ VISA
closed 8 to 22 August, Sunday dinner and Monday dinner – **M** 120 b.i./200 b.i..

XX **Relais de St-Cucufa,** 114 r. Gén.-Miribel ✆ 749.79.05, ☂ – AE ⓓ VISA
closed 6 to 20 August, Sunday dinner and Monday dinner – **st. : M** a la carte 140/230.

at Nanterre N : 2 km – ✉ **92000** Nanterre :

XXX **Ile de France,** 83 av. Mar. Joffre ✆ 724.10.44, ☂ – Ⓟ. AE ⓓ VISA
closed August and Sunday – **M** a la carte 150/200.

Rungis 94150 Val-de-Marne 101 ㉖ – pop. 2 650 – alt. 80 - Main wholesale produce market for Paris – ✪ 1.

Paris 13 – Antony 5,5 – Corbeil-Essonnes 26 – Créteil 11 – Longjumeau 10.

Frantel Rungis Orly Ⓜ Access : from Paris, Highway A6 and take Orly Airport exi, from outside of Paris, A6 and Rungis-Orly exit, 20 av. Ch.-Lindbergh ✉ 94656 ✆ 687.36.36, Telex 260738, ⩤, ⛆ – |‡| ▤ TV ☎ ♿ ⇔ Ⓟ – 🛆 50 - 300. AE ⓓ E VISA
st. : rest. **La Rungisserie M** a la carte 160/225 – ☐ 39 – **206 rm** 390/520.

Holiday Inn Ⓜ Access : from Paris, Highway A6 and take Orly Airport exit, from outside of Paris, A6 and Rungis-Orly exit ✆ 687.26.66, Telex 204679, ⛆ – |‡| ▤ TV ☎ ♿ Ⓟ – 🛆 50 - 250. AE ⓓ E VISA
st. : M 65/115 – ☐ 40 – **170 rm** 391/449.

XXX **Le Charolais,** 13 r. N-Dame at Rungis Ville ✆ 686.16.42 – AE ⓓ VISA
closed 15 August-15 September, Saturday and Sunday – **M** a la carte 155/220.

XX Le Gd Pavillon, M.I.N. building 6 quai Lorient (opposite the Pavillon de la marée) ✆ 687.58.58.

Saclay 91400 Essonne 101 ㉓ – pop. 1 865 – alt. 157 – ✪ 6.

⛳18 St-Aubin ✆ 941.25.19, SW : 2,5 km.

Paris 21 – Arpajon 22 – Chartres 68 – Evry 28 – Rambouillet Versailles – 11 .

Novotel Ⓜ, near Christ-de-Saclay circle ✆ 941.81.40, Telex 691856, ☂, ⛆, ✗ – |‡| ▤ TV ☎ ♿ Ⓟ – 🛆 300. AE ⓓ E VISA
M (coffee shop only) a la carte approx. 95 ♁ – ☐ 30 – **134 rm** 277/293.

St-Cloud 92210 Hauts-de-Seine ⑩①① ⑭ – pop. 28 760 – alt. 60 – ✪ 1.

See : Park ★★ — Eglise Stella Matutina ★.

🇮🇸 🇮🇸 ✆ 701.01.85, Buzenval Park at Garches, W : 4 km.

Paris 12 — Nanterre 5 — Rueil-Malmaison 5,5 — St-Germain 16 — Versailles 10.

XXX ✿ **Le Florian** (Mᵐᵉ Carini), 14 r. Eglise ✆ 771.29.90 – AE VISA ⚙️
closed 10 to 31 August, Saturday lunch and Sunday – st. : **M** a la carte 190/250
Spec. Gâteau de lapereau, Ragoût de St-Jacques au Noilly, Mignon de veau "Irène".

St-Germain-en-Laye 78100 Yvelines ⑩①① ⑫ – pop. 40 829 – alt. 78 – ✪ 3.

See : Terrace★★ BY — English Garden★ BY — Château ★ BZ : Museum of National
Antiquities ★★ — Priory Museum ★ AZ — 🇮🇸 ; 🇮🇸 ✆ 451.75.90 by ④ : 3 km ; 🇮🇸 ; 🇮🇸 ; 🇮🇸 of
Fourqueux ✆ 451.41.47 by r. de Mareil AZ - 4 km — 🛈 1 bis r. République ✆ 451.05.12.

Paris 21 ② — Beauvais 73 ① — Chartres 81 ③ — Dreux 70 ③ — Mantes-la-J. 34 ④ — Versailles 13 ③.

ST-GERMAIN EN-LAYE

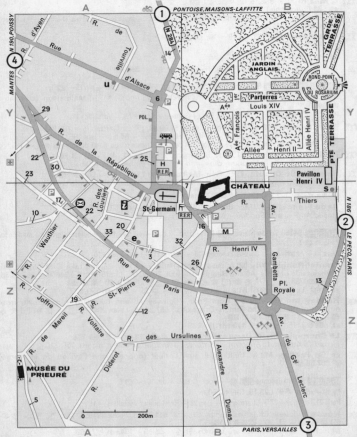

🏨 **Pavillon Henri IV** Ⓜ ⤶, 21 r. Thiers 🞵 451.62.62, Telex 695822, ≤ Paris and the River Seine, 🞹, 🞲 – 🛗 🕭 ♿ 🅿 – 🔬 200. ⒶⒺ ⓄⒹ 𝗩𝗜𝗦𝗔
st. : **M** a la carte 210/340 – **42 rm** ⊡ 500/1 400, 3 apartments.
BZ **s**

🏨 **Le Cèdre** ⤶, 7 r. Alsace 🞵 451.84.35, 🞲 – 🖃wc ⊛. 🞾
closed 1 February-10 March – st. : **M** 81/93 – **31 rm** ⊡ 115/245 – P 235/340.
AY **u**

XXX **Le 7 Rue des Coches**, 7 r. Coches 🞵 973.66.40 – ⒶⒺ ⓄⒹ Ⓔ 𝗩𝗜𝗦𝗔
closed 4 to 27 August, 3 to 11 March, Sunday dinner and Monday – st. : **M** a la carte 185/235.
AZ **e**

X **Petite Auberge**, 119 bis r. L.-Desoyer by r. Joffre - AZ - 🞵 451.03.99
closed 15 to 25 March, 1 to 30 July, Tuesday dinner and Wednesday – st. : **M** (booking essential) a la carte 90/130.

X **La Résidence**, 149 r. Pdt Roosevelt 🞵 451.03.07, 🞹 – 𝗩𝗜𝗦𝗔
closed Sunday dinner and Monday – st. : **M** a la carte 130/190.

to the NW by ① : 2,5 km on N 284 and route des Mares – ✉ 78100 St-Germain-en-Laye :

🏨 **La Forestière** Ⓜ ⤶, 1 av. Prés.-Kennedy 🞵 973.36.60, Telex 696055, 🞲 – 🛗 📺 ☎ 🅿
– 🔬 40. 𝗩𝗜𝗦𝗔
st. : **M** Rest. see Cazaudehore below – ⊡ 36 – **24 rm** 465/530, 6 apartments 635/690.

XXX ❀ **Cazaudehore**, 1 av. Prés.-Kennedy 🞵 451.93.80, 🞹, « Rustic decor, flower garden in woods » – 🅿. 𝗩𝗜𝗦𝗔
closed Monday except Bank Holidays – **M** a la carte 160/220
Spec. Foie gras de canard, Saumon rôti à l'aneth, Aiguillettes de canard à l'orange.

Vélizy-Villacoublay 78140 Yvelines 📖📖📖 ㉓ – pop. 23 886 – alt. 174 – ✿ 3.
Paris 18 – Antony 11 – Chartres 79 – Meudon 7,5 – Versailles 6,5.

🏨 **Ramada** Ⓜ, av. Europe, near commercial centre Vélizy II 🞵 946.96.98, Telex 696537, 🖾
– 🛗 🍽 📺 ☎ 🅿 – 🔬 300. ⒶⒺ ⓄⒹ 𝗩𝗜𝗦𝗔
st. : **M** 150/179 ⅛ – ⊡ 44 – **183 rm** 460/575.

Versailles Ⓟ 78000 Yvelines 📖📖📖 ㉒ – pop. 95 240 – alt. 132 – ✿ 3.
See : Château★★★ Y – Gardens★★★ fountain display★★★ (grandes eaux) and illuminated night performances★★★ (grandes fêtes de nuit) in summer – Grand Canal★★ – The Trianons★★ – Lambinet Museum★ Y M.
📗📗📗 Racing Club France 🞵 950.59.41 by ③ : 2,5 km.
🖪 7 r. Réservoirs 🞵 950.36.22.
Paris 22 ① – Beauvais 92 ⑦ – Dreux 62 ⑥ – Évreux 85 ⑦ – Melun 59 ③ – Orléans 121 ③.

Plan on next page

🏨 **Trianon Palace** ⤶, 1 bd Reine 🞵 950.34.12, Telex 698863, 🞹, park – 🛗 📺 ☎ ♿ 🅿 –
🔬 80. ⒶⒺ ⓄⒹ Ⓔ 𝗩𝗜𝗦𝗔. 🞾 rest
st. : **M** 145/200 – ⊡ 45 – **120 rm** 400/770, 8 apartments – P 563/691.
X **r**

🏨 **Mercure** Ⓜ without rest, r. Marly-le-Roi at the Chesnay, across from Parly 2 Shopping mall ✉ 78150 Le Chesnay 🞵 955.11.41, Telex 695205 – 🛗 📺 🖃wc ☎ 🚗 🅿. ⒶⒺ ⓄⒹ Ⓔ
𝗩𝗜𝗦𝗔
st. : ⊡ 25 – **78 rm** 302/327.

🏨 **Bellevue** Ⓜ without rest, 12 av. Sceaux 🞵 950.13.41, Telex 695613 – 🛗 📺 🖃wc 🛏 ☎.
ⒶⒺ ⓄⒹ Ⓔ 𝗩𝗜𝗦𝗔
st. : ⊡ 19 – **24 rm** 160/240.
Z **a**

🏨 **Le Versailles** without rest, r. Ste-Anne (Petite Place) 🞵 950.64.65 – 🛗 📺 🖃wc ⊛
🚗. ⒶⒺ 𝗩𝗜𝗦𝗔
st. : ⊡ 16 – **48 rm** 211/286.
Y **m**

XXXX ❀❀ **Trois Marches** (Vié), 3 r. Colbert 🞵 950.13.21, 🞹, « Elegant 18C hotel » – 🍽. ⒶⒺ
ⓄⒹ Ⓔ 𝗩𝗜𝗦𝗔
closed Sunday and Monday – **M** a la carte 240/310
Spec. Flan chaud de foie gras aux huîtres et écrevisses, Gibier (season), Gâteau au chocolat et au café.
Y **u**

XXX **Rescatore**, 27 av. St-Cloud 🞵 950.23.60 – ⒶⒺ 𝗩𝗜𝗦𝗔
closed Saturday lunch and Sunday – **M** a la carte 180/240.
Y **s**

XXX **Boule d'Or**, 25 r. Mar.-Foch 🞵 950.22.97 – ⒶⒺ ⓄⒹ 𝗩𝗜𝗦𝗔
closed Sunday dinner and Monday – **M** a la carte 145/215.
Y **a**

Viry-Châtillon 91170 Essonne 📖📖📖 ㊱ – pop. 30 290 – alt. 36 – ✿ 6.
Paris 26 – Corbeil-Essonnes 11 – Évry 8,5 – Longjumeau 8,5 – Versailles 29.

XX ❀ **La Dariole de Viry** (Richard), 21 r. Pasteur 🞵 944.22.40 – 🍽. ⒶⒺ 𝗩𝗜𝗦𝗔
closed 1 to 22 September, Saturday lunch, Sunday and Bank Holidays – st. : **M** a la carte 165/230
Spec. Blinis aux escargots de Bourgogne, Rouelles de rognon de veau à la crème d'échalotes, Coupe "Béatrice".

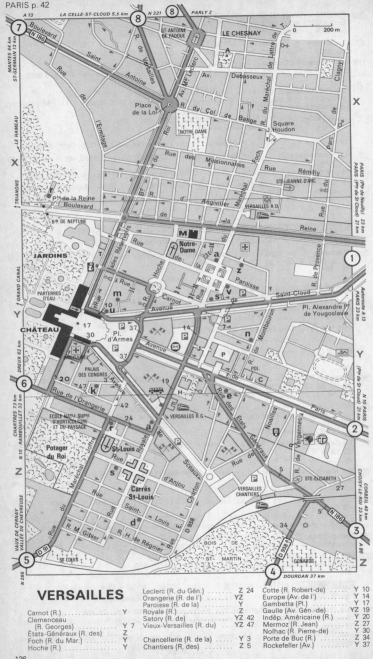

VERSAILLES

and beyond...

Fère-en-Tardenois 02130 Aisne 🗧🗧 ⑭⑮ – pop. 3 295 – alt. 125 – ✪ 23.
See : Château de Fère★ : Monumental bridge★★ N: 3 km.
Paris 110 – Château-Thierry 26 – Laon 54 – Reims 45 – Soissons 26.

to the N : 3 km by D 967 – ✉ 02130 Fère-en-Tardenois :

🏨 ✿✿ **Host. du Château** 🗧 by forester road, ✆ 82.21.13, Telex 145526, ≼, « Attractive
16C mansion, park », 🗧 – 📺 ☎ 🕭 🅿 – 🕭 30. 🅰🅴 🅴 🆅🆂🅰 . 🗧 rest
closed 1 January-1 March – **st.** : **M** (booking essential) 220/330 and a la carte – 🖙 38 –
13 rm 350/680, 8 apartments 700/900
Spec. Foie gras chaud aux bigorneaux, Rissoles de turbot au foie gras et langoustines, Farandole des
desserts. **Wines** Crémant, Bouzy.

La Ferté-sous-Jouarre 77260 S.-et-M. 🗧🗧 ⑬, 🄸🄾🄶 ㉔ – pop. 7 020 – alt. 62 – ✪ 6.
See : Jouarre : crypt★ of the abbey (S : 3 km).
Paris 66 – Melun 63 – Reims 82 – Troyes 117.

🗴🗴🗴🗴 ✿✿ **Auberge de Condé** (Tingaud), 1 av. Montmirail ✆ 022.00.07 – 🅿. 🅰🅴 🅾 🅴 🆅🆂🅰
closed 11 to 27 February, Monday dinner and Tuesday – **M** (booking essential on Sunday)
200/270 and a la carte
Spec. Mousseline d'écrevisses en chartreuse, Filet de bar sauce ciboulette, Blanc de volaille aux deux
sauces.

Rheims ◁▷ 51100 Marne 🗧🗧 ⑥⑯ – pop. 181 985 – alt. 83 – ✪ 26.
See : Cathédral★★★ : tapestries★★ – St-Remi Basilica★★ : interior★★★ – Palais du
Tau★★ : treasure★★ – Champagne cellars★ – Place Royale★ – Porte Mars★ – Hôtel
de la Salle★ – Foujita Chapel★ – Hôtel le Vergeur Museum★ – St-Denis Museum★.
Envir. : Fort de la Pompelle : German helmets ★ 9 km to the SE by N 44.
🏌 ✆ 03.60.14 at Gueux to the NW by N 44 : 9,5 km.
✈ ✆ 88.50.50.
🛈 and Accueil de France (Information facilities and hotel reservations - not more than 5 days in
advance) 1 r. Jadart ✆ 47.04.60, Telex 830631 A.C. 7 bd Lundy ✆ 47.34.76.
Paris 142 – Bruxelles 214 – Châlons-sur-Marne 45 – Lille 205 – Luxembourg 232.

🏨 ✿✿✿ **Boyer "Les Crayères"** 🗧, 64 bd Vasnier ✆ 82.80.80, Telex 830959, ≼, 🗧,
« Elegant mansion in park », 🗧, – 🖛 🅿. 🅰🅴 🅾 🅴 🆅🆂🅰
closed 23 December-12 January – **M** (closed Tuesday lunch and Monday) (booking
essential) a la carte 230/290 – 🖙 50 – **16 rm** 630/950
Spec. Soufflé de St-Pierre sauce coraline, Grenadin de veau au homard, Délices de Marjorie. **Wines** Tauxieres,
Vertus.

Vézelay 89450 Yonne 🗧🗧 ⑮ – pop. 582 – alt. 302 – Pilgrimage (22 July) – ✪ 86.
See : Ste-Madeleine Basilica★★★ : tower ❄★.
Envir. : Site★ of Pierre-Perthuis SE : 6 km.
🛈 r. St-Pierre (season) ✆ 33.23.69.
Paris 225 – Auxerre 51 – Avallon 15 – Château-Chinon 60 – Clamecy 23.

at St-Père SE : 3 km by D 957 – alt. 148 – ✉ 89450 Vézelay :
See : Church of N.-Dame★.

🏨 ✿✿✿ **Espérance** (Meneau), ✆ 33.20.45, Telex 800005, ≼, « country garden » – 📺 🅿.
🅰🅴 🅾 🆅🆂🅰
closed early January to early February – **M** (closed Wednesday lunch and Tuesday)
(booking essential) 180 (lunch only)/350 and a la carte – 🖙 50 – **19 rm** 400/700
Spec. Ambroisie de volaille au foie gras, Salmis de pigeon à la "Conti", Desserts. **Wines** Chablis, Irancy.

BORDEAUX

■ BORDEAUX ■ ⓟ 33000 Gironde **☷** ⑨ – pop. 211 197 – Greater Bordeaux 617 705 – alt. 5 – ✿ 56.

See : Grand Théâtre★★ CDVX – Cathedral★ and Pey Berland Belfry★ CX **E** – Place de la Bourse★ DX – St-Michel Basilica★ DY **F** – Place du Parlement★ DX **65** – Façade★ of Ste-Croix Church DY **K** – Façade★ of the church of N.-Dame CX **D** – Fine Arts Museum★★ (Musée des Beaux Arts) CX **M1** – The mint★ of Pessac (Établissement monétaire de Pessac).

⌖₈ Golf Bordelais ♂ 28.56.04, to the NW by D 109 : 4 km ; ⌖₈ de Bordeaux ♂ 50.92.72, to the N by D2 : 10 km ; ⌖₉⌖₅ de Cameyrac ♂ 30.96.79, to the NE by N 89 : 18 km.

✈ of Bordeaux-Mérignac : ♂ 34.32.32 to the W : 11 km.

🚈 ♂ 92.50.50.

ℤ and Accueil de France, (Information, exchange facilities and hotel reservations - not more than 5 days in advance) 12 cours 30 - juillet ♂ 44.28.41. Telex 570362 - A.C. 8 pl. Quinconces ♂ 44.22.92 – Bordeaux wine Exhibition (Maison du vin de Bordeaux), 1 cours 30-juillet (Information, wine-tasting - closed Saturday afternoon and Sunday) – ♂ 52.82.82 CV **Z**.

Paris 579 – Lyon 545 – Nantes 325 – Strasbourg 1 060 – Toulouse 244.

Plan on preceding pages

🏨 **Frantel** Ⓜ, 5 r. R-Lateulade ♂ 90.92.37, Telex 540565 – 🛗 ▤ 📺 ☎ ♿ – 🛄 350. 🎫 ⓞ **Ε** **VISA**. ⅙ rest BX **w**
st. : rest. **Le Mériadeck M** a la carte 130/220 ♗ – ⌑ 39 – **196 rm** 385/495.

🏨 **Gd H. and Café de Bordeaux** without rest, 2 pl Comédie ♂ 90.93.44, Telex 541658 – 🛗 ▤ rm 📺 ☎ – 🛄 30-50. 🎫 ⓞ **Ε** **VISA** CVX **b**
st. : ⌑ 25 – **95 rm** 290/393, 3 apartments 687.

🏨 **Normandie** without rest, 7 cours 30-Juillet ♂ 52.16.80, Telex 570481 – 🛗 📺 ☎. 🎫 ⓞ **Ε** **VISA** CV **z**
st. : ⌑ 25 – **100 rm** 160/300.

🏨 **Majestic** without rest, 2 r. Condé ♂ 52.60.44 – 🛗 📺 ☎ ⇦. **VISA** DV **b**
st. : ⌑ 22 – **50 rm** 183/280.

🏨 **Terminus**, at St-Jean Railway station ✉ 33800 ♂ 92.71.58, Telex 540264 – 🛗 📺 ☎ ⓟ – 🛄 60. 🎫 ⓞ **Ε** **VISA**
M 85 bi/120 ♗ – ⌑ 28 – **80 rm** 199/344 – P 495/570.

🏨 **Royal Médoc** Ⓜ without rest, 3 r. Sèze ♂ 81.72.42, Telex 571042 – 🛗 ⇔wc �🚿wc ☎. **Ε** **VISA**. ⅙ CV **u**
st. : ⌑ 25 – **45 rm** 150/250.

🏨 **Tour Intendance** Ⓜ without rest, 16 r. Vieille Tour ♂ 81.46.27 – 🛗 ⇔wc �🚿wc ☎. 🎫 ⓞ **VISA** CX **t**
closed 26 July-26 August – st. : ⌑ 20 – **20 rm** 135/225.

🏨 **Sèze** without rest, 23 allées Tourny ♂ 52.65.54 – 🛗 ⇔wc ☎. 🎫 ⓞ **VISA** CV **u**
st. : ⌑ 24 – **25 rm** 100/255.

🏨 **Français** without rest, 12 r. Temple ♂ 48.10.35, Telex 550587 – 🛗 ⇔wc �🚿wc ☎. 🎫 ⓞ **VISA** CX **u**
st. : ⌑ 20 – **36 rm** 132/250.

🏠 **Bayonne** without rest, 4 r. Martignac ♂ 48.00.88 – 🛗 ⇔wc �🚿wc ☎. 🎫 CX **p**
st. : ⌑ 20 – **37 rm** 105/210.

🏠 **Modern'H** ⌂ without rest, 21 r. P.-Loti ✉ 33800 ♂ 91.66.11, 🚗 – �🚿wc. ⅙
st. : ⌑ 17 – **16 rm** 103/152.

XXXX ✿ **Dubern**, 42 allées Tourny ♂ 48.03.44 – 🎫 ⓞ **Ε** **VISA** CV **s**
closed Saturday lunch, Sunday and Bank Holidays – **M** a la carte 200/250
Spec. Écrevisses à la bordelaise, Pigeon en bécasse, Magret et foie gras frais. Wines Quinsac, Bordeaux blanc.

XXX ✿ **Le Rouzic** (Gautier), 34 Cours du Chapeau rouge ♂ 44.39.11 – 🎫 ⓞ **VISA** DX **b**
closed Saturday lunch and Sunday lunch – st. : **M** 160/260
Spec. Ravioles d'huîtres au curry, Queues de langoustines en feuilleté aux morilles et ris d'agneau, Râble de lapereau au romarin. Wines Médoc, Premières côtes de Bordeaux.

XXX ✿ **Clavel** (Garcia), 44 r. Ch.-Domercq ✉ 33800 ♂ 92.91.52 – 🎫 ⓞ **VISA**. ⅙
closed 7 to 30 July, February Holidays, Sunday and Monday – st. : **M** 220/250
Spec. Gratin d'huîtres au foie gras, Gaspacho de homard (from 1 June to 15 September), Lapereau à la royale.

XXX ✿ **Christian Clément**, 58 r. Pas St-Georges ♂ 81.01.39 DX **k**
closed 24 August-2 September, 21 to 26 December, Saturday lunch and Sunday – st. : **M** (booking essential) a la carte 190/260
Spec. Huîtres tièdes au sabayon de citron vert, Paupiettes de saumon frais, Pigeon au caramel d'épices. Wines Médoc, St-Estèphe.

XXX ✿ **La Chamade** (Carrere), 20 r. Piliers de Tutelle ♂ 48.13.74 – 🎫 DX **d**
closed Sunday lunch from 14 July to 15 August – st. : **M** 125/185 a la carte dinner
Spec. Salade "Chamade", Panaché de poissons de mer, Pavé de filet de boeuf poëlé.

XXX ✿ **Ramet**, 7 pl. J. Jaurès ♂ 44.12.51. **VISA** DV **u**
closed Easter, 12 to 25 August, February Holidays, Saturday and Sunday – st. : **M** a la carte 170/250
Spec. Feuilleté d'huîtres tièdes, Jambonnette de volaille, Ragoût de St-Jacques (November to March). Wines Podensac, Haut-Médoc.

XX **Le Vieux Bordeaux**, 27 r. Buhan ♂ 52.94.36 – 🎫 ⓞ **VISA**. ⅙ DY **a**
closed August, February Holidays, Saturday lunch and Sunday – st. : **M** 89/170.

XX **Le Buhan,** 28 r. Buhan 🖉 52.80.86 – 🖭 ⑩, ⬥   DY x
closed Saturday lunch and Sunday – **st. : M** 80/190.

XX **La Jabotière,** 86 r. Bègles ⬚ 33800 🖉 91.69.43 – 🖭 ⑩ 𝗩𝗜𝗦𝗔
closed August, Saturday lunch and Sunday – **st. : M** 90/140.

X **Tupina,** 6 r. Porte de la Monnaie 🖉 91.56.37 – 𝗩𝗜𝗦𝗔   DY q
closed Sunday – **M** a la carte 90/140.

X **l'Alhambra,** 111 bis r. Judaïque 🖉 96.06.91 – ⬥   BX e
closed 14 July-15 August, Saturday lunch, Sunday and Bank Holidays – **st. : M** a la carte 95/150.

X **Chez le Chef,** 57 r. Huguerie 🖉 81.67.07, ⌂, 🖭 ⑩ 𝗩𝗜𝗦𝗔   CV a
closed 1 to 15 October, 1 to 15 February, Sunday dinner and Monday – **st. : M** 55/160.

at Parc des Expositions : North of the town – ⬚ 33300 Bordeaux :

🏨 **Sofitel** Ⓜ, 🖉 50.90.14, Telex 540097, ⌂, ⌂, ⬥ – 🛗 ▤ 📺 ☎ & 🅿 – 🔏 120. 🖭 ⑩ E 𝗩𝗜𝗦𝗔
rest. **La Pinasse M** a la carte 120/165 – ⬚ 39 – **95 rm** 375/490, 5 apartments 800.

🏨 **Sofitel Aquitania** Ⓜ, 🖉 50.83.80, Telex 570557, ≤, ⌂ – 🛗 ▤ 📺 ☎ & 🅿 – 🔏 25-600.
🖭 ⑩ E 𝗩𝗜𝗦𝗔
rest. **Les Acanthes** *(closed August and Sunday)* **M** a la carte 120/170 – **le Pub M** a la carte approx. 90 ⅃ – ⬚ 39 – **204 rm** 345/480, 8 apartments 620/800.

🏨 **Novotel-Bordeaux le Lac** Ⓜ, 🖉 50.99.70, Telex 570274, ⌂, ⌂ – 🛗 ▤ 📺 ☎ & 🅿 –
🔏 350. 🖭 ⑩ E 𝗩𝗜𝗦𝗔
M a la carte approx. 110 ⅃ – ⬚ 29 – **173 rm** 255/279.

🏨 **Mercure** Ⓜ, 🖉 50.90.30, Telex 540077 – 🛗 ▤ 📺 ⌂wc ☎ & 🅿 – 🔏 250. 🖭 ⑩ E 𝗩𝗜𝗦𝗔
M a la carte approx. 100 ⅃ – ⬚ 27 – **108 rm** 291/346.

at Bouliac – ⬚ 33270 Floirac :

XXX ⊛⊛ **Le St-James** (Amat), pl. C. Hosteins, near church 🖉 20.52.19, ≤, ⌂, ⌲ – 🖭 ⑩
𝗩𝗜𝗦𝗔.
closed 15 January-28 February – **M** 100/190 and a la carte
Spec. Terrine d'aubergines au cumin, Langoustines aux ravioli d'huîtres, Pigeon rôti safrané. **Wines** Graves, 1ᵉᵉˢ Côtes de Bordeaux.

to the S :

at Talence : 6 km – ⬚ 33400 Talence :

🏛 **Guyenne** (Hotel School) Ⓜ, av. F.-Rabelais 🖉 80.75.08 – 🛗 📺 ⌂wc ☎ 🅿. ⬥
closed 29 March-15 April and 15 June-29 September – **st. : M** *(closed Saturday dinner and Sunday)* (booking essential) 62/91 – ⬚ 19,50 – **30 rm** 130/182, 3 apartments 284.

To the W :

at l'Alouette : 9 km – ⬚ 33600 Pessac :

🏨 ⊛ **La Réserve** Ⓜ ⬥, av. Bourgailh 🖉 07.13.28, Telex 560585, ⬥, « park » – 📺 🅿 – 🔏 70. 🖭 ⑩ E 𝗩𝗜𝗦𝗔
29 March-4 November – **M** 130/220 – ⬚ 28 – **20 rm** 175/445
Spec. Mousse de persil, Paupiettes de sole, Magret aux framboises. **Wines** Graves, Médoc.

at the airport : 11 km by D 106E – ⬚ 33700 Mérignac :

🏨 **Novotel-Mérignac** Ⓜ, 🖉 34.10.25, Telex 540320, ⌂, ⌂, ⌲ – ▤ 📺 ☎ & 🅿 – 🔏 25-200. 🖭 ⑩ E 𝗩𝗜𝗦𝗔
M (coffee shop only) a la carte approx. 95 ⅃ – ⬚ 29 – **100 rm** 276/297.

▭ **Eugénie-les-Bains** 40 Landes 🎱🎲 ① – pop. 408 – alt. 90 – Spa (8 March-31 Oct.) – ⬚ 40320 Geaune – ✪ 58.

Bordeaux 152.

🏨 ⊛⊛⊛ **Les Prés d'Eugénie** (Guérard) Ⓜ ⬥, 🖉 51.19.01, Telex 540470, « 19C mansion, elegant decor, park », ⌂, ⬥ – 🛗 📺 ☎ & 🅿. 🖭. ⬥
28 March-4 November – **M** (low-calorie menu for residents only) 125/150 – **rest. Michel Guérard M** (booking essential) 270/320 and a la carte – ⬚ 48 – **28 rm** 580/670, 7 apartments 810/880
Spec. Raviole de truffe, Caneton rôti à l'ail et au citron, Le dessert du roi. **Wines** Blanc de pays, Tursan.

▭ **Margaux** 33460 Gironde 🎱🎲 ⑧ – pop. 1 371 – ✪ 56.

Bordeaux 22.

XXX ⊛⊛ **Relais de Margaux** ⬥ with rm, 🖉 88.38.30, parc, ⌂, ⬥ – 🅿. 🖭 ⑩ E 𝗩𝗜𝗦𝗔
M 130/380 – ⬚ 40 – **18 rm** 500/800, 3 apartments
Spec. Homard à la vapeur et sa mousseline d'estragon, Gâteau chaud d'huîtres et de caviar, Foie de canard. **Wines** Médoc.

CANNES 06400 Alpes-Mar. 84 ⑨. 195 ㉟⑯ — pop. 72 787 — Casinos : Les Fleurs BZ, Palm Beach X, Municipal BZ — ⬡ 93.

See : Boulevard de la Croisette★★ BCZ — Pointe de la Croisette★ X — ≼★ from the Mount Chevalier Tower AZ **V** — La Castre Museum★ (Musée de la Castre) AZ **M** — Super Cannes Observatory ✳★★★ E : 4 km, VX **B** — Tour into the Hills★ (Chemin des Collines) NE : 4 km V — The Croix des Gardes V **E** ≼★ **W** : 5 km then 15 mn.

⛳ Country-Club of Cannes-Mougins 🕿 75.79.13 by ⑤ : 9 km ; ⛳ ⛳ Golf Club of Cannes-Mandelieu 🕿 49.55.39 by ② : 6,5 km ; ⛳ Biot 🕿 65.08.48 by ⑤ : 14 km ; ⛳ Valbonne 🕿 42.00.08 by ⑤ : 15 km.

🅱 and Accueil de France (Information, exchange facilities and hotel reservations - not more than 5 days in advance), Railway Station S.N.C.F. 🕿 99.19.77, Télex 470795 and Palais des Festivals et des Congrès, La Croisette 🕿 39.24.53, Télex 470749 - A.C. 21 quai St-Pierre 🕿 39.38.94.

Paris 901 ③ — Aix-en-Provence 146 ③ — Grenoble 316 ⑤ — Marseille 158 ③ — Nice 32 ⑤ — Toulon 123 ③.

CANNES - LE CANNET - VALLAURIS

André (R. du Cdt)	CZ	Dollfus (R. Jean)	AZ 22	Observatoire (Bd de l')	X 54
Antibes (R. d')	BCZ	Ferrare (Bd de la)	BYZ 23	Oxford (Bd d')	V 55
Belges (R. des)	BZ 5	Fiesole (Av.)	V 24	Pastour (R. L.)	AZ 56
Chabaud (R.)	CZ 15	Fournas (Av. de)	V 26	Perier (Bd du)	V 57
Croisette (Bd de la)	BCZ	Gambetta (Bd)	V 27	Perrissol (R. L.)	AZ 59
Félix-Faure (R.)	ABZ	Gaulle (Pl. du Gén.-de)	BZ 28	Pins (Bd des)	X 60
Foch (R. du Mar.)	BZ 25	Grasse (av. de)	V 29	République	
Hôtel-de-Ville (Pl. de l')	AZ 33	Haddad-Simon (R. J.)	CY 30	(Bd de la)	X 62
Joffre (R. du Mar.)	BZ 35	Hôpital (Av. de l')	V 32	Roi-Albert-1er	
Riouffe (R. du Mar.)	BZ 64	Isnard (Pl. Paul)	V 34	(Av. du)	DZ 65
		Lacour (Bd A.)	V 36	Rouguière (R.)	BZ 66
Alexandre-III (Bd)	X 2	Lattre-de-Tassigny		Roumier (Bd M.)	V 67
Amouretti (R. F.)	CZ 3	(Av. J.-de)	ABY 37	St-Charles (⊕)	V 69
Beau-Soleil (Bd)	V 4	Leader (Bd)	VX 38	St-Joseph (⊕)	AY 70
Bellevue (Pl.)	V 6	Lérins (Av. de)	X 39	St-Nicolas (Av.)	BY 71
Bréguières (Ch. des)	V 7	Macé (R.)	BZ 41	St-Sauveur (R.)	V 72
Broussailles (Av. des)	V 8	Monod (Bd Jacques)	V 42	Ste-Philomène (⊕)	V 73
Buttura (R.)	BZ 10	Montaigne (R.)	BY 43	Sardou (R. L.)	V 74
Carnot (Bd)	V 13	Mont-Chevalier (R. du)	AZ 44	Serbes (R. des)	BZ 75
Castre (Pl. de la)	AZ 14	Montfleury (Bd)	X 45	Souvenir (⊕)	CY 76
Christ-Roi (⊕)	V 16	Myron-T.-Herrik (Bd)	V 46	Tapis-Vert (Av. du)	V 77
Clemenceau (Av. G.)	V 17	N.-D.-de-		Tuby (Bd Victor)	AZ 78
Coteaux (Av. des)	V 18	Bon-Voyage (⊕)	BZ 49	Vallauris (Av. de)	V 79
Dr-Pierre-		N.-D.-d'Espérance (⊕)	AZ 50	Victor-Hugo (R.)	V 80
Gazagnaire (R.)	AZ 20	N.-D.-des-Pins (⊕)	DZ 52	Vidal (R. du Cdt)	CZ 82

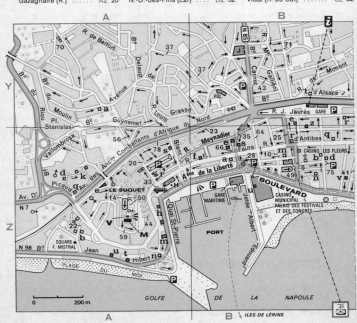

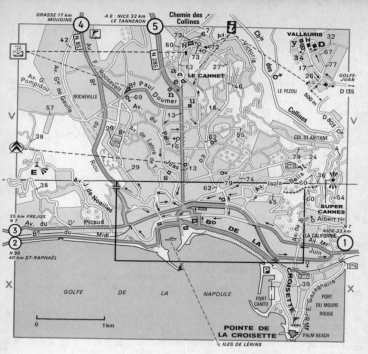

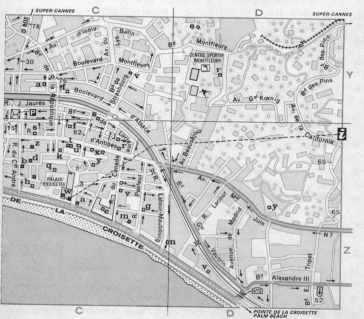

🏨🏨🏨 **Carlton**, 58 bd Croisette ℰ 68.91.68, Telex 470720, ≤, ⩙ – 🛗 ☰ 📺 ☎ ⅙ ⛱ – 🅰
80. 🆎 ⓞ Ε 𝘝𝘐𝘚𝘈, ⅋ rest
CZ **e**
   M *(closed November)* 250 – **Grill** a la carte approx. 220 – ⊑ 50 – **295 rm** 680/1 425, 30 apartments – P 1 007/1 931.

🏨🏨🏨 **Majestic** 🅼, bd Croisette ℰ 68.91.00, Telex 470787, ≤, 🎇, ⤳, ⩙, ⛱ – 🛗 ☰ 📺 ☎
   ⛱ – 🅰 30-120. 🆎 ⓞ Ε 𝘝𝘐𝘚𝘈, ⅋ rest
BZ **n**
   closed 8 November-15 December – **M** (dinner only in summer) a la carte 185/240 – **Grill** *(closed November-mid December)* **M** (lunch only) a la carte approx. 220 – ⊑ 45 – **248 rm** 950/1 450, 12 apartments.

🏨🏨🏨 **Martinez-Concorde**, 73 bd Croisette ℰ 68.91.91, Telex 470708, ≤, 🎇, ⤳, ⩙, ⛱ – 🛗
   ☰ rm 📺 ☎ ⅙ ℗ – 🅰 40-700
CDZ **n**
   421 rm.

🏨🏨🏨 **Gray d'Albion** 🅼, 38 r. Serbes ℰ 48.54.54, Telex 470744, 🎇, ⩙ – 🛗 ☰ 📺 ☎ – 🅰
   30-200. 🆎 ⓞ Ε 𝘝𝘐𝘚𝘈
BZ **d**
   st. : M rest see **Royal Gray** below - **Les 4 Saisons M** a la carte approx. 160 – ⊑ 50 –
   173 rm 900/1 225, 14 apartments.

🏨🏨🏨 **Sofitel Méditerranée** 🅼, 2 bd J.-Hibert ℰ 99.22.75, Telex 470728, ≤, « Roof-top swimming pool and terrace ≤ bay of Cannes » – 🛗 ☰ 📺 ☎ ⛱ – 🅰 150. 🆎 ⓞ Ε 𝘝𝘐𝘚𝘈,
   ⅋ rest
AZ **n**
   closed 20 November-20 December – **st. : M** a la carte 130/200 – ⊑ 39 – **145 rm** 390/860,
   5 apartments.

🏨🏨🏨 **Montfleury** 🅼 ⌔, 25 av. Beauséjour ℰ 68.91.50, Telex 470039, ≤, 🎇, « Garden », ⤳
   – 🛗 ☰ 📺 ⛱ ℗ – 🅰 400. 🆎 ⓞ Ε 𝘝𝘐𝘚𝘈
DY **r**
   closed 25 November-3 January – **st. : M** 175 – ⊑ 50 – **229 rm** 670/1 140, 6 apartments.

🏨🏨🏨 **Gd Hôtel** ⌔, 45 bd Croisette ℰ 38.15.45, Telex 470727, ≤, ⩙ – 🛗 ☰ 📺 ☎ ⅙ ℗ 🆎
   M rest see **Lamour** below – ⊑ 50 – **74 rm** 600/1 000 – P 725/1 230.
CZ **q**

🏨🏨🏨 **Frantel Beach** 🅼 without rest, 13 r. Canada ℰ 38.22.32, Telex 470034, ⤳ – 🛗 ☰ 📺 ☎
   ⅙ ⛱ – 🅰 30-60. 🆎 ⓞ Ε 𝘝𝘐𝘚𝘈
CZ **v**
   closed 1 November-25 January – **st. :** ⊑ 45 – **86 rm** 560/825, 9 apartments 990.

🏨🏨 **Splendid** without rest, 4 r. F.-Faure ℰ 99.53.11, Telex 470990, ≤ – 🛗 kitchenette 📺 ☎.
   🆎 ⓞ Ε 𝘝𝘐𝘚𝘈
BZ **a**
   st. : 63 rm ⊑ 250/550.

🏨🏨 **Victoria** 🅼 without rest, 122 r. d'Antibes ℰ 99.36.36, Telex 470817, ⤳ – 🛗 ☰ 📺 ☎
   ⛱ 🆎 ⓞ Ε 𝘝𝘐𝘚𝘈
CZ **x**
   closed November-December – **st. : 25 rm** ⊑ 355/600.

🏨🏨 **Fouquet's** 🅼 without rest, 2 Rd-Pt Duboys-d'Angers ℰ 38.75.81 – ☰ 📺 ⛱ 🆎 Ε
   closed 20 October-19 December – **st. : 10 rm** ⊑ 540/850.
CZ **y**

🏨🏨 **Solhotel and rest. Le Trident** 🅼, 61 av. Dr Picaud by ③ ✉ 06150 Cannes La Bocca ℰ
   47.63.00, Telex 970956, 🎇, ⤳, ⛱ – 🛗 kitchenette ☰ 📺 ☎ ⛱ – 🅰 150. 🆎 ⓞ 𝘝𝘐𝘚𝘈
   closed 1 November-15 December – **st. : M** 94/120 – ⊑ 20 – **101 rm** 325/470 – P 464/574.

🏨🏨 **Gonnet et de la Reine**, 42 bd Croisette ℰ 38.40.00, ≤ – 🛗 🆎 𝘝𝘐𝘚𝘈, ⅋
CZ **h**
   1 April-1 October – **st. : M** (residents only) – **50 rm** ⊑ 300/600, 4 apartments 900.

🏨🏨 **Paris** without rest, 34 bd d'Alsace ℰ 38.30.89, Telex 470995, ⤳, ⛱ – 🛗 ☰ ☎ – 🅰 40.
   ⓞ Ε 𝘝𝘐𝘚𝘈, ⅋
CY **a**
   closed 4 November-20 January – **st. :** ⊑ 20 – **48 rm** 368/416.

🏨🏨 **Beau Séjour** 🅼, 5 r. Fauvettes ℰ 39.63.00, Telex 470975, ⤳, ⛱ – 🛗 📺 ☎ ⛱ 🆎 ⓞ
   Ε 𝘝𝘐𝘚𝘈, ⅋ rest
AZ **d**
   closed 1 November-15 December – **st. : M** 85 – **46 rm** ⊑ 235/460 – P 387/550.

🏨🏨 **Century** 🅼 without rest, 133 r. d'Antibes ℰ 99.37.64, Telex 470090 – 🛗 📺 ☎ ⛱
   🆎 ⓞ 𝘝𝘐𝘚𝘈
CZ **r**
   closed 20 November-10 January – **st. :** ⊑ 24 – **35 rm** 340/400.

🏨🏨 **Abrial** 🅼 without rest, 24 bd Lorraine ℰ 38.78.82, Telex 470761 – 🛗 ☰ ⅙ ⛱ 🆎 ⓞ
   𝘝𝘐𝘚𝘈
CY **s**
   20 January-15 November – **st. : 48 rm** ⊑ 260/410.

🏨🏨 **Embassy and rest. As de Carreau**, 6 r. Bône ℰ 38.79.02, Telex 470081 – 🛗 ☰ 📺 ☎
   ⛱ 🆎 ⓞ Ε 𝘝𝘐𝘚𝘈
CZ **j**
   st. : M 85 – **60 rm** ⊑ 370/410 – P 300.

🏨🏨 **Canberra** without rest, 120 r. d'Antibes ℰ 38.20.70, Telex 470817 – 🛗 ☰ ☎ ℗ 🆎 ⓞ Ε
   𝘝𝘐𝘚𝘈
CZ **u**
   st. : 37 rm ⊑ 280/522.

🏨 **Licorn' H. and rest. Les Saisons** 🅼, 23 av. Fr.-Tonner by ③ ✉ 06150 Cannes-La-Bocca ℰ 47.18.46, Telex 470818 – 🛗 ☰ rest 📺 ⌁wc ▥wc ☎ ℗. 🆎 ⓞ Ε 𝘝𝘐𝘚𝘈
   closed November – **st. : M** 82/135 – **45 rm** ⊑ 255/400 – P 298/370.

🏨 **Ruc Hôtel** without rest, 15 bd Strasbourg ℰ 38.64.32 – 🛗 ☰ 📺 ⌁wc ☎. 🆎 Ε 𝘝𝘐𝘚𝘈
CY **v**
   closed 1 November to 24 December – **st. : 30 rm** ⊑ 240/390.

🏨 **La Madone** ⌔ without rest, 5 av. Justinia ℰ 43.57.87, « fine setting », ⤳, 🛗
   kitchenette 📺 ⌁wc ▥wc ☎ ℗. 🆎 ⓞ Ε 𝘝𝘐𝘚𝘈
DZ **y**
   st. : ⊑ 25 – **22 rm** 330/450.

🏨 **Acapulco** 🅼, 16 bd Alsace ℰ 99.16.16, Telex 470929, ⤳ – 🛗 ☰ 📺 ⌁wc ▥wc ☎ ⛱
   🆎 ⓞ Ε 𝘝𝘐𝘚𝘈, ⅋ rest
BY **t**
   st. : M *(closed 18 November-23 December)* 68/80 – **59 rm** ⊑ 350/468 – P 394/604.

Les Orangers, 1 r. des Orangers $\mathscr{C}$ 39.99.92, Telex 470873, $\leqslant$, 🛋, 🏊, 🌲 – 🛗 ⇌wc
🛁wc 🅿. 🎴 ⓸ 🅴 𝗩𝗜𝗦𝗔, 🧳 rest   AZ **k**
closed 1 November-20 December – **st.** : **M** 95 – **40 rm** ⇌ 250/395 – P 360.

Host. de L'Olivier without rest, 90 r. G.-Clemenceau $\mathscr{C}$ 39.53.28, 🏊, 🌲 – ⇌wc 🛁wc
☎ 🅿. 🎴 ⓸ 𝗩𝗜𝗦𝗔   AZ **k**
st. : **23 rm** ⇌ 200/380.

Provence, 9 r. Molière $\mathscr{C}$ 38.44.35, 🏡 – 🛗 ▤ rm 📺 ⇌wc 🛁wc 🎴 ⓸ 🅴 𝗩𝗜𝗦𝗔
🧳 rest   CZ **t**
st. : **M** *(closed 1 November-22 December and Sunday)* a la carte 105/130 – ⇌ 20 – **30 rm**
150/300.

Château de la Tour 🦢, 10 av. Font-de-Veyre by ③ ✉ 06150 Cannes-La-Bocca
$\mathscr{C}$ 47.32.23, Telex 470906, 🌲 – 🛗 ⇌wc 🛁wc 🅿 🅿. 🎴 ⓸. 🧳 rest
st. : **M** 86 – **42 rm** ⇌ 240/390 – P 350/420.

Univers Ⓜ, 2 r. Mar.-Foch $\mathscr{C}$ 39.59.19, Telex 470972 – 🛗 ▤ rm 📺 ⇌wc 🛁wc ☎. 🎴
⓸ 🅴 𝗩𝗜𝗦𝗔   BZ **r**
st. : **M** (6th floor) 65/75 – **68 rm** ⇌ 296/426 – P 307/363.

Palma without rest, 77 bd Croisette $\mathscr{C}$ 94.22.16, Telex 470826, $\leqslant$ – 🛗 ⇌wc 🛁wc 🅿 🅿.
🎴 ⓸ 🅴 𝗩𝗜𝗦𝗔   DZ **v**
52 rm ⇌ 230/520.

Toboso 🦢 without rest, 7 allée des Oliviers $\mathscr{C}$ 38.20.05, 🌲 – kitchenette 📺 ⇌wc ☎
🅿   DY **e**
st. : ⇌ 21 – **10 rm** 350.

El Puerto 🦢, 45 av. Petit-Juas $\mathscr{C}$ 68.39.75, 🌲 – ⇌wc 🛁wc 🅿 🅿. 🧳   V **s**
closed 1 October-15 December – **st.** : **M** *(closed Monday)* 90 – ⇌ 20 – **22 rm** 165/280 –
P 195/255.

Cheval Blanc without rest, 3 r. de-Maupassant $\mathscr{C}$ 39.88.60 – 📺 ⇌wc 🛁wc 🅿   AY **a**
st. : ⇌ 15,50 – **16 rm** 199/210.

Athénée without rest, 6 rue Lecerf $\mathscr{C}$ 38.69.54 – 📺 ⇌wc 🛁wc   CZ **f**
16 rm.

Wagram, 140 r. d'Antibes $\mathscr{C}$ 94.55.53, 🌲 – 🛗 ▤ rm ⇌wc 🛁wc 🅿. 🧳   CZ **x**
st. : **M** 75 – ⇌ 19 – **23 rm** 158/378 – P 327/457.

Roches Fleuries without rest, 92 r. G.-Clemenceau $\mathscr{C}$ 39.28.78, 🌲 – 🛗 ⇌wc 🛁wc 🅿
🅿. 🧳   AZ **q**
closed 15 November-27 December – **st.** : **24 rm** ⇌ 100/206.

Festival without rest, 3 r. Molière $\mathscr{C}$ 38.69.45 – kitchenette 🛁wc ☎   CZ **k**
closed 25 November-20 December – **st.** : ⇌ 15 – **17 rm** 130/300.

Campanile, Aérodrome de Cannes-Mandelieu by ③ : 6 km ✉ 06150 Cannes-La-Bocca
$\mathscr{C}$ 48.69.41, Telex 461570 – 📺 ⇌wc 🅿 🅿. 𝗩𝗜𝗦𝗔
st. : **M** 59 b.i./78 b.i. – 🍷 22 – **48 rm** 188.

🍴🍴🍴🍴 ✿✿ **Royal Gray** 2 r. des Etats-Unis, $\mathscr{C}$ 48.54.54, 🏡, « Tasteful, contemporary decor »
– ▤. 🎴 ⓸ 🅴 𝗩𝗜𝗦𝗔   BZ **d**
closed February, Sunday except July-August and Monday – **M** a la carte 230/300
Spec. Salade de St-Jacques tiède, Fricassée de homard aux mousserons, Gâteau chaud de noix à la crème.
Wines Flassans, Vidauban.

🍴🍴🍴🍴 Bistingo, Palais des Festivals $\mathscr{C}$ 38.12.11 – ▤   BZ **u**

🍴🍴🍴 **Félix,** 63 bd Croisette $\mathscr{C}$ 94.00.61, $\leqslant$, 🏡 – ▤. 🎴   CZ **m**
closed end October-25 December and Wednesday – **M** a la carte 160/220.

🍴🍴🍴 **Gaston-Gastounette,** 7 quai St-Pierre $\mathscr{C}$ 39.47.92, $\leqslant$, 🏡 – 🎴 ⓸ 𝗩𝗜𝗦𝗔   AZ **h**
closed 1 to 23 December and 3 to 20 January – **M** 155.

🍴🍴🍴 **Reine Pédauque,** 6 r. Mar.-Joffre $\mathscr{C}$ 39.40.91 – ▤. 𝗩𝗜𝗦𝗔   BZ **s**
closed 1 to 20 December and Monday – **M** (booking essential) 130/240.

🍴🍴🍴 **Poêle d'Or,** 23 r. États-Unis $\mathscr{C}$ 39.77.65 – ▤. 🎴 ⓸ 𝗩𝗜𝗦𝗔   BZ **v**
closed November and Monday – **st.** : **M** 120.

🍴🍴🍴 **Le Festival,** 52 bd Croisette $\mathscr{C}$ 38.04.81, 🏡 – ▤. 🎴 ⓸   CZ **a**
closed December – **M** a la carte 150/200.

🍴🍴🍴 **Rescator,** 7 r. Mar.-Joffre $\mathscr{C}$ 39.44.57 – ▤. 𝗩𝗜𝗦𝗔   BZ **e**
closed Monday out of season – **M** (dinner only in July and August) 160/350.

🍴🍴🍴 **Lamour,** 45 bd Croisette $\mathscr{C}$ 99.49.60, 🏡, 🍽 – 🅿. 🎴 𝗩𝗜𝗦𝗔   CZ **q**
M 130.

🍴🍴 **Blue Bar,** Former festival Centre $\mathscr{C}$ 39.03.04, 🏡 – ▤   CZ **w**
closed 27 June-6 July and Tuesday except July-August – **M** a la carte 125/170.

🍴🍴 **Le Croquant,** 18 bd J.-Hibert $\mathscr{C}$ 39.39.79, $\leqslant$ – ▤. 🎴 ⓸ 🅴 𝗩𝗜𝗦𝗔   AZ **u**
closed 1 to 15 February, Sunday dinner except from 15 June to 15 September and Monday
– **M** (from 15 September to 15 May: open Sunday lunch and weeknights) a la carte
140/180.

🍴🍴 **Caveau Provençal,** 45 r. Félix-Faure $\mathscr{C}$ 39.06.33, 🏡 – ▤. 🎴 ⓸ 𝗩𝗜𝗦𝗔   BZ **f**
M 75/160.

XX **Voile au Vent,** 17 quai St-Pierre ℰ 39.27.84, ≼, 🍴 — 🆎 ⓞ 𝗩𝗜𝗦𝗔   AZ **m**
closed 3 November-25 December and Thursday out of season — **M** a la carte 120/170.

XX **Monsieur Madeleine,** 12 bd Jean Hibert ℰ 39.72.22, ≼, 🍴 — 𝗩𝗜𝗦𝗔   AZ **t**
closed January, Wednesday dinner and Thursday except July-August — **st. : M** 125/160.

XX **Mère Besson,** 13 r. Frères-Pradignac ℰ 39.59.24, Provençal cuisine — 🆎 𝗩𝗜𝗦𝗔   CZ **d**
closed Sunday except Bank Holidays — **st. : M** a la carte 140 a 200.

X **L'Olivier,** 9 r. Rouguière ℰ 39.91.63 — 🆎 ⓞ E 𝗩𝗜𝗦𝗔   BZ **e**
closed 10 December-15 January and Monday — **st. : M** 65/100.

X **Le Monaco,** 15 r. 24-août ℰ 38.37.76   BY **e**
closed 1 November-10 December and Sunday — **st. : M** 60/80 🍷.

X **Aux Bons Enfants,** 80 r. Meynadier — 🍴   AZ **r**
closed April and 1 to 15 July, Wednesday dinner and Sunday — **st. : M** 60 🍷.

route de Pégomas : 8 km — ✉ 06150 Cannes-la-Bocca :

XXX **L'Oriental,** 286 av. M.-Jourdan ℰ 47.43.99, « Moorish décor », North African cuisine —
🆎 ⓞ
closed January, lunch from 15 June to 15 September, Sunday dinner and Monday from 15 september to 15 June — **st. : M** 185.

Antibes 06600 Alpes-Mar. 🟦🟦 ⑨. 🟥🟥🟥 ㉟㊵ — ⊛ 93.
Cannes 11.

on N 7 N : 4 km, quartier de la Brague — ✉ 06600 Antibes :

XXXXX ✿✿ **La Bonne Auberge** (Rostang), ℰ 33.36.65, Telex 470989, 🍴, « Provençal style dining room and flowered terrace » — ⓟ 🆎 𝗩𝗜𝗦𝗔
closed 10 November-15 December, 1 to 8 March and Monday except July, August — **M** 300/380 and a la carte
Spec. Safari de rougets et millefeuille de fenouil, Minute de loup grillé, Salade d'artichauts et de langoustines. **Wines** Palette, Côteaux d'aix.

Mougins 06250 Alpes-Mar. 🟦🟦 ⑨. 🟥🟥🟥 ㉔㊳ — pop. 10 197 — alt. 260 — ⊛ 93.
Cannes 7.

XXXX ✿✿ **Moulin de Mougins** (Vergé) 🛏 with rm, at Notre-Dame-de-Vie SE :2,5 km by D 3 ℰ 75.78.24, Telex 970732, ≼, 🍴, 🌳 — ▤ rest 📺 ☎🔲wc ☎ ⓟ 🆎 ⓞ 𝗩𝗜𝗦𝗔
closed 15 November-23 December and 15 February-25 March — **M** *(closed Thursday lunch and Monday)* 363 and à la carte — ⊠ 59 — **3 rm** 503/603
Spec. Poupeton de truffes, Noisettes d'agneau à la fleur de thym, Terrine de fruits. **Wines** Gassin, Rians.

La Napoule-Plage 06 Alpes-Mar. 🟦🟦 ⑧. 🟥🟥🟥 ㉔㊲ — ✉ 06210 Mandelieu-La-Napoule — ⊛ 93.
Cannes 8.

XXXX ✿✿ **L'Oasis** (Outhier), ℰ 49.95.52, « Shaded and flowered patio » — ▤
closed end October to 20 December, Monday dinner and Tuesday — **M** 320/340 and a la carte
Spec. Truffe surprise, St-Pierre au vin, Langoustine aux herbes thaï. **Wines** Cassis, Bandol.

LYONS ⓟ 69000 Rhône 🟦🟦 ⑪⑫ — pop. 418 476 Greater Lyons 1 173 797 — alt. 169 — ⊛ 7.

See : Site★★★ — Old Lyons★ (Vieux Lyon) BX : Jewry Street★ (rue Juiverie) 65, rue St-Jean★ 92, Hotel de Gadagne★ **M1** , Maison du Crible★ **D** — St-Jean★ : Chancel★★ — Basilica of N.-D.-de-Fourvière ❄★★, ≼★ BX — Capitals★ of the Basilica St-Martin d'Ainay BYZ — Lanterne tower★ of St-Paul Church BV — Virgin with Child★ in the St-Nizier Church CX — Park of the Tête d'Or★ : Rose-garden★ (roseraie) — Fountain★ of the Place des Terreaux CV — Traboules★ of Quartier Croix-Rousse — Arches of Chaponost★ - Montée de Garillan★ BX — Punch and Judy Show (Théâtre de Guignol) BX **N** — Museums : Textile★★★ CZ**M2**, Gallo-Roman Civilization★★ (claudian table★★★) BX **M3**, Fine-Arts★★ CV **M4**, — Decorative Arts★★ CZ **M5**, Printing and Banking★★ CX**M6** , Guimet of Natural history★ — Puppet★ BX**M1**, Historic★ : lapidary★ BX **M1**, Apothecary's Shop★ (Civil Hospitals) CY **M8**.

Envir. : Rochetaillée : Automobile Museum Henri Malartre★ : 12 km.

🔲🔲🔲 Villette d'Anthon ℰ 831.11.33 to the E : 21 km.

✈ of Lyon-Satolas ℰ 871.92.21 to the E : 27 km.

🚃 ℰ 892.50.50.

🅱 and Accueil de France (Information, exchange facilities, hotel reservations - not more than 5 days in advance), pl. Bellecour ℰ 842.25.75, Télex 330032 and Centre d'Echange de Perrache ℰ 842.22.07 - A.C. 7 r. Grolée ℰ 842.51.01.

Paris 460 — Bâle 387 — Bordeaux 545 — Genève 159 — Grenoble 104 — Marseille 315 — St-Étienne 63 — Strasbourg 480 — Torino 300 — Toulouse 534.

Plan on following pages

Hotels

Town Centre (Bellecour-Terreaux) :

Sofitel M, 20 quai Gailleton, ✉ 69002, ✆ 842.72.50, Telex 330225, ← – ⧉ ▤ TV ☎ ♿ 🚗 – 🏛 25 - 200. AE ⊕ E VISA. ✻ rest CY **k**
st. : rest. **Les Trois Dômes** (8th floor) **M** a la carte 195/255 - **Sofi Shop** (ground floor) **M** a la carte approx. 100 – ☕ 45 – **196 rm** 475/830.

Gd Hôtel Concorde, 11 r. Grolée, ✉ 69002, ✆ 842.56.21, Telex 330244 – ⧉ ▤ TV ☎ 🚗 – 🏛 80. AE ⊕ E VISA. ✻ rest DX **e**
st. : **Le Fiorelle** (Grill) *(closed Sunday)* **M** 65/95 – ☕ 33 – **140 rm** 290/590, 12 apartments 650/900.

Royal, 20 pl. Bellecour, ✉ 69002, ✆ 837.57.31, Telex 310785 – ⧉ TV ☎ – 🏛 40. AE ⊕ E VISA CY **d**
st. : **M** Grill *(closed Saturday and Sunday)* 75/100 – ☕ 29 – **90 rm** 237/585, 5 apartments.

Gd H. des Beaux-Arts without rest, 75 r. Prés.-E.-Herriot, ✉ 69002, ✆ 838.09.50, Telex 330442 – ⧉ TV ☎. AE ⊕ E VISA CX **t**
st. : ☕ 22 – **80 rm** 188/286.

Carlton without rest, 4 r. Jussieu, ✉ 69002, ✆ 842.56.51, Telex 310787 – ⧉ TV ☎. AE ⊕ E VISA CX **y**
st. : ☕ 23 – **90 rm** 126/320.

La Résidence without rest, 18 r. Victor-Hugo, ✉ 69002, ✆ 842.63.28, Telex 900950 – ⧉ TV 🛁wc 🚿wc ☎. AE VISA CY **s**
st. : **62 rm** ☕ 180/200.

Globe et Cécil without rest, 21 r. Gasparin ✉ 69002 ✆ 842.58.95, Telex 305184 – ⧉ 🛁wc 🚿wc ☎ – 🏛 60. AE ⊕ VISA CY **b**
☕ 18 – **65 rm** 107/223.

Gd H. des Terreaux without rest, 16 r. Lanterne ✉ 69001 ✆ 827.04.10, Telex 310273 – ⧉ TV 🛁wc 🚿wc ☎. AE ⊕ E VISA CV **u**
st. : ☕ 23 – **50 rm** 86/234.

Moderne without rest, 15 r. Dubois, ✉ 69002, ✆ 842.21.83 – ⧉ TV 🚿wc ☎ CX **n**
st. : ☕ 18 – **31 rm** 79/210.

Bayard without rest, 23 pl. Bellecour, ✉ 69002, ✆ 837.39.64 – 🛁wc 🚿wc ☎. ✻ CY **g**
st. : ☕ 17 – **15 rm** 117/148.

Perrache :

Terminus Perrache without rest, Perrache railway station, 12 cours Verdun, ✉ 69002, ✆ 837.58.11, Telex 330500 – ⧉ ▤ TV ☎ 🚗 P – 🏛 200. AE ⊕ E VISA BZ **s**
st. : **140 rm** ☕ 165/417.

Bristol without rest, 28 cours Verdun, ✉ 69002, ✆ 837.56.55, Telex 330584 – ⧉. AE ⊕ VISA. ✻ BZ **y**
st. : **131 rm** ☕ 105/273.

Bordeaux et Parc without rest, 1 r. Bélier, ✉ 69002, ✆ 837.58.73, Telex 330355 – ⧉ TV ☎. AE ⊕ E VISA BZ **y**
st. : ☕ 20 – **87 rm** 160/247.

Axotel M, 12 r. Marc-Antoine Petit ✉ 69002 ✆ 842.17.18, Telex 380736, 🌳 – ⧉ TV 🛁wc ☎ P – 🏛 25 - 100
130 rm.

Normandie without rest, 3 r. Bélier ✉ 69002 ✆ 837.31.36 – ⧉ 🛁wc 🚿wc ☎. AE ⊕ E VISA BZ **e**
st. : **38 rm** ☕ 97/169.

La Croix Rousse :

Lyon Métropole, 85 quai J.-Gillet ✉ 69004 ✆ 829.20.20, 🌳, 🏊, 🎾 – ⧉ ▤ rest TV ☎ ♿ 🚗 P – 🏛 650. AE ⊕ E VISA
st. : **Les Eaux Vives M** 90/160 - **Le Grill M** a la carte approx 85 – ☕ 21 – **119 rm** 300/350.

Les Brotteaux :

Roosevelt M without rest, 25 r. Bossuet ✉ 69006, ✆ 852.35.67, Telex 300295 – ⧉ ▤ TV ☎ 🚗 P – 🏛 60. AE ⊕ E VISA
st. : ☕ 24 – **87 rm** 235/292, 3 apartments 357.

Olympique without rest, 62 r. Garibaldi ✉ 69006 ✆ 889.48.04 – ⧉ 🛁wc 🚿wc ☎. AE VISA
☕ 15 – **25 rm** 153/174.

Britania without rest, 17 r. Prof.-Weill, ✉ 69006, ✆ 852.86.52 – ⧉ 🛁wc 🚿wc ☎
st. : ☕ 15,50 – **22 rm** 127/173.

La Part-Dieu :

Frantel M 🍷, 129 r. Servient (30th floor) ✉ 69003 ✆ 862.94.12, Telex 380088, ← Lyons, Valley of the Rhône – ⧉ ▤ TV ☎ – 🏛 250. AE ⊕ E VISA
st. : rest. **L'Arc-en-Ciel** *(closed 12 July-21 August, Monday lunch and Sunday)* **M** a la carte 165/240 - **La Ripaille** (Grill) (ground floor) *(closed Friday dinner and Saturday)* **M** 65 /100 – ☕ 42 – **241 rm** 445/530.

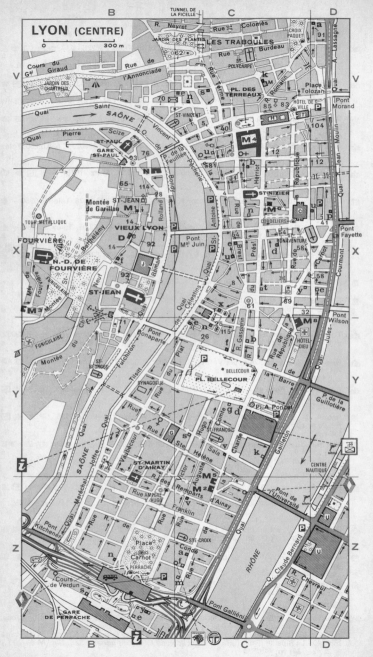

STREET INDEX TO LYON TOWN PLAN

🏨🏨 **Mercure** Ⓜ, 47 bd Vivier Merle ⊠ 69003 ℰ 234.18.12, Telex 306469 — 🔄 🗏 📺 ☎ 🔥 🍽 — 🖴 50-140. 🆌 ⓞ 🄴 📶
M a la carte approx. 95 — � 27 — **124 rm** 307/376.

🏨 **Athéna La Part-Dieu** Ⓜ without rest, 45 bd Vivier Merle ⊠ 69003 ℰ 233.70.04, Telex 306412 — 🔄 ⌷wc 🎵wc ☎ 🍽. 📶
st. : ⊒ 24 — **122 rm** 215/235.

🏨 **Créqui** Ⓜ without rest, 158 r. Créqui ⊠ 69003 ℰ 860.20.47 — 🔄 📺 ⌷wc ☎. 📶
st. : ⊒ 24 — **28 rm** 204/245.

La Guillotière :

🏨 **Urbis Université** Ⓜ without rest, 51 r. Université, ⊠ 69007, ℰ 872.78.42, Telex 340455 — 🔄 🗏 📺 ⌷wc 🎵wc ☎ 🍽 🄴 📶
st. : ⊒ 22 — **53 rm** 205/250.

Gerland :

🏨🏨 **Mercure** Ⓜ, 70 av. leclerc ⊠ 69007 ℰ 858.68.53, Telex 305484, 🏊 — 🔄 🗏 📺 🔥 🍽 — 🖴 350. 🆌 ⓞ 🄴 📶
M a la carte approx. 95 — ⊒ 27 — **194 rm** 307/354.

Monchat-Monplaisir :

🏨🏨 **Park H. P.L.M** Ⓜ, 4 r. Prof.-Calmette, ⊠ 69008, ℰ 874.11.20, Telex 380230, � — 🔄 📺 📺 ⌷wc 🖴 35. 🆌 ⓞ 📶
st. : le Patio *(closed Saturday, Sunday and Bank Holidays)* M 80 b.i. — ⊒ 28 — **70 rm** 255/280.

🏨 **Lyon-Est** Ⓜ without rest, 104 rte Genas, ⊠ 69003, ℰ 854.64.53 — 🔄 🗏 ⌷wc 🎵wc ☎ 🔥 🍽 🄿 🆌 ⓞ 🄴 📶
st. : ⊒ 20 — **42 rm** 115/200.

à Villeurbanne :

🏨🏨 **Congrès** Ⓜ, pl. Cdt Rivière ⊠ 69100 Villeurbanne ℰ 889.81.10, Telex 370216 — 🔄 🗏 📺 ☎ 🍽 🄿 — 🖴 50 - 100. 🆌 ⓞ 🄴 📶
st. : **M** rest. see Le Grand Camp below — ⊒ 18 — **132 rm** 230.

🏨 **Athena-Tolstoï** Ⓜ, 90 cours Tolstoï ⊠ 69100 Villeurbanne ℰ 868.81.21, Telex 330574 — 🔄 ⌷wc ☎ 🄿 — 🖴 50 - 200
138 rm.

🏨 **Athena-Zola** Ⓜ, 163 cours E.-Zola ⊠ 69100 Villeurbanne ℰ 885.32.33, Telex 380608 — 🔄 kitchenette ⌷wc 🎵wc ☎ 🍽 — 🖴 120 — **108 rm**.

Restaurants

XXXXX ⬧⬧⬧ **Paul Bocuse** bridge of Collonges, 12 km by the banks of the River Saône (D43, D51) ⊠ 69660 Collonges-au-Mont-d'Or, ℰ 822.01.40, Telex 375382, « Tasteful decor » — 🗏 🄿 🆌 ⓞ 📶
closed 5 to 21 August — **M** 260/380 and a la carte
Spec. Soupe aux truffes noires, Loup en croûte, Volaille de Bresse en vessie. Wines Pouilly-Fuissé, Brouilly.

XXXX **Roucou La Mère Guy**, 35 quai J.-J. Rousseau ⊠ 69350 La Mulatière ℰ 851.65.37, Telex 310241 — 🆌 ⓞ 📶
closed August, February Holidays, Sunday dinner and Monday — **M** 140/250.

XXX ❀ **Tour Rose** (Chavent), 16 r. Boeuf, ✉ 69005, 𝒫 837.25.90, « 17C house in the old part
of Lyons » – 🍽 ⚿ ⓞ 🅴 𝗩𝗜𝗦𝗔   BX **e**
closed Sunday – **M** 170/300
Spec. Saumon mi-cuit au fumoir, Rouget barbet poêlé aux artichauts, Noisettes de lapereau. **Wines** St-Véran,
Brouilly.

XXX ❀❀ **Orsi**, 3 pl. Kléber, ✉ 69006, 𝒫 889.57.68 – 🍽 ⚿ ⓞ 𝗩𝗜𝗦𝗔
*closed August, Saturday except lunch from 1 September to 30 April, Sunday and Bank
Holidays* – **st. : M** 170 and a la carte
Spec. Foie de canard poêlé, Pêche bretonne au homard, filets de loup et rouget, Pigeonneau de Bresse en
cocotte. **Wines** St-Véran, St-Amour.

XXX ❀❀ **Vettard**, 7 pl. Bellecour, ✉ 69002, 𝒫 842.07.59 – 🍽 ⚿ ⓞ 𝗩𝗜𝗦𝗔   CY **f**
closed 28 July-26 August, Saturday dinner from May to August and Sunday – **M** (at rest.)
210/310 and a la carte - **Café Neuf M** a la carte approx. 120
Spec. Loup à l'huile de basilic et vinaigre de Xérès, Quenelle de brochet, Paupiette de saumon au citron vert
(May-end September). **Wines** Beaujolais-Villages, St-Joseph.

XXX ❀ **Henry**, 27 r. Martinière, ✉ 69001, 𝒫 828.26.08, mural paintings – 🍽 ⚿ ⓞ 𝗩𝗜𝗦𝗔
closed Saturday lunch and Monday except Bank Holidays – **M** 100/180   CV **n**
Spec. Salade de homard, Turbot rôti, Charolais aux truffes et oranges. **Wines** Fleurie, Volnay.

XXX ❀❀ **Nandron**, 26 quai J.-Moulin, ✉ 69002, 𝒫 842.10.26 – 🍽 ⚿ ⓞ 🅴 𝗩𝗜𝗦𝗔   DX **p**
closed 28 July-25 August, Friday dinner and Saturday – **M** 150/280 and a la carte
Spec. Quenelles de brochet, Terrine de champignons, Côte de boeuf à la moelle. **Wines** Morgon, St-Véran.

XXX ❀ **Bourillot**, 8 pl. Célestins, ✉ 69002, 𝒫 837.38.64 – 🍽 ⚿ ⓞ 𝗩𝗜𝗦𝗔   CY **n**
closed July, 23 December-3 January, Sunday and Bank Holidays – **M** 135/195
Spec. Etuvée de homard, Ragoût de ris de veau et rognons, Soufflé glacé au chocolat.. **Wines** Mâcon,
Brouilly.

XXX ❀ **Mère Brazier**, 12 r. Royale, ✉ 69001, 𝒫 828.15.49, typical local establishment – 🍽
⚿ 𝗩𝗜𝗦𝗔   DV **a**
closed August, Saturday lunch and Sunday – **M** (🍽 1st floor) 160/180
Spec. Quenelle pochée sauce homard, Volaille demi-deuil, Crêpes aux truffes fraîches (December to March).
Wines Chiroubles, Côtes du Rhône.

XXX ❀❀ **Léon de Lyon** (Lacombe), 1 r. Pleney, ✉ 69001, 𝒫 828.11.33, typical local establishment – 🍽 ⚿   CVX **b**
closed 23 December-6 January, Monday lunch and Sunday – **M** 140/290 and a la carte
Spec. Quenelle de brochet Nantua, Filets de rouget poêlés, Aile de poularde farcie au foie gras. **Wines**
Chiroubles, Côteaux du Lyonnais.

XXX ❀ **Aub. de Fond-Rose** (Brunet), 23 quai Clemenceau, ✉ 69300, Caluire 𝒫 829.34.61,
🌳, « Garden » – ⓟ ⚿ ⓞ 🅴 𝗩𝗜𝗦𝗔
closed Monday from November to Easter and Sunday dinner – **M** 140/260
Spec. Marinade de rouget, Fruits de mer (in season), Cuisses de canard aux poires. **Wines** Mâcon-Villages.

XXX ❀ **Daniel et Denise** (Léron), 2 r. Tupin, ✉ 69002, 𝒫 837.49.98 – 🍽 ⚿ ⓞ 🅴 𝗩𝗜𝗦𝗔
closed August, Sunday, Monday lunch and Bank Holidays – **M** 98/165   CX **e**
Spec. Terrine de homard, Soufflé de turbotin florentine, Filet d'agneau en croûte. **Wines** Chiroubles,
St-Joseph.

XXX ❀ **Les Fantasques**, 47 r. Bourse, ✉ 69002, 𝒫 837.36.58 – 🍽 ⚿ 𝗩𝗜𝗦𝗔   DX **u**
closed 10 to 27 August and Sunday – **M** 135/200
Spec. Terrine de homard, Rouget en papillote, Bouillabaisse. **Wines** Mâcon, Brouilly.

XXX **Cazenove**, 75 r. Boileau, ✉ 69006 𝒫 889.82.92 – 🍽 ⚿ ⓞ 𝗩𝗜𝗦𝗔
*closed August, Saturday except lunch from 1 September to 30 April, Sunday and Bank
Holidays* – **st. : M** a la carte 140/200.

XXX **Beluga**, Commercial centre La Part-Dieu, porte des Cuirassiers ✉ 69003 𝒫 860.67.24 –
🍽 ⚿ ⓞ 🅴 𝗩𝗜𝗦𝗔
closed Sunday and Bank Holidays – **M** 92/130.

XXX **Le Rocher**, quartier St-Rambert, 8 quai R.-Carrié, ✉ 69009, 𝒫 883.99.72, ≤, 🌳 – ⓟ
𝗩𝗜𝗦𝗔
*closed 9 August-3 September, 21 December-2 January, Saturday (except dinner from May
to October) and Sunday* – **st. : M** 100/280.

XXX **Le Grand Camp**, pl. Cdt-Rivière ✉ 69100 Villeurbanne 𝒫 889.48.45 – 🍽
closed Sunday and Bank Holidays – **M** 100/165 ♨.

XX ❀ **Le Quatre Saisons** (Bertoli), 15 r. Sully ✉ 69006 𝒫 893.76.07 – 🍽 ⚿ ⓞ
*closed August, Saturday except dinner from 1 September to 31 May, Sunday and Bank
Holidays* – **M** 150/260
Spec. Foie gras, Rognon de veau cuit dans sa graisse, Gibier (season). **Wines** Chiroubles, St-Véran.

XX **Le Gourmandin**, 156 r. P.-Bert ✉ 69003 𝒫 862.78.77 – 🍽 ⓟ ⚿ ⓞ 𝗩𝗜𝗦𝗔
closed 26 July-26 August, Saturday, Sunday and Bank Holidays – **st. : M** 105/220.

XX **Garioud**, 14 r. Palais Grillet ✉ 69002 𝒫 837.04.71 – 🍽 ⚿ ⓞ   CX **d**
closed August, 1 to 6 January, Saturday lunch and Sunday – **st. : M** 96/142.

XX **Les Grillons**, 18 r. D.-Vincent at Champagne-au-Mont-d'Or ✉ 69410 Champagne,
𝒫 835.04.78, 🌳 – ⓟ ⚿ ⓞ 🅴 𝗩𝗜𝗦𝗔
closed November, 4 to 16 March, Sunday dinner and Monday – **M** 88/175.

XX ✿ **Chez Gervais** (Lescuyer), 42 r. P.-Corneille, ⊠ 69006, ℰ 852.19.13 — ▤. ℡ ① E 𝘝𝘐𝘚𝘈
closed July, Saturday from May to end September, Sunday and Bank Holidays — **st. : M**
150/300
Spec. Salade de ris de veau, Gratin de queues d'écrevisses (July to March) Coupe Florence. **Wines** Mâcon
blanc, St-Joseph.

XX **Au Petit Col,** 68 r. Charité, ⊠ 69002, ℰ 837.25.18 — ▤. ℡ 𝘝𝘐𝘚𝘈
closed 21 July-19 August, Sunday dinner and Monday — **st. : M** 69/127.   CZ **a**

X **Chevallier,** 40 r. du Sergent-Blandan, ⊠ 69001, ℰ 828.19.83   CV **s**

X **La Bonne Auberge ''Chez Jo'',** 48 av. Félix-Faure, ⊠ 69003, ℰ 860.00.57 — ▤. ℡
① 𝘝𝘐𝘚𝘈
closed August, Saturday dinner and Sunday — **st. : M** 60/115.

X **Pied de Cochon,** 9 r. St-Polycarpe, ⊠ 69001, ℰ 828.15.31, typical local establishment
— ℡ ①   CV **k**
closed August, Saturday, Sunday and Bank Holidays — **st. : M** 70/105.

Environs

at Tassin-la-Demi-Lune 5 km by D 407 — pop. 15 034 — ⊠ **69160** Tassin-la-Demi-Lune :

XXX **Les Tilleuls,** 146 av. Ch.-de-Gaulle ℰ 834.19.58, 🍴 — ⓟ. ℡ 𝘝𝘐𝘚𝘈
*closed 16 to 26 August, February Holidays, Sunday dinner and Monday except Bank
Holidays* — **st. : M** 83/200 🍷.

at Bron — pop. 41 500 . — ⊠ **69500** Bron :

🏨 **Novotel** Ⓜ, r. Lionel Terray ℰ 826.97.48, Telex 340781, ⌇ — 📶 ▤ ℡ ☎ ⅄ ⓟ — 🕍
25 - 700. ℡ ① E 𝘝𝘐𝘚𝘈
M a la carte approx. 110 🍷 — ⊊ 34 — **196 rm** 295.

🏨 **Dau Ly** Ⓜ ⌂ without rest, 28 r. de Prévieux ℰ 826.04.37 — ℡ ⌐wc 🛁wc 🅿 ⇌ ⓟ.
℡ 𝘝𝘐𝘚𝘈
st. : ⊊ 15,50 — **22 rm** 152/203.

to the NE :

at Crépieux-la-Pape : 7 km by N 83 and N 84 — ⊠ **69140** Rillieux-la-Pape :

XX ✿ **Larivoire** (Constantin), ℰ 888.50.92, ≤, 🍴 — ⓟ. ℡ ① 𝘝𝘐𝘚𝘈
closed 2 to 8 September, in February, Monday dinner and Tuesday — **st. : M** 108/200
Spec. Huîtres chaudes au Montagnieu (October to April), Oeufs en cocotte aux écrevisses et aux truffes,
Fricassée de volaille au vinaigre. **Wines** Montagnieu, Côteaux du Lyonnais.

by the SE :

at the airport of Satolas : 27 km by A 43 — ⊠ **69125** Lyon Satolas Airport :

🏨 **Méridien** Ⓜ, 3rd floor ℰ 871.91.61, Telex 380480 — 📶 ▤ ℡ ☎ — 🕍 25 - 250. ℡ ① E
𝘝𝘐𝘚𝘈
st. : M rest. see **La Gde Corbeille** — ⊊ 34 — **120 rm** 365/430.

XXX **La Gde Corbeille,** 1st floor ℰ 871.91.62, ≤ — ▤. ℡ ① 𝘝𝘐𝘚𝘈
closed August and Saturday — **st. : M** 145/180.

at St-Priest : 12 km by N 6 and D 148 — pop. 42 913 — ⊠ **69800** St-Priest :

🏨 **Moderne** Ⓜ without rest, 64 rte Heyrieux ℰ 820.47.46 — 📶 ℡ ⓟ. ℡ ① 𝘝𝘐𝘚𝘈
st. : ⊊ 22 — **35 rm** 210/300.

to the W :

at Charbonnières-les-Bains : 8 km by N 7 — pop. 3 973 — alt. 240 — Spa — Casino —
⊠ **69260** Charbonnières-les-Bains :

🏨 **Mercure** Ⓜ without rest, N 7 ℰ 834.72.79, Telex 900972, ⌇ — 📶 ℡ ⌐wc ☎ ⓟ — 🕍
30 - 150. ℡ ① E 𝘝𝘐𝘚𝘈
st. : ⊊ 24 — **60 rm** 229/260.

🏨 **Domaine des Pins** Ⓜ, N 7 ℰ 887.03.14, Telex 330060, ≤, park, ⌇, ⅊ — 📶 ℡ ⌐wc
☎ ⅄ ⓟ — 🕍 25 - 250. ℡ ① E 𝘝𝘐𝘚𝘈
st. : M 114/165 — ⊊ 21 — **82 rm** 195/225.

🏨 **Beaulieu** Ⓜ without rest, 19 av. Gén.-de-Gaulle ℰ 887.12.04 — 📶 ⌐wc 🅿 ⓟ — 🕍 100.
℡ ① — **st. :** ⊊ 16,50 — **40 rm** 132/159.

XX **Gigandon,** 5 av. Gén.-de-Gaulle ℰ 887.15.51 — ℡ 𝘝𝘐𝘚𝘈
closed August, 24 December-3 January, Sunday dinner and Monday — **st. : M** 68/160.

Porte de Lyon - motorway junction A 6 N 6 Exit road signposted Limonest N : 10 km —
⊠ **69260** Dardilly :

🏨 **Novotel Lyon-Nord** Ⓜ ⌂, ℰ 835.13.41, Telex 330962, ⌇ — 📶 ▤ ℡ ☎ ⓟ — 🕍
25 - 120. ℡ ① E 𝘝𝘐𝘚𝘈
M (coffee shop only) a la carte approx 95 🍷 — ⊊ 33 — **107 rm** 280/305.

🏨 **Holiday Inn** Ⓜ, ℰ 835.70.20, Telex 900006, ⊠ — 📶 ▤ ℡ ☎ ⅄ ⓟ — 🕍 25 - 400. ℡ ①
E 𝘝𝘐𝘚𝘈
st. : Grill la Braise **M** 110/170 — ⊊ 30 — **204 rm** 273/300.

🏨 **Mercure** Ⓜ, ℰ 835.28.05, Telex 330045, ⌇, ⅊ — ▤ rest ℡ ☎ ⓟ — 🕍 25 - 120. ℡ ①
E 𝘝𝘐𝘚𝘈
M a la carte approx 100 🍷 — 🍽 25 — **169 rm** 205/264.

🏢 **Campanile** ⬦, 🕿 835.48.44, Telex 310155 — 🛌wc ℗. VISA
st. : **M** 59 b.i./78 b.i. — 🍴 22 — **43 rm** 188.

XXX Le Panorama, at Dardilly-le-Haut, near the church, ✉ 69570 Dardilly, 🕿 847.40.19, �,
🌲 — ℗.

Chagny 71150 S.-et-L. 69 ⑨ — pop. 5 604 — alt. 216 — ✪ 85.
Lyon 143.

🏨 ✪✪✪ **Lameloise** Ⓜ, pl. d'Armes 🕿 87.08.85, « Old Burgundian house, tasteful decor »
— TV 🕿 🚗, VISA. 🍴 rest
  closed 17 to 25 July, 4 December-2 January, Thursday lunch and Wednesday — **M** (booking
  essential) a la carte 200/250 — � 30 — **25 rm** 200/380
  Spec. Ravioli d'escargots, Pigeon de Bresse en vessie, Assiette du chocolatier,. **Wines** Rully, Givry.

Condrieu 69420 Rhône 74 ⑪ — pop. 3 158 — alt. 150 — ✪ 74.
Lyon 40.

🏨 ✪✪ **Hôt. Beau Rivage** (Mme Castaing) Ⓜ, 🕿 59.52.24, Telex 308946, 🌅, « Terrace
with view of Rhône River », 🌲 — 🕿 ℗. AE ① E VISA
  closed 5 January-15 February — **M** 150/230 a la carte — ⊒ 31 — **22 rm** 190/315
  Spec. Salade de ris de veau, Turbot aux écrevisses, Foie gras chaud à l'embeurrée de choux. **Wines** Crozes
  Hermitage, St-Joseph.

Fleurie 69820 Rhône 74 ① — pop. 1 151 — alt. 295 — ✪ 74.
Lyon 58.

XXX ✪✪ **Aub. du Cep** (Cortembert), pl. de l'Eglise 🕿 04.10.77, 🌅 — AE VISA
  closed December, Sunday dinner and Monday except Bank Holidays — **st. : M** (dinner :
  booking essential) 150/350 and a la carte
  Spec. Mousseline de sandre, Fricassée de volaille au Fleurie, Entremets glacé moka nougatine. **Wines**
  Beaujolais, Fleurie.

Mionnay 01 Ain 74 ② — pop. 796 — alt. 288 — ✉ 01390 St-André-de-Corcy — ✪ 7.
Lyon 20.

XXXX ✪✪✪ **Alain Chapel** with rm, 🕿 891.82.02, 🌅, « flowered garden » — 🛌wc 🅿️ ℗
  closed January, Tuesday lunch and Monday except Bank Holidays — **M** 275/360 and a la
  carte — ⊒ 68 — **13 rm** 500/675
  Spec. Trois petites salades (June-October), Cuisses de grenouilles à la crème (August-January), Poulette de
  Bresse en vessie. **Wines** Blanc de blancs du Bugey, Mondeuse.

Montrond-les-Bains 42210 Loire 73 ⑱ — pop. 3 194 — alt. 356 — ✪ 77.
Lyon 68.

🏨 ✪✪ **Host. La Poularde** (Randoing), 🕿 54.40.06 — TV ℗ — 🅰️ 40. AE ① VISA. 🍴 rest
  closed 2 to 15 January, Monday dinner except Bank Holidays and Tuesday lunch — **st. : M**
  (Sunday : booking essential) 130/320 and a la carte — ⊒ 30 — **15 rm** 160/300
  Spec. Feuilleté d'amourettes, ris de veau et crêtes de coq, Marguerite de l'océan au beurre nantais, Coeur de
  charolais au Fleurie. **Wines** Chassagne-Montrachet, Fleurie.

Rive-de-Gier 42800 Loire 73 ⑲ — pop. 15 850 — alt. 242 — ✪ 77.
Lyon 37.

XXX ✪✪ **Host. Renaissance** (Laurent) with rm, 41 r. A.-Marrel 🕿 75.04.31, 🌅, 🌲 —
🛌wc 🅿️ ℗ — 🅰️ 25. AE ① E VISA
  closed February Holidays, Sunday dinner and Monday out of season (except Bank Holidays)
  — **st. : M** 150/350 — ⊒ 50 — **10 rm** 160/280
  Spec. Galette de sarrazin aux primeurs (except Winter), Pigeon en ballotine, Rêve d'enfant sage (dessert).
  Wines Viognier, St-Joseph.

Roanne ℗ 42300 Loire 73 ⑦ — pop. 49 638 — alt. 279 — ✪ 77.
Lyon 86.

🏨 ✪✪✪ **H. des Frères Troisgros** Ⓜ, pl. Gare 🕿 71.66.97, Telex 307507 — 🛗 ▤ rest TV
🕿 ℗. AE ① VISA
  closed 6 to 21 August, January, Wednesday lunch and Tuesday — **M** (booking essential)
  200/365 and a la carte — ⊒ 50 — **24 rm** 380/480, 6 apartments 700/850
  Spec. Cuisses de grenouilles aux cucurbitacées, Opus de fromage de chèvre, Feuillet au chocolat mousse.
  Wines Vins de Bourgogne.

Valence ℗ 26000 Drôme 77 ⑫ — pop. 68 157 — alt. 123 — ✪ 75.
Lyon 99.

XXXX ✪✪✪ **Pic** with rm 285 av. Victor-Hugo, Motorway exit signposted Valence-Sud 🕿 44.
15.32, « Shaded garden » — ▤ rest TV 🛌wc 🕿 ℗. AE ①
  closed 1 to 28 August, February Holidays, Sunday dinner and Wednesday — **st. : M**
  (Sunday : booking essential) 300/380 — ⊒ 40 — **5 rm** 300/750
  Spec. Menu Rabelais. **Wines** Crozes-Hermitage, St Péray.

Vienne <SP> **38200** Isère **74** ⑪⑫ – pop. 29 050 – alt. 158 – ✪ 74.
Lyon 30.

XXXX ✿✿✿ **Pyramide** (Mme Point), bd F.-Point ✆ 53.01.96, « flowered garden » – ▤ Ⓟ. AE ⓓ
closed 1 February-1 March, Monday dinner and Tuesday – **M** (booking essential) 315/365 and a la carte
Spec. Assiette de marée, Turbot au champagne,. **Wines** Condrieu, Côte Rôtie.

Vonnas **01540** Ain **74** ② – pop. 2 505 – alt. 189 – ✪ 74.
Lyon 66.

✿✿✿ **Georges Blanc** Ⓜ, ✆ 50.00.10, Telex 380776, ⛱, ⛨, % – ▤ rest TV ☎ 🚗 Ⓟ. AE ⓓ VISA
closed 2 January-10 February – **M** *(closed Thursday except dinner from 15 June to 15 September and Wednesday except Bank Holidays)* (booking essential) 210/320 and a la carte – ☕ 39 – **25 rm** 320/900, 6 apartments
Spec. St-Jacques à la coque (October-April), Bar à la marinière, Poularde de Bresse aux gousses d'ail et au foie gras. **Wines** Montagnieu, Chiroubles.

MARSEILLES Ⓟ **13** B.-du-R. **84** ⑬ – pop. 878 689 – ✪ 91.

See : N.-D.-de-la-Garde Basilica ✱★★★ BY – La Canebière★★ CV – Old Port★★ ABVX – Corniche Président-J.-F.-Kennedy★★ – Modern Port★★ – Palais Longchamp★ DU – St-Victor Basilica★ : crypt★★ AX – Old Major Cathedral★ AU N – Pharo Parc ≤★ AX – St-Laurent Belvedere ≤★ AV E – Museum : Grobet-Labadié★★ DU M4, Cantini★ : Marseilles and Moustiers pottery★★ (galerie de la Faïence de Marseille et de Moustiers) – Fine Arts★ and Natural History Museum★ (Longchamp Palace) DU M, Mediterranean Archeology★ Egyptian antiquities★★ (Château Borely), Roman Docks★ ABV M2, Old Marseilles★ AV M1 – Envir. : Corniche road★★ of Callelongue S : 13 km.

Exc. : Château d'If★★ (✱★★★) 1 h 30.

18 of Aix-Marseilles ✆ 24.20.41 to the North : 22 km.

✈ Marseille-Marignane Air France ✆ 89.92.12 to the North : 28 km.

🚗 ✆ 08.50.50.

⛴ for Corsica : Société Nationale Maritime Corse-Méditerranée, 61 bd des Dames (2e) ✆ 91.92.20 AU.

ℹ and Accueil de France (Information and hotel reservations - not more than 5 days in advance, 4 Canebière, 13001, ✆ 54.91.11, Telex 430402 - and at St-Charles railway Station ✆ 50.59.18 A.C. 143 cours Lieutaud, 13006, ✆ 47.86.23.

Paris 776 – Lyon 315 – Nice 187 – Torino 407 – Toulon 64 – Toulouse 404.

Plan on following pages

Sofitel Vieux Port Ⓜ, **36 bd Ch.-Livon,** ✉ **13007,** ✆ **52.90.19, Telex 401270, panoramic restaurant** ≤ **old port,** ⛱ – |‡| ▤ TV ☎ ♿ 🚗 Ⓟ – 🎤 100 - 450. AE ⓓ E VISA AX **n**
rest. **les Trois Forts** *(closed August)* **M** a la carte 190/250 - **Le Jardin** *(closed Saturday and Sunday from October to 15 may)* **M** a la carte approx. 110 🌡 – ☕ 40 – **219 rm** 395/810, 3 apartments.

Frantel Ⓜ, **r. Neuve St-Martin,** ✉ **13001,** ✆ **91.91.29, Telex 401886,** ⛨ – |‡| ▤ TV ☎ ♿ 🚗 – 🎤 400. AE ⓓ E VISA BUV **g**
st. : rest. **L'Oursinade** *(closed 22 July-26 August, Sunday and Bank Holidays)* **M** a la carte 180/240 - **L'Oliveraie** (Grill) **M** a la carte approx. 100 – ☕ 39 – **200 rm** 395/485.

P.L.M. Beauvau without rest, **4 r. Beauvau** ✉ **13001** ✆ **54.91.00, Telex 401778** – |‡| ▤ TV ☎. AE ⓓ E VISA BV **r**
st. : ☕ 40 – **71 rm** 410/520.

Concorde-Prado Ⓜ, **11 av. Mazargues,** ✉ **13008,** ✆ **76.51.11, Telex 420209** – |‡| ▤ TV ☎ 🚗 – 🎤 80. AE ⓓ E VISA
st. : M a la carte 115/140 🌡 – ☕ 37 – **100 rm** 402/448.

Résidence Bompard ⛰ without rest, **2 r. Flots-Bleus,** ✉ **13007,** ✆ **52.10.93, Telex 400430,** ⛨ – |‡| kitchenette TV ☎ ♿ Ⓟ – 🎤 40. AE ⓓ
st. : ☕ 20 – **47 rm** 190/255.

Gd H. Noailles without rest, **66 Canebière,** ✉ **13001,** ✆ **54.91.48, Telex 430609** – |‡| ▤ rm TV ☎ – 🎤 30 - 60. AE ⓓ E VISA CV **x**
st. : ☕ 30 – **70 rm** 250/420, 4 apartments 500.

Gd H. Genève without rest, **3 bis r. Reine-Élisabeth,** ✉ **13001,** ✆ **90.51.42, Telex 440672** – |‡| TV. ⓓ VISA. ✗ BV **e**
st. : ☕ 19 – **44 rm** 118/268, 4 apartments 315.

Castellane Ⓜ without rest, **31 r. Rouet** ✉ **13006** ✆ **79.27.54** – |‡| TV ⛀wc ☎ 🚗. AE VISA DY **f**
st. : ☕ 25 – **55 rm** 205/270.

Européen Ⓜ without rest, **115 r. Paradis,** ✉ **13006,** ✆ **37.77.20** – |‡| ▤ ⛀wc ⛆wc ☎
closed August – **st. :** ☕ 16 – **43 rm** 111/167. CY **u**

Manhattan Ⓜ, **3 pl. Rome,** ✉ **13006,** ✆ **54.35.95** – |‡| TV ⛀wc ⛆wc ☎ – 🎤 80. AE ⓓ E VISA CX **w**
st. : M *(closed August, Saturday and Sunday)* 60/250 🌡 – ☕ 22 – **41 rm** 180/280.

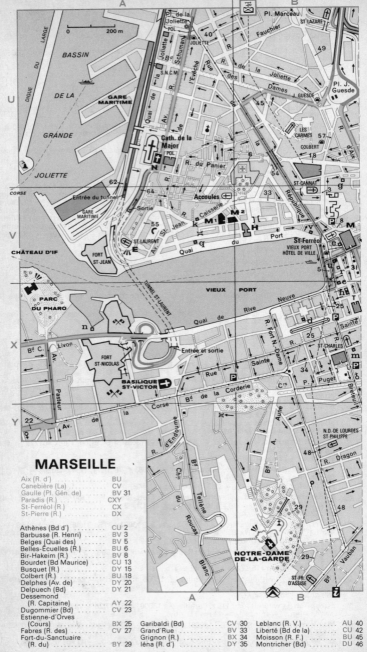

MARSEILLE

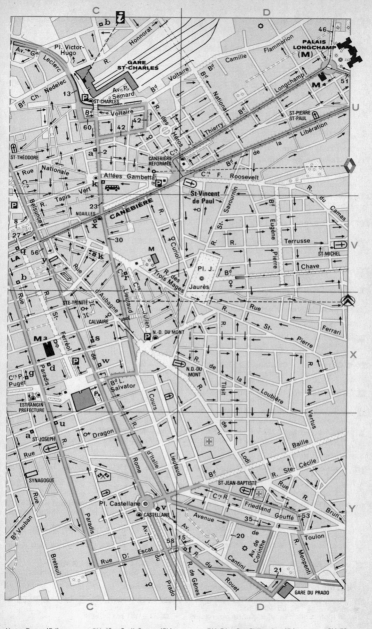

🏨 **Rome et St Pierre** without rest, 7 cours St-Louis, ⊠ 13001, 🖉 54.19.52, Telex 430641 — 🛗 📺 🛏wc 🛢wc ☎. 🗚 ① E ᴠɪsᴀ
CV **y**
st. : 🖵 19 — **63 rm** 110/255.

🏨 **Petit Louvre,** 19 Canebière, ⊠ 13001, 🖉 90.13.78 — 🛗 🔲 📺 🛏wc 🛢wc ☎. 🗚 ① E
ᴠɪsᴀ ⅙ rest
CV **q**
st. : **M** (closed 2 January-15 February and Sunday from 1 November to 31 March) 73/110 —
🖵 19 — **33 rm** 140/255 — P 290/330.

🏨 **Ibis** Ⓜ, 6 r. Cassis ⊠ 13008 🖉 78.59.25, Telex 400362 — 🛗 🔲 🛏wc ☎ ఉ. ☞ — 🅰 40.
E ᴠɪsᴀ ⅙ rest
st. : **M** a la carte approx. 70 🍷 — 🍺 19.50 — **119 rm** 189/207.

🏨 **Sud** without rest, 18 r. Beauvau ⊠ 13001 🖉 54.38.50 — 🛗 🛏wc ⊜
BX **n**
st. : 🖵 15 — **24 rm** 155/185.

🏨 **Martini** without rest, 5 bd G.-Desplaces, ⊠ 13003, 🖉 64.11.17 — 🛗 🛏 🛢wc ☎ ☞. 🗚
CU **b**
st. : 🖵 17 — **40 rm** 101/178.

XXX ❀ **Jambon de Parme,** 67 r. La Palud, ⊠ 13006, 🖉 54.37.98 — ▪. 🗚 ① E ᴠɪsᴀ
CX **s**
closed 12 July-20 August, Sunday dinner and Monday — **M** a la carte 150/210
Spec. Salade aux deux saumons, Filets de chapon au safran, Blancs de volaille au sabayon de poireaux.
Wines Gassin, Rousset.

XXX **Georges Mavro,** 2 Canebière ⊠ 13001 🖉 33.00.94, ≤ old port — ▪. 🗚 ① ᴠɪsᴀ
BV **u**
closed 3 to 31 August, Saturday in July, Monday lunch from September to June and
Sunday — **st. : M** 185/270.

XXX **Max Caizergues,** 11 r. G.-Ricard, ⊠ 13006 🖉 33.58.07 — ▪. 🗚 ① ᴠɪsᴀ. ⅙
CX **g**
closed 13 July-16 August, Saturday lunch and Sunday — **st. : M** a la carte 170/230.

XXX **Au Pescadou,** 19 place Castellane, ⊠ 13006, 🖉 78.36.01, Seafood — ▪.
CY **v**
closed July, August and Sunday dinner from November to end June — **st. : M** a la carte
150/210.

XXX **La Ferme,** 23 r. Sainte, ⊠ 13001, 🖉 33.21.12 — ▪. ᴠɪsᴀ
BX **m**
closed August, Saturday lunch, Sunday and Bank Holidays — **st. : M** a la carte 145/205.

XXX **Le Bellecour,** 26 cours Julien ⊠ 13006 🖉 42.23.14 — ▪. 🗚 ① ᴠɪsᴀ
CV **r**
closed 15 to 31 July, Saturday lunch and Sunday — **st. : M** 85/150.

XXX **Brasserie New-York Vieux Port,** 7 quai Belges ⊠ 13001 🖉 33.60.98 — ▪. 🗚 ① E
ᴠɪsᴀ
BX **e**
st. : **M** a la carte approx. 150 🍷.

XX ❀ **Michel,** 6 r. Catalans, ⊠ 13007, 🖉 52.64.22, ≤ — ᴠɪsᴀ
closed July, Tuesday and Wednesday — **M** a la carte 200/275
Spec. Bouillabaisse, Bourride, Poissons grillés. Wines Cassis, Bandol.

XX ❀ **Calypso,** 3 r. Catalans, ⊠ 13007, 🖉 52.64.00, ≤ — ᴠɪsᴀ
closed August, Sunday and Monday — **M** a la carte 200/270
Spec. Bouillabaisse, Bourride, Poissons grillés. Wines Bandol, Cassis.

XX **Chez Caruso,** 158 quai Port, ⊠ 13002, 🖉 90.94.04, ≤, �, italian specialities — 🗚
AV **q**
closed 15 October-15 November, Sunday dinner and Monday — **st. : M** 130/170.

XX **Miramar,** 12 quai Port, ⊠ 13002, 🖉 91.10.40, � — ▪. 🗚 ① E ᴠɪsᴀ
BV **v**
closed 3 to 26 August, 23 December-6 January and Sunday — **M** a la carte 130/200 🍷.

X **La Charpenterie,** 22 r. Paix ⊠ 13001 🖉 54.22.89 — 🗚 ① E ᴠɪsᴀ
BX **d**
closed 13 July-16 August, Saturday lunch and Sunday — **st. : M** a la carte 75/125.

at the Corniche :

🏨 **Concorde-Palm Beach** Ⓜ ⅍, 2 promenade Plage, ⊠ 13008, 🖉 76.20.00, Telex 401894,
≤, �, 🏊, 🐎 — 🛗 🔲 📺 ☎ ☞ ℗ — 🅰 450. 🗚 ① E ᴠɪsᴀ
st. : **La Réserve M** 128 - grill **Les Voiliers M** 95/105 🍷 — 🖵 32 — **145 rm** 382/
425, 3 apartments.

🏨 ❀❀ **Le Petit Nice** (Passedat) Ⓜ ⅍, anse de Maldormé (turn off when level with no 160
Corniche Kennedy) ⊠ 13007, 🖉 52.14.39, Telex 401565, �, « Villas overlooking the sea,
refined decor », 🏊 — 🛗 ▪ rm 📺 ☎ ☞ ℗. 🗚 ᴠɪsᴀ. ⅙ rest
closed 1 January-8 February — **M** (closed Tuesday lunch from 15 October to end March
and Monday) 310 and a la carte — 🖵 57 — **8 rm** 600/900, 8 apartments
Spec. Loup de ligne en huile d'olive, Ragoût phocéen aux pistils de safran, Feuillant de fruits rouges
(season). Wines Bandol, Coteaux d'Aix.

XX **Chez Fonfon,** 140 vallon des Auffes, ⊠ 13007, 🖉 52.14.38, ≤ — 🗚 ① ᴠɪsᴀ
closed October, 24 December-1 January, Saturday and Sunday — **M** a la carte approx. 200.

to the E 10 km, exit road signposted La Penne-St-Menet :

🏨 **Novotel** Ⓜ, at St-Menet, ⊠ 13011, 🖉 43.90.60, Telex 400667, �, 🏊, ⅛ — 🛗 ▪ 📺 ☎
ఉ. ℗ — 🅰 250. 🗚 ① E ᴠɪsᴀ
M (coffee shop only) a la carte 95 🍷 — 🖵 29 — **131 rm** 249/285.

Ensure that you have up to date **Michelin** maps in your car.

Les Baux-de-Provence 13 B.-du-R. 84 ① – pop. 433 – alt. 280 – ⊠ **13520** Maussane-les-Alpilles – ✿ 90.
Marseille 86.

in the Vallon :

XXXXX ✿✿✿ **Oustaù de Baumanière** (Thuilier) M ⌿ with rm, ✆ 97.33.07, Telex 420203, ≤
« Tastefully decorated mansions, flowered terraces, ⌸, ❄, ⌁, Riding club », ⌖ –
≣ rm ⊡ ⌂wc ☎ ⇔ ℗ ⌶ ⓞ ⱸ VISA
closed 15 January-1 March, Thursday lunch and Wednesday from 31 October to 31 March
– **M** a la carte 260/350 – ⊐ 60 – **15 rm** 660, 11 apartments 925
Spec. Filets de rougets au vin rouge, Noisettes d'agneau Beaumanière, Gratin de fruits frais. **Wines** Gigondas,
Coteaux des Baux.

XXX ✿ **La Riboto de Taven,** ✆ 97.34.23, ⌸, « Shaded terrace and flowered garden near
the rocks » – ℗. ⌶ VISA
closed 10 January-24 February, Sunday dinner out of season and Monday – **st. : M** a la
carte 210/280
Spec. Huîtres de Bouzigues en feuillantine, Filet de loup à l'huile d'olive et gros sel, Selle d'agneau farcie à
la truffe. **Wines** Coteaux des Baux, Châteauneuf-du-Pape.

XXX ✿ **La Cabro d'Or** M ⌿ with rm, ✆ 97.33.21, Telex 401810, ≤, ⌸, « Shaded terraces,
lake », ⌁, ⌖ – ⊡ ⌂wc ☎ ℗ – ⌸ 80. ⌶ ⓞ ⱸ VISA
*closed 18 November-20 December, Tuesday lunch and Monday from 15 October to 31
March* – **st. : M** 180/210 – ⊐ 42 – **22 rm** 350/550 – P 600/710
Spec. Foie gras chaud au vinaigre, Filet de loup en papillote, Noisettes d'agneau aux primeurs. **Wines**
Coteaux des Baux.

MONACO (Principality of) 84 ⑩, 195 ㉗㉘ – pop. 27 800 – alt. 65 – Casino – ✿ 93.
Paris 958 – Menton 9 – Nice (by the Moyenne Corniche) 18 – San Remo 44.

Monaco Capital of the Principality – ⊠ Monaco.

See : Tropical Garden⋆⋆ (Jardin exotique) : ≤⋆ – Observatory Caves⋆ (Grotte de
l'Observatoire) – St-Martin Gardens⋆ – Early paintings of the Nice School⋆⋆ in Cathedral – Recumbent Christ⋆ in the Misericord Chapel – Place du Palais⋆ – Prince's
Palace⋆ – Museums : oceanographic⋆⋆ (aquarium⋆⋆, ≤⋆⋆ from the terrace), Prehisto-
ric Anthropology⋆ – Museum of Napoleon and Monaco History⋆.

Urban racing circuit - A.C. 23 bd Albert-1er ✆ 30.32.20, Télex 469003.

Monte-Carlo Fashionable resort of the Principality - Grand casino, Casino of Sporting Club, Casino
Loews – ⊠ Monte-Carlo.

See : Terrace⋆⋆ of the Grand casino – Museum of Dolls and Automata⋆.
⌁ Monte-Carlo Golf Club ✆ 41.09.11 to the S by N7 : 11 km.
🛈 Direction Tourisme et Congrès, 2 a bd Moulins ✆ 30.87.01, Télex 469760.

🏨 ✿ **Paris,** pl. Casino ✆ 50.80.80, Telex 469925, ≤, ⌸, « Empire style dining room », ⌁,
⌖ – ⌸ ≣ rm ⊡ ☎ & ℗ – ⌸ 50. ⌶ ⓞ ⱸ VISA. ⌿ rest
M *(closed 30 September-23 December and Wednesday except July-August)* 300/450 – ⊐
65 – **220 rm** 1 200/1 500, 34 apartments
Spec. Soufflé de langouste, Médaillon de turbot aux encornets de saumon, Fricassée de veau aux écrevisses.
Wines Cuers, La Londe.

🏨 **Hermitage,** square Beaumarchais ✆ 50.67.31, Telex 479432, ≤, ⌸, « Dining room in
Baroque style », ⌁ – ⌸ ⱨ ≣ ⊡ ☎ ℗ – ⌸ 80. ⌶ ⓞ ⱸ VISA. ⌿ rest
M 205/270 – ⊐ 65 – **200 rm** 800/1 250, 9 apartments.

🏨 **Loews** M ⌿, av. Spélugues ✆ 50.65.00, Telex 479435, ≤, Casino and cabaret, ⌁ – ⱨ
≣ ⊡ ⊡ ☎ ⇔ – ⌸ 50-1 100. ⌶ ⓞ ⱸ VISA. ⌿ rest
st. : Le Foie Gras (dinner only) **M** a la carte 260/350 - L'Argentin (dinner only) **M** a la carte
190/280 - Le Pistou (dinner only) **M** 190/240 - Café de la mer (coffee shop only) **M** a la
carte approx. 120 – ⊐ 65 – **550 rm** 1 100/1 400, 68 apartments.

🏨 **Mirabeau** M, 1 av. Princesse-Grace ✆ 25.45.45, Telex 479413, ≤, ⌁ – ⱨ ≣ ⊡ ☎ ⇔
– ⌸ 80. ⌶ ⓞ ⱸ VISA. ⌿ rest
M 165/240 – ⊐ 60 – **96 rm** 600/1 050, 5 apartments.

🏨 **Beach Plaza** M, av. Princesse-Grace, à la Plage du Larvotto ✆ 30.98.80, Telex 479617,
≤, ⌸, « Fashionable resort with good bathing facilities », ⌁, ⌖ – ⱨ ≣ ⊡ ☎ & ⇔
– ⌸ 30-300. ⌶ ⓞ ⱸ VISA. ⌿ rest
st. : **M** 150/220 – ⊐ 48 – **311 rm** 480/1 125, 9 apartments.

🏨 **Balmoral** ⌿ without rest, 12 av. Costa ✆ 50.62.37, Telex 479436, ≤ – ⱨ ≣ rm ⊡ ☎. ⌶
ⓞ ⱸ VISA. ⌿
st. : ⊐ 28 – **67 rm** 210/430.

🏨 **Louvre** without rest, 16 bd Moulins ✆ 50.65.25, Telex 479645 – ⱨ ⊡ ⌂wc ☎. ⓞ ⱸ
VISA. ⌿
st. : ⊐ 28 – **35 rm** 366/402.

🏨 **Alexandra** without rest, 35 bd Princesse-Charlotte ✆ 50.63.13 – ⱨ ⌂wc ⌁wc ⇔. ⌶
ⓞ VISA
st. : ⊐ 27.50 – **55 rm** 187/360.

MONACO (Principality of) - Monte-Carlo

XXXX ❀ **Dominique Le Stanc,** 18 bd Moulins ℘ 50.63.37 — 🅰🅴 ⓪ 𝗩𝗜𝗦𝗔
closed Sunday and Monday — **M** 280/380
Spec. Chausson d'écrevisses aux petits légumes, Aiguillettes de canard au basilic, Pêche rôtie aux pistaches.

XXX **Grill de l'Hôtel de Paris,** pl. Casino ℘ 50.80.80, « Roof-top grill (open air) with ≤ over
the Principality » — 🅿 🅰🅴 ⓪ 𝗘
closed 6 to 30 January and Monday except 15 July to end August — **M** a la carte 300/360.

XXX **Bec Rouge,** 11 av. Gde Bretagne ℘ 30.74.91 — 🅰🅴 ⓪ 𝗘
closed January — **M** a la carte 170/230.

XX **Toula,** 20 bd de Suisse ℘ 50.02.02, 😄, Italian cuisine — 🅰🅴 ⓪
closed January and Monday except June, July and August — **M** a la carte 190/280.

XX **Rampoldi,** 3 av. Spélugues ℘ 30.70.65 — 🔲.

XX **Chez Gianni,** 39 av. Princesse Grace ℘ 30.46.33, Italian cuisine — 🔲. 🅰🅴 ⓪ 𝗩𝗜𝗦𝗔
closed February and Tuesday — **st. : M** a la carte 170/250.

XX **du Port,** quai Albert 1er ℘ 50.77.21, ≤, Italian cuisine — 🔲. 🅰🅴 ⓪ 𝗘 𝗩𝗜𝗦𝗔
closed 4 November-4 December and Monday — **st. : M** 150/250.

X **La Calanque,** 33 av. St-Charles ℘ 50.63.19, Seafood — 🅰🅴 ⓪ 𝗘 𝗩𝗜𝗦𝗔
closed 15 March-15 April and Sunday — **st. : M** a la carte 195/260.

at Monte-Carlo Beach (06 Maritime Alps) at : 2,5 km — ✉ 06190 Roquebrune-Cap-Martin :

🏨 **Monte-Carlo Beach H.** 🅼 ⬙, ℘ 78.21.40, ≤ sea and Monaco, « Fashionable resort
with good bathing facilities, ⟋, ⟋, ⟋ — 🛏 🔲 rm 🆃🆅 ☎ 🅿 — 🚗 30. 🅰🅴 ⓪ 𝗘 𝗩𝗜𝗦𝗔.
🍽 rest
29 March-14 september — **M** a la carte 210/290 — 🍽 65 — **46 rm** 1 100/1 250.

NICE 🅿 06000 Maritime Alps 🎯 ⑨⑩. 🎯 ㉖㉗ — pop. 338 486 — alt. at château 92 — Casino-Club
GYZ **T** — ❀ 93.

See : Site★★ — Promenade des Anglais★★ EFZ — Old Nice★ : Château ≤★★ JZ, Interior★ of
church of St-Martin and St-Augustin HY D, Balnstraded staircase★ of the Palais Lascaris HZ K,
Interior★ of Ste-Reparate Cathedral HZ L, St-Jacques Church★ HZ N, Decoration of St-Giaumes
Chapel HZ R — Mosaic★ by Chagall in Law Faculty DZ U — Cimiez : Monastery★ (Master-
pieces★★ of the early Nice School in the church) HV Q, Roman Ruins★ HV — Museums : Marc
Chagall★★ GX, Matisse★ HV M2, Fine Arts Museum★★ DZ M, Masséna★ FZ M1, International
Naive Style Museum★ — Carnival★★★ (before Shrove Tuesday) — Mount Alban ≤★★ 5 km —
Mount Boron ≤★ 3 km — St-Pons Church★ : 3 km.

Envir. : St-Michel Plateau ≤★★ 9,5 km.

🏌 Biot ℘ 65.08.48 : 22 km.

✈ of Nice-Côte d'Azur ℘ 72.30.30 : 7 km.

🚉 ℘ 87.50.50.

🚢 for Corsica : Société Nationale Maritime Corse-Méditerranée, 3 av. Gustave-V ℘ 89.60.63
FZ **D.**

🅱 Accueil de France (hotel reservations - not more than 5 days in advance) av. Thiers ℘ 87.07.07, Telex
460042 ; Palais des Congrès, Esplanade Kennedy ℘ 92.80.80, Télex 461861 ; 5 av. Gustave-V ℘ 87.60.60
and Nice-Parking near the Airport ℘ 83.32.64 - A.C. 9 r. Massenet ℘ 87.18.17.

Paris 931 — Cannes 32 — Genova 194 — Lyon 470 — Marseille 187 — Turino 220.

Plan on following pages

🏨 **Négresco,** 37 prom. des Anglais ℘ 88.39.51, Telex 460040, ≤, « Public rooms and
bedrooms, in period style : 16C and 18C, Empire and Napoléon III » — 🛏 🔲 🆅 ☎ 🅰
— 🚗 50-400. 🅰🅴 ⓪ 𝗘 𝗩𝗜𝗦𝗔
FZ **k**
st. : La Rotonde M a la carte 125/165 ⛟ and see rest. **Chantecler** below — 🍽 65 — **140 rm**
1 010/1 645, 10 apartments.

🏨 **Sofitel Splendid** 🅼, 50 bd Victor-Hugo ℘ 88.69.54, Telex 460938, « ⟋ on 8th floor, ≤
Nice » — 🛏 🔲 🆅 ☎ ❀ — 🅰🅴 ⓪ 𝗘 𝗩𝗜𝗦𝗔. 🍽 rest
FYZ **g**
st. : M a la carte 110/150 ⛟ — **126 rm** 🍽 420/740, 12 apartments 800/950 — P 590/660.

🏨 **Méridien** 🅼, 1 prom. des Anglais ℘ 82.25.25, Telex 470361, 😄, « Roof-top swimming
pool, ≤ bay » — 🛏 🔲 🆅 ☎ — 🚗 30-400. 🅰🅴 ⓪ 𝗘 𝗩𝗜𝗦𝗔
FZ **d**
st. : M a la carte 150/220 — 🍽 60 — **314 rm** 650/1 200, 21 apartments.

🏨 **Beach Régency** 🅼, 223 prom. des Anglais ℘ 83.91.51, Telex 461635, ≤ bay, 😄, ⟋ —
🛏 🔲 🆅 ☎ ❀ — 🚗 50-400. 🅰🅴 ⓪ 𝗘 𝗩𝗜𝗦𝗔
st. : Rendez Vous M a la carte 170/260 - **La Promenade** (coffee shop only) a la carte
approx. 170 — 🍽 55 — **301 rm** 600/850, 10 apartments.

🏨 **Plaza H.,** 12 av. Verdun ℘ 87.80.41, Telex 460979, ≤, « Roof-top terrace » — 🛏 🔲 🆅
☎ — 🚗 30-500. 🅰🅴 ⓪ 𝗘 𝗩𝗜𝗦𝗔. 🍽 rest
GZ **f**
st. : M 110 — 🍽 45 — **186 rm** 400/700 — P 620/1 140.

🏨 **Frantel** 🅼 without rest, 28 av. Notre-Dame ℘ 80.30.24, Telex 470662, « ⟋ on 8th floor,
hanging gardens on 2nd floor, ≤ » — 🛏 🔲 🆅 ☎ ❀ ⟋ — 🚗 25-120. 🅰🅴 ⓪ 𝗘 𝗩𝗜𝗦𝗔
st. : 🍽 32 — **200 ch** 350/490.
FXY **s**

🏨 **Westminster Concorde,** 27 prom. des Anglais ℘ 88.29.44, Telex 460872, ≤, 😄 —
🆅 ☎ — 🚗 40-350. 🅰🅴 ⓪ 𝗘 𝗩𝗜𝗦𝗔
FZ **m**
st. : Le Farniente *(closed November-10 December)* **M** 130 — 🍽 40 — **110 rm** 450/800.

🏨 **Continental-Masséna** Ⓜ without rest, 58 r. Gioffredo 🖉 85.49.25, Telex 470192 – 🕼
🖿 Ⓣⓥ ☎ 🚗 – ⚒ 60. Ⓐ🄴 ⓪ 🄴 𝘝𝘐𝘚𝘈
st. : ⊑ 25 – **116 rm** 173/407.
GZ **k**

🏨 **Ambassador** Ⓜ without rest, 8 av. Suède 🖉 87.90.19, Telex 460025, ≼ – 🕼 Ⓣⓥ ☎ ዿ. Ⓐ🄴
⓪ 🄴 𝘝𝘐𝘚𝘈
closed 15 November-15 December – st. : **45 rm** ⊑ 340/410.
FZ **x**

🏨 **La Pérouse** ⍐, 11 quai Rauba-Capeù ✉ 06300 🖉 62.34.63, Telex 461411, « ≼ Nice and
promenade des Anglais », ⍤, 🌫 – 🕼 🖿 rm Ⓣⓥ ☎ – ⚒ 30. Ⓐ🄴 ⓪ 🄴 𝘝𝘐𝘚𝘈. ⍰ rest
st. : **M** (*coffee shop only in summer*) – **65 rm** ⊑ 300/800.
HZ **k**

🏨 **La Malmaison**, 48 bd V.-Hugo 🖉 87.62.56, Telex 470410 – 🕼 🖿 Ⓣⓥ ☎. Ⓐ🄴 ⓪ 🄴 𝘝𝘐𝘚𝘈
⍰ rest
st. : **M** (*closed Tuesday*) 95/140 – **50 rm** ⊑ 260/370 – P 375/485.
FYZ **e**

🏨 **Grand H. Aston** Ⓜ, 12 av. F.-Faure 🖉 80.62.52, Telex 470290, 🌫, « Roof-top terrace »
– 🕼 🖿 Ⓣⓥ ☎ ዿ. – ⚒ 50-180. Ⓐ🄴 ⓪ 🄴 𝘝𝘐𝘚𝘈
st. : **M** 85/108 – ⊑ 40 – **155 rm** 540/640.
HZ **u**

🏨 **Napoléon** without rest, 6 r. Grimaldi 🖉 87.70.07, Telex 460949 – 🕼 🖿 Ⓣⓥ ☎ ዿ. Ⓐ🄴 ⓪ 🄴
𝘝𝘐𝘚𝘈
closed November – st. : ⊑ 18,50 – **80 rm** 235/357.
FZ **r**

🏨 **Atlantic,** 12 bd Victor-Hugo 🖉 88.40.15, Telex 460840 – 🕼 Ⓣⓥ ☎ Ⓟ – ⚒ 30-80. Ⓐ🄴 ⓪
🄴 𝘝𝘐𝘚𝘈
st. : **M** 85 – ⊑ 25 – **123 rm** 300/410 – P 365/500.
FY **d**

🏨 **Park and rest. Le Passage,** 6 av. de Suède 🖉 87.80.25, Telex 970 176, ≼ – 🕼 🖿 rest
Ⓣⓥ ☎ ዿ – ⚒ 80. Ⓐ🄴 ⓪ 🄴 𝘝𝘐𝘚𝘈
st. : **M** (*closed Sunday and Bank Holidays*) 100 – ⊑ 35 – **150 rm** 360/510 – P 455/525.
FZ **x**

🏨 **Gd Hôtel de Florence** Ⓜ without rest, 3 r. P.-Deroulède 🖉 88.46.87, Telex 470652 – 🕼
🖿 Ⓣⓥ ☎ ዿ. ⍰
st. : **53 rm** ⊑ 250/360.
GY **r**

🏨 **Victoria** without rest, 33 bd V.-Hugo 🖉 88.39.60, Telex 461337, 🌫 – 🕼 Ⓣⓥ ☎. Ⓐ🄴 ⓪ 🄴
𝘝𝘐𝘚𝘈
st. : **40 rm** ⊑ 260/350.
FYZ **z**

🏨 **Locarno** without rest, 4 av. Baumettes 🖉 96.28.00, Telex 970015 – 🕼 🖿 Ⓣⓥ 🚗
– ⚒ 50. Ⓐ🄴 ⓪ 🄴 𝘝𝘐𝘚𝘈
st. : ⊑ 16 – **48 rm** 185/270.
DEZ **t**

🏨 **Gounod** without rest, 3 r. Gounod 🖉 88.26.20, Telex 461705 – 🕼 🖿 Ⓣⓥ 🛏wc 🛁wc ☎
🚗. Ⓐ🄴 ⓪ 𝘝𝘐𝘚𝘈
st. : **45 rm** ⊑ 280/360, 5 apartments 460.
FYZ **g**

🏨 **New York** without rest, 44 av. Mar.-Foch 🖉 92.04.19, Telex 470215 – 🕼 🛏wc 🛁wc ☎.
Ⓐ🄴 ⓪ 𝘝𝘐𝘚𝘈
st. : ⊑ 20 – **52 rm** 231/267.
GY **g**

🏨 **Georges** Ⓜ ⍐, without rest, 3 r. H.-Cordier 🖉 86.23.41 – 🕼 🛏wc 🚗. Ⓐ🄴
DZ **e**
st. : ⊑ 14 – **18 rm** 161/255.

🏨 **Suisse** without rest, 15 quai Rauba-Capeu ✉ 06300 🖉 62.33.00, ≼ – 🕼 🛏wc 🛁wc 🚗
st. : ⊑ 15 – **39 rm** 126/235.
HZ **r**

🏨 **Avenida** without rest, 41 av. J.-Médecin 🖉 88.55.03 – 🕼 kitchenette 🖿 Ⓣⓥ 🛏wc 🛁wc
🚗. Ⓐ🄴 𝘝𝘐𝘚𝘈. ⍰
st. : ⊑ 14 – **34 rm** 143/188.
FY **m**

🏨 **Lausanne,** 36 r. Rossini 🖉 88.85.94, Telex 461269 – 🕼 Ⓣⓥ 🛏wc 🛁wc ☎. Ⓐ🄴 ⓪ 🄴 𝘝𝘐𝘚𝘈
st. : **M** (*closed November and Wednesday*) 85 (except Bank Holidays)/180 – **40 rm**
⊑ 290/390 – P 480/570.
FY **t**

🏨 **Windsor** without rest, 11 r. Dalpozzo 🖉 88.59.35, Telex 970072, ⍤, 🌫 – 🕼 Ⓣⓥ 🛏wc
🛁wc ☎. Ⓐ🄴 ⓪ 🄴 𝘝𝘐𝘚𝘈
st. : **59 rm** ⊑ 220/340.
FZ **f**

🏨 **Carlton** without rest, 26 bd V.-Hugo 🖉 88.87.83 – 🕼 🛏wc 🛁wc 🚗. Ⓐ🄴 ⓪ 🄴 𝘝𝘐𝘚𝘈
st. : ⊑ 15 – **29 rm** 116/260.
FY **f**

🏨 **Brice,** 44 r. Mar.-Joffre 🖉 88.14.44, Telex 470658, 🌫, 🌫 – 🕼 Ⓣⓥ 🛏wc 🛁wc 🚗 ዿ.
⚒ 30. ⓪ 🄴 𝘝𝘐𝘚𝘈. ⍰ rest
st. : **M** 92 – **65 rm** ⊑ 245/400 – P 370/440.
FZ **b**

🏨 **Chatham** without rest, 9 r. A.-Karr 🖉 87.80.61 – 🕼 🛏wc 🛁wc 🚗. Ⓐ🄴 ⓪ 🄴 𝘝𝘐𝘚𝘈
FY **x**
st. : – **50 rm** ⊑ 200/275.

🏨 **Midi** Ⓜ without rest, 16 r. Alsace-Lorraine 🖉 88.49.17, Telex 970565 – 🕼 🖿 Ⓣⓥ 🛏wc
🛁wc ☎. ⍰
st. : **40 rm** ⊑ 350.
FX **n**

🏨 **Durante** ⍐, without rest, 16 av. Durante 🖉 88.84.40, 🌫 – kitchenette 🛏wc 🛁wc 🚗
Ⓟ. ⍰
closed 26 October-2 December – st. : ⊑ 20 – **30 rm** 120/200.
FY **b**

🏨 **Cigognes** without rest, 16 r. Maccarani 🖉 88.65.02 – 🕼 Ⓣⓥ 🛏wc 🛁wc ☎. ⍰
st. : – **32 rm** ⊑ 180/250.
FY **s**

🏨 **Trianon** without rest, 15 av. Auber 🖉 88.30.69 – 🕼 🛏wc 🛁wc 🚗. Ⓐ🄴 ⓪ 🄴 𝘝𝘐𝘚𝘈
FY **u**
st. : ⊑ 14 – **32 rm** 149/187.

🏨 **Star H.** Ⓜ without rest, 14 r. Biscarra 🖉 85.19.03 – 🛏wc 🛁wc ☎
st. : ⊑ 15 – **20 rm** 112/195.
GY **k**

NICE

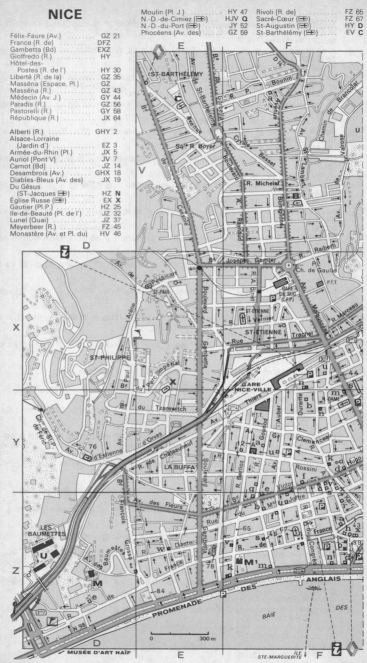

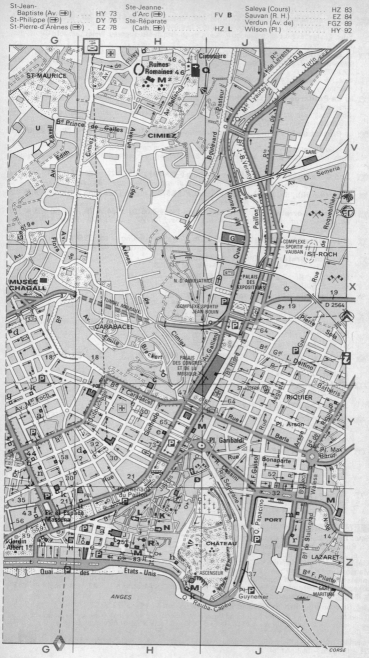

XXXX ۞۞ **Chantecler** (Maximin), 37 prom. des Anglais ℰ 88.39.51 — 🍽. �æ ⓞ E 𝘝𝘐𝘚𝘈   FZ **k**
closed November — **st. : M** 250/400 and a la carte
Spec. Courgettes aux truffes, Saumon frais au gros sel, Tian de filet d'agneau. **Wines** Cassis, Le Cannet-des-Maures.

XXX ۞ **Ane Rouge** (Vidalot), 7 quai Deux-Emmanuel ⊠ 06300 ℰ 89.49.63 — �æ ⓞ 𝘝𝘐𝘚𝘈
closed 14 July-1 September, Saturday dinner, Sunday and Bank Holidays — **M** a la carte
170/270   JZ **m**
Spec. Huîtres plates au champagne, Petits choux farcis au homard, St-Pierre Mascareignes. **Wines** Bellet, Palette.

XXX ۞ **La Poularde chez Lucullus** (Normand), 9 r. Deloye ℰ 85.22.90 — 🍽. �æ ⓞ E 𝘝𝘐𝘚𝘈
closed 12 July-18 August and Wednesday — **M** 135/190   GY **n**
Spec. Langouste grillée aux herbes (15 March-15 October), Rougets à la sauvage, Capilotade de volaille.
Wines Gassin, Bellet.

XXX ۞ **Bistrot de la Promenade,** 7 promenade des Anglais ℰ 81.63.48, ≼, 🏤 — 🍽. �æ ⓞ
𝘝𝘐𝘚𝘈   FZ **n**
closed 15 January-15 February and Sunday — **M** a la carte 195/290
Spec. Goujonnettes de sole aux pâtes vertes, Selle d'agneau à la crème d'ail, Mousseline de fruits de la
passion.

XXX **Los Caracolès,** 5 r. St-François-de-Paule ⊠ 06300 ℰ 80.98.23 — 🍽. �æ E 𝘝𝘐𝘚𝘈   HZ **e**
closed July, February holidays, Sunday dinner and Wednesday — **st. : M** 140/150.

XX **Don Camillo,** 5 r. Ponchettes ⊠ 06300 ℰ 85.67.95, cuisine italienne — 🍽. �æ ⓞ E 𝘝𝘐𝘚𝘈
closed July and Sunday — **M** a la carte 110/170   HZ **h**

XX **Gourmet Lorrain** 🐌 with rm, 7 av. Santa-Fior ⊠ 06100 ℰ 84.90.78 — 🍽 📺 ⇔ 🐾. �æ
M *(closed August, Sunday dinner and Monday)* 70/120 — 🖵 12,50 — **15 rm** 110/170 — P
120/160.   FV **a**

XX **Chez Rolando,** 3 r. Desboutins ℰ 85.76.79, Italian cooking — 🍽. �æ 𝘝𝘐𝘚𝘈   GZ **n**
closed July, Sunday and at lunch in August — **M** a la carte 110/165 🍺.

XX **Bon Coin Breton,** 5 r. Blacas ℰ 85.17.01 — 🍽   GY **v**
closed Sunday dinner and Monday — **st. : M** 59/138.

X **Rivoli,** 9 r. Rivoli ℰ 88.12.62 — 🍽. �æ 𝘝𝘐𝘚𝘈   FZ **v**
closed 15 June-15 July and Monday — **st. : M** 80 b.i./120.

X **La Nissarda,** 17 r. Gubernatis ℰ 85.26.29 — �æ   HY **d**
closed July, Tuesday and Wednesday — **st. : M** 43/75.

X **Mireille,** 19 bd Raimbaldi ℰ 85.27.23 🍽. 𝘝𝘐𝘚𝘈   GX **d**
closed June, Monday and Tuesday except July and August — **st. : M** one dish only : paella
a la carte 85 approx..

at the airport 7 km — ⊠ 06200 Nice :

🏨 **Holiday Inn** Ⓜ, on N 7 ℰ 83.91.92, Telex 970202, 🏤, 🏊 — 🛗 🍽 📺 ☎ 🕭 🚗 — 🔺
250. �æ ⓞ E 𝘝𝘐𝘚𝘈
st. : M 100 — 🖵 44 — **154 rm** 550/650.

XXX **Ciel d'Azur,** 2nd floor in Airport ℰ 72.36.36, Telex 970011 — 🍽. �æ ⓞ 𝘝𝘐𝘚𝘈
M 130/185.

at the Cap 3000 to the SW : 8 km — ⊠ 06700 St-Laurent-du-Var :

🏨 **Novotel** Ⓜ, ℰ 31.61.15, Telex 470643, 🏤, 🏊 — 🛗 🍽 📺 ☎ 🕭 🅿 — 🔺 300. �æ ⓞ E
𝘝𝘐𝘚𝘈 — **M** (coffee shop only) a la carte approx. 95 🍺 — 🖵 33 — **103 rm** 320/378.

at St-Pancrace N : 8 km by D 914 — alt. 302 — ⊠ 06100 Nice :

XXX ۞ **Rôtisserie de St-Pancrace** (Teillas), ℰ 84.43.69, ≼ — 🅿. 𝘝𝘐𝘚𝘈
closed 5 January-5 February and Monday except from 26 May to September — **M** a la
carte 170/245
Spec. Ravioles au foie gras, Pot au feu à la riche (September-June), Gibiers (September-February). **Wines**
Bellet, Bandol.

XX **Cicion,** ℰ 84.49.29, ≼ Nice and seaside, 🏤 — 🅿
*closed 15 October-25 November, dinners (except July-August and school holidays) and
Wednesday* — **M** 110/130.

STRASBOURG Ⓟ 67000 B.-Rhin 🖽 ⑩ — pop. 252 264 Greater Strasbourg 409 161 alt. 139 — ۞ 88.

See : Cathédral★★★ : Astronomical clock★, ≼★ CX — Old City★★★ BCX : la Petite France★★
BX, Rue du Bain-aux-Plantes★★ BX **7,** Place de la Cathédrale★★ CX **17,** — Maison Kammerzell★
CX **e,** Château des Rohan★ CX, Cour du Corbeau★ CX **18,** — Ponts couverts★ BX **B,** Place
Kléber★, Hôtel de Ville★ CV **H,** rue Mercière — ≼★ CX **53** — Barrage Vauban ⚘★★ BX **D** —
Mausoleum★★ in St-Thomas Church CX **E** — Orangery★ — Boat trips on the Ill river and the
canals★ CX — Guided tours of the Port★ by boat — Museum : Oeuvre N.-Dame★★★ CX **M1,**
collections de céramiques★★ du château des Rohan CX, Alsatian★ CX **M2,** Historical★ CX **M3** —
🮰 Illkirch-Graffenstaden ℰ 66.17.22.

✈ Strasbourg-Entzheim ℰ 78.40.99 by D 392 : 12 km — 🚆 ℰ 22.50.50.

🖽 and Accueil de France (Information and hotel reservations, not more than 5 days in advance), Palais des
Congrès av. Schutzenberger ℰ 35.03.00, Télex 870860 ; pl. Gare ℰ 32.51.49 and pl. Gutenberg ℰ 32.57.07
— Bureau d'accueil, pont Europe (exchange facilities) ℰ 61.39.23 - A.C. 5 av. Paix ℰ 36.04.34.

Paris 488 — Bâle 145 — Bonn 360 — Bordeaux 1 060 — Frankfurt 218 — Karlsruhe 81 — Lille 505 — Luxembourg
221 — Lyon 480 — Stuttgart 154.

STRASBOURG

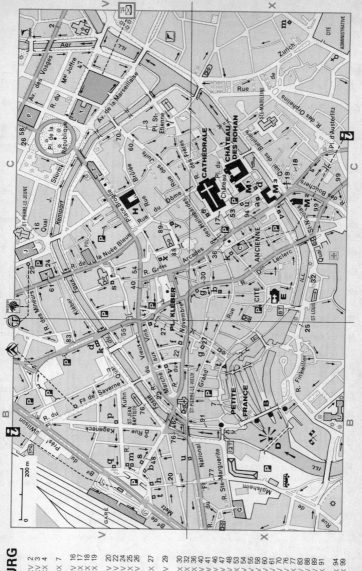

163

🏨🏨🏨 ⚜ **Hilton** Ⓜ, av. Herrenschmidt ℰ 37.10.10, Telex 890363, ☕ – 🕴 kitchenette 🖥 📺 ☎
      🔥 🏊 – 🔬 30-250 ⒶⒺ ⓄⒹ Ε 𝘝𝘐𝘚𝘈
      st. : Le Jardin M a la carte approx. 120 ⅃ - **La Maison du Bœuf** *(closed 5 to 25 August and Saturday lunch)* **M** a la carte 170/240 – ⌖ 39 – **247 rm** 450/595, 5 apartments
      Spec. Soupière de grenouilles aux petits légumes, Filet de bœuf au pinot noir à la moëlle, Chariot de gourmandises.

🏨🏨 **Sofitel** Ⓜ, pl. St-Pierre-le-Jeune ℰ 32.99.30, Telex 870894, patio – 🕴 🖥 📺 ☎ 🔥 🚗
      – 🔬 30-100. ⒶⒺ ⓄⒹ Ε 𝘝𝘐𝘚𝘈 ⅍ rest   CV s
      st. : Le Chateaubriand *(closed 1 to 15 August and Sunday)* **M** a la carte 160/230 ⅃ – ⌖ 42
      – **180 rm** 425/605, 5 apartments 950.

🏨🏨 **Holiday Inn** Ⓜ, 20 pl. Bordeaux ℰ 35.70.00, Telex 890515, 🔲 – 🕴 🖥 📺 ☎ 🔥 🅿 – 🔬
      50-600. ⒶⒺ ⓄⒹ Ε 𝘝𝘐𝘚𝘈
      st. : La Louisiane M 105 ⅃ – ⌖ 43 – **168 rm** 455/527.

🏨🏨 **Terminus-Gruber,** 10 pl. Gare ℰ 32.87.00, Telex 870998 – 🕴 📺 🔥 – 🔬 60. ⒶⒺ
      Ε 𝘝𝘐𝘚𝘈   BV m
      rest. **Cour de Rosemont** *(closed 22 December-6 January)* **M** 110/150 ⅃ – ⌖ 33 – **72 rm** 210/440, 6 apartments 500/560 – P 360/470.

🏨🏨 **Novotel** Ⓜ, quai Kléber ℰ 22.10.99, Telex 880700 – 🕴 🖥 📺 ☎ 🔥 🅿 – 🔬 30-200. ⒶⒺ
      ⓄⒹ Ε 𝘝𝘐𝘚𝘈   BV k
      M (coffee shop only) a la carte approx. 95 ⅃ – ⌖ 31 – **97 rm** 361/410.

🏨🏨 **France** Ⓜ without rest, 20 r. Jeu-des-Enfants ℰ 32.37.12, Telex 890084 – 🕴 📺 ☎ 🚗
      – 🔬 30. ⒶⒺ ⓄⒹ Ε 𝘝𝘐𝘚𝘈   BV v
      st. : ⌖ 22 – **70 rm** 258/339.

🏨🏨 **Monopole-Métropole** without rest, 16 r. Kuhn ℰ 32.11.94, Telex 890366, « Alsatian
      decor » – 🕴 📺 ☎ 🚗 ⒶⒺ ⓄⒹ Ε 𝘝𝘐𝘚𝘈   BV p
      closed Christmas Day-1 January – **st. :** ⌖ 19 – **98 rm** 200/315.

🏨🏨 **Gd Hôtel** without rest, 12 pl. Gare ℰ 32.46.90, Telex 870011 – 🕴 🔥 ⒶⒺ ⓄⒹ 𝘝𝘐𝘚𝘈   BV m
      st. : ⌖ 30 – **90 rm** 275/380, 4 apartments 380.

🏨🏨 **des Rohan** Ⓜ without rest, 17 r. Maroquin ℰ 32.85.11 – 🕴 📺 ☎. ⅍   CX u
      st. : ⌖ 24 – **36 rm** 205/340.

🏨🏨 **Nouvel H. Maison Rouge** without rest, 4 r. F.-Bourgeois ℰ 32.08.60, Telex 880130 –
      🕴 📺 ☎. ⒶⒺ ⓄⒹ Ε 𝘝𝘐𝘚𝘈   CX g
      st. : ⌖ 22 – **130 rm** 132/305, 6 apartments 425.

🏨 **Villa d'Est** Ⓜ without rest, 12 r. J.-Kablé ℰ 36.69.02 – 🕴 📺 🛁wc ☎ 🔥. ⒶⒺ ⓄⒹ Ε 𝘝𝘐𝘚𝘈
      closed 23 December-1 January – **st. :** ⌖ 21 – **32 rm** 269/281.

🏨 **La Dauphine** Ⓜ without rest, 30 r. 1ᵉ Armée ℰ 36.26.61, Telex 880766 – 🕴 📺 🛁wc
      🚿wc ☎ 🚗. ⒶⒺ ⓄⒹ 𝘝𝘐𝘚𝘈
      closed 23 December-2 January – **st. :** ⌖ 21 – **45 rm** 265/275.

🏨 **Hannong** without rest, 15 r. 22-Novembre ℰ 32.16.22, Telex 890551 – 🕴 📺 🛁wc 🚿wc
      ☎ 🅿 – 🔬 50. ⒶⒺ ⓄⒹ Ε 𝘝𝘐𝘚𝘈   BV f
      closed 23 to 30 December – **st. :** ⌖ 21 – **70 rm** 199/322.

🏨 **Bristol,** 4 pl. Gare ℰ 32.00.83, Telex 890317 – 🕴 🛁-rest 🛁wc 🚿wc ☎. ⒶⒺ ⓄⒹ Ε 𝘝𝘐𝘚𝘈
      st. : M 72/94 ⅃ – ⌖ 25 – **38 rm** 195/270.   BV h

🏨 **Europe** without rest, 38 r. Fossé-des-Tanneurs ℰ 32.17.88, Telex 890220 – 🕴 📺 🛁wc
      🚿wc ☎ 🔥. ⒶⒺ ⓄⒹ Ε 𝘝𝘐𝘚𝘈   BX g
      st. : ⌖ 18,50 – **60 rm** 97/240.

🏨 **Continental** without rest, 14 r. Maire Kuss ℰ 22.28.07, Telex 880881 – 🕴 📺 🛁wc ☎.
      ⒶⒺ ⓄⒹ Ε 𝘝𝘐𝘚𝘈   BV s
      st. : ⌖ 16,50 – **48 rm** 178/235.

🏨 **Ibis,** 1 pl. Halles ℰ 22.14.99, Telex 880399 – 🕴 📺 🛁wc ☎ – 🔬 50. Ε 𝘝𝘐𝘚𝘈   BV d
      st. : M a la carte approx. 70 ⅃ – ⚑ 18,50 – **97 rm** 203.

🏨 **Vendôme** without rest, 9 pl. Gare ℰ 32.45.23, Telex 890850 – 🕴 🛁wc 🚿wc ☎. ⒶⒺ ⓄⒹ
      Ε 𝘝𝘐𝘚𝘈   BV b
      st. : ⌖ 16 – **48 rm** 130/200.

🍴🍴🍴🍴 ⚜⚜ **Crocodile** (Jung), 10 r. Outre ℰ 32.13.02 – 🖥. ⒶⒺ ⓄⒹ Ε. ⅍   CV x
      closed 7 July-5 August, 22 December-1 January, Sunday and Monday – **st. : M** 195 and a la carte
      Spec. Flan de cresson aux grenouilles, Gratin de langouste, Canard sauvage à la presse (season). Wines Riesling, Kaefferkopf.

🍴🍴🍴 ⚜⚜ **Buerehiesel** (Westermann), Set in the Orangerie Park ℰ 61.62.24, « Attractive Alsatian mansion in a park » – 🅿. ⒶⒺ ⓄⒹ
      closed 8 to 23 August, 23 December-6 January, February holidays, Tuesday dinner and Wednesday – **st. : M** 170/280 and a la carte
      Spec. Eminçé de saumon et lotte en terrine, Soupe de grenouilles et ravioli, Poêlée de Sot-l'y-laisse aux truffes. Wines Muscat, Sylvaner.

🍴🍴🍴 ⚜ **Valentin-Sorg** (14th floor), 6 pl. Homme-de-Fer ℰ 32.12.16, ⩽ Strasbourg – ⒶⒺ ⓄⒹ
      𝘝𝘐𝘚𝘈   BV r
      closed 15 to 31 August, 15 to 28 February, Sunday dinner and Tuesday – **st. : M** 130/200
      Spec. Foie chaud "Fritz Kobus", Suprême de sole Newbourg, Ris de veau Demidoff. Wines Riquewihr, Pinot blanc.

XXX ✿ **Maison Kammerzell**, 16 pl. Cathédrale ℘ 32.42.14, Telex 890221, « Attractive 16C
Alsatian house » — ▥ ⓸ ☰ 𝘝𝘐𝘚𝘈 CX e
st. : Leo Schnug (ground floor) **M** 165 b.i./143 ♧ - upstairs **M** 196/302
Spec. Parfait de foie gras frais, Choucroute, Matelote d'anguilles. Wines Sylvaner, Riesling.

XXX **Maison des Tanneurs dite ''Gerwerstub''**, 42 r. Bain-aux-Plantes ℘ 32.79.70, « Old
Alsatian house on the banks of the River III » — ▥ ⓸ BX t
closed 26 June-9 July, 22 December-23 January, Sunday and Monday — st. : **M** a la carte
120/200.

XXX **La Volière**, 1 av. Gén.-de-Gaulle ℘ 61.05.79 — ▤. ▥ ⓸ ☰ 𝘝𝘐𝘚𝘈
closed 14 July-13 August, Saturday lunch and Sunday — st. : **M** 146/218.

XX **Zimmer**, 8 r. Temple-Neuf ℘ 32.35.01 — ▤. ▥ 𝘝𝘐𝘚𝘈 CV y
closed August, Saturday and Sunday — st. : **M** 140/200.

XX **Gourmet sans Chiqué**, 15 r. Ste-Barbe ℘ 32.04.07 — ▥ ⓸ 𝘝𝘐𝘚𝘈 CX b
closed Sunday and Monday — st. : **M** 160/200.

XX ✿ **La Table Gourmande** (Reix), 43 rte Gén.-de-Gaulle ⊠ 67300 Schiltigheim ℘ 83.61.67
— ▤. ▥ ⓸ 𝘝𝘐𝘚𝘈
closed 29 July-21 August, 24 December-8 January, Monday lunch and Sunday — st. : **M**
210
Spec. Feuilleté chaud de tourteaux à l'oseille, Filet de barbue à la vinaigrette tiède d'orange, Confit de
canard ''périgourdine''.

X **A l'Ancienne Douane**, 6 r. Douane ℘ 32.42.19, « Riverside terrace ». ▥ CX v
st. : **M** 56/90 ♧.

X **Strissel**, pl. Grande-Boucherie ℘ 32.14.73, Restaurant with wine tasting, rustic decor
— 𝘝𝘐𝘚𝘈 CX a
closed 8 to 31 July, February holidays, Sunday and Monday except Bank Holidays — st. :
M 35/69 ♧.

at pont de l'Europe :

🏨 **P.L.M. Motel du Pont de l'Europe** Ⓜ ⅖, ℘ 61.03.23, Telex 870833, 🍽 — 📺 ☎ Ⓟ
— 🔬 100-400. ▥ ⓸ ☰ 𝘝𝘐𝘚𝘈
st. : **M** 49/150 ♧ — ⊡ 25 — **88 rm** 240/277, 5 apartments 356.

at Illkirch-Graffenstaden 8 km — ⊠ 67400 Illkirch-Graffenstaden :

🏨 **Alsace** Ⓜ, 187 rte Lyon ℘ 66.41.60 — 🛗 ⌷wc ☎ Ⓟ — 🔬 60. 𝘝𝘐𝘚𝘈 ⌘ rm
closed 24 December-2 January — st. : **M** (closed Saturday lunch and Sunday) 75/125 ♧ —
⊡ 18 — **40 rm** 189/205 — P 260.

near Colmar interchange A 35 10 km — ⊠ 67400 Illkirch-Graffenstaden :

🏨 **Novotel** Ⓜ, ℘ 66.21.56, Telex 890142, 🍽, ⛱, 🌳 — ▤ rest 📺 ☎ ♧ Ⓟ. ▥ ⓸ ☰ 𝘝𝘐𝘚𝘈
M (coffee shop only) a la carte approx. 95 ♧ — ⊡ 30 — **76 rm** 280/307.

🏨 **Mercure** Ⓜ, ℘ 66.03.00, Telex 890277, 🍽, ⛱, 🌳 — 🔬 200. ▥ ⓸ ☰ 𝘝𝘐𝘚𝘈
M a la carte approx. 100 ♧ — ⊡ 30 — **91 rm** 276/318.

at La Wantzenau NE by D 468 — pop. 4 084 — ⊠ 67610 La Wantzenau :

🏨 **H. Au Moulin** without rest, S : 1,5 km by D 468 ℘ 96.27.83 — 🛗 ⌷wc ▥wc ☎ Ⓟ. ▥
𝘝𝘐𝘚𝘈
closed 24 December-1 January — st. : ⊡ 23 — **19 rm** 155/220.

🏠 **A la Gare**, 32 r. Gare ℘ 96.63.44 — ⌷wc ▥wc ☎ Ⓟ. 𝘝𝘐𝘚𝘈 ⌘ rm
st. : **M** (closed 29 July-18 August, 1 to 10 March, Sunday dinner and Friday) a la carte
approx. 110 ♧ — ☞ 15 — **19 rm** 105/145.

XXX ✿ **A la Barrière** (Aeby), 3 rte Strasbourg ℘ 96.20.23 — Ⓟ. ▥ ⓸ 𝘝𝘐𝘚𝘈
closed 15 August-6 September, February holidays, Wednesday dinner and Thursday —
st. : **M** (booking essential) a la carte 180/250
Spec. Foie gras d'oie, Filet de bar marinière, Râble de lièvre aux cèpes (October to December). Wines
Riesling, Pinot noir.

XX ✿ **Zimmer**, 23 r. Héros ℘ 96.62.08 — Ⓟ. ▥ ⓸ ☰ 𝘝𝘐𝘚𝘈
closed 1 to 18 August, Sunday dinner and Monday — st. : **M** 80/160 ♧
Spec. Salade gourmande, Sandre aux petits légumes, Noisette de chevreuil (June to February). Wines Pinot
noir, Edelzwicker.

�**Ammerschwihr** 68770 H.-Rhin ⑥② ⑱⑲ — pop. 1 639 — alt. 230 — ✿ 89.
Strasbourg 74.

XXX ✿✿ **Aux Armes de France** (Gaertner) with rm, ℘ 47.10.12 — ⌷wc ☎ Ⓟ. ▥ ⓸ ☰
𝘝𝘐𝘚𝘈 ⌘ rm
closed January, Thursday lunch and Wednesday — **M** (booking essential) 150/270 and a la
carte — ☞ 28 — **8 rm** 170/230
Spec. Foie gras frais, Gratin de queues d'écrevisses, Canette de Barbarie aux épices et au miel. Wines
Riesling, Gewurztraminer.

Illhaeusern 68 H.-Rhin 🄑🄑 ⑲ – pop. 557 – alt. 176 – ✉ 68150 Ribeauvillé – ✪ 89.
Strasbourg 60.

🏨 **La Clairière** Ⓜ ⬙ without rest, rte Guémar ℰ 71.80.80, ✵ – 🛗 📺 ☎ 🄿
closed January, February and Monday evening in November, December and March – st. :
🗙 24 – **24 rm** 230/320.

XXXX ✿✿✿ **Aub de l'Ill** (Haeberlin), ℰ 71.83.23, « Tasteful decor, set on the banks of the
River Ill, ≼ over flower gardens » – 🔲 🄿
closed 1 to 7 July, February, Monday except at lunch from 1 April to 31 October and
Tuesday – **M** (booking essential) a la carte 200/260
Spec. Salade de langouste au curry et à la mangue, Mousseline de grenouilles et filets de poissons au
Riesling, Feuilleté de pigeonneau aux choux et truffes. **Wines** Riesling, Sylvaner.

🚐 *There is no paid publicity in this Guide.*

TOURS

Tours P 37000 I.-et-L. 64 ⑮ – pop. 136 483 Greater Tours 251 320 – alt. 48 – ✪ 47.

See : Cathedral quarter★★ : Cathédrale★★ EX, Fine Arts Museum★★ EXY **M2**, The Psa-
lette★ EX **F**, – Place Grégoire de Tours★ EX47 – Old Tours★★ : Place Plumereau★ CY 67,
hôtel Gouin★ CX **M4**, rue Briçonnet★ CX 15 – St-Julien quater★ : Craft Guilds Museum★★
(Musée du Compagnonnage) DX **M5**, Beaune-Semblançay Gardens★ DX **B**, – Staircase
banister★ of hôtel Mame DY **D** – St-Cosme Priory★ W : 3 km – Meslay Tithe Barn★
(Grange de Meslay) NE : 10 km – ┌n┐ of Touraine ℰ 53.20.28 ; domaine de la Touche at
Ballan-Miré : 14 km – ✈ of Tours-St-Symphorien : ℰ 54.19.46 NE : 7 km.

🚗 ℰ 20.23.43 – 🅱 and Accueil de France (Information, exchange facilities and hotel reservations - not more than 5 days in advance), pl. Mar. Leclerc ℰ 05.58.08, Télex 75008 – Automobile
Club de l'Ouest 4 pl. J.-Jaurès ℰ 05.50.19.

Paris 234 – Angers 108 – Bordeaux 345 – Chartres 140 – Clermont-Ferrand 307 – Limoges 204
– Le Mans 82 – Orléans 112 – Rennes 236 – St-Étienne 424.

St-Pierre (⇥)	FX	Simon (R. Jules)	EY
St-Saturnin (⇥)	CX	Tanneurs (R. des)	BX 94
Ste-Jeanne d'Arc (⇥)	CZ	Thiers (Bd et Pl.)	CDZ
Salengro (R. Roger)	CDZ	Thomas (R. A.)	EX
Sicard (Pl. François)	EY 92	Ursulines (R. des)	EXY

Vaillant (R. E.)	EFYZ
Victoire (R. de la)	BXY
Victor-Hugo (R.)	BCY
Voltaire (R.)	DXY 96
Zola (R. Émile)	DY

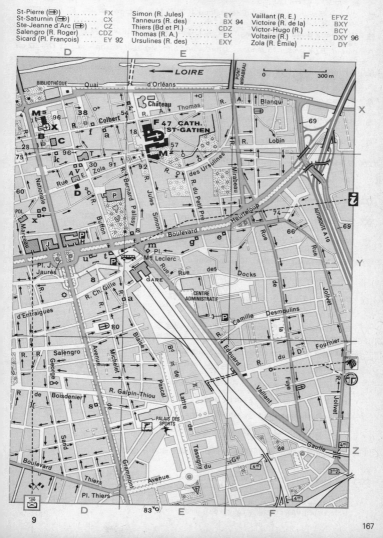

9

🏨🏨 **Méridien** Ⓜ ⤴, 292 av. Grammont ⊠ 37200 ℘ 28.00.80, Telex 750922, ≼, 🏊, 🎾, ✂ — 🛗 🗄 📺 ☎ 🅿 — 🔬 40-200. 🖭 ⓓ Ⅽ 𝘝𝘐𝘚𝘈
st. : **M** *(closed Sunday out of season)* 100 — ⌓ 34 — **119 rm** 350/460, 6 apartments.

🏨🏨 **Univers and rest. la Touraine,** 5 bd Heurteloup ℘ 05.37.12, Telex 751460 — 🛗 📺 ☎ ⟵ — 🔬 30. 🖭 ⓓ Ⅽ 𝘝𝘐𝘚𝘈   DY **u**
st. : **M** *(closed February and Saturday)* 95/136 — ⌓ 29 — **88 rm** 229/324, 3 apartments 520.

🏨🏨 **Royal** Ⓜ without rest, 65 av. Grammont ℘ 64.71.78 — 🛗 ⟵. 🖭 ⓓ 𝘝𝘐𝘚𝘈. ❄   DZ **s**
st. : ⌓ 24 — **35 rm** 220/256.

🏨🏨 **Bordeaux,** 3 pl. Mar.-Leclerc ℘ 05.40.32, Telex 750414 — 🛗 📺 ☎. 🖭 ⓓ 𝘝𝘐𝘚𝘈. ❄ rm   DY **t**
M 75/100 — **53 rm** ⌓ 258/280 — P 330/490.

🏨 **Central H.** without rest, 21 r. Berthelot ℘ 05.46.44, Telex 751173 — 🛗 ⌂wc 📶wc ☎ & ⟵ 🅿. 🖭 ⓓ Ⅽ 𝘝𝘐𝘚𝘈   DY **k**
st. : ⌓ 20 — **42 rm** 120/245.

🏨 **Criden** Ⓜ without rest, 65 bd Heurteloup ℘ 20.81.14 — 🛗 ⌂wc ☎ ⟵. 🖭 ⓓ Ⅽ 𝘝𝘐𝘚𝘈   EY **g**
st. : ⌓ 20 — **33 rm** 215.

🏨 **Châteaux de la Loire** without rest, 12 r. Gambetta ℘ 05.10.05 — 🛗 ⌂wc 📶wc 🖭 ⓓ Ⅽ 𝘝𝘐𝘚𝘈   DY **x**
closed 15 December-15 January, Saturday and Sunday out of season — st. : ⌓ 17 — **32 ch** 89/192.

🏨 **Europe** without rest, 12 pl. Mar.-Leclerc ℘ 05.42.07, « Paintings and antique furniture » — 🛗 ⌂wc 📶wc ☎   EY **m**
st. : ⌓ 18 — **54 rm** 100/210.

🏨 **Balzac** without rest, 47 r. Scellerie ℘ 05.40.87 — ⌂wc 📶wc ☎. 🖭 ⓓ Ⅽ 𝘝𝘐𝘚𝘈   DY **v**
st. : ⌓ 16 — **18 rm** 75/185.

🏨 **Italia** without rest, 19 r. Devilde ⊠ 37100 ℘ 54.43.01 — ⌂wc 📶wc 🅿. 𝘝𝘐𝘚𝘈. ❄
closed 1 to 15 September and 25 December-5 January — st. : ⌓ 18 — **20 rm** 95/170.

🏨 **Rosny** without rest, 19 r. B. Pascal ℘ 05.23.54 — ⌂wc 📶wc 🅿. 𝘝𝘐𝘚𝘈   DEY **a**
closed 20 December-5 January — st. : ⌓ 16,50 — **22 rm** 79/207.

XXXX ❀ **Barrier,** 101 av. Tranchée ⊠ 37100 ℘ 54.20.39, flowered patio — ▤ 🅿. 🖭 ⓓ 𝘝𝘐𝘚𝘈
closed January, 5 to 11 August, Sunday dinner and Monday — **M** 295/355
Spec. Feuilleté de petits gris à la coriandre, Brochet croustillant au vinaigre, Canard de Challans rosé. **Wines** Bourgueil, Chinon.

XXX **La Rôtisserie Tourangelle,** 23 r. Commerce ℘ 05.71.21, 🍽 — 🖭 ⓓ 𝘝𝘐𝘚𝘈   CX **z**
closed 15 July-6 August, Sunday dinner and Monday — **M** 120/200.

XXX **Au Gué de Louis XI,** 36 quai Loire ⊠ 37100 ℘ 54.00.43 — 🖭 ⓓ 𝘝𝘐𝘚𝘈
closed Sunday dinner and Monday — **M** 70/150.

XX **Bistro 17,** 17 pl. Victoire ℘ 39.61.72 — 🖭 ⓓ Ⅽ 𝘝𝘐𝘚𝘈   BY **k**
closed August and Sunday except Bank Holidays — **M** a la carte 130/200.

XX ❀ **Les Tuffeaux** (Devaux), 19 r. Lavoisier ℘ 47.19.89   EX **r**
closed 15 to 27 January, 5 to 9 May, Sunday and Monday — st. : **M** a la carte 165/220
Spec. Foie gras de canard, Blanc de turbot au melon (June-October), Emincé de canard à la mangue (October-July).

XX **Coq d'Or,** 272 av. Grammont ℘ 20.39.51 — 𝘝𝘐𝘚𝘈
closed 5 to 25 August, 9 to 18 February, Saturday lunch, Sunday dinner and Monday — st. : **M** 80.

XX **Relais Buré,** 1 pl. Résistance ℘ 05.67.74 — 𝘝𝘐𝘚𝘈   CXY **w**
closed Monday — st. : **M** (1st floor) 85/107 & - (ground floor) **M** a la carte approx. 100.

exit road to Poitiers : interchange Tours Sud — ⊠ 37170 Chambray-les-Tours :

🏨🏨 **Novotel** Ⓜ, ℘ 27.41.38, Telex 751206, 🍽, 🏊, 🎾 — 🛗 ▤ 📺 ☎ & 🅿 — 🔬 200. 🖭 ⓓ Ⅽ 𝘝𝘐𝘚𝘈
M snack a la carte approx. 95 & — ⌓ 32 — **91 rm** 245/302.

at Joué-lès-Tours SW : 5 km by D 86 — ⊠ 37300 Joué-lès-Tours :

🏨 **Château de Beaulieu** ⤴, rte Villandry ℘ 53.20.26, ≼, park — ⌂wc 📶 ☎ 🅿 — 🔬 50. 𝘝𝘐𝘚𝘈
st. : **M** 135/260 — ⌓ 27 — **17 rm** 185/350 — P 355/425.

Bracieux 41250 L.-et-Ch. 🔲 ⑱ — pop. 1 150 — alt. 81 — ✿ 54.
Tours 81.

XXXX ❀❀ **Le Relais** (Robin), 1 av. Chambord ℘ 46.41.22, ≼ — 🅿. 🖭 ⓓ 𝘝𝘐𝘚𝘈
closed 20 December-25 January, Monday dinner and Tuesday — st. : **M** (booking essential) 100/268 and a la carte
Spec. Carpe à la Chambord (10 September-30 May), Filets de pigeonneau au citron, Gibier (25 September-15 December). **Wines** Cheverny, Côteaux du Giennois.

Montbazon 37250 I.-et-L. 64 ⑮ G. Châteaux de la Loire — pop. 3 011 — alt. 71 — ☺ 47.

🆔 Mairie ℰ 26.01.30.

Paris 248 — Châtellerault 60 — Chinon 41 — Loches 32 — Montrichard 40 — Saumur 67 — Tours 13.

🏨 ✿ **Château d'Artigny** ⟋, SW : 2 km by D 17 ℰ 26.24.24, Telex 750900, « Garden, park, ≼ River Indre, riverside annex with 8 rm 🏊 », ✵ — 🛗 ☎ ❷ — 🔨 30-80. 𝘝𝘐𝘚𝘈
closed 1 December-11 January — **st. : M** 180/300 — ☷ 48 — **48 rm** 420/875, 7 apartments 600/995

Spec. Ravioli de homard, Rouget barbet rôti, Epigrammes d'agneau. **Wines** Sauvignon de Touraine, Chinon.

🏨 ✿ **Domaine de la Tortinière** ⟋, N : 2 km by N 10 and D 287 ℰ 26.00.19, « in a parc ≼ valley of River Indre », 🏊 — ☎ ❷ — 🔨 30. 🇪 𝘝𝘐𝘚𝘈 ✵ rest
1 March-15 November — **st. : M** *(closed Tuesday lunch and Monday in march and from 15 October to 15 November)* a la carte 160 to 225 — ☷ 36 — **14 rm** 275/495, 7 apartments 520/635

Spec. Escalope de sandre à la julienne de légumes, Sauté de boeuf au Champigny, Crèpes fourrées aux fraises cuites.

🏨 **Relais de Touraine** Ⓜ, N : 2 km rte Tours ℰ 26.06.57, 🍴, park — 🛏wc 🛁wc ☎ ❷ — 🔨 50. 🇦🇪 🇪 𝘝𝘐𝘚𝘈
st. : M *(closed Sunday dinner, Monday and 1 to 14 August)* 95/195 — ☷ 27 — **21 rm** 210/260 — P 360/380.

✕✕ ✿ **La Chancelière** wirh rm, 1 pl. Marronniers ℰ 26.00.67 — 🛏wc 🛁. 🇦🇪 𝘝𝘐𝘚𝘈
closed 1 to 5 July, 10 November-2 December, 2 to 6 January, Sunday dinner and Monday except Bank Holidays — **st. : M** a la carte 170/240 — ☷ 22 — **4 rm** 140/220
Spec. Ris de veau à l'huile de noisettes (June-September), Dos de saumon poelé, Noisettes d'agneau à la crème d'ail. **Wines** Chinon, Bourgueil.

to W : 5 km by N 10, D 287 and D 87 — ✉ 37250 Montbazon :

✕✕ **Moulin fleuri** ⟋ with rm, ℰ 26.01.12, ≼, « Terrace overlooking the River Indre », 🍴 — 🛁 ❷. 🇦🇪 𝘝𝘐𝘚𝘈
closed 15 to 30 October, 1 to 20 February and Monday except Bank Holidays — **st. : M** a la carte 100/180 — ☷ 23 — **10 rm** 56/163 — P 173/250.

Romorantin-Lanthenay ⬦ 41200 L.-et-Ch. 64 ⑱ — pop. 18 187 — alt. 88 — ☺ 54.

Tours 90.

🏨 ✿✿ **Gd H. Lion d'Or** Ⓜ, 69 r. Clemenceau ℰ 76.00.28, Telex 750990, « flowered terrace » — 🛗 📺 ☎ ♿ ❷ — 🔨 50. 🇦🇪 ⓞ 🇪 𝘝𝘐𝘚𝘈
closed early January-mid February — **st. : M** (booking essential) 200/330 and a la carte — ☷ 40 — **8 rm** 300/400

Spec. Langoustines rôties, Ris de veau braisés, Soufflé chaud aux fruits. **Wines** Vouvray, Bourgueil.

Germany
Deutschland

Berlin
Cologne
Düsseldorf
Frankfurt am Main
Hamburg
Hanover
Munich
Stuttgart

PRACTICAL INFORMATION

LOCAL CURRENCY

Deutsche Mark : 100 DM = 31.497 US $ (Jan. 85)

FOREIGN EXCHANGE

Is possible in banks, saving banks and at exchange offices.

Hours of opening from Monday to Friday 8.30am to 12.30pm and 2.30pm to 4pm except Thursday 2.30pm to 6pm.

TOURIST INFORMATION

Deutsche Zentrale für Tourismus (DZT)
Beethovenstr. 69, 6000 Frankfurt 1, ☎ 7 57 20
Telex Y4189178

Hotel booking service
Allgemeine Deutsche Zimmerreservierung (ADZ)
Beethovenstr. 69, 6000 Frankfurt 1, ☎ 74 07 67
Telex 416666

BREAKDOWN SERVICE

ADAC : for the addresses see text of the towns mentioned

AvD : Lyoner Str. 16, 6000 Frankfurt 71-Niederrad, ☎ 069/6 60 63 00

In Germany the ADAC, and the AvD, make a special point of assisting foreign motorists. They have motor patrols covering main roads.

GERMAN AIRLINES

Deutsche Lufthansa AG
Von-Gablenz-Str. 2
5000 Köln 21, ☎ 0221/82 61

SHOPPING

In the index of street names, those printed in red are where the principal shops are found.

TIPPING

In Germany, prices include service and taxes. You may choose to leave a tip if you wish but there is no obligation to do so.

SPEED LIMITS

The speed limit, generally, in built up areas is 50 km/h - 31 mph and on all other roads it is 100 km/h - 62mph. On motorways and dual carriageways, the recommended speed limit is 130 km/h - 80 mph.

SEAT BELTS

The wearing of seat belts is compulsory for drivers and front seat passengers.

BERLIN

SIGHTS

West Berlin

Kurfürstendamm★★ BDX and Memorial Church (Kaiser-Wilhelm-Gedächtniskirche) DEV – Brandenburg Gate★★ (Brandenburger Tor) (East-Berlin) GU – Zoological Park★★ (Zoologischer Garten, Aquarium) EV .
Dahlem Museums (Museum Dahlem)★★★ (Painting Gallery, Ethnographic Museum★★) – Chateau of Charlottenburg★★ (Schloß Charlottenburg) BU (at the Knobelsdorff-Wing : Painting Collection★★, Golden Gallery★★, Museum of Decorative Arts★ with Guelph treasure★★) – Antique Museum★ (Antikenmuseum) (ancient treasure★★★) BU M3 – Egyptian Museum★ (Ägyptisches Museum) bust of Queen Nefertiti★) BU M4 – National Gallery★ (Nationalgalerie) FV M6.
Olympic Stadium★ (Olympia-Stadion) – Radio Tower★★ (Funkturm) AV – Botanical Gardens★★ (Botanischer Garten).
Havel★ and Peacock Island★ (Pfaueninsel) – Wannsee★★.
Church of Maria Regina Martyrum★ (Maria-Regina-Martyrum-Kirche) BU D and Plötzensee Memorial (Gedenkstätte von Plötzensee) DU.

East-Berlin

Brandenburg Gate★★ (Brandenburger Tor) GU – Unter den Linden★ GUV (State Opera House★ GHU C, Neue Wache★ HU D, Arsenal★★ GHU) – Platz der Akademie★ GV
Museum Island (Museuminsel) (Pergamon-Museum★★★ GHU M7 with Pergamon-Altar, National Gallery★★ HU M8).
Alexanderplatz★★ HU – Television Tower★★ (Fernsehturm) (✵) HU K – Karl-Marx-Allee★ HU – Soviet Memorial★ (Sowjetisches Ehrenmal).

BERLIN West Berlin 1000. **987** ⑰ – Pop. 1 964 000 – alt. 40 m – ✪ 030.

✈ Tegel, ℘ 4 10 01.

🚇 Berlin - Wannsee, ℘ 3 13 81 30.

Exhibition Grounds (Messegelände) AV, ℘ 3 03 81, Telex 182908.

🛈 Berlin Tourist-Information, Europa-Center (Budapester Straße), ℘ 7 82 30 31/2 62 60 31, Telex 18 3356 ;

🛈 Tourist Information, at Tegel Airport, ℘ 41 01 31 45.

ADAC, Berlin-Wilmersdorf, Bundesallee 29 (B 31), ℘ 8 68 61, Telex 183513.

BERLIN

Continued p. 8

177

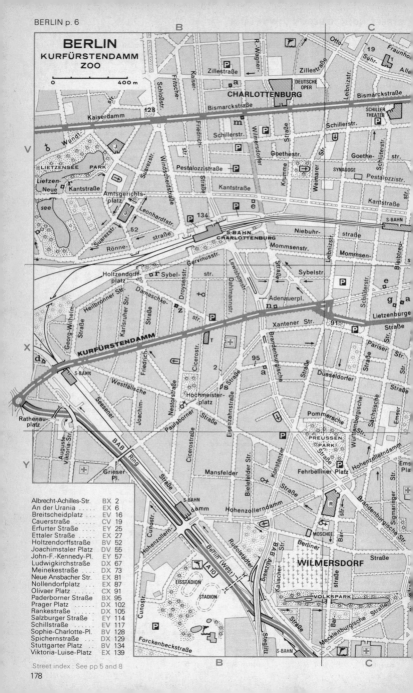

BERLIN
KURFÜRSTENDAMM
ZOO

0   400 m

Street index : See pp 5 and 8

178

The reference (B 15) at the end of the address is the postal district : Berlin 15

at Kurfürstendamm and near Kurfürstendamm :

Bristol-H. Kempinski ⌂, Kurfürstendamm 27 (B 15), ℰ 88 10 91, Telex 183553, Massage, ⌂, ◻ – ❙ ☰ ⯐ ☷ ♿ ⬛ ᴁ ⊙ E 𝖵𝖨𝖲𝖠 ❊ rest   DV **n**
Restaurants : – **Kempinski-Grill M** a la carte 43/90 – **Kempinski-Rest.** *(closed Monday)*
M a la carte 34/79 – **Kempinski-Eck M** a la carte 25/50 – **358 rm** 174/328.

❀ **Steigenberger Berlin - Park-Rest.** ⬛, Los Angeles-Platz 1 (B 30), ℰ 2 10 80, Telex 181444, Massage, ⌂, ◻ – ❙ ☰ ⯐ ⇔ ♿ ᴁ ⊙ E 𝖵𝖨𝖲𝖠   EX **d**
M a la carte 41/80 – **Berliner Stube M** a la carte 25/49 – **396 rm** 184/328 Bb
Spec. Terrine von Steinbutt und Lachs, Dessert vom Wagen.

Mondial ⬛ ⌂, Kurfürstendamm 47 (B 15), ℰ 88 41 10, Telex 182839, Massage, ◻ – ❙
☰ rest ⯐ ♿ ᴁ ⊙ E 𝖵𝖨𝖲𝖠 ❊ rest   CX **e**
M a la carte 25/55 – **75 rm** 139/180 Bb.

Am Zoo without rest, Kurfürstendamm 25 (B 15), ℰ 88 30 91, Telex 183835 – ❙ ⯐
⬛wc ☎ ℗ ♿ ᴁ ⊙ E 𝖵𝖨𝖲𝖠   DV **z**
145 rm 98/170.

Eurotel Arosa, Lietzenburger Str. 79 (B 15), ℰ 88 00 50, Telex 183397, ⌸ – ❙ ⯐ ⇔wc
⬛wc ☎ ⇔ ♿ ᴁ ⊙ E 𝖵𝖨𝖲𝖠 ❊ rest   DX **y**
M *(closed Sunday)* a la carte 26/55 – **90 rm** 98/175 Bb.

Meineke without rest, Meinekestr. 10 (B 15), ℰ 882811 – ❙ ⯐ ⇔wc ⬛wc ☎. ᴁ ⊙
E 𝖵𝖨𝖲𝖠   DX **q**
60 rm 90/140 Bb.

Domus without rest, Uhlandstr. 49 (B 15), ℰ 88 20 41, Telex 185975 – ❙ ⬛wc ☎ ℗ ᴁ
⊙ E 𝖵𝖨𝖲𝖠 – **76 rm** 88/160.   DX **a**

Ristorante Anselmo, Damaschkestr. 17 (B 31), ℰ 3 23 30 94, « Modern Italian rest. »
    BX **z**

Tessiner Stuben, Bleibtreustr. 33 (B 15), ℰ 8 81 36 11 – ᴁ ⊙ E 𝖵𝖨𝖲𝖠   CX **a**
closed Saturday and Sunday lunch, and 29. July - 28. August – **M** a la carte 36/77
(booking essential).

XX **Kopenhagen** (Danish Smörrebröds), Kurfürstendamm 203 (B 15), ℰ 8 83 25 03 — ▤. 🖭 ⓞ 🗲
   M a la carte 25/53.   DX **k**

XX **Hongkong** (Chinese rest.), Kurfürstendamm 210 (2nd floor, 🛗) (B 15), ℰ 8 81 57 56 —
   🖭 ⓞ 🗲   DX **t**
   M a la carte 23/38.

X **Friesenhof**, Uhlandstr. 185 (B 12), ℰ 8 83 60 79 — ▤. 🛠
   M a la carte 21/52.   DV **m**

near Memorial Church and Zoological Park :

🏨 **Inter-Continental**, Budapester Str. 2 (B 30), ℰ 2 60 20, Telex 184380, Massage, 🛋, 🔲
   — 🛗 ▤ 🖭 ⓞ ⓟ 🅰 🖭 ⓞ 🗲 🆅🆂🅰 🛠 rest   EV **a**
   M a la carte 41/72 — **600 rm** 170/345 Bb.

🏨 **Schweizerhof**, Budapester Str. 25 (B 30), ℰ 2 69 61, Telex 185501, Massage, 🛋 — 🛗
   ▤ rest 🖭 ♿ ⟸ ⓟ 🅰. 🛠 rest   EV **w**
   431 rm.

🏨 **Berlin Penta H.** 🅼 🛎, Nürnberger Str. 65 (B 30), ℰ 24 00 11, Telex 182877, Massage,
   🛋, 🔲 — 🛗 ▤ 🖭 ♿ ⟸ ⓟ 🅰. 🖭 ⓞ 🗲 🆅🆂🅰. 🛠 rest   EV **t**
   M a la carte 27/66 — **425 rm** 166/217 Bb.

🏨 **Alsterhof**, Augsburger Str. 5 (B 30), ℰ 21 99 60, Telex 183484, Massage, 🛋, 🔲 — 🛗
   🖭 ⟸ ⓟ 🅰. 🖭 ⓞ 🗲 🆅🆂🅰   EX **q**
   M a la carte 23/60 — **139 rm** 103/188.

🏨 **Palace**, Budapester Str. 42 (Europa-Centre) (B 30), ℰ 26 20 11, Telex 184825 — 🛗 ▤ rest
   🖭 ⓟ 🅰. 🖭 ⓞ 🗲 🆅🆂🅰. 🛠 rest   EV **k**
   M a la carte 23/60 — **175 rm** 161/250.

🏨 **Berlin Exelsior-H.**, Hardenbergstr. 14 (B 12), ℰ 3 19 93, Telex 184781 — 🛗 ▤ rest 🖭
   ⓟ 🅰. 🖭 ⓞ 🗲 🛠 rest   DV **b**
   M a la carte 27/59 — **320 rm** 135/185 Bb.

🏨 **Hotel Berlin**, Kurfürstenstr. 62 (B 30), ℰ 26 92 91, Telex 184332 — 🛗 ▤ rest 🖭 ⓟ 🅰.
   🖭 ⓞ 🗲. 🛠 rest   EV **b**
   M a la carte 27/60 (see also **Berlin Grill**) — **255 rm** 105/178 Bb.

🏨 **Ambassador**, Bayreuther Str. 42 (B 30), ℰ 21 90 20, Telex 184259, Massage, 🛋, 🔲 —
   🛗 ▤ rest 🖭 ⟸ ⓟ 🅰. 🖭 ⓞ 🗲 🆅🆂🅰. 🛠 rest   EV **z**
   Restaurants : — **Küchenstube M** a la carte 22/45 — **Conti-Fischstuben** *(closed Sunday)* **M**
   a la carte 36/75 — **120 rm** 118/220 Bb.

🏨 **Savoy**, Fasanenstr. 9 (B 12), ℰ 31 06 54, Telex 184292 — 🛗 🖭 🛁wc ☎. 🖭 ⓞ 🗲 🆅🆂🅰.
   🛠 rest   DV **s**
   M a la carte 24/56 — **115 rm** 118/300 Bb.

🏨 **Hamburg**, Landgrafenstr. 4 (B 30), ℰ 26 91 61, Telex 184974 — 🛗 🖭 🛁wc ☎ ⟸ ⓟ
   🅰. 🖭 ⓞ 🗲 🆅🆂🅰. 🛠 rest   EV **s**
   M a la carte 22/52 — **240 rm** 107/162 Bb.

🏨 **Sylter Hof**, Kurfürstenstr. 116 (B 30), ℰ 2 12 00, Telex 183317 — 🛗 🖭 🛁wc ☎ ⓟ 🅰.
   🖭 ⓞ 🗲 🆅🆂🅰   EV **d**
   M *(closed Sunday dinner)* a la carte 32/56 — **131 rm** 100/280 Bb.

🏨 **President** without rest, An der Urania 16 (B 30), ℰ 21 90 30, Telex 184018, 🛋 — 🛗 🖭
   🛁wc 🚿wc ☎ ⓟ. 🖭 ⓞ 🗲 🆅🆂🅰   EX **t**
   60 rm 100/200.

🏨 **Remter** without rest, Marburger Str. 17 (B 30), ℰ 24 60 61, Telex 183497 — 🛗 🖭 🛁wc
   🚿wc ☎. ⓞ 🗲 🆅🆂🅰   EVX **c**
   33 rm 70/130 Bb.

🏨 **Astoria** without rest, Fasanenstr. 2 (B 12), ℰ 3 12 40 67, Telex 181745 — 🛗 🖭 🛁wc ☎.
   🖭 ⓞ 🗲 🆅🆂🅰   DV **a**
   32 rm 55/125.

XXX 🕸 **Berlin-Grill**, Kurfürstenstr. 62 (at Berlin H.) (B 30), ℰ 26 92 91 — ▤ ⓟ. 🖭 ⓞ 🗲 🆅🆂🅰.
   🛠   EV **b**
   closed Sunday — **M** a la carte 43/84 (booking essential)
   Spec. Kartoffelcremesuppe mit frischen Pilzen, Schneckenragout im Spinatnest, Kalbslendchen mit
   Hummermedaillons und Spitzmorcheln.

XXX **Ritz**, Rankestr. 26 (B 30), ℰ 24 72 50 — 🖭 ⓞ 🗲. 🛠   DX **e**
   closed 4 weeks July - August, Sunday and Bank Holidays — **M** a la carte 38/68.

XX **Du Pont**, Budapester Str. 1 (B 30), ℰ 2 61 88 11 — 🖭 ⓞ 🗲   EV **x**
   closed 24 December - 2 January, Saturday lunch, Sunday and Bank Holidays — **M** a la
   carte 35/66.

XX **Daitokai** (Japanese rest.), Tauentzienstr. 9 (Europa Centre, 1st floor) (B 30), ℰ 2 61 80 99
   — 🖭 ⓞ 🗲   EV **n**
   closed Monday — **M** 31/58.

XX **Ristorante Il Sorriso** (Italian rest.), Kurfürstenstr. 76 (B 30), ℰ 2 62 13 13 — 🖭 ⓞ 🗲.
   🛠   EV **r**
   closed Sunday — **M** a la carte 27/50.

at Berlin-Charlottenburg :

🏨 **Seehof** ⑤, Lietzensee-Ufer 11 (B 19), ℰ 32 00 20, Telex 182943, ≼, ☆, ⧖ – 🛗 📺
⟨with 🍽⟩. 🅰🅴 ⓪ 🖪 𝘝𝘐𝘚𝘈, ℅ rest
M a la carte 36/72 – **77 rm** 120/210 Bb.
BV **r**

🏨 **Kanthotel** without rest, Kantstr. 111 (B 12), ℰ 32 30 26, Telex 183330 – 🛗 📺 ⌷wc
🛗wc ☎ 🅿. 🅰🅴 ⓪ 🖪 𝘝𝘐𝘚𝘈
55 rm 114/164 Bb.
BV **e**

🏨 **Apartment-H. Heerstraße**, Heerstr. 80 (B 19), ℰ 3 05 50 51, ⧖, ▨ – 🛗 📺 ⌷wc ☎
🛗. 🅿. 🅰🅴 ⓪ 🖪 𝘝𝘐𝘚𝘈
M a la carte 35/64 – **38 rm** 115/220.
LS **t**

🏨 **Ibis** without rest, Messedamm 10 (B 19), ℰ 30 20 11, Telex 182882 – 🛗 ⌷wc 🛗wc ☎
🛗
191 rm Bb.
AV **b**

🏨 **Kardell**, Gervinusstr. 24 (B 12), ℰ 3 24 10 66 – 🛗 ⌷wc 🛗wc ☎ 🅿. 🅰🅴 ⓪ 🖪 𝘝𝘐𝘚𝘈
M (closed Saturday lunch) a la carte 28/63 – **30 rm** 80/150 Bb.
BX **r**

XX **Pullman**, Messedamm 11 (Congress Centre) (B 19), ℰ 30 38 39 46 – 🛗 🍽 🛗. 🅰🅴 ⓪ 🖪.
℅
closed Sunday dinner and July – **M** a la carte 30/56.
AV **s**

at Berlin-Dahlem by ② EZ :

🏨 **Forsthaus Paulsborn** ⑤, Am Grunewaldsee (B 33), ℰ 8 13 80 10, ☆ – 📺 ⌷wc
🛗wc ☎ 🅿. 🅰🅴 ⓪ 🖪
closed 14 January - 15 February – **M** (closed Monday) a la carte 25/54 – **11 rm** 85/120.

XXXX ✿ **Maître**, Podbielskiallee 31 (B 33), ℰ 8 32 60 04, « Villa with elegant installation » –
🍽. 🅰🅴 ⓪ 🖪
closed Monday, Tuesday - Saturday dinner only, Sunday lunch only – **M** 108/148 (booking essential).

at Berlin-Hermsdorf by Seilerstr. FU :

XXX ✿ **Rockendorf's Restaurant**, Düsterhauptstr. 1 (B 28), ℰ 4 02 30 99
closed Sunday, Monday, Bank Holidays, 3 weeks July - August and Christmas - 1 January
– **M** a la carte 46/90 (booking essential)
Spec. Lachsparfait mit Dillvinaigrette, Bresse-Täubchen in Balsam-Essig mit Linsengemüse, Roggennudeln mit Lauch und Kaninchenfilet.

at Berlin-Reinickendorf by Seilerstr. FU :

🏨 **Rheinsberg am See**, Finsterwalder Str. 64 (B 26), ℰ 4 02 10 92, Telex 185972, ☆,
Massage, ⧖, ☒, ☞ – 🛗 📺 🛗wc ☎ 🅿
M a la carte 22/52 – **70 rm** 80/138 Bb.

at Berlin-Siemensstadt by Siemensdamm AU :

🏨 **Novotel**, Ohmstr. 4 (B 13), ℰ 38 10 61, Telex 181415, ☒ – 🛗 🍽 rest 📺 ⌷wc ☎ 🛗. 🅰🅴
⓪ 🖪 𝘝𝘐𝘚𝘈
M a la carte 21/55 – **119 rm** 111/164 Bb.

at Berlin-Steglitz by Hauptstr. EYZ :

🏨 **Steglitz International** Ⓜ, Albrechtstr. 2 (B 41), ℰ 79 10 61, Telex 183545, Massage,
⧖ – 🛗 📺 ₺ 🛗. 🅰🅴 ⓪ 🖪 𝘝𝘐𝘚𝘈
M a la carte 29/55 – **212 rm** 115/190 Bb.

at Berlin-Tegel by Jakob-Kaiser-Platz BU :

🏨 **Gästehaus am Tegeler See**, Wilkestr. 2 (B 27), ℰ 4 38 40 (hotel) 4 38 43 33 (rest.) – 🛗 📺
🛗wc ☎ ⟨⟩ 🅿
39 rm Bb.

at Berlin-Wilmersdorf :

🏨 **Crest Motor Hotel** without rest, Güntzelstr. 14 (B 31), ℰ 87 02 41, Telex 182948 – 🛗
📺 ⌷wc 🛗wc ☎ ⟨⟩. 🅰🅴 ⓪ 🖪 𝘝𝘐𝘚𝘈
110 rm 132/172 Bb.
DY **t**

🏨 **Franke**, Albrecht-Achilles-Str. 57 (B 31), ℰ 8 92 10 97, Telex 184857 – 🛗 ⌷wc ☎ 🅿. 🅰🅴
⓪ 🖪 𝘝𝘐𝘚𝘈
M a la carte 18,50/36 – **67 rm** 87/145.
BX **s**

Do not mix up :

Comfort of hotels : 🏨🏨🏨 ... 🏠, 🏡

Comfort of restaurants : XXXXX ... X

Quality of the cuisine : ✿✿✿, ✿✿, ✿

COLOGNE (KÖLN) 5000. Nordrhein-Westfalen **987** ㉓ ㉔ — pop. 1 008 700 — alt. 65 m — 🌀 0221.

See : Cathedral (Dom)★★★ (Magi's Shrine★★★) DV — Roman-Germanic Museum (Römisch-Germanisches Museum)★★★ (Dionysos Mosaic) DV — Wallraf-Richartz-Museum (14 - 16 C pictures by Cologne Masters) and Museum Ludwig★★★ DVX — Schnütgen-Museum★★ (Madonnas of Cologne) DX **M2** — St. Columbia (St. Kolumba)★ DX **V** — St. Alban the New (Neu St. Alban)★ — St. Maria of the Capitol (St. Maria im Kapitol) (wooden doors★★) DX **D** — Holy Apostles (St. Aposteln) (apse★) CX **N** — St. Severinus (St. Severin) (inside★) DY **K** — Rhine Park (Rheinpark)★.

🛫 Köln-Bonn at Wahn (SE : 17 km), 𝒫 (02203) 4 01.

🚗 𝒫 1 41 52 89.

Exhibition Centre (Messegelände), 𝒫 82 11, Telex 8873426.

🛈 Tourist office (Verkehrsamt), Am Dom, 𝒫 2 21 33 40, Telex 8883421.

ADAC, Köln 51-Bayenthal, Alteburger Str. 375, 𝒫 3 79 90.

Düsseldorf 43 — Aachen 70 — Bonn 28 — Essen 68.

Plans on following pages

🏨 **Excelsior H. Ernst - Rest. Hanse-Stube**, Trankgasse 1, 𝒫 27 01, Telex 8882645 — 🛗 📺 🕭
🛗. 🌾 rest
166 rm.   DV **a**

🏨 **Inter-Continental**, Helenenstr. 14, 𝒫 26 51, Telex 8882313, Massage, 🕿, 🏊 — 🛗 🍽 📺
🕭 🅿 🛗. 🌾 rest
300 rm Bb.   CV **p**

🏨 **Dom-H.** 🐾, Domkloster 2a, 𝒫 23 37 51, Telex 8882919, « Terrace with ≤ » — 🛗 📺 🕭
M a la carte 34/90 — **135 rm** 185/370 Bb.   DV **d**

🏨 **Consul**, Belfortstr. 9, 𝒫 73 10 51, Telex 8885242, 🕿, 🏊 — 🛗 📺 🅿 🛗. 🖭 ⓞ 🇪 𝗩𝗜𝗦𝗔
🌾 rest
M (closed Sunday and Bank Holidays) a la carte 27/54 — **80 rm** 132/235 Bb.   DU **v**

🏨 **Mondial**, Bechergasse 10, 𝒫 21 96 71, Telex 8881932 — 🛗 📺 🚗 🛗. 🖭 ⓞ 🇪 𝗩𝗜𝗦𝗔
🌾 rest
M a la carte 32/62 — **204 rm** 134/205 Bb.   DV **f**

🏨 **Savoy** without rest, Turiner Str. 9, 𝒫 12 04 66, Telex 8886360 — 🛗 📺 ➰wc 🛁wc 🕿 🖭
69 rm 105/240 Bb.   DU **s**

🏨 **Haus Lyskirchen**, Filzengraben 28, 𝒫 23 48 91, Telex 8885449, 🏊 — 🛗 📺 🛁wc 🕿 🚗
🛗. 🖭 ⓞ 🇪 𝗩𝗜𝗦𝗔   DY **u**
closed 23 December - 2 January — **M** (dinner only, closed Sunday and Bank Holidays) a la carte 28/58 — **95 rm** 85/190 Bb.

🏨 **Bristol** without rest, Kaiser-Wilhelm-Ring 48, 𝒫 12 01 95, Telex 8881146, « Antique furnished rooms » — 🛗 ➰wc 🛁wc 🕿 🛗. 🖭 ⓞ 🇪 𝗩𝗜𝗦𝗔   CU **m**
44 rm 90/205.

🏨 **Königshof** without rest, Richartzstr. 14, 𝒫 23 45 83, Telex 8881318 — 🛗 📺 ➰wc 🛁wc
🕿. 🖭 ⓞ 🇪 𝗩𝗜𝗦𝗔
95 rm 95/290 Bb.   DV **n**

🏨 **Eden am Dom** without rest, Am Hof 18, 𝒫 23 61 23, Telex 8882889 — 🛗 ➰wc 🛁wc 🕿.
🖭 ⓞ 🇪 𝗩𝗜𝗦𝗔
33 rm 138/215 Bb.   DV **w**

🏨 **Kolpinghaus International**, St.-Apern-Str. 32, 𝒫 21 03 53 — 🛗 🛁wc 🕿 🅿 🛗. 🖭
ⓞ   CV **q**
M a la carte 17/50 — **48 rm** 77/107.

🏨 **Kommerz-H.** without rest, Breslauer Platz, 𝒫 12 40 86, 🕿 — 🛗 📺 ➰wc 🛁wc 🕿. 🖭
ⓞ 🇪 𝗩𝗜𝗦𝗔   DV **r**
54 rm 105/190.

🏨 **Senats-H.**, Unter Goldschmied 9, 𝒫 23 38 61, Telex 8881765 — 🛗 ➰wc 🕿 🛗. 🖭 ⓞ
🇪   DX **r**
M a la carte 31/71 — **53 rm** 135/235 Bb.

🏨 **Altstadt H.** without rest, Salzgasse 7, 𝒫 23 41 87, 🕿 — 🛗 ➰wc 🛁wc 🕿. 🖭 ⓞ 🇪
𝗩𝗜𝗦𝗔   DX **p**
closed 21 December - 2 January and July — **27 rm** 68/120.

🏨 **Coellner Hof**, Hansaring 100, 𝒫 12 20 75, Telex 8885264 — 🛗 📺 ➰wc 🛁wc 🕿 🛗. 🖭
ⓞ 🇪   DU **k**
closed Saturday — **M** a la carte 20/55 — **67 rm** 65/175 Bb.

🏨 **Windsor** without rest, Von-Werth-Str. 36, 𝒫 13 40 31 — 🛗 🛁wc 🕿. 🖭 ⓞ 🇪 𝗩𝗜𝗦𝗔
closed 20 December - 1 January — **37 rm** 75/170.   CU **e**

🏨 **Intercity-H. Ibis Köln** without rest, Bahnhofsvorplatz, 𝒫 13 20 51, Telex 8881002 —
🛗 🛁wc 🕿. 🖭 ⓞ 🇪 𝗩𝗜𝗦𝗔   DV **u**
66 rm 80/140 Bb.

KÖLN

0 [____] 200 m

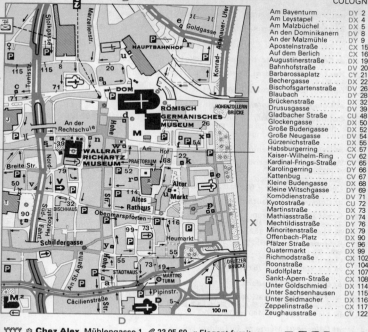

XXXX ✿ **Chez Alex**, Mühlengasse 1, ☎ 23 05 60, « Elegant furniture » – ▪ ⚼ ⊙ E   DX **k**
closed Saturday lunch, Sunday and Bank Holidays – **M** a la carte 53/110 (booking essential)
Spec. Rissole de truffes et foie gras, Poêlée d'écrevisses au basilic, Poularde farcie en croûte de sel.

XXX ✿ **Rino Casati**, Ebertplatz 3, ☎ 72 11 08 – ⚼ ⊙ E VISA ✷   DU **t**
closed Sunday and 3 weeks June - July – **M** a la carte 38/90 (booking essential)
Spec. Nudelgerichte, Babysteinbutt mit Champagnersauce, Ente mit Pflaumensauce.

XXX **Die Bastei**, Konrad-Adenauer-Ufer 80, ☎ 12 28 25, ≤ Rhein – ⚼ ⊙ E. ✷   DU **b**
closed Saturday lunch – **M** a la carte 43/90.

XXX **Franz Kellers Rest.**, Aachener Str. 21, ☎ 21 95 49, 斎 – ⚼ ⊙ E. ✷
closed 31 March - 9 April, and Sunday – **M** *(dinner only)* a la carte 55/90 (booking essential) – **Kellers Keller M** (lunch also) a la carte 30/50.   by Rudolfplatz CX

XXX ✿ **La Poêle d'or im Weinhaus Wolff**, Komödienstr. 52, ☎ 13 41 00 – ⊙ E   DV **c**
closed Monday lunch, Sunday, Bank Holidays, 2 weeks July and Christmas to New Year –
M a la carte 56/96
Spec. Salade de canard, de caille et de foie gras, Le homard aux poireaux, Le ris de veau à la crème de foie gras.

XX **Kranzler an der Oper**, Brüderstr. 2, ☎ 23 32 91, 斎 – ⚼ ⊙ E   DX **t**
M a la carte 30/59.

XX **Daitokai** (Japanese rest.), Kattenbug 2, ☎ 12 00 48 – ▪ ⚼ ⊙ E. ✷   CV **e**
closed Monday – **M** a la carte 31/61.

XX **Börsen-Rest.**, Unter Sachsenhausen 10, ☎ 13 56 26 – ▪ ⚼ ⚼ ⊙ E. ✷   CV **r**
closed Sunday and Bank Holidays – **M** a la carte 39/75.

XX **Ristorante Alfredo**, Tunisstr. 3, ☎ 24 43 01   DX **v**
closed Sunday, Saturday dinner and 3 weeks July – **M** a la carte 41/70.

XX **Weinhaus im Walfisch** (17 C house), Salzgasse 13, ☎ 21 95 75 – ⊙ E. ✷   DX **p**
closed Sunday and Bank Holidays – **M** a la carte 35/75 (booking essential).

X **China - Rest. Tchang**, Große Sandkaul 19, ☎ 21 76 51   DX **y**
M a la carte 25/50.

X **Le Gaulois**, Roonstr. 8, ☎ 24 62 39 – ⊙ E   CY **v**
closed Sunday – **M** a la carte 38/56.

at Cologne 41-Braunsfeld by Rudolfplatz CX :

🏨 **Regent**, Melatengürtel 15, 𝒫 5 49 91, Telex 8881824 — 🛗 🍽 rest 📺 🛏wc 🛗wc ☎ 🅿
🔬. 🅰🅴 ⓘ 🄴 𝘝𝘐𝘚𝘈
closed 24 December - 1 January — **M** a la carte 21/50 — **190 rm** 110/210 Bb.

at Cologne 21-Deutz by Deutzer Brücke DX :

XX **Rest. im Messeturm**, Kennedy-Ufer (18th floor, 🛗), 𝒫 88 10 08, ≼ Cologne — 🍽 🅰🅴
ⓘ 🄴 ⚭
closed July and Thursday — **M** a la carte 35/70.

at Cologne 30-Ehrenfeld by Erftstr. CU :

XX **Colonius-Turmrest.**, Innere Kanalstr. 100 (🛗, 3,50 DM), 𝒫 52 20 61, ☀ Cologne,
« Revolving rest. at 166 m » — 🍽 🅿. ⓘ 🄴 𝘝𝘐𝘚𝘈. ⚭
dinner only, Sunday and Bank Holidays lunch also, closed Monday — **M** a la carte 33/68.

at Cologne 50-Immendorf by Bonner Str. DZ :

XX **Weinstuben Bitzerhof** with rm (farmyard from 1821), Immendorfer Hauptstr. 21,
𝒫 (02236) 6 19 21, 🍽, « Country house atmosphere » — 📺 🛗wc ☎ ⚭. ⚭ rm
*closed Saturday lunch, Sunday dinner, Monday, mid July - mid August and 2 weeks
December - January* — **M** a la carte 31/57 — **3 rm** 75/130.

at Cologne 41-Lindenthal by Rudolfplatz CX :

🏨 **Crest H. Köln**, Dürener Str. 287, 𝒫 46 30 01, Telex 8882516, « Garden with 🍽 » — 🛗
🍽 rest 📺 🔬 ⚭ 🔬. 🅰🅴 ⓘ 🄴 𝘝𝘐𝘚𝘈 ⚭ rest
M a la carte 32/70 — **152 rm** 173/235 Bb.

🏨 **Bremer**, Dürener Str. 225, 𝒫 40 50 13, Telex 8882063, 🔲 — 🛗 🍽 rest 📺 🛏wc 🛗wc ☎
⚭. 🅰🅴 ⓘ 🄴. ⚭
closed 20 December - 4 January — **M** a la carte 38/78 (booking essential) — **König-Pub :**
M a la carte 25/56 — **75 rm** 95/145.

at Cologne 40-Marsdorf

🏨 **Novotel Köln-Westkreuz**, Horbeller Str. 1, 𝒫 (02234) 1 60 81, Telex 8886355, 🍽, 🔲
— 🛗 🍽 rest 📺 🔬 🅿 🔬 with 🍽. 🅰🅴 ⓘ 🄴 𝘝𝘐𝘚𝘈
M a la carte 32/62 — **140 rm** 141/185.

at Cologne 91-Merheim by Deutzer Brücke DX :

XXXX ✿✿✿ **Goldener Pflug**, Olpener Str. 421 (B 55), 𝒫 89 55 09 — 🅿
closed Saturday lunch, Sunday, Bank Holidays and 3 weeks June - July — **M** a la carte
75/155
Spec. Bretonischer Hummer in weißer Buttersauce, mit Langostinos gefüllte Spinat-Ravioli auf
Hummersauce, Kalbsbries mit Trüffeln.

at Cologne 90- Porz-Wahnheide SE : 17 km by A 59 – ✪ 02203 :

🏨 **Holiday Inn**, Waldstr. 255, 𝒫 56 12 30, Telex 8874665, 🛋, 🔲, 🖼 — 🛗 🍽 🛏wc ☎
🅿 🔬. 🅰🅴 ⓘ 🄴 𝘝𝘐𝘚𝘈. ⚭ rest
M a la carte 26/57 — **113 rm** 167/217 Bb.

Aachen 5100. Nordrhein-Westfalen 🔢🔢🔢 ③. 🔢🔢🔢 ⑪ — pop. 245 000 — alt. 174 m —
✪ 0241.

Köln 70.

XXXX ✿✿ **Gala**, Monheimsallee 44 (at Casino), 𝒫 15 30 13, « Modern-elegant furniture » —
🍽. ⓘ 🄴 𝘝𝘐𝘚𝘈
dinner only, closed Monday — **M** a la carte 55/110 (booking essential)
Spec. Rinderfilet in Kürbisvinaigrette, Hummerravioli, Sambucaeis in Malzbierteig gebacken.

DÜSSELDORF 4000. Nordrhein-Westfalen 🔢🔢🔢 ③㉔ — pop. 569 000 — alt. 40 m — ✪ 0211.

See : Königsallee★ — Hofgarten★ — Hetjensmuseum★ BX **M2** — Land Economic Museum
(Landesmuseum Volk u. Wirtschaft)★ BV **M1** — Goethemuseum★ CV **M3** — Thyssen building
(Thyssenhaus)★ CVX **E.**

Envir. : Chateau of Benrath (Schloß Benrath) (Park★) S : 10 km by Kölner Str. DXY

🛬 Düsseldorf-Lohausen (N : 8 km), 𝒫 42 12 23.

🚂 𝒫 3 68 04 68.

Exhibition Centre (Messegelände), 𝒫 4 56 01, Telex 8584853.

🛈 Tourist office, K.-Adenauer-Pl. 12 and at the main station, 𝒫 35 05 05, Telex 8587785.

ADAC, Kaiserswerther Str. 207, 𝒫 43 49 49.

Amsterdam 225 — Essen 31 — Köln 43 — Rotterdam 237.

Plan on following pages

🏨🏨🏨 **Breidenbacher Hof**, Heinrich-Heine-Allee 36, ✆ 86 01, Telex 8582630 – 🛗 🖷 📺 🏊
🕮 ⓔ 𝘝𝘐𝘚𝘈 ✖
BX a
Restaurants : – **Grill Royal** *(closed Saturday lunch and Sunday)* **M** a la carte 53/95 –
Breidenbacher Eck M a la carte 35/70 – **160 rm** 220/410.

🏨🏨 **Nikko** Ⓜ, Immermannstr. 41, ✆ 86 61, Telex 8582080, Massage, ⇔s, 🔲 – 🛗 🖷 📺
⇔ 🏊 🕮 ⓞ ⓔ 𝘝𝘐𝘚𝘈 ✖ rest
DX a
Restaurants : – **Benkay** (Japanese rest.) **M** a la carte 30/80 – **Travellers M** a la carte
37/75 – **301 rm** 248/437 Bb.

🏨🏨 **Steigenberger Parkhotel**, Corneliusplatz 1, ✆ 86 51, Telex 8582331, ☞ – 🛗 📺 🅿
🏊 🕮 ⓞ ⓔ 𝘝𝘐𝘚𝘈 ✖ rest
CX p
M a la carte 36/87 – **160 rm** 169/340 Bb.

🏨🏨 **Excelsior** without rest, Kapellstr. 1, ✆ 48 60 06, Telex 8584737 – 🛗 📺 🕮 ⓞ ⓔ 𝘝𝘐𝘚𝘈
65 rm 138/258.
CV a

🏨🏨 **Holiday Inn**, Graf-Adolf-Platz 10, ✆ 37 70 53, Telex 8586359, ⇔s, 🔲 – 🛗 🖷 📺 🅿 🏊
🕮 ⓞ ⓔ 𝘝𝘐𝘚𝘈
CY r
Restaurants : – **Suppentopf** *(lunch only, closed Sunday)* **M** a la carte 21/38 – **La Rhenane**
M a la carte 30/70 – **120 rm** 202/290 Bb.

🏨🏨 **Savoy**, Oststr. 128, ✆ 36 03 36, Telex 8584215, Massage, ⇔s, 🔲 – 🛗 🖷 rest 📺 🅿 🏊
🕮 ⓞ ⓔ 𝘝𝘐𝘚𝘈
CX w
M a la carte 32/70 – **130 rm** 160/290 Bb.

🏨🏨 **Uebachs**, Leopoldstr. 5, ✆ 36 05 66, Telex 8587620 – 🛗 📺 ⇔ 🏊 🕮 ⓞ ⓔ 𝘝𝘐𝘚𝘈
✖ rest
DX r
M a la carte 29/65 – **82 rm** 126/220 Bb.

🏨 **Börsenhotel** without rest, Kreuzstr. 19a, ✆ 36 30 71, Telex 8587323 – 🛗 📺 ⇌wc
⑂wc ☎ 🏊 🕮 ⓞ ⓔ
CX n
80 rm 120/200 Bb.

🏨 **Graf Adolf** ☜ without rest, Stresemannplatz 1, ✆ 36 05 91, Telex 8587844 – 🛗 📺
⇌wc ⑂wc ☎ 🏊 🕮 ⓞ
CX e
closed 23 December - 1 January – **100 rm** 68/177 Bb.

🏨 **Eden**, Adersstr. 29, ✆ 38 10 60, Telex 8582530 – 🛗 📺 ⇌wc ⑂ ☎ 🕮 ⓞ ⓔ 𝘝𝘐𝘚𝘈
CY m
M *(bar lunch)* a la carte 20/50 – **90 rm** 127/190 Bb.

🏨 **Lindenhof** without rest, Oststr. 124, ✆ 36 09 63, Telex 8587012 – 🛗 📺 ⇌wc ⑂wc ☎
🕮 ⓞ ⓔ
CX u
43 rm 120/185.

🏨 **National** without rest, Schwerinstr. 16, ✆ 49 90, Telex 8586597 – 🛗 📺 ⇌wc ⑂wc ☎
🅿 🕮 ⓞ ⓔ
by Duisburger Str. CV
35 rm 105/200 Bb.

🏨 **Centralhotel**, Luisenstr. 42, ✆ 37 90 01, Telex 858215 – 🛗 📺 ⇌wc ⑂wc ☎ 🕮 ⓞ ⓔ
𝘝𝘐𝘚𝘈
CY v
80 rm 130/200 Bb.

🏨 **Acon** without rest, Mintropstr. 23, ✆ 37 70 20 – 🛗 ⇌wc ☎ 🕮 ⓞ ⓔ 𝘝𝘐𝘚𝘈
CDY x
24 rm 100/240.

🏨 **Astor** without rest, Kurfürstenstr. 23, ✆ 36 06 61, ⇔s – 📺 ⑂wc ☎ 🕮 ⓔ
DX k
16 rm 75/145.

🏨 **Großer Kurfürst** without rest, Kurfürstenstr. 18, ✆ 35 76 47 – 🛗 📺 ⇌wc ⑂wc ☎ 🕮
DX s
22 rm 75/145.

🏨 **Vossen am Karlplatz**, Bilker Str. 2, ✆ 32 50 10, Telex 8586605 – 🛗 ⇌wc ⑂wc ☎ 🕮
ⓞ ⓔ 𝘝𝘐𝘚𝘈 ✖ rm
BX v
M *(closed 28 June - 27 July)* a la carte 14,50/49 – **51 rm** 59/190.

XXXX ✿ **Orangerie**, Bilker Str. 30, ✆ 37 37 33
BX e
(booking essential)
Spec. Lachs mit Caviar, Zandertäschchen mit Filderkraut in Krebsrahmsauce, Wachtel mit Leberspätzle und
Steinpilzen.

XXX **Schadowstuben**, Königsallee 14 (1st floor 🛗), ✆ 32 68 32 – 🕮 ⓞ ⓔ
CX y
closed Sunday and Bank Holidays – **M** a la carte 45/82.

XXX ✿ **Victorian**, Königstr. 3a (1st floor), ✆ 32 02 22 – 🖷 🕮 ⓞ ⓔ ✖
CX c
closed Sunday and Bank Holidays – **M** a la carte 35/77
Spec. Carpaccio von Thunfisch mit Caviar, Gratin von Hummer und Seezunge, Rinderfilet in Kräutersenfsauce.

XXX **Müllers und Fest** Ⓚ Ⓓ, Königsallee 12, ✆ 32 60 01, ☞ – 🕮 ⓞ ⓔ ✖
CX y
closed Sunday and Bank Holidays – **M** a la carte 39/83.

XX **Riccione**, Pionierstr. 6, ✆ 37 99 87 – 🅿 ⓞ ⓔ ✖
CY z
closed Sunday and Bank Holidays except exhibitions – **M** a la carte 32/75.

XX **Nippon Kan** (Japanese rest.), Immermannstr. 35, ✆ 35 31 35 – 🕮 ⓞ ⓔ 𝘝𝘐𝘚𝘈 ✖
CX g
M a la carte 29/58.

XX **Daitokai** (Japanese rest), Mutter-Ey-Str. 1, ✆ 32 50 54 – 🖷 🕮 ⓞ ⓔ ✖
BX z
closed Sunday – **M** a la carte 38/85 (booking essential).

X **Mandarin** (Chinese rest), Steinstr. 23 (1st floor), ✆ 32 81 96 – ⓞ ⓔ 𝘝𝘐𝘚𝘈
CX s
M a la carte 21/47.

at Düsseldorf 31-Angermund N : 15 km by Flinger Str. BV :

🏠 **Haus Litzbrück**, Bahnhofstr. 33, ℰ (0203) 7 44 81, « Terrace », ⚓, ⬛, 🐎 — 📺 🚗
🅿 🏛 ⓐ⑩
closed July - 3 August — **M** a la carte 33/67 — **23 rm** 106/175.

at Düsseldorf 13-Benrath by Kölner Str. DXY :

🏨 **Rheinterrasse**, Benrather Schloßufer 39, ℰ 71 20 70, « Terrace with ≼ » — 📺 🚽wc
🚿wc 🅿 🏛 ⓐ E
M a la carte 26/65 — **19 rm** 95/150.

XX **Pigage** with rm, Schloßallee 28, ℰ 71 40 66 — 📺 🚽wc 🚿wc ☎ 🅿 ⑩ E 𝑽𝑰𝑺𝑨
Restaurants : — **Rotisserie M** a la carte 32/73 — **Dante M** a la carte 28/64 — **10 rm** 60/140.

XX **Lignano** (Italian rest.), Hildener Str. 43, ℰ 71 19 36 — 🏛 ⑩ E 𝑽𝑰𝑺𝑨 ⚓
closed Saturday lunch, Sunday, 26 May - 9 June and 1 to 15 September — **M** a la carte
29/58.

at Düsseldorf 30-Derendorf by Prinz-Georg-Str. CV :

🏨 **Gildors H.** without rest, Collenbachstr. 51, ℰ 48 80 05, Telex 8584418 — ▮ 📺 🚽wc
🚿wc ☎. 🏛 ⑩ E 𝑽𝑰𝑺𝑨
35 rm 135/200 Bb.

XXX **Amalfi** (Italian rest.), Ulmenstr. 122, ℰ 43 38 09 — 🏛 ⑩ E
closed Sunday and July — **M** a la carte 33/83.

at Düsseldorf 13-Eller by Kölner Str. DXY :

🏨 **Novotel Düsseldorf Süd**, Am Schönenkamp 9, ℰ 74 10 92, Telex 8584374, ⬛ (heated),
🐎 — ▮ 🍴 📺 🚽wc ☎ ⅋ 🅿 🏛 ⓐ ⑩ E 𝑽𝑰𝑺𝑨
M a la carte 23/57 — **120 rm** 139/176 Bb.

at Düsseldorf 30-Golzheim by Flinger Str. CV :

🏨 **Inter-Continental** Ⓜ, Karl-Arnold-Platz 5, ℰ 4 55 30, Telex 8584601, Massage, ⚓, ⬛ —
▮ 🍽 📺 🍴 ⇦⇨ 🅿 🏛. ⚓ rest
310 rm Bb.

🏨 **Düsseldorf Hilton**, Georg-Glock-Str. 20, ℰ 43 49 63, Telex 8584376, 🌻, Massage, ⚓,
⬛, 🐎 — ▮ 🍽 📺 ⅋ 🅿 🏛. 🏛 ⑩ E 𝑽𝑰𝑺𝑨. ⚓ rest
Restaurants : — **Hofgarten M** a la carte 30/55 (see also **San Francisco** below) — **83 rm**
211/455.

🏨 **Golzheimer Krug** ⚓, Karl-Kleppe-Str. 20, ℰ 43 44 53, Telex 8588919, 🌻 — 📺 🚽wc
🚿wc 🅿 ⑩ E 𝑽𝑰𝑺𝑨
M *(closed Friday except exhibitions)* a la carte 35/65 — **27 rm** 115/220 Bb.

XXXX ✪ **San Francisco**, Georg-Glock-Str. 20 (at Hilton-Hotel), ℰ 43 49 63 — 🍽 🅿. 🏛 ⑩ E
𝑽𝑰𝑺𝑨. ⚓
M a la carte 50/103 (booking essential)
Spec. Salat mesclin mit gefüllter Stubenkükenbrust, Kaninchenfilet in Olivensauce, Lachsmedaillons in
weißem Portwein.

XX **Fischer-Stuben-Mulfinger**, Rotterdamer Str. 15, ℰ 43 26 12, « Terrace »
closed Friday dinner and Saturday — **M** a la carte 34/70 (booking essential).

XX **Rosati** (Italian rest), Felix-Klein-Str. 1, ℰ 43 65 03 — 🅿. ⑩. ⚓
closed Saturday — **M** a la carte 39/70 (booking essential).

at Düsseldorf 31-Kaiserswerth by Flinger Str. CV :

🏠 **Barbarossa** without rest, Niederrheinstr. 365 (B 8), ℰ 40 27 19 — ▮ 🚽wc ☎ 🅿. 🏛 ⑩
E
33 rm 78/135.

XXX ✪✪ **Im Schiffchen** (1733 house with beautiful facade), Kaiserswerther Markt 9,
ℰ 40 10 50 — 🏛 E
dinner only, closed Sunday, Bank Holidays and 4 weeks July - August — **M** a la carte
67/100 (booking essential)
Spec. Gefüllte Canelloni in Trüffelbutter, kleiner Hummer in Kamillenblüten gedämpft, Eisauflauf mit
Bergkräutern.

XX **Alte Rheinfähre**, Fährerweg 22, ℰ 40 11 34, Terrace with ≼ — 🅿
M a la carte 24/56.

at Düsseldorf 30-Lohausen by Kaiserstr. CV :

XX **Flughafen Grill Rest.**, Terminal 2 (4th floor ▮), ℰ 4 21 60 97, ≼ — ⚓
M a la carte 30/70.

at Düsseldorf 30-Mörsenbroich by Rethelstr. DV :

🏨 **Ramada-Renaissance-H.** Ⓜ, Nördlicher Zubringer 6, ℰ 6 21 60, Telex 172114001,
Massage, ⚓, ⬛ — ▮ 🍽 📺 ⅋ ⇦⇨ 🅿 🏛. 🏛 ⑩ E 𝑽𝑰𝑺𝑨. ⚓ rest
M a la carte 33/70 — **250 rm** 189/343 Bb.

at Düsseldorf 11-Oberkassel by Hofgartenrampe BV :

🏨 **Ramada**, Am Seestern 16, ℰ 59 10 47, Telex 8585575, ⇌, 🔲 – 🛗 🛗 📺 🅿 ⑩ Ε 𝗩𝗜𝗦𝗔.
※ rest
M a la carte 42/82 — **222 rm** 165/280 Bb.

🏨 **Rheinstern-Penta-Hotel**, E.-Leutze-Str. 17, ℰ 5 99 70, Telex 8584242, ⇌, 🔲 – 🛗
▤ rest 📺 🅿 🏋 (with ▤). 🅰Ε ⑩ Ε 𝗩𝗜𝗦𝗔 ※ rest
M a la carte 31/64 — **176 rm** 186/282 Bb.

🏨 **Hanseat** without rest, Belsenstr. 6, ℰ 57 50 69 – 📺 🏚wc ☎. 🅰Ε ⑩ Ε 𝗩𝗜𝗦𝗔
28 rm 100/180.

🏨 **Arosa** without rest, Sonderburgstr. 48, ℰ 55 40 11, Telex 8582242 – 🛗 🛏wc 🏚wc ☎
⇌ 🅿 🅰Ε ⑩
closed 23 December - 4 January — **32 rm** 100/160.

XXX **De' Medici** (Italian rest.), Amboßstr. 3, ℰ 59 41 51 – 🅰Ε ⑩ Ε 𝗩𝗜𝗦𝗔
closed 4 weeks June - July except exhibitions, Saturday lunch, Sunday and Bank Holidays
— **M** a la carte 30/70.

at Düsseldorf 1-Unterbilk :

XXX **Frickhöfer**, Stromstr. 47, ℰ 39 39 31 – 🅰Ε ⑩   by Stromstr. BY
closed Sunday and Bank Holidays except exhibitions — **M** a la carte 45/91.

XX **Rheinturm Top 180**, Stromstr. 20, ℰ 84 85 80, ⁂ Düsseldorf and Rhein, « Revolving
restaurant at 172 m ». (🛗, 4 DM) – ▤ 🅰Ε ⑩ Ε ※   BY **a**
M a la carte 36/72.

Grevenbroich 4048. Nordrhein-Westfalen 𝟵𝟴𝟳 ㉓ – pop. 57 000 – alt. 60 m –
🕿 02181.

Düsseldorf 28.

XXX ❀❀ **Zur Traube** with rm, Bahnstr. 47, ℰ 6 87 67, wine list with more than 300 wines –
🏚wc ☎ ⇌ 🅿 🅰Ε ⑩ Ε
closed 31 March - 6 April, 2 weeks June - July and 23 December - 16 January — **M** (closed
Sunday and Monday) a la carte 44/87 (booking essential) — **13 rm** 45/165
Spec. Parfait vom Stör mit Kaviar, Gefüllte Wachtel mit Trüffelsauce, Variationen von der Birne.

FRANKFURT AM MAIN 6000. Hessen 𝟵𝟴𝟳 ㉓ – pop. 614 700 – alt. 91 m – 🕿 069.

See : Zoo★★★ FX — Goethe's House (Goethehaus)★★ and Goethemuseum★ DEY **M1** —
Cathedral (Dom)★ (Tower★★, Treasure★, Choir-stalls★) EY — Tropical Garden (Palmengarten)★
CV — Senckenberg-Museum★ (Palaeontology department★★) CX **M8** — Städel
Museum (Städelsches Kunstinstitut)★ (Collection★★ of flemish Primitives and German Masters
of the 16 C) DY **M2** — Museum of Applied Arts (Museum für Kunsthandwerk)★ EY **M4** — St.
Catherine's Church (Katharinenkirche) (windows★) EX **A** — Henninger Turm ⁂★ DZ.

🛬 Rhein-Main (by ⑤ : 12 km), ℰ 6 90 25 95.

🚗 at Neu-Isenburg, ℰ (06102) 85 75.

Exhibition Centre (Messegelände) (CY), ℰ 7 57 51, Telex 411558.

🮲 Tourist Information, main station (Hauptbahnhof), ℰ 23 10 55.

ADAC, Schumannstr. 4, ℰ 7 43 02 70.

Wiesbaden 39 ⑤ — Bonn 176 ⑤ — Nürnberg 223 ④ — Stuttgart 205 ⑤.

Plans on following pages

🏨 **Steigenberger-H. Frankfurter Hof**, Bethmannstr. 33, ℰ 2 02 51, Telex 411806 – 🛗
▤ rest 📺 & 🏋 🅰Ε ⑩ Ε 𝗩𝗜𝗦𝗔 ※ rest   DY **e**
M (closed Saturday) a la carte 32/74 — **400 rm** 185/340 Bb.

🏨 **Frankfurt Intercontinental**, Wilhelm-Leuschner-Str. 43, ℰ 23 05 61, Telex 413639, ⩽
Frankfurt, Massage, ⇌, 🔲 – 🛗 ▤ 📺 & 🏋 🅰Ε ⑩ Ε 𝗩𝗜𝗦𝗔 ※ rest   CY **a**
Restaurants : — Rôtisserie (closed Sunday lunch) **M** a la carte 44/90 — **Brasserie M** a la
carte 25/58 — **Bierstube** (closed Saturday, Sunday and Bank Holidays) **M** a la carte 17/25
— **800 rm** 280/395 Bb.

🏨 **Hessischer Hof**, Friedrich-Ebert-Anlage 40, ℰ 7 54 00, Telex 411776, « Rest. with
collection of Sèvres porcelain » – 🛗 📺 🅿 🏋 🅰Ε ⑩ Ε 𝗩𝗜𝗦𝗔 ※ rest   CY **p**
M a la carte 37/85 — **161 rm** 179/418.

🏨 **Parkhotel Frankfurt**, Wiesenhüttenplatz 36, ℰ 2 69 70, Telex 412808, Massage, ⇌ –
🛗 ▤ 📺 & ⇌ 🅿 🏋 🅰Ε ⑩ Ε 𝗩𝗜𝗦𝗔 ※ rest   CY **k**
Restaurants : — **La Truffe** (closed Saturday lunch, Sunday and Bank Holidays) **M** a la carte
45/90 — **Die Parkstube M** a la carte 27/60 — **280 rm** 190/350 Bb.

🏨 **CP Frankfurt Plaza H.** 🅼, Hamburger Allee 2, ℰ 77 07 21, Telex 412573, ⩽ Frankfurt,
⇌ – 🛗 ▤ 📺 & 🏋 🅰Ε ⑩ Ε 𝗩𝗜𝗦𝗔 ※ rest   CX **a**
Restaurants : — **Geheimratsstube** (closed Saturday lunch and Sunday) **M** a la carte 39/77
— **Bäckerei M** a la carte 26/56 — **591 rm** 190/390 Bb.

🏨 **National**, Baseler Str. 50, ℰ 23 48 41, Telex 412570 – 🛗 📺 🏋 🅰Ε ⑩ Ε 𝗩𝗜𝗦𝗔 ※ rest
M a la carte 27/52 — **95 rm** 65/195 Bb.   CY **x**

🏨 **Savigny**, Savignystr. 14, ℰ 7 53 30, Telex 412061 – 🛗 📺 🏋 🅰Ε ⑩ Ε 𝗩𝗜𝗦𝗔   CY **f**
closed 20 to 31 December — **M** a la carte 28/72 — **122 rm** 140/300 Bb.

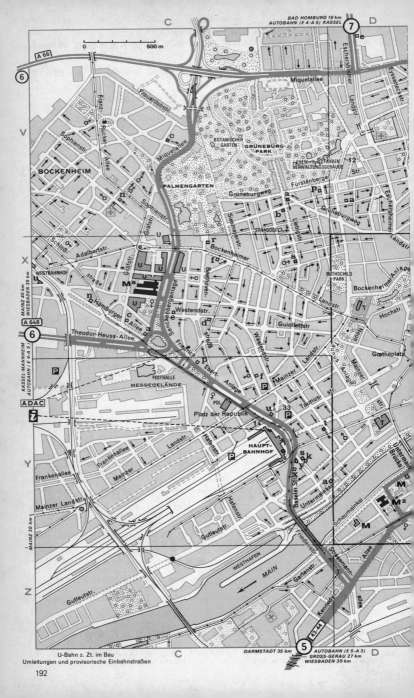

FRANKFURT AM MAIN

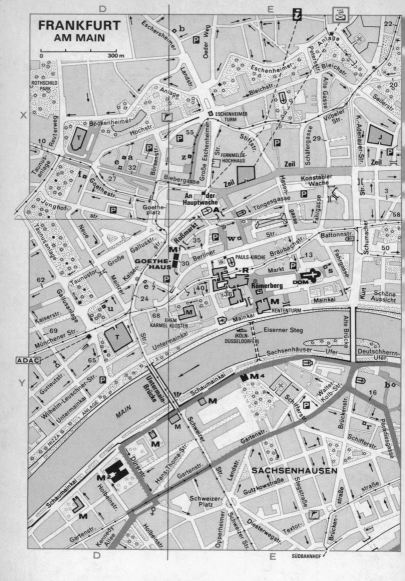

FRANKFURT
AM MAIN

0   300 m

ⓜ **Savoy**, Wiesenhüttenstr. 42, ℰ 23 05 11, Telex 413694, Massage, ≘s, ◫ − ⌷ ≡ rest ⊡
⌷wc ⌷wc ☎ ⇔ ⌷. ⅍
M a la carte 38/70 − **151 rm** 148/198.
CY **s**

ⓜ **Turm-Hotel** without rest, Eschersheimer Landstr. 20, ℰ 55 00 01 − ⌷ ⊡ ⌷wc ☎ ⓟ
ℼ ⓞ ⅀ ⓥⓘⓢⓐ
75 rm 92/140 Bb.
EX **b**

ⓜ **Continental**, Baseler Str. 56, ℰ 23 03 41, Telex 412502 − ⌷ ⊡ ⌷wc ⌷wc ☎ ⓟ. ℼ
ⓞ ⅀ ⓥⓘⓢⓐ. ⅍
M (closed Sunday and Bank Holidays) a la carte 17/45 − **80 rm** 91/160.
CY **y**

ⓜ **Mozart** without rest, Parkstr. 17, ℰ 55 08 31 − ⌷ ⌷wc ⌷wc ☎. ℼ ⓞ ⅀
closed 22 December - 2 January − **35 rm** 99/185.
CV **p**

ⓜ **An der Messe** without rest, Westendstr. 102, ℰ 74 79 79, Telex 4189009 − ⌷ ⊡ ⌷wc
⌷wc ☎ ⇔. ℼ ⓞ ⅀ ⓥⓘⓢⓐ
46 rm 130/230 Bb.
CX **e**

ⓜ **Am Zoo** without rest, Alfred-Brehm-Platz 6, ℰ 49 07 71, Telex 4170082 − ⌷ ⌷wc ⌷wc
☎ ⓟ. ℼ ⓞ ⅀
closed 24 December - 3 January − **85 rm** 53/114.
FX **q**

ⓜ **Tatra** without rest, Kreuznacher Str. 37, ℰ 77 20 71 − ⌷ ⌷wc ⌷wc ☎ ⇔. ℼ ⓞ ⅀
ⓥⓘⓢⓐ. ⅍
closed 24 December - 3 January − **25 rm** 95/140 Bb.
CX **u**

ⓜ **Am Dom** without rest, Kannengießergasse 3, ℰ 28 21 41, Telex 414955 − ⌷ ⌷wc
⌷wc ☎. ℼ ⅀
34 rm 100/150 Bb.
EY **s**

ⓜ **Admiral** without rest, Hölderlinstr. 25, ℰ 44 80 21 − ⌷ ⊡ ⌷wc ⌷wc ☎ ⓟ. ℼ ⓞ ⅀
52 rm 65/130.
FX **w**

ⓜ **Henninger Hof**, Hanauer Landstr. 127, ℰ 43 91 15, Telex 411091 − ⌷ ⊡ ⌷wc ⌷ ☎.
ℼ ⓞ ⅀ ⓥⓘⓢⓐ
closed 21 December - 5 January − **M** (closed Friday dinner, Saturday and Sunday except
exhibitions) a la carte 19/46 − **64 rm** 70/158 Bb.
FY **m**

ⅩⅩⅩⅩ ⌾ **Rest. Français**, Bethmannstr. 33 (at Steigenberger-H. Frankfurter Hof), ℰ 2 02 51 −
≡. ℼ ⓞ ⅀ ⅍
closed mid July - mid August, 23 December - 7 January, Sunday and Bank Holidays − **M**
a la carte 40/90 (booking essential)
Spec. Terrine von Kalbsbries und Gänseleber, Hummernavarin mit Pimento-Buttersauce, Kalbsmedaillons
pochiert mit Kaviarsauce.
DY **e**

ⅩⅩⅩ **Weinhaus Brückenkeller**, Schützenstr. 6, ℰ 28 42 38, « Old vaulted cellar with
precious antiques » − ⓟ. ℼ ⓞ ⅀
closed Sunday and Bank Holidays except exhibitions − **M** a la carte 42/92 (booking
essential).
FY **a**

ⅩⅩⅩ ⌾ **Humperdinck**, Grüneburgweg 95, ℰ 72 21 22 − ℼ ⓞ ⅀ ⓥⓘⓢⓐ
closed Saturday lunch and Sunday − **M** a la carte 47/83
Spec. Seeteufel in Balsamessig mit roten Zwiebeln, Pochierter Lammrücken auf Lauchstreifen, Galette von
Mandeln mit Fruchtmark.
CV **a**

ⅩⅩⅩ **Le Midi**, Liebigstr. 47, ℰ 72 14 38 − ℼ ⓞ ⅀ ⓥⓘⓢⓐ
closed Saturday lunch, Sunday and 2 weeks August − **M** a la carte 38/84.
CV **b**

ⅩⅩ **Da Bruno** (Italian rest.), Elbestr. 15, ℰ 23 34 16 − ≡. ℼ ⓞ ⅀
closed Sunday, Bank Holidays and mid July - mid August − **M** a la carte 35/65.
CY **t**

ⅩⅩ **Frankfurter Stubb** (Rest. in the vaulted cellar of Hotel Frankfurter Hof), Bethmannstr.
33, ℰ 21 56 79 − ≡. ℼ ⓞ ⅀ ⅍
closed Sunday, Bank Holidays and 23 December - 1 January − **M** a la carte 24/54 (booking
essential).
DY **e**

ⅩⅩ **La Galleria** (Italian rest.), Theaterplatz 2 (BFG-Haus), ℰ 23 56 80 − ≡. ℼ ⓞ ⅀ ⓥⓘⓢⓐ
closed Sunday, Bank Holidays and 24 December - 2 January − **M** a la carte 46/70 (booking
essential).
DY **u**

ⅩⅩ **Firenze** (Italian rest.), Berger Str. 30, ℰ 43 39 56 − ≡. ℼ ⓞ ⅀ ⅍
closed Monday except exhibitions − **M** a la carte 37/72.
FX **s**

ⅩⅩ **Börsenkeller**, Schillerstr. 11, ℰ 28 11 15 − ≡ ⓟ. ℼ ⓞ ⅀ ⓥⓘⓢⓐ
closed Sunday − **M** a la carte 20/60.
EX **z**

ⅩⅩ ⌾ **Ernos Bistro** (French rest.), Liebigstr. 15, ℰ 72 19 97, 🌞 − ℼ ⓞ ⅀ ⓥⓘⓢⓐ
closed Saturday and Sunday except exhibitions and 15 June - 21 July − **M** a la carte 50/94
(booking essential)
Spec. Foie d'oie frais, Filet de sandre au Pinot noir, Canard de Challans aux baies de Cassis.
CX **s**

at Frankfurt 80-Griesheim by ⑥ :

ⓜ **Ramada-Caravelle**, Oeserstr. 180, ℰ 3 90 50, Telex 416812, ≘s, ◫ − ⌷ ≡ rest ⊡ ⓟ
ⓟ. ℼ ⓞ ⅀ ⓥⓘⓢⓐ. ⅍ rest
M a la carte 35/71 − **236 rm** 150/265 Bb.

at Frankfurt 71-Niederrad by ⑤ :

ⓜ **Arabella-H. Frankfurt**, Lyoner Str. 44, ℰ 6 63 30, Telex 416760, 🌞, ≘s, ◫ − ⌷ ≡
⊡ ⓟ ⓟ ⓟ. ℼ ⓞ ⅀ ⓥⓘⓢⓐ. ⅍ rest
M a la carte 27/69 − **400 rm** 140/250 Bb.

195

🏨🏨 **Crest-H. Frankfurt**, Isenburger Schneise 40, 𝄞 6 78 40, Telex 416717 — 📶 🔳 📺 👤 📶 🅿
🏇 ⚿ 🆎 ⓪ 📧 *VISA*
M a la carte 27/65 — **283 rm** 165/235 Bb.

XX **Weidemann**, Kelsterbacher Str. 66, 𝄞 67 59 96, 🍴 — 🅿. 🆎 ⓪ 📧 *VISA*
Saturday, Sunday and Bank Holidays dinner only, closed 24 December - 2 January — **M** a
la carte 40/70 (booking essential).

at Frankfurt 70 - Sachsenhausen :

🏨🏨 **Holiday Inn-City Tower** 🅼, Mailänder Str. 1, 𝄞 68 00 11, Telex 411805, 🏊 — 📶 📶
📺 🅿 🏇 ⚿ 🆎 ⓪ 📧 *VISA*   by ④
M a la carte 28/60 — **405 rm** 175/285 Bb.

🏛 **Mühlberg** without rest, Offenbacher Landstr. 56, 𝄞 61 30 63 — 📶 🚻wc ☎ 🚙. 🆎 ⓪
closed 2 weeks December - January — **69 rm** 50/120.   FY **h**

XX **Bistrot 77** (modern Bistro - rest.), Ziegelhüttenweg 1, 𝄞 61 40 40, 🍴 — 🆎 ⓪ 📧
closed Saturday lunch, Sunday, 4 weeks July - August and 2 weeks December - January
— **M** a la carte 51/86.   EZ **a**

X Henninger Turm - Museum Stubb (height 101 m, 📶 DM 2), Hainer Weg 60, 𝄞 6 06 36 00,
≤ Frankfurt — 🔳 🅿   FZ

at Eschborn 6236 NW : 12 km :

🏛 **Novotel**, Philipp-Helfmann-Str. 10, 𝄞 (06196) 4 28 12, Telex 415655, 🌊 — 📶 🔳 rest 📺
🛏🚻wc ☎ 👤 🏇 ⚿. 🆎 ⓪ 📧   by A 66 CV
M a la carte 25/46 — **227 rm** 129/161.

near Main-Taunus-Einkaufszentrum W : 14 km by ⑥ :

🏨🏨 **Holiday Inn**, Am Main-Taunus-Zentrum 1, ✉ 6231 Sulzbach, 𝄞 (06196) 78 78,
Telex 410373, 🏊, 🌊 — 📶 🔳 📺 🅿 🏇. 🆎 ⓪ 📧 *VISA*
M a la carte 32/64 — **291 rm** 170/240 Bb.

at Neu-Isenburg 2-Gravenbruch 6078 SE : 11 km :

🏨🏨🏨 **Gravenbruch-Kempinski-Frankfurt** 🅼, 𝄞 (06102) 50 50, Telex 417673, 🍴, « Park »,
Massage, 🏊, 🌊 (heated), 🌊, 🎾, 🛝 — 📶 🔳 📺 👤 🛏 🚙 🅿 🏇. 🆎 ⓪ 📧 *VISA*. 🛝 rest
M a la carte 36/71 — **317 rm** 161/321.

XXXX ⚙ **Gourmet Rest.** (at Gravenbruch-Kempinski H.), 𝄞 (06102) 50 50 — 🅿 🏇. 🆎 ⓪ 📧
VISA. 🛝
*dinner only, closed Saturday, Sunday and Bank Holidays except exhibitions and 4 weeks
July - August* — **M** a la carte ragout mit Nudeln, Pot au feu von Steinbutt und Fenchel, Ente mit Rhabarbersauce.
Spec. Hummerragout mit Nudeln, Pot au feu von Steinbutt und Fenchel, Ente mit Rhabarbersauce.

near Rhein-Main airport SW : 12 km by ⑤ (near motorway Flughafen exit) — ⚙ 069 :

🏨🏨 **Sheraton** 🅼, Am Flughafen (Terminal Mitte), ✉ 6000 Frankfurt 75, 𝄞 6 97 70,
Telex 4189294, 🏊, 🌊 — 📶 🔳 📺 👤 🏇. 🛝 rest
819 rm.

🏨🏨 **Steigenberger Airporthotel**, Unterschweinstiege 16, ✉ 6000 Frankfurt 75, 𝄞 6 98 51,
Telex 413112, 🏊, 🌊 — 📶 🔳 📺 👤 🏇. 🆎 ⓪ 📧 *VISA*
Restaurants — **Grill-Rest.** *(closed Sunday)* **M** a la carte 35/70 — **Pergola** **M** a la carte
27/52 — **350 rm** 169/270 Bb.

XX **Waldrestaurant** Unterschweinstiege, Flughafenstraße, ✉ 6000 Frankfurt 75, 𝄞 69 25 03,
« Terrace, country house atmosphere » — 🔳 🅿. 🛝 — (booking essential).

at Rhein-Main airport SW : 12 km by ⑤ :

XX **Rötisserie 5 Continents**, Ankunft Ausland B (Besucherhalle, Ebene 3), ✉ 6000
Frankfurt 75, 𝄞 (069) 6 90 34 44, ≤ — 🔳. 🆎 ⓪ 📧 *VISA*
M a la carte 32/73.

*on the road from Neu-Isenburg to Götzenhain by ④ : 13 km by A 661 and
motorway-exit Dreieich :*

XXX Gutsschänke Neuhof, ✉ 6072 Dreieich-Götzenhain, 𝄞 (06102) 32 14, « Country house
atmosphere, terrace » — ⚿ 🅿 🏇.

at Maintal 6457 by ② : 13 km :

XXX ⚙ **Hessler**, Am Bootshafen 4 (Dörnigheim), 𝄞 (06181) 49 29 51 — 🅿
dinner only, closed Monday and 3 weeks July - August — **M** a la carte 50/89
Spec. Rotbarbe in Austernsauce, Lammrücken in Thymiankruste, Dreierlei von Mousse au chocolat.

Wertheim 6980. Baden-Württemberg 🔟🔟🔟 ㉘ — pop. 20 000 — alt. 142 m — ⚙ 09342.
Frankfurt am Main 87.

XXX ⚙⚙ **Schweizer Stuben** 🥄 with rm, at Wertheim-Bettingen (E : 10 km),
Geiselbrunnweg 11, 𝄞 43 51, Telex 689123, ≤, 🍴, 🏊, 🌊, 🚗, 🛝 (indoor) — 📺 🛏wc
🚻wc ☎ 🅿
M *(closed Monday lunch, Sunday and 7 to 31 January)* a la carte 74/122 (booking essential)
— **16 rm** 148/270
Spec. Gugelhupf von Gänsestopfleber mit Weinbeerensauce, Steinbutt mit gefüllter Zucchiniblüte und
Pimentosauce, Gefüllter Ochsenschwanz.

See : Rathausmarkt★ and Jungfernstieg★ DY — Außenalster★★★ (trip by boat★★★) EX — Hagenbeck Zoo (Tierpark Hagenbeck)★★ — Television Tower (Fernsehturm)★★ (✲✲★) BX — Art Gallery (Kunsthalle)★★ (19C German painting) EY **M1** — St. Michael's church (St. Michaelis)★ (tower ✲✲★) BZ — Stintfang (≤★) BZ — Port (Hafen)★★ (trip by boat★★) BZ.

✈ Hamburg-Fuhlsbüttel (N: 15 km), ℰ 50 81, City-Centre Airport Air Terminal, Brockesstraße (at ZOB FY) ℰ 50 85 57.

🚗 ℰ 39 18 65 56.

Exhibition Centre (Messegelände) (BX), ℰ 3 56 91, Telex 212609.

🛈 Tourist-Information, Hachmannplatz 1, ℰ 24 87 00, Telex 2163036.

🛈 Tourist-Information at the airport (Ankunftshalle), ℰ 24 87 00.

ADAC, Amsinckstr. 39 (H 1), ℰ 2 39 91.

Berlin 297 — Bremen 118 — Hannover 152.

The reference (H 15) at the end of the address is the postal district :Hamburg 15

Plan on following pages

near Hauptbahnhof, at St. Georg, east of the Außenalster :

🏨 **Atlantic-H. Kempinski**, An der Alster 72 (H 1), ℰ 24 80 01, Telex 2163297, ≤ Außenalster, Massage, ≐s, 🔲 — 🛗 ▤ rest 📺 🚙 🅿 🏛 (with ▤), 🆀 ⓓ 🔤 *VISA*, ✻ rest
M a la carte 50/92 — **320 rm** 259/378. EX **a**

🏨 **Europäischer Hof**, Kirchenallee 45 (H 1), ℰ 24 81 71, Telex 2162493 — 🛗 ▤ rest 📺 🚙 🏛, 🆀 ⓓ 🔤 *VISA*
M a la carte 29/63 — **350 rm** 118/258 Bb. FY **e**

🏨 **Reichshof**, Kirchenallee 34 (H 1), ℰ 24 83 30, Telex 2163396 — 🛗 📺 🚙 🏛, 🆀 ⓓ 🔤 *VISA*, ✻ rest
M a la carte 25/68 — **319 rm** 128/228 Bb. FY **d**

🏨 **Berlin**, Borgfelder Str. 1 (H 26), ℰ 25 16 40, Telex 213939 — 🛗 ▤ rest 📺 🚙 🅿 🏛 (with ▤), 🆀 ⓓ 🔤 *VISA*, ✻ rest by Kurt-Schumacher-Allee FY
M a la carte 27/69 — **93 rm** 135/200 Bb.

🏨 **Prem**, An der Alster 9 (H 1), ℰ 24 54 54, Telex 2163115, « Garden » — 🛗 📺, 🆀 ⓓ 🔤 *VISA*, ✻ rest
M a la carte 39/68 — **48 rm** 140/260 Bb. FX **c**

🏨 **Ambassador**, Heidenkampsweg 34 (H 1), ℰ 23 40 41, Telex 2162398, Massage, ≐s, 🔲 — 🛗 ▤ rest 📺 🚙 🅿 🏛 (with ▤), 🆀 ⓓ 🔤 *VISA*, ✻ by Nordkanalstr. FZ
closed 23 to 30 December — M a la carte 34/60 — **123 rm** 85/190 Bb.

🏨 **Senator**, Lange Reihe 18 (H 1), ℰ 24 12 03, Telex 2174002 — 🛗 📺 ➘wc 🝔wc ☎ 🅿, 🆀 ⓓ 🔤 *VISA*
(only dinner for residents) — **56 rm** 120/160 Bb. FY **u**

🏨 **St. Raphael**, Adenauer-Allee 41 (H 1), ℰ 24 11 91, Telex 2174733 — 🛗 📺 🝔wc ☎ 🅿 🏛, ✻ rest
(dinner only) — **120 rm** Bb. FY **m**

🏨 **Fürst Bismarck** without rest, Kirchenallee 49 (H 1), ℰ 2 80 91, Telex 2162980 — 🛗 📺 ➘wc 🝔wc ☎, 🆀 ⓓ 🔤 *VISA*
59 rm 75/140. FY **x**

🏨 **Merkur** without rest, Bremer Reihe 12 (H 1), ℰ 24 33 83 — 🛗 📺 ➘wc 🝔wc ☎, 🆀 ⓓ 🔤 *VISA*
55 rm 60/125. FY **z**

🏨 **Dänischer Hof**, Holzdamm 4 (H 1), ℰ 24 55 56, Telex 2162760 — 🛗 ➘wc 🝔wc ☎ 🅿, 🆀 ⓓ 🔤 *VISA*
(Rest. for residents only) — **44 rm** 80/170. EXY **d**

🏨 **Wedina** ⤢ without rest, Gurlittstr. 23 (H 1), ℰ 24 30 11, ≐s, 🔟, ⋙ — ➘ 🝔wc ☎, 🆀 ⓓ 🔤 *VISA*
closed 17 December - 5 February — **23 rm** 50/112. FX **n**

XX **Peter Lembcke**, Holzdamm 49 (H 1), ℰ 24 32 90 — 🆀 ⓓ FY **t**
closed Sunday, Bank Holidays and 20 July - 10 August — M a la carte 38/81.

XX ✿ **Le Delice** (modern rest. in communication centre), Klosterwall 9 (Markthalle) (H 1), ℰ 32 77 27 — ✻ FYZ **n**
dinner only, closed Sunday, Bank Holidays and July — M a la carte 48/98 (booking essential)
Spec. Lachstatar, pochierte Entenstopfleber in Caramel, Pot au feu vom Lamm.

at Binnenalster, Altstadt, Neustadt :

🏨 ✿ **Vier Jahreszeiten - Rest. Haerlin**, Neuer Jungfernstieg 9 (H 36), ℰ 3 49 41, Telex 211629, ≤ Binnenalster — 🛗 📺 🚙 🏛, 🆀 ⓓ 🔤 *VISA*, ✻ DY **v**
M a la carte 46/100 — **187 rm** 215/516
Spec. Meeresfrüchte im Kräutersud, Meerwolf mit Estragonbuttersauce, Stubenküken gefüllt mit Gänseleber und Kalbsbries.

🏨 **Ramada Renaissance Hotel** Ⓜ, Große Bleichen (H 36), ℰ 34 91 80, Massage, ≐s — 🛗 ▤ 📺 ⅙ 🅿 🏛, 🆀 ⓓ 🔤 *VISA*, ✻ rest CY **e**
M a la carte 42/79 — **211 rm** 247/385 Bb.

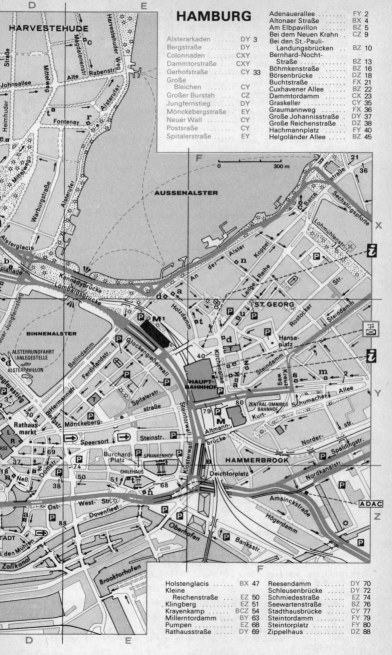

HAMBURG

CP Hamburg Plaza Ⓜ, Marseiller Str. 2 (H 36), *𝒫* 3 50 20, Telex 214400, ≼ Hamburg, 🅰, ⛾ – 📶 ▤ ⇔ ふ ⇦ 🅰. 🖭 ⓞ 🄴 𝘝𝘐𝘚𝘈. ⁓ rest
CX **a**
Restaurants : – **Englischer Grill** *(closed Saturday lunch and Sunday)* **M** a la carte 35/75 –
Vierländerstube M a la carte 27/50 – **570 rm** 188/316 Bb.

Hafen Hamburg, Seewartenstr. 9 (H 11), *𝒫* 31 15 25, Telex 2161319, ≼ – 📶 ⇔wc
📶wc ☎ 🅿. 🖭 ⓞ 🄴 𝘝𝘐𝘚𝘈
BZ **y**
M *(closed Sunday dinner and Monday)* a la carte 25/72 – **160 rm** 85/150 Bb.

Alster-Hof without rest, Esplanade 12 (H 36), *𝒫* 35 00 70, Telex 213843 – 📶 🖭 ⇔wc
📶wc ☎ ふ. 🖭 ⓞ 🄴 𝘝𝘐𝘚𝘈
DX **x**
closed 20 December- 2 January – **120 rm** 60/180.

Baseler Hospiz, Esplanade 11 (H 36), *𝒫* 34 19 21, Telex 2163707 – 📶 ⇔wc 📶wc ☎ ふ.
⁓
DX **x**
160 rm.

Ratsweinkeller, Gr. Johannisstr. 2 (H 11), *𝒫* 36 41 53, « 1896 Hanseatic rest. » – ふ.
🖭 ⓞ 🄴
DY **r**
closed Sunday and Bank Holidays – **M** a la carte 22/78.

Zum alten Rathaus (with entertainment-rest. Fleetenkieker), Börsenbrücke 10 (H 11),
𝒫 36 75 70 – 🖭 ⓞ 🄴 𝘝𝘐𝘚𝘈
DZ **n**
closed Saturday lunch and Sunday – **M** a la carte 30/68 (booking essential).

Ehmke, Grimm 14 (H 11), *𝒫* 32 71 32 – 🖭 ⓞ 🄴 𝘝𝘐𝘚𝘈. ⁓
DZ **a**
closed Saturday lunch and Sunday – **M** a la carte 32/69.

Mövenpick - Café des Artistes, Große Bleichen 36 (H 36), *𝒫* 35 16 35 – 📶. 🖭 ⓞ 🄴
𝘝𝘐𝘚𝘈
CY **r**
M a la carte 34/66 – **Mövenpick-Rest. M** a la carte 20/44.

Harmonie, Ost-West-Str. 12 (H 1), *𝒫* 32 71 91 – ⓞ
EZ **n**
closed Sunday and Bank Holidays – **M** a la carte 40/79.

Rest. im Finnlandhaus, Esplanade 41 (12th floor, 📶) (H 36), *𝒫* 34 41 33, ≼ Hamburg,
Binnen- and Außenalster – ▤. 🖭 ⓞ 🄴 𝘝𝘐𝘚𝘈. ⁓
DX **b**
closed Sunday and Bank Holidays for dinner and Saturday – **M** a la carte 33/67.

Schümann's Austernkeller, Jungfernstieg 34 (H 36), *𝒫* 34 62 65, « Rest. from the
turn of the century with private dining rooms » – ⁓
CY **a**
closed Sunday and Bank Holidays – **M** a la carte 42/128.

Deichgraf, Deichstr. 2 (H 11), *𝒫* 36 42 08 – 🖭 ⓞ 🄴 𝘝𝘐𝘚𝘈
CZ **a**
closed Saturday lunch, Sunday and Bank Holidays – **M** a la carte 37/96 (booking essential).

Überseebrücke, Vorsetzen (H 11), *𝒫* 31 33 33, ≼ Port and Docks – ▤. 🖭 ⓞ 🄴 𝘝𝘐𝘚𝘈
BZ **b**
M a la carte 29/73.

at Hamburg-Altona by Reeperbahn BY :

Raphael H. Altona, Präsident-Krahn-Str. 13 (H 50), *𝒫* 38 12 39 – 📶 📶wc ☎ 🅿. 🖭 ⓞ
🄴. ⁓ rest
M *(dinner only, closed Saturday and Sunday)* a la carte 19/32 – **54 rm** 55/140 Bb.

❀ **Landhaus Scherrer**, Elbchaussee 130 (H 50), *𝒫* 8 80 13 25 – 🅿. 🖭 ⓞ
closed Sunday – **M** 55/105 (booking essential) – **Bistro-Rest.** *(lunch only)* **M** a la carte
30/60
Spec. Hausgeräucherter Seeteufel auf Gartenkräutern, Roulade von Lachs und Zander in Wirsing, Vierländer
Ente auf Rhabarber.

Fischereihafen-Rest. Hamburg, Große Elbstr. 143 (H 50), *𝒫* 38 18 16, ≼ – 🅿. ⓞ
M a la carte 30/93 (booking essential).

Hanse-Grill, Elbchaussee 94 (H 50), *𝒫* 39 46 11 – 🅿.

at Hamburg-Billstedt by Nordkanalstr. FZ :

Panorama Ⓜ without rest, Billstedter Hauptstr. 44 (H 74), *𝒫* 73 17 01, Telex 212162, 🅽
– 📶 🖭 ⇔ 🅿 ふ. 🖭 ⓞ 🄴 𝘝𝘐𝘚𝘈
111 rm 110/200 Bb.

at Hamburg-Blankenese W : 16 km by Reeperbahn BY :

Strandhotel ⑳, Strandweg 13 (H 55), *𝒫* 86 09 93, ≼, 🍴, « Villa with elegant
installation, painting collection », ⇦ – 🖭 ⇔wc 📶wc ☎ 🅿. 🖭 ⓞ 🄴 𝘝𝘐𝘚𝘈
M *(closed Sunday dinner and Monday)* a la carte 41/76 – **13 rm** 100/230.

Süllberg, Süllbergterrasse 2 (H 55), *𝒫* 86 16 86, « Terraced garden with ≼ » – 🅿 ふ.
🖭 ⓞ 🄴 𝘝𝘐𝘚𝘈
M a la carte 32/76.

Sagebiels Fährhaus, Blankeneser Hauptstr. 107 (H 55), *𝒫* 86 15 14, « Garden with ≼ »
– 🅿. 🖭 ⓞ 🄴
closed Monday October - March – **M** a la carte 26/75.

Strandhof, Strandweg 27 (H 55), *𝒫* 86 52 36, ≼, 🍴 – 🖭 ⓞ
dinner only, closed October - May, Monday and 15 November - 15 December – **M** a la
carte 40/75.

at Hamburg-City Nord by Buchtstr. FX :

🏨🏨 **Crest-H. Hamburg**, Mexicoring 1 (H 60), ☏ 6 30 50 51, Telex 2174155 — 🛗 ☰ rest 📺 ⇦ 🅿 ♿ . 🆎 ① 🅴 💳. 🍽 rest
M a la carte 30/60 — **185 rm** 155/240 Bb.

at Hamburg-Eppendorf by Grindelallee CX :

XXX ❀ **Le Canard**, Martinistr. 11 (H 20), ☏ 4 60 48 30 — 🆎 🍽
closed Sunday — M a la carte 57/95 (booking essential)
Spec. Kaninchensülze, Steinbutt auf Rote Beete, Barbarieentenbrust in Rotweinsauce.

XX **Fisch Sellmer**, Ludolfstr. 50 (H 20), ☏ 47 30 57 — 🅿. 🍽
M a la carte 38/70.

at Hamburg-Harvestehude :

🏨🏨🏨 **Inter-Continental**, Fontenay 10 (H 36), ☏ 41 41 50, Telex 211099, ⩽ Hamburg and Alster,
« Terrace », Massage, ⇆, 🔲 — 🛗 📺 ♿ ⇦ 🅿 ♿. 🆎 ① 🅴 💳. 🍽 rest   EX **r**
Restaurants : — **Fontenay-Grill** (closed Saturday lunch) M a la carte 44/96 —
Hulk-Brasserie (buffet lunch and dinner) M a la carte 32/55 — **300 rm** 230/330 Bb.

🏨🏨 **Smolka**, Isestr. 98 (H 13), ☏ 47 50 50, Telex 215275 — 🛗 ⇦ ♿ 🆎 ① 🅴 💳. 🍽 rest
M (closed Saturday dinner, Sunday and Bank Holidays) a la carte 24/63 — **40 rm** 99/198
Bb.   by Rothenbaumchaussee CX

🏨 **Mittelweg** without rest, Mittelweg 59 (H 13), ☏ 45 32 51 — 📺 ⇦wc ♿ ☎ 🅿. 🆎
38 rm 92/169.   by Mittelweg DX

🏨 **Garden H. Pöseldorf** 🐦 without rest, Magdalenenstr. 60 (H 13), ☏ 44 99 59,
Telex 212621, « Elegantly furnished », 🌿 — 🛗 📺 ⇦wc 🏠wc ☎. 🆎 ① 🅴 💳   EX **c**
70 rm 112/304.

XX **Daitokai** (Japanese rest.), Milchstr. 1 (H 13), ☏ 4 10 10 61 — 🆎 ① 🅴
M a la carte 33/65 (booking essential).   by Mittelweg DX

XX **La vite** (Italian rest.), Heimhuder Str. 5 (H 13), ☏ 45 84 01, 🍽 — 🆎 ① 🅴. 🍽   DX **e**
closed Sunday and 23 December - 2 January — M a la carte 37/62 (booking essential).

at Hamburg-Nienstedten W : 13 km :

XXX **Jacob** with rm, Elbchaussee 401 (H 52), ☏ 82 93 52, ⩽, « Elbe-side setting terrace » —
📺 ⇦wc ☎ 🅿 ♿. 🆎 ① 🅴
M a la carte 40/77 — **14 rm** 110/214.

XX ❀ **Landhaus Dill**, Elbchaussee 404 (H 52), ☏ 82 84 43 — 🅿. 🆎 ① 💳
Tuesday to Friday dinner only,closed Monday January - October — M a la carte 42/84
Spec. Hausgebeizter Lachs mit Reibekuchen und Schnittlauchsauce, Kalbsmedaillons mit Krebsen in
Kerbelsauce, Lammrücken mit Basilikum.

at Hamburg-Rotherbaum :

XX ❀ **L'auberge française** (French rest.), Rutschbahn 34 (H 13), ☏ 4 10 25 32 — 🍽
closed Saturday, Sunday and July — M a la carte 41/70.   by Grindelhof CX

XX **Skyline-Turm-Rest.**, Lagerstr. 2 (🛗, 3,75 DM) (H 6), ☏ 43 80 24, 🌤 Hamburg,
« Revolving rest. at 132 m » — ☰ 🅿. 🆎 ① 🅴. 🍽
M a la carte 30/70 (booking essential).   BX

at Hamburg-St. Pauli :

XX **Bavaria-Blick**, Bernhard-Nocht-Str. 99 (7th floor, 🛗) (H 4), ☏ 31 48 00, ⩽ port — ☰. 🆎
① 🅴 💳
M a la carte 34/68 (booking essential).   BZ **m**

at Hamburg-Schnelsen by Grindelallee CX :

🏨🏨 **Novotel**, Oldesloer Str. 166 (H 61), ☏ 5 50 20 73, Telex 212923, 🏊, 🌿 — 🛗 📺 ⇦wc ☎
♿ 🅿 ♿. 🆎 ① 🅴 💳
M a la carte 23/45 — **124 rm** 131/172 Bb.

at Hamburg-Stillhorn by Amsinckstraße FZ :

🏨 **Autobahn Rasthaus und Motel**, Eastside, ✉ 2102 Hamburg, ☏ 7 54 00 20 — 🏠wc ☎
⇦ 🅿
M a la carte 18/40 — **62 rm** 57/111.

at Hamburg-Uhlenhorst by Buchtstraße FX :

🏨🏨 **Parkhotel Alster Ruh** 🐦 without rest, Am Langenzug 6 (H 76), ☏ 22 45 77 — 📺
⇦wc 🏠wc ☎
27 rm 87/185.

X **Ristorante Roma** (Italian rest.), Hofweg 7 (H 76), ☏ 22 25 54 — 🆎 ①
closed Sunday lunch and Saturday — M a la carte 30/54.

202

HANNOVER

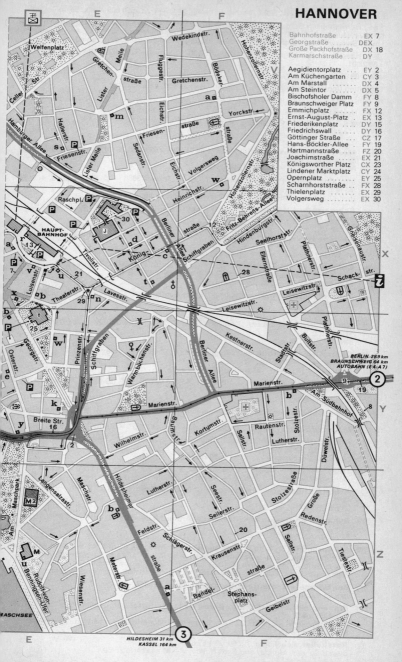

BERLIN 289 km
BRAUNSCHWEIG 64 km
AUTOBAHN (E 4-A 7)

HILDESHEIM 31 km
KASSEL 164 km

HANOVER (HANNOVER) 3000. Niedersachsen 987 ⑮ — pop. 550 000 — alt. 55 m — ✪ 0511.

See : Herrenhausen Gardens (Herrenhäuser Gärten)★★ (Großer Garten★★, Berggarten★) CV — Kestner-Museum★ DY **M1** — Market Church (Marktkirche) (Altarpiece★★) DY **A** — Museum of Lower Saxony (Niedersächsisches Landesmuseum) (Prehistorical department★) EZ **M2**.

🛬 Hanover-Langenhagen (① : 11 km), ✆ 7 30 51, City-Air-Terminal, Raschplatz 1PQ, ✆ 1 68 28 01.

🚗 1 98 54 52.

Exhibition Centre (Messegelände), (by ② and B 6) ✆ 8 91, Telex 922728.

🛈 Tourist office, Ernst-August-Platz 8, ✆ 1 68 23 19.

ADAC, Hindenburgstr. 37. ✆ 8 50 00.

Berlin 289 ② — Bremen 123 ① — Hamburg 151 ①.

Plan on preceding pages

🏨 **Maritim** Ⓜ, Hildesheimer Str. 34, ✆ 1 65 31, Telex 9230268, 🚗, 🔲 — 🛗 🗐 📺 & 🅿️ 👤 EZ **b**
AE ⓘ E VISA ⚛ rest
M a la carte 31/72 — **293 rm** 134/278 Bb.

🏨 **Inter-Continental**, Friedrichswall 11, ✆ 1 69 11, Telex 923656 — 🛗 🗐 rest 📺 & 🚗 👤 DY **a**
⚛ rest
Restaurants : — Brasserie — Prinz Taverne — Bierstube — **285 rm**.

🏨 **Schweizerhof Hannover - Schu's Rest.** Ⓜ, Hinüberstr. 6, ✆ 3 49 50, Telex 923359 EX **d**
— 🛗 📺 🅿️ 👤 AE ⓘ E
M a la carte 50/80 — **Gourmet's Buffet M** a la carte 25/50 — **84 rm** 181/297.

🏨 **Kastens H. Luisenhof**, Luisenstr. 2, ✆ 1 61 51, Telex 922325 — 🛗 📺 & 🚗 🅿️ 👤 AE EX **r**
ⓘ E VISA ⚛ rest
M (closed Sunday July to August) a la carte 36/67 — **200 rm** 127/250 Bb.

🏨 **Congress-H. am Stadtpark** Ⓜ, Clausewitzstr. 6, ✆ 81 00 51, Telex 921263, « Terrace by ②
with ≤ », Massage, 🚗, 🔲 — 🛗 📺 & 🚗 🅿️ 👤 AE ⓘ E VISA
M a la carte 26/64 — **252 rm** 119/218 Bb.

🏨 **Grand H. Mussmann** 📖 without rest, Ernst-August-Platz 7, ✆ 32 79 71, Telex 922859 — EX **v**
🛗 📺 🅿️ 👤
100 rm Bb.

🏨 **Königshof** Ⓜ without rest, Königstr. 12, ✆ 31 20 71, Telex 922306 — 🛗 📺 ⌾wc 🚿wc EX **c**
☎ 🅿️ AE E
84 rm 90/180 Bb.

🏨 **Central-H. Kaiserhof**, Ernst-August-Platz 4, ✆ 32 78 11, Telex 922810 — 🛗 📺 ⌾wc EX **a**
🚿wc ☎ 👤 AE ⓘ E VISA ⚛ rest
M a la carte 18,50/45 — **67 rm** 96/186 Bb.

🏨 **Am Funkturm** without rest, Hallerstr. 34, ✆ 31 70 33 — 🛗 📺 ⌾wc 🚿wc & 🅿️ AE E EV **s**
VISA
40 rm 74/140 Bb.

🏨 **Hospiz Loccumer Hof**, Kurt-Schumacher-Str. 16, ✆ 32 60 51 — 🛗 📺 ⌾wc 🚿wc ☎ DX **s**
👤 👤 AE ⓘ E VISA ⚛
M (closed Saturday and Sunday for dinner) a la carte 21/57 — **70 rm** 70/160 Bb.

🏨 **Am Thielenplatz** without rest, Thielenplatz 2, ✆ 32 76 91, Telex 922665 — 🛗 ⌾wc EX **n**
🚿wc ☎ AE ⓘ E VISA
closed 23 December - 1 January — **90 rm** 60/120.

🏨 **Thüringer Hof** without rest, Osterstr. 37, ✆ 32 64 37 — 🛗 ⌾wc 🚿wc ☎. AE ⓘ E EY **e**
closed 24 December - 1 January — **59 rm** 55/200.

🏨 **Atlanta** without rest, Hinüberstr. 1, ✆ 34 29 39, Telex 924603 — 🛗 ⌾wc 🚿wc ☎. E. EX **t**
⚛
39 rm 55/110.

XXX **Bakkarat im Casino am Maschsee**, Arthur-Menge-Ufer 3 (1st floor), ✆ 80 10 20, ≤, DZ **a**
🍴 — 🅿️ AE ⓘ E VISA
M a la carte 30/60.

XXX ❀ **Georgenhof** 📖 with rm, Herrenhäuser Kirchweg 20, ✆ 70 22 44, wine-list with more CV
than 200 wines, « Lower Saxony country house in park, terrace » — ⌾wc 🚿wc ☎ 🅿️
M a la carte 40/102 — **17 rm** 65/180   by Engelbosteler Damm
Spec. Carpaccio von geräucherter Ochsenlende, Roulade vom Steinbutt, Saltimbocca vom Lammrücken.

XXX **Zur Brügge's Restaurant**, Bödekerstr. 29, ✆ 31 90 05 FV **a**
closed Saturday lunch — **M** a la carte 37/79.

XXX **Mövenpick Café Kröpcke - Baron de la Mouette**, Georgenstr. 35, ✆ 32 62 85, 🍴 EX **x**
— 🗐 AE ⓘ E VISA
Café Kröpcke M a la carte 23/52 — **Baron de la Mouette M** a la carte 26/60 — **Backstube M** a la carte 17/30.

XX **Ratskeller**, Köbelinger Str. 60, ✆ 1 53 63 — 👤 DY **n**
closed Sunday, Monday and Bank Holidays — **M** a la carte 22/60.

204

XX ❀ **Clichy**, Weiße Kreuzstr. 31, ℰ 31 24 47   EV **m**
  closed Saturday lunch, Sunday and Bank Holidays — **M** a la carte 39/71 (booking essential)
  Spec. Ententerrine mit Gänsestopfleber, Lachsroulade in Sauerampfersauce, Kaninchenrücken in Blätterteig.

XX **Stern's Rest. Härke-Stuben**, Marienstr. 104, ℰ 81 73 22 — ⟨AE⟩ ⟨O⟩ **E**   FY **b**
  closed Saturday — **M** a la carte 41/91.

XX **Leineschloss**, H.-Wilhelm-Kopf-Platz 1, ℰ 32 66 93, 🌤 — 🅿 🏛   DY **k**
  M a la carte 23/62.

X **Härke Klause** (brewery - inn), Ständehausstr. 4, ℰ 32 11 75   EY **b**

X **Wein-Wolf**, Rathenaustr. 2, ℰ 32 07 88 — ⟨AE⟩ ⟨O⟩ **E**   EY **w**
  closed July for dinner, Sunday and Bank Holidays — **M** a la carte 22/58.

X **Dalmatia Grill** (Yugoslavian rest.), Hildesheimer Str. 117, ℰ 88 81 17 — ⟨AE⟩ ⟨O⟩ **E** ⟨VISA⟩
  closed Monday and 15 July - 30 August — **M** a la carte 20/35.   by ③

  at Hanover 51-Bothfeld by Celler Str. EV :

🏠 **Halberstadt** 🐾 without rest, Im Heidkampe 80, ℰ 64 01 18 — 🚿wc 🛁wc ☎ 📟 🅿.
  ⟨AE⟩ ⟨VISA⟩
  closed 23 December - 2 January — **36 rm** 65/140.

XXX ❀ **Witten's Hop**, Gernsstr. 4, ℰ 64 88 44, « Country house atmosphere » — 🅿. 🦌
  Monday to Saturday dinner only, closed Tuesday, 16 February - 12 March and 17 to 24
  April — **M** a la carte 55/96 (booking essential)
  Spec. Feuilleté von St. Petersfisch und Hummer mit Orangenbutter, Heidschnucken-Gerichte.

  at Hanover 51-Buchholz by Celler Str. EV :

🏨 **Föhrenhof** Ⓜ, Kirchhorster Str. 22, ℰ 6 17 21, Telex 923448, 🌤 — 🔼 📺 ⚙ 🅿 🏛.
  🦌 rest
  77 rm Bb.

  at Hanover 81-Döhren by ③ :

XXX **Wichmann**, Hildesheimer Str. 230, ℰ 83 16 71, « Courtyard » — 🅿
  closed Sunday, Monday, Bank Holidays and 3 weeks July - August — **M** a la carte 38/78.

XX **Die Insel - Maschseeterrassen**, Rudolf-von-Bennigsen-Ufer 81, ℰ 83 12 14, ≤, 🌤
  — 🅿 🏛
  closed Monday and 2 to 21 January — **M** a la carte 22/55.

  at Hanover 42-Flughafen by ① : 11 km :

🏨 **Holiday Inn**, Am Flughafen, ℰ 73 01 71, Telex 924939, ⟨≋s⟩, 🔲 — 🔼 🍽 📺 ⚙ 🅿 🏛. ⟨AE⟩
  ⟨O⟩ **E** ⟨VISA⟩
  M a la carte 26/64 — **146 rm** 185/235 Bb.

  at Hanover 71-Kirchrode by ② and B 65 :

🏨 **Crest-H. Hannover**, Tiergartenstr. 117, ℰ 52 30 92, Telex 922748 — 🔼 📺 📟 🅿 🏛.
  ⟨AE⟩ ⟨O⟩ **E** ⟨VISA⟩
  M a la carte 28/60 — **108 rm** 155/205 Bb.

  at Hanover 71-Kleefeld by ② and B 65 :

XX **Alte Mühle**, Hermann-Löns-Park 3, ℰ 55 94 80, ≤, « Converted lower Saxony
  farm-house, terrace » — ⚙ 🅿. ⟨AE⟩ ⟨O⟩
  closed Thursday and 3 weeks August — **M** a la carte 22/68.

  at Hanover 72-Messe (near exhibition Centre) by ② :

🏨 **Parkhotel Kronsberg**, Messeschnellweg, ℰ 861086, Telex 923448, 🔲, 🎴, 🍴 — 🔼
  🍽 rest 📺 📟 🅿 🏛 (with 🍽). ⟨AE⟩ ⟨O⟩ **E** ⟨VISA⟩. 🦌 rest
  M a la carte 26/72 — **105 rm** 96/200 Bb.

  at Garbsen 4-Berenbostel 3008 by ⑥ : 13 km :

🏨 **Landhaus Köhne am See** 🐾, Seeweg 19, ℰ (05131) 60 11, ≤, « Lakeside setting,
  terrace », ⟨≋s⟩, 🔲, 🎴, 🍴 — 🍽 rest 📺 🚿wc 🛁wc ☎ 🅿
  M a la carte 31/64 — **19 rm** 76/120 Bb.

👉 *The hotels have entered into certain undertakings*
   towards the readers of this Guide.
   Make it plain that you have the most recent Guide.

   If you write to a hotel abroad,
   enclose an International Reply Coupon
   (available from Post Offices).

MUNICH (MÜNCHEN) 8000. Bayern 987 ㊲, 426 ④ ⑰ – pop. 1 297 000 – alt. 520 m – ☎ 089.

See : Marienplatz★ KLY – Church of Our Lady (Frauenkirche)★★ (tower ★) KY – Old Pinakothek (Alte Pinakothek)★★★ KY – German Museum (Deutsches Museum)★★ LZ **M1** – The Palace (Residenz)★ (Treasury★★ Palace Theatre★) LY – (Church of the Asam Brothers (Asamkirche) ★ KZ **A** – National Museum of Bavaria (Bayerisches Nationalmuseum)★★ HV – New Pinakothek (Neue Pinakothek)★ GU – City Historical Museum (Münchener Stadtmuseum)★ (Moorish Dancers★★) KZ **M2** – Villa Lenbach Collections (Städt. Galerie im Lenbachhaus) (Portraits by Lenbach★) KY **M5** – Antique Collections (Staatl. Antikensammlungen)★(Etruscan trinkets★) KY **M6** – Glyptothek★ KY **M7** – German Hunting Museum (Deutsches Jagdmuseum)★ KY **M8** – Olympic Park (Olympia-Park) (Olympic Tower ★★★) – New Town Hall (Neues Rathaus)★ LY **R** – Church of the Theatines (Theatinerkirche)★(Choir and Cupola★) LY **D** – English Garden (Englischer Garten)(view from Monopteros Temple★) HU.

Envir. : Nymphenburg★★ (castle★, park★, Amalienburg★★, Botanical Gardens★★).

✈ München-Riem (③ : 11 km), ℰ 92 11 21 27.

ℰ 5 90 42 90.

Exhibition Centre (Messegelände) (EX), ℰ 5 10 71, Telex 5212086.

ℹ Tourist office in the main station, ℰ 2 39 11, Telex 524801.

ℹ Tourist office in the airport München-Riem, ℰ 2 39 12 66.

ADAC, Sendlinger-Tor-Platz 9, ℰ 59 39 79.

The reference (M 15) at the end of the address is the postal district: Munich 15

Plans on following pages

✿ **Vier Jahreszeiten Kempinski - Rest. Walterspiel**, Maximilianstr. 17 (M 22), ℰ 23 03 90, Telex 523859, Massage, ≘s, ▣ – ▮ ▤ ▢ ⇔ ♨. AE ⓓ E VISA. ✻ rest
M *(closed Monday lunch, Saturday lunch and August)* a la carte 64/110 – **Jahreszeiten-Eck** *(closed Sunday)* **M** a la carte 32/65 – **365 rm** 183/416 LY **a**
Spec. Salat von Krustentieren und Edelfischen, Timbale vom Fasan mit Rahmmorcheln, Lammnüßchen mit Gorgonzolasauce.

✿ **Königshof**, Karlsplatz 25 (M 2), ℰ 55 84 12, Telex 523616 – ▮ ▤ ▢ ⓟ ♨. AE ⓓ E VISA. ✻ rest KY **s**
M a la carte 43/106 (booking essential) – **120 rm** 162/234
Spec. Warme Terrine von Lachs und Jacobsmuscheln mit weißer Hummersauce, Suprême vom Loup de mer mit Lauch und Trüffel, Aiguillettes vom Milchlammrücken mit Krebsen und Morchelcreme.

Hilton, Am Tucherpark 7 (M 22), ℰ 34 00 51, Telex 5215740, beer-garden, Massage, ≘s, ▣ – ▮ ▤ ▢ ♿ ⓟ ♨. AE ⓓ E VISA HU **n**
Restaurants : – **Hilton Grill M** a la carte 36/80 – **Isar-Terrassen M** a la carte 26/56 – **485 rm** 186/377 Bb.

Bayerischer Hof-Palais Montgelas, Promenadeplatz 6 (M 2), ℰ 2 12 00, Telex 523409, Massage, ≘s, ▣ – ▮ ▤ rest ♿ ⇔ ♨. AE ⓓ E VISA KY **y**
Restaurants : – **Grill M** a la carte 33/75 – **Trader Vic's** *(dinner only)* **M** a la carte 28/70 – **Palais Keller M** a la carte 17/48 – **442 rm** 163/413.

Continental, Max-Joseph-Str. 5 (M 2), ℰ 55 79 71, Telex 522603, ☂, « Antique furniture » – ▮ ▢ ⇔ ♨. AE ⓓ E VISA KY **f**
M a la carte 43/83 – **160 rm** 196/320 Bb.

Excelsior, Schützenstr. 11 (M 2), ℰ 55 79 06, Telex 52419 – ▮ ▤ rest ▢ ♨. AE ⓓ E VISA JY **z**
M a la carte 31/65 – **118 rm** 152/224.

Eden-Hotel-Wolff, Arnulfstr. 4 (M 2), ℰ 55 82 81, Telex 523564 – ▮ ▢ ⇔ ♨. AE ⓓ E VISA JY **p**
M a la carte 25/57 – **214 rm** 140/280 Bb.

Drei Löwen - Rest.Strawberry, Schillerstr. 8 (M 2), ℰ 59 55 21, Telex 523867 – ▮ ▢ ⇔ ⓟ ♨. AE ⓓ E VISA. ✻ rest JY **e**
M *(closed Sunday)* a la carte 26/50 – **130 rm** 112/194 Bb.

Metropol, Bayerstr. 43, (Entrance Goethestr.) (M 2), ℰ 53 07 64, Telex 522816 – ▮ ▤ rest ♨. AE ⓓ E JY **k**
M a la carte 21/50 – **272 rm** 67/145.

Germania, Schwanthaler Str. 28 (M 2), ℰ 5 16 80, Telex 523790 – ▮ ▢ ⊟wc ⋒wc ☎ ♿ ♨. AE ⓓ E VISA JY **a**
M *(grill rest.)* a la carte 20/44 – **100 rm** 134/194 Bb.

Bundesbahnhotel, Bahnhofplatz 2 (M 2), ℰ 55 85 71, Telex 523174 – ▮ ▢ ⊟wc ⋒wc ☎ ♨. AE E JY **u**
M a la carte 22/56 – **228 rm** 80/170.

Reinbold without rest, Adolf-Kolping-Str. 11 (M 2), ℰ 59 79 45, Telex 522539 – ▮ ▤ ▢ ⊟wc ☎ ⇔. AE ⓓ E VISA JY **t**
56 rm 77/184.

Deutscher Kaiser, Arnulfstr. 2 (M 2), ℰ 55 83 21, Telex 522650, rest. on the 15th floor with ≤ Munich – ▮ ⊟wc ⋒wc ☎ ♿ ⓟ ♨. AE ⓓ E VISA. ✻ rest JY **s**
M a la carte 32/60 – **156 rm** 112/195 Bb.

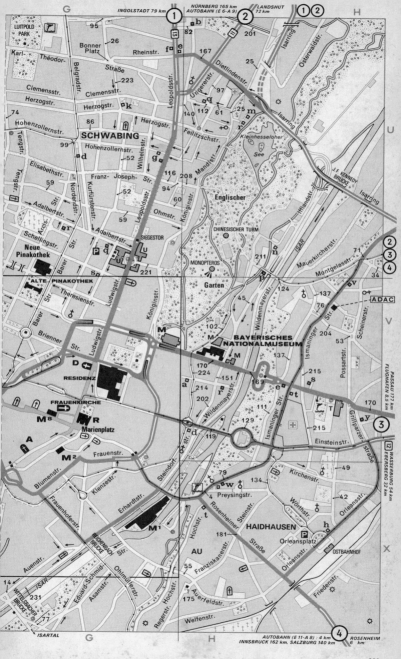

STREET INDEX TO MÜNCHEN TOWN PLANS

Continued after town plan

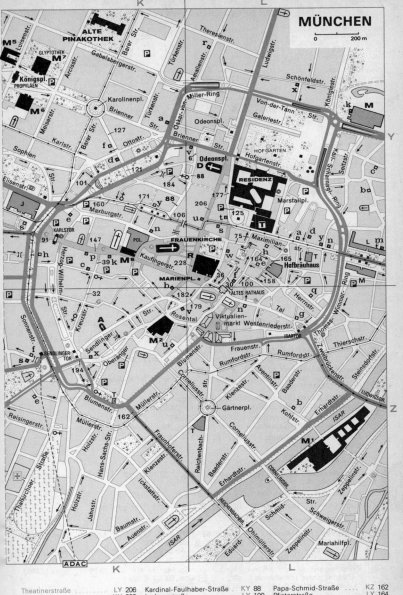

STREET INDEX TO MÜNCHEN TOWN PLANS (Concluded)

XX **Zum Bürgerhaus**, Pettenkoferstr. 1 (M 2), 🕿 59 79 09, 🍴, « Bavarian farm-house furniture » – ❶ 🖃   KZ **s**
closed Saturday, Sunday and Bank Holidays – **M** a la carte 26/70 (booking essential).

XX **Dallmayr**, Dienerstr. 14 (1st floor) (M 2), 🕿 2 13 51 00 – 🖭 ❶   LY **w**
closed Saturday dinner, Sunday and for lunch in August – **M** a la carte 27/70.

XX **Halali**, Schönfeldstr. 22 (M 22), 🕿 28 59 09   LY **x**
closed Saturday lunch, Sunday, Bank Holidays and 15 to 30 June – M a la carte 29/55 (booking essential).

X **Goldene Stadt** (Bohemian cooking), Oberanger 44 (M 2), 🕿 26 43 82 – 🖭 ❶ 🖃
closed Sunday – **M** a la carte 20/53 (booking essential for dinner).   KZ **x**

X **Zum Klösterl**, St.-Anna-Str. 2 (M 22), 🕿 22 50 86   LY **m**
dinner only,closed Saturday and Bank Holidays – **M** a la carte 20/55 (booking essential).

X **Ratskeller**, Marienplatz 8 (M 2), 🕿 22 03 13 – 🖭   LY **R**
M a la carte 18/42.

Brewery - inns :

XX Spatenhaus-Bräustuben, Residenzstr. 12 (M 2), 🕿 22 78 41, 🍴, « Furnished in traditional alpine style »   LY **t**

X Franziskaner - Fuchs'n-Stub'n, Perusastr. 5 (M 2), 🕿 22 50 02, 🍴   LY **s**

X Augustiner-G., Neuhauser Str. 16 (M 2), 🕿 2 60 41 06, « Beer-garden »   KY **p**

at Munich-Bogenhausen :

🏨 **Sheraton**, Arabellastr. 6 (M 81), 🕿 92 40 11, Telex 522391, ≼ Munich, beer-garden, Massage, ⛊s, 🏊, 🍴 – 🛗 🖃 📺 🕭 ⇔ 🚗. 🖭 ❶ 🖃 🆅🆂🅰   by Isarring HU
Restaurants : – **Atrium M** a la carte 33/79 – **Alt Bayern Stube** *(dinner only)* **M** a la carte 29/64 – **Sandwich Bar M** a la carte 19/36 – **650 rm** 155/320.

🏨 **Prinzregent** 🅼 without rest, Ismaninger Str. 42 (M 80), 🕿 4 70 20 81, Telex 524403, « Elegant, rustic installation », ⛊s – 🛗 📺 ⇔. 🖭 ❶ 🖃 🆅🆂🅰   HV **t**
closed Christmas - 6 January – **66 rm** 160/250 Bb.

🏨 **Crest-H.**, Effnerstr. 99 (M 81), 🕿 98 25 41, Telex 524757 – 🛗 🖃 📺 🅿 🚗. 🖭 ❶ 🖃 🆅🆂🅰 🚿 rest   by Isarring HU
M a la carte 26/54 – **155 rm** 162/217 Bb.

🏨 **Arabella-H.**, Arabellastr. 5 (M 81), 🕿 9 23 21, Telex 529987, ≼ Munich, Massage, ⛊s, 🏊 – 🛗 🖃 rest 📺 🕭 ⇔ 🚗 (with 🖃). 🖭 ❶ 🖃 🆅🆂🅰   by Isarring HU
M a la carte 26/55 – **285 rm** 135/240 Bb – 90 apartments 240/320.

XXX ✿ **Käfer-Schänke**, Schumannstr. 1 (M 80), ✆ 4 16 81, Telex 523073, ⛱, « Rustic and elegant installations » – AE ◑ E. ✈ HV **s**
closed Sunday and Bank Holidays – **M** a la carte 38/81 (booking essential)
Spec. Vorspeisen vom Schaubuffet, Krusten- und Schalentiere, Das große Dessert Maison Käfer.

XXX **Da Pippo** (Italian rest.), Mühlbauerstr. 36 (M 80), ✆ 4 70 48 48, ⛱ – ◑ E. ✈
closed 1 to 21 August, Sunday and Bank Holidays – **M** a la carte 32/65.
by Prinzregentenstr. HV

XX **Tai Tung** (Chinese rest.), Prinzregentenstr. 60 (Villa Stuck) (M 80), ✆ 47 11 00 – ◑ E
closed 3 weeks August, June - September Sunday and Monday, October - May Sunday dinner and Monday – **M** a la carte 25/50. HV **e**

XX **Mifune** (Japanese rest.), Ismaninger Str. 136 (M 80), ✆ 98 75 72 – AE ◑ E. ✈ HV **v**
closed Sunday – **M** a la carte 18/60.

X **Zum Klösterl**, Schneckenburger Str. 31 (M 80), ✆ 47 61 98 HV **y**
closed Saturday – **M** a la carte 20/55.

at Munich 80-Haidhausen :

Preysing (see also **Preysing-Keller** rest. below), Preysingstr. 1, ✆ 48 10 11, Telex 529044, « Rustic, elegant installation », ≘s, ⊠ – |♦| ▤ TV ⇔ ⛹ HX **w**
closed 23 December - 7 January – **Preysing-Pub** *(dinner only, closed Sunday and Bank Holidays)* **M** a la carte 37/65 – **73 rm** 130/380.

München Penta Hotel, Hochstr. 3, ✆ 4 48 55 55, Telex 529046, Massage, ≘s, ⊠ – |♦| ▤ TV P ⛹. AE ◑ E VISA HX **t**
M a la carte 31/68 – **83 rm** 131/256 Bb.

XXX ✿ **Preysing-Keller**, Innere-Wiener-Str. 6, ✆ 48 10 15, wine-list with 480 wines, « Vaulted cellar, country-house furniture » – ▤ HX **w**
dinner only, closed Sunday, Bank Holidays and 23 December - 7 January – **M** a la carte 40/77
Spec. Geräucherter Lachs (warm) auf Schnittlauch-Vinaigrette, Krebse in Dillsud, Pot-au-feu vom Lamm.

at Munich 83-Neu Perlach by ④ :

Orbis Hotel München M, Karl-Marx-Ring 87, ✆ 6 32 70, Telex 5213357, ≘s, ⊠ – |♦| ▤ rest TV ⇔ P ⛹ (with ▤). AE ◑ E VISA
M a la carte 19/51 – **185 rm** 120/180 Bb.

at Munich 40-Oberwiesenfeld by Schleissheimer Str. FU :

Olympiapark-H., Helene-Mayer-Ring 12, ✆ 3 51 60 71, Telex 5215231, free entrance to the ⊠ in the recreation centre – |♦| TV P ⛹. AE ◑ E VISA. ✈ rest
closed 24 December - 2 January – **M** a la carte 19/42 – **100 rm** 120/190 Bb.

at Munich 40-Schwabing :

Holiday Inn, Leopoldstr. 194, ✆ 34 09 71, Telex 5215439, Massage, ≘s, ⊠ – |♦| ▤ TV ⇔ ⛹. AE ◑ E VISA by ①
Restaurants : – **Almstuben-Grill** *(dinner only)* **M** a la carte 32/63 – **Oma's Küche M** a la carte 22/44 – **360 rm** 213/296 Bb.

Residence, Arthur-Kutscher-Platz 4, ✆ 39 90 41, Telex 529788, ⛱, ⊠ – |♦| ⇔ ⛹. AE ◑ E VISA. ✈ rest HU **q**
M a la carte 29/60 – **150 rm** 170/230.

Weinfurtners Garden-H. without rest, Leopoldstr. 132, ✆ 36 80 04, Telex 5214315 – |♦| TV ⇔wc ⋔wc ☎ ⇔ P ⛹ GU **e**
180 rm 88/190.

International-H. Auer without rest, Hohenzollernstr. 5, ✆ 33 30 43, Telex 529148 – |♦| TV ⇔wc ☎ ⇔ GU **g**
70 rm 150/200.

Biederstein ♨ without rest, Keferstr. 18, ✆ 39 50 72, ⛱ – |♦| ⇔wc ☎ ⇔. AE HU **m**
31 rm 85/130.

Gästehaus Englischer Garten ♨ without rest, Liebergesellstr. 8, ✆ 39 20 34, ⛱ – TV ⇔wc ☎ ⇔ HU **r**
14 rm 62/140 – 14 apartments.

Lettl ♨ without rest, Amalienstr. 53, ✆ 28 30 26 – |♦| TV ⇔wc ⋔wc ☎ ⇔ P GU **s**
closed 23 December - 2 January – **26 rm** 63/140.

XXXX ✿✿✿ **Tantris**, Johann-Fichte-Str. 7, ✆ 36 20 61, ⛱, « Modern rest., fashionable decoration » – ▤ P. AE ◑ E. ✈ HU **b**
Monday and Saturday dinner only, closed Sunday, Bank Holidays and 1 to 8 January – **M** a la carte 69/116 (booking essential)
Spec. Wildlachs in Petersiliensauce mit Pfifferlingen, Nantaiser Ente mit Sauce von Senfkörnern, Nuß-Soufflé mit weißem mousse-au-chocolat und Himbeersauce.

XXX ✿ **La Mer**, Schraudolphstr. 24, ✆ 2 72 24 39, « Opulent decor » – AE ◑ E. ✈ GU **r**
dinner only, closed Monday and end July - end August – **M** a la carte 50/95 (booking essential)
Spec. Marinierte Stopfgansleber mit Trüffeln, Seezungenfilets auf Nudeln mit Austernpilzen, Lammfilet in Thymiansauce.

XXX ❀ **Savarin**, Schellingstr. 122, ℰ 52 53 11 — ⓪ **E** FU **t**
closed Saturday lunch, Sunday, Monday and 3 weeks August — **M** a la carte 40/70 (booking essential)
Spec. Seezungenröllchen gefüllt mit Langustinenschaum, Zicklein mit Rosmarinsauce, Rehnüßchen in Wacholderrahm.

XX **Walliser Stuben**, Leopoldstr. 33, ℰ 34 80 00, Beer-garden — **AE** ⓪ **E** **VISA** GU **g**
dinner only, closed Sunday and Bank Holidays — **M** a la carte 30/56.

XX **Daitokai** (Japanese rest), Nordendstr. 64 (entrance Kurfürstenstr.), ℰ 2 71 14 21 — ▤. **AE** ⓪ **E** ✿ GU **d**
closed Sunday — **M** a la carte 37/72.

XX **Bistro Terrine** (French rest), Amalienstr. 89 (Amalien-Passage), ℰ 28 17 80 — **AE E**
Monday and Saturday dinner only, closed Sunday and Bank Holidays — **M** a la carte 32/60 (booking essential). GU **q**

X **Ristorante Bei Grazia**, Ungererstr. 161, ℰ 36 69 31 by ②
closed Friday dinner and Saturday — **M** a la carte 20/45 (booking essential).

STUTTGART 7000. Baden-Württemberg 9⒏7 ㉟ — pop. 578 000 — alt. 245 m — ✿ 0711.

See : Site (Lage)★★ — Killesberg Park (Höhenpark Killesberg)★★ BU — Television Tower (Fernsehturm)★★ (❀★★) DZ — Birkenkopf ❀★★ AY — Congress- and Concert Hall (Liederhalle)★ BX — Old Castle (Altes Schloß) (Renaissance courtyard★) CX — Stuttgart State Gallery (Staatsgalerie)★ CX **M1** — Collegiate Church (Stiftskirche) (Commemorative monuments of dukes★) CX **A** — Württemberg Regional Museum (Württembergisches Landesmuseum) (Medieval art objects★★) CX **M2** — Daimler-Benz Museum★ EX **M** — Porsche-Museum★ by ⑧.

Envir. : Bad Cannstatt Spa Park (Kurpark)★ E : 4 km EU.

✈ Stuttgart-Echterdingen, by ③ ℰ 7 90 11, City Air Terminal, Stuttgart, Lautenschlagerstr. 14, ℰ 22 12 64. .

Exhibition Centre (Messegelände Killesberg) (BU), ℰ 2 09 31, Telex 722584.

🛈 Tourist-Information, Klett-Passage (subway to the main Station), ℰ 2 22 82 40, Telex 723854.

ADAC, Am Neckartor 2, ℰ 2 80 00.

Frankfurt am Main 205 ⑧ — Karlsruhe 82 ⑥ — München 219 ④ — Strasbourg 154 ⑥.

Plans on following pages

🏨 ❀ **Steigenberger-H. Graf Zeppelin** ⟨S⟩, Arnulf-Klett-Platz 7, ℰ 29 98 81, Telex 722418, Massage, ⟨≘⟩, ▨ — ⌷ ▤ ⬚ 🅰 🗗 **AE** ⓪ **E** **VISA** CX **s**
M *(closed Saturday, Sunday, Bank Holidays and 29 July - 25 August)* a la carte 39/85 (booking essential) — **280 rm** 169/350 Bb
Spec. Roulade von Seezunge und Salm in der Spinathülle, Barbarie-Entenbrust mit Olivensauce, Lammrückenfilet mit Zitronenmelisse und Schupfnudeln.

🏨 **Am Schloßgarten**, Schillerstr. 23, ℰ 29 99 11, Telex 722936, « Terrace with ≤ » — ⌷ ⬚ 🅰 ⟨≕⟩ 🗗 **AE** ⓪ **E** **VISA** CX **u**
M a la carte 33/75 — **125 rm** 155/250.

🏨 **Royal**, Sophienstr. 35, ℰ 62 50 50, Telex 722449 — ⌷ ▤ rest ⬚ ⟨≕⟩ 🅿 🗗 **AE** ⓪ **E** BY **b**
M a la carte 32/60 — **85 rm** 160/240.

🏨 **Park-H.**, Villastr. 21, ℰ 28 01 61, Telex 723405, ☆ — ⌷ ▤ rest ⬚ 🅿 🗗 **AE** ⓪ **E** DV **r**
M a la carte 35/61 — **Radiostüble** *(dinner only)* **M** a la carte 21/49 — **81 rm** 70/210 Bb.

🏨 **Ruff**, Friedhofstr. 21, ℰ 25 01 61, Telex 721645, ⟨≘⟩, ▨ — ⌷ ⬚ ⊟wc 🍴wc ☎ ⟨≕⟩ 🅿 🗗. **AE** ⓪ **E** **VISA** CV **a**
closed 21 December - 3 January — **M** *(closed Saturday)* a la carte 20/49 — **85 rm** 80/140 Bb.

🏨 **Intercity-H.** without rest, Arnulf-Klett-Platz 2, ℰ 29 98 01, Telex 723543 — ⌷ ⬚ ⊟wc 🍴wc ☎ 🅿 🗗. **AE** ⓪ **E** **VISA** CX **p**
104 rm 70/160.

🏨 **Kronen-H.** ⟨S⟩ without rest, Kronenstr. 48, ℰ 29 96 61, Telex 723632, ⟨≘⟩ — ⌷ ⬚ 🍴wc ☎ ⟨≕⟩ 🗗. **AE** ⓪ **E** **VISA** BX **m**
closed 20 December - 7 January — **90 rm** 80/160 Bb.

🏨 **Azenberg** ⟨S⟩, Seestr. 116, ℰ 22 10 51, Telex 721819, ▨ — ⌷ ⊟wc 🍴wc ☎ ⟨≕⟩ 🅿. **AE** ⓪ **E** **VISA** AV **e**
(dinner for residents only) — **55 rm** 95/170.

🏨 **Unger** without rest, Kronenstr. 17, ℰ 29 40 41, Telex 723995 — ⌷ ⊟wc 🍴wc ☎ ⟨≕⟩ 🗗. **AE** ⓪ **E** **VISA** CX **a**
80 rm 92/170 Bb.

🏨 **Rieker** without rest, Friedrichstr. 3, ℰ 22 13 11 — ⌷ ⬚ ⊟wc 🍴wc ☎. **AE E** CX **d**
63 rm 85/152.

🏨 **Am Feuersee**, Johannesstr. 2, ℰ 62 61 03 — ⌷ ⬚ 🍴wc ☎. **AE** AY **t**
closed 21 December - 10 January — **M** *(dinner only, closed Saturday, Sunday and Bank Holidays)* a la carte 18/47 — **38 rm** 95/140 Bb.

🏨 **Wörtz-Zur Weinsteige** ⟨S⟩, Hohenheimer Str. 30, ℰ 24 53 96, Telex 723821, « Terrace » — ⬚ ⊟wc 🍴wc ☎. **AE** ⓪ **E** **VISA** CY **p**
closed 20 December - 15 January — **M** *(closed Saturday, Sunday and Bank Holidays)* a la carte 13,50/52 — **25 rm** 54/145.

⌂ **Mack und Pflieger**, Kriegerstr. 7, ℰ 29 19 27 — 🛗 🛠wc ☎ 🅿
(dinner only) — **94 rm**.
CX **h**

⌂ **Haus von Lippe** without rest, Rotenwaldstr. 68, ℰ 63 15 11 — 🛗 ➚wc 🛠wc ☎ ➾ 🅿
36 rm 46/98.
AY **s**

⌂ **Ketterer**, Marienstr. 3, ℰ 29 41 51, Telex 722340 — 🛗 ➚wc 🛠wc ☎. 🖭 ⓸ ⓔ 𝗩𝗜𝗦𝗔
M *(closed Saturday)* a la carte 19,50/48 — **75 rm** 87/145.
BY **y**

⌂ **Buchenhof** without rest, Hasenbergsteige 90, ℰ 65 20 18, ≼ Stuttgart — 🛗 ➚wc 🛠
☎ ➾ 🅿 🖭 ⓔ
closed Christmas - 13 January — **15 rm** 41/94.
AY **w**

XXX ۞ **Alte Post**, Friedrichstr. 43, ℰ 29 30 79 — ⓸
closed Sunday, Bank Holidays, end July - mid August and for lunch Monday and Saturday
— **M** a la carte 47/88 (booking essential)
Spec. Roulade von Petersfisch in Meursault, Ausgebeinter Ochsenschwanz in Portweinsauce, Suprême von
Poularde in Gänselebercrème.
CX **e**

XXX **Mövenpick-Rôtisserie Baron de la Mouette**, Kleiner Schloßplatz 11 (entrance
Theodor-Heuss-Str.), ℰ 22 00 34 — 🗏. 🖭 ⓸ ⓔ 𝗩𝗜𝗦𝗔
M a la carte 32/70 — **Boulevard Café M** a la carte 19/48.
BX **a**

XX **Der Goldene Adler**, Böheimstr. 38, ℰ 64 17 62 — 🅿. 🖭 ⓸ ⓔ
closed Monday and June — **M** a la carte 23/55.
AY **e**

XX **Schwyzer Eck**, Neckarstr. 246, ℰ 26 58 90 — ⓔ
closed Monday and 1 to 8 January — **M** a la carte 35/65.
DV **a**

XX **Greiner Stuben**, Arnulf-Klett-Platz 1, ℰ 29 51 21 — 🖭 ⓸ ⓔ
M a la carte 25/51 — **Bräustüble M** a la carte 13,50/37.
CX **t**

XX **Zeppelin-Stüble-Maukenescht** (Swabian specialities), Lautenschlagerstr. 2 (at Graf
Zeppelin H.), ℰ 22 40 13, 🛠 — 🗏. 🖭 ⓸ ⓔ 𝗩𝗜𝗦𝗔
M a la carte 19/54 (booking essential).
CX **s**

XX **China Garden** (Chinese rest.), Königstr. 17 (2nd floor), ℰ 22 38 66 — 🖭 ⓸ ⓔ 𝗩𝗜𝗦𝗔
M a la carte 17,50/40.
CX **n**

X **Börse**, Heustr. 1, ℰ 29 26 98 — 🖭 ⓸ ⓔ
closed Saturday, Sunday, Bank Holidays and 15 July - 10 August — **M** a la carte 18,50/48.
BX **e**

X **Kupferschmiede**, Christophstr. 45, ℰ 23 35 30, Terrace — 🖭 ⓸ ⓔ
closed Sunday, Bank Holidays and 1 to 10 January — **M** a la carte 22/58 ♨.
CY **a**

at Stuttgart 50 - Bad Cannstatt :

🏨 **Spahr** 🅼 without rest, Waiblinger Str. 63 (B 14), ℰ 55 20 08, Telex 7254608 — 🛗 📺
➚wc 🛠wc ☎ & ➾ 🅿. 🖭 ⓸ ⓔ
59 rm 100/180.
EU **a**

XX **Alt Cannstatt**, Königsplatz 1 (Kursaal), ℰ 56 11 15, 🛠 — ♨
EU

at Stuttgart 70 - Degerloch :

🏨 **Waldhotel Degerloch**, Guts-Muths-Weg 18, ℰ 76 50 17, Telex 7255728, 🛠, ⚭ — 🛗
📺 ➚wc 🛠wc ☎ & 🅿 ♨. 🖭 ⓸ ⓔ 𝗩𝗜𝗦𝗔
M a la carte 22/50 — **52 rm** 80/180 Bb.
by Guts-Muths-Weg DZ

XX **Turmrestaurant** (Television Tower, 144 m 🛗 4 DM), Jahnstr. 120, ℰ 24 61 04, ☀
Stuttgart and environs — 🗏 🅿. 🖭 ⓸ ⓔ 𝗩𝗜𝗦𝗔
M a la carte 21/50.
DZ

at Stuttgart 30 - Feuerbach :

🏨 **Europe**, Siemensstr. 26, ℰ 81 50 91, Telex 723650 — 🛗 🗏 📺 ➾ ♨. 🖭 ⓸ ⓔ 𝗩𝗜𝗦𝗔.
⚭ rest
M a la carte 29/63 — **200 rm** 140/180 Bb.
CU **z**

XX ۞ **Lamm**, Mühlstr. 24, ℰ 85 36 15 — ⚭
closed Saturday lunch, Sunday, Bank Holidays and 23 December - 10 January — **M** a la
carte 55/85 (booking essential)
Spec. Pasteten, Lachsfilet auf Sauerampfer, Brust von Barbarie-Ente in Himbeeressigsauce.
AU **n**

at Stuttgart 23 - Flughafen ③ : 15 km :

🏨 **Airport-Hotel Mövenpick**, Randstraße, ℰ 7 90 70, Telex 725677 — 🛗 🗏 rest 📺 ➚wc
☎ 🅿 ♨. 🖭 ⓸ ⓔ 𝗩𝗜𝗦𝗔. ⚭ rest
M a la carte 23/45 — **128 rm** 148/296.

XX **Flughafen-Rest. Schwabenstube**, Randstraße (at the Airport), ℰ 79 02 11, ≼, 🛠 — 🅿
♨.

at Stuttgart 80 - Möhringen ④ : 7 km :

🏨 **Stuttgart International**, Plieninger Str. 100, ℰ 7 20 21, Telex 7255763, entrance to the
Römerbad — 🛗 🗏 rest 📺 ➾ 🅿 ♨. 🖭 ⓸ ⓔ 𝗩𝗜𝗦𝗔. ⚭ rest
Restaurants : — **Kopenhagen** *(lunch only)* **M** a la carte 25/62 — **Paris Grill** *(dinner only)* **M**
33/73 — **Schwabenbräu-Stuben M** a la carte 15,50/48 — **200 rm** 148/285 Bb.

🏨 **Neotel** 🅼 without rest, Vaihinger Str. 151, ℰ 7 80 06 35, Telex 7255179 — 🛗 📺 ➚wc
🛠wc ☎ & 🅿. 🖭 ⓸ ⓔ 𝗩𝗜𝗦𝗔
71 rm 114/184 Bb.

STUTTGART

🏠 **Gloria**, Sigmaringer Str. 59, ℰ 71 30 59, 🍴 – 🛗 📺 🚿wc ☎ ⇦ 🅿 🏧 🖭 ⑩
M a la carte 17/35 – **70 rm** 78/113 Bb.

🏠 **Anker**, Vaihinger Str. 76, ℰ 71 30 31 – 🛗 🚿wc ⇦ 🖭 ⑩ **E** 🎯
closed 2 weeks August – **M** *(Swabian specialities, closed saturday)* a la carte 15/42 🔔 –
24 rm 72/120 Bb.

XX ❀ **Hirsch-Weinstuben**, Maierstr. 3, ℰ 71 13 75 – 🅿 🖭
closed Saturday lunch, Sunday, Bank Holidays and 2 weeks April – **M** a la carte 27/64
(booking essential)
Spec. Kuttelsülze mit Spätzlesalat, Lachs mit Kräuterkruste auf Lauchcrème.

XX **Landgasthof Riedsee** 🦢 with rm, Elfenstr. 120, ℰ 71 24 84, 🍴 – 🚿wc 🚿wc ☎ 🅿
🖭 ⑩ **E** 𝐕𝐈𝐒𝐀
closed 2 to 14 January – **M** *(closed Sunday dinner and Monday)* a la carte 30/62 – **12 rm**
55/110.

at Stuttgart 50 - Mühlhausen by Neckartalstraße EU :

XX ❀ **Öxle's Löwen**, Veitstr. 2, ℰ 53 22 26
Monday and Saturday dinner only, closed Sunday and Bank Holidays – **M** a la carte
43/72.

at Stuttgart 61 - Obertürkheim by ② :

X **Weinstube Paule**, Augsburger Str. 643, ℰ 32 14 71 – 🅿 🖭
closed end July - mid August, Thursday and every last Sunday in the month – **M** a la
carte 23/53.

X **Wirt am Berg**, Uhlbacher Str. 14, ℰ 32 12 26
closed 4 weeks August - September, Sunday, Bank Holidays and every first Saturday in
month – **M** a la carte 27/52.

at Stuttgart 70 - Plieningen ③ : 13 km :

🏨 ❀ **Traube**, Brabandtgasse 2, ℰ 45 48 33 – 🚿wc 🚿wc ☎ 🅿
closed 3 weeks August – **M** *(closed Saturday and Sunday)* a la carte 31/80 (booking
essential) – **22 rm** 65/180
Spec. Maultaschen nach altem Familienrezept, Wildlachs in Safransauce, Milchlammnüßchen mit
Knoblauchsprossen.

🏠 **Fissler-Post**, Schoellstr. 4, ℰ 45 50 74 – 🚿wc 🚿wc ☎ ⇦ 🅿 🏧 🖭 ⑩ **E** 𝐕𝐈𝐒𝐀
closed 27 to 30 December – **M** *(closed Sunday dinner)* a la carte 28/54 (booking essential)
– **63 rm** 68/105.

XX **Recknagel's Nagelschmiede**, Brabandtgasse 1, ℰ 45 74 54 – 🅿
Monday to Saturday dinner only.

at Stuttgart 40 - Stammheim by ⑧ :

🏨 **Novotel**, Korntaler Str. 207, ℰ 80 10 65, Telex 7252137, 🍴, 🏊 – 🛗 ▤ 📺 🚿wc ☎ 🚿
🅿 🏧 🖭 ⑩ **E** 𝐕𝐈𝐒𝐀
M a la carte 22/46 – **117 rm** 130/165 Bb.

🏠 **Strobel**, Korntaler Str. 35a, ℰ 80 15 32 – 🚿wc 🅿
closed 5 to 27 August – **M** *(closed Saturday and Sunday)* a la carte 18/46 – **23 rm** 37/75.

at Fellbach 7012 by ① : 8 km :

🏠 **Am Kappelberg** without rest, Karlstr. 37, ℰ (0711) 58 50 41, Telex 7254486, 🍴, 🔲 –
🛗 ▤ 📺 🚿wc ☎ ⇦ 🅿 🖭 ⑩ **E**
closed 22 December - 10 January – **41 rm** 100/155 Bb.

XX **Alt Württemberg**, Tainer Str. 7 (Schwabenlandhalle), ℰ (0711) 58 00 88 – ▤ 🅿 🖭
⑩ **E** 𝐕𝐈𝐒𝐀 – **M** a la carte 26/57.

219

at Gerlingen 7016 ⑦ : 14 km :

🏨 **Krone**, Hauptstr. 28, 𝒫 (07156) 2 10 04 − 劇 ▥ ⇔wc 📶wc ☎ ⇔ 🅿 🏊 ▥ ⓘ **E**
M *(closed Wednesday dinner, Sunday, Bank Holidays and 5 to 22 August)* a la carte 27/64
(booking essential) − **35 rm** 92/175 Bb.

at Korntal-Münchingen 2 7015 ⑧ : 9 km, near motorway exit S-Zuffenhausen :

🏨 **Mercure**, Siemensstr. 50, 𝒫 (07150) 1 31, Telex 723589, ⇔, ▧ − 劇 ▤ ▥ ᕦ 🅿 🏊
215 rm Bb.

🏨 **Strohgäu Hotel**, Stuttgarter Str. 60, 𝒫 (07150) 60 81 − 📶wc ☎ 🅿 🏊 ▥ ⓘ **E** **VISA**
M a la carte 20/47 − **22 rm** 92/130 Bb.

at Leinfelden-Echterdingen 3 - Stetten 7022 ④ 13 km :

🏨 **Nödingerhof**, Unterer Kasparswald 22, 𝒫 (0711) 79 90 67, ≤, 🎇 − 劇 ▥ 📶wc ☎ ⇔
🅿 🏊 ▥ ⓘ **E** **VISA**
M a la carte 18,50/54 − **24 rm** 82/130.

Baiersbronn 7292. Baden-Württemberg **987** ㉟ − pop. 15 600 − alt. 550 m −
✪ 07442.
Stuttgart 100.

XXXX ✿✿ **Rest. Bareiss**, Gärtenbühlweg 14 (Mitteltal), 𝒫 4 71, ≤, wine-list with 350 wines −
▤ 🅿 ⓘ 🍸
closed Monday, Tuesday, 28 May - 14 June and 27 November - 24 December − **M** a la
carte 45/84
Spec. Hummerterrine in Safrangelee, Täubchen auf Lauch und Trüffel, St. Petersfisch mit Pimentos.

XXXX ✿✿ **Schwarzwaldstube in der Traube-Tonbach**, Tonbachstr. 237 (Tonbach),
𝒫 49 20, ≤ − 🅿 ▥ ⓘ **E**
closed Friday lunch, Thursday and 14 January- 14 February − **M** a la carte 43/92 (booking
essential)
Spec. Terrine von Kalbsbries und Gänseleber, Hummerauflauf auf gedämpfter Brunnenkresse,
Kaninchenrückenfilet auf sautierten Träuschlingen.

Bühl 7580. Baden-Württemberg **987** ㉞, **57** ㉙ − pop. 22 100 − alt. 135 m − ✪ 07223.
Stuttgart 117.

XXX ✿✿ **Burg Windeck**, Kappelwindeckstr. 104 (SE : 4 km, near the castle ruins Altwindeck),
𝒫 2 36 71, ≤ Bühl and Rhine-plain, 🎇 − 🅿 ⓘ
closed Monday, Tuesday and January - 25 February − **M** a la carte 53/108
Spec. Zander-Nocken und Flußkrebse auf Mangold-Gemüse, Kaninchenrücken mit Lauch und Morcheln,
Perlhuhnbrust mit Orangensensauce.

Republic of Ireland

Dublin

PRACTICAL INFORMATION

LOCAL CURRENCY

Punt (Irish Pound) : 1 punt = 0.984 US $ (Jan. 85)

TOURIST INFORMATION

The telephone number and address of the Tourist Information office is given in the text under **ℹ**.

TIPPING

Many hotels and restaurants include a service charge but where this is not the case an amount equivalent to between 10 and 15 per cent of the bill is customary. Additionally doormen, baggage porters and cloakroom attendants are generally given a gratuity.

Taxi drivers are customarily tipped between 10 and 15 per cent of the amount shown on the meter in addition to the fare.

FOREIGN EXCHANGE

Banks are open 10am to 12.30pm and 1.30pm to 3pm on weekdays only.

CAR HIRE

The international car hire companies have branches in each major city. Your hotel porter will be able to give details and help you with your arrangements.

SPEED LIMITS

The maximum permitted speed in the Republic is 55 mph (88 km/h) except where a lower speed limit is signposted.

SEAT BELTS

The wearing of seat belts is compulsory for drivers and front seat passengers.

SHOPPING IN DUBLIN

In the index of street names those printed in red are where the principal shops are found.

DUBLIN

DUBLIN Dublin 𝟗𝟖𝟔 ㉖ and ㊲ — pop. 567 866 — ✆ 01.

🏌 Edmondstown, Rathfarnham ✆ 907461, S : 3 m. by N 81 — 🏌 Elm Park, Nutley House, Donnybrook ✆ 693438, S : 3 m. — 🏌 Lower Churchtown Rd, Milltown ✆ 977060, S : by T 43.

✈ ✆ 379900, N : 5 ½ m. by N 1 — **Terminal :** Busaras (Central Bus Station) Store St.

⛴ to Liverpool (B & I Line) 1 nightly (8 h) — to Holyhead (B & I Line) 1 daily (3 h 30 mn) — to the Isle of Man : Douglas (Isle of Man Steam Packet Co.) June to September 1-3 weekly (4 h 30 mn).

🛈 14 Upper O'Connell St. ✆ 747733 — Dublin Airport ✆ 376387 and 375533.

Belfast 103 — Cork 154 — Londonderry 146.

DUBLIN

Anne Street South	BY	2
Dawson Street	BY	
Duke Street	BY	27
Grafton Street	BY	
Henry Street	BY	
Irish Life Mall Centre	BY	
O'Connell Street	BXY	
Belvidere Place	BX	4
Blessington Street	BX	6
Brunswick Street North	BY	8
Bull Alley	BY	9
Chancery Street	BY	13
Charlotte Street	BZ	15
College Street	BY	19
Denmark Street	BX	23
D'Olier Street	BY	24
Essex Quay	BY	30
Fitzgibbon Street	BX	31
Fitzwilliam Place	BZ	32
Frederick Street North	BX	33
Gardiner Place	BX	35
George's Quay	BY	36
Golden Lane	BY	39
Harrington Street	BZ	44
Kevin Street Upper	BZ	47
Kildare Street	BYZ	48
King Street South	BY	49
Malborough Street	BY	53
Merchants Quay	BY	56
Montague Street	BZ	59
Mountjoy Street	BX	62
Nicholas Street	BY	64
Parnell Square East	BX	67
Parnell Square North	BX	68
Parnell Square West	BX	69
Stephen Street	BY	80
Tara Street	BY	81
Townsend Street	BY	89
Wellington Quay	BY	95
Westland Row	BY	96
Westmoreland Street	BY	97
Wexford Street	BZ	99
Winetavern Street	BY	100
Wood Quay	BY	103

Berkeley Court, Lansdowne Rd, Ballsbridge, ℘ 601711, Telex 30554, – AE VISA
M 12.75/16.50 **t.** 4.50 – 6.00 – **210 rm** 68.00/82.00 **t.**

Jury's, Pembroke Rd, Ballsbridge, ℘ 605000, Telex 25304, heated, – AE VISA
M 12.00/15.00 **t.** 7.50 – 7.50 – **314 rm** 69.50/77.50 **t.**

Shelbourne (T.H.F.), 27 St. Stephen's Green, ℘ 766471, Telex 25184 – AE VISA BZ **s**
M 15.50/18.00 **t.** 4.00 – 7.50 – **167 rm** 70.00/110.00 **t.**

Blooms, Anglesea St., ℘ 715622, Telex 31688 – AE VISA BY **e**
M 9.00/11.50 **t.** 4.25 – 5.50 – **86 rm** 60.00/70.00 **t.**

Le Coq Hardi, 35 Pembroke Rd, ℘ 689070 – AE VISA
closed Saturday lunch, Sunday, 2 weeks August, 2 weeks Christmas and Bank Holidays – **M** a la carte 17.00/27.50 **t.** 5.00.

Patrick Guilbaud, 46 St. James's Pl., St. James' St., off Lower Baggot St., ℘ 764192, French rest. – AE VISA BZ **n**
closed Saturday lunch, Sunday and Bank Holidays – **M** a la carte 14.95/27.15 **t.**

Bailey, 2-4 Duke St., ℘ 770600 – AE VISA BY **a**
closed Saturday lunch, Sunday, 2 weeks Easter and 2 weeks Christmas – **M** a la carte 17.50/26.00 **t.** 5.95.

Locks, 1 Windsor Terr., Portobello, ℘ 752025 – AE VISA BZ **u**
closed Saturday lunch, Sunday, 25 December-3 January and Bank Holidays – **M** a la carte 13.95/17.35 **t.** 3.75.

Old Dublin, 90-91 Francis St., ℘ 751173, Scandinavian rest. – AE VISA BY **i**
closed Saturday lunch, Sunday and Bank Holidays – **M** 8.50/13.95 **t.** 4.25.

Lord Edward, 23 Christchurch Pl., ℘ 752557, Seafood – AE VISA BY **c**
closed Saturday lunch, Sunday, 1 week Christmas and Bank Holidays – **M** a la carte 16.25/30.75 **t.**

Celtic Mews, 109a Lower Baggot St., ℘ 760796 – AE VISA BZ **z**
closed Sunday and last 2 weeks July – **M** (dinner only) a la carte 21.00/25.00 **t.**

Small Home, 41-43 Shelbourne Rd, Ballsbridge, ℘ 608087 – AE VISA
closed Saturday lunch, Sunday, Easter, Christmas and Bank Holidays – **M** a la carte 11.25/15.25 **t.** 4.00.

Mitchell's Cellars, 21 Kildare St., ℘ 680367 – AE VISA BZ **x**
closed Sunday, 25 December-2 January and Bank Holiday weekends – **M** (lunch only) a la carte 8.60 **t.** 3.75.

at Dublin Airport N : 6 ½ m. by N 1 – ✉ 01 Dublin :

Dublin International (T.H.F.), ℘ 379211, Telex 24612 – wc AE VISA
M 14.00/17.00 **st.** 4.75 – 6.00 – **195 rm** 52.00/75.00 **st.**

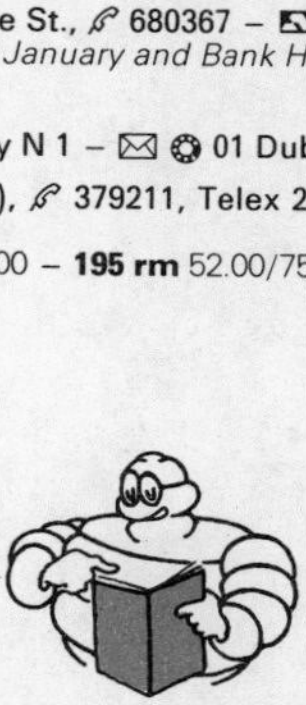

Italy

Italia

Rome
Florence
Milan
Naples - Capri
Turin
Venice
Sicily: Palerme, Taormina

PRACTICAL INFORMATION

LOCAL CURRENCY

Italian Lire : 1000 lire = 0.512 US $ (Jan. 85)

TOURIST INFORMATION

Welcome Office (Ente Provinciale per il Turismo), closed Saturday and Sunday :
— Via Parigi 5 - 00185 ROMA, ☎ 06/46 37 48
— Via Marconi 1 - 20123 MILANO, ☎ 02/808813
See also telephone number and address of other Tourist Information offices in the text of the towns under 🛈.
American Express :
— Piazza di Spagna 38 - 00187 ROMA, ☎ 06/67641
— Via Vittor Pisani 19 - 20124 MILANO, ☎ 02/6709061

FOREIGN EXCHANGE

Money can be changed at the Banca d'Italia, other banks and authorised exchange offices (Banks close at 1.15pm and at weekends)

POSTAL SERVICES

Local post offices : open Monday to Saturday 8.00am to 2.00pm
General Post Office (open 24 hours only for telegrams) :
— Piazza San Silvestro 00187 ROMA — Piazza Cordusio 20123 MILANO

SHOPPING

In the index of street names those printed in red are where the principal shops are found. In Rome, the main shopping streets are : Via del Babuino, Via dei Condotti, Via Frattina, Via Vittorio Veneto ; in Milan : Via Dante, Via Manzoni, Via Monte Napoleone, Corso Vittorio Emanuele.

AIRLINES

ALITALIA : Via Bissolati 13 - 00187 ROMA, ☎ 06/4688
Piazzale Pastore o dell'Arte (EUR) - 00144 ROMA, ☎ 06/5454
Via Albricci 5 - 20122 MILANO, ☎ 02/6281
AIR FRANCE : Via Barberini 11 - 00187 ROMA, ☎ 06/4718
Piazza Cavour 2 - 20121 MILANO, ☎ 02/7738
PAN AM : Via Bissolati 46 - 00187 ROMA, ☎ 06/4773
Piazza Velasca 5 - 20122 MILANO, ☎ 02/877262
TWA : Via Barberini 59/67 - 00187 ROMA, ☎ 06/47211
Corso Europa 9/11 - 20122 MILANO, ☎ 02/77961

BREAKDOWN SERVICE

Certain garages in the centre and outskirts of towns operate a 24 hour breakdown service. If you breakdown the police are usually able to help by indicating the nearest one.
A free car breakdown service (a tax is levied) is operated by the A.C.I. for foreign motorists carrying the fuel card (Carta Carburante). The A.C.I. also offers telephone information in English (8am to 5pm) for road and weather conditions and tourist events : 06/4212.

TIPPING

As well as the service charge, it is the custom to tip employees. The amount can vary with the region and the service given.

SPEED LIMITS

Speed limits applicable on trunk roads and motorways are according to engine capacity : 80-90 km/h or 50-56 mph (600 cc) to 110-140 km/h or 68-87 mph (over 1300 cc).

ROME

SIGHTS

Rome's most famous sights are indicated on the town plans pp. 2 to 5. For a more complete visit see the Green Guide to Italy.

ROME (ROMA) 00100 988 ⑳ – Pop. 2 834 094 – alt. 20 – ✆ 06.

▮ₙ (closed Monday) at Acquasanta ⊠ 00178 Roma ✆ 783407, SE : 12 km.

▮ₙ Fioranello (closed Wednesday) at Santa Maria delle Mole ⊠ 00040 Roma ✆ 6009403.

▮ₙ and ▮ₙ (closed Monday) at Olgiata ⊠ 00123 Roma ✆ 3788040.

✈ Ciampino SE : 15 km ✆ 600251 and Leonardo da Vinci di Fiumicino ✆ 6012 – Alitalia, via Bissolati 13 ⊠ 00187 ✆ 4688 and piazzale Pastore o dell'Arte (EUR) ⊠ 00144 ✆ 5454.

🚗 Termini ✆ 464923 – Tiburtina ✆ 4956626.

🛈 via Parigi 5 ⊠ 00185 ✆ 463748 at Termini station ✆ 465461 : on the motorways : A1 Roma North ✆ 6919958 and A2 Roma South ✆ 9464341.

A.C.I. via Cristoforo Colombo 261 ⊠ 00147 ✆ 5106 and via Marsala 8 ⊠ 00185 ✆ 4998. Telex 610686.

Distances from Rome are indicated in the text of the other towns listed in this Guide.

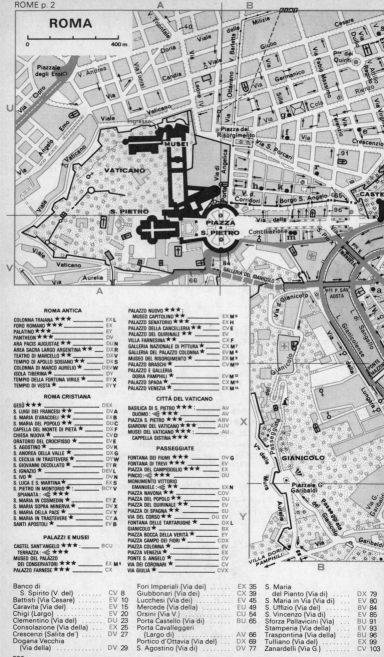

ROMA

0   400 m

ROMA ANTICA

COLONNA TRAIANA ★★★	EX L
FORO ROMANO ★★★	EX
PALATINO ★★★	EY
PANTHEON ★★★	DV
ARA PACIS AUGUSTAE ★★	DU N
AREA SACRA LARGO ARGENTINA ★★	DX R
TEATRO DI MARCELLO ★★	DX V
TEMPIO DI APOLLO SOSIANO ★★	DX S
COLONNA DI MARCO AURELIO ★	DEV W
ISOLA TIBERINA ★	DY
TEMPIO DELLA FORTUNA VIRILE ★	EY X
TEMPIO DI VESTA ★	EY Y

ROMA CRISTIANA

GESÙ ★★★	DEX
S. LUIGI DEI FRANCESI ★★	DV A
S. MARIA D'ARACOELI ★★	EX B
S. MARIA DEL POPOLO ★★	DU C
CAPELLA DEL MONTE DI PIETÀ ★	DX F
CHIESA NUOVA ★	CVD
ORATORIO DEL CROCIFISSO ★	EV E
S. AGOSTINO ★	DV K
S. ANDREA DELLA VALLE ★	DX G
S. CECILIA IN TRASTEVERE ★	DY W
S. GIOVANNI DECOLLATO ★	EY R
S. IGNAZIO ★	DEV L
S. IVO ★	DV N
S. LUCA E S. MARTINA ★	EX S
S. PIETRO IN MONTORIO ★ :	BCY V
SPIANATA : ← ★★	
S. MARIA IN COSMEDIN ★	EY Z
S. MARIA SOPRA MINERVA ★	DV X
S. MARIA DELLA PACE ★	CV Y
S. MARIA IN TRASTEVERE ★	CY A
SANTI APOSTOLI ★	EV B

PALAZZI E MUSEI

CASTEL SANT'ANGELO ★★★	BCU
TERRAZZA : ← ★★★	
MUSEO DEL PALAZZO DEI CONSERVATORI ★★★	EX M 5
PALAZZO FARNESE ★★★	CX

PALAZZO NUOVO ★★★ :

MUSEO CAPITOLINO ★★	EX M 6
PALAZZO SENATORIO ★★★	EX H
PALAZZO DELLA CANCELLERIA ★★	CV E
PALAZZO DEL QUIRINALE ★★	EV
VILLA FARNESINA ★★	CX F
GALLERIA NAZIONALE DI PITTURA ★	CX M 7
GALLERIA DEL PALAZZO COLONNA ★	EV M 8
MUSEO DEL RISORGIMENTO ★	EX M 9
PALAZZO BRASCHI ★	CV M 10
PALAZZO E GALLERIA DORIA PAMPHILI ★	EV M 12
PALAZZO SPADA ★	DX M 13
PALAZZO VENEZIA ★	EX M 14

CITTÀ DEL VATICANO

BASILICA DI S. PIETRO ★★★ :	AV
DUOMO : ← ★★★	AV
PIAZZA S. PIETRO ★★★	ABV
GIARDINI DEL VATICANO ★★★	AUV
MUSEI DEL VATICANO ★★★	AU
CAPPELLA SISTINA ★★★	

PASSEGGIATE

FONTANA DEI FIUMI ★★★	DV G
FONTANA DI TREVI ★★★	EV
PIAZZA DEL CAMPIDOGLIO ★★★	EX
PINCIO : ← ★★	DU
MONUMENTO VITTORIO EMANUELE : ← ★★	EX N
PIAZZA NAVONA ★★	CDV
PIAZZA DEL POPOLO ★★	DU
PIAZZA DEL QUIRINALE ★★	EV
PIAZZA DI SPAGNA ★★	EU
VIA DEL CORSO ★	DU V
FONTANA DELLE TARTARUGHE ★	DX L
GIANICOLO ★	BX
PIAZZA BOCCA DELLA VERITÀ ★	EY
PIAZZA CAMPO DEI FIORI ★	CDX
PIAZZA COLONNA ★	DV
PIAZZA VENEZIA ★	EX
PONTE S. ANGELO ★	CV
VIA DEI CORONARI ★	CV
VIA GIULIA ★	CVX

Banco di S. Spirito (V. del)	CV 8	
Battisti (Via Cesare)	EV 10	
Caravita (Via del)	EV 15	
Chigi (Largo)	EV 20	
Clementino (Via del)	DU 23	
Consolazione (Via della)	EX 25	
Crescenzi (Salita de')	DV 27	
Dogana Vecchia (Via della)	DV 29	
Fori Imperiali (Via dei)	EX 35	
Giubbonari (Via dei)	CX 39	
Lucchesi (Via dei)	EV 45	
Mercede (Via della)	EU 49	
Orsini (Via V.)	CU 54	
Porta Castello (Via di)	BU 65	
Porta Cavalleggeri (Largo di)	AV 66	
Portico d'Ottavia (Via del)	DX 69	
S. Agostino (Via di)	DV 77	
S. Maria del Pianto (Via di)	DX 79	
S. Maria in Via (Via di)	EV 80	
S. Uffizio (Via del)	BV 84	
S. Vincenzo (Via di)	EV 85	
Sforza Pallavicini (Via)	BU 91	
Stamperia (Via della)	EV 93	
Trastontina (Via della)	EV 96	
Tulliano (Via del)	EX 99	
Zanardelli (Via G.)	CV 103	

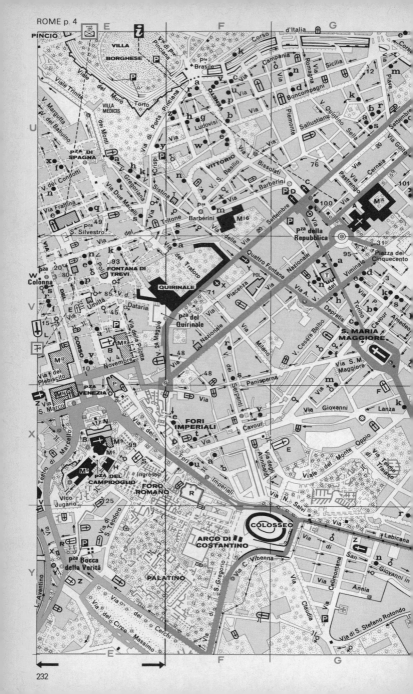

ROMA

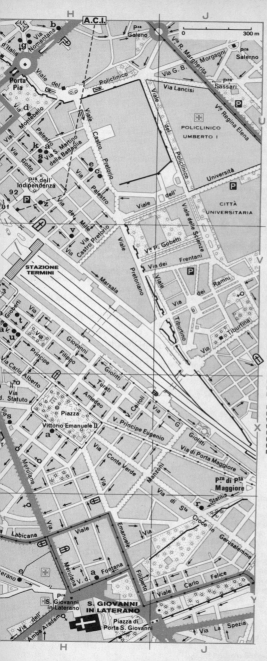

ROMA ANTICA

ARCO DI COSTANTINO ★★★	FY
BASILICA DI MASSENZIO ★★★	FX R
COLONNA TRAIANA ★★★	EX L
COLOSSEO ★★★	FGY
FORI IMPERIALI ★★★	FX
FORO ROMANO ★★★	EX
PALATINO ★★★	EX
TEATRO DI MARCELLO ★★	EX V
COLONNA DI MARCO AURELIO ★	EV W
TEMPIO DELLA FORTUNA VIRILE ★	EY X
TEMPIO DI VESTA ★	EY Y

ROMA CRISTIANA

GESÙ ★★★	EX Z
S. GIOVANNI IN LATERANO ★★★	HY
S. MARIA MAGGIORE ★★★	GV
S. ANDREA AL QUIRINALE ★★	FV X
S. CARLO ALLE QUATTRO FONTANE ★★	FV Y
S. CLEMENTE ★	GY Z
S. MARIA DEGLI ANGELI ★★	GU A
S. MARIA D'ARACOELI ★★	EX B
S. MARIA DELLA VITTORIA ★★	GU C
S. SUSANNA ★★	GU D
ORATORIO DEL CROCIFISSO ★	EV E
S. IGNAZIO ★	EV L
S. GIOVANNI DECOLLATO ★	EY R
S. LUCA E S. MARTINA ★	EX S
S. MARIA IN COSMEDIN ★	EY Z
S. PIETRO IN VINCOLI ★	GX E
S. PRASSEDE ★	GVX F
SANTI APOSTOLI ★	EV B

PALAZZI E MUSEI

MUSEO NAZIONALE ROMANO ★★★	GU M¹⁵
MUSEO DEL PALAZZO DEI CONSERVATORI ★★★	EX M⁵
PALAZZO NUOVO ★★★ : MUSEO CAPITOLINO ★★	EX M⁶
PALAZZO SENATORIO ★★	EX H
PALAZZO BARBERINI ★★	FU M¹⁶
PALAZZO DEL QUIRINALE ★★	EV
GALLERIA DEL PALAZZO COLONNA ★	EV M⁸
MUSEO DEL RISORGIMENTO ★	EX M⁹
PALAZZO E GALLERIA DORIA PAMPHILI ★	EV M¹²
PALAZZO VENEZIA ★	EX M¹⁴

PASSEGGIATE

FONTANA DI TREVI ★★★	EV
PIAZZA DEL CAMPIDOGLIO ★★★	EX
MONUMENTO VITTORIO EMANUELE : ⋘ ★★	EX N
PIAZZA DEL QUIRINALE ★★	FV
PIAZZA DI SPAGNA ★★	EU
VIA VITTORIO VENETO ★★	FU
PIAZZA BOCCA DELLA VERITÀ ★	EY
PIAZZA COLONNA ★	EV
PIAZZA DI PORTA MAGGIORE ★	JX
PIAZZA VENEZIA ★	EX
PORTA PIA ★	HU

North area Monte Mario, Stadio Olimpico, via Flaminia-Parioli, Villa Borghese, via Salaria, via Nomentana (Plans : Rome pp. 2 to 5)

🏨🏨 **Cavalieri Hilton** 🦢, via Cadlolo 101 ⊠ 00136 ℰ 3151, Telex 610296, ≤ town, « Terraces and park », 🛁, ⚒ – 🛗 🗏 📺 ☎ 🚗 ℗ – 🔬   by via Trionfale   AU
387 rm.

🏨🏨 **Lord Byron** 🦢, via De Notaris 5 ⊠ 00197 ℰ 3609541, Telex 611217, 🌿 – 🛗 🗏 📺 ☎.   🖭 ⓘ Ε 𝘝𝘐𝘚𝘈   by lungotevere in Augusta   DU
M rest. see Le Jardin below – ⚏ 16000 – **55 rm** 250/300000.

🏨🏨 **Aldrovandi Palace Hotel** without rest., via Aldrovandi 15 ⊠ 00197 ℰ 841091, Telex 616141, 🌿 – 🛗 🗏 📺 ☎ ℗ – 🔬. 🖭 ⓘ 𝘝𝘐𝘚𝘈. 🛦   by viale Trinità   EU
139 rm ⚏ 140/195000.

🏨🏨 **Borromini** without rest., via Lisbona 7 ⊠ 00198 ℰ 841321, Telex 680485 – 🛗 🗏 📺 ☎ 🚗 – 🔬. 🖭 ⓘ Ε 𝘝𝘐𝘚𝘈. 🛦   by viale Regina Margherita   JU
⚏ 9000 – **75 rm** 125/147000.

🏨🏨 **Albani** without rest., via Adda 41 ⊠ 00198 ℰ 84991, Telex 612414 – 🛗 🗏 📺 ☎ & 🚗 – 🔬. 🖭 ⓘ 𝘝𝘐𝘚𝘈   by via Piave   GU
157 rm ⚏ 110/170000.

🏨🏨 **Parco dei Principi**, via Frescobaldi 5 ⊠ 00198 ℰ 841071, Telex 610517, « Small park with 🛁 » – 🛗 🗏 ☎ & 🚗 – 🔬. 🖭 ⓘ 𝘝𝘐𝘚𝘈. 🛦 rest   by via Piemonte   GU
M (residents only) 35000 – ⚏ 11000 – **203 rm** 144/215000 – P 155/200000.

🏨 **Fleming** without rest., piazza Monteleone di Spoleto 20 ⊠ 00191 ℰ 3276741, Telex 610640 – 🛗 🗏 📺 🚿wc 🛁wc 🕾 – 🔬. 🖭 ⓘ 𝘝𝘐𝘚𝘈   by lungotevere in Augusta   DU
270 rm ⚏ 72/115000.

🏨 **Panama** without rest., via Salaria 336 ⊠ 00199 ℰ 862558, Telex 620189, 🌿 – 🛗 🗏 🚿wc 🛁wc ☎. 🛦   by viale Regina Margherita   JU
43 rm ⚏ 65/120000, 🗏 9000.

🏨 **Degli Aranci**, via Oriani 11 ⊠ 00197 ℰ 870202, « Orange-grove terrace » – 🛗 🚿wc 🛁wc 🕾 – 🔬. 🖭   by lungotevere in Augusta   DU
M 26000 – **46 rm** ⚏ 64/102000.

XXXX ⚘ **Le Jardin**, via De Notaris 5 ⊠ 00197 ℰ 3609541, Elegant rest. – 🗏. 🖭 ⓘ Ε 𝘝𝘐𝘚𝘈. 🛦
closed Sunday – **M** (booking essential) a la carte 53/77000
Spec. Terrina di rombo e pescatrice salsa finocchio (October-March), Ravioli di anatra al Pernod e mirtilli (June-September), Filetto con funghi spugnoli. **Wines** Marino, Fiorano.
                         by lungotevere in Augusta   DU

XX **Al Fogher**, via Tevere 13/b ⊠ 00198 ℰ 837032, Typical Venetian rest. – 🗏. 🖭 ⓘ
closed Sunday – **M** a la carte 26/42000.   by via Piave   GU

XX **La Vigna dei Cardinali**, piazzale Ponte Milvio 34 ⊠ 00191 ℰ 3965846, « Summer service in garden » – ℗. 🖭 ⓘ 𝘝𝘐𝘚𝘈   by lungotevere in Augusta   DU
closed Saturday – **M** a la carte 22/35000.

XX **La Mousse**, via dei Parioli 103 ⊠ 00197 ℰ 805136, « Outdoor service in Summer » – 🗏
                        by lungotevere in Augusta   DU

X **Al Ceppo**, via Panama 2 ⊠ 00198 ℰ 8449696, Typical rest. – 🗏. 🖭 ⓘ 𝘝𝘐𝘚𝘈
closed Monday and August – **M** a la carte 21/33000.   by viale Regina Margherita   JU

X **Delle Vittorie**, via Monte Santo 62/64 ⊠ 00195 ℰ 386847 – 🖭 ⓘ Ε 𝘝𝘐𝘚𝘈. 🛦   **M** a la carte 20/33000.
closed Sunday, Saturday in August and 20 December-10 January –   by Marcantonio Colonna   CU

Middle-western area San Pietro (Vatican City), Gianicolo, corso Vittorio Emanuele, piazza Venezia, Pantheon and Quirinale, Pincio and Villa Medici, piazza di Spagna, Palatino and Fori (Plan : Rome pp. 2 and 3)

🏨🏨🏨 **Hassler-Villa Medici**, piazza Trinità dei Monti 6 ⊠ 00187 ℰ 6792651, Telex 610208, ≤ town from roof-garden rest. – 🛗 🗏 ☎ &. 🛦   EU   **a**
M a la carte 65/105000 – ⚏ 15000 – **106 rm** 210/395000.

🏨🏨 **Eden**, via Ludovisi 49 ⊠ 00187 ℰ 4743551, Telex 610567, « Roof-garden rest. with ≤ town » – 🛗 🗏 📺 ☎. 🛦   EU   **y**
M a la carte 40/56000 – ⚏ 12000 – **110 rm** 180/280000.

🏨🏨 **D'Inghilterra** without rest., via Bocca di Leone 14 ⊠ 00187 ℰ 672161, Telex 614552 – 🛗 🗏 📺 ☎ &. 🖭 ⓘ Ε 𝘝𝘐𝘚𝘈. 🛦   EU   **n**
⚏ 14000 – **102 rm** 148/188000.

🏨🏨 **Jolly Leonardo da Vinci**, via dei Gracchi 324 ⊠ 00192 ℰ 39680, Telex 611182 – 🛗 🗏 📺 ☎ 🚗 – 🔬. 🖭 ⓘ Ε 𝘝𝘐𝘚𝘈. 🛦 rest   CU   **r**
M 38000 – **245 rm** ⚏ 130/180000 – P 200000.

🏨🏨 **Plaza** without rest., via del Corso 126 ⊠ 00186 ℰ 672101, Telex 624669 – 🛗 🗏 ☎ – 🔬. 🖭 ⓘ. 🛦   DU   **d**
⚏ 10000 – **207 rm** 97/150000, 🗏 7500.

🏨🏨 **Gd H. de la Ville**, via Sistina 69 ⊠ 00187 ℰ 6733, Telex 620836 – 🛗 🗏 ☎ 🚗 – 🔬. 🖭 ⓘ Ε 𝘝𝘐𝘚𝘈. 🛦   EU   **h**
M a la carte 35/60000 – **189 rm** ⚏ 145/213000.

🏨 Visconti Palace without rest., via Cesi 37 ☒ 00193 ℰ 3684, Telex 680407 – 🛗 🗐 📺 ☎
🖘 – 🔬. 🅰🅴 🅾 🅴 𝐕𝐈𝐒𝐀. ⚘
        CU **u**
247 rm ⥮ 130/180000.

🏨 Cicerone without rest., via Cicerone 55 ☒ 00193 ℰ 3576, Telex 680514 – 🛗 🗐 📺 ☎
🖘 – 🔬. 🅰🅴 🅾 🅴 𝐕𝐈𝐒𝐀. ⚘
        CU **t**
⥮ 15000 – **237 rm** 150/180000.

🏨 Colonna Palace without rest., piazza Montecitorio 12 ☒ 00186 ℰ 6781341, Telex 621467
– 🛗 🗐 📺 ☎. 🅰🅴 🅾 𝐕𝐈𝐒𝐀. ⚘
        DV **s**
⥮ 10000 – **100 rm** 132/176000.

🏨 Giulio Cesare without rest., via degli Scipioni 287 ☒ 00192 ℰ 310244, Telex 613010 – 🛗
🗐 📺 ☎ 🅿 – 🔬. 🅰🅴 🅾 𝐕𝐈𝐒𝐀. ⚘
        CU **s**
⥮ 18000 – **86 rm** 125/175000. 🗐 6000.

🏨 Atlante, via Vitelleschi 34 ☒ 00193 ℰ 6564196, Telex 680258, « Roof-garden rest. with
≼ St. Peter's Basilica » – 🛗 🗐 rm 📺. 🅰🅴 🅾 🅴 𝐕𝐈𝐒𝐀. ⚘ rest
        BU **r**
M *(closed January-February)* 25/40000 – **61 rm** ⥮ 160/220000.

🏨 Delle Nazioni without rest., via Poli 7 ☒ 00187 ℰ 6792441, Telex 614193 – 🛗 🗐 📺 ☎
🔥. 🅰🅴 🅾 🅴 𝐕𝐈𝐒𝐀. ⚘
        EV **e**
75 rm ⥮ 142/209000.

🏨 Gregoriana without rest., via Gregoriana 18 ☒ 00187 ℰ 6794269 – 🛗 🗐 ⇔wc 🛁wc 🖘
🔥.
        EU **t**
19 rm ⥮ 78/125000.

🏨 Columbus, via della Conciliazione 33 ☒ 00193 ℰ 6565435, Telex 620096, « Beautiful
decor in 15C style building » – 🛗 ⇔wc 🛁wc ☎ 🔥 🅿 – 🔬. 🅰🅴 🅾 🅴 𝐕𝐈𝐒𝐀. ⚘ rest
        BV **m**
M a la carte 30/42000 – **107 rm** ⥮ 75/115000 – P 95/105000.

🏨 Internazionale without rest., via Sistina 79 ☒ 00187 ℰ 6793047, Telex 614333 – 🛗 🗐
⇔wc 🛁wc 🖘. 🅰🅴 🅾 🅴 𝐕𝐈𝐒𝐀. ⚘
        EU **k**
38 rm ⥮ 102/150000.

🏨 Gerber without rest., via degli Scipioni 241 ☒ 00192 ℰ 3595148 – 🛗 ⇔wc 🛁wc 🖘 🔥.
🅰🅴 🅾 🅴 𝐕𝐈𝐒𝐀. ⚘
        BU **s**
28 rm ⥮ 45/75000.

🏨 Della Torre Argentina without rest., corso Vittorio Emanuele 102 ☒ 00186 ℰ 6548251
– 🛗 ⇔wc 🛁wc ☎ 🔥. 🅰🅴 🅾 𝐕𝐈𝐒𝐀. ⚘
        DX **e**
⥮ 7000 – **32 rm** 58/91000.

🏨 Bologna without rest., via di Santa Chiara 4/a ☒ 00186 ℰ 6568951, Telex 621124 – 🛗
⇔wc 🛁wc 🖘. ⚘
        DV **z**
⥮ 9500 – **117 rm** 72/108000.

🏨 Senato without rest., piazza della Rotonda 73 ☒ 00186 ℰ 6793231, ≼ Pantheon – 🛗
⇔wc 🛁wc 🖘.
        DV **y**
⥮ 5500 – **48 rm** 33/73000.

🏨 Mozart without rest., via dei Greci 23/b ☒ 00187 ℰ 6787422 – 🛗 🗐 📺 ⇔wc 🛁wc ☎.
🅰🅴 🅾 🅴 𝐕𝐈𝐒𝐀. ⚘
        DU **h**
31 rm ⥮ 51/75000.

🏨 Adriano without rest., via di Pallacorda 2 ☒ 00186 ℰ 6542451 – 🛗 ⇔wc 🛁wc ☎. 🅰🅴
🅾 𝐕𝐈𝐒𝐀. ⚘
        DV **c**
⥮ 6000 – **82 rm** 46/82000.

🏨 Cesàri without rest., via di Pietra 89/a ☒ 00186 ℰ 6792386 – 🛗 ⇔wc 🖘 🔥. 🅰🅴 🅾 🅴
𝐕𝐈𝐒𝐀
        EV **r**
⥮ 6500 – **51 rm** 58/72000.

XXXXX Hostaria dell'Orso, via Monte Brianzo 93 ☒ 00186 ℰ 6564250, Elegant rest. - night
club, « Building and decorations in 15C style » – 🗐. 🅰🅴 🅾 🅴 𝐕𝐈𝐒𝐀. ⚘
        CV **n**
closed Sunday and August – **M** (dinner only) (booking essential) a la carte 50/85000.

XXXX ⚘ El Toulà, via della Lupa 29 ☒ 00186 ℰ 6781196, Elegant rest. – 🗐. 🅰🅴 🅾 🅴 𝐕𝐈𝐒𝐀. ⚘
closed Saturday lunch, Sunday, August and 24 to 26 December – **M** (booking essential)
        DU **e**
a la carte 42/56000 (15%)
Spec. Risotto al nero di seppia, Filetto di San Pietro al pepe verde, Fegato di vitello alla veneta. **Wines**
Sauvignon, Refosco.

XXX ⚘ Passetto, via Zanardelli 14 ☒ 00186 ℰ 6543696 – 🗐. 🅰🅴 🅾 𝐕𝐈𝐒𝐀. ⚘
        CV **v**
closed Sunday – **M** a la carte 30/52000
Spec. Fettuccine alla crema con funghi, Orata al cartoccio, Scaloppine Passetto. **Wines** Frascati, Chianti.

XXX Ranieri, via Mario de' Fiori 26 ☒ 00187 ℰ 6791592 – 🗐. 🅰🅴 🅾 🅴 𝐕𝐈𝐒𝐀
        EU **f**
closed Sunday – **M** (booking essential) a la carte 32/64000.

XXX 4 Colonne, via della Posta 4 ☒ 00186 ℰ 6547152 – 🗐. ⚘
        DV **n**
closed Sunday and 5 to 31 August – **M** (booking essential) a la carte 31/46000.

XX ⚘ Piperno, Monte de' Cenci 9 ☒ 00186 ℰ 6540629, Roman rest. – 🗐. ⚘
        DX **d**
closed Sunday dinner, Monday, Easter, August and 23 December-2 January – **M**
a la carte 27/42000
Spec. Carciofi alla giudia, Filetti di baccalà con fritto vegetariano, Coda alla vaccinara. **Wines** Frascati, Rosso
Tapino.

XX Mastrostefano, piazza Navona 94 ☒ 00186 ℰ 6541669, Rest.-American bar, « Outdoor
service in Summer with ≼ Bernini fountain » – 🗐
        DV **d**

XX **Taverna Giulia,** vicolo dell'Oro 23 ⊠ 00186 ℰ 6569768, Ligurian rest. – ▤. 🆎 ⓪
closed Sunday and August – **M** (booking essential) a la carte 30/40000. BV **a**

XX Dal Bolognese, piazza del Popolo 1 ⊠ 00187 ℰ 3611426, Bolognese rest., « Collection of
paintings » – ▤ DU **z**

XX **Alfredo alla Scrofa,** via della Scrofa 104 ⊠ 00186 ℰ 6540163 – ▤. 🆎 ⓪ 🇪 𝘝𝘐𝘚𝘈
closed Tuesday – **M** a la carte 27/45000 (13%). DV **r**

XX **Eau Vive,** via Monterone 85 ⊠ 00186 ℰ 6541095, Catholic missionaries; international
cuisine, « 16C building » – ▤. 🎄
closed Sunday and August – **M** a la carte 20/33000. DV **f**

XX **La Maiella,** piazza Sant'Apollinare 45/46 ⊠ 00186 ℰ 6564174, Abruzzi rest. – ▤. 🆎 ⓪
🇪 𝘝𝘐𝘚𝘈. 🎄 CDV **x**
closed Sunday and 10 to 20 August – **M** a la carte 28/42000.

X ✿ **Carmelo alla Rosetta,** via della Rosetta 9 ⊠ 00187 ℰ 6561002, Sicilian and seafood
trattoria – ▤. 🆎 ⓪. 🎄 DV **e**
closed Sunday, Monday lunch and August – **M** a la carte 40/50000
Spec. Zuppa alla Nostromo, Pappardelle ai frutti di mare, Pesce spada alla messinese (April-June). **Wines**
Regaleali, Gavi.

X **Al 59,** via Brunetti 59 ⊠ 00186 ℰ 3619019, Bolognese rest. – ▤. 🎄 DU **y**
closed August, Sunday and Saturday from June to July – **M** a la carte 27/42000.

X **Al Salanova,** via Florida 23 ⊠ 00186 ℰ 6561409 – 🆎 ⓪ 𝘝𝘐𝘚𝘈 DX **v**
closed Monday, 4 to 20 January and 4 to 20 September – **M** a la carte 20/40000 (10%).

X **Al Moro,** vicolo delle Bollette 13 ⊠ 00187 ℰ 6783495, Roman trattoria – ▤. 🎄 EV **p**
closed Sunday and August – **M** (booking essential) a la carte 31/48000.

X **La Cantinella,** via Crispi 19 ⊠ 00187 ℰ 6795069, Habitués' trattoria with Sardinian
specialities – ▤. 🆎 ⓪ 🇪 𝘝𝘐𝘚𝘈. 🎄 EU **s**
closed Wednesday and August – **M** a la carte 19/28000 (12%).

Central eastern area via Vittorio Veneto, via Nazionale, Viminale, Santa Maria Maggiore,
Colosseum, Porta Pia, via Nomentana, Stazione Termini, Porta San Giovanni (Plan : Rome
pp. 4 and 5) :

🏨🏨 **Le Grand Hotel,** via Vittorio Emanuele Orlando 3 ⊠ 00185 ℰ 4709, Telex 610210 – 🛗
▤ 📺 ☎ – 🏃. 🆎 ⓪ 🇪 𝘝𝘐𝘚𝘈 GU **t**
M a la carte 60/100000 – 😐 16500 – **160 rm** 303/428000.

🏨🏨 Excelsior, via Vittorio Veneto 125 ⊠ 00187 ℰ 4708, Telex 610232 – 🛗 ▤ 📺 ☎ – 🏃
363 rm. FU **b**

🏨🏨 **Ambasciatori Palace,** via Vittorio Veneto 70 ⊠ 00187 ℰ 473831, Telex 610241 – 🛗 ▤
📺 ☎ ♿ – 🏃. 🆎 ⓪ 𝘝𝘐𝘚𝘈 FU **e**
M rest. see Grill Bar ABC below – 😐 14500 – **145 rm** 193/308000.

🏨🏨 **Bernini Bristol,** piazza Barberini 23 ⊠ 00187 ℰ 463051, Telex 610554 – 🛗 ▤ 📺 ☎ –
🏃. 🆎 ⓪ 🇪. FU **m**
M *(closed Sunday dinner and Monday)* a la carte 41/63000 – 😐 12000 – **126 rm** 210/275000.

🏨🏨 **Jolly Vittorio Veneto,** corso d'Italia 1 ⊠ 00198 ℰ 8495, Telex 612293 – 🛗 ▤ 📺 ☎
⇔ – 🏃. 🆎 ⓪ 🇪 𝘝𝘐𝘚𝘈 🎄 rest FU **k**
M 40000 – **200 rm** 😐 145/200000 – P 215000.

🏨🏨 **Regina Carlton,** via Vittorio Veneto 72 ⊠ 00187 ℰ 476851, Telex 620863 – 🛗 ▤. 🆎 ⓪
🇪 𝘝𝘐𝘚𝘈. 🎄 FU **e**
M a la carte 40/60000 – 😐 10000 – **134 rm** 139/200000.

🏨🏨 **Mediterraneo,** via Cavour 15 ⊠ 00184 ℰ 464051 – 🛗 ▤ 📺 ☎ – 🏃. 🆎 ⓪ 🇪 𝘝𝘐𝘚𝘈. 🎄
M *(closed Friday and Saturday)* 27000 – **272 rm** 😐 138/198000. GV **k**

🏨🏨 **Victoria,** via Campania 41 ⊠ 00187 ℰ 473931, Telex 610212 – 🛗 ▤ 📺 ☎ ♿. 🆎 🇪. 🎄 rest
M a la carte 31/47000 – **110 rm** 😐 127/214000, ▤ 7000 – P 140/147000. FU **c**

🏨🏨 **Genova** without rest., via Cavour 33 ⊠ 00184 ℰ 476951, Telex 621599 – 🛗 ▤ 📺 ☎ ♿.
🆎 ⓪ 𝘝𝘐𝘚𝘈. 🎄 GV **b**
91 rm 😐 150/210000.

🏨🏨 **Londra e Cargill,** piazza Sallustio 18 ⊠ 00187 ℰ 473871, Telex 680412 – 🛗 ▤ 📺 ☎
⇔ – 🏃. 🆎 ⓪. 🎄 GU **k**
M a la carte 30/40000 – **105 rm** 😐 140/195000 – P 155/195000.

🏨🏨 **Massimo D'Azeglio,** via Cavour 18 ⊠ 00184 ℰ 460646, Telex 610556 – 🛗 ▤ 📺 ☎ –
🏃. 🆎 ⓪ 🇪 𝘝𝘐𝘚𝘈. 🎄 GV **s**
M *(closed Sunday)* 27000 – **210 rm** 😐 118/170000.

🏨🏨 **Quirinale,** via Nazionale 7 ⊠ 00184 ℰ 4707, Telex 610332 – 🛗 ▤ ☎ ♿. 🆎 ⓪ 🇪.
🎄 rest GV **x**
M 30/35000 – **193 rm** 😐 142/196000 – P 134/195000.

🏨🏨 **Forum,** via Tor de' Conti 25 ⊠ 00184 ℰ 6792446, Telex 622549, « Roof-garden rest. with
≼ Imperial Forums » – 🛗 ▤ ☎ ⇔ – 🏃. 🆎 ⓪. 🎄 FX **t**
M *(closed Sunday)* a la carte 40/58000 – 😐 12000 – **81 rm** 150/205000.

🏨🏨 **Eliseo,** via di Porta Pinciana 30 ⊠ 00187 ℰ 460556, Telex 610693, « Roof-garden rest.
with ≼ Villa Borghese » – 🛗 ▤ 📺 ☎ ♿ – 🏃. 🆎 ⓪ 🇪 𝘝𝘐𝘚𝘈. 🎄 FU **r**
M a la carte 31/53000 – **50 rm** 😐 121/185000.

🏨 **P.L.M. Etap Boston,** via Lombardia 47 ⌧ 00187, 𝒫 473951, Telex 680460 – 📳 🍽 ☎ ↻.
🆎 ⓘ **E**. 🛇 rest
M 25000 – **121 rm** ⌂ 120/190000 – P 145000.
FU **z**

🏨 **Imperiale,** via Vittorio Veneto 24 ⌧ 00187, 𝒫 4756351, Telex 621071 – 📳 🍽 ☎
84 rm.
FU **n**

🏨 **Napoleon,** piazza Vittorio Emanuele 105 ⌧ 00185, 𝒫 737646, Telex 611069 – 📳 🍽 – 🏛.
🆎 **E** 𝘝𝘐𝘚𝘈. 🛇
M (dinner only) 20000 – ⌂ 7000 – **80 rm** 65/101000.
HX **a**

🏨 **San Giorgio** without rest., via Amendola 61 ⌧ 00185, 𝒫 4751341 – 📳 🍽 📺. 🆎 ⓘ **E**
𝘝𝘐𝘚𝘈. 🛇
186 rm ⌂ 102/146000.
GV **s**

🏨 **Mondial** without rest., via Torino 127 ⌧ 00184, 𝒫 472861, Telex 612219 – 📳 🍽 📺 ☎ ↻.
🆎 **E**. 🛇
⌂ 9000 – **77 rm** 105/153000.
GV **a**

🏨 **Atlantico** without rest., via Cavour 23 ⌧ 00184, 𝒫 485951 – 📳 🍽 📺 ☎. 🆎 ⓘ **E** 𝘝𝘐𝘚𝘈.
🛇
83 rm ⌂ 102/146000.
GV **k**

🏨 **Universo,** via Principe Amedeo 5 ⌧ 00185, 𝒫 476811, Telex 610342 – 📳 🍽 – 🏛.
🛇 rest
M (closed Saturday dinner) 23/29000 – **206 rm** ⌂ 111/167000 – P 125/168000.
GV **e**

🏨 **Commodore** without rest., via Torino 1 ⌧ 00184, 𝒫 485656, Telex 612170 – 📳 🍽 ☎. 🆎
ⓘ **E** 𝘝𝘐𝘚𝘈. 🛇
⌂ 8000 – **65 rm** 75/118000.
GV **c**

🏩 **La Residenza** without rest., via Emilia 22 ⌧ 00187, 𝒫 6799592 – 📳 🍽 📺 ⇔wc 🕌wc ☎
ⓟ – **30 rm** ⌂ 74/115000.
FU **w**

🏩 **Britannia** without rest., via Napoli 64 ⌧ 00184, 𝒫 463153, Telex 611292 – 📳 🍽 ⇔wc
🕌wc ☎ ☎. 🆎 ⓘ **E** 𝘝𝘐𝘚𝘈. 🛇
32 rm ⌂ 95/147000.
GV **t**

🏩 **Diana,** via Principe Amedeo 4 ⌧ 00185, 𝒫 4751541, Telex 611198 – 📳 🍽 rest ⇔wc
🕌wc ☎. 🆎 **E** 𝘝𝘐𝘚𝘈. 🛇 rest
M (residents only) 21/23000 – ⌂ 7000 – **187 rm** 52/82000.
GV **e**

🏩 **Nord-Nuova Roma** without rest., via Amendola 3 ⌧ 00185, 𝒫 465441 – 📳 🍽 ⇔wc
🕌wc ☎. 🆎 ⓘ **E** 𝘝𝘐𝘚𝘈. 🛇
156 rm ⌂ 75/114000.
GV **d**

🏩 **Sitea** without rest., via Vittorio Emanuele Orlando 90 ⌧ 00185, 𝒫 4743647, Telex 614163
– 📳 🍽 ⇔wc 🕌wc ☎
37 rm ⌂ 100/150000.
GU **t**

🏩 **Milani** without rest., via Magenta 12 ⌧ 00185, 𝒫 4940051, Telex 614356 – 📳 ⇔wc 🕌wc
☎. 🛇
⌂ 10000 – **78 rm** 56/84000.
HU **z**

🏩 **Globus** without rest., viale Ippocrate 119 ⌧ 00161, 𝒫 4940001, Telex 616322 – 📳 🍽
⇔wc 🕌wc ☎ ↻ – 🏛. 🆎 ⓘ **E** 𝘝𝘐𝘚𝘈
by viale Regina Elena   JU
96 rm ⌂ 76/125000.

🏩 **Alpi** without rest., via Castelfidardo 84/a ⌧ 00185, 𝒫 464618, Telex 611677 – 📳 🍽 ⇔wc
☎. 🆎 ⓘ **E** 𝘝𝘐𝘚𝘈. 🛇
46 rm ⌂ 69/94000.
HU **s**

🏩 **Galles** without rest., viale Castro Pretorio 66 ⌧ 00185, 𝒫 4954741, Telex 613126 – 📳 🍽
⇔wc 🕌wc ☎ ↻. 🆎 ⓘ **E** 𝘝𝘐𝘚𝘈. 🛇
45 rm ⌂ 60/94000.
HU **c**

🏩 **Edera** without rest., via Poliziano 75 ⌧ 00184, 𝒫 738355, Telex 621472, 🌿 – 📳 ⇔wc
🕌wc ☎ ⓟ. 🆎 𝘝𝘐𝘚𝘈. 🛇
38 rm ⌂ 80/110000.
GY **r**

🏩 **Siviglia** without rest., via Gaeta 12 ⌧ 00185, 𝒫 4750004, Telex 612225 – 📳 ⇔wc 🕌wc
☎. 🆎 ⓘ **E** 𝘝𝘐𝘚𝘈. 🛇
41 rm ⌂ 60/93000.
HU **k**

🏠 **Igea** without rest., via Principe Amedeo 97 ⌧ 00185, 𝒫 7311212 – 📳 🕌wc ☎. 🛇
HV **u**
⌂ 4000 – **42 rm** 29/45000.

🏠 **Centro** without rest., via Firenze 12 ⌧ 00184, 𝒫 464142, Telex 612125 – 📳 ⇔wc 🕌wc
☎. 🆎 ⓘ 𝘝𝘐𝘚𝘈. 🛇
36 rm ⌂ 68/102000.
GV **n**

🏠 **Canada** without rest., via Vicenza 58 ⌧ 00185, 𝒫 4941097, Telex 613037 – 📳 🍽 ⇔wc
🕌wc ☎. 🆎 ⓘ **E** 𝘝𝘐𝘚𝘈. 🛇
48 rm ⌂ 50/80000.
HU **e**

🏠 **Alba** without rest., via Leonina 12 ⌧ 00184, 𝒫 484471 – 📳 ⇔wc 🕌wc ☎ ↻ – 🏛. 🆎 ⓘ
E 𝘝𝘐𝘚𝘈
FX **v**
⌂ 5000 – **25 rm** 40/50000.

🏠 **Flavio** without rest., via Frangipane 34 ⌧ 00184, 𝒫 6797203 – 📳 🕌wc ↻. 🛇
FX **x**
⌂ 3500 – **23 rm** 17/36000.

🏠 **Buenos Aires** without rest., via Clitunno 9 ⌧ 00198, 𝒫 864854 – 🍽 ⇔wc 🕌wc ☎ ⓟ.
🆎 ⓘ **E** 𝘝𝘐𝘚𝘈
by viale Regina Margherita   JU
23 rm ⌂ 43/76000, 🍽 4000.

XXXX ❀ **Sans Souci,** via Sicilia 20/24 ⊠ 00187 ✆ 493504, Elegant tavern-late night dinners – FU **p**
    ᴀᴇ ⑩ E ᴠɪsᴀ. ⅍
    closed Monday and August – **M** (dinner only) (booking essential) a la carte 50/75000
    Spec. I nostri risotti, Filetti di sogliola al Berlucchi e fragole, Medaglioni di vitella al Nero di Norcia. **Wines** Sauvignon del Collio, Rubesco.

XXX **Grill Bar ABC,** via Vittorio Veneto 66 ⊠ 00187 ✆ 4740950, Elegant rest. – 🝙. ᴀᴇ ⑩ E
    ᴠɪsᴀ. ⅍ – **M** (booking essential) a la carte 44/70000. FU **e**

XXX **Harry's Bar,** via Vittorio Veneto 150 ⊠ 00187 ✆ 4745832 – ᴀᴇ ⑩. ⅍ FU **a**
    M (booking essential) a la carte 36/54000.

XX **Cesarina,** via Piemonte 109 ⊠ 00187 ✆ 460828, Bolognese rest. – 🝙. ᴀᴇ ⑩ ᴠɪsᴀ. ⅍
    closed Sunday – **M** a la carte 27/47000. GU **n**

XX **Loreto,** via Valenziani 19 ⊠ 00187 ✆ 4742154, Seafood – 🝙. ⅍ GU **m**
    closed Sunday and 10 to 28 August – **M** a la carte 30/43000.

XX **Leon d'Oro,** via Cagliari 25 ⊠ 00198 ✆ 861847, Seafood – 🝙. ᴀᴇ ⑩ E ᴠɪsᴀ. ⅍
    closed Sunday – **M** a la carte 26/37000.   by viale Regina Margherita JU

XX **Andrea,** via Sardegna 28 ⊠ 00187 ✆ 493707 – 🝙. ᴀᴇ ⑩ E ᴠɪsᴀ FU **v**
    closed Sunday and 1 to 20 August – **M** (booking essential) a la carte 27/46000.

XX ❀ **Girarrosto Toscano,** via Campania 29 ⊠ 00187 ✆ 493759, Modern tavern – 🝙. ᴀᴇ
    ⑩ ᴠɪsᴀ. ⅍ FU **v**
    closed Wednesday – **M** a la carte 31/50000
    Spec. Antipasto misto della Casa, Costoletta d'abbacchio a scottadito, Bistecca alla fiorentina. **Wines** Frascati, Chianti.

X **Tullio,** via di San Nicola da Tolentino 26 ⊠ 00187 ✆ 4758564, Tuscan trattoria – 🝙. ᴀᴇ
    ⑩ ᴠɪsᴀ. ⅍ FU **x**
    closed Sunday and August – **M** a la carte 23/35000.

X **La Matriciana,** via del Viminale 40/44 ⊠ 00184 ✆ 461775 – 🝙. ᴀᴇ ⑩ ᴠɪsᴀ GV **h**
    closed Saturday and 11 to 16 August – **M** a la carte 18/31000.

X **Cannavota,** piazza San Giovanni in Laterano 20 ⊠ 00184 ✆ 775007, Roman trattoria –
    ᴀᴇ ⑩. ⅍ HY **a**
    closed Wednesday and 1 to 20 August – **M** a la carte 17/27000.

Southern area Aventino, Porta San Paolo, Terme di Caracalla, via Appia Nuova (Plans : Rome pp. 2 to 5) :

🏨 Santa Prisca, largo Manlio Gelsomini 25 ⊠ 00153 ✆ 571917 – ➔│🛗 🝙 rest 🚾wc ☎ ②
    45 rm.   by lungotevere Aventino DEY

🏨 Villa San Pio without rest., via di Sant'Anselmo 19 ⊠ 00153 ✆ 5781325, ✍ – ➔│🛗 🚾wc
    🚾wc ⓟ ᴄ. ⅍   by lungotevere Aventino DEY
    59 rm ⊃ 45/65000.

🏨 Domus Maximi ⑤ without rest., via Santa Prisca 11/b ⊠ 00153 ✆ 5782565 – 🚾wc
    🚾wc ☎. ⅍   by via del Circo Massimo EY
    21 rm ⊃ 51/77000.

🏨 Sant'Anselmo without rest., piazza Sant'Anselmo 2 ⊠ 00153 ✆ 573547 – 🚾wc ⓟ.
    ⅍ – **26 rm** ⊃ 45/65000.   by lungotevere Aventino DY

XX **Severino,** piazza Zama 5/c ⊠ 00183 ✆ 7550872 – 🝙   by via dell'Amba Aradam HY
    closed Sunday dinner, Monday, 1 to 22 August and 24 to 30 December – **M**
    a la carte 29/45000.

XX **Apuleius,** via Tempio di Diana 15 ⊠ 00153 ✆ 572160, « Ancient Rome style decor
    tavern » – ᴀᴇ. ⅍   by via del Circo Massimo EY
    closed Sunday and 13 to 28 August – **M** a la carte 23/36000.

Trastevere area (typical district) (Plan : Rome p. 3) :

XX ❀ **Alberto Ciarla,** piazza San Cosimato 40 ⊠ 00153 ✆ 5818668 – 🝙. ᴀᴇ ⑩ ᴠɪsᴀ. ⅍
    closed Sunday, 13 to 31 August and 23 December-10 January – **M** (dinner only) (booking
    essential) a la carte 50/60000 CY **u**
    Spec. Insalate di pesce al crudo, Zuppa di pasta e fagioli ai frutti di mare, Filetti di spigola alle mandorle. **Wines** Marino superiore.

XX **Corsetti-il Galeone,** piazza San Cosimato 27 ⊠ 00153 ✆ 5816311, Typical seafood
    rest. and pizzeria – 🝙. ᴀᴇ ⑩ E ᴠɪsᴀ. ⅍ CY **g**
    closed Wednesday and 2 to 26 July – **M** a la carte 21/37000.

XX **Sabatini a Santa Maria in Trastevere,** piazza di Santa Maria in Trastevere 10 ⊠
    00153 ✆ 582026, Roman and seafood rest. – ᴀᴇ ⑩ CY **n**
    closed Wednesday – **M** a la carte 35/60000.

XX **Galeassi,** piazza di Santa Maria in Trastevere 3 ⊠ 00153 ✆ 5803775, Roman and
    seafood rest. – 🝙. ᴀᴇ ⑩ ᴠɪsᴀ CY **f**
    closed Monday and 20 December-10 January – **M** a la carte 25/42000.

XX **Checco er Carettiere,** via Benedetta 10 ⊠ 00153 ✆ 5817018, Typical Roman and
    seafood rest. – 🝙 CX **k**
    closed Sunday dinner, Monday and 10 August-1 September – **M** a la carte 23/37000.

X **Romolo,** via di Porta Settimiana 8 ⊠ 00153 ✆ 5818284, Typical trattoria, « Summer
    service in a cool little court-yard » – ᴀᴇ ᴠɪsᴀ CX **a**
    closed Monday and August – **M** a la carte 29/41000.

Outskirts of Rome

on national road 1 - Aurelia :

Villa Pamphili, via della Nocetta 105 ⊠ 00164 ℰ 5862, Telex 611675, ⤒ (covered in winter), ℛ, ℀ – ⋈ ▤ ℡ ☎ ♿ ℗ – ⚐. ℀ ⓪ Ε 𝘝𝘐𝘚𝘈. ℀ rest   by via Garibaldi BY
M 35000 – **253 rm** ☲ 104/157000.

Holiday Inn St. Peter's, via Aurelia Antica 415 ⊠ 00165 ℰ 5872, Telex 680195, ⤒, ℛ, ℀ – ⋈ ▤ ℡ ☎ ♿ ℗ – ⚐. ℀ ⓪ Ε 𝘝𝘐𝘚𝘈. ℀ rest   by via Garibaldi BY
M a la carte 30/50000 – ☲ 8000 – **330 rm** 108/160000.

Motelagip, ⊠ 00163 ℰ 6379001, Telex 613699, ⤒, ℛ – ⋈ ▤ ⌇wc ☎ ♿ ℗ – ⚐. ℀
⓪ Ε 𝘝𝘐𝘚𝘈. ℀   by via Aurelia AV
M 18500 – **222 rm** ☲ 56/88000 – P 83/90000.

La Maielletta, via Aurelia Antica 270 ⊠ 00165 ℰ 6374957, ⌲, Typical Abruzzi rest. –
℗. ℀ ⓪   by via Aurelia AV
closed Monday – **M** a la carte 19/32000.

on the Ancient Appian way :

Cecilia Metella, via Appia Antica 125/127 ⊠ 00179 ℰ 5136743, ⌲, « Shaded garden »
– ℗. ℀ Ε. ℀   by via Claudia GY
closed Monday – **M** a la carte 22/33000.

Quo Vadis, via Appia Antica 38 ⊠ 00179 ℰ 5136795, ⌲ – ℗. ⓪. ℀
          by via Claudia GY
closed Tuesday and 2 to 22 August – **M** (lunch only) a la carte 24/35000.

on via Cristoforo Colombo :

Caravel without rest., via Colombo 124/c ⊠ 00147 ℰ 5115046 – ⋈ ⌇wc ⌇wc ☎. ℀
83 rm ☲ 65/92000.   by via Claudia GY

to E.U.R. Garden City :

Sheraton, viale del Pattinaggio ⊠ 00144 ℰ 5453, Telex 614223, ⤒, ℀ – ⋈ ▤ ℡ ☎ ♿
⊜ ℗ – ⚐. ℀ Ε 𝘝𝘐𝘚𝘈. ℀   by via di San Gregorio FY
M a la carte 33/51000 – **615 rm** ☲ 153/272000.

Shangri Là-Corsetti, viale Algeria 141 ⊠ 00144 ℰ 5916441, Telex 614664, ⤒ heated,
ℛ – ▤ ℡ ☎ ♿ – ⚐. ℀ ⓪ Ε 𝘝𝘐𝘚𝘈. ℀   by via di San Gregorio FY
M a la carte 21/37000 – ☲ 7500 – **52 rm** 102/135000.

Dei Congressi without rest., viale Shakespeare 29 ⊠ 00144 ℰ 5926021, Telex 614140 –
⋈ ▤ ☎ ♿. ℀ ⓪ Ε 𝘝𝘐𝘚𝘈. ℀   by via di San Gregorio FY
96 rm ☲ 80/120000.

Vecchia America-Corsetti, piazza Marconi 32 ⊠ 00144 ℰ 5926601, Typical rest. and
ale house – ℀ ⓪ Ε 𝘝𝘐𝘚𝘈. ℀   by via di San Gregorio FY
closed Tuesday – **M** a la carte 20/33000.

on the motorway to Fiumicino close to the ring-road :

Holiday Inn-Parco dei Medici, viale Castello della Magliana 65 ⊠ 00148 ℰ 5475,
Telex 613302, ⤒, ℛ, ℀ – ⋈ ▤ ℡ ☎ ♿ ℗ – ⚐. ℀ ⓪ Ε 𝘝𝘐𝘚𝘈. ℀
M 31000 – ☲ 10000 – **324 rm** 110/158000 – P 150/181000.   by viale Trastevere CY

FLORENCE (FIRENZE) 50100 𝟘𝟠𝟠 ⑮ – pop. 444 294 – alt. 49 – ✆ 055.

See : Monuments of Piazza del Duomo★★★ : Cathedral★★ (exterior of the apse★★★, dome★★★ :
❄★★ – ball tower★★ (❄★★) – Baptistry★★ (doors★★★, mosaics★★★) – Museum of the Cathedral building and its possessions★★ (Pietà★★ by Michelangelo, choristers' tribunes★★★ by
Luca della Robbia and Donatello, bas-reliefs★★ from the ball tower) – Uffizi Gallery★★★ (Botti-
celli room★★★) – Piazza della Signoria★★ : Palazzo Vecchio★★ (cabinet★★) – Loggia della
Signoria★★ (Perseus★★ by B. Cellini) – Ponte Vecchio★ – Pitti Palace★★ : Palatine Gallery★★
(collection★★★ of Titian and Raphael) – The Bargello Palace and museum★★ (courtyard★★,
works by Donatello★★★) – Museum of St. Mark★★ (works by Fra Angelico★★★) – Academy
Gallery★★ (works by Michelangelo★★★) – San Lorenzo★ : church★, Laurentian Library★★,
Medici chapels★★ (Medici tombs★★★) – Santa Maria Novella★★ : church★ (frescoes★★★ of the
chapel by Domenico Ghirlandaio, Crucifix★★ by Brunelleschi); Spaniard's chapel (frescoes★★)
– Santa Croce★★ : church★ (interior★★ : bas relief of the Annunciation★ by Donatello, frescoes
by Giotto depicting the life of St. Francesco★★) ; Pazzi chapel★★ – Medici Riccardi Palace★★
(frescoes★★★ by Benozzo Gozzoli, Luca Giordano Gallery★★) – Strozzi Palace★★ BY F – Trip to
the Hills★★ : from Piazzale Michelangiolo ❄★★; church of San Miniato al Monte★★ DZ – Boboli
Garden★, ❄★★ from the Citadel Belvedere ABZ – Orsanmichele★ (tabernacle★★ by Orcagna)
BCY G – Church of Santa Maria del Carmine : frescoes★★ by Masaccio AY Z.

🏌 Dell'Ugolino (closed Monday), to Grassina ⊠ 50015 ℰ 2051009, S : 12 km.

✈ Galileo Galilei of Pisa to ⑦ : 95 km ℰ (050) 28088 – Alitalia, lungarno Acciaiuoli 10/12,
⊠ 30123 ℰ 263051.

🛈 via Manzoni 16 ⊠ 50121 ℰ 678841 – via de' Tornabuoni 15 ⊠ 50123 ℰ 216544, Telex 572263.
A.C.I. viale Amendola 36 ⊠ 50121 ℰ 27841, Telex 571202.

Roma 277 ③ – Bologna 105 ⑧ – Milano 298 ⑧.

FIRENZE

0   300 m

★★ S. LORENZO
★★ STA MA NOVELLA

MICHELIN

PONTE VECCHIO
PALAZZO PITTI

240

FIRENZE

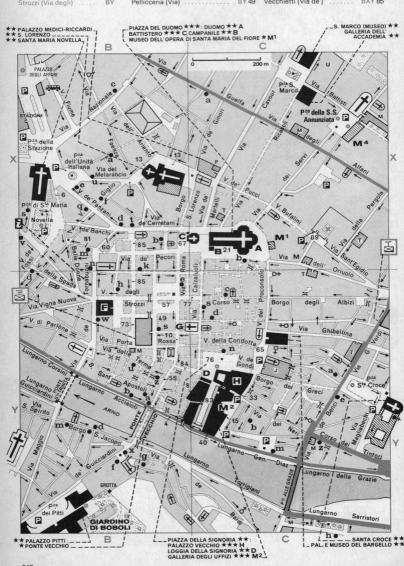

★★ PALAZZO MEDICI-RICCARDI
★★ S. LORENZO
★★ SANTA MARIA NOVELLA

PIAZZA DEL DUOMO ★★★: DUOMO ★★ A
BATTISTERO ★★★ C CAMPANILE ★★ B
MUSEO DELL'OPERA DI SANTA MARIA DEL FIORE ★ M¹

S. MARCO (MUSEO) ★★
GALLERIA DELL'
ACCADEMIA ★★

★★ PALAZZO PITTI
★ PONTE VECCHIO

PIAZZA DELLA SIGNORIA ★★:
PALAZZO VECCHIO ★★★ H
LOGGIA DELLA SIGNORIA ★★ D
GALLERIA DEGLI UFFIZI ★★★ M²

SANTA CROCE ★★
PAL. E MUSEO DEL BARGELLO ★★

242

🏨🏨🏨🏨🏨 **Excelsior,** piazza Ognissanti 3 ✉ 50123 ✆ 264201, Telex 570022, « Rest. with summer service on terrace with < » – ⇅ ▤ 📺 ☎ ♿ – 👥. AE ◑ E VISA. ⊘ rest AY **g**
M 65/100000 – ☕ 16000 – **205 rm** 274/441000.

🏨🏨🏨🏨🏨 **Savoy,** piazza della Repubblica 7 ✉ 50123 ✆ 283313, Telex 570220 – ⇅ ▤ 📺 ☎ ♿ – 👥. AE ◑ E VISA. ⊘ rest BY **e**
M a la carte 50/70000 – ☕ 14000 – **101 rm** 240/300000.

🏨🏨🏨🏨🏨 **Villa Medici,** via Il Prato 42 ✉ 50123 ✆ 261331, Telex 570179, 🏊 – ⇅ ▤ 📺 ☎ – 👥. AE ◑ E AX **g**
M rest. see **Lorenzaccio** below – ☕ 13000 – **107 rm** 200/330000.

🏨🏨🏨🏨 **Baglioni,** piazza Unità Italiana 6 ✉ 50123 ✆ 218441, Telex 570225, « Roof-garden rest. with < » – ⇅ ▤ 📺 ☎ ♿ – 👥. AE ◑ E VISA. ⊘ rest BX **e**
M a la carte 35/47000 – **195 rm** ☕ 143/205000.

🏨🏨🏨🏨 **Jolly,** piazza Vittorio Veneto 4/a ✉ 50123 ✆ 2770, Telex 570191, « 🏊 on panoramic terrace » – ⇅ ▤ 📺 ☎ – 👥. AE ◑ E VISA. ⊘ rest AX **u**
M 35000 – **167 rm** ☕ 117/185000 – P 185000.

🏨🏨🏨🏨 **Majestic,** via del Melarancio 1 ✉ 50123 ✆ 264021, Telex 570628 – ⇅ ▤ 📺 ☎ 🚗 – 👥. AE E VISA. ⊘ rest BX **u**
M *(closed Sunday)* 30/35000 – ☕ 15000 – **104 rm** 132/176000 – P 170/200000.

🏨🏨🏨🏨 **Regency,** piazza Massimo D'Azeglio 3 ✉ 50121 ✆ 245247, Telex 571058 – ▤ 📺 ☎ Ⓟ. AE ◑ E VISA. ⊘ rest DX **c**
M *(closed Sunday)* a la carte 38/52000 – ☕ 15000 – **31 rm** 210/280000 – P 375000.

🏨🏨🏨 **Plaza Hotel Lucchesi,** lungarno della Zecca Vecchia 38 ✉ 50122 ✆ 264141, Telex 570302, < – ⇅ ▤ ☎ ♿ – 👥. AE ◑ E VISA. ⊘ rest DY **f**
M a la carte 30/45000 (15%) – **104 rm** ☕ 149/209000.

🏨🏨🏨 **Gd H. Minerva,** piazza di Santa Maria Novella 16 ✉ 50123 ✆ 284555, Telex 570414, 🏊 – ⇅ ▤ 📺 ☎ ♿ – 👥. ⊘ rest BX **s**
M a la carte 31/46000 – ☕ 15500 – **107 rm** 132/176000 – P 137/197000.

🏨🏨🏨 **Etap Astoria,** via del Giglio 9 ✉ 50123 ✆ 298095, Telex 571070 – ⇅ ▤ 📺 ☎ ♿. AE ◑ E VISA. ⊘ rest BX **f**
M a la carte 31/51000 – **90 rm** ☕ 120/190000.

🏨🏨🏨 **De la Ville,** piazza Antinori 1 ✉ 50123 ✆ 261805, Telex 570518 – ⇅ ▤ 📺 ☎ ♿. AE ◑ VISA. ⊘ rest BX **n**
M *(closed lunch and Sunday)* a la carte 35/51000 – ☕ 15000 – **75 rm** 133/178000.

🏨🏨🏨 **Croce di Malta and Rest. il Coccodrillo,** via della Scala 7 ✉ 50123 ✆ 282600, Telex 570540, 🏊, 🌳 – ⇅ ▤ 📺 ☎ ♿ – 👥. AE. ⊘ rest BX **v**
M *(closed Sunday and Monday lunch)* a la carte 28/45000 – ☕ 14000 – **100 rm** 132/176000 – P 134/200000.

🏨🏨🏨 **Augustus** without rest., piazzetta dell'Oro 5 ✉ 50123 ✆ 283054, Telex 570110 – ⇅ ▤ 📺 ☎ ♿ – 👥. AE ◑ E VISA. ⊘ BY **a**
☕ 10000 – **67 rm** 110/160000.

🏨🏨🏨 **Kraft,** via Solferino 2 ✉ 50123 ✆ 284273, Telex 571523, « Roof-garden rest. with < », 🏊 – ⇅ ▤ 📺 ☎ – 👥. AE ◑ E VISA. ⊘ rest AX **c**
M 35000 – ☕ 14000 – **66 rm** 118/170000 – P 145/180000.

🏨🏨🏨 **Anglo American,** via Garibaldi 9 ✉ 50123 ✆ 282114, Telex 570289 – ⇅ ▤ ☎ ♿ – 👥. AE ◑ E VISA. ⊘ rest AX **d**
M *(closed Sunday)* 34/40000 – **118 rm** ☕ 140/197000.

🏨🏨🏨 **Londra,** via Jacopo da Diacceto 16 ✉ 50123 ✆ 262791, Telex 571152 – ⇅ ▤ 📺 ☎ ♿ 🚗 – 👥. AE E VISA. ⊘ rest AX **n**
M a la carte 31/54000 – ☕ 15500 – **105 rm** 134/170000 – P 134/193000.

🏨🏨🏨 **Lungarno** without rest., borgo Sant'Jacopo 14 ✉ 50125 ✆ 264211, Telex 570129, <, « Collection of modern pictures » – ⇅ ▤ 📺 ☎ – 👥. AE ◑ E VISA. ⊘ BY **d**
☕ 10000 – **71 rm** 110/160000.

🏨🏨🏨 **Michelangelo,** via Fratelli Rosselli 2 ✉ 50123 ✆ 278711, Telex 571113 – ⇅ ▤ 📺 ☎ 🚗 – 👥. AE ◑ E VISA. ⊘ rest AX **w**
M a la carte 30/41000 – **138 rm** ☕ 145/198000 – P 187000.

🏨🏨🏨 **Crest and Rest. la Tegolaia,** viale Europa 205 ✉ 50126 ✆ 686841, Telex 570376, 🏊 heated, 🌳 – ⇅ ▤ 📺 ☎ ♿ Ⓟ – 👥. AE ◑ E VISA. ⊘ rest by ③
M a la carte 30/45000 – ☕ 12000 – **92 rm** 140/170000.

🏨🏨🏨 **Principe** without rest., lungarno Vespucci 34 ✉ 50123 ✆ 284848, Telex 571400, <, 🌳 – ⇅ ▤ Ⓟ. AE ◑ E VISA – ☕ 12000 – **21 rm** 84/132000. AX **b**

🏨🏨 **Montebello** without rest., via Montebello 60 ✉ 50123 ✆ 298051, Telex 574009, 🌳 – ⇅ ▤ 🛁wc ☎ ♿. AE ◑ E. ⊘ – ☕ 15000 – **45 rm** 105/155000. AX **e**

🏨🏨 **Continental** without rest., lungarno Acciaiuoli 2 ✉ 50123 ✆ 282392, « Flower terrace with < » – ⇅ ▤ 🛁wc 🚿wc ☎ ♿. AE ◑ E VISA BY **a**
☕ 10000 – **62 rm** 71/104000.

🏨🏨 **Alexander,** viale Guidoni 101 ✉ 50127 ✆ 4378951, Telex 574026 – ⇅ ▤ 📺 🛁wc 🚿wc ☎ Ⓟ. AE ◑ E VISA. ⊘ by ⑧
M a la carte 27/43000 – ☕ 12500 – **88 rm** 87/131000 – P 125/137000.

🏨🏨 **Ville sull'Arno** without rest., lungarno Colombo 5 ✉ 50136 ✆ 670971, Telex 573297, <, 🏊 heated – ▤ 🛁wc 🚿wc ☎ 🚗 Ⓟ. AE ◑ VISA by ②
☕ 12000 – **47 rm** 95/155000.

🏨 **Calzaiuoli** without rest., via Calzaiuoli 6 🖂 50122 🖉 212458 – 🛗 ⇔wc ☎ 🕭. 🝣 ⓪ 🖪
VISA. 🛠 – ⤢ 7000 – **37 rm** 59/87000.
CY **s**

🏨 **Golf** without rest., viale Fratelli Rosselli 56 🖂 50123 🖉 293088, Telex 571630 – 🛗 🗏
⇔wc ⇑wc ☜ 🕭. 🅿. 🝣 ⓪ 🖪 **VISA**
AV **k**
⤢ 9500 – **39 rm** 69/106000.

🏨 **Columbus**, lungarno Colombo 22/a 🖂 50136 🖉 677251, Telex 570273 – 🛗 🗏 ⇔wc
⇑wc ☜ 🅿. 🝣 ⓪ **VISA**. 🛠 rest
by ②
M 28000 – ⤢ 9000 – **99 rm** 62/97000.

🏨 **Helvetia e Bristol** without rest., via de' Pescioni 2 🖂 50123 🖉 287814 – 🛗 ⇔wc ⇑wc
☜ 🕭. 🝣 ⓪ 🖪 **VISA**
BY **h**
⤢ 6500 – **62 rm** 58/92000.

🏨 **Balestri** without rest., piazza Mentana 7 🖂 50122 🖉 214743 – 🛗 🗏 ⇔wc ⇑wc ☜ 🕭.
🝣 **VISA**. 🛠
CY **m**
March-November – ⤢ 9000 – **49 rm** 57/87000, 🗏 5000.

🏨 **David** without rest., via Michelangelo 1 🖂 50125 🖉 6811696, Telex 574553 – 🛗 🗏
⇑wc ☎ 🕭. 🅿. 🝣 ⓪ 🖪 **VISA**.
DZ **a**
⤢ 8000 – **26 rm** 58/88000, 🗏 5000.

🏛 **Franchi** without rest., via Sgambati 28 🖂 50127 🖉 372425 – 🛗 ⇑wc ☜ 🕭. 🅿. 🝣 🖪 **VISA**
by ⑧
⤢ 7000 – **35 rm** 38/57000.

🏛 **Rapallo**, via di Santa Caterina d'Alessandria 7 🖂 50129 🖉 472412, Telex 574251 – 🛗 🗏
⇔wc ⇑wc ☜ ⇑. 🝣 ⓪ 🖪 **VISA**. 🗏 5000.
CV **s**
M (residents only) 21000 – ⤢ 6500 – **31 rm** 55/84000, – P 73/93000.

🏛 **Astor**, viale Milton 41 🖂 50129 🖉 483391, Telex 573155 – 🛗 🗏 rest ⇔wc ⇑wc ☎ 🕭.
🝣 🖪 **VISA**. 🛠 rest
CV **u**
M (residents only) 25000 – ⤢ 9000 – **25 rm** 48/70000, – P 92000.

🏛 **Fiorino** without rest., via Osteria del Guanto 6 🖂 50122 🖉 210579 – 🗏 ⇔wc ⇑wc ☜
⤢ 7500 – **23 rm** 34/51000, 🗏 4500.
CY **b**

🏛 **Orcagna** without rest., via Orcagna 57/59 🖂 50121 🖉 675959 – 🛗 ⇔wc ⇑wc ☜. 🖪
⤢ 6000 – **18 rm** 36/53000.
DY **n**

🏛 **Jane** without rest., via Orcagna 56 🖂 50121 🖉 677383 – 🛗 🗏 ⇔wc ⇑wc ☜. 🛠
DY **m**
⤢ 6000 – **28 rm** 36/55000, 🗏 5000.

🏛 **San Remo** without rest., lungarno Serristori 13 🖂 50125 🖉 213390 – 🛗 🗏 ⇔wc ⇑wc
☜. 🝣 🖪. 🛠 – **17 rm** 44/70000, 🗏 4000.
DZ **e**

XXXX **Sabatini**, via de' Panzani 9/a 🖂 50123 🖉 282802, Elegant traditional decor – 🝣 ⓪
🖪 **VISA**. 🛠
BX **q**
closed Monday – **M** a la carte 37/51000 (13%).

XXX **Doney**, via de' Tornabuoni 46 r 🖂 50123 🖉 214348, Elegant rest. – 🗏. 🝣 ⓪ **VISA**
BY **w**
closed August – **M** a la carte 25/39000 (15%).

XXX ⊛⊛ **Enoteca Pinchiorri**, via Ghibellina 87 🖂 50122 🖉 242777, « Summer service in a
cool court-yard » – 🝣
CDY **x**
closed Sunday, Monday lunch, August and 25 to 27 December – **M** (booking essential)
a la carte 75/85000 (12%)
Spec. Seasonal specialities.

XXX **Da Dante-al Lume di Candela**, via delle Terme 23 r 🖂 50123 🖉 294566 – 🗏. 🝣 ⓪
VISA. 🛠
BY **u**
closed Sunday, Monday lunch and 10 to 25 August – **M** (booking essential)
a la carte 27/37000 (16%).

XXX **Harry's Bar**, lungarno Vespucci 22 r 🖂 50123 🖉 296700 – 🗏. 🝣
AY **x**
closed Sunday and 10 December-15 January – **M** (booking essential) a la carte 35/52000
(16%).

XXX Lorenzaccio, via Rucellai 1/a 🖂 50123 🖉 217100 – 🗏
AX **g**

XX **La Posta**, via de' Lamberti 20 r 🖂 50123 🖉 212701 – 🗏. 🝣 ⓪ 🖪 **VISA**. 🛠
BY **s**
closed Tuesday – **M** a la carte 25/40000 (13%).

XX **Al Campidoglio**, via del Campidoglio 8 r 🖂 50123 🖉 287770 – 🗏. 🝣 ⓪ 🖪 **VISA**. 🛠
BXY **h**
closed Thursday and August – **M** a la carte 23/30000 (12%).

XX **La Loggia**, piazzale Michelangiolo 1 🖂 50125 🖉 287032, « Outdoor service in Summer
with ⩽ » – 🅿. 🝣 ⓪ **VISA**. 🛠
DZ **r**
closed Wednesday and 10 to 25 August – **M** a la carte 22/33000 (13%).

XX **Il Profeta**, borgo Ognissanti 93 r 🖂 50123 🖉 212265 – 🗏. 🝣 🖪 **VISA**. 🛠
AX **r**
closed Sunday, Monday and August – **M** a la carte 21/28000 (12%).

XX **Buca Lapi**, via del Trebbio 1 r 🖂 50123 🖉 213768, Typical tavern – 🗏. 🝣 🖪 **VISA**.
BX **m**
closed Sunday and Monday lunch – **M** a la carte 23/35000 (12%).

XX **Paoli**, via dei Tavolini 12 r 🖂 50122 🖉 216215, Typical rest., « Reproduction 14C style
decor » – 🝣 ⓪ 🖪 **VISA**. 🛠
CY **d**
closed Tuesday – **M** a la carte 23/36000 (12%).

XX **13 Gobbi**, via del Porcellana 9 r 🖂 50123 🖉 298769, Tuscan rest. – 🝣 **VISA**
AX **v**
closed Sunday, Monday and 28 July-29 August – **M** a la carte 22/33000 (10%).

XX **La Greppia**, lungarno Ferrucci 8 🖂 50126 🖉 6812341, Rustic rest. and pizzeria, « Summer
service on terrace with ⩽ » – 🝣 ⓪ **VISA**. 🛠
DZ **u**
closed Monday and August – **M** a la carte 20/33000 (12%).

✗ **Celestino,** piazza Santa Felicita 4 r ⊠ 50125 ℰ 296574 – ▤   BY **x**
closed Sunday and 30 July-23 August – **M** a la carte 23/34000 (12%).

✗ **Il Tirabusciò,** via de' Benci 34 r ⊠ 50122 ℰ 246225   CY **e**
closed Wednesday and Thursday – M (booking essential) a la carte 15/27000 (12%).

✗ **Bordino,** via Stracciatella 9 r ⊠ 50125 ℰ 213048, Typical trattoria – ▤. ⒶⒺ ⓞ Ⓔ 𝘝𝘐𝘚𝘈
closed lunch Sunday, Monday, July and 23 to 31 December – **M** a la carte 19/39000.   BY **g**

✗ ⚘ **Cammillo,** borgo Sant'Jacopo 57 r ⊠ 50125 ℰ 212427, Typical florentine trattoria –
▤. ⒶⒺ ⓞ Ⓔ 𝘝𝘐𝘚𝘈   BY **m**
closed Wednesday, Thursday, 20 December-15 January and 1 to 20 August – **M**
a la carte 25/50000
Spec. Trippa alla fiorentina, Petti di pollo alla Cammillo, Scaloppine Capriccio. **Wines** Chianti.

✗ **Cavallino,** via delle Farine 6 r ⊠ 50122 ℰ 215818, Habitués' rest., « Outdoor service in
Summer with ◄ » – ▤. 🌿   CY **n**
closed Tuesday dinner, Wednesday and 1 to 26 August – **M** a la carte 22/31000 (12%).

on the hills S : 3 km :

🏨 **Gd H. Villa Cora and Rest. Taverna Machiavelli** 🐦, viale Machiavelli 18 ⊠ 50125
ℰ 2298451, Telex 570604, « Floral park with 🏊 » – 🛗 ▤ 📺 ☎ Ⓟ – 🔬
M a la carte 40/50000 – 🍽 14000 – **48 rm** 195/310000.   by viale Machiavelli ABZ

🏨 **Villa Belvedere** 🐦, via Benedetto Castelli 3 ⊠ 50124 ℰ 222501, ◄ town and hills,
« Garden-park with 🏊 », 🌿 – 🛗 ▤ ⓦc 🍽 ♿ Ⓟ. 🌿   by ④
March-November – **M** coffee shop only – 🍽 8500 – **27 rm** 70/110000.

🏨 **Villa Carlotta** 🐦, via Michele di Lando 3 ⊠ 50125 ℰ 220530, Telex 573485, « Beautiful
garden – 🛗 ▤ ⓦc ⓯wc ☎ Ⓟ – 🔬. ⒶⒺ ⓞ 𝘝𝘐𝘚𝘈. 🌿 rest   AZ **a**
M *(closed 15 November-1 March)* 32000 – 🍽 12000 – **26 rm** 87/131000 – P 110/131000.

at Arcetri S : 5 km – ⊠ 50125 Firenze :

✗ **Omero,** via Pian de' Giullari 11 r ℰ 220053, Rustic trattoria with ◄, « Summer service on
terrace »   by viale Galileo CDZ
closed Tuesday and August – **M** a la carte 18/28000 (13%).

at Candeli – ⊠ 50010 :

🏨 **Villa La Massa and Rest. Il Verrocchio** 🐦, ℰ 630051, Telex 573555, ◄, « House
and furnishing in 18C style », 🏊 heated, 🚗, 🌿 – 🛗 ▤ 📺 ☎ ♿ Ⓟ – 🔬. ⒶⒺ ⓞ Ⓔ 𝘝𝘐𝘚𝘈.
🌿 rest
M *(closed Monday, Tuesday lunch and November-March)* a la carte 30/50000 – 🍽 14000
– **43 rm** 146/268000, ▤ 5500 – P 213/256000.

towards Trespiano N : 7 km :

🏨 **Villa le Rondini** 🐦, via Bolognese Vecchia 224 ⊠ 50139 Firenze ℰ 400081, ◄ town,
« Among the olive trees », 🏊, 🚗, 🌿 – ⓦc ⓯wc ☎ ♿ Ⓟ – 🔬. ⒶⒺ ⓞ Ⓔ 𝘝𝘐𝘚𝘈. 🌿 rest
M 25/30000 – 29 rm 🍽 63/92000 – P 118/133000.

MILAN (MILANO) 20100 ⑨⑧⑧ ③, ②①⑨ ⑲ – pop. 1 580 810 – alt. 122 – ✪ 02.

See : Cathedral★★★ (Duomo), Tour of the Cathedral terraces★★★ – Brera exhibition hall and
art gallery★★★ – Sforza castle★★ (municipal Art collections★★) – Poldi-Pezzoli museum★★
(Golden Hall : portrait of a woman★★★, Persian carpet★, Ecce Homo★★ by G. Bellini) CU M1 –
Via and piazza Mercanti★ – La Scala Theatre★ – Church of St. Maria delle Grazie (dome★,
Leonardo da Vinci's Last Supper★★★) – Basilica of St. Ambrogio★ (atrium★★) – Galleria Vittorio
Emanuele★ CV – Ambrosian Library★ (art gallery★★, two portraits★★ by Leonardo da Vinci,
Raphael's cartoons★★★ for the fresco of the Athenian School, the Manger★★ by Barocci, the
Mouse with a rose★ by Velvet Breughel) BV – Leonardo da Vinci museum of Science and
Technology★ AV M1 – Church of St. Eustorgio★ (Portinari Chapel★★) BY B – Church of St.
Satiro★ CV C – Maggiore Hospital★ DX U – Church of St. Maurizio (frescoes by Luini★) BV E –
Parco Sempione★.

Envir. : Chiaravalle Abbey★ SE : 7 km – N : Lakes : Lake Como★★★, Lake Maggiore★★★, Lake
Lugano★★.

🏌, 🏌 (closed Monday) in Monza Park ⊠ 20052 Monza ℰ (039) 303081, by ② : 20 km;
🏌 Barlassina (closed Monday) in Birago di Camnago ⊠ 20030 ℰ (0362) 560621, by ① : 26 km;
🏌 Le Rovedine in Noverasco di Opera ⊠ 20090 Opera ℰ (02) 5442730, S : 8 km by via Ripamonti.
Motor-Racing circuit in Monza Park by ② : 20 km, ℰ (039) 22366.

✈ Forlanini of Linate E : 8 km ℰ 6281 and Malpensa through ⑱ : 45 km ℰ (0331) 868020 –
Alitalia, viale Luigi Sturzo 37 ⊠ 20154 ℰ 6281 and via Albricci 5 ⊠ 20122 ℰ 6281.

🚄 Porta Garibaldi ℰ 228274.

🛈 via Marconi 1 ⊠ 20123 ℰ 808813 – Central Station ⊠ 20124 ℰ 206030.

A.C.I. corso Venezia 43 ⊠ 20121 ℰ 7745.

Roma 572 ⑦ – **Genève** 323 ⑱ – **Genova** 142 ⑨ – **Torino** 140 ⑱.

MILANO

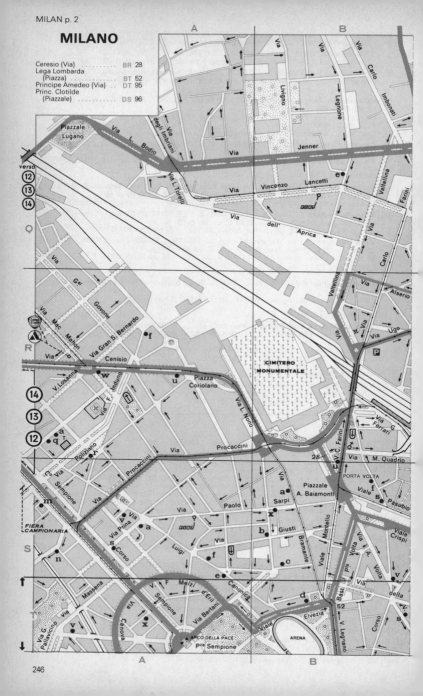

MILANO

★ PARCO SEMPIONE
★★ CASTELLO SFORZESCO
★ SANT'AMBROGIO
S⁴ M⁴ DELLE GRAZIE

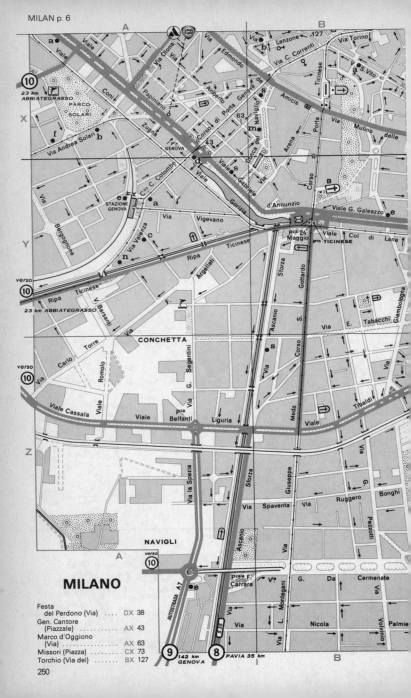

MILANO

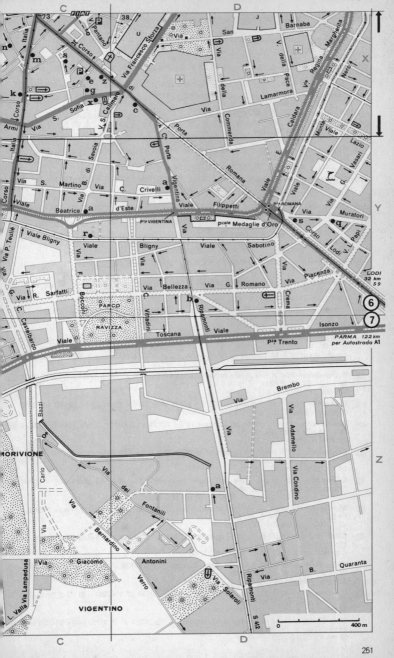

Northern area Piazza della Repubblica, Central Station, viale Zara, Stazione Porta Garibaldi, Porta Volta, corso Sempione (Plan : Milan pp. 2 and 3, except where otherwise stated)

🏨🏨🏨 **Principe e Savoia,** piazza della Repubblica 17 ⊠ 20124 ℰ 6230, Telex 310052 – 📳 🗏 📺
☎ 🅿 – 🏯.
284 rm.
DS x

🏨🏨🏨 **Palace,** piazza della Repubblica 20 ⊠ 20124 ℰ 6336, Telex 311026 – 📳 🗏 📺 ☎ 📞 🅿 –
🏯. 🝙 ⓪ 🅴 𝗩𝗜𝗦𝗔. ℅ rest
DS t
M Casanova rest. (closed Saturday) a la carte 60/75000 – 🖙 16500 – **203 rm** 236/354000.

🏨🏨🏨 **Excelsior Gallia,** piazza Duca d'Aosta 9 ⊠ 20124 ℰ 6277, Telex 311160 – 📳 🗏 📺 ☎ 📞
– 🏯. 🝙 ⓪ 🅴 𝗩𝗜𝗦𝗔. ℅ rest
DR a
M 50000 – 🖙 15000 – **252 rm** 252/320000.

🏨🏨🏨 **Milano Hilton,** via Galvani 12 ⊠ 20124 ℰ 6983, Telex 330433 – 📳 🗏 📺 ☎ 📞 🚗 –
🏯. 🝙 ⓪ 🅴 𝗩𝗜𝗦𝗔. ℅ rest
DR t
M a la carte 47/77000 – 🖙 19000 – **339 rm** 230/286000.

🏨🏨 **Executive,** viale Luigi Sturzo 45 ⊠ 20154 ℰ 6294, Telex 310191 – 📳 🗏 📺 ☎ 📞 – 🏯.
🝙 ⓪ 🅴 𝗩𝗜𝗦𝗔. ℅ rest
CRS v
M 35000 – **420 rm** 🖙 165/210000.

🏨🏨 **Michelangelo,** via Scarlatti 33 ⊠ 20124 ℰ 6755, Telex 340330 – 📳 🗏 📺 ☎ 🚗 – 🏯.
🝙 ⓪ 🅴 𝗩𝗜𝗦𝗔. ℅ rest
DR c
M 50/70000 – **280 rm** 🖙 200/250000.

🏨🏨 **Anderson** without rest., piazza Luigi di Savoia 20 ⊠ 20124 ℰ 2043741, Telex 321018 –
📳 🗏 📺 ☎ 🚗. 🝙 🅴 𝗩𝗜𝗦𝗔
DR v
closed August – 🖙 8500 – **102 rm** 115/148000.

🏨🏨 **Jolly Touring,** via Tarchetti 2 ⊠ 20121 ℰ 6335, Telex 320118 – 📳 🗏 📺 ☎ – 🏯. 🝙 ⓪
🅴 𝗩𝗜𝗦𝗔. ℅ rest
DT v
M 40000 – **270 rm** 🖙 138/188000 – P 212000.

🏨🏨 **Auriga** without rest., via Pirelli 7 ⊠ 20124 ℰ 6592851 – 📳 🗏 📺 ☎. ℅
DR f
closed August – 🖙 8500 – **65 rm** 103/129000.

🏨🏨 **Windsor** without rest., via Galilei 2 ⊠ 20124 ℰ 6346, Telex 330562 – 📳 🗏 📺 ☎ – 🏯.
🝙 ⓪ 🅴
DS j
🖙 11000 – **114 rm** 118/146000.

🏨🏨 **Atlantic** without rest., via Napo Torriani 24 ⊠ 20124 ℰ 2043941, Telex 321451 – 📳 🗏
📺 ☎ 📞 🚗. 🝙 🅴 𝗩𝗜𝗦𝗔. ℅
DS q
🖙 11000 – **62 rm** 131/180000.

🏨🏨 **Royal,** via Cardano 1 ⊠ 20124 ℰ 6709151, Telex 333167 – 📳 🗏 ☎ 📞 – 🏯. 🝙 ⓪ 🅴
𝗩𝗜𝗦𝗔. ℅
DR b
closed August – **M** (residents only) (closed Saturday and Sunday) 30000 – 🖙 10000 –
110 rm 115/155000.

🏨🏨 **Splendido** without rest., viale Andrea Doria 4 ⊠ 20124 ℰ 2050, Telex 321413 – 📳 🗏 📺
☎ – 🏯. 🝙 ⓪ 🅴 𝗩𝗜𝗦𝗔
DR x
129 rm 🖙 145/228000.

🏨🏨 **Bristol** without rest., via Scarlatti 32 ⊠ 20124 ℰ 203751 – 📳 🗏 📺 – 🏯. 🝙 ⓪ 🅴. ℅
DR u
closed August – 🖙 9500 – **71 rm** 113/152000.

🏨🏨 **Berna** without rest., via Napo Torriani 18 ⊠ 20124 ℰ 2046441, Telex 334695 – 📳 🗏
☎ – 🏯. 🝙 ⓪ 🅴 𝗩𝗜𝗦𝗔. ℅
DS a
🖙 9500 – **83 rm** 96/132000.

🏨🏨 **Europeo** without rest., via Canonica 38 ⊠ 20154 ℰ 344041, Telex 321237, 🚗 – 📳 🗏 📺
☎ 🚗 – 🏯. 🝙 🅴 𝗩𝗜𝗦𝗔. ℅
AS f
🖙 15000 – **45 rm** 80/120000.

🏨 **Lancaster** without rest., via Abbondio Sangiorgio 16 ⊠ 20145 ℰ 344705 – 📳 🗏 📺
🚿wc 🛁wc 📞. 🝙 🅴 𝗩𝗜𝗦𝗔
AT v
closed July and August – 🖙 15000 – **29 rm** 76/107000.

🏨 **Mediolanum** without rest., via Mauro Macchi 1 ⊠ 20124 ℰ 6705312, Telex 310448 – 📳
🗏 📺 🚿wc 🛁wc ☎ 📞. 🝙 𝗩𝗜𝗦𝗔
DS r
🖙 12000 – **52 rm** 75/108000.

🏨 **Club Hotel** without rest., via Copernico 18 ⊠ 20125 ℰ 606128, Telex 323816 – 📳 🗏 📺
🚿wc 🛁wc 🚗. 🝙
DR n
closed August – 🖙 10000 – **53 rm** 70/95000.

🏨 **Augustus** 🝤 without rest., via Napo Torriani 29 ⊠ 20124 ℰ 6575741, Telex 333112 – 📳
🗏 🚿wc 🛁wc ☎. 🝙 ⓪ 🅴 𝗩𝗜𝗦𝗔
DS h
🖙 9000 – **56 rm** 64/91000.

🏨 **Alexander,** without rest., via Napo Torriani 9 ⊠ 20124 ℰ 654006 – 📳 🗏 🚿wc 🛁wc ☎
🚗
DS v
65 rm.

🏨 **San Carlo** without rest., via Napo Torriani 28 ⊠ 20124 ℰ 203022, Telex 314324 – 📳 🗏
🚿wc 🛁wc ☎. 🝙 ⓪ 🅴 𝗩𝗜𝗦𝗔
DS s
62 rm 🖙 69/106000.

🏛 **Flora** without rest., via Napo Torriani 23 ⊠ 20124 ℰ 650242, Telex 312547 – 📶 ⬛ 📺
⇌wc ⊞wc ☎. 🅰🅴 ⓪ 𝘝𝘐𝘚𝘈. ⅗
DS **h**
⊊ 9000 – **45 rm** 67/98000.

🏛 **New York** without rest., via Pirelli 5 ⊠ 20124 ℰ 650551, Telex 325057 – 📶 ⇌wc ☎. 🅰🅴
⓪ 🅴 𝘝𝘐𝘚𝘈
DR **f**
closed 8 to 28 August – ⊊ 7000 – **71 rm** 65/93000.

🏛 **Cervo**, without rest., piazzale Principessa Clotilde 10 ⊠ 20121 ℰ 666112 – 📶 ⇌wc ⊞wc
⊜
DS **d**
58 rm.

🏛 **Gala** without rest., viale Zara 89 ⊠ 20159 ℰ 6890867 – 📶 ⬛ ⇌wc ⊞wc ⊛. 🅴 𝘝𝘐𝘚𝘈
closed August – ⊊ 8000 – **22 rm** 35/80000.
DQ **j**

XXX **Romani,** via Trebazio 3 ⊠ 20145 ℰ 340738 – ⬛. 🅰🅴 ⓪
AS **m**
closed Saturday lunch, Sunday and August – **M** a la carte 35/51000.

XXX **Grattacielo,** via Vittor Pisani 6 ⊠ 20124 ℰ 6592359, ⌖, « Collection of paintings by
well-known artists » – ⬛. 🅰🅴 ⓪ 𝘝𝘐𝘚𝘈
DS **y**
closed Friday dinner, Saturday, August and 26 December-4 January – **M** a la carte 25/43000
(11%).

XX **Tre Pini,** via Tullo Morgagni 19 ⊠ 20125 ℰ 6898464, « Pergola-garden » – 🅰🅴 𝘝𝘐𝘚𝘈. ⅗
closed Friday lunch, Saturday and 5 to 31 August – **M** a la carte 26/40000.
DQ **n**

XX ✿ **A Riccione,** via Taramelli 70 ⊠ 20124 ℰ 6086807, Seafood – ⬛ 🅿. 🅰🅴 ⓪ 🅴 𝘝𝘐𝘚𝘈
closed Monday – **M** (booking essential) a la carte 50/70000
DQ **a**
Spec. Paella valenciana e di solo pesce, Fritto misto e grigliata mista di pesce alla brace. Wines del Collio,
Barbaresco.

XX **Da Lino Buriassi,** via Lecco angolo via Casati 12 ⊠ 20124 ℰ 273383 – ⬛. 🅰🅴 𝘝𝘐𝘚𝘈
closed Saturday lunch, Sunday and 4 to 19 August – **M** (booking essential)
a la carte 25/35000.
DT **g**

XX **Cavallini,** via Mauro Macchi 2 ⊠ 20124 ℰ 200297, ⌖ – ⬛. 🅰🅴 ⓪ 🅴 𝘝𝘐𝘚𝘈
DS **p**
closed Saturday lunch, Sunday, August and 24 December-3 January – **M**
a la carte 22/34000 (12%).

XX ✿ **Alfredo-Gran San Bernardo,** via Borgese 14 ⊠ 20154 ℰ 389000 – ⬛
AR **f**
closed Sunday, August and 21 December-19 January – **M** (booking essential)
a la carte 30/39000
Spec. Risotto alla milanese ed al salto, Costoletta alla milanese, Foiolo (trippa). Wines Barbera, Barbaresco.

XX **Altopascio,** via Gustavo Fara 17 ⊠ 20124 ℰ 6702458, Tuscan rest. – ⬛. 🅰🅴 🅴
DS **e**
closed Saturday, Sunday lunch and August – **M** a la carte 18/30000 (11%).

X **Antica Trattoria della Pesa,** viale Pasubio 10 ⊠ 20154 ℰ 665741, Old Milan typical
trattoria with Lombardy specialities – ⬛
BS **s**
closed Sunday and August – **M** a la carte 24/36000.

X ✿ **Casa Fontana,** piazza Carbonari 5 ⊠ 20124 ℰ 6892684 – ⬛. 🅰🅴 𝘝𝘐𝘚𝘈. ⅗
DQ **s**
closed 1 to 20 August, Saturday lunch, Sunday and 15 June - 31 July – **M** (booking
essential) a la carte 25/36000 (15%)
Spec. Risotti della Casa, Rognoncini di vitello al Cognac, Filetti alla menta. Wines Trebbiano, Sizzano.

X **Pechino,** via Cenisio 7 ⊠ 20154 ℰ 384668, Chinese rest. with Pekinese specialities – ⬛
closed Monday, 15 July-22 August and 20 December-4 January – **M** a la carte 20/27000
(12%).
AR **u**

Central area Duomo, Scala, Sempione Park, Sforza Castle, Public gardens, corso Venezia,
via Manzoni, North Station, corso Magenta, Porta Vittoria (Plan : Milan pp. 4 and 5)

🏨 **Gd H. Duomo,** via San Raffaele 1 ⊠ 20121 ℰ 8833, Telex 312086 – 📶 ⬛ ☎ ᵹ. 🅴 𝘝𝘐𝘚𝘈
⅗
CV **m**
M 30/40000 – ⊊ 10000 – **160 rm** 135/210000 – P 155/195000.

🏨 **Jolly President,** largo Augusto 10 ⊠ 20122 ℰ 7746, Telex 312054 – 📶 ⬛ 📺 ☎ – 🏛.
🅰🅴 ⓪ 🅴 𝘝𝘐𝘚𝘈. ⅗ rest
DV **t**
M 45000 – **201 rm** ⊊ 170/210000 – P 250000.

🏨 **Galileo** without rest., corso Europa 9 ⊠ 20122 ℰ 7743, Telex 322095 – 📶 ⬛ 📺 ☎. ⅗
76 rm ⊊ 190/275000.
DV **a**

🏨 **Plaza** without rest., piazza Diaz 3 ⊠ 20123 ℰ 8058452, Telex 321162 – 📶 ⬛ 📺 ☎ – 🏛.
🅰🅴 ⓪. ⅗
CV **r**
closed 1 to 21 August – ⊊ 14000 – **118 rm** 176/225000.

🏨 **Carlton Hotel Senato,** via Senato 5 ⊠ 20121 ℰ 798583, Telex 331306 – 📶 ⬛ 📺 ☎
⇌. 🅰🅴 🅴 𝘝𝘐𝘚𝘈. ⅗ rest
DU **q**
closed August – **M** (closed Saturday and Sunday) a la carte 31/47000 – ⊊ 9500 – **73 rm**
115/143000.

🏨 **Grand Hotel et de Milan,** without rest., via Manzoni 29 ⊠ 20121 ℰ 870757, Telex 334505
– 📶 ⬛ ☎ – 🏛
CDU **f**
90 rm.

🏨 **Cavour,** via Fatebenefratelli 21 ⊠ 20121 ℰ 650983, Telex 320498 – 📶 ⬛ 📺 ☎ ᵹ. 🅰🅴
⓪ 🅴 𝘝𝘐𝘚𝘈. ⅗ rest
DU **n**
M (closed Friday dinner, Saturday and Sunday lunch) 36000 – ⊊ 11000 – **113 rm**
119/138000.

Select without rest., via Baracchini 12 ⊠ 20123 𝒫 8843, Telex 312256 – 🛗 🗐 📺 ☎ –
🏠. 🖭 ⓘ E 𝘝𝘐𝘚𝘈   CV **s**
140 rm ⊊ 135/180000.

Dei Cavalieri without rest., piazza Missori 1 ⊠ 20123 𝒫 8857, Telex 312040 – 🛗 🗐 📺
☎ – 🏠. 🖭 ⓘ E 𝘝𝘐𝘚𝘈   CVX **c**
⊊ 9000 – **175 rm** 111/155000.

Manin, via Manin 7 ⊠ 20121 𝒫 6596511, Telex 320385, 🌫 – 🛗 🗐 📺 🗐 ᬶ – 🏠. 🖭
𝘝𝘐𝘚𝘈. 🍴 rest   DU **b**
closed 3 to 19 August – **M** (closed Saturday and Sunday) a la carte 31/48000 – ⊊ 12000
– **106 rm** 125/160000 – P 150/195000.

De la Ville without rest., via Hoepli 6 ⊠ 20121 𝒫 867651, Telex 312642 – 🛗 🗐 📺 ☎. 🖭
E 𝘝𝘐𝘚𝘈. 🍴   CV **v**
⊊ 12000 – **105 rm** 145/175000.

Gran Duca di York without rest., via Moneta 1/a ⊠ 20123 𝒫 874863 – 🛗 🗐 📺 ᬶ –
🏠. 🍴   BV **s**
closed August – ⊊ 7000 – **33 rm** 65/95000.

Ariosto without rest., via Ariosto 22 ⊠ 20145 𝒫 490995 – 🛗 🗐 – 🏠. 🖭 ⓘ E 𝘝𝘐𝘚𝘈. 🍴
⊊ 6500 – **53 rm** 68/97000.   AU **c**

Manzoni without rest., via Santo Spirito 20 ⊠ 20121 𝒫 705700 – 🛗 ⌂wc 🗐wc ☎ ⇦.
🍴   DU **g**
⊊ 7000 – **52 rm** 67/97000.

Casa Svizzera without rest., via San Raffaele 3 ⊠ 20121 𝒫 802246, Telex 316064 – 🛗
🗐 📺 ⌂wc 🗐wc ☎. 🖭 ⓘ E 𝘝𝘐𝘚𝘈   CV **m**
closed 28 July-24 August – **45 rm** ⊊ 72/106000.

Lord Internazionale without rest., via Spadari 11 ⊠ 20123 𝒫 803028 – 🛗 🗐 ⌂wc
🗐wc ⇦. 🖭   CV **t**
⊊ 6000 – **46 rm** 69/98000.

Centro without rest., via Broletto 46 ⊠ 20121 𝒫 875232, Telex 332632 – 🛗 🗐 ⌂wc
🗐wc ⇦. 🖭 ⓘ E 𝘝𝘐𝘚𝘈. 🍴   BU **e**
54 rm ⊊ 76/112000.

Star without rest., via dei Bossi 5 ⊠ 20121 𝒫 871703 – 🛗 🗐 🗐wc ⇦. 🍴   CU **b**
closed August – ⊊ 6000 – **28 rm** 55/82000, 🗐 5500.

XXXXX ❀ **Savini,** galleria Vittorio Emanuele II° ⊠ 20121 𝒫 8058343, Elegant traditional decor,
« Winter garden » – 🗐. 🖭 ⓘ E 𝘝𝘐𝘚𝘈   CV **n**
closed Sunday, 10 to 19 August and 23 December-3 January – **M** (booking essential)
a la carte 52/82000 (15%)
Spec. Risotto alla milanese ed al salto, Costoletta alla milanese, Filetto di bue all'Armagnac. **Wines** Pinot,
Barbera.

XXXX **El Toulà,** piazza Paolo Ferrari 6 ⊠ 20121 𝒫 870302, Elegant installation – 🗐. 🖭 ⓘ E
𝘝𝘐𝘚𝘈   CU **z**
closed 6 July-21 August, Saturday and Sunday in June-August – **M** a la carte 44/65000
(13%).

XXXX **St. Andrews,** via Sant'Andrea 23 ⊠ 20121 𝒫 793132, Elegant installation, late night
dinners – 🗐. 🖭 ⓘ E 𝘝𝘐𝘚𝘈. 🍴   DU **y**
closed Sunday and August – **M** (booking essential) a la carte 45/68000 (20%).

XXXX **Biffi Scala,** piazza della Scala ⊠ 20121 𝒫 876332, Tea-room and late night dinners –
🗐. 🖭 ⓘ E 𝘝𝘐𝘚𝘈   CU **z**
closed Sunday and August – **M** a la carte 35/60000 (13%).

XXX **Suntory,** via Verdi 6 ⊠ 20121 𝒫 862210, Japanese rest. – 🗐. 🖭 ⓘ 𝘝𝘐𝘚𝘈. 🍴   CU **n**
closed Sunday and 12 to 19 August – **M** a la carte 39/63000.

XXX **Prospero,** via Chiossetto 20 ⊠ 20122 𝒫 701345 – 🗐. 🖭 ⓘ E 𝘝𝘐𝘚𝘈   DV **e**
closed Saturday, Sunday and August – **M** a la carte 23/35000.

XXX **Luciano,** via Ugo Foscolo 1 ⊠ 20121 𝒫 866818 – 🗐. 🖭 ⓘ E 𝘝𝘐𝘚𝘈   CV **a**
closed Saturday and 10 to 28 August – **M** a la carte 37/45000 (12%).

XXX **Alfio,** via Senato 31 ⊠ 20121 𝒫 780731 – 🗐. 🖭 ⓘ E 𝘝𝘐𝘚𝘈   DU **a**
closed Saturday, Sunday lunch, 9 to 26 August and 23 December-3 January – **M**
a la carte 35/48000.

XXX **Crispi,** corso Venezia 3 ⊠ 20121 𝒫 782010, 🌤 – 🗐. 🖭 ⓘ E 𝘝𝘐𝘚𝘈   DU **v**
closed Monday and 11 to 31 August – **M** a la carte 36/45000 (12%).

XXX **Rigoletto,** via Vincenzo Monti 33 ⊠ 20123 𝒫 4988687, Rest. and piano-bar – 🗐. 🖭 ⓘ
𝘝𝘐𝘚𝘈   AU **b**
closed Sunday and August – **M** a la carte 27/42000.

XXX L'Innominato, via Fiori Oscuri 3 ⊠ 20121 𝒫 8690552, Rest. and piano-bar – 🗐   CU **r**

XXX **Barbarossa,** via Cerva 10 ⊠ 20122 𝒫 781418, Old Milan-style setting – 🗐. 🖭 ⓘ 𝘝𝘐𝘚𝘈.
🍴   DV **f**
closed August, Sunday and in July also Saturday – **M** a la carte 27/38000.

XXX 4 Mori, via San Giovanni sul Muro 2 ⊠ 20121 𝒫 870617, « Summer service in garden » –
🗐   BU **d**

XXX **Boeucc,** piazza Belgioioso 2 ✉ 20121 ℰ 790224, 🍽 – 🍴. 🆎. ✘ CDU **x**
    closed Friday dinner, Saturday and August – **M** (booking essential) a la carte 28/43000.

XXX **Peck,** via Victor Hugo 4 ✉ 20123 ℰ 87677 – 🍴. 🆎 ⓪ Ⓔ 𝗩𝗜𝗦𝗔 CV **b**
    closed Sunday – **M** a la carte 31/47000.

XX **La Lanterna,** via Novati 2 ✉ 20123 ℰ 8052497 – 🍴 BX **b**
    closed Monday lunch and August – **M** (booking essential) a la carte 36/48000.

XX **Kota Radja,** piazzale Baracca 6 ✉ 20123 ℰ 468850, Chinese rest. – 🍴. 🆎 ⓪ 𝗩𝗜𝗦𝗔 AU **a**
    closed Monday – **M** a la carte 15/48000 (12%).

XX **Bagutta,** via Bagutta 14 ✉ 20121 ℰ 702767, 🍽, Artists' meeting place, « Typical
   paintings and caricatures » – 🆎 ⓪ Ⓔ 𝗩𝗜𝗦𝗔 DU **e**
    closed Sunday, 7 to 31 August and 23 December-5 January – **M** a la carte 28/42000 (12%).

XX **Al Mercante,** piazza Mercanti 17 ✉ 20123 ℰ 8052198, « Outdoor service in summer »
   – 🆎. CV **k**
    closed Saturday lunch, Sunday and 5 to 25 August – **M** a la carte 24/34000.

XX **Boccondivino,** via Carducci 17 ✉ 20123 ℰ 866040, Typical pork-butcher's meat, cheese
   and wines – 🍴. AV **e**
    closed Sunday and August – **M** (dinner only) (booking essential) a la carte 24/34000.

XX **Albric,** via Albricci 3 ✉ 20122 ℰ 806356, « Collection of paintings » – 🍴. 🆎 ⓪ Ⓔ 𝗩𝗜𝗦𝗔.
   ✘ CV **q**
    closed Sunday and 25 July-25 August – **M** a la carte 28/41000.

XX **I Matteoni,** piazzale 5 Giornate 6 ✉ 20129 ℰ 588293, Habitués' rest. – 🍴. 🆎 Ⓔ 𝗩𝗜𝗦𝗔 DV **s**
    closed Sunday and August – **M** a la carte 22/34000.

X **Trattoria dell'Angolo,** via Formentini 9 ✉ 20121 ℰ 8058495 – 🍴 CU **e**
    closed Saturday lunch, Sunday and 10 to 26 August – **M** a la carte 21/32000.

X **Trattoria al Piccolo Teatro,** via Rovello angolo via Cusani 9 ✉ 20121 ℰ 877127,
   Typical rest. – 🍴 BU **v**
    closed Saturday lunch, Sunday and August – **M** (booking essential) a la carte 29/35000.

X **Francesco,** via Festa del Perdono 4 ✉ 20122 ℰ 8053071 – 🍴. 🆎 ⓪ Ⓔ 𝗩𝗜𝗦𝗔. ✘ DV **n**
    closed Sunday, 12 to 24 August and 23 to 31 December – **M** a la carte 21/36000.

X **Allo Scudo,** via Mazzini 7 ✉ 20123 ℰ 8052761, Habitués' rest. – 🍴. 🆎 ⓪. ✘ CV **e**
    closed Sunday and August – **M** a la carte 17/32000 (10%).

X **Al Chico,** via Sirtori 24 ✉ 20129 ℰ 2716883, 🍽, Tuscan rest. – 𝗩𝗜𝗦𝗔 DU **s**
    closed Saturday lunch, Sunday, 31 July-24 August and 24 December-3 January – **M**
    a la carte 23/41000.

Southern area Porta Ticinese, Porta Romana, Genova Station, Navigli, Ravizza Park,
Vientino (Plan : Milan pp. 6 and 7) :

🏨 **Lloyd** without rest., corso di Porta Romana 48 ✉ 20122 ℰ 867971, Telex 335028, « Collection of paintings by well-known artists » – 📶 🍴 📺 ☎ – 🅰. 🆎 Ⓔ 𝗩𝗜𝗦𝗔 CX **z**
   ⊠ 10000 – **52 rm** 110/150000.

🏨 **Ascot** without rest., via Lentasio 3 ✉ 20122 ℰ 862946, Telex 311303 – 📶 🍴 ☎ 🚗. 🆎
   ⓪ Ⓔ 𝗩𝗜𝗦𝗔. ✘ CX **e**
    closed August – ⊠ 13000 – **56 rm** 108/154000.

🏨 **Crivi's** without rest., corso di Porta Vigentina 46 ✉ 20122 ℰ 5463341, Telex 313255 – 📶 🍴
   📺 ☎ 🚗 – 🅰. DY **a**
    closed August – ⊠ 10000 – **62 rm** 112/150000.

🏨 **D'Este** without rest., viale Bligny 23 ✉ 20136 ℰ 5461041, Telex 324216 – 📶 🍴 📺 ☎ 👤
   – 🅰. 🆎 Ⓔ 𝗩𝗜𝗦𝗔 CY **r**
   ⊠ 10000 – **54 rm** 62/88000.

🏨 **Sant'Ambroeus** without rest., viale Papiniano 14 ✉ 20123 ℰ 4697451, Telex 313373 –
   📶 🍴 👤 – 🅰. 🆎 ⓪ Ⓔ 𝗩𝗜𝗦𝗔 AX **a**
    closed August – ⊠ 7000 – **52 rm** 73/97000.

🏨 **Ambrosiano** without rest., via Santa Sofia 9 ✉ 20122 ℰ 580445 – 📶 🍴 ☎ Ⓟ. 🆎 ⓪ Ⓔ
   𝗩𝗜𝗦𝗔. ✘ CX **x**
    closed 20 July-26 August and 24 December-7 January – ⊠ 7000 – **68 rm** 63/91000.

🏨 **Mediterraneo** without rest., via Muratori 14 ✉ 20135 ℰ 5488151, Telex 335812 – 📶 🍴
   📺 ⌂wc 🍴wc ☎ – 🅰. 🆎 Ⓔ 𝗩𝗜𝗦𝗔 DY **q**
   ⊠ 6500 – **93 rm** 70/101000, 🍴 2500.

🏨 **Adriatico** without rest., via Conca del Naviglio 20 ✉ 20123 ℰ 8324141 – 📶 🍴 📺 ⌂wc
   🍴wc 🅿. 🆎 ⓪ Ⓔ 𝗩𝗜𝗦𝗔 BX **m**
   ⊠ 6500 – **105 rm** 68/98000.

🏨 **Imperial** without rest., corso di Porta Romana 68 ✉ 20122 ℰ 5468241 – 🍴 📺 ⌂wc
   🍴wc ☎ 👤 Ⓟ. 🆎 Ⓔ 𝗩𝗜𝗦𝗔. ✘ DX **c**
   ⊠ 9000 – **36 rm** 62/90000.

🏨 **Garden** without rest., via Rutilia 6 ✉ 20141 ℰ 537368 – 🍴wc 🅿️ Ⓟ DZ **a**
    closed August – ⊠ 5000 – **23 rm** 36/50000.

XXX La Nôs, via Amedei 2 ✉ 20123 ☎ 8058759, Elegant old Milan-style meeting-place, « 19C decor » – ▤ CX n

XXX **Vecchia Milano,** viale Gian Galeazzo 25 ✉ 20136 ☎ 8397365, Arabian rest. – ▤. ⓓ E VISA. ✻ BY e
closed Monday and 1 to 20 August – **M** a la carte 28/44000 (12%).

XXX **Malatesta,** via Bianca di Savoia 19 ✉ 20122 ☎ 5461079 – ▤. AE VISA. ✻ CY a
closed Saturday, Sunday and August – **M** a la carte 40/45000.

XXX ✲ **San Vito da Nino,** via San Vito 5 ✉ 20123 ☎ 8377029 – ▤. VISA. ✻ BX a
closed Monday and August – **M** (booking essential) a la carte 40/56000 (13%)
Spec. Gingillo tartufato, Pollo allo Champagne, Costa di manzo alla bourguignonne. **Wines** Fiano, Barbaresco.

XXX ✲✲ **Scaletta,** piazzale stazione Porta Genova ✉ 20144 ☎ 8350290 – ▤. ✻ AY a
closed Sunday, Monday, 5 to 16 April, August and 24 December-7 January – **M** (booking essential) a la carte 60/70000
Spec. Risotto con porcini e mirtilli, Animella all'aglio, Insalata di scampi. **Wines** Pinot di Franciacorta, Monte Vertine.

XX ✲ **Al Porto,** piazzale Generale Cantore ✉ 20123 ☎ 8321481, Seafood – ▤ AXY d
closed Sunday, Monday lunch, August and 24 December-3 January – **M** (booking essential) a la carte 33/46000
Spec. Orata al pepe rosa, Scamponi gratinati, Branzino al verde. **Wines** Franciacorta Pinot, Riesling.

XX **Giordano,** via Torti angolo corso Genova 3 ✉ 20123 ☎ 8350824, Neo rustic Bolognese cuisine – ▤. AE ⓓ BX s
closed Sunday and 5 to 28 August – **M** a la carte 23/32000 (12%).

XX **Osteria del Binari,** via Tortona 1 ✉ 20144 ☎ 8399428, ☂, Old Milan atmosphere
closed Sunday and August – **M** (dinner only) (booking essential) a la carte 30/35000. AY e

XX **La Tavolozza,** via Solari 7 ✉ 20144 ☎ 8390084, ☂ – ▤. AE ⓓ E VISA AX b
closed Sunday and August – **M** a la carte 23/38000.

X **Osteria Via Pré,** via Casale 4 ✉ 20144 ☎ 8373869, Typical trattoria Ligurian cuisine – ▤ – *closed Monday, Tuesday and July* – **M** a la carte 23/32000. AY c

Districts : Città Studi, Monforte, corso 22 Marzo, viale Corsica – E : by : Linate Airport, Idroscalo, strada Rivoltana :

🏨 **Zefiro** without rest., via Gallina 12 ✉ 20129 ☎ 7384253 – |☰| ▤ ⌂wc ⋒wc ☎ – 🅰. ✻
closed 27 July-1 September – ☕ 7000 – **55 rm** 63/90000. by corso Concordia DU

🏨 **Vittoria** without rest., via Pietro Calvi 32 ✉ 20129 ☎ 5459695 – |☰| ▤ ⌂wc ⋒wc ☎. AE. ✻ by corso 22 Marzo DV
closed 27 July-27 August and 23 December-1 January – ☕ 6000 – **18 rm** 52/76000, ▤ 2000.

🏨 **Città Studi** without rest., via Saldini 24 ✉ 20133 ☎ 744666 – |☰| ⌂wc ⋒wc ☎. AE
☕ 4500 – **45 rm** 36/52000. by corso Concordia DU

XXXX ✲ **Giannino,** via Amatore Sciesa 8 ✉ 20135 ☎ 5452948, Traditional style, « Original decor; winter garden » – Ⓟ. AE ⓓ E VISA. ✻ by corso 22 Marzo DV
closed Sunday and August – **M** a la carte 48/73000
Spec. Risotto alla Giannino, Baccalà in tre modi, Ossobuco del buongustaio. **Wines** Gavi, Dolcetto.

XXXX ✲✲ **Gualtiero Marchesi,** via Bonvesin de la Riva 9 ✉ 20129 ☎ 741246, Elegant installation – ▤. AE. ✻ by corso 22 Marzo DV
closed Sunday (in July also Saturday), Monday lunch, 1 to 6 January, 1 to 7 April and August – **M** (booking essential) a la carte 60/90000
Spec. Lasagne fresche al burro di basilico noci di capesante, Filetti di triglia impanati e sedani brasati, Medaglioni di vitello e verdure brasate in agrodolce. **Wines** Prosecco, Settefilari.

XX **La Bella Pisana,** via Pasquale Sottocorno 17 ✉ 20129 ☎ 708376, ☂ – ▤. AE VISA
closed Sunday, Monday lunch, 4 to 31 August and 25 December-5 January – **M** a la carte 25/38000. by corso Concordia DU

XX **La Pesa-da Rino,** via Morosini 12 ✉ 20135 ☎ 592058, Habituès' rest. – ▤. AE ⓓ E VISA by corso 22 Marzo DV
closed Wednesday and 1 to 28 August – **M** a la carte 24/35000.

XX **Palazzo del Ghiaccio,** via Piranesi 14 ✉ 20137 ☎ 7398 – ▤. ✻
closed Monday and August – **M** a la carte 20/29000. by corso 22 Marzo DV

X **Il Palio di Siena,** via Turroni 4 ✉ 20129 ☎ 7387928, ☂, Tuscan trattoria – VISA
closed Sunday dinner, Monday and August – **M** a la carte 21/32000. by corso Concordia DU

X **Al Grissino,** via Tiepolo 54 ✉ 20129 ☎ 730392 – ▤ by corso Concordia DU
closed Sunday dinner, Wednesday and August – **M** a la carte 31/45000.

Districts : Fiera Campionaria, San Siro, Porta Magenta – NW : by ⑩ and ⑪ : Novara, Torino :

🏨 **Gd H. Fieramilano,** viale Boezio 20 ✉ 20145 ☎ 3105, Telex 331426 – |☰| ▤ 📺 ☎ ♿ – 🅰. AE ⓓ E VISA. ✻ rest by via Vincenzo Monti AT
M 35000 – **238 rm** ☕ 165/210000.

🏨 **Gd H. Brun,** via Caldera ✉ 20153 ☎ 45271, Telex 315370 – |☰| ▤ 📺 ☎ ♿ – 🅰. AE ⓓ E VISA by corso Sempione AS
M a la carte 35/59000 – **330 rm** ☕ 165/220000.

🏨 **Rubens** without rest., via Rubens 21 ✉ 20148 ℘ 405051, Telex 333503 – 🛗 🗐 📺 ☎ 🅿
– 🛡. 🅰🅴 🅴 *VISA* 🕸.   by corso Vercelli   AV
closed 1 to 21 August – ⊷ 8000 – **76 rm** 73/107000.

🏨 **Montebianco** without rest., via Monte Rosa 90 ✉ 20149 ℘ 4697941 – 🛗 🗐 ☎ & 🅿. 🅰🅴
🅾🅴 *VISA* 🕸.   by ⑪
closed August and Christmas – ⊷ 7000 – **44 rm** 74/105000.

🏨 **Capitol** without rest., via Cimarosa 6 ✉ 20144 ℘ 4988851, Telex 316150 – 🛗 🗐 📺 ☎ –
🛡. 🅰🅴 🅾🅴 🅴   by corso Vercelli   AV
96 rm ⊷ 102/142000.

🏩 **Fiera** without rest., via Spinola 9 ✉ 20149 ℘ 432374, « Little garden » – 🛗 ⇌wc 🚿wc
☎ ⟷ – 🛡. 🕸   by ⑪
⊷ 7000 – **29 rm** 65/94000.

🏩 **Astoria**, viale Murillo 9 ✉ 20149 ℘ 4046646, Telex 334201 – 🛗 🗐 ⇌wc 🚿wc ☎ – 🛡.
🅰🅴 🅾🅴 🅴 *VISA* 🕸   by ⑪
M *(closed Sunday)* 18/30000 – **72 rm** ⊷ 75/125000 – P 90/140000.

🏩 **Wagner** without rest., via Buonarroti 13 ✉ 20149 ℘ 4696051 – 🛗 🗐 ⇌wc 🚿wc 🕸. 🅰🅴
🅾🅴 🅴 *VISA*   by ⑪
⊷ 6500 – **49 rm** 64/92000, 🗐 4500.

XXX **La Corba,** via dei Gigli 14 ✉ 20147 ℘ 4158977, �, « Summer service in garden »
closed Sunday dinner, Monday and 8 to 24 August – **M** a la carte 28/40000.   by ⑩

XX **Raffaello**, via Raffaello Sanzio 8 ✉ 20149 ℘ 495227, � – 🅰🅴 🅾🅴 🅴 *VISA*
closed Friday, Saturday lunch and 5 to 22 August – **M** a la carte 24/43000.   by ⑪

XX ✿ **Da Aimo**, via Montecuccoli 6 ✉ 20147 ℘ 416886, � – 🗐. 🅰🅴. 🕸   by ⑩
closed Saturday lunch, Sunday and August – **M** a la carte 35/51000
Spec. Calamari ripieni con erbe e formaggi freschi, Risotto con fiori di zucca e tartufi bianchi, Filetto di
manzo in insalata.

XX **Da Gino e Franco,** largo Domodossola 2 ✉ 20145 ℘ 312003 – 🗐. 🕸
closed Monday and 25 July-25 August – **M** a la carte 24/40000 (12%).
     by corso Sempione   AS

XX **Ribot,** via Cremosano 41 ✉ 20148 ℘ 390646, « Summer service in garden » – 🅿. *VISA*.
     by ⑪
closed Monday and August – **M** a la carte 27/39000.

XX **Al Garfagnino**, via Cherubini 8 ✉ 20145 ℘ 495191 – 🗐. 🅰🅴 🅾🅴 🅴 *VISA*. 🕸   by ⑪
closed Monday and July – **M** a la carte 18/29000.

X **Pace,** via Washington 74 ✉ 20146 ℘ 468567, Habitués' rest. – *VISA*. 🕸   by ⑩
closed Tuesday dinner, Wednesday and August – **M** a la carte 19/31000.

Districts : Sempione-Bullona, viale Certosa – NW : by ⑫ ⑬ and ⑭ : Varese, Como,
Torino, Malpensa Airport :

🏨 **Raffaello** without rest., viale Certosa 108 ✉ 20156 ℘ 3270146, Telex 315499 – 🛗 🗐 📺
☎ – 🛡. 🅰🅴 🅴 *VISA*.   by via Cenisio   AR
⊷ 7000 – **109 rm** 60/87000.

🏩 **Berlino** without rest., via Plana 33 ✉ 20155 ℘ 367732, Telex 312609 – 🛗 🗐 ⇌wc 🚿wc
☎ – 🛡. 🅴 *VISA*   by via Cenisio   AR
⊷ 6000 – **47 rm** 62/89000.

🏠 **Mac Mahon** without rest., via Mac Mahon 45/a ✉ 20155 ℘ 341281 – 🛗 ⇌wc 🚿wc 🕸.
🅰🅴.   by via Mac Mahon   AR
closed August – ⊷ 6000 – **27 rm** 42/65000.

XX **La Pobbia,** via Gallarate 92 ✉ 20151 ℘ 305641, Neo rustic rest., « Outdoor service in
summer » – 🅿. 🅰🅴.   by via Cenisio   AR
closed Sunday and August – **M** a la carte 26/40000 (12%).

X **Da Stefano il Marchigiano,** via Plana angolo via Arimondi 1 ✉ 20155 ℘ 390863 – 🅰🅴
VISA. 🕸   by via Cenisio   AR
closed Friday dinner, Saturday and August – **M** a la carte 22/37000.

X **Al Vöttantott,** corso Sempione 88 ✉ 20154 ℘ 3182114, Habitués trattoria – 🗐. 🅰🅴
closed Sunday and August – **M** a la carte 21/29000.   by corso Sempione   AS

Abbiategrasso 20081 Milano 🖳🖳🖳 ③, 🖳🖳🖳 ⑱ – pop. 27 264 – ✪ 02.
Roma 590 – Alessandria 74 – Milano 23 – Novara 29 – Pavia 33.

at Cassinetta di Lugagnano N : 3 km – ✉ 20081 :

XXX ✿✿ **Antica Osteria del Ponte,** ℘ 9420034 – 🗐 🅿. 🅰🅴. 🕸
closed Sunday, Monday, 1 to 15 January and August – **M** (booking essential)
a la carte 60/80000
Spec. e. Wines Chef's recommandation.

EUROPE on a single sheet **Michelin** map no 🖳🖳🖳.

NAPOLI

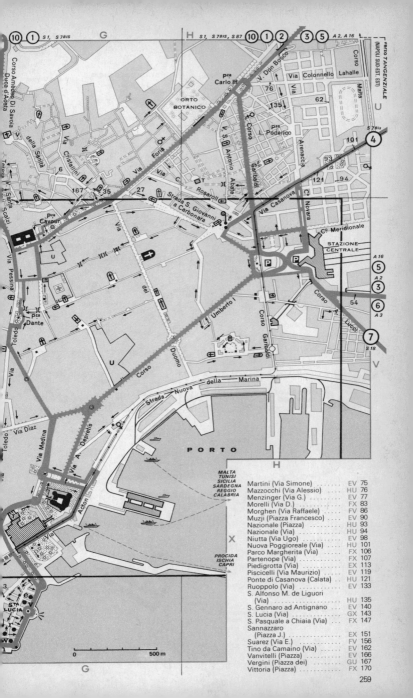

259

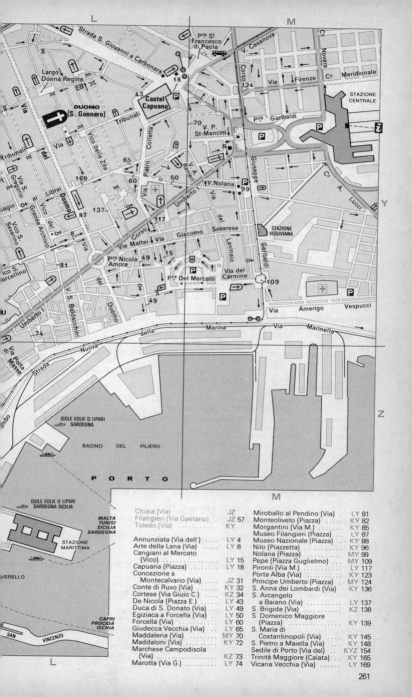

NAPLES (NAPOLI) 80100 **□□□** ㉗ – pop. 1 209 086 – h.s. April-October – **✿** 081.

See : On the sea-front : Castel Nuovo★★ (triumphal arc★★) KZ, San Carlo Theatre★ KZ **T**, piazza del Plebiscito★ JKZ, Royal Palace★ KZ – Port of Santa Lucia★★ (≤★★★ of the gulf) – Mergellina★ (≤★★ of the gulf).

National Archaeological Museum★★★ KY : Graeco-Roman sculptures★★★; mosaics★★; collections★★ of small bronzes, paintings and various objects from Herculaneum and Pompeii – Carthusian Monastery of St. Martin★★ JZ : historical collections (presepi★★), from Belvedere (room n° 25) ≤★★★ of the Bay of Naples, Baroque church★ (the monks' chancel★★) – Capodimonte Palace and National Galleries★★ : picture gallery★★, Royal apartments (the porcelain room★★).

Spacca-Napoli quarter★★ KY : St. Chiara Church★ KY**C** (tomb★★ of King Robert the Wise, the cloisters★) – Cathedral : Chapel of San Gennaro★ LY.

Envir. : Island of Capri★★★ – Island of Ischia★★★ – Vesuvius★★★ (ascent of the volcano★★★, ※★★★), E : 23 km and chairlift – Pompeii★★★ (excavations), SE : 24 km – Herculaneum★★ (excavations), SE : 9 km.

✈ Ugo Niutta of Capodichino NE : 6 km ✆ 312211 – Alitalia, via Miguel Cervantes 78 ✉ 80133 ✆ 325325.

⛴ to Capri March-October daily (1 h 30 mn about) – Navigazione Libera del Golfo, molo Beverello ✆ 325589; to Capri, Ischia and Procida daily (1 h 30 mn) – Agency De Luca, molo Beverello ✆ 313882; to Cagliari Wednesday and Sunday (15 h) and Palermo daily (10 h); to Reggio di Calabria (10,30 h), Catania (15 h) and Siracusa (19 h) : Thursday – Tirrenia Navigazione, Stazione Marittima, molo Angioino ✉ 80133 ✆ 312181, Telex 710030; to Ischia daily (1 h 15 mn) – Libera Navigazione Lauro, via Caracciolo 11 ✆ 991889, Telex 720354 and Agency de Luca, molo Beverello ✆ 313882.

⛴ to Capri, Ischia and Procida daily (30/45 mn) – Agency De Luca, molo Beverello ✆ 313882; to Capri daily (45 mn), Sorrento 15 June-15 September daily (25 mn) and Ischia daily (45 mn) – Alilauro, via Caracciolo 11 ✆ 682017, Telex 720354; to Capri daily (30/45 mn) – SNAV, via Caracciolo 10 ✆ 660444, Telex 720446.

🛈 via Partenope 10/a ✉ 80121 ✆ 406289 – piazza del Plebiscito (Royal Palace) ✉ 80132 ✆ 418744 – Central Station ✉ 80142 ✆ 268779 – Capodichino Airport ✉ 80133 ✆ 7805761.

A.C.I. piazzale Tecchio 49/d ✉ 80125 ✆ 611084.

Roma 219 ③ – Bari 261 ⑤.

Plans on preceding pages

🏨🏨🏨 **Excelsior,** via Partenope 48 ✉ 80121 ✆ 417111, Telex 710043, ≤ gulf, Vesuvio and Castel dell'Ovo – 🛗 ▤ 📺 ☎ – 🔬 – 🔬. 🅰🅴 ⓞ 🄴 𝗩𝗜𝗦𝗔. ※ GX **w**
   M a la carte 61/91000 – ⵚ 14500 – **137 rm** 202/310000.

🏨🏨 **Vesuvio,** via Partenope 45 ✉ 80121 ✆ 417044, Telex 710127, « Roof-garden rest. with ≤ gulf and Castel dell'Ovo » – 🛗 ▤ 📺 ☎ – 🔬 – 🔬. 🅰🅴 ⓞ 🄴 𝗩𝗜𝗦𝗔. ※ rest FX **n**
   M a la carte 32/45000 – **179 rm** ⵚ 132/186000.

🏨🏨 **Jolly,** via Medina 70 ✉ 80133 ✆ 416000, Telex 720335, « Roof-garden rest. with ≤ town » – 🛗 ▤ 📺 ☎ – 🔬. 🅰🅴 ⓞ 🄴 𝗩𝗜𝗦𝗔. ※ rest KZ **s**
   M 35000 – **278 rm** ⵚ 110/140000 – P 160000.

🏨🏨 Royal, via Partenope 38 ✉ 80121 ✆ 400244, Telex 710167, ≤ gulf, Posillipo and Castel dell'Ovo, ⌇ – 🛗 ▤ 📺 ☎ – ⭤ – 🔬 – **300 rm**. FX **n**

🏨🏨 **Britannique,** corso Vittorio Emanuele 133 ✉ 80121 ✆ 660933, Telex 722281, ≤, 🌁 – 🛗 ▤ ⭤ – 🔬. 🅰🅴 ⓞ 🄴 𝗩𝗜𝗦𝗔. ※ rest EX **r**
   M 25000 – ⵚ 9000 – **80 rm** 90/140000 – P 110/120000.

🏨🏨 **San Germano,** via Beccadelli 41 ✉ 80125 ✆ 7605422, Telex 720080, « Beautiful garden-park », ⌇ – 🛗 ▤ 🅿 – 🔬. ※ by ⑧
   M 26000 – ⵚ 7000 – 107 **rm** 68/107000.

🏨 **Serius,** viale Augusto 74 ✉ 80125 ✆ 614844 – 🛗 ▤ ⌇wc 🎞wc 🅿 ⭤. ※ by ⑧
   M 20000 – ⵚ 6000 – **69 rm** 46/65000, ▤ 5000 – P 78000.

🏨 **Palace Hotel,** piazza Garibaldi 9 ✉ 80142 ✆ 264575 – 🛗 ▤ ⌇wc 🎞wc 🅿. 🅰🅴 ⓞ 𝗩𝗜𝗦𝗔. ※ rest MY **s**
   M a la carte 22/31000 – ⵚ 5000 – **102 rm** 43/63000, ▤ 6000 – P 71/80000.

🏨 **Rex** without rest., via Palepoli 12 ✉ 80132 ✆ 416388 – 🛗 ▤ ⌇wc 🎞wc 🅶. ⓞ 🄴 𝗩𝗜𝗦𝗔 GX **r**
   ⵚ 4000 – **40 rm** 40/63000.

🏨 **Domitiana** without rest., viale Kennedy 143 ✉ 80125 ✆ 610560 – 🛗 ⌇wc 🅿 🅶. 🅰🅴 ⓞ 🄴 𝗩𝗜𝗦𝗔 by ⑧
   ⵚ 7000 – **40 rm** 52/80000.

🏨 **Miramare** without rest., via Nazario Sauro 24 ✉ 80132 ✆ 427388 – 🛗 ▤ ⌇wc 🎞wc ☎. 🅰🅴 ⓞ 🄴 𝗩𝗜𝗦𝗔 GX **e**
   26 rm ⵚ 75/95000.

XXX La Sacrestia, via Orazio 116 ✉ 80122 ✆ 664186, ≤, Elegant rest., �─ – ▤ FX
   by via Caracciolo

XX **Harry's Bar,** via Lucilio 11 ✉ 80132 ✆ 407810 – ▤. 🅰🅴. ※ GX **a**
   closed Sunday and August – **M** (booking essential) a la carte 20/30000.

XX ✿ **Giuseppone a Mare,** via Ferdinando Russo 13-Capo Posillipo ✉ 80123 ✆ 7696002, Seaside rest. with ≤, « In little harbour » – 🅿. 🅰🅴 ⓞ 🄴 𝗩𝗜𝗦𝗔. ※
   closed Sunday and 23 to 31 December – **M** a la carte 35/46000 (12%)
   Spec. Cocktail di gamberi e frutti di mare, Linguine Riva Fiorita, Polipetti al pignatello. **Wines** Greco di Tufo, Tiberio. by via Caracciolo FX

262

XX ✿ **La Cantinella,** via Cuma 42 ✉ 80132 ✆ 404884, Typical seaside rest. – AE ⓓ VISA. ✻
closed Sunday and August – **M** a la carte 21/40000 (12%) GX **v**
Spec. Linguine con scampi e frutti di mare, Grigliata mista di pesce. **Wines** Falerno.

XX **Don Salvatore,** strada Mergellina 4/a ✉ 80122 ✆ 681817, Rest. and pizzeria – ▤. AE ⓓ VISA by via Caracciolo FX
closed Wednesday – **M** a la carte 22/35000 (12%).

X Al Sarago, piazza Sannazzaro 201/b ✉ 80122 ✆ 685587 EX **a**

X **Sbrescia,** rampe Sant'Antonio a Posillipo 109 ✉ 80122 ✆ 669140, Typical Neapolitan trattoria with ≤ – ✻ by via Caracciolo FX
closed Monday – **M** a la carte 20/33000 (12%).

X **Umberto,** via Alabardieri 30 ✉ 80121 ✆ 418555, Rest. and pizzeria – ▤. AE ⓓ E VISA. ✻ JZ **e**
closed Wednesday and August – **M** a la carte 19/27000 (12%).

Island of Capri 80073 Napoli 988 ㉗ – pop. 7 443 – ✪ 081.

Gd H. Quisisana, via Camerelle 2 ✆ 8370788, Telex 710520, ≤ sea and Certosa, « Garden with heated ⛱ » – |✦| ▤ ☎ – 🏋. AE ⓓ E VISA. ✻
April-October – **M** 45/60000 – 140 rm (dinner included) 197/272000, low season 152/227000.

Scalinatella ⛰ without rest., via Tragara 8 ✆ 8370633, Telex 721204, ≤ sea and Certosa, ⛱ heated – |✦| ▤ ☎
15 March-October – ☕ 15000 – **28 rm** 100/200000, ▤ 10000.

Luna ⛰, viale Matteotti 3 ✆ 8370433, Telex 721247, ≤ sea, Faraglioni and Certosa, « Terraces and garden with ⛱ » – |✦| ▤ rm ☎ – 🏋. AE ⓓ E VISA. ✻ rest
April-October – **M** a la carte 36/46000 – ☕ 11000 – 48 rm 70/155000, ▤ 6000 – P 120/160000, low season 100/140000.

La Palma, via Vittorio Emanuele 32 ✆ 8370133, Telex 722015 – |✦| ▤ TV ☎ ♿ – 🏋. AE ⓓ E VISA. ✻ rest
April-October – **M** 40/50000 – 80 rm ☕ 111/212000, ▤ 7000 – P 138/160000, low season 110/132000.

Regina Cristina ⛰, via Serena 20 ✆ 8370303, Telex 710531, ⛱, 🌴 – |✦| ▤ rm – 🏋. AE ⓓ VISA. ✻ rest
M 30000 – 55 rm ☕ 56/160000, ▤ 9000 – P 100/130000, low season 90/120000.

L'a Pazziella ⛰ without rest., via Giuliani 4 ✆ 8370044, ≤ sea, 🌴 – ▤ 🛁wc 🚿wc ☎. AE. ✻
April-September – ☕ 15000 – **19 rm** 80/145000, ▤ 10000.

Villa delle Sirene, via Camerelle 51 ✆ 8370102, ≤ sea, « Lemon-grove » – |✦| ▤ 🛁wc 🚿wc ☎. AE ⓓ E VISA. ✻ rest
April-October – **M** *(closed Tuesday)* a la carte 25/35000 – 35 rm ☕ 67/105000, ▤ 5000 – P 105000, low season 102000.

La Pineta ⛰ without rest., via Tragara 6 ✆ 8370644, Telex 710011, ≤ sea and Certosa, « Floral terraces in pine-wood », ⛱ – ▤ 🛁wc ☎. AE ⓓ E VISA
April-October – **54 rm** ☕ 91/144000, ▤ 7000.

Gatto Bianco, via Vittorio Emanuele 32 ✆ 8370446, « Summer rest. service under pergola » – |✦| ▤ rm 🛁wc 🚿wc ☎ ♿. AE ⓓ E VISA. ✻
April-October – **M** 25/35000 – 44 rm ☕ 55/99000, ▤ 6000 – P 90/120000.

Villa Sarah ⛰ without rest., via Tiberio 3/a ✆ 8377817, ≤, « Shaded garden » – 🛁wc 🚿wc ☎. AE. ✻
Easter-October – **28 rm** ☕ 40/66000.

Flora ⛰ without rest., via Serena 26 ✆ 8370211, ≤ sea and Certosa, « Floral terrace » – ▤ 🛁wc ☎. ⓓ E VISA
April-October – **25 rm** ☕ 62/100000.

La Vega ⛰ without rest., via Occhio Marino 10 ✆ 8370481, ≤ sea, « Panoramic terrace with ⛱ » – 🛁wc 🚿wc ☎. AE ⓓ VISA
15 March-October – **24 rm** ☕ 65/102000.

XX ✿ **La Capannina,** via Le Botteghe 14 ✆ 8370732 – ▤. AE. ✻
15 March-10 November; closed Wednesday (except August) – **M** a la carte 24/34000 (13%)
Spec. Ravioli alla caprese, Linguine al sugo di scorfano, Grigliata mista di pesce. **Wines** Capri, Greco di Tufo.

XX **La Pigna,** via Lo Palazzo 30 ✆ 8370280, ≤ gulf of Napoli, 🌳 – AE ⓓ E VISA. ✻
Easter-October; closed Tuesday during low season – **M** a la carte 23/33000 (15%).

XX Faraglioni, via Camerelle 75 ✆ 8370320, ≤ – ▤
seasonal.

XX **Aurora Grill,** via Le Botteghe 46 ✆ 8377642 – AE ⓓ E VISA
closed Monday, January, February and March – **M** a la carte 20/34000 (12%).

X **La Sceriffa,** via Acquaviva 29 ✆ 8377953, ≤
April-October; closed Tuesday – **M** a la carte 19/31000.

X **Da Gemma,** via Madre Serafina 6 ✆ 8370461, ≤ – AE ⓓ E VISA
closed Monday and November-5 December – **M** a la carte 17/29000 (15%).

TURIN **(TORINO) 10100** 988 ⑫ – pop. 1 093 384 – alt. 239 – ☎ 011.

See : Piazza San Carlo★★ – Academy of Science (galleria Sabauda★★, Gualino collection★, Egyptian museum★★) – St. John's cathedral (chapel of the Holy Shroud★) – Palazzo Madama (museum of ancient Art★) CX **A** – Royal Palace (Royal Armoury★) CDX **B** – Valentino Park (Mediaeval Village★) CZ – Carlo Biscaretti di Ruffia Car Museum★.

Envir. : Superga (basilica★, ≤★★★) E : 10 km – Stupinigi : Hunting villa (houses a furniture museum)★ SW : 11 km.

18 and 9 I Roveri (closed January, February and Monday) at La Mandria ✉ 10070 Fiano ✆ 9235683, by ① : 18 km;

18 and 9 Torino (closed January, February and Monday), at Fiano ✉ 10070 ✆ 9235440, by ① : 20 km;

9 of Stupinigi, corso Unione Sovietica 506/bis ✉ 10135 ✆ 343975.

✈ Turin Airport by ① : 15 km ✆ 5778361 – Alitalia, via Lagrange 35 ✉ 10123 ✆ 5769.

✆ 537766.

ℹ via Roma 226 (piazza C.L.N.) ✉ 10121 ✆ 535889 – Porta Nuova Railway station ✉ 10125 ✆ 531327.

A.C.I. via Giovanni Giolitti 15 ✉ 10123 ✆ 57791.

Roma 669 ⑦ – Briançon 108 ⑪ – Chambéry 209 ⑪ – Genève 252 ③ – Genova 170 ⑦ – Grenoble 224 ⑪ – Milano 140 ③ – Nice 220 ⑨.

Plans on following pages

Jolly Principi di Piemonte, via Gobetti 15 ✉ 10123 ✆ 519693, Telex 221120 – ▯ ▤ TV ☎ – ⛟. AE ◑ E VISA. ✗ rest — CY **z**
M 39000 – **107 rm** ☕ 153/195000 – P 220000.

Turin Palace Hotel, via Sacchi 8 ✉ 10128 ✆ 515511, Telex 221411 – ▯ ▤ TV ☎ ♿ 🚗 – ⛟. AE ◑ E VISA. ✗ rest — CY **u**
M a la carte 27/48000 – ☕ 12000 – **125 rm** 120/165000 – P 150/180000.

Jolly Ambasciatori, corso Vittorio Emanuele 104 ✉ 10121 ✆ 5752, Telex 221296 – ▯ ▤ TV ☎ 🚗 – ⛟. AE ◑ E VISA. ✗ rest — BX **a**
M 35000 – **197 rm** ☕ 126/155000 – P 180000.

City without rest., via Juvarra 25 ✉ 10122 ✆ 540546 – ▯ ▤ TV. AE VISA. ✗ — BV **e**
☕ 12000 – **40 rm** 120/160000.

Majestic without rest., via Rattazzi 12 ✉ 10123 ✆ 539153 – ▯ ▤ TV ♿. AE ◑ E VISA — CY **k**
closed August – **93 rm** ☕ 98/140000, ▤ 7000.

Gd H. Sitea without rest., via Carlo Alberto 35 ✉ 10123 ✆ 5570171, Telex 220229 – ▯ ▤ TV ☎ – ⛟. AE ◑ E VISA. ✗ — CY **t**
☕ 10000 – **114 rm** 98/157000.

Concord, via Lagrange 47 ✉ 10123 ✆ 5576756, Telex 221323 – ▯ ▤ TV ☎ 🚗 – ⛟. AE ◑ E VISA. ✗ rest — CY **s**
M 25/35000 – **140 rm** ☕ 121/153000 – P 130000.

Royal, corso Regina Margherita 249 ✉ 10144 ✆ 748444, Telex 220259, 🎾 – ▯ ▤ TV ☎ 🚗 – ⛟. AE ◑ E VISA. ✗ rest — BV **u**
closed August – **M** *(closed Saturday and Sunday dinner)* a la carte 23/35000 – ☕ 7500 – **65 rm** 73/98000.

Luxor without rest., corso Stati Uniti 7 ✉ 10128 ✆ 531529 – ▯ ▤ TV 🛁wc 🚿wc ☎. AE ◑ VISA — CZ **s**
☕ 5000 – **63 rm** 51/71000, ▤ 5000.

Victoria without rest., via Nino Costa 4 ✉ 10123 ✆ 553710, Telex 212580 – ▯ 🛁wc 🚿wc ☎. AE ◑ VISA. ✗ — CY **v**
☕ 7000 – **75 rm** 50/70000.

Genio without rest., via Vittorio Emanuele 47 ✉ 10152 ✆ 6505771, Telex 220308 – 🛁wc 🚿wc ☎ ♿. AE ◑ E VISA. ✗ — CYZ **w**
☕ 7000 – **80 rm** 52/72000.

Stazione Genova without rest., via Sacchi 14 ✉ 10128 ✆ 545323, Telex 224242 – ▯ TV 🛁wc 🚿wc ☎ ♿. AE ◑ E VISA. ✗ — CZ **b**
☕ 7500 – **40 rm** 51/71000.

Gran Mogol without rest., via Guarini 2 ✉ 10123 ✆ 540287 – ▯ 🛁wc 🚿wc ☎. AE ◑ E VISA — CY **r**
closed August – ☕ 7000 – **45 rm** 52/72000.

Lancaster without rest., corso Filippo Turati 8 ✉ 10128 ✆ 501720 – ▯ ▤ 🛁wc 🚿wc ☎ — BZ **r**
closed 15 to 31 August – ☕ 4500 – **81 rm** 52/72000.

Cairo without rest., via La Loggia 6 ✉ 10134 ✆ 352003 – ▯ 🚿wc ☎ P. ✗ — by ⑩
closed 1 to 28 August – ☕ 5000 – **36 rm** 39/52000.

Eden without rest., via Donizetti 22 ✉ 10126 ✆ 659545 – ▯ 🛁wc 🚿wc ☎ ♿. ◑ VISA — CZ **f**
closed August – ☕ 2500 – **26 rm** 38/50000.

Cristallo 🌿 without rest., corso Traiano 28/9 ✉ 10135 ✆ 618383 – 🚿wc ☎ — by ⑩
closed 3 to 26 August – ☕ 3500 – **21 rm** 35/49000.

Smeraldo without rest., piazza Carducci 169 ✉ 10126 ✆ 634577 – 🛁wc 🚿wc ☎ ♿. AE ◑ VISA — CZ **q**
closed August – ☕ 4000 – **12 rm** 36/48000.

XXXX ✿ **Villa Sassi-El Toulà** 🌿 with rm, strada al Traforo del Pino 47 ✉ 10132 ℰ 890556, « 18C Country house in a spacious park » – ▤ rest ⌂wc 📱wc ☜ 🅿 – ⚖. 🅰🅴 ① 🅴 VISA ✂
by ⑤
closed August – **M** *(closed Sunday)* a la carte 44/64000 – ⌘ 12000 – **12 rm** 135/175000 – P 200000
Spec. Salmone marinato al pepe rosa, Risotto verde allo Champagne, Petto d'anatra alle erbe. **Wines** Arneis, Carema.

XXXX ✿ **Del Cambio,** piazza Carignano 2 ✉ 10123 ℰ 546690, Elegant traditional decor, « 19C Decoration » – ▤. 🅰🅴 ① VISA ✂
CX **a**
closed Sunday and 28 July-31 August – **M** (booking essential) a la carte 38/55000 (15%)
Spec. Risotto al verde, Fonduta con crostini e carne cruda all'albese, Brasato al Barolo. **Wines** Dolcetto, Grignolino.

XXXX **Tiffany,** piazza Solferino 16/h ✉ 10121 ℰ 540538 – ▤. 🅰🅴
CX **x**
closed Sunday and August – **M** a la carte 26/44000 (15%).

XXX **Vecchia Lanterna,** corso Re Umberto 21 ✉ 10128 ℰ 537047, Elegant installation – ▤. 🅴 VISA
CY **x**
closed Saturday lunch, Sunday and August – **M** (booking essential) a la carte 42/60000 (10%).

XXX **Ferrero,** corso Vittorio Emanuele 54 ✉ 10123 ℰ 547225, Elegant installation – ▤. 🅰🅴 ① 🅴 VISA
CY **k**
closed Monday – **M** (booking essential) a la carte 29/46000.

XXX ✿ **Al Gatto Nero,** corso Filippo Turati 14 ✉ 10128 ℰ 590414, Typical Tuscan decor and cuisine – ▤. 🅰🅴
BZ **z**
closed Sunday, Monday lunch and August – **M** a la carte 35/50000
Spec. Insalata di pesce Gatto Nero, Costata di manzo alla fiorentina, Misto mare alla brace. **Wines** bianco e rosso Montecarlo.

XXX **Al Saffi,** via Aurelio Saffi 2 ✉ 10138 ℰ 442213, Elegant installation – ▤. 🅰🅴 ① VISA
AV **n**
closed Sunday and August – **M** (booking essential) a la carte 40/48000.

XXX **Due Lampioni,** via Carlo Alberto 45 ✉ 10123 ℰ 546721 – ▤. ✂
CY **n**
closed Sunday and August – **M** a la carte 33/50000.

XX **Bridge,** via Giacosa 2 bis ✉ 10125 ℰ 687609 – ▤
CZ **v**

XX **La Smarrita,** corso Unione Sovietica 244 ✉ 10134 ℰ 390657 – ▤. 🅰🅴 ① VISA ✂ by ⑩
closed Monday and 5 to 30 August – **M** (booking essential) a la carte 30/50000.

XX **Plessis,** via Mazzini 31 ✉ 10123 ℰ 882110, also french cooking – ▤. ✂
DYZ **a**
closed Monday – **M** a la carte 19/38000.

XX **La Cloche,** strada al Traforo del Pino 106 ✉ 10132 ℰ 894213, Typical atmosphere – ▤ 🅿. 🅰🅴 ① VISA ✂
by ⑤
closed Monday – **M** (surprise menu) 23/45000.

XX **Al Dragone,** via Pomba 14 ✉ 10123 ℰ 547019 – ✂
CY **m**
closed Saturday, Sunday and August – **M** a la carte 25/39000.

XX **Al Bue Rosso,** corso Casale 10 ✉ 10131 ℰ 830753 – ▤. 🅰🅴 ① VISA
DY **e**
closed Monday, Saturday lunch and August – **M** a la carte 23/35000 (10%).

XX **Al Camin,** corso Francia 339 ✉ 10142 ℰ 724033, New rustic rest. – ▤
by ⑪
closed Saturday lunch, Sunday and August – **M** a la carte 22/36000.

XX **Il Papavero,** corso Raffaello 5 ✉ 10126 ℰ 6505168 – 🅰🅴 ①
CZ **d**
closed Sunday and 20 June-10 July – **M** (booking essential) a la carte 21/34000.

X **La Cuccagna,** corso Casale 371 ✉ 10132 ℰ 890069, Typical Romagnese rest.
by ⑤
closed Monday and August – **M** (surprise menu) 15/25000.

X **Porta Rossa,** corso Appio Claudio 227 ✉ 10146 ℰ 790963, 🏖 – 🅰🅴 VISA ✂ by ⑪
closed Saturday lunch, Sunday and August – **M** (booking essential) a la carte 21/40000.

X ✿ **Ostu Bacu,** corso Vercelli 226 ✉ 10155 ℰ 264579, Modern Piedmontese trattoria – ▤
closed Sunday and August – **M** a la carte 26/43000   by corso Vercelli DV
Spec. Assaggi di pasta, Fritto misto piemontese, Dolci piemontesi. **Wines** Grignolino, Dolcetto.

X **C'era una volta,** corso Vittorio Emanuele 41 ✉ 10125 ℰ 655498, Typical Piedmontese rest. – 🅰🅴 ① 🅴 VISA
CZ **k**
closed lunch, Sunday and August – **M** (surprise menu-booking essential) 25/30000.

X **Da Mauro,** via Maria Vittoria 21 ✉ 10123 ℰ 8397811, Tuscan habitués' trattoria – ▤. ✂
DY **h**
closed Monday and July – **M** a la carte 15/25000.

X **Da Lallo e Virginia,** strada delle Ghiacciaie 78 ✉ 10143 ℰ 734341, Rustic Piedmontese trattoria, « Summer service on terrace » – 🅿. ✂
AV **e**
closed Saturday lunch, Sunday and August – **M** a la carte 22/30000.

X **Trattoria della Posta,** strada Mongreno 16 ✉ 10132 ℰ 890193, Habitués' trattoria Piedmontese cheese – ▤. ✂
by ⑤
closed Sunday dinner, Monday and 10 July-20 August – **M** a la carte 16/26000.

X **Da Giudice,** strada Valsalice 78 ✉ 10131 ℰ 682488, « Summer service under pergola » – 🅿. 🅴. ✂
by ⑤
closed Tuesday, Wednesday lunch and August – **M** a la carte 22/33000.

TORINO

DUOMO
PAL. D. ACCADEMIA
DELLE SCIENZE
PIAZZA SAN CARLO ★★

CHIERI 18 km
ASTI 56 km

TORINO

S 29, A 21, S 393, A 6

A.C.I.

VENICE (VENEZIA) 30100 🔡🔡🔡 ⑤ – pop. 342 514 – h.s. April-October and Christmas – ✪ 041.

See : St. Mark's square★★★ CY : St. Mark's basilica★★★ (mosaics★★★, Pala d'oro★★★, Treasury★★★), Bell tower★ (❈★★), Clock tower★, Law courts★, Correr Museum★★, Doges Palace★★★, Piazzetta★★★ (Old library★) – Bridge of sighs★ CY.
Grand Canal★★★ : Palazzo Venier (modern art gallery★) BZ, Palazzo Rezzonico★ (Museum of Eighteenth-Century Venetian Art) AY, Rialto bridge★ CX, Cà d'Oro★★ BX – Academy of fine arts★★★ ABZ.
School of St. Rocco★★★ (paintings by Tintoretto★★★) AX – School of St. Giorgio degli Schiavoni★ (paintings by Carpaccio★★) DX – School of Carmini★ (paintings by Tiepolo★) AY – Church of St. Maria della Salute★ BZ – Church of St. Giorgio Maggiore★ CZ – Church of St. Zanipolo★, Equestrian statue of Bartolomeo Colleoni★★ CX – Church of St. Maria Gloriosa dei Frari★ AX – Church of St. Zaccaria★ CY – Church of St. Maria dei Miracoli★ CX – Church of St. Sebastiano (ceiling by Veronese★) AY.

Envir. : Lido★★★ SE : 15 mn by boat – Murano★ (Glass-making Museum★) NE : 15 mn by boat – Burano★ NE : 30 mn by boat – Torcello★★ (Cathedral of St. Maria Assunta★, Church of St. Fosca★) NE : 45 mn by boat – Riviera del Brenta★★, W : departure by boat and return by coach (whole day).

🏌 (closed Monday) al Lido Alberoni ⊠ 30011 ☎ 731015, 15 mn by boat and 9 km.

✈ Marco Polo di Tessera, NE : 13 km ☎ 661111 – Alitalia, campo San Moisè 1483 ⊠ 30124 ☎ 700355.

🚂 at Mestre ☎ 929472.

⛴ to Lido - San Nicolò from piazzale Roma (Tronchetto) daily (35 mn) – San Nicolò from piazzale Roma (Tronchetto) daily (35 mn).

⛴ to Punta Sabbioni from riva degli Schiavoni daily (45 mn); to island of Pellestrina-Santa Maria del Mare from Lido Alberoni daily (10 mn); to islands of Murano (10 mn), Burano (45 mn) and Torcello (50 mn) daily, from fondamenta Nuove – Information : ACTV - Venetian Transport Union, San Marco corte dell'Albero 3880 ⊠ 30124 ☎ 89620.

🛈 San Marco Ascensione 71/c ⊠ 30124 ☎ 26356 – piazzale Roma 540/d ⊠ 30125 ☎ 27402 – Santa Lucia Railway station ⊠ 30121 ☎ 715016.

A.C.I. piazzale Roma ⊠ 30125 ☎ 700300.

Roma 528 ① – Bologna 152 ① – Milano 267 ① – Trieste 158 ①.

Plans on following pages

🏨🏨 **Cipriani** ≫, isola della Giudecca 10 ⊠ 30123 ☎ 707744, Telex 410162, ≤, ⤳ heated, 🚗
– 🛗 ▤ 📺 ☎ 🕭 – 🕍. 🖭. ✾ rest　　　　　　　　　　　　　　　　　　CZ **h**
15 February-16 November – **M** a la carte 75/100000 – **94 rm** ⇌ 370/550000.

🏨🏨 **Gritti Palace,** campo Santa Maria del Giglio 2467 ⊠ 30124 ☎ 794611, Telex 410125, ≤
Grand Canal – 🛗 ▤ 📺 ☎ 🕭 – 🕍. 🖭 ⓞ 🗲 𝗩𝗜𝗦𝗔. ✾ rest　　　　　　　　　BY **a**
M a la carte 75/100000 – **99 rm** ⇌ 380/522000.

🏨🏨 **Danieli,** riva degli Schiavoni 4196 ⊠ 30122 ☎ 26480, Telex 410077, ≤ canale di San Marco, « Hall in a small Venetian-style courtyard » – 🛗 ▤ 📺 ☎ – 🕍. 🖭 ⓞ 🗲 𝗩𝗜𝗦𝗔.
✾ rm　　　　　　　　　　　　　　　　　　　　　　　　　　　　　　　CY **a**
M a la carte 68/103000 – **242 rm** ⇌ 268/464000.

🏨🏨 **Bauer Grünwald e Grand Hotel,** campo San Moisè 1459 ⊠ 30124 ☎ 707022, Telex 410075, ≤ Grand Canal, 🏖 – 🛗 ▤ 🕭 – 🕍. 🖭 ⓞ 🗲 𝗩𝗜𝗦𝗔. ✾ rest　　　CY **h**
M a la carte 60/85000 – **214 rm** ⇌ 215/358000.

🏨🏨 **Monaco e Grand Canal,** calle Vallaresso 1325 ⊠ 30124 ☎ 700211, Telex 410450, ≤ Grand Canal – 🛗 ▤ 📺 ☎ – 🕍. 🖭 𝗩𝗜𝗦𝗔. ✾ rest　　　　　　　　　　CY **e**
M Grand Canal Rest. (closed Tuesday from October to June) a la carte 68/98000 – ⇌ 14000 – **80 rm** 200/315000.

🏨🏨 **Europa e Regina,** calle larga 22 Marzo 2159 ⊠ 30124 ☎ 700477, Telex 410123, ≤ Grand Canal – 🛗 ▤ 📺 ☎ 🕭 – 🕍. 🖭 ⓞ 🗲 𝗩𝗜𝗦𝗔. ✾ rest　　　　　　CY **d**
200 rm.

🏨🏨 **Metropole,** riva degli Schiavoni 4149 ⊠ 30122 ☎ 705044, Telex 410340, ≤ canale di San Marco – 🛗 ▤ 📺 – 🕍. 🖭 ⓞ 🗲 𝗩𝗜𝗦𝗔. ✾ rest　　　　　　　　　　DY **t**
M Zodiaco Grill (closed Tuesday) a la carte 36/64000 – ⇌ 14000 – **65 rm** 150/230000.

🏨🏨 **Londra Palace,** riva degli Schiavoni 4171 ⊠ 30122 ☎ 700533, Telex 431315, ≤ canale di San Marco – 🛗 ▤ 📺 ☎ – 🕍. 🖭 ⓞ 🗲 𝗩𝗜𝗦𝗔　　　　　　　　　　　CY **t**
M rest. see **Do Leoni** below – **69 rm** ⇌ 162/274000.

🏨🏨 **Gd H. Luna,** calle larga dell'Ascensione 1243 ⊠ 30124 ☎ 89840, Telex 410236 – 🛗 ▤ 📺 ☎ – 🕍. 🖭. ✾ rest　　　　　　　　　　　　　　　　　　CY **p**
M 46000 – ⇌ 15000 – **125 rm** 160/275000 – P 230/252000.

🏨🏨 **Etap-Park Hotel,** giardini Papadopoli ⊠ 30125 ☎ 85394, Telex 410310 – 🛗 ▤ 📺 ☎ – 🕍. 🖭 🗲 𝗩𝗜𝗦𝗔. ✾ rest　　　　　　　　　　　　　　　　　AX **k**
M a la carte 34/50000 – **100 rm** ⇌ 140/230000.

🏨🏨 **Splendid-Suisse,** San Marco-Mercerie 760 ⊠ 30124 ☎ 700755, Telex 410590 – 🛗 ▤ 📺 ☎ 🕭 – 🕍. 🖭 ⓞ 🗲 𝗩𝗜𝗦𝗔. ✾ rest　　　　　　　　　　　　CX **n**
M a la carte 40/60000 – ⇌ 14000 – **155 rm** 170/250000.

🏨🏨 **Saturnia-International and Rest. il Cortile,** calle larga 22 Marzo 2398 ⊠ 30124 ☎ 708377, Telex 410355, « 14C Patrician building; outdoor rest. service in Summer » – 🛗 ▤ 📺 ☎ – 🕍. 🖭 ⓞ 🗲 𝗩𝗜𝗦𝗔　　　　　　　　　　　　　　　　　　BY **n**
M (closed Wednesday) a la carte 42/62000 – **99 rm** ⇌ 160/260000.

270

🏛️ **La Fenice et des Artistes** without rest., campiello de la Fenice 1936 ⊠ 30124 𝒞 32333, Telex 411150 – |🔆| 📺 🌺
🗠 8000 – **68 rm** 85/122000, 🍴 7000.
BY **v**

🏛️ **Cavalletto e Doge Orseolo**, calle del Cavalletto 1107 ⊠ 30124 𝒞 700955, Telex 410684, ≼ – |🔆| 📺 🗚
M 48000 – **81 rm** 🗠 97/146000.
CY **f**

🏛️ **Gabrielli Sandwirth**, riva degli Schiavoni 4110 ⊠ 30122 𝒞 31580, Telex 410228, ≼ canale di San Marco, « Small courtyard and garden » – |🔆| 🍴 🗚 ⓪ E 𝘝𝘐𝘚𝘈 🌺 rest
15 March-15 November – **M** 35/50000 – **110 rm** 🗠 174/288000 – P 249000.
DY **b**

🏛️ **Concordia** without rest., calle larga San Marco 367 ⊠ 30124 𝒞 706866, Telex 411069 – |🔆| ⌂wc 🗚 𝘝𝘐𝘚𝘈
60 rm 🗠 99/150000.
CY **k**

🏛️ **Flora** 🌿 without rest., calle larga 22 Marzo 2283/a ⊠ 30124 𝒞 705844, « Small flower garden » – |🔆| 🍴 ⌂wc 🍴wc 🐾 🕹 🗚 ⓪ E 𝘝𝘐𝘚𝘈
February-15 November – **44 rm** 🗠 85/138000, 🍴 8000.
BY **c**

🏛️ **Panada**, San Marco-calle dei Specchieri 646 ⊠ 30124 𝒞 709088, Telex 410153 – |🔆| ⌂wc 🍴wc 🐾. 🗚 ⓪ E 𝘝𝘐𝘚𝘈
M rest. see **Panada** below – **45 rm** 🗠 99/150000 – P 131000, low season 119000.
CY **k**

🏛️ **San Cassiano** without rest., Santa Croce 2232 ⊠ 30125 𝒞 23051, Telex 223479, ≼ – 🍴 📺 🍴wc 🐾 🕹 🗚 ⓪. 🌺
35 rm 🗠 95/142000.
BX **f**

🏛️ **Santa Chiara** without rest., Santa Croce 548 𝒞 706955, Telex 215621 – |🔆| 🍴 📺 🍴wc ☎ 🗚
28 rm 🗠 94/140000.
AX **c**

🏛️ **Ala** without rest., campo Santa Maria del Giglio 2494 ⊠ 30124 𝒞 708333, Telex 410275 – |🔆| 🍴 ⌂wc 🍴wc ☎ 🗚 ⓪ E 𝘝𝘐𝘚𝘈
80 rm 🗠 95/140000, 🍴 7000.
BY **e**

🏛️ **Abbazia** without rest., calle Priuli 66 ⊠ 30121 𝒞 717333, 🐾 – ⌂wc 🍴wc ☎ 🕹 AX **a**
37 rm 🗠 48/80000.

🏛️ **Casanova** without rest., San Marco-Frezzeria 1284 ⊠ 30124 𝒞 706855 – |🔆| 🍴 ⌂wc 🍴wc ☎ 🕹. 🗚
45 rm 🗠 99/150000, 🍴 10000.
CY **u**

🏛️ **Montecarlo** without rest., calle dei Specchieri 463 ⊠ 30124 𝒞 28026, Telex 411098 – |🔆| 🍴 ⌂wc 🍴wc 🐾. 🗚 E 𝘝𝘐𝘚𝘈
🗠 14000 – **48 rm** 85/122000, 🍴 10000.
CY **q**

🏛️ **Bonvecchiati**, calle Goldoni 4488 ⊠ 30124 𝒞 85017, Telex 410560, « Modern art picture collection » – |🔆| 🍴 ⌂wc 🍴wc ☎ 🕹. 🗚 E. 🌺 rest
M a la carte 30/48000 – 🗠 9000 – **86 rm** 85/122000, 🍴 8500 – P 103/134000, low season 76/100000.
CY **w**

🏛 **Scandinavia** without rest., Santa Maria Formosa 5240 ⊠ 30122 𝒞 23507 – ⌂wc 🍴wc 🐾
31 rm 🗠 49/86000.
CX **s**

🏛 **Torino**, without rest., calle delle Ostreghe 2356 ⊠ 30124 𝒞 705222 – 🍴 🍴wc 🐾 BY **z**
20 rm.

🏛 **Nuovo Teson** without rest., calle de la Pescaria 3980 ⊠ 30122 𝒞 705555 – 🍴wc 🐾. 🗚 ⓪ E 𝘝𝘐𝘚𝘈. 🌺
30 rm 🗠 48/80000.
DY **s**

🏛 **Serenissima** without rest., calle Goldoni 4486 ⊠ 30124 𝒞 700011 – ⌂wc 🍴wc 🐾. 🗚 ⓪
10 March-5 November – **34 rm** 🗠 45/78000.
CY **w**

🏛 **Basilea** without rest., rio Marin 817 ⊠ 30125 𝒞 718477 – ⌂wc 🍴wc 🕹. 🗚 𝘝𝘐𝘚𝘈. 🌺
🗠 7500 – **30 rm** 40/66000.
AX **d**

🏛 **La Residenza** without rest., campo Bandiera e Moro 3608 ⊠ 30122 𝒞 85315, « 14C building » – 🍴 📺 ⌂wc 🍴wc ☎. 🗚 ⓪ 𝘝𝘐𝘚𝘈. 🌺
closed 8 January - 15 February and 16 November - 7 December – **14 rm** 🗠 41/67000, 🍴 3500.
DY **n**

XXXX ❀ **Antico Martini**, campo San Fantin 1983 ⊠ 30124 𝒞 24121, Elegant rest. – 🍴. 🗚 ⓪ E 𝘝𝘐𝘚𝘈. 🌺
March-November; closed Tuesday and Wednesday lunch – **M** a la carte 55/85000 (15%)
Spec. Blinis di salmone, Filetti di San Pietro alla Betty, Chicche del nonno. Wines Malvasia, Cabernet.
BY **x**

XXX ❀❀ **Harry's Bar**, calle Vallaresso 1323 ⊠ 30124 𝒞 36797, American bar-rest. – 🍴. ⓪ E 𝘝𝘐𝘚𝘈
closed Monday and 3 January-13 February – **M** a la carte 54/88000 (20%)
Spec. Taglierini con seppioline (15 July-15 October), Pesce fresco con verdure di stagione, Pasticceria della Casa. Wines Pinot, Cabernet.
CY **e**

XXX ❀ **La Caravella**, calle larga 22 Marzo 2397 ⊠ 30124 𝒞 708901, Typical rest. – 🍴. 🗚 ⓪ E 𝘝𝘐𝘚𝘈. 🌺
closed Wednesday – **M** (booking essential) a la carte 52/78000
Spec. Bigoli in salsa, Scampi allo Champagne, Filetto di bue Caravella. Wines Barchessa, Venegazzù.
BY **n**

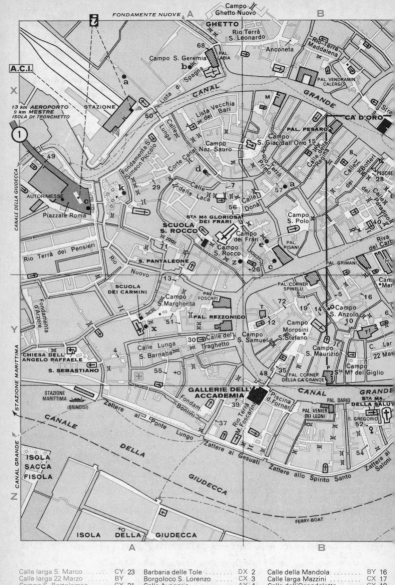

273

XXX **Do Leoni,** riva degli Schiavoni 4175 ⊠ 30122 𝒫 25032, Elegant rest., « Summer service on the bank of the canal » – 🗐. 𝐀𝐄 ⓪ 🇪 𝘝𝘐𝘚𝘈. 🍽   CY **t**
closed Tuesday and 15 November-15 December – **M** (booking essential) a la carte 60/92000.

XXX **Taverna La Fenice,** San Marco 1938 ⊠ 30124 𝒫 23856, 🍴, Elegant rest. – 🗐. 𝐀𝐄 ⓪ 🇪 𝘝𝘐𝘚𝘈   BY **v**
closed Sunday, Monday lunch and 7 January-11 February – **M** a la carte 36/61000 (15%).

XXX **Al Campiello,** colle dei Fuseri 4346 ⊠ 30124 𝒫 706396, Rest.-American-bar-late night dinners – 🗐. 𝐀𝐄 ⓪ 🇪 𝘝𝘐𝘚𝘈   CY **z**
closed Monday and 8 to 22 August – **M** (booking essential) a la carte 33/47000 (13%).

XXX **Do Forni,** calle dei Specchieri 457/468 ⊠ 30124 𝒫 32148, New rustic rest. – 🗐. 𝐀𝐄 ⓪ 🇪 𝘝𝘐𝘚𝘈   CX **c**
closed Thursday and 22 November-5 December – **M** a la carte 38/56000.

XX **Malamocco,** campiello del Vin 4650 ⊠ 30122 𝒫 27438 – 🗐   CY **n**
closed Thursday and 9 January-14 February – **M** a la carte 41/65000 (15%).

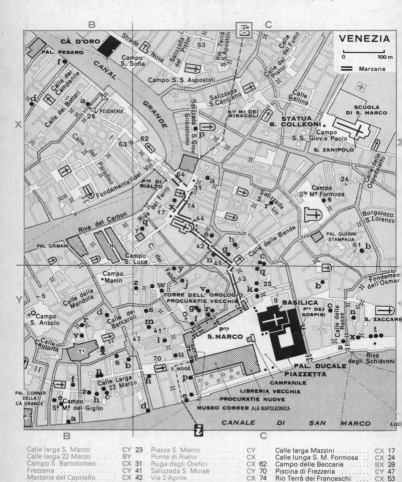

XX ❀ **Al Graspo de Uva,** calle dei Bombaseri 5094 ⌧ 30124 ℰ 23647, Typical tavern – ▤.
ÆE ⓞ E 𝑽𝑰𝑺𝑨   CX x
  closed Monday, Tuesday and 20 December-3 January – **M** a la carte 28/45000 (12%)
  Spec. Zuppa di pesce alla chioggiotta con crostini, Bisato alla gondoliera con polenta, Braciola di vitello alla
  vetraia. **Wines** Valpolicella, Soave.

XX **Panada,** calle larga San Marco 656 ⌧ 30124 ℰ 27358, « Typical decor » – ▤. ❀
  closed Sunday dinner and Monday – **M** a la carte 28/42000.   CY k

XX **La Colomba,** piscina di Frezzeria 1665 ⌧ 30124 ℰ 23817, Typical trattoria, « Modern
  art picture collection » – ÆE ⓞ E 𝑽𝑰𝑺𝑨   CY m
  closed Tuesday and 7 November-17 December – **M** a la carte 37/55000 (12%).

XX ❀ **Noemi** with rm, calle dei Fabbri 909 ⌧ 30124 ℰ 25238 – ▤ rest ☎. ÆE ⓞ E 𝑽𝑰𝑺𝑨
  M *(closed Sunday dinner, Monday and 7 January-19 February)* a la carte 39/55000 (12%) –
  ⚌ 6500 – **15 rm** 29/50000   CY g
  Spec. Cannelloni Smeraldina, Vermicelli neri alle seppie, Filetti di sogliola Casanova e Salmone fresco alla
  Sultanina. **Wines** Verduzzo, Cabernet.

XX **Osteria da Fiore,** San Polo-calle del Scaleter 2202 ⌧ 30125 ℰ 37208, Typical rest. –
  ▤. E. ❀   BX a
  closed Sunday, Monday, 5 August-2 September and 23 December-1 January – **M** (seafood
  only) (booking essential) a la carte 28/53000 (10%).

X **Madonna,** calle della Madonna 594 ⌧ 30125 ℰ 23824, Venetian trattoria – ▤. ❀
  closed Wednesday, 24 December-31 January and 4 to 17 August – **M** a la carte 19/31000
  (11%).   BX e

X **Da Bruno,** Castello-calle del Paradiso 5731 ⌧ 30122 ℰ 21480, Habitués' trattoria – ▤
  closed Tuesday and 15 to 30 July – **M** a la carte 19/27000.   CX r

X **Antica Carbonera,** calle Bembo 4648 ⌧ 30124 ℰ 25479, Venetian trattoria – ▤. ❀
  closed Sunday, July and August – **M** a la carte 20/36000 (12%).   CX q

X **Antica Trattoria Poste Vecie,** Pescheria 1608 ⌧ 30125 ℰ 23822, Typical Venetian
  trattoria   BX a
  closed Monday dinner, Tuesday and 20 November-20 December – **M** a la carte 25/43000
  (12%).

  in Lido : 15 mn by boat from San Marco CY – ⌧ **30126** Venezia Lido.

  🖫 Gran Viale S. M. Elisabetta 6 ℰ 765721 :

🏨🏨🏨 **Excelsior,** lungomare Marconi 41 ℰ 760201, Telex 410023, ≤, ⤬ heated, ▲₆, ❀, Ⅰ₈ –
  🛗 ▤ ▥ ☎ & – ▵. ÆE ⓞ E 𝑽𝑰𝑺𝑨. ❀ rest
  15 April-20 October – **M** a la carte 67/105000 – ⚌ 18000 – **231 rm** 356/441000 –
  P 328/511000.

🏨🏨🏨 **Des Bains,** lungomare Marconi 17 ℰ 765921, Telex 410142, ≤, « Flower garden with
  heated ⤬ and ❀ », ▲₆, Ⅰ₈ – 🛗 ▤ ▥ ☎ & ₱ – ▵. ÆE ⓞ E 𝑽𝑰𝑺𝑨. ❀
  April-October – **254 rm**.

🏨🏨 **Quattro Fontane** ❀, via 4 Fontane 16 ℰ 768814, ⤬, ❀ – ☎ ₱ ÆE 𝑽𝑰𝑺𝑨
  20 April-September – **M** 50/70000 – ⚌ 14000 – **70 rm** 130/220000 – P 190/235000, low
  season 170/210000.

🏨🏨 **Villa Mabapa,** riviera San Nicolò 16 ℰ 760590, Telex 440170, « Summer rest. in garden »,
  ⤬ – 🛗 ▤ ⇌wc ⫚wc ☎ & ÆE ⓞ E 𝑽𝑰𝑺𝑨. ❀ rest
  M *(closed 3 November-15 March)* a la carte 35/48000 – **62 rm** ⚌ 110/180000 – P 90/130000,
  low season 70/100000.

🏨🏨 **Villa Otello** without rest., via Lepanto 12 ℰ 760048 – 🛗 ⇌wc ⫚wc ☎ ₱. ❀
  22 April-15 October – ⚌ 7500 – **34 rm** 84/124000.

🏨 **Byron Central Hotel,** via Bragadin 30 ℰ 760052, ⤬ – 🛗 ▤ ⇌wc ⫚wc ☎ &. ÆE 𝑽𝑰𝑺𝑨.
  ❀ rest
  April-15 October – **M** 28/32000 – **36 rm** ⚌ 75/112000, ▤ 10000 – P 110000, low season 77000.

🏨 **Vianello,** località Alberoni ⌧ 30011 ℰ 731072, ⤬ – ⇌wc ⫚wc. ❀ rest
  April-September – **M** *(closed April, May and September)* 15000 – **20 rm** ⚌ 38/70000 –
  P 39/49000.

XX **Al Porticciolo-da Danilo,** verso Malamocco ℰ 768384, « Summer service in garden »
  – ▤ ₱. ÆE
  April-October; closed Wednesday – **M** a la carte 25/45000 (12%).

X **Trattoria da Ciccio,** via San Gallo 241-in direction of Malamocco ℰ 765489, ⌂ – ₱
  closed Tuesday and 15 to 30 November – **M** a la carte 25/40000 (12%).

  in Torcello 50 mn by boat from fondamenta Nuove CX – ⌧ **30012** Burano :

XX ❀ **Locanda Cipriani** ❀, ℰ 730757, Typical rest., « Floral setting » – ÆE 𝑽𝑰𝑺𝑨. ❀
  19 March-10 November; closed Tuesday – **M** a la carte 55/83000 (15%)
  Spec. Risotto alla torcellana, Scampi alla Carlina, Zuppa di pesce. **Wines** Soave, Cabernet.

XX **Osteria al Ponte del Diavolo,** ℰ 730401, ⌂ – ÆE
  March-15 November; closed Thursday and dinner (except Saturday) – **M**
  a la carte 30/49000 (10%).

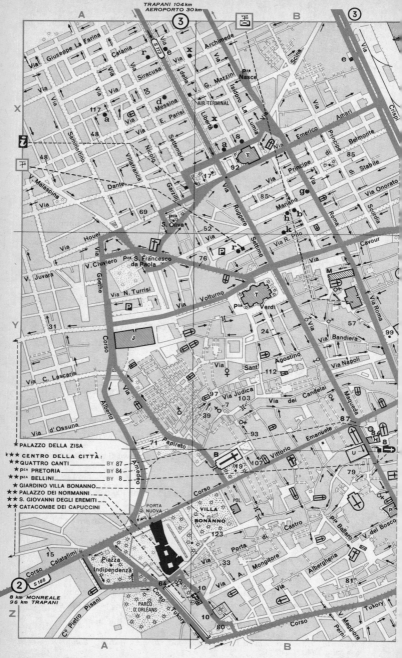

TRAPANI 104 km
AEROPORTO 30 km

TRAPANI 104 km

A   ③   B   ③

X

Y

Z

Via Giuseppe La Farina
Via Catania
Via Siracusa
Via Messina
Via E. Parisi
Via Settembre
Via Nicolo
Via Villafranca
Via Sammartino
V. Malaspina
Via Dante
Via Houel
V. Ciuviero
V. Juvara
V. C. Lascaris
Via d' Ossuna
Via Goethe
Corso Alberto

Archimede
Via G. Mazzini
Isidoro
AIR TERMINAL
Via della Libertà
P.za Nasce
Scina
Sciuti
Via Emerico Amari
Via Amari
Principe di Belmonte
Via di Stabile
Via Onorato
Scordia
Via Roma
Cavour
Via Principe di Scordia
Mariano
Via R. Pilo
Via Settimo
Via Ruggero
P.za S. Francesco da Paola
Via N. Turrisi
Volturno
P.za Verdi
Via Bandiera
Via Roma
Via Napoli
Sant'Agostino
Via dei Candelai
Via Judica
Via Maqueda
Corso Vittorio Emanuele
Papireto
Amedeo
Corso
Corso
VILLA BONANNO
POL
Porta di Castro
P.za Ballaró
V. del Bosco
Albergheria
Porta NUOVA
PIAZZA Independenza
Corso Calatafimi
Cso Pietro Pisani
PARCO D'ORLEANS
Corso Tukory
V. A. Mongitore
Via
Corso
V. Maghore
V. Tukory
Peni

★ PALAZZO DELLA ZISA
★★★ CENTRO DELLA CITTÀ:
  ★★ QUATTRO CANTI _____ BY 87
  ★ P.za PRETORIA _____ BY 84
  ★★ P.za BELLINI _____ BY 8
★ GIARDINO VILLA BONANNO __ BY
★ PALAZZO DEI NORMANNI __
★★ S. GIOVANNI DEGLI EREMITI __
★★ CATACOMBE DEI CAPPUCCINI

2   S 186
8 km MONREALE
96 km TRAPANI

A   B

276

PALERMO

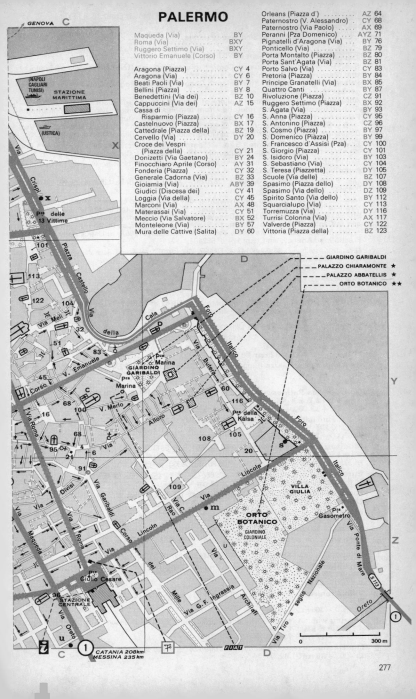

GIARDINO GARIBALDI
PALAZZO CHIARAMONTE ★
PALAZZO ABBATELLIS ★
ORTO BOTANICO ★★

CATANIA 208km
MESSINA 235km

0   300 m

🚣 see : Palerme.

🚢 to Sicily see : Naples; from Sicily see : Palerme.

Palerme 90100 988 ㉟ – pop. 707 721 – ✪ 091.

See : Town centre★★★ : Quattro Canti★★, piazza Pretoria★ (fountain★★), piazza Bellini★★ (the Martorana★★, church of St. Cataldo★★) – Church of St. John of the Hermits★★ – Palace of the Normans★★ (the palatine Chapel★★★, King Roger's Room★★) – Botanical garden★★ – Capuchin catacombs★★.
Abbatellis Palace★ : National Gallery of Sicily★★ (fresco of Death Triumphant★★★) – Archaeological Museum★ (metopes from temples at Selinus★★) BY M – Chiaramonte Palace★ – Palazzo della Zisa★ (temporarily closed for restoration work) – Cathedral★ BZ B – St. Lawrence Oratory★ CY C – St. Mary of the Chain★ DY D – Garden of the Villa Bonanno★ – Garibaldi gardens (ficus magnolioides★★) – Villa Giulia (garden★) DZ.
Envir. : Park of the Favourite★ 3 km – Monte Pellegrino (picturesque landscapes★★ and ≤★★) N : 14 km – Monreale : Cathedral★★★ (mosaics★★★), Cloister★★★ 8 km by ②.
Exc : Ustica Island (ensemble ≤★★, Blue grotto★) 2 h by boat-service or 1 h 15 mn by hydrofoil speedboat (seasonal).

🛫 Punta Raisi by ③ : 30 km 𝒫 237025 – Alitalia, via della Libertà 29 ✉ 90139 𝒫 584533.

🚢 to Genova : Tuesday, Friday and Sunday (22 h) and to Livorno : Monday, Wednesday and Friday (18 h) – Grandi Traghetti, via Mariano Stabile 179 𝒫 587832, Telex 910098; to Napoli daily (10 h), to Genova Monday, Wednesday, Friday and Sunday (23 h) and to Cagliari Friday from 18 June to September and Monday in other months (12,30 h) – Tirrenia Navigazione, via Roma 385 𝒫 585733, Telex 910057; to Ustica daily (2,30 h) – Prestifilippo Agency, via Crispi 124 𝒫 582403.

🛈 piazza Castelnuovo 35 ✉ 90141 𝒫 583847, Telex 910179 – Punta Raisi Airport 𝒫 591405 – Central Station ✉ 90127 𝒫 233808.

A.C.I. viale delle Alpi 6 ✉ 90144 𝒫 266393.

Messina 235 ①.

Plan on preceding pages

🏨 **Villa Igiea Gd H.** ⑤, salita Belmonte 1 ✉ 90142 𝒫 543744, Telex 910092, ≤, « Floral terraces overlooking the sea », ⌁ heated, 🚗, ⚒ – 🛗 ▤ 📺 ☎ 🅿 – 🔺 AE ⊙ E VISA ⚒
    by via Crispi BX
M 45000 – ⌸ 14000 – **120 rm** 130/200000 – P 180/192000.

🏨 **President**, via Crispi 230 ✉ 90133 𝒫 580733, Telex 910359, « Roof-garden Rest. » – 🛗 ▤ 📺 ☎ 🅿 – 🔺 VISA   BX e
M 16000 – ⌸ 4000 – **129 rm** 55/70000 – P 72000.

🏨 **Politeama Palace**, piazza Ruggero Settimo 15 ✉ 90139 𝒫 322777, Telex 911053 – 🛗 ▤ 📺 ☎ – 🔺   BX a
102 rm.

🏨 **Gd H. et des Palmes**, via Roma 398 ✉ 90139 𝒫 583933, Telex 911082 – 🛗 ▤ 📺 ☎ ♿ – 🔺 AE ⊙ E VISA ⚒ rest   BX g
M 28000 – ⌸ 9000 – 184 rm 68/88000 – P 88/99000.

🏨 **Jolly**, Foro Italico 22 ✉ 90133 𝒫 235842, Telex 910076, ≤, ⌁, 🚗 – 🛗 ▤ 📺 ☎ 🅿 – 🔺 AE ⊙ E VISA ⚒ rest   DY s
M 30000 – **290 rm** ⌸ 85/120000 – P 140000.

🏨 **Mediterraneo**, via Rosolino Pilo 44 ✉ 90139 𝒫 581133 – 🛗 ▤ 📺 ☎ ♿ ⇆ – 🔺 AE ⊙ E VISA   BX k
M a la carte 19/25000 – ⌸ 6000 – **106 rm** 43/68000 – P 65/73000.

🏨 **Europa**, via Agrigento 3 ✉ 90141 𝒫 266673 – 🛗 ▤ 📺 ☎. AE ⊙ E VISA ⚒ rest   AX r
M (residents only) 20000 – ⌸ 6000 – **73 rm** 43/68000.

🏨 **Ponte**, via Crispi 99 ✉ 90133 𝒫 583744 – 🛗 ▤ 📺 ⌂wc 🛁wc ☎   CX x
136 rm.

🏨 **Motelagip**, viale della Regione Siciliana 2620 ✉ 90145 𝒫 552033, Telex 911196 – 🛗 ▤ 🛁wc ☎ ♿ 🅿 – 🔺 AE ⊙ E VISA ⚒   by ③
M 18500 – **100 rm** ⌸ 46/85000 – P 75000.

🏨 **Metropol**, via Turrisi Colonna 4 ✉ 90141 𝒫 588608 – ▤ ⌂wc 🛁wc ☜. AE ⊙ E VISA ⚒ rest   AX a
M (residents only) 16/17000 – ⌸ 6000 – **44 rm** 32/55000. ▤ 5500 – P 52/58000.

🏨 **Sausele** without rest., via Vincenzo Errante 12 ✉ 90127 𝒫 237524 – 🛗 ⌂wc 🛁wc ☜ ⇆. AE ⊙ E VISA   CZ u
⌸ 5000 – **40 rm** 21/42000.

🏨 **Villa Archirafi** without rest., via Lincoln 30 ✉ 90133 𝒫 285827, 🚗 – 🛗 🛁wc ☜ ♿ 🅿 E   DZ m
⌸ 4500 – **30 rm** 29/44000.

🏨 **Touring** without rest., via Mariano Stabile 136 ✉ 90139 𝒫 584444 – 🛗 ▤ ⌂wc 🛁wc ☜. AE ⊙ E VISA ⚒   BX h
⌸ 5000 – **22 rm** 33/48000, ▤ 5000.

🏨 **Liguria** without rest., via Mariano Stabile 128 ✉ 90139 𝒫 581588 – 🛁wc ☜. ⚒   BX b
⌸ 4000 – **16 rm** 21/42000.

XXXX ✿ **Charleston,** piazzale Ungheria 30 ☒ 90141 ✆ 321366 – ☰. 🅰🅴 ⓪ 🄴 *VISA*. ⅍ BY **r**
closed Sunday and 16 June-25 September – **M** a la carte 37/53000
Spec. Melanzana Charleston (March-December). Involtini siciliani alla brace, Capriccio gelati Conca d'Oro.
Wines Regaleali, Corvo.

XXXX ✿ **Gourmand's,** via della Libertà 37/e ☒ 90139 ✆ 323431 – ☰. 🅰🅴 ⓪ 🄴 *VISA*. ⅍
closed Sunday – **M** a la carte 32/47000 AX **e**
Spec. Aneletti alla siciliana, Costoletta Arciduca, Millefoglie al mandarino. **Wines** Carboj, Libecchio.

XXX **Chamade,** via Torrearsa 22 ☒ 90139 ✆ 322204 – ☰. 🅰🅴 ⓪. ⅍ BX **x**
15 October-May; closed Monday – **M** a la carte 25/42000 (15%).

XXX **Trattoria Trittico,** largo Montalto 7 ☒ 90147 ✆ 294809 – ☰ ⓟ. 🅰🅴 ⓪ *VISA*. ⅍ by ③
closed Sunday – **M** a la carte 27/41000.

XXX **Friend's Bar** via Brunelleschi 138 ☒ 90145 ✆ 201401 – ☰ ⓟ. 🅰🅴 ⓪ by ③
closed Monday – **M** a la carte 24/32000.

XX **Regine,** via Trapani 4/a ☒ 90141 ✆ 586566 – ☰. 🅰🅴 ⓪ *VISA*. ⅍ AX **d**
closed Sunday and August – **M** a la carte 18/25000.

XX **Trattoria L'Angolo,** via Simone Corleo 1 ☒ 90139 ✆ 585318 – ☰. 🅰🅴 ⓪. ⅍ AX **x**
closed Sunday – **M** a la carte 16/23000.

X Lo Scudiero, via Turati 7 ☒ 90139 ✆ 581628 – ☰ BX **s**

Taormina 98039 Messina 🄆🄆🄆 ㊲ – pop. 10 211 – alt. 250 – Health and seaside resort
(at Mazzarò) – ✆ 0942.

See : Picturesque site★★★ – Greek Theatre★★ (≤★★★) B – Public gardens★★ B – Corso
Umberto★ A – Piazza 9 Aprile★ (≤★★) A – Castle★ (≤★★) A – Belvedere★ A.

Envir. : Castelmola (picturesque site★) NW : 5 km A – **Exc :** Tour of Etna★★.

🄸 (June-September) corso Umberto 144 ✆ 23751 – largo Santa Caterina (Corvaja palace)
✆ 23243, Telex 980062.

Catania 52 ② – Enna 135 ② – Messina 52 ① – Palermo 255 ② – Siracusa 111 ② – Trapani 359 ②.

TAORMINA

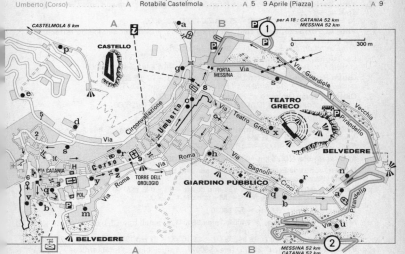

🏨🏨 **San Domenico Palace** ⬗, piazza San Domenico 5 ✆ 23701, Telex 980013, « Floral
garden with ≤ sea, coast and Etna », ⊴ heated – ⧮ ☰ 📺 ☎ 🖑 – 🍴. 🅰🅴 ⓪ 🄴 *VISA*.
⅍ rest A **m**
M 50000 – ☲ 14000 – **117 rm** 138/240000 – P 225/258000.

🏨🏨 **Jolly** ⬗, via Bagnoli Croce 75 ✆ 23312, Telex 980028, ≤ sea, coast and Etna, ⊴, 🚗 –
⧮ ⓟ. 🅰🅴 🄴 *VISA*. ⅍ rest B **q**
M 35000 – **103 rm** ☲ 90/140000 – P 155000.

🏨🏨 **Excelsior Palace** ⬗, via Toselli 8 ✆ 23975, Telex 980185, ≤ sea, coast and Etna,
« heated ⊴ on panoramic terrace », 🚗 – ⧮ ☰ 📺 ☎ 🖑 ⓟ – 🍴. ⓪ *VISA*. ⅍ A **v**
15 March-October – **M** 20/25000 – 87 rm ☲ 60/95000 – P 78/90000.

🏨 **Timèo** ⓢ, via Teatro Greco 59 🏶 23801, Telex 980073, ≤ sea, coast and Etna, « Large garden and floral terraces » – |齒| 🅟 – **55 rm**.　B **x**

🏨 **Bristol Park Hotel,** via Bagnoli Croce 92 🏶 23006, Telex 980005, ≤ sea, coast and Etna, ⤓ – |齒| ▤ ☎ ♨ ⟵, ⤋ rest　B **r**
March-October – **M** 30000 – 54 rm ☲ 65/130000 – P 70/100000.

🏨 **Méditerranée,** via Circonvallazione 61 🏶 23901, Telex 980175, ≤ sea, coast and Etna, « Floral terraces with ⤓ » – |齒| 🅟 – **50 rm**.　A **d**

🏨 **Vello d'Oro,** via Fazzello 🏶 23789, Telex 980186, ≤ – |齒| ▤. ⤋　A **r**
15 March-October – **M** *(dinner only)* 22000 – ☲ 7000 – **59 rm** 38/65000.

🏨 **Villa Paradiso,** via Roma 2 🏶 23922, ≤ sea, coast and Etna – |齒| ▤ ⌷wc ▥wc ☎ ♿. ⒶⒺ ⓪ Ⅹ 𝓥𝓘𝓢𝓐. ⤋ rest　B **h**
closed November-18 December – **M** 21/25000 – ☲ 9000 – 33 rm 39/77000 – P 65/87000.

🏨 **Villa Fiorita** without rest., via Pirandello 39 🏶 24122, ≤ sea and coast, ⤓, ⤐ – |齒| ▤ ⑨ ⌷wc ▥wc ⬚ ⟵　B **s**
☲ 5000 – **22 rm** 77000.

🏨 **Villa Riis** ⓢ, via Rizzo 13 🏶 24874, ≤ sea, coast and Etna, ⤓, ⤐ – |齒| ▤ ⌷wc ▥wc ☎ 🅟. ⒶⒺ 𝓥𝓘𝓢𝓐. ⤋ rest　A **b**
April-October – **M** *(dinner only)* 27000 – 30 rm ☲ 48000.

🏨 **Villa San Michele,** via Damiano Rosso 11 bis 🏶 24327, ≤ sea and bay of Naxos – |齒| ▤ ⌷wc ▥wc ⬚. ⒶⒺ ⓪ Ⅹ 𝓥𝓘𝓢𝓐. ⤋ rest　A **q**
M (residents only) – ☲ 7500 – **23 rm** 37/68000.

🏨 **Sole-Castello,** Rotabile Castelmola 83 🏶 28036, ≤ sea, coast and Etna, ⤓ – |齒| ▤ ⌷wc ▥wc ⟵ ♿. ⤐ Ⅹ 𝓥𝓘𝓢𝓐　A **p**
15 March-October – **M** *(dinner only)* – 57 rm (dinner included) 32/45000.

🏨 **Villa Belvedere** without rest., via Bagnoli Croce 79 🏶 23791, ≤ gardens, sea and Etna, « ⤓ on panoramic terrace », ⤐ – |齒| ⌷wc ▥wc ⬚ ♿ 🅟. Ⅹ 𝓥𝓘𝓢𝓐　B **b**
23 March-October – **40 rm** ☲ 43/75000.

🏠 **La Campanella** without rest., via Circonvallazione 3 🏶 23381 – ⌷wc ▥wc. ⤋　A **g**
12 rm ☲ 27/48000.

🏠 **Villa Kristina,** Rotabile Castelmola 🏶 24679, ≤, ⤓ – |齒| ▤ ⌷wc ▥wc ⬚ ⟵. ⒶⒺ ⓪ 𝓥𝓘𝓢𝓐. ⤋ rest – *closed January* – 32 rm (dinner included) 30/35000.　A **e**

🏠 **Villa Carlotta** without rest., via Pirandello 81 🏶 23732, ≤ sea and coast, ⤐ – ▤ ⌷wc ▥wc ☎.　B **a**
15 March-October – ☲ 6500 – **21 rm** 23/43000, ▤ 4000.

🗙🗙🗙 **Villa le Terrazze,** corso Umberto 172 🏶 23913, « Summer service on terrace with ≤ sea and coast » – ⒶⒺ ⓪ Ⅹ 𝓥𝓘𝓢𝓐　A **z**
April-October; closed Monday – **M** a la carte 33/50000.

🗙🗙 **La Griglia,** corso Umberto 54 🏶 23980 – ⤋　A **c**
closed Tuesday and 11 November-20 December – **M** a la carte 21/34000.

🗙 **Giova Rosy Senior,** corso Umberto 38 🏶 24411 – ⒶⒺ ⓪ 𝓥𝓘𝓢𝓐. ⤋　A **c**
closed Monday and 8 January-14 February – **M** a la carte 25/37000.

🗙 **Ciclope,** corso Umberto 🏶 23263 – ▤. ⒶⒺ ⓪ Ⅹ 𝓥𝓘𝓢𝓐　A **y**
closed Wednesday and 10 to 31 January – **M** a la carte 19/28000.

at Capo Taormina by ② : 3 km – ✉ **98030** Mazzarò :

🏨 **Grande Alb. Capotaormina,** 🏶 24000, Telex 980147, ≤ sea, ⤓ heated, ⩙⬡ – |齒| ▤ ☎ ♿ ♨ 🅟 – ⚐. ⒶⒺ ⓪ Ⅹ 𝓥𝓘𝓢𝓐　A
April-October – **M** 46000 – ☲ 13000 – 208 rm 66/132000 – P 174000.

at Castelmola NO : 5 km A – alt. 550 – ✉ **98030** :

🗙 **Il Faro,** contrada Pretalia 🏶 28193, ≤ sea and coast – 🅟
closed Wednesday – **M** a la carte 14/23000.

🗙 **Terrazza Auteri,** 🏶 28219, ≤ sea and coast – ⒶⒺ ⓪ Ⅹ 𝓥𝓘𝓢𝓐. ⤋
closed Monday and September – **M** a la carte 17/25000.

at Mazzarò by ② : 5,5 km – ✉ **98030** :

🏨 **Mazzarò Sea Palace,** 🏶 24004, Telex 980041, ≤ small bay, ⤓ heated, ⩙⬡ – |齒| ▤ 📺 ♿ – ⚐. ⒶⒺ ⓪ 𝓥𝓘𝓢𝓐. ⤋ rest
April-October – **M** a la carte 54/75000 – ☲ 16000 – **81 rm** 130/210000 – P 113/182000.

🏨 **Villa Sant'Andrea,** 🏶 23125, Telex 980077, ≤ small bay, « Floral terraces », ⩙⬡, ⤐ – ▤ rm 🅟. ⒶⒺ ⓪ Ⅹ 𝓥𝓘𝓢𝓐
M 40/45000 – ☲ 13000 – **48 rm** 61/123000, ▤ 4500 – P 150000.

🗙 ⚘ **Il Pescatore,** 🏶 23460, ≤ sea and cliffs – 🅟
3 March-October; closed Monday – **M** a la carte 20/33000
Spec. Cannelloni alla Giovanni, Riso alla pescatora, Cernia alla marinara. **Wines** Villagrande.

🗙 **Il Delfino-da Angelo,** 🏶 23004, ≤ small bay, ⌂ – ⓪
15 March-October – **M** a la carte 19/29000.

🗙 **Da Giovanni,** 🏶 23531, ≤ sea – ⤋
closed Monday – **M** a la carte 20/30000.

at Lido di Spisone by ② : 7 km – ✉ **98030** Mazzarò :

🏨 Lido Méditerranée, 🏶 24422, ≤, ⩙⬡ – |齒| ▤ 🅟 – *seasonal* – **72 rm**.

Norway

Norge

Oslo

PRACTICAL INFORMATION

LOCAL CURRENCY

Norwegian Kroner : 100 N-Kr = 10.916 US $ (Jan. 85)

TOURIST INFORMATION

The telephone number and address of the Tourist Information office is given in the text under ⊞.

FOREIGN EXCHANGE

In the Oslo area banks are usually open between 8.15am and 3.30pm, but in summertime, 15.5 - 31/8, they close at 3pm. Thursdays they are open till 5pm. Saturdays closed.

Most large hotels, main airports and railway stations have exchange facilities. At Fornebu Airport the bank is open from 6.30am to 10.30pm on weekdays and 7.00am to 10pm on Sundays, all the year round.

CAR HIRE

The international car hire companies have branches in each major city. Your hotel porter will be able to give details and help you with your arrangements.

SPEED LIMITS

The maximum permitted speed within congested areas is 50 km/h - 31mph. Outside congested areas it is 80 km/h - 50mph. Where there are other speed limits (lower or higher) it is signposted.

SEAT BELTS

The wearing of seat belts in Norway is compulsory for drivers and front seat passengers. All cars registered in Norway after 1/1-84 have got to have seat belts in the back seat too, and after 1/3-85 it is compulsory to use them.

SHOPPING IN OSLO
(Knitted ware - silver ware)

Your hotel porter will be able to help you and give you information.

TIPPING IN NORWAY

A service charge is included in hotel and restaurant bills and it is up to the customer to give something in addition if he wants to.

The cloakroom is sometimes included in the bill, sometimes you pay a certain amount.

Taxi drivers and baggage porters have no claim to be tipped.
It is up to you if you want to give a gratuity.

OSLO

📠 Oslo Golfklubb 🖉 50 44 02.

SIGHTS

See : Bygdøy Museum★★ AZ : Viking Ships★★★ (Vikingeskipene), Folk Museum★★ (Norsk Folkemuseum), Kon-Tiki Museum★ (Kon-Tiki Museet), Fram Museum★ (Fram Museet), Maritime Museum★ (Norsk Sjøfartsmuseum) ; Frognerparken★ (Vigeland Sculptures★★) AX ; City Hall★ (Rådhuset) BY H ; Munch Museum★ (Munchmuseet) CY ; National Gallery★ (Nasjonalgalleriet) BY **M1** ; Akershus Castle★ (Akershus Festning) BZ ; Historical Museum★ (Historisk Museum) BY **M2**.

Outskirts : Holmenkollen★★ (NW : 10 km) : Ski Jump★, Ski Museum★ AX ; Tryvann Tower★★ (Tryvannstårnet) (NW : 14 km) : ☀★★ AX ; Sonja Henie-Onstad Centre★ (Henie-Onstads Kunstsenter) (W : 12 km) AY.

OSLO Norge 🎕🎔🎕 K 2 – pop. 448 775 – ✆ 02.

✈ Fornebu SW : 8 km 🖉 59 67 16 – SAS : Ruseløkkveien 6 🖉 42 75 00 (Europe and Overseas) 42 79 00 (Domestics and Scandinavia). – Air Terminal : Havnegata, main railway station.

⛴ Copenhagen, Frederikshavn, Kiel : contact tourist information centre (see below).

🛈 Oslo Tourist Information, City Hall, seaside 🖉 42 71 70 — **KNA** (Kongelig Norsk Automobilklub) Royal Norwegian Automobile Club 🖉 56 26 90 — **NAF** (Norges Automobil Forbund) 🖉 42 94 00.

Hamburg 888 – København 583 – Stockholm 522.

OSLO

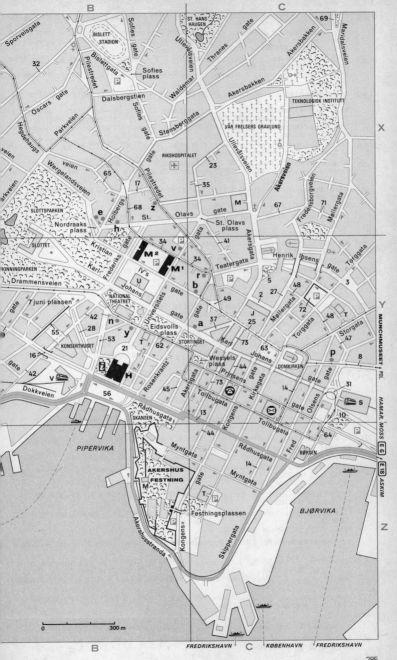

285

🏨 **Grand,** Karl Johansgt. 31, Oslo 1, ℰ 42 93 90, Telex 71683, 🛎, 🖼 – 🛗 ▤ 📺 ☎. ♨. ᴁᴱ
⓪ Ε 𝘝𝘐𝘚𝘈. ⚘
CY **a**
closed 21 December-2 January – **M** (see **Grand Café** below) – **Etoile** (buffet lunch) 105 a
la carte approx. 360 – **Fritzuer Grill** *(closed lunch Saturday and summer and Sunday)* a la
carte 182/246 – **310 rm** ⊡ 720/1210.

🏨 **SAS Scandinavia** Ⓜ, Holbergsgate 30, Oslo 1, ℰ 11 30 00, Telex 19090, 🛎, 🖼 – 🛗 ▤
📺 ☎. ⇆. ♨. ᴁᴱ ⓪ Ε 𝘝𝘐𝘚𝘈
BX **e**
M (see **Charley's** below) – **Holberg** (dinner only) a la carte 212/351 – ⊡ 67 – **490 rm**
855/990.

🏨 ❀ **Continental,** Stortingsgaten 24-26, Oslo 1, ℰ 41 90 60, Telex 71012 – 🛗 📺 ☎. ♨.
ᴁᴱ ⓪ Ε 𝘝𝘐𝘚𝘈. ⚘
BY **n**
M (see **Theatercaféen** below) - **Annen Etage** *(closed Sunday lunch, Saturday, 21
December-2 January and Bank Holidays)* a la carte 190/395 – **170 rm** ⊡ 680/825
Spec. Mousse de homard au jus de truffe, Escalope de saumon aux oeufs de truite et sauce Sabayon, Filet
de Renne aux champignons des bois.

🏨 **Bristol,** Kristian 4 des gate 7, Oslo 1, ℰ 41 58 40, Telex 71668 – 🛗 📺 ☎. ♨.
CY **b**
M (grill rest only) – **El Toro** (dinner only) – **143 rm**.

🏨 **Kna,** Parkveien 68, Oslo 2, ℰ 56 26 90, Telex 71763 – 🛗 📺 ☎. ♨. ᴁᴱ ⓪ Ε 𝘝𝘐𝘚𝘈. ⚘
AY **f**
closed Easter and Christmas – **M** (buffet lunch) 130 a la carte 170/360 – **148 rm** ⊡ 700/890.

🏨 **Sara,** Biskop Gunnerus gate 3, Oslo 1, ℰ 42 94 10, Telex 71342 – 🛗 ▤ 📺 ☎ ☎. ♨. ᴁᴱ
⓪ Ε 𝘝𝘐𝘚𝘈. ⚘
CY **p**
M (buffet lunch) 95 a la carte 151/291 – **319 rm** ⊡ 660/850.

🏨 **Gabelshus** ⑳, Gabelsgate 16, Oslo 2, ℰ 56 25 90, 🍴 – 🛗 ▤ 🛁wc 🛁wc ☎ ⓟ. ♨. ᴁᴱ
. ⚘
AY **m**
closed Easter and Christmas – **M** a la carte 155/192 – **45 rm** ⊡ 450/600.

🏨 **Europa** Ⓜ without rest., St. Olavsgate 31, Oslo 1, ℰ 20 99 90, Telex 71512 – 🛗 📺 🛁wc
🛁wc ☎. ♨. ᴁᴱ ⓪ Ε 𝘝𝘐𝘚𝘈. ⚘
BX **h**
closed Easter and Christmas – **140 rm** ⊡ 590/690.

🏨 **Ambassadeur,** Camilla Colletts vei 15, Oslo 2, ℰ 44 18 35, Telex 71446, 🛎, 🖼 – 🛗 📺
🛁wc 🛁wc ⊛. ♨. ᴁᴱ ⓪ Ε 𝘝𝘐𝘚𝘈. ⚘
AX **t**
closed 21 December-2 January – **M** *(closed Saturday and Sunday)* (buffet lunch) 155
a la carte 130/288 – **33 rm** ⊡ 695/895.

🏨 **Stefan,** Rosenkrantzgate 1, Oslo 1, ℰ 42 92 50, Telex 19809 – 🛁wc ☎ ♿. ᴁᴱ ⓪ Ε 𝘝𝘐𝘚𝘈.
⚘ – *closed Easter and Christmas* – **M** (unlicensed) – **126 rm** ⊡ 600/700.
CY **r**

🏨 **Carlton Rica** ⑳, Parkveien 78, Oslo 2, ℰ 56 30 90, Telex 71902 – 🛗 🛁wc ☎
AY **q**
50 rm.

🏨 **Norum,** Bygdøy Allé 53, ℰ 44 79 90 – 🛗 🛁wc 🛁wc ☎. ♨. – **60 rm**.
AX **s**

🏨 **Savoy** without rest., Universitetsgt. 11, Oslo 1, ℰ 20 26 55, Telex 76418 – 🛗 📺 🛁wc
☎. ᴁᴱ ⓪ Ε 𝘝𝘐𝘚𝘈. ⚘ – **65 rm** ⊡ 260/590.
BY **v**

XXX **Bagatelle,** Bygdøy Allé 3, Oslo 2, ℰ 44 63 97 – ▤. ᴁᴱ ⓪ Ε 𝘝𝘐𝘚𝘈
AY **x**
closed Saturday, Sunday, Easter, 6 July-4 August and 22 December-2 January – **M** a la
carte 130/350.

XXX **Mølla,** Sagveien 21, Oslo 4, ℰ 37 54 50, « Old water-mill » – ▤. ᴁᴱ ⓪ Ε 𝘝𝘐𝘚𝘈
closed Sunday and Bank Holidays – **M** a la carte 190/285.   by Maridalsveien CX

XXX **3 Kokker,** Drammensveien 30, Oslo 2, ℰ 44 26 50 – ▤. ᴁᴱ ⓪ Ε 𝘝𝘐𝘚𝘈
AY **k**
closed Sunday – **M** a la carte 140/300.

XX **Frascati Rotisserie,** Stortingsgaten 20, Oslo 1, ℰ 41 68 76 – ▤
BY **y**

XX **La Mer,** Pilestredet 31, Oslo 1, ℰ 20 34 45, Seafood – ▤. ᴁᴱ 𝘝𝘐𝘚𝘈
BX **z**
closed Sunday and Bank Holidays – **M** (dinner only) a la carte 200/285.

XX **Theatercaféen** (at Continental H.), Stortingsgaten 24-26, Oslo 1, ℰ 41 90 60, Telex
71012 – ᴁᴱ ⓪ Ε 𝘝𝘐𝘚𝘈
BY **n**
M a la carte 130/236.

XX **Grand Café** (at Grand H.), Karl Johansgt. 31, Oslo 1, ℰ 33 48 70 – ▤. ᴁᴱ ⓪ Ε 𝘝𝘐𝘚𝘈
M a la carte 113/163.
CY **a**

X **Charlys** (at SAS Scandinavia H.), St. Olavs gate 33, Oslo 1, ℰ 11 30 00, Telex 19090 – ᴁᴱ
⓪ Ε 𝘝𝘐𝘚𝘈
BX **e**
M (buffet lunch) 49/a la carte 89/121.

at Holmenkollen NW : 7 km by Bogstadveien – AX – and Holmenkollveien – ✉ ❀ 02
Oslo :

🏨 **Holmenkollen Park** Ⓜ ⑳, Kongeveien 26, Oslo 3, NW : 7 km by Hegdehaugsveien
ℰ 14 60 90, Telex 72094, ≤ Oslo and fjord, 🛎, 🖼 – 🛗 ▤ 📺 ☎ ⇆ ⓟ. ♨. ᴁᴱ ⓪ Ε
𝘝𝘐𝘚𝘈. ⚘ – *closed 22 December-2 January* – **M De fem Stuer** a la carte 217/298 – **Bakeriet**
a la carte 135/218 – **200 rm**.

XXX **Frognerseteren,** Holmenkollveien 200, Oslo 3, NW : 10 km by Holmenkollveien ℰ
14 37 36, ≤ Oslo and fjord – ▤ ⓟ
M a la carte 181/241.

at Fornebu Airport SW : 8 km by E 18 – AY – and Snarøyveien – ✉ ❀ 02 Oslo :

🏨 **SAS Globetrotter** ⑳, Oslo-N-1324, Lysaker ℰ 12 02 20, Telex 18745, 🛎, park, ⚔ – 🛗
▤ 📺 ☎ ⓟ. ♨. – **150 rm**.

Portugal

Lisbon

PRACTICAL INFORMATION

LOCAL CURRENCY

Escudo : 100 Esc. = 0.586 US $ (Jan. 85)

FOREIGN EXCHANGE

Hotels, restaurants and shops do not always accept foreign currencies and the tourist is therefore advised to change cheques and currency at banks, saving banks and exchange offices - The general opening times are as follows: banks 9.30am to noon and 2 to 4pm (closed on Saturdays), money changers 9.30am to 6pm (usually closed on Saturday afternoons and Sundays).

SHOPPING IN LISBON

Shops and boutiques are generally open from 9am to 1pm and 3 to 7pm - In Lisbon, the main shopping streets are: Rua Augusta, Rua do Carmo, Rua Garrett (Chiado), Rua do Ouro, Rua da Prata.

TIPPING

A service charge is added to all bills in hotels, restaurants and cafés. It is usual, however, to give an additional tip for personal service ; 10 % of the fare or ticket price is also the usual amount given to taxi drivers and cinema and theatre usherettes.

SPEED LIMITS

The speed limit on motorways is 130 km/h - 80 mph, on other roads 90 km/h - 56 mph and in built up areas 60 km/h - 37 mph.

SEAT BELTS

It is compulsory for drivers and front seat passengers to wear seat belts.

THE FADO

The Lisbon Fado (songs) can be heard in restaurants in old parts of the town such as the Alfama, the Bairro Alto and the Mouraria. A selection of fado cabarets will be found at the end of the Lisbon restaurant list.

LISBON

SIGHTS

See : View : ★★ from the Suspension Bridge (Ponte de 25 Abril), ※ ★★ from Christ in Majesty (Cristo-Rei) S : 3,5 km.

CENTRE : POMBALINE LISBON
See : Rossio★ (square) GY — Avenida da Liberdade★ FX — Edward VII Park★ (Cold Greenhouse) EX — St. Rock★ (Igreja São Roque) FY **M¹** — Terreiro do Paço (square) GZ.

MEDIAEVAL LISBON
See : St. George's Castle★★ (Castelo de São Jorge) GY — Cathedral★ (Sé) GZ — Santa Luzia Belvedere★ (Miradouro de Santa Luzia) JY — Alfama★★ JYZ.

MANUELINE LISBON
See : Hieronymite Monastery★★ (Mosteiro dos Jerónimos : church★★, cloister★★★) — Belém Tower★★ (Torre de Belém) — Monument to the Discoveries★ (Padrão dos Descobrimentos).

MUSEUMS
Museum of Ancient Art★★ (Museu Nacional de Arte Antiga : polyptych by Nuno Gonçalves★★★) — Calouste Gulbenkian Museum★★★ (Art collection) — Azulejo Museum★ and Church of the Mother of God★★ (Igreja da Madre de Deus) — Coach Museum★★ (Museu Nacional dos Coches) — Maritime Museum★★ (Museu de Marinha).

LISBON **(LISBOA)** 1100 **37** ⑫ e ⑰ — Pop. 826 140 — alt. 111 — ✆ 01.

🏌, 🏌 Estoril Golf Club W : 25 km ✆ 268 01 76 Estoril — 🏌 Lisbon Sports Club NW : 20 km ✆ 96 00 77 — 🏌 Club de Campo de Lisboa S : 15 km ✆ 24 57 17 Aroeira, Fonte da Telha.

✈ Lisboa Airport N : 8 km from city centre — T.A.P., Praça Marquês de Pombal 3, ⊠ 1200, ✆ 53 88 52 and airport ✆ 88 91 81.

🚃 ✆ 87 60 27 and 87 70 92.

🚢 to Madeira : E.N.M., Rua de São Julião 5, ⊠ 1100, ✆ 87 30 28, and Rocha Conde de Óbidos, ⊠ 1300, ✆ 66 25 47.

🛈 Palácio Foz, Praça dos Restaudores ✆ 36 36 24, jardim de Regedor ✆ 36 35 21 and airport ✆ 89 43 23 — A.C.P. Rua Rosa Araújo 24, ⊠ 1200, ✆ 56 39 31. Telex 12581 — A.C.P. Av. Barbosa du Bocage 23, ⊠ 1000, ✆ 77 54 75, Telex 14070.

Madrid 648 — Bilbao 902 — Paris 1814 — Porto 330 — Sevilla 409.

LISBOA

291

🏨 **Ritz Inter-Continental,** Rua Rodrigo da Fonseca 88, ✉ 1000, 𝒫 69 20 20, Telex 12589,
≼, 🍴 – ⧆ 🔲 ⇔ 🅿 – 🕭. 🖭 ⓘ 🗄 𝘝𝘐𝘚𝘈 ✖️ EX **b**
M a la carte 1 550/2 920 – **300 rm** ☐ 11 400/13 600.

🏨 **Sheraton** Ⓜ, Rua Latino Coelho 1, ✉ 1000, 𝒫 57 57 57, Telex 12774, ≼, 🍴, ⬛ heated
– ⧆ 🔲 ⇔ – 🕭. 🖭 ⓘ 🗄 𝘝𝘐𝘚𝘈 ✖️ rest by Av. Fontes Pereira de Melo EFX
M (closed Saturday and Sunday) 2 550/4 050 – **390 rm** ☐ 12 000/14 500.

🏨 **Altis** Ⓜ, Rua Castilho 11, ✉ 1200, 𝒫 52 24 96, Telex 13314 – ⧆ 🔲 ⇔ – 🕭. 🖭 ⓘ 🗄
𝘝𝘐𝘚𝘈. ✖️ rest EX **z**
M 1 500/2 250 – **225 rm** ☐ 9 700/11 500.

🏨 **Tivoli,** Av. da Liberdade 185, ✉ 1200, 𝒫 53 01 81, Telex 12588, 🍴, ⬛ heated, ✖️ – ⧆
🔲 ⇔ – 🕭. 🖭 ⓘ 🗄 𝘝𝘐𝘚𝘈. ✖️ FX **d**
M 1 500 – **344 rm** ☐ 6 600/7 600 – P 9 300/13 000.

🏨 **Alfa Lisboa,** Av. Columbano Bordalo Pinheiro 𝒫 72 21 21, Telex 18477, ≼ – ⧆ 🔲 ⇔ 🅿.
🖭 ⓘ 🗄 𝘝𝘐𝘚𝘈. ✖️ rest NW : by Av. A. Augusto de Aguiar EX
260 rm ☐ 7 300/9 100 – P 7 250/10 500.

🏨 **Avenida Palace,** without rest., Rua 1° de Dezembro 123, ✉ 1200, 𝒫 36 01 51, Telex
12815 – ⧆. 𝘝𝘐𝘚𝘈 FY **n**
100 rm ☐ 5 000/7 000.

🏨 **Lutécia,** Av. Frei Miguel Contreiras 52, ✉ 1700, 𝒫 80 31 21, Telex 12457, ≼ – ⧆ 🔲 –
🕭. 🖭 ⓘ 🗄 𝘝𝘐𝘚𝘈. N : by Av. Almirante Reis GX
M 1 200 – **151 rm** ☐ 4 900/5 800 – P 4 800/6 000.

🏠 **Dom Manuel I** without rest., av, Duque d'Ávila 189, ✉ 1000, 𝒫 57 61 60, Telex 43558,
« Tasteful decor » – ⧆ 🔲. 🖭 ⓘ 🗄 𝘝𝘐𝘚𝘈. ✖️ N : by Av. Fontes Pereira de Melo EFX
64 rm ☐ 4 200/4 800.

🏠 **Tivoli Jardim,** Julio Cesar Machado 7, ✉ 1200, 𝒫 53 99 71, Telex 12172, ⬛ heated, ✖️
– ⧆ 🔲 ⇔ 🅿. 🖭 ⓘ 🗄 𝘝𝘐𝘚𝘈. ✖️ FX **e**
M 1 300 – **119 rm** ☐ 6 900/7 200 – P 9 900/13 200.

🏠 **Diplomático,** Rua Castilho 74, ✉ 1200, 𝒫 56 20 41, Telex 13713 – ⧆ 🔲 🅿 – 🕭. 🖭 ⓘ
🗄 𝘝𝘐𝘚𝘈. ✖️ EX **c**
M 1 300 – **90 rm** ☐ 3 600/4 800 – P 7 500/11 000.

🏠 **Flórida** without rest., Rua Duque de Palmela 32, ✉ 1200, 𝒫 57 61 45, Telex 12256 – ⧆
🔲 – 🕭. 🖭 ⓘ 🗄 𝘝𝘐𝘚𝘈. ✖️ EX **x**
120 rm ☐ 4 300/5 400.

🏠 **Mundial,** Rua D. Duarte 4, ✉ 1100, 𝒫 86 31 01, Telex 12308, ≼ – ⧆ 🔲 🅿 – 🕭. 🖭 ⓘ 🗄
𝘝𝘐𝘚𝘈. ✖️ rest GY **c**
M 1 300 – **147 rm** ☐ 4 500/7 000.

🏠 **Fénix and Rest. El Bodegón,** Praça Marquês de Pombal 8, ✉ 1200, 𝒫 53 51 21, Telex
12170 – ⧆ 🔲 – 🕭. 🖭 ⓘ 🗄 𝘝𝘐𝘚𝘈. ✖️ EX **g**
M (closed Saturday dinner and Sunday) a la carte 1 800/2 800 – **112 rm** ☐ 4 200/4 900.

🏠 **Lisboa Penta,** Av. dos Combatentes, ✉ 1600, 𝒫 72 50 50, Telex 18437, ⬛ – ⧆ 🔲 ⇔
🅿 – 🕭. 🖭 ⓘ 🗄 𝘝𝘐𝘚𝘈 NW : by Av. A. Augusto de Aguiar EX
M 2 270 – **588 rm** ☐ 7 810/9 625 – P 12 350/14 165.

🏠 **Roma,** Av. de Roma 33, ✉ 1700, 𝒫 76 77 61, Telex 16586, ≼, 🔲 – ⧆ 🔲 – 🕭. 🖭 ⓘ 🗄
𝘝𝘐𝘚𝘈. ✖️ N : by Av. Almirante Reis GX
M 1 000 – **263 rm** ☐ 3 000/4 000 – P 3 800/4 700.

🏠 **Lisboa Plaza,** Travessa do Salitre 7, ✉ 1200, 𝒫 36 39 22, Telex 16402 – ⧆ 🔲 🅿. 🖭 ⓘ
🗄 𝘝𝘐𝘚𝘈. ✖️ FX **b**
M 1 200/1 800 – **93 rm** ☐ 4 900/5 800 – P 7 500/11 000.

🏠 **Dom Carlos,** without rest., Av. Duque de Loulé 121, ✉ 1000, 𝒫 53 90 71, Telex 16468 –
⧆ 🔲. 🖭 🗄 𝘝𝘐𝘚𝘈. ✖️ EX **s**
☐ 200 – **73 rm** 3 500/4 600.

🏠 **Embaixador** without rest., Av. Duque de Loulé 73, ✉ 1000, 𝒫 53 01 71, Telex 13773, ≼
– ⧆ 🔲 – 🕭. 🖭 ⓘ 🗄 𝘝𝘐𝘚𝘈. ✖️ FX **a**
96 rm ☐ 3 600/4 800.

🏡 **Miraparque,** Av. Sidónio Pais 12, ✉ 1000, 𝒫 57 80 70, Telex 16745 – ⧆ 🔲 rest 🛏wc
🛉wc ☎. ✖️ rest EX **k**
M 1 100 – **100 rm** ☐ 3 000/3 500 – P 3 550/5 200.

🏡 **Britânia** without rest., Rua Rodrigues Sampaio 17, ✉ 1100, 𝒫 57 50 95, Telex 13733 – ⧆
🔲 🛏wc ☎. 🖭 ⓘ 🗄 𝘝𝘐𝘚𝘈. ✖️ FX **y**
30 rm ☐ 3 200/4 200.

🏡 **Príncipe Real,** without rest., Rua da Alegria 53, ✉ 1200, 𝒫 36 01 16, « Tasteful decor » –
⧆ 🛏wc ☎ EX **q**
24 rm.

🏡 **Eduardo VII,** Av. Fontes Pereira de Melo 5, ✉ 1000, 𝒫 53 01 41, Telex 18340, ≼ – ⧆ 🔲
🛏wc 🛉wc ☎. 🖭 🗄 𝘝𝘐𝘚𝘈. ✖️ EX **p**
M 1 200/1 500 – **110 rm** ☐ 3 000/3 900 – P 4 350/5 400.

🏡 **York House,** Rua das Janelas Verdes 32, ✉ 1200, 𝒫 66 25 44, « Former 16C Convent,
Portuguese decor » – 🛏wc 🛉wc ☎. 🖭 ⓘ 🗄 𝘝𝘐𝘚𝘈. ✖️ rest
M 900/1 200 – **58 rm** ☐ 3 800/5 000 – P 5 600/8 200.
W : by calçada M. de Abrantes EZ

🏠 **Botánico,** without rest, Rua Mãe d'Água 16, ✉ 1200, 𝒫 32 03 92, Telex 12308 – 🛗 🗏
🚿wc 🛁wc 🅟
30 rm. FX **s**

🏠 **Vip,** without rest., Rua Fernão Lopes 25, ✉ 1000, 𝒫 57 89 23, Telex 14194 – 🛗 🚿wc
🅟 – 🔬
54 rm. FX **n**

🏠 **Principe,** Av. Duque d'Ávila 201, ✉ 1000, 𝒫 53 61 51, Telex 43565 – 🛗 🗏 🚿wc 🅟 🅿.
🆎 ⓞ 🗈 𝘝𝘐𝘚𝘈 🍴 NW : by Av. A. Augusto de Aguiar EX
M 800 – **67 rm** ☴ 2 500/3 500 – P 3 250/4 000.

🏠 **Do Reno** without rest., Av. Duque d'Ávila 195, ✉ 1000, 𝒫 54 81 81, Telex 15893 – 🛗
🚿wc 🛁wc 🅟 🅿. 🆎 ⓞ 🗈 𝘝𝘐𝘚𝘈 NW : by Av. A. Augusto de Aguiar EX
54 rm ☴ 2 500/3 500.

🏠 **Excelsior,** Rua Rodrigues Sampaio 172, ✉ 1100, 𝒫 53 71 51, Telex 14223 – 🛗 🗏 rest
🚿wc 🛁wc 🅟. 🆎 ⓞ 🗈 𝘝𝘐𝘚𝘈 🍴 EX **d**
M 850 – **80 rm** ☴ 2 700/3 500 – P 3 450/4 400.

🏠 **Nazareth,** 4th floor, without rest., Av. António Augusto de Aguiar 25, ✉ 1000, 𝒫 54 20 16
– 🛗 🚿wc 🅟 EX **y**
32 rm.

🏠 **São Pedro** without rest., Rua Pascoal de Melo 130, ✉ 1000, 𝒫 57 87 65 – 🛗 🚿wc 🛁wc
🅟. 🍴 N : by Av. Almirante Reis GX
40 rm ☴ 2 500.

🏠 **Insulana,** 2nd floor, without rest., Rua da Assunção 52, ✉ 1100, 𝒫 32 80 13 – 🛗 🚿wc
🛁wc 🅟 GY **e**
32 rm.

🏠 **Imperador** without rest., Av. 5 de Outubro 55, ✉ 1000, 𝒫 57 48 84 – 🛗 🚿wc 🛁wc 🅟.
🍴 N : by Av. Fontes Pereira de Melo EFX
43 rm ☴ 2 300/2 580.

🏠 **Roma** 1st floor, without rest., Travessa da Glória 22-A, ✉ 1200, 𝒫 36 05 57 – 🚿wc
🛁wc 🅟. 🆎 ⓞ 🗈 𝘝𝘐𝘚𝘈 FY **t**
24 rm ☴ 2 450/3 300.

🏠 **Americano** without rest., Rua 1° de Dezembro 73, ✉ 1200, 𝒫 32 75 19 – 🛗 🚿wc 🛁wc
🅟 FY **c**
49 rm ☴ 975/2 750.

XXXX **Aviz,** Rua Serpa Pinto 12-B, ✉ 1200, 𝒫 32 53 72 – 🗏. 🆎 ⓞ 🗈 𝘝𝘐𝘚𝘈 FZ **x**
closed Saturday lunch and Sunday – **M** a la carte 2 000/3 600.

XXXX ✸ **Tágide,** Largo da Academia Nacional de Belas Artes 18, ✉ 1200, 𝒫 32 07 20, ≼ – 🗏.
🆎 ⓞ 🗈 𝘝𝘐𝘚𝘈 FZ **z**
closed Saturday dinner and Sunday – **M** a la carte 2 140/3 500
Spec. Paté de salmão, Cherne, Churrasco de cabrito finas ervas.

XXXX **António Clara,** av. da República 38, ✉ 1000, 𝒫 76 63 80, Telex 62506, « Former old
palace » – 🗏 🅿. 🆎 ⓞ 🗈 𝘝𝘐𝘚𝘈 🍴 N : by Av. Fontes Pereira de Melo EFX
M a la carte 1 700/2 930.

XXXX **Clara,** Campo dos Martires da Patria 49, ✉ 1000, 𝒫 55 73 41 – 🗏. 🆎 ⓞ 🗈 𝘝𝘐𝘚𝘈 🍴
M 1 600/2 300. FX **f**

XXXX **Tavares,** Rua da Misericórdia 37, ✉ 1200, 𝒫 37 09 06, Late 19C decor – 🗏. 🆎 ⓞ 𝘝𝘐𝘚𝘈
🍴 FZ **t**
closed Saturday and Sunday lunch – **M** a la carte 1 790/3 490.

XXX **Cota D'Armas,** Beco de São Miguel 7, ✉ 1100, 𝒫 86 86 82, 🌳, Tasteful decor and Fado
cabaret at night – 🗏 JZ **d**

XXX **Gambrinus,** Rua das Portas de Santo Antão 25, ✉ 1100, 𝒫 32 14 66 – 🗏. 🆎 🗈 𝘝𝘐𝘚𝘈
M a la carte 2 460/4 700. GY **n**

XXX **Escorial,** Rua das Portas de Santo Antão 47, ✉ 1100, 𝒫 36 44 29, Modern decor – 🗏.
🆎 ⓞ 🗈 𝘝𝘐𝘚𝘈 GY **n**
M a la carte 2 020/3 600.

XXX **Pabe,** Rua Duque de Palmela 27-A, ✉ 1200, 𝒫 53 74 84, English pub style – 🗏. 🆎 ⓞ
🗈 𝘝𝘐𝘚𝘈 EX **u**
M a la carte 1 880/3 340.

XXX ✸ **Casa da Comida,** Travessa das Amoreiras 1, ✉ 1200, 𝒫 68 53 76, « Patio with
plants » – 🗏. 🆎 ⓞ 🗈 𝘝𝘐𝘚𝘈 🍴 EX **e**
closed Saturday lunch, Sunday and August – **M** a la carte 1 990/4 100
Spec. Pregado com pimento verde, Mariscada Casa da Comida, Cabrito assado.

XXX **Chester,** Rua Rodrigo da Fonseca 87-D, ✉ 1000, 𝒫 68 78 11, Meat specialities – 🗏. 🆎
ⓞ 🗈 𝘝𝘐𝘚𝘈 EX **w**
closed Sunday – **M** a la carte 1 200/3 000.

XXX **Saraiva's,** Rua Eng. Canto Rosende 3, ✉ 1000, 𝒫 53 19 87, Modern decor – 🗏. 🆎 ⓞ
🗈 𝘝𝘐𝘚𝘈 N : by Av. A. Augusto de Aguiar EX
closed Saturday and Bank Holidays – **M** a la carte 1 550/3 100.

XXX **Conventual,** Praça das Flores 45, ✉ 1200, 𝒫 60 91 96, Monastic decor and atmosphere,
Traditional Portuguese cuisine – 🗏. 🆎 ⓞ 🗈 𝘝𝘐𝘚𝘈 EY **m**
closed Sunday – **M** 1 310/2 720.

XXX O Faz Figura, Rua do Paraíso 15 B, ⊠ 1100, ✆ 86 89 31, ≤, 🍴 – 🍽   HY **n**

XXX **Bachus** Largo da Trindade 9, ⊠ 1200, ✆ 32 28 28 – 🍽. **AE** ⓞ **E** **VISA**. ⚶   FY **s**
     M a la carte 1 490/2 830.

XX A Góndola, Av. de Berna 64, ⊠ 1000, ✆ 77 04 26, 🍴 – 🍽. **E** **VISA**
     closed Saturday dinner and Sunday.   N : by Av. A. Augusto de Aguiar   EX

XX **Michel**, Largo de Santa Cruz do Castelo 5, ⊠ 1100, ✆ 86 43 38, French rest. – 🍽. **AE** ⓞ
     E **VISA**   GY **b**
     closed Saturday lunch, Sunday and Bank Holidays – **M** a la carte 1 960/3 060.

XX São Jerónimo, Rua dos Jerónimos 12, ⊠ 1400, ✆ 64 87 96 – 🍽
                               W : by Av. 24 de Julho   EZ

XX Casa do Leão, Castelo de Jorge, ⊠ 1100, ✆ 87 59 62, ≤ – 🍽   GY **s**
     M (lunch only).

XX **Petite Folie,** Av. António Augusto de Aguiar 74, ⊠ 1000, ✆ 52 19 48, 🍴, French rest.
     – **AE** ⓞ **E** **VISA**   EX **m**
     M a la carte 1 050/1 950.

XX **Espelho d'Água,** av. de Brasilia, ⊠ 1300, ✆ 61 73 73, ≤, 🍴, Modern decor – 🍽. **AE**
     ⓞ **E** **VISA**   W : by Av. 24 de Julho   EZ
     closed Sunday – **M** a la carte 1 350/2 430.

XX **Sancho,** Travessa da Glória 14, ⊠ 1200, ✆ 36 97 80 – 🍽. **AE** ⓞ **E** **VISA**   FX **t**
     closed Sunday and Bank Holidays – **M** a la carte 910/2 025.

X O Vicentinho, Rua Voz do Operario 1 B, ⊠ 1100, ✆ 86 46 95 – 🍽   HY **a**

X **Xêlê Bananas,** Praça das Flores 29, ⊠ 1200, ✆ 67 05 15, Tropical style decor – 🍽. **AE**
     ⓞ **E** **VISA**. ⚶   EY **n**
     closed Sunday – **M** a la carte 980/2 420.

X **Sua Excelência,** Rua do Conde 42, ⊠ 1200, ✆ 60 36 14 – 🍽. **AE** ⓞ **E** **VISA**
     closed Wednesday and September – **M** a la carte 1 200/3 475.
                     W : by calçada M. de Abrantes   EY

X **António,** Rua Tomás Ribeiro 63, ⊠ 1000, ✆ 53 87 80 – 🍽. **AE** ⓞ **E** **VISA**. ⚶
     M a la carte 1 450/2 740.   N : by Av. A. Augusto de Aguiar   EX

X Mestre Cuco, Rua Nova S. Mamede 16, ⊠ 1200, ✆ 67 57 23 – 🍽   EX **y**

Typical restaurants.

XX O Faia, Rua da Barroca 56, ⊠ 1200, ✆ 32 67 42, Telex 13649, Fado cabaret – 🍽   FY **f**
     M (dinner only).

XX **A Severa,** Rua das Gáveas 51, ⊠ 1200, ✆ 36 40 06, Fado cabaret – 🍽. **AE** ⓞ **E** **VISA**. ⚶
     closed Thursday – **M** a la carte 1 700/3 000.   FY **b**

XX Lisboa à Noite, Rua das Gáveas 69, ⊠ 1200, ✆ 36 85 57, Fado cabaret at dinner – 🍽
                FY **x**

XX **Sr. Vinho,** Rua do Meio - à - Lapa 18, ⊠ 1200, ✆ 67 26 81, Fado cabaret – 🍽. **AE** ⓞ **E**
     VISA. ⚶   EZ **r**
     closed Sunday – **M** (dinner only) a la carte 2 200/2 800.

X **Adega Machado,** Rua do Norte 91, ⊠ 1200, ✆ 36 00 95, Fado cabaret – 🍽. **AE** ⓞ **E**
     VISA. ⚶   FY **k**
     closed Monday from October to May – **M** (dinner only) a la carte 1 450/2 870.

X O Forcado, Rua da Rosa 221, ⊠ 1200, ✆ 36 85 79, Fado cabaret – 🍽   FY **r**
     M (dinner only).

X Parreirinha de Alfama, Beco do Espírito Santo 1, ⊠ 1100, ✆ 86 82 09, Fado cabaret
     M (dinner only).   in Alfama

Spain
España

Madrid
Barcelona
Malaga - Marbella
Sevilla
Valencia

PRACTICAL INFORMATION

LOCAL CURRENCY

Peseta : 100 ptas = 0.572 US $ (Jan. 85)

TOURIST INFORMATION

The telephone number and address of the Tourist Information offices is given in the text of the towns under **🛈**.

FOREIGN EXCHANGE

Banks are open from 9am to 2pm (12.30pm on Saturdays).
Exchange offices in Sevilla and Valencia airports open from 9am to 2pm, in Barcelona airport from 9am to 2pm and 7 to 11pm. In Madrid and Malaga airports, offices operate a 24 hour service.

TRANSPORT

Taxis may be hailed when showing the green light or sign "Libre" on the windscreen. Madrid and Barcelona have a Metro (subway) network. In each station complete information and plans will be found.

SHOPPING

In the index of street names, those printed in red are where the principal shops are found.
The big stores are easy to find in town centres; they are open from 10am to 8pm.
Exclusive shops and boutiques are open from 10am to 2pm and 5 to 8pm - In Madrid they will be found in Serrano, Princesa and the Centre; in Barcelona, Passeig de Gracia, Diagonal and the Rambla de Catalunya.
Second-hand goods and antiques: El Rastro (Flea Market), Las Corts, Serrano in Madrid; in Barcelona, Los Encantes (Flea Market), Barrio Gótico.

"TAPAS"

Bars serving "tapas" (typical spanish food to be eaten with a glass of wine or an aperitif) will usually be found in central, busy or old quarters of towns. In Madrid, idle your way to the Calle de la Cruz (Puerta del Sol) or to the Calle de Cuchilleros (Plaza Mayor).

TIPPING

Hotel, restaurant and café bills always include service in the total charge. Nevertheless it is usual to leave the staff a small gratuity which may vary with the district and the service given. Doormen, porters and taxi-drivers are used to being tipped.

SPEED LIMITS

The maximum permitted speed on motorways is 120 km/h - 74 mph, and 90 km/h - 56 mph on other roads.

SEAT BELTS

The wearing of seat belts is compulsory for drivers and front seat passengers.

MADRID

SIGHTS

See : The Prado Museum★★★ (Museo del Prado) NZ — Parque del Buen Retiro★★ HY — Paseo del Prado (Plaza de la Cibeles) NXYZ — Paseo de Recoletos NVX — Paseo de la Castellana NV — Puerta del Sol and Calle de Alcalá LMNY — Plaza Mayor★ KYZ — Royal Palace (Palacio Real)★★ KY — Descalzas Reales Convent★★ (Convento de las Descalzas Reales) KY L — San Antonio de la Florida (fresco by Goya★) DX **R.**

Other Museums : Archeological Museum★★ (Arqueológico Nacional) NV M²² — Lázaro Galdiano★★ HV M⁷ — The Américas Museum★ DV M⁸ — Museum of Contemporary Spanish Art★ — Army Museum (del Ejército★) NY M².

Envir. : El Pardo (Palacio★) NW : 13 km by C 601.

MADRID 444 y 447 K 19 — Pop. 3 188 297 — alt. 646 — ✿ 91 — Bullring.

Racecourse of the Zarzuela — 🏌, 🏌 Puerta de Hierro ✆ 216 17 45 — 🏌, 🏌 Club de Campo ✆ 207 03 95 — 🏌 La Moraleja by ① : 11 km ✆ 650 07 00 — 🏌 Club Barberán by ⑥ : 10 km ✆ 218 85 05 — 🏌, 🏌 Las Lomas — El Bosque by ⑥ : 18 km ✆ 464 32 15 — 🏌 Real Automóvil Club de España by ① : 28 km ✆ 652 26 00 — 🏌 Nuevo Club de Madrid, Las Matas by ⑦ : 26 km ✆ 630 08 20 — 🏌 Somosaguas W : 10 km by Casa de Campo ✆ 212 16 47.

✈ Madrid-Barajas by ② : 13 km ✆ 222 11 65 — Iberia : pl. de Cánovas 5, ⊠ 28014, ✆ 429 74 43 and Aviaco, Modesto Lafuente 76, ⊠ 28003, ✆ 254 51 19 — ➞ Atocha ✆ 228 52 37 — Chamartín ✆ 733 11 22 — Príncipe Pío ✆ 248 87 16.

Shipping Companies : Cía. Trasmediterránea, Pedro Muñoz Seca 2 NX, ⊠ 1, ✆ 431 07 00, Telex 23189.

🅿 Princesa 1, ⊠ 28008, ✆ 241 23 25, Maria de Molina 50, ⊠ 28006, ✆ 411 43 36 pl. Mayor 3, ⊠ 28012, ✆ 266 48 74, Caballero de Gracia 7, ⊠ 28013, ✆ 231 44 57 and Barajas airport ✆ 205 86 56 — R.A.C.E. José Abascal 10, ⊠ 28003, ✆ 447 32 00, Telex 27341.

Paris (by Irún) 1317 ① — Barcelona 626 ② — Bilbao 401 ① — La Coruña 601 ⑦ — Lisboa 648 ⑥ — Málaga 546 ④ — Porto 602 ⑦ — Sevilla 547 ④ — Valencia 354 ③ — Zaragoza 321 ②.

Centre : Paseo del Prado, Puerta del Sol, Gran Vía, Alcalá, Paseo de Recoletos, Plaza Mayor, Leganitos (plan pp. 6 and 7).

Palace, pl. de las Cortes 7, ✉ 28014, ✆ 429 75 51, Telex 22272 – 🛗 ▤ 🚗 – 🏛. AE ⓓ E VISA. ✗ rest MY **e**
M 3 500 – ☕ 800 – **510 rm** 10 400/13 700.

Princesa Plaza Ⓜ, Princesa 40, ✉ 28008, ✆ 242 21 00, Telex 44378 – 🛗 ▤ 🚗 – 🏛. AE ⓓ E VISA. ✗ KV **c**
M 3 175 – ☕ 690 – **406 rm** 9 800/12 250.

Plaza without rest. coffee shop only, pl. España, ✉ 28013, ✆ 247 12 00, Telex 27383, ≤, 🏊 – 🛗 ▤ – 🏛. AE ⓓ E VISA. ✗ KV **s**
☕ 550 – **306 rm** 7 250/9 050.

Emperador without rest, Gran Vía 53, ✉ 28013, ✆ 247 28 00, Telex 46261, 🏊 – 🛗 ▤ – 🏛. AE ⓓ E VISA. ✗ KX **n**
☕ 400 – **231 rm** 5 500/6 870.

Liabeny, Salud 3, ✉ 28013, ✆ 232 53 06, Telex 49024 – 🛗 ▤ 🚗. AE VISA. ✗ LY **e**
M 1 100 – ☕ 450 – **158 rm** 4 000/6 100.

Suecia and Rest. Bellman, Marqués de Casa Riera 4, ✉ 28014, ✆ 231 69 00, Telex 22313 – 🛗 ▤. AE ⓓ E VISA. ✗ MY **b**
M *(closed Saturday dinner, Sunday and August)* 2 000 – ☕ 500 – **64 rm** 6 900/8 500 – P 8 750/11 400.

Victoria, pl. del Angel 7, ✉ 28012, ✆ 231 45 00 – 🛗 ▤. AE ⓓ E VISA. ✗ LZ **u**
M 1 250 – ☕ 250 – **110 rm** 3 100/4 750 – P 4 875/5 600.

Arosa without rest, coffee shop only, Salud 21, ✉ 28013, ✆ 232 16 00, Telex 43618 – 🛗 ▤. AE ⓓ E VISA LX **q**
☕ 410 – **126 rm** 4 740/7 150.

El Prado without rest, Prado 11, ✉ 28014, ✆ 429 35 68 – 🛗 ▤ 🚗. AE ⓓ VISA LZ **z**
☕ 350 – **45 rm** 5 500/6 500.

Mayorazgo without rest, coffee shop only, Flor Baja 3, ✉ 28013, ✆ 247 26 00, Telex 45647 – 🛗 ▤ 🚗 – 🏛. AE ⓓ E VISA. ✗ KX **b**
☕ 350 – **200 rm** 4 500/6 000.

El Coloso, Leganitos 13, ✉ 28013, ✆ 248 76 00, Telex 47017 – 🛗 ▤ 🚗. AE ⓓ E VISA. ✗ KX **y**
M 1 200 – ☕ 400 – **84 rm** 5 460/8 575.

Casón del Tormes without rest, Río 7, ✉ 28013, ✆ 241 97 46 – 🛗 ▤ 🛁wc ☎ 🚗. VISA. ✗ KX **v**
61 rm ☕ 2 875/4 325.

Mercator without rest, coffee shop only, Atocha 123, ✉ 28012, ✆ 429 05 00, Telex 46129 – 🛗 ▤ 🛁wc ☎ Ⓟ. AE ⓓ E VISA NZ **b**
☕ 260 – **90 rm** 2 650/3 990.

Atlántico 3rd floor, without rest, Gran Via 38, ✉ 28013, ✆ 222 64 80 – 🛗 ▤ 🛁wc ☎. ⓓ E VISA. ✗ LX **e**
☕ 250 – **62 rm** 2 800/4 200.

Lope de Vega 9th floor, without rest, Gran Via 59, ✉ 28013, ✆ 247 70 00, ≤ – 🛗 🛁wc 🚿wc ☎. ⓓ. ✗ KX **b**
☕ 200 – **50 rm** 1 750/3 100.

Carlos V without rest, Maestro Vitoria 5, ✉ 28013, ✆ 231 41 00, Telex 48547 – 🛗 ▤ 🛁wc 🚿wc ☎. AE ⓓ E VISA. ✗ KY **f**
☕ 225 – **67 rm** 3 300/4 400.

Moderno without rest., Arenal 2, ✉ 28013, ✆ 231 09 00 – 🛗 ▤ 🛁wc ☎. AE VISA. ✗ LY **d**
☕ 180 – **98 rm** 2 600/4 000.

Reyes Católicos without rest, Angel 18, ✉ 28005, ✆ 265 86 00, Telex 44474 – 🛗 ▤ 🛁wc ☎. AE. ✗ KZ **w**
☕ 290 – **38 rm** 2 445/3 790.

Fontela 2nd floor, without rest, Gran Vía 11, ✉ 28013, ✆ 221 64 00 – 🛗 ▤ 🛁wc 🚿 ☎. AE E VISA. ✗ LX **u**
☕ 180 – **64 rm** 1 600/3 200.

California without rest, Gran Vía 38, ✉ 28013, ✆ 222 47 03 – 🛗 🛁wc ☎. AE ⓓ E VISA. ✗ LX **e**
☕ 215 – **27 rm** 2 250/3 600.

Amberes 7th floor, without rest, Gran Via 68, ✉ 28013, ✆ 247 61 00 – 🛗 🛁wc ☎. AE ⓓ VISA. ✗ KX **x**
☕ 200 – **42 rm** 3 220.

XXX ✿ **Clara's,** Arrieta 2, ✉ 28013, ✆ 242 09 45, Telex 23307, « Tasteful decor » – ▤. E VISA. ✗ KY **s**
closed Sunday – **M** a la carte 2 450/3 750
Spec. Fondos de alcachofas al higado fresco, Escalope de salmón con acederas, Magret de pato a las 3 pimientas.

XXX **El Cenador del Prado,** Prado 4, ✉ 28014, ✆ 429 15 49 – ▤. AE ⓓ E VISA. ✗ LZ **n**
closed Sunday, Saturday dinner and August – **M** a la carte 2 300/3 930.

MADRID

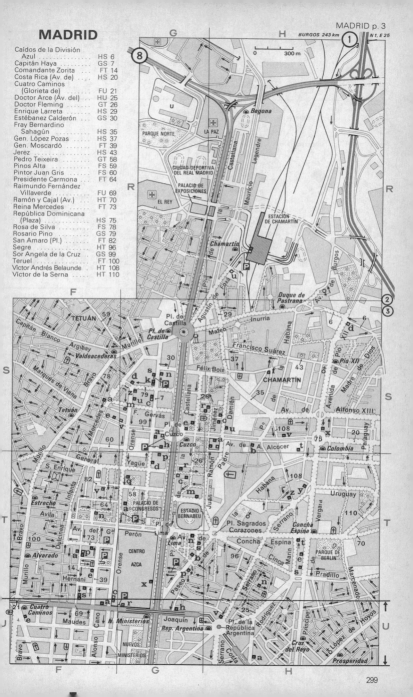

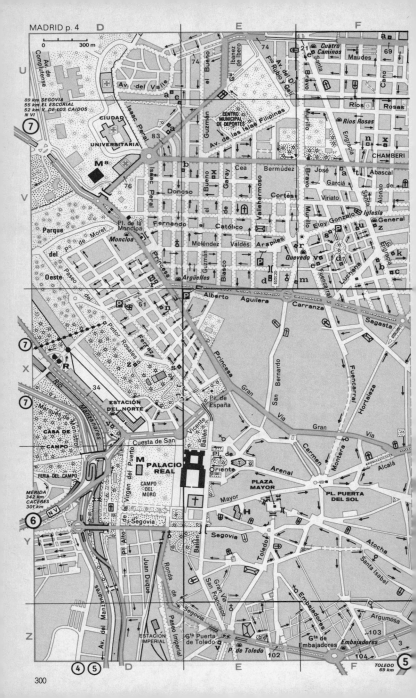

MADRID

301

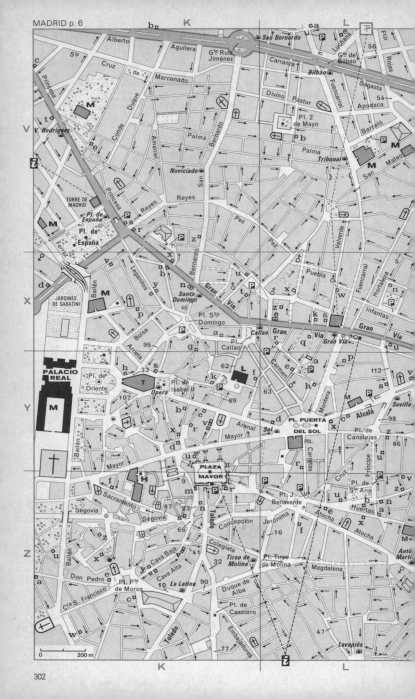

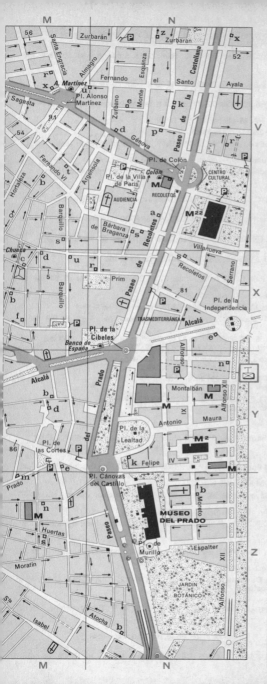

When driving through towns

use the plans

in the **Michelin Guide**

Features indicated include :

throughroutes

and by-passes ;

traffic junctions and

major squares,

new streets,

car parks,

pedestrian streets...

All this information

is revised annually.

XXX **Korynto,** Preciados 36, ⊠ 28013, ℰ 221 59 65, Seafood – ▤. AE ① E VISA. ⍟   KX **a**
M a la carte 2 200/4 350.

XXX **Bajamar,** Gran Vía 78, ⊠ 28013, ℰ 248 48 18, Telex 22818, Seafood – ▤. AE ① E VISA.
⍟   KV **r**
M a la carte 2 450/4 700.

XXX **El Escuadrón,** Tamayo y Baús 8, ⊠ 28004, ℰ 419 28 30 – ▤. AE ① E VISA. ⍟   NV **s**
M a la carte 1 825/3 915.

XXX **El Landó,** pl. Gabriel Miró 8, ⊠ 28005, ℰ 266 76 81, Tasteful decor – ▤. AE ① E VISA.
⍟   KZ **a**
closed Sunday and August – M a la carte 2 250/3 650.

XXX Medinaceli, Prado 27, ⊠ 28014, ℰ 429 13 92 – ▤   MZ **m**

XXX **Irizar** 1st floor, Jovellanos 3, ⊠ 28014, ℰ 231 45 69, Basque and French rest. – ▤. AE
① VISA.   MY **d**
closed Saturday lunch, Sunday and August – M a la carte 2 150/3 950.

XX **El Espejo,** paseo de Recoletos 31, ⊠ 28004, ℰ 410 25 25, « Old Parisian café style » –
▤. AE ① E VISA. ⍟   NV **a**
M a la carte 1 800/2 950.

XX **El Descubrimiento,** pl. Colón 1, ⊠ 28046, ℰ 410 28 51 – ▤. AE ① VISA. ⍟   NV **m**
closed Sunday – M a la carte 1 855/3 325.

XX Platerías, pl. de Santa Ana 11, ⊠ 28012, ℰ 429 70 48, Early 20C café style – ▤   LZ **b**
M (booking essential).

XX **La Grillade,** Jardines 3, ⊠ 28013, ℰ 221 22 17, Telex 43618 – ▤. AE ① E VISA. ⍟   LY **p**
M a la carte 2 065/3 260.

XX **Valentín,** San Alberto 3, ⊠ 28013, ℰ 221 16 38 – ▤. AE ① E VISA. ⍟   LY **h**
M a la carte 2 375/3 360.

XX ✿ **Gure-Etxea,** pl. de la Paja 12, ⊠ 28005, ℰ 265 61 49, Basque rest. – ▤. AE ① VISA. ⍟
closed Sunday and August – M a la carte 1 825/3 475   KZ **x**
Spec. Piperrada, Merluza Gure-Etxea, Xangurro a la donostiarra.

X Pepe Botella, San Andrés 12, ⊠ 28004, ℰ 222 52 78, French cuisine – ▤   LV **b**

X **Pazo de Monterrey,** Alcalá 4, ⊠ 28014, ℰ 222 30 10, Galician rest. – ▤. ① VISA. ⍟
M a la carte 1 900/2 950.   LY **c**

X **Casa Lucio,** Cava Baja 35, ⊠ 28005, ℰ 265 32 52, Castilian decor – ▤. AE ① VISA. ⍟
closed Saturday lunch and August – M a la carte 2 200/3 700.   KZ **y**

X **La Gran Tasca,** Ballesta 1, ⊠ 28004, ℰ 231 00 44 – AE ① E VISA. ⍟   LX **x**
closed Sunday and July-August – M a la carte 1 700/3 400.

X **Berrio,** San Marcos 8, ⊠ 28004, ℰ 221 20 35 – ▤. AE ① E VISA   LX **n**
closed Sunday and August – M a la carte 1 600/2 175.

X **El Schotis,** Cava Baja 11, ⊠ 28005, ℰ 265 32 30 – ▤. AE ① VISA. ⍟   KZ **v**
closed Sunday dinner and August – M a la carte 1 600/2 925.

Typical atmosphere

XX **Café de Chinitas,** Torija 7, ⊠ 28013, ℰ 248 51 35, Flamenco cabaret – ▤. AE E. ⍟
closed Sunday and 24 December – M (dinner only) a la carte 2 875/4 950
(extra charge for show 1 900).   KX **p**

XX **Sixto Gran Mesón** 1st floor, Cervantes 28, ⊠ 28014, ℰ 429 22 55, Castilian decor – ▤.
AE ① E VISA. ⍟   MZ **n**
closed Sunday dinner – M a la carte 1 750/3 000.

XX **Posada de la Villa,** Cava Baja 9, ⊠ 28005, ℰ 266 18 60, Castilian decor – ▤. AE ①
VISA. ⍟   KZ **v**
closed Sunday dinner and mid July-mid August – M a la carte 1 275/3 000.

XX **Botín,** Cuchilleros 17, ⊠ 28005, ℰ 266 42 17, Old Madrid decor, Typical bodega – ▤.
AE ① E VISA   KZ **n**
closed 24 December dinner – M a la carte 1 935/3 405.

X **Corral de la Morería,** Morería 17, ⊠ 28005, ℰ 265 84 46, Flamenco cabaret – ▤. AE
① VISA. ⍟   KZ **u**
M (dinner only) a la carte 2 600/4 900.

XX **Las Cuevas de Luis Candelas,** Cuchilleros 1, ⊠ 28012, ℰ 266 54 28, Old Madrid
decor - Staff in bandit costume – ▤. AE ① E VISA. ⍟   KZ **m**
M a la carte 1 225/3 675.

X **Taberna del Alabardero,** Felipe V - 6, ⊠ 28013, ℰ 247 25 77, Typical tavern – ▤. AE
① VISA. ⍟   KY **h**
M a la carte 1 725/3 650.

X **El Cosaco,** Alfonso VI - 4, ⊠ 28005, ℰ 265 35 48, Russian rest. – ①   KZ **z**
M (dinner only) a la carte 1 545/2 955.

X **Esteban,** Cava Baja 36, ⊠ 28005, ℰ 265 90 91, Old Madrid decor – ▤. AE ①. ⍟
M a la carte 2 300/3 250.   KZ **y**

Retiro-Salamanca-Ciudad Lineal Castellana, Velázquez, Serrano, Goya, Príncipe de Vergara, Narvaez, Don Ramón de la Cruz (plan p. 5 except where otherwise stated)

Ritz, pl. de la Lealtad 5, ⊠ 28014, ℰ 221 28 57, Telex 43986 – 🛗 ▤ 🚗 (in Palace H.). ⚑ ⓘ 🆅🅸🆂🅰 ℀ rest   plan p. 7   NY **k**
M a la carte 4 200/7 500 – ⊊ 1100 – **156 rm** 20 000/25 000.

Villa Magna 🅼, paseo de la Castellana 22, ⊠ 28046, ℰ 261 49 00, Telex 22914 – 🛗 ▤ 🚗 – 🔬 ⚑ ⓘ   plan p. 7   NV **x**
M 4 700 – ⊊ 975 – **200 rm** 15 500/21 500.

Wellington, Velázquez 8, ⊠ 28001, ℰ 275 44 00, Telex 22700, 🏊 – 🛗 ▤ 🚗 ⚑ ⓘ ⋿ 🆅🅸🆂🅰   HX **t**
M (rest see **El Fogón** below) – ⊊ 650 – **291 rm** 6 800/10 850.

Sanvy without rest, Goya 3, ⊠ 28001, ℰ 276 08 00, 🏊 – 🛗 ▤ 🚗 ⚑ ⓘ ⋿ 🆅🅸🆂🅰 ℀
⊊ 450 – **108 rm** 5 300/6 700.   plan p. 7   NV **r**

Convención without rest, coffee shop only, O'Donnell 53, ⊠ 28009, ℰ 274 68 00, Telex 45248 – 🛗 ▤ 🚗 – 🔬 ⚑ ⓘ ⋿ 🆅🅸🆂🅰 ℀   JX **a**
⊊ 430 – **780 rm** 4 750/6 300.

Los Galgos and Rest. La Almoraima, Claudio Coello 139, ⊠ 28006, ℰ 262 42 27, Telex 43957 – 🛗 ▤ 🚗 – 🔬 ⚑ ⓘ ⋿ 🆅🅸🆂🅰   HV **a**
M 2 000 – ⊊ 550 – **361 rm** 6 450/9 900 – P 8 590/10 090.

G. H. Velázquez, Velázquez 62, ⊠ 28001, ℰ 275 28 00, Telex 22779 – 🛗 ▤ 🚗 ⚑ ⓘ ⋿ 🆅🅸🆂🅰 ℀   HX **s**
M 1 600 – ⊊ 375 – **144 rm** 5 200/6 800 – P 6 400/7 000.

G. H. Colón, Pez Volador II, ⊠ 28007, ℰ 273 86 00, Telex 22984 – 🛗 ▤ 🚗 – 🔬 ⚑ ⓘ ⋿ 🆅🅸🆂🅰 ℀ rest   JY **x**
M 1 300/1 500 – ⊊ 300 – **220 rm** 3 500/5 000 – P 5 305/6 305.

Alcalá and Rest. Basque, Alcalá 66, ⊠ 28009, ℰ 435 10 60, Telex 48094 – 🛗 ▤ 🚗 ⚑ ⓘ ⋿ 🆅🅸🆂🅰   HX **w**
closed 22 December - 8 January – **M** (closed Sunday dinner) 1 750 – ⊊ 435 – **153 rm** 4 200/6 500.

Pintor without rest, coffee shop only, Goya 79, ⊠ 28001, ℰ 435 75 45, Telex 23281 – 🛗 ▤ 🚗 – 🔬 ⚑ ℀   HX **c**
⊊ 430 – **176 rm** 4 370/6 300.

Emperatriz, without rest, coffee shop only, López de Hoyos 4, ⊠ 28006, ℰ 413 65 11, Telex 43640 – 🛗 ▤ 🚗 ⚑ ⓘ ⋿ 🆅🅸🆂🅰 ℀   GV **z**
⊊ 360 – **170 rm** 4 510/7 345.

Agumar without rest, coffee shop only, paseo Reina Cristina 7, ⊠ 28014, ℰ 252 69 00, Telex 45248 – 🛗 ▤ 🚗 ⚑ ⓘ ⋿ 🆅🅸🆂🅰 ℀   HZ **a**
⊊ 430 – **252 rm** 4 590/5 750.

Serrano without rest, Marqués de Villamejor 8, ⊠ 28006, ℰ 435 52 00 – 🛗 ▤ ⚑ ⓘ ⋿ 🆅🅸🆂🅰 ℀   HV **b**
34 rm ⊊ 5 150/6 800.

Claridge without rest, coffee shop only, pl. del Conde de Casal 6, ⊠ 28001, ℰ 251 94 00, Telex 45585 – 🛗 ▤ 🚿wc 🛁wc 🚗 ⚑ ⓘ ⋿ 🆅🅸🆂🅰   JZ **a**
⊊ 260 – **150 rm** 2 250/3 825.

Abeba without rest, Alcántara 63, ⊠ 28006, ℰ 401 16 50 – 🛗 ▤ 🚿wc 🚗 🚗 ⚑ ⓘ ⋿ 🆅🅸🆂🅰 ℀   HV **r**
⊊ 260 – **90 rm** 2 920/4 140.

Don Diego 5th floor, without rest, Velázquez 45, ⊠ 28001, ℰ 435 07 60 – 🛗 🛁wc 🚿. ℀   HX **x**
⊊ 345 – **58 rm** 3 565/5 065.

🅇🅇🅇🅇 ۞ **Horcher,** Alfonso XII - 6, ⊠ 28014, ℰ 222 07 31, « Tasteful decor » – ▤. ⚑ ⓘ. ℀
closed Sunday – **M** a la carte 2 625/5 035   plan p. 7   NY **n**
Spec. Ragoût de crangrejos, Perdíz a la prensa, Riñones con setas al vino blanco.

🅇🅇🅇 ۞ **Club 31,** Alcalá 58, ⊠ 28014, ℰ 231 00 92 – ▤. ⚑ ⓘ ⋿ 🆅🅸🆂🅰 ℀   plan p. 7   NX **e**
closed August – **M** a la carte 2 950/4 200
Spec. Fricase de cigalas y langostinos con verduras tiernas, Popietas de lenguado Club 31 con nouilles verdes, Entrecote de cebón con granos de pimienta verde.

🅇🅇🅇 ۞ **El Amparo,** Puigcerdá 8, ⊠ 28001, ℰ 431 64 56, Basque and French cuisine – ▤. ⚑ 🆅🅸🆂🅰 ℀   HX **h**
closed Saturday lunch, Sunday, 1 week at Easter and August – **M** a la carte 3 100/4 800
Spec. Charlota de cordero con verduras, Lubina al tomillo con compote de tomate, Hojaldre de peras Williams caramelizadas.

🅇🅇🅇 **El Circo,** Ortega y Gasset 29, ⊠ 28006, ℰ 276 01 44, Modern decor, Pianist at dinner – ▤. ⚑ ⓘ ⋿ 🆅🅸🆂🅰 ℀   HV **f**
M a la carte 2 430/4 010.

🅇🅇🅇 **Villa y Corte de Madrid,** Serrano 110, ⊠ 28006, ℰ 261 29 77, Elegant decor – ▤. ⚑ ⓘ 🆅🅸🆂🅰 ℀   HV **a**
M a la carte 2 025/3 425.

🅇🅇🅇 **El Gran Chambelán,** Ayala 46, ⊠ 28001, ℰ 431 77 45 – ▤   HX **r**

🅇🅇🅇 **Balzac,** Moreto 7, ⊠ 28014, ℰ 239 19 22 – ▤. ⚑ ⓘ 🆅🅸🆂🅰 ℀   plan p. 7   NZ **b**
closed Saturday lunch and Sunday – **M** a la carte 2 380/4 150.

XX **St.-James,** Juan Bravo 26, ✉ 28020, ☎ 275 60 10, 🍴, Rice rest. – ▤. AE. ✗ HV **t**
closed Sunday – **M** a la carte 1 525/3 200.

XX **Caruso,** Serrano 70, ✉ 28001, ☎ 435 52 62 – ▤. AE ⓓ VISA. ✗ HVX **p**
closed Sunday and Bank Holidays – **M** a la carte 1 600/2 725.

XX **Schwarzwald (Selva Negra),** O'Donnel 46, ✉ 28009, ☎ 409 56 13, « Original decor » – ▤. AE ⓓ E VISA. ✗ JX **n**
M a la carte 1 675/2 675.

XX **Al Mounia,** Recoletos 5, ✉ 28001, ☎ 435 08 28, « Oriental atmosphere », North African rest. – ▤. AE ⓓ VISA. ✗ plan p. 7 NX **s**
closed Sunday, Monday lunch and August – **M** a la carte 1 600/3 930.

XX **La Fonda,** Lagasca 11, ✉ 28001, ☎ 403 83 07, Catalonian rest – ▤. AE ⓓ E VISA. ✗ HX **f**
M a la carte 1 890/2 700.

XX **Ponteareas,** Claudio Coello 96, ✉ 28006, ☎ 275 58 73, Galican rest – ▤. AE ⓓ VISA. ✗ HV **w**
closed Sunday, Bank Holidays and August – **M** a la carte 1 860/3 835.

XX **El Fogón,** Villanueva 34, ✉ 28001, ☎ 275 44 00, « Spanish rustic style decor » – ▤. AE ⓓ E VISA. ✗ HX **t**
M a la carte 2 245/3 890.

X **La Abuelita,** av. de Badajoz 25, ✉ 28027, ☎ 405 49 94 – ▤. AE ⓓ VISA. ✗ by ②
closed Sunday, Bank Holiday dinner and August – **M** a la carte 1 535/2 570.

X **Asador Velate,** Jorge Juan 91, ✉ 28009, ☎ 435 10 24, Basque rest. – ▤. VISA HJX **x**
closed Sunday and August to September – **M** a la carte 2 000/2 925.

X ✿ **El Pescador,** José Ortega y Gasset 75, ✉ 28006, ☎ 402 12 90, 🍴, Seafood – ▤. ✗ JV **t**
closed Sunday and 10 August-15 September – **M** a la carte 1 850/2 600
Spec. Sopa El Pescador, Lenguado Evaristo, Langosta a la americana.

X ✿ **La Trainera,** Lagasca 60, ✉ 28001, ☎ 275 47 17, Seafood – ▤. VISA. ✗ HX **k**
closed Sunday and August – **M** a la carte 1 600/3 350
Spec. Crema de mariscos, Langosta americana, Pescados a la plancha.

Arganzuela, Carabanchel, Villaverde : Antonio López, paseo de las Delicias, Santa María de la Cabeza.

🏨 **Praga** without rest, coffee shop only, Antonio López 65, ✉ 28019, ☎ 469 06 00, Telex 45248 – |‡| ▤ 🚗. AE ⓓ E VISA. ✗ by ⑤
☕ 350 – **428 rm** 2 500/3 800.

🏨 **Aramo** without rest, coffee shop only, paseo Santa María de la Cabeza 73, ✉ 28045, ☎ 473 91 11, Telex 45885 – |‡| ▤ 🚗. AE ⓓ E VISA by ⑤
☕ 300 – **105 rm** 3 500/5 200.

🏨 **Puerta de Toledo,** glorieta Puerta de Toledo 4, ✉ 28005, ☎ 474 71 00, Telex 22291 – |‡| ▤ 🚗. AE ⓓ E VISA. ✗ plan p. 4 EZ **v**
M (rest see **Puerta de Toledo** below) – ☕ 250 – **152 rm** 2 500/4 600.

🏨 Carlton, paseo de las Delicias 26, ✉ 28045, ☎ 239 71 00, Telex 42598 – |‡| ▤ plan p. 5 GZ **n**
133 rm.

XX **Puerta de Toledo,** glorieta Puerta de Toledo 4, ✉ 28005, ☎ 474 12 69 – ▤. ⓓ E VISA. ✗ plan p. 4 EZ **v**
M a la carte 1 450/2 800.

Moncloa : Princesa, Rosales, paseo Florida, Casa de Campo (plan p. 4 except where otherwise stated)

🏨 **Meliá Madrid** Ⓜ, Princesa 27, ✉ 28028, ☎ 241 82 00, Telex 22537, 🍴 – |‡| ▤ – 🏛. AE ⓓ E VISA. ✗ plan p. 6 KV **t**
M 2 900 – ☕ 730 – **250 rm** 9 350/11 700 – P 11 400/14 900.

🏨 **Florida Norte** Ⓜ, paseo de la Florida 5, ✉ 28008, ☎ 241 61 90, Telex 23675 – |‡| ▤ 🚗. AE ⓓ E VISA. ✗ rest DX **v**
M 1 300 – ☕ 350 – **399 rm** 4 400/6 100 – P 6 000/7 350.

🏨 **Príncipe Pío,** cuesta de San Vicente 16, ✉ 28008, ☎ 247 08 00, Telex 42183 – |‡| ▤ 🚗. AE E VISA. ✗ rest plan p. 6 KX **d**
M 1 075 – ☕ 325 – **157 rm** 2 975/4 390 – P 4 275/5 055.

🏨 **Tirol** without rest., coffee shop only and no ☕, Marqués de Urquijo 4, ✉ 28008, ☎ 248 19 00 – |‡| ▤ 🛁wc ☎ 🚗. E VISA. ✗ DV **r**
93 rm 2 780/4 100.

XXX Café Viena, Luisa Fernanda 23, ✉ 28008, ☎ 248 15 91, Pianist at dinner, « Old style café » – ▤ DX **s**

XXX **Los Porches,** paseo Pintor Rosales 1, ✉ 28008, ☎ 247 70 53, 🍴 – ▤. AE ⓓ E VISA. ✗ DX **z**
M a la carte 2 160/3 300.

Chamberí : San Bernardo, Fuencarral, Alberto Aguilera, Santa Engracia (plan pp. 4 to 7).

🏨🏨 **Miguel Angel** Ⓜ, Miguel Angel 31, ✉ 28010, 𝒸 442 00 22, Telex 44235, 🔲 – 🛗 ▦
GV c
M 3 100 – ☑ 700 – **305 rm** 7 500/13 900.

🏨🏨 **Mindanao,** paseo de San Francisco de Sales 15, ✉ 28003, 𝒸 449 55 00, Telex 22631, 🏯,
🔲, ⬛ ▦ 🍴 – 🛗 ▦ 🍴 ▦ 🔲 ● 🄴 𝖵𝖨𝖲𝖠.
DV a
M 2 350 – ☑ 550 – **289 rm** 8 100/10 100 – P 9 250/12 300.

🏨🏨 **Luz Palacio,** paseo de la Castellana 57, ✉ 28046, 𝒸 442 51 00, Telex 27207 – 🛗 ▦
● ▦ 🍴 🄰 🄴 ● 🄴 𝖵𝖨𝖲𝖠.
GV p
M 2 760 – ☑ 600 – **182 rm** 8 700/13 100 – P 11 750/13 900.

🏰 **Castellana** without rest, coffee shop only, paseo de la Castellana 49, ✉ 28046, 𝒸
410 02 00, Telex 27686 – 🛗 ▦ 🍴 – 🄰 🄴 ● 🄴 𝖵𝖨𝖲𝖠. 🍴
GV a
☑ 1200 – **311 rm** 10 750/12 750.

🏨🏨 **Escultor** Ⓜ, Miguel Angel 3, ✉ 28010, 𝒸 410 42 03, Telex 44285 – 🛗 ▦ 🚗 🄰 ● 🄴
𝖵𝖨𝖲𝖠
GV s
M 2 300 – ☑ 525 – **82 apartments** 5 400/8 900 – P 9 250/10 200.

🏨🏨 **Las Alondras,** without rest, coffee shop only, José Abascal 8, ✉ 28003, 𝒸 447 40 00,
Telex 49454 – 🛗 ▦ 🄰 🄴 ● 🄴 𝖵𝖨𝖲𝖠. 🍴
FV a
☑ 350 – **72 rm** 5 600/7 000.

🏛 **Bretón** without rest, coffee shop only, Bretón de los Herreros 29, ✉ 28003, 𝒸 442 83 00
– 🛗 ▦ 🚿wc 🛁wc 🄰 ● 🄴 𝖵𝖨𝖲𝖠. 🍴
FV n
☑ 350 – **56 rm** 3 630/5 600.

🏛 **Conde Duque** without rest, coffee shop only, pl. Conde Valle de Suchil 5, ✉ 28015, 𝒸
447 70 00, Telex 22058 – 🛗 🚿wc 🄰 🄴 ● 🄴 𝖵𝖨𝖲𝖠
EV d
☑ 270 – **138 rm** 2 580/4 400.

🏛 **Zurbano,** Zurbano 79, ✉ 28003, 𝒸 441 55 00, Telex 27578 – 🛗 ▦ 🚿wc 🄰 🚗 🄰 🄴
𝖵𝖨𝖲𝖠. 🍴 rest
GV x
M 1 350 – ☑ 325 – **261 rm** 3 500/5 500 – P 5 200/5 950.

🏛 **Embajada** without rest, Santa Engracia 5, ✉ 28010, 𝒸 447 33 00 – 🛗 🚿wc 🄰 𝖵𝖨𝖲𝖠. 🍴
MV r
☑ 250 – **65 rm** 2 700/3 700.

🏛 **Trafalgar** without rest, Trafalgar 35, ✉ 28010, 𝒸 445 62 00 – 🛗 ▦ 🚿wc 🛁wc 🄰 🄴
● 🄴 𝖵𝖨𝖲𝖠. 🍴
FV s
☑ 175 – **45 rm** 2 250/3 800.

XXXX ❀ **Jockey,** Amador de los Rios 6, ✉ 28010, 𝒸 419 24 35, « Tasteful decor » – ▦. 🄰 ●
🄴 𝖵𝖨𝖲𝖠. 🍴
NV k
closed Sunday and August – **M** a la carte 2 500/4 350
Spec. Codorníz escabechada a la gelée de tomillo, Rape braseado en hoja de col tierna, Pato con higos y maiz en leche.

XXX **Lur Maitea,** Fernando el Santo 4, ✉ 28010, 𝒸 419 09 38, Basque rest. – ▦. 🄰 ● 🄴.
🍴
MNV u
closed Saturday dinner, Bank Holidays and August – **M** a la carte 2 450/3 650.

XX **Aymar,** Fuencarral 138, ✉ 28010, 𝒸 445 57 67, Seafood – ▦. 🄰 ● 🄴 𝖵𝖨𝖲𝖠. 🍴 FV e
M a la carte 2 000/3 500.

XX **Las Reses,** Orfila 3, ✉ 28010, 𝒸 419 33 15, Meat rest. – ▦. 🄰. 🍴 NV v
closed Sunday, Bank Holidays and August – **M** a la carte 1 600/3 000.

X **Quattrocento,** General Ampudia 18, ✉ 28003, 𝒸 234 91 06, Italian rest. – ▦. 🄰 ●
𝖵𝖨𝖲𝖠. 🍴
DU a
closed Sunday dinner – **M** a la carte 1 535/1 940.

X La Parra, Monte Esquinza 34, ✉ 28010, 𝒸 419 54 98 – ▦ NV z

X **Casa Félix,** Bretón de los Herreros 39, ✉ 28003, 𝒸 441 24 79 – ▦. ● 𝖵𝖨𝖲𝖠. 🍴 FV x
M a la carte 1 690/2 925.

Chamartín, Tetuán : Capitán Haya, Orense, Alberto Alcocer, paseo de la Habana (plan p. 3 except where otherwise stated)

🏨🏨 **Eurobuilding** Ⓜ, Padre Damián 23, ✉ 28036, 𝒸 457 17 00, Telex 22548, « Garden with
🔲 » – 🛗 ▦ 🚗 – 🄰 🄰 ● 🄴 𝖵𝖨𝖲𝖠. 🍴
HS a
M (rest see **Balthasar and La Taberna** below) – ☑ 700 – **555 rm** 9 200/12 300.

🏨🏨 **Meliá Castilla** Ⓜ, Capitán Haya 43, ✉ 28020, 𝒸 270 80 00, Telex 23142, 🔲 – 🛗 ▦ 🅿 –
🄰 🄰 ● 🄴 𝖵𝖨𝖲𝖠. 🍴
GS c
1 000 rm ☑ 8 900/11 140.

🏨🏨 **Cuzco** without rest, coffee shop only, paseo de la Castellana 133, ✉ 28046, 𝒸 456 06 00,
Telex 22464 – 🛗 ▦ 🚗 🅿 – 🄰. 🄰 ● 🄴 𝖵𝖨𝖲𝖠. 🍴
GS a
☑ 500 – **330 rm** 6 150/8 000.

🏨🏨 **Chamartín** without rest, estación de Chamartín (railway station), ✉ 28036, 𝒸 733 90 11,
Telex 49201 – 🛗 ▦ – 🄰. 🄰 ● 🄴 𝖵𝖨𝖲𝖠. 🍴
HR
☑ 450 – **378 rm** 4 800/6 700.

🏨🏨 **Foxá 32** Ⓜ without rest, coffee shop only, 28036, ✉ 28036, 𝒸 733 10 60, Telex 49366 –
🛗 ▦ 🚗 – 🄰. 🄰 ● 🄴 𝖵𝖨𝖲𝖠
HR u
☑ 200 – **161 rm** 4 300/5 300.

🏨 **El Gran Atlanta** without rest, Comandante Zorita 34, ⊠ 28020, 𝒫 253 59 00, Telex
45210 – |钅| 🗏 ⊲⇒ – ⚿. ⚏ ⓞ ⊑ 𝖵𝖨𝖲𝖠. ※ FT **p**
⟟ 450 – **180 rm** 4 300/6 600.

🏨 **Aitana** without rest, coffee shop only, paseo de la Castellana 152, ⊠ 28046, 𝒫 250 71 07,
Telex 49186 – |钅| 🗏. ⚏ ⓞ 𝖵𝖨𝖲𝖠. ※ GT **c**
⟟ 330 – **111 rm** 4 000/6 200.

🏨 **Foxá 32** without rest, coffee shop only, Agustín de Foxá 32, ⊠ 16, 𝒫 733 10 60, Telex
49366 – |钅| 🗏 ⊲⇒. ⚏ ⓞ 𝖵𝖨𝖲𝖠. ※ HR **u**
⟟ 200 – **161 rm** 3 700/4 600.

🏛 **Aristos and Rest El Chaflán**, av. Pío XII-34, ⊠ 28016, 𝒫 457 04 50, 🍽 – |钅| 🗏 ☐wc
☜. ⚏ ⓞ 𝖵𝖨𝖲𝖠. ※ rest HS **d**
M *(closed Sunday)* a la carte 1 625/2 825 – ⟟ 250 – **25 rm** 3 300/5 400.

🏵🏵 ✦✦ **Zalacaín**, Álvarez de Baena 4, ⊠ 28006, 𝒫 261 48 40, 🍽, « Elegant decor » – 🗏
⊲⇒. ⚏ ※ plan p. 5 GV **b**
closed Saturday lunch, Sunday and 25 July - 5 September – **M** a la carte 5 000/7 000.

🏵🏵🏵🏵 ✦ **Balthasar**, Juan Ramón Jiménez 8, ⊠ 28036, 𝒫 457 91 91, Telex 22548, « Tasteful
classic decor » – 🗏 ⊲⇒. ⚏ ⓞ ⊑ 𝖵𝖨𝖲𝖠. HS **a**
closed Sunday, Bank Holidays, 1 week at Easter and August – **M** a la carte 2 750/4 900.

🏵🏵🏵🏵 **Mayte Commodore**, pl. República Argentina 5, ⊠ 28002, 𝒫 261 86 06, 🍽, « Elegant
decor » – 🗏 HU **v**

🏵🏵🏵🏵 ✦ **El Bodegón**, Pinar 15, ⊠ 28006, 𝒫 262 31 37 – 🗏. ⚏ ⓞ ⊑ 𝖵𝖨𝖲𝖠. ※ plan p. 5 GV **q**
closed Sunday, Bank Holidays and August – **M** a la carte 2 490/3 370
Spec. Salmón ahumado por el jefe, Brocheta de rape y langostinos, Filet mignón al estragón.

🏵🏵🏵🏵 ✦ **Príncipe de Viana**, Manuel de Falla 5, ⊠ 28036, 𝒫 259 14 48, Basque rest. – 🗏. ⚏.
※ GT **c**
closed Saturday lunch, Sunday and 25 July - 5 August – **M** a la carte 3 100/5 000.

🏵🏵🏵🏵 **Wallis**, Raimondo Fernández Villaverde 65 - edificio Windsor, ⊠ 28003, 𝒫 456 71 70 –
🗏 ⓟ. ⚏ ⓞ ⊑ 𝖵𝖨𝖲𝖠. ※ GU **r**
closed Saturday lunch, Sunday and August – **M** a la carte 2 850/3 725.

🏵🏵🏵 **Nicolasa**, Velázquez 150, ⊠ 28006, 𝒫 261 99 85 – 🗏. ⚏ ⓞ ⊑ 𝖵𝖨𝖲𝖠. ※ HU **a**
closed Sunday and August – **M** a la carte 2 175/4 340.

🏵🏵🏵 **Nuevo Valentín**, Concha Espina 8, ⊠ 28036, 𝒫 259 74 16, 🍽 – 🗏. ⚏ ⓞ ⊑ 𝖵𝖨𝖲𝖠. ※
M a la carte 1 865/3 200. GT **n**

🏵🏵🏵 **O'Pazo**, Reina Mercedes 20, ⊠ 28020, 𝒫 234 37 48, Seafood – 🗏. ※ FT **p**
closed Sunday and August – **M** a la carte 1 700/4 225.

🏵🏵🏵 **L'Albufera**, Capitán Haya 45, ⊠ 28020, 𝒫 279 63 74, Pianist at dinner – 🗏. ⚏ ⊑ 𝖵𝖨𝖲𝖠.
※ GS **c**
closed August – **M** a la carte 2 150/3 575.

🏵🏵🏵 **La Gabarra**, Santo Domingo de Silos 6, ⊠ 28036, 𝒫 458 78 97, Basque rest. – 🗏. ⚏
ⓞ ⊑ 𝖵𝖨𝖲𝖠. ※ GT **s**
closed Sunday and August – **M** a la carte 2 575/4 050.

🏵🏵🏵 **La Máquina**, Sor Angela de la Cruz 22, ⊠ 28020, 𝒫 270 61 23 – 🗏. ⚏ ⓞ ⊑ 𝖵𝖨𝖲𝖠. ※
closed Sunday – **M** a la carte 2 250/3 200. FS **e**

🏵🏵🏵 **José Luis**, Rafael Salgado 11, ⊠ 28036, 𝒫 457 50 36, 🍽 – 🗏. ⚏ ⓞ ⊑ 𝖵𝖨𝖲𝖠. ※ GT **m**
closed Sunday and August – **M** a la carte 1 800/3 050.

🏵🏵🏵 **La Boucade**, Capitán Haya 30, ⊠ 28020, 𝒫 456 02 45 – 🗏. ⚏ ⓞ ⊑ 𝖵𝖨𝖲𝖠. ※ GS **a**
closed Sunday and Bank Holidays – **M** a la carte 2 450/3 650.

🏵🏵🏵 **Cota 13**, estación de Chamartín (railway station), ⊠ 28036, 𝒫 215 10 83, 🍽 – 🗏. ⚏
ⓞ ⊑ 𝖵𝖨𝖲𝖠 HR
M a la carte 1 450/2 650.

🏵🏵🏵 **Bogavante**, Capitán Haya 20, ⊠ 28020, 𝒫 456 21 14, Seafood – 🗏. ⚏ ⓞ ⊑ 𝖵𝖨𝖲𝖠. ※
closed Sunday and August – **M** a la carte 1 675/3 300. GT **d**

🏵🏵🏵 **Itxaso**, Capitán Haya 58, ⊠ 28020, 𝒫 450 64 64, Basque rest. – 🗏. ⚏ ⓞ ⊑ 𝖵𝖨𝖲𝖠. ※
closed Sunday – **M** a la carte 2 400/3 700. JS **n**

🏵🏵🏵 **Señorío de Bertiz**, Comandante Zorita 6, ⊠ 28020, 𝒫 233 27 57 – 🗏. ⚏ ⓞ 𝖵𝖨𝖲𝖠. ※
closed Saturday lunch, Sunday and August – **M** a la carte 2 225/3 750. FT **s**

🏵🏵🏵 **Señorío de Alcocer**, Alberto Alcocer 1, ⊠ 28036, 𝒫 457 16 96 – 🗏 GS **e**

🏵🏵🏵 **Gaztelupe**, Comandante Zorita 37, ⊠ 28020, 𝒫 233 01 85 – 🗏 FT **a**

🏵🏵🏵 **La Taberna**, Alberto Alcocer 18, ⊠ 28036, 𝒫 457 17 00 (ext. 9830), Telex 22548 – 🗏
M a la carte 1 995/3 800. HS **a**

🏵🏵 **El Hostal**, Príncipe de Vergara 285, ⊠ 28023, 𝒫 259 11 94 – 🗏 HS **e**

🏵🏵 ✦ **Cabo Mayor**, Juan Hurtado de Mendoza 11 (back), ⊠ 28036, 𝒫 250 87 76, « Original
decor » – 🗏. ⚏ ⓞ 𝖵𝖨𝖲𝖠. ※ GHS **r**
closed Sunday, 1 week at Easter, 15 to 30 August and Christmas – **M** a la carte 2 100/3 400
Spec. Bogavante a la ciboulette, Sopa de ostras al azafrán, Filetes de hígado y pechuga de pato al cassis.

🏵🏵 **El Faisán de Oro**, Bolivia 11, ⊠ 28016, 𝒫 259 30 76 – 🗏 HS **t**

🏵🏵 **Fass**, Rodríguez Marín 84, ⊠ 28022, 𝒫 457 22 02, Bavarian decor, German cuisine – 🗏.
⚏ ⓞ ⊑ 𝖵𝖨𝖲𝖠. ※ HT **t**
M a la carte 2 755/2 800.

XX **Rugantino,** Velázquez 136, ✉ 28006, ℰ 261 02 22, Italian rest. – 📺. 🖭 ⓪ E 𝗩𝗜𝗦𝗔. ❅
M a la carte 1 670/2 930. plan p. 5 HV **e**

XX **De Funy,** Serrano 213, ✉ 28016, ℰ 259 72 25, ㊟, Lebanese rest., pianist at dinner –
📺. 🖭 ⓪ E 𝗩𝗜𝗦𝗔. ❅ HT **z**
closed Monday – M a la carte 1 800/3 300.

XX **Rheinfall,** Padre Damián 44, ✉ 28036, ℰ 457 82 88, German cuisine, « Regional decor »
– 📺. 🖭 ⓪ E 𝗩𝗜𝗦𝗔. ❅ HS **u**
M a la carte 1 700/3 000.

X El Pajar, Orense 35, ✉ 28020, ℰ 455 00 09 – 📺 FT **b**

X **Asador Donostiarra,** Pedro Villar 14, ✉ 28020, ℰ 279 73 40, Basque rustic decor – 📺.
🖭 ⓪ E 𝗩𝗜𝗦𝗔 FS **a**
closed Sunday dinner – M a la carte 1 400/3 350.

X Los Borrachos de Velázquez, Príncipe de Vergara 205, ✉ 28002, ℰ 458 10 76, Andalusian
rest. – 📺 HT **s**

Environs

at Ciudad Puerta de Hierro by ⑦ : 8 km by N VI and road to El Pardo – ✉ 28035
Madrid – ⊛ 91 :

🏩 **Monte Real** ⟆, Arroyofresno 17, ✉ 28035, ℰ 216 21 40, Telex 22089, ㊟, « Elegant
decor, garden », 🏊 – 🖃 📺 ☎ ❷ – 🔬. 🖭 ⓪ E 𝗩𝗜𝗦𝗔. ❅ rest
M 3 400 – ⇌ 690 – **79 rm** 9 000/14 000 – P 14 200/16 000.

by ② *: N II* and Coslada - San Fernando Road E : 12 km – ✉ 28022 Madrid – ⊛ 91 :

XX **Rancho Texano,** av. Aragón 364, ✉ 28022, ℰ 747 47 44, ㊟, Grill rest., « Terrace » –
🖃 ❷. 🖭 ⓪ E 𝗩𝗜𝗦𝗔. ❅
closed Sunday dinner – M a la carte 1 800/2 890.

on the road to the Airport : 12,5 km – ✉ 28022 Madrid – ⊛ 91 :

🏨 **Eurotel Madrid** without rest, Galeón 27 (Alameda de Osuna), ✉ 28042, ℰ 747 13 55,
Telex 45688, 🏊, – 🖃 – 🔬. 🖭 ⓪ E 𝗩𝗜𝗦𝗔.
⇌ 290 – **271 apartments** 5 250/6 550.

at Barajas by ② : 14 km – ⊛ 91 :

🏨 **Barajas** Ⓜ, av. de Logroño 305, ✉ Madrid 28042, ℰ 747 77 00, Telex 22255, ㊟, « Large
lawn with 🏊 » – 🖃 📺 ❷ – 🔬. 🖭 ⓪ E 𝗩𝗜𝗦𝗔. ❅ rest
M 2 375 – ⇌ 575 – **230 rm** 7 950/11 950 – P 10 500/12 475.

🏨 **Alameda** Ⓜ, av. de Logroño 100, ✉ Madrid 28042, ℰ 747 48 00, Telex 43809, 🖼 – 🖃 📺
⇌ ❷ – 🔬. 🖭 ⓪ E 𝗩𝗜𝗦𝗔. ❅ rest
M 2 150 – ⇌ 495 – **145 rm** 6 800/9 500 – P 8 825/10 875.

at San Sebastián de los Reyes by ① : 17 km – ✉ San Sebastián de los Reyes – ⊛ 91

XXX **Mesón Tejas Verdes,** carret. NI ℰ 652 73 07, ㊟, « Typical Castilian tavern, garden »
– 🖃 ❷. 🖭 𝗩𝗜𝗦𝗔
closed Sunday, Bank Holiday dinner and August – M a la carte 1 750/3 000.

BARCELONA 08000 ⓸⓷ ⑱ and ⓽⓽⓪ ⑳ – pop. 1 754 900 – ⊛ 93 – Bullring.

See : Gothic Quarter★★ (Barrio Gótico) : Cathedral★★ MR , Federic Marés Museum★★ (Museo
F. Marés) MR, Provincial Council★ (Palau de la Generalitat) MR – Montjuïc★ (≼★) : Museum of
Catalonian Art★★ (Museo d'Art de Catalunya) : Romanesque and Gothic department★★★,
ceramic Museum★ – Archeological Museum (Museo Arqueológico), Spanish Village★ (Pueblo
Español), Joan Miró Foundation★ – Zoo★ (Parque Zoológico) LV – Tibidabo★ (⊹★★) – Mari-
time Museum★★ (Drassanes i Museo Maritim) KZ M6 – Cambo Collection (Palau de la Virreina)★
JX M7 – Picasso Museum★ KV M8 – Church of the Holy Family★ (Sagrada Familia) JU L.

🏌, 🏌 of Prat by ⑤ : 16 km ℰ 379 02 78 – 🏌 of Sant Cugat by ⑦ : 20 km ℰ 674 39 58 – 🏌 of
Vallromanas by ④ : 25 km ℰ 568 03 62.

✈ Barcelona by ⑤ : 12 km ℰ 317 01 12 – Iberia : pl. Espanya, ✉ 08004, ℰ 325 60 00 EZ
Aviaco : aeropuerto ℰ 379 24 58.

🚄 ℰ 310 00 30.

🚢 to the Balearic islands : Cía. Trasmediterránea, via Laietana 2, ✉ 08003, ℰ 319 82 12,
Telex 54629 KX.

🛈 Gran Vía de les Corts Catalanes 658, ✉ 08010, ℰ 301 74 43, 317 22 46 - Palacio de Congresos, av. María
Cristina, ✉ 08004, ℰ 323 31 01 and at Airport ℰ 325 58 29 – R.A.C.C. Santaló 8, ✉ 08006, ℰ 200 33 11,
Telex 53056.

Madrid 626 ⑥ – Bilbao 606 ⑥ – Lérida/Lleida 169 ⑥ – Perpignan 185 ② – Tarragona 108 ⑥ – Toulouse 387
② – Valencia 361 ⑥ – Zaragoza 307 ⑥.

Plans on following pages

🏨 **Princesa Sofía** Ⓜ, pl. del Papa Pius XII, ✉ 08028, ℰ 330 71 11, Telex 51032, ≼, 🖼 – 🖃
🖃 ⇌ – 🔬. 🖭 ⓪ E 𝗩𝗜𝗦𝗔. ❅ by ⑥
M 2 800 – ⇌ 10 200/13 200 – P 11 300/14 900.

🏨 **G. H. Sarriá** Ⓜ, av. de Sarriá 50, ✉ 08029, ℰ 239 11 09, Telex 51033, ≼ – 🖃 🖃 ⇌
❷ – 🔬. 🖭 ⓪ E 𝗩𝗜𝗦𝗔. ❅ EU **n**
M 2 300 – ⇌ 520 – **314 rm** 8 050/11 150 – P 9 675/12 150.

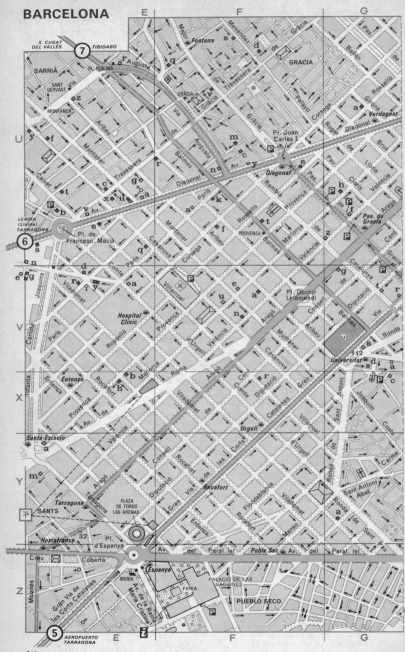

BARCELONA

BARCELONA

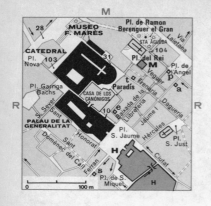

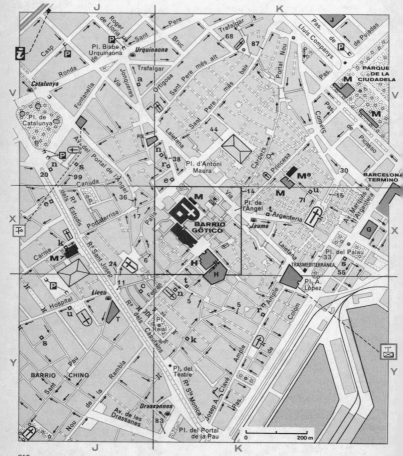

🏨 **Avenida Palace,** Gran Via 605, 🖂 08007, 🖉 301 96 00, Telex 54734, Pianist at dinner –
🍴 🔲 – 🏛 🖭 ⓪ 🖬 *VISA*. 🕸 rest
GV **r**
M 2 390 – **211 rm** 🖵 9 700/12 470 – P 10 260/13 725.

🏨 **Ritz,** Gran Via de les Corts Catalanes 668, 🖂 08010, 🖉 318 52 00, Telex 52739, 🍴 – 🍴
🔲 – 🏛 🖭 ⓪ 🖬 *VISA*. 🕸 rest
JU **p**
M 3 000 – 🖵 850 – **203 rm** 9 600/14 400 – P 18 250/23 050.

🏨 **Presidente** without rest, av. de la Diagonal 570, 🖂 08029, 🖉 200 21 11, Telex 52180, ⤳
– 🍴 🔲 🚗 – 🏛 🖭 ⓪ 🖬 *VISA*
EU **u**
161 rm 🖵 9 025/11 600.

🏨 **Majestic,** passeig de Grácia 70, 🖂 08008, 🖉 215 45 12, Telex 52211, ⤳ – 🍴 🔲 🚗 – 🏛
340 rm
GU **f**

🏨 **Diplomatic and Rest. la Salsa,** Pau Claris 122, 🖂 08009, 🖉 317 31 00, Telex 54701, ⤳ – 🍴
🔲 🚗 ⓟ – 🏛
213 rm
GU **e**

🏨 **Calderón,** rambla Catalunya 26, 🖂 08007, 🖉 301 00 00, Telex 51549, ⤳ – 🍴 🔲 🚗 –
🏛 🖭 ⓪ 🖬 *VISA*. 🕸
GV **t**
M 1 450/2 600 – 🖵 600 – **244 rm** 6 200/8 900.

🏨 **Colón,** av. de la Catedral 7, 🖂 08002, 🖉 301 14 04, Telex 52654 – 🍴 🔲 ⓟ – 🏛 🖭 ⓪ 🖬
VISA. 🕸 rest
KV **e**
M 1 675 – **161 rm** 🖵 4 445/7 950 – P 7 325/7 745.

🏨 **Hesperia** Ⓜ 🕭 without rest, Los Vergós 20, 🖂 08017, 🖉 204 55 51, Telex 98403 – 🍴 🔲
🚗 – 🏛 🖭 ⓪ 🖬 *VISA*
by ⑦
🖵 500 – **144 rm** 4 400/7 500.

🏨 **Derby** without rest, Loreto 21, 🖂 08029, 🖉 322 32 15, Telex 97429 – 🍴 🔲 🚗 – 🏛 🖭
⓪ 🖬 *VISA*
by ⑥
🖵 500 – **116 rm** 5 000/7 850.

🏨 **Cristal,** Diputació 257, 🖂 08007, 🖉 301 66 00, Telex 54560 – 🍴 🔲 🚗 – 🏛 🖭 ⓪ 🖬 *VISA*.
🕸 rest
GV **t**
147 rm 🖵 6 350/8 200.

🏨 **Gran Derby** Ⓜ without rest, Loreto 28, 🖂 08029, 🖉 322 32 15, Telex 97429 – 🍴 🔲
🚗 – 🏛 🖭 ⓪ 🖬 *VISA*
EV **g**
🖵 500 – **36 rm** 9 350.

🏨 **Nuñez Urgel,** without rest, coffee shop only, Comptes de Urgell 232, 🖂 08036, 🖉
322 41 53 – 🍴 🔲 🚗
EV **a**
121 rm

🏨 **Royal** without rest, Ramblas 117, 🖂 08002, 🖉 301 94 00, Telex 97565 – 🍴 🔲 🚗 🖭 ⓪
🖬 *VISA*. 🕸
JX **e**
🖵 350 – **108 rm** 4 300/6 800.

🏨 **Balmoral** without rest, coffee shop only, via Augusta 5, 🖂 08006, 🖉 217 87 00, Telex
54087 – 🍴 🔲 🚗 – 🏛 🖭 ⓪ 🖬 *VISA*. 🕸
FU **n**
🖵 440 – **94 rm** 4 950/7 650.

🏨 **Regente,** rambla de Catalunya 76, 🖂 08008, 🖉 215 25 70, Telex 51939, ⤳ – 🍴 🔲 🖭 ⓪
🖬 *VISA*. 🕸
GU **z**
M 1 500 – 🖵 350 – **78 rm** 5 000/7 500 – P 7 100/8 350.

🏨 **Condor,** without rest, coffee shop only, via Augusta 127, 🖂 08006, 🖉 209 45 11, Telex
52925 – 🍴 🔲 🚗
EU **z**
78 rm

🏨 **Arenas** without rest, coffee shop only for dinner, Capitán Arenas 20, 🖂 08034, 🖉
204 03 00 – 🍴 🔲 🚗 – 🏛 🖭 ⓪ 🖬 *VISA*. 🕸
by ⑥
59 rm 🖵 6 750/8 700.

🏨 **Astoria** without rest, coffee shop only, París 203, 🖂 08036, 🖉 209 83 11, Telex 97429 –
🍴 🔲 🖭 ⓪ 🖬 *VISA*
FU **a**
🖵 300 – **108 rm** 3 000/5 000.

🏨 **G. H. Cristina** without rest, coffee shop only, av. de la Diagonal 458, 🖂 08006, 🖉
217 68 00, Telex 54328 – 🍴 🔲 🖭 ⓪ 🖬 *VISA*
FU **y**
🖵 350 – **123 rm** 5 000/7 000.

🏨 **Dante** without rest, Mallorca 181, 🖂 08036, 🖉 323 22 54, Telex 52588 – 🍴 🔲 🚗 – 🏛
🖭 ⓪ 🖬 *VISA*. 🕸
FV **e**
🖵 350 – **81 rm** 3 800/6 550.

🏨 **Numáncia** without rest, coffee shop only, Numància 74, 🖂 08015, 🖉 322 44 51 – 🍴 🔲
🚗 – 🏛 🖭 ⓪ 🖬 *VISA*. 🕸
by ⑤
🖵 350 – **140 rm** 3 300/5 200.

🏨 **Ficus,** without rest, Mallorca 163, 🖂 08036, 🖉 253 35 00, Telex 98203 – 🍴 🔲
FV **u**
74 rm

🏨 **Expo H.** without rest, coffee shop only, Mallorca 1, 🖂 08014, 🖉 325 12 12, Telex 54147,
⤳ – 🍴 🔲 🚗 – 🏛 🖭 ⓪ 🖬 *VISA*. 🕸
EY **m**
432 rm 🖵 3 800/6 300.

🏨 **Euro-Park,** without rest, coffee shop only, Aragó 325, 🖂 08009, 🖉 257 92 05 – 🍴 🔲
66 rm
JU **e**

🏨 **Mitre** without rest, Bertrán 15, ⊠ 08023, ℰ 212 11 04, Telex 51531 – 🛗 🗐 ⏥wc 🅿️
🚗 ⚠️ ⓪ 🇪 𝗩𝗜𝗦𝗔.
⟷ 330 – **57 rm** 3 850/5 600.

🏨 **Gala Placidia**, via Augusta 112, ⊠ 08006, ℰ 217 82 00, Telex 98820 – 🛗 🗐 rest ⏥wc
🅿️. ⚠️ ⓪ 🇪 𝗩𝗜𝗦𝗔. ⌘ rest
M 1 200 – ⟷ 475 – **28 apartments** 4 500/6 500 – P 5 250/6 500.

🏨 **Condado**, Aribau 201, ⊠ 08021, ℰ 200 23 11, Telex 54546 – 🛗 🗐 rest ⏥wc 🗐wc 🅿️.
⚠️ ⓪ 🇪 𝗩𝗜𝗦𝗔. ⌘
M 1 250 – ⟷ 275 – **89 rm** 2 970/5 365 – P 5 035/5 320.

🏨 **Taber** without rest, Aragó 256, ⊠ 08007, ℰ 318 70 50 – 🛗 ⏥wc 🅿️. ⚠️ ⓪ 🇪 𝗩𝗜𝗦𝗔. ⌘
65 rm ⟷ 3 125/5 600.

🏨 **Terminal** 7th floor, without rest, coffee shop only for dinner, Provença 1, ⊠ 08029, ℰ
321 53 50, Telex 98213 – 🛗 🗐 ⏥wc 🅿️ 🚗. ⚠️ ⓪ 🇪 𝗩𝗜𝗦𝗔. ⌘
75 rm ⟷ 4 700/6 100.

🏨 **Tres Torres** without rest, Calatrava 32, ⊠ 08017, ℰ 247 73 00, Telex 54990 – 🛗 ⏥wc
🅿️ 🚗. ⚠️ ⓪ 🇪 𝗩𝗜𝗦𝗔. ⌘
⟷ 350 – **56 rm** 4 400/5 500.

🏨 **Covadonga** without rest, coffee shop only, av. de la Diagonal 596, ⊠ 08021, ℰ 209 55 11
– 🛗 🗐 ⏥wc 🗐wc 🅿️. ⚠️ ⓪ 🇪 𝗩𝗜𝗦𝗔
⟷ 275 – **76 rm** 3 100/5 050.

🏨 **Regencia Colón** without rest, Sagristans 13, ⊠ 08002, ℰ 318 98 58, Telex 98175 – 🛗 🗐
⏥wc 🗐wc 🅿️. ⚠️ ⓪ 🇪 𝗩𝗜𝗦𝗔. ⌘
⟷ 285 – **55 rm** 2 730/4 420.

🏨 **Wilson** without rest, av. de la Diagonal 568, ⊠ 08021, ℰ 209 25 11, Telex 54134 – 🛗 🗐
⏥wc 🅿️. ⚠️ ⓪ 𝗩𝗜𝗦𝗔
52 rm ⟷ 4 700/6 100.

🏨 **Gótico** without rest, Jaime I - 14, ⊠ 08002, ℰ 315 22 11, Telex 97206 – 🛗 🗐 ⏥wc 🅿️.
⚠️ ⓪ 🇪 𝗩𝗜𝗦𝗔.
⟷ 280 – **72 rm** 3 050/5 100.

🏨 **Las Corts** without rest, coffee shop only, Travessera de Les Corts 292, ⊠ 08029, ℰ
322 08 11, Telex 59001 – 🛗 🗐 ⏥wc 🗐wc 🅿️ 🅿️. ⓪ 🇪 𝗩𝗜𝗦𝗔. ⌘
⟷ 250 – **80 rm** 3 000/4 400.

🏨 **Bonanova Park**, without rest, Capitán Arenas 51, ⊠ 08034, ℰ 204 09 00, Telex 54990 – 🛗
⏥wc 🗐wc 🅿️ 🚗
60 rm.

🏠 **Lleó**, Pelai 24, ⊠ 08001, ℰ 318 13 12, Telex 98338 – 🛗 ⏥wc 🅿️. ⌘ rest
M 750 – ⟷ 200 – **42 rm** 1 800/3 100 – P 2 990/3 240.

🏠 **Torelló** without rest, Ample 31, ⊠ 08002, ℰ 315 40 11, Telex 54606 – 🛗 ⏥wc 🗐wc 🅿️.
⌘
⟷ 225 – **72 rm** 1 600/2 700.

🏠 **Cortés**, Santa Ana 25, ⊠ 08002, ℰ 317 91 12, Telex 98215 – 🛗 🗐 rest ⏥wc 🗐wc 🅿️.
⚠️ 𝗩𝗜𝗦𝗔. ⌘
M (closed Sunday) 695 – ⟷ 275 – **46 rm** 2 200/3 650 – P 3 325/3 700.

🏠 **L'Alguer** without rest, passeig Pedro Rodriguez 20, ⊠ 08028, ℰ 334 60 50 – 🛗 🗐wc 🅿️.
🇪 𝗩𝗜𝗦𝗔. ⌘
⟷ 225 – **33 rm** 1 725/3 000.

Classical and modern restaurants

🍴🍴🍴🍴 ✿ **Ama Lur**, Mallorca 275, ⊠ 08008, ℰ 215 30 24, 🍽️, « Garden-terrace » – 🗐. ⚠️ ⓪
🇪 ⌘
closed Sunday, Bank Holidays and 23 to 27 December – **M** a la carte 3 700/5 900
Spec. Crudites de verduras con centollo frío, Troncón de merluza, Medallones de ternera con foie gras y
trufa (November-March).

🍴🍴🍴🍴 ✿ **Reno**, Tuset 27, ⊠ 08006, ℰ 200 91 29, « Elegant classical decor » – 🗐 🅿️. ⚠️ ⓪ 🇪
𝗩𝗜𝗦𝗔. ⌘
M a la carte 3 100/4 500
Spec. Hojaldre de lenguado y salmón ahumado, Brochette de langostinos a las finas hierbas, Solomillo al
tuétano y a las trufas.

🍴🍴🍴🍴 ✿ **Vía Veneto**, Ganduxer 10, ⊠ 08021, ℰ 250 31 00, « Early 20C style » – 🗐 🅿️. ⚠️ ⓪
🇪 𝗩𝗜𝗦𝗔.
M a la carte 2 515/4 260
Spec. Salmón fresco marinado al coriandro y vinagre de frambuesas, Filetes de lenguado al Martini, Filetes
de buey a la mostaza de hierbas.

🍴🍴🍴 **Finisterre**, av. de la Diagonal 469, ⊠ 08036, ℰ 239 55 76 – 🗐. ⚠️ ⓪ 🇪 𝗩𝗜𝗦𝗔
M a la carte 3 850/5 600.

🍴🍴🍴 **Germán**, Dr Rizal 8, ⊠ 08006, ℰ 217 71 85 – 🗐

🍴🍴🍴 **Gueridón**, pasaje Permanyer 2, ⊠ 08009, ℰ 318 09 94 – 🗐

🍴🍴🍴 ✿✿ **Neichel**, av. de Pedralbes 16 bis, ⊠ 08034, ℰ 203 84 08 – 🗐. ⚠️ ⓪ 🇪 𝗩𝗜𝗦𝗔
closed Sunday, Bank Holidays, Easter, Christmas and August – **M** (booking essential)
a la carte 2 700/4 200
Spec. Pastas frescas caseras al foie gras caliente y trufas, Fricase de bogavante y cigalas, Hojaldre de lomo
de cordero con pimientos del pico.

XXX **Hostal del Sol** 1st floor, passeig de Gràcia 44, ✉ 08007, ☎ 215 62 25, Pianist at dinner – ▤. AE ⓓ E VISA. ⛔ GU **n**
M a la carte 1 895/3 345.

XXX **El Túnel de Muntaner,** Sant Mario 22, ✉ 08022, ☎ 212 60 74 – ▤ Ⓟ. AE ⓓ E VISA. ⛔
closed Saturday lunch, Sunday, Bank Holidays and 25 July-25 August – **M** a la carte 2 400/3 800. by ⑥

XXX ❁ **Botafumeiro,** Major de Grácia 81, ✉ 08012, ☎ 218 42 30, Seafood – ▤ Ⓟ. AE ⓓ E VISA. ⛔ FU **v**
closed Monday except Bank Holidays, day before Bank Holidays and August – **M** a la carte 1 600/3 950.

XX ❁ **La Odisea,** Copons 7, ✉ 08002, ☎ 302 37 88, Pianist at dinner – ▤. VISA KV **n**
closed Sunday, 2 weeks at Easter and August – **M** a la carte 1 880/3 115
Spec. La gran marmita de la casa, Flan de sesos con trufa Teresa, Filete de buey con hortalizas al calvados.

XX **El Gran Café,** Avinyó 9, ✉ 08002, ☎ 318 79 86, Pianist at dinner, « Early 20C style » – AE ⓓ E VISA KY **t**
closed Sunday and August – **M** a la carte 1 725/3 675.

XX ❁ **Azulete,** Vía Augusta 281, ✉ 08017, ☎ 203 59 43, 🏠, « Conservatory terrace with plants » – AE ⓓ E VISA by ⑦
closed Saturday lunch, Sunday, Bank Holidays and November – **M** a la carte 2 325/3 550
Spec. Brazo de gitano de pasta y verduras arlequín, Escalopa de lubina con juliana de cebollas al hinojo, Corona de naranja.

XX ❁ **Ara-Cata,** Dr Ferràn 33, ✉ 08034, ☎ 204 10 53 – ▤. AE ⓓ VISA. ⛔ by ⑥
closed Easter, 3 to 31 August, Saturday and Bank Holidays dinner, Saturday and Bank Holidays lunch in Summer – **M** a la carte 2 150/3 250
Spec. Setas Ara Cata, Brandada a la catalana, Tournedo José Torres.

XX ❁ Eldorado Petit, Dolors Monserdá 51, ✉ 08017, ☎ 204 51 53, 🏠, « Agradable terraza » – ▤ by ⑦

XX **Aitor,** Carbonnell 5, ✉ 08003, ☎ 319 94 88, Basque rest. – ▤. VISA LXY **m**
closed Sunday and 15 August-15 September – **M** a la carte 2 050/3 650.

XX **Las Indias,** passeig Manuel Girona 38 bis, ✉ 08034, ☎ 204 48 00 – ▤. AE E VISA. ⛔
closed Sunday dinner – **M** a la carte 2 050/4 100. by ⑥

XX **El Dento,** Loreto 32, ✉ 08029, ☎ 321 67 56, Seafood – ▤. AE ⓓ E VISA. ⛔ EV **g**
closed Saturday and 2 August-2 September – **M** a la carte 2 300/3 775.

XX **Quo Vadis,** Carme 7, ✉ 08001, ☎ 317 74 47 – ▤. AE ⓓ E VISA JX **k**
closed Sunday – **M** a la carte 1 850/3 720.

XX **Chévere,** rambla del Prat 14, ✉ 08012, ☎ 217 03 59 – ▤ Ⓟ. AE ⓓ E VISA. ⛔ FU **q**
closed Saturday lunch, Sunday and August – **M** a la carte 1 800/3 675.

XX **Cathay,** Santaló 86, ✉ 08021, ☎ 209 37 86, Chinese rest., « Elegant decor » – ▤. VISA. ⛔ EU **f**
closed Monday and August – **M** a la carte 940/2 080.

XX ❁ **Jaume de Provença,** Provença 88, ✉ 08029, ☎ 230 00 29, Modern decor – ▤. AE ⓓ E VISA. ⛔ EX **h**
closed Sunday dinner, Monday 1 week at Easter and August – **M** a la carte 1 850/3 450
Spec. Canelones de espinacas, Espardenyes con mariscos marinera, Flan de mejillones con lenguado.

XX **Alt Berlín,** Diagonal 633, ✉ 08028, ☎ 339 01 66, German rest. – ▤. AE ⓓ E VISA by ⑥
M a la carte 2 150/3 850.

XX ❁ **Hostal Sant Jordi,** Travessera de Dalt 123, ✉ 08024, ☎ 213 10 37 – ▤. AE ⓓ VISA. ⛔ by Travessera de Gràcia FU
closed Sunday dinner and August – **M** a la carte 1 890/2 880
Spec. Chipirones con cebolla, Filete de lenguado Hostal Sant Jordi, Fricandó con setas del tiempo.

X **La Balsa,** Infanta Isabel 4, ✉ 08022, ☎ 211 50 48, 🏠 – AE ⓓ VISA by ⑦
closed Sunday and Monday lunch – **M** a la carte 1 790/3 200.

X Tinell, Freneria 8, ✉ 08002, ☎ 315 46 04 – ▤ MR **t**

X **Chicoa,** Aribau 71, ✉ 08036, ☎ 253 11 23, Rustic decor – ▤. AE E VISA FV **a**
closed Sunday and August – **M** a la carte 1 775/3 350.

X **La Senyora Grill,** Bori i Fontesta 45, ✉ 08017, ☎ 259 05 00, 🏠 – ▤. AE VISA. ⛔ by ⑥
M a la carte 1 650/3 275.

X **Portofino 2,** Ganduxer 50, ✉ 08021, ☎ 201 00 09, Italian rest. – ▤. VISA. ⛔ by ⑥
closed Saturday and Sunday dinner – **M** a la carte 1 800/3 100.

Typical atmosphere restaurants

XX La Dida, Roger de Flor 230, ✉ 08025, ☎ 207 20 04, « Regional decor » – ▤ 🚗 Ⓟ JU **c**

XX **Agut d'Avignon,** Trinidad 3 (Aviño 8), ✉ 08022, ☎ 302 60 34, « Regional decor » – ▤. AE ⓓ E VISA. ⛔ KY **n**
closed Sunday and 1 week at Easter – **M** a la carte 1 700/3 300.

XX **Font del Gat,** passeig Santa Madrona, Montjuic, ✉ 08004, ☎ 224 02 24, 🏠, Regional decor – Ⓟ. AE ⓓ. ⛔ by av. Reina María Cristina EZ
M a la carte 1 575/3 150.

✗ **La Cuineta,** Paradís 4, ⌧ 08002, 🏠 315 01 11, « In a 17C cellar » – 🍽. 🖭 ⓞ 🅴 𝖵𝖨𝖲𝖠
closed Monday except Bank Holidays – **M** a la carte 1 700/3 325.　　　　　　　MR **e**

✗ **Los Caracoles,** Escudellers 14, ⌧ 08002, 🏠 301 20 41, Rustic regional decor – 🍽. 🖭
ⓞ 🅴 𝖵𝖨𝖲𝖠. 🍴　　　　　　　　　　　　　　　　　　　　　　　　　　　　　　　　KY **k**
M a la carte 1 565/2 790.

✗ **Can Culleretes,** Quintana 5, ⌧ 08002, 🏠 317 64 85 – 🍽　　　　　　　　　JY **c**
closed Sunday dinner and Monday – **M** a la carte 1 150/1 800.

✗ **Pá i Trago,** Parlamento 41, ⌧ 08015, 🏠 241 13 20 – 🍽 ⓟ. 🅴 𝖵𝖨𝖲𝖠. 🍴　　　　GY **a**
closed Monday except Bank Holidays and 24 June-23 July – **M** (booking essential)
a la carte 1 400/2 700.

✗ **A la Menta,** passeig Manuel Girona 50, ⌧ 08035, 🏠 204 15 49, Tavern – 🍽. 🖭 ⓞ 𝖵𝖨𝖲𝖠.
🍴　　　　　　　　　　　　　　　　　　　　　　　　　　　　　　　　　　　　　　by ⑥
closed Sunday in August and Sunday dinner all year – **M** (booking essential)
a la carte 1 625/3 050.

✗ **L'Alberg,** Ramón y Cajal 13, ⌧ 08012, 🏠 214 10 25, Rustic decor – 🍽. 🅴 𝖵𝖨𝖲𝖠. 🍴
closed Sunday – **M** a la carte 1 850/2 750.　　　　　　　　　　　　　　　　　FU **d**

✗ **Del Teatre** 1st floor, Montseny 47, ⌧ 08012, 🏠 218 67 38　　　　　　　　　FU **s**
closed Sunday, Monday and August – **M** a la carte 1 350/2 180.

at Esplugues de Llobregat by ⑥ – ⌧ Esplugues de Llobregat – ⓢ 93 :

✗✗✗ **La Masía,** av. Paisos Catalans 58 🏠 371 37 42, ☂, « Terrace under pine-trees » – 🍽
ⓟ. 🖭 ⓞ 🅴 𝖵𝖨𝖲𝖠. 🍴
M a la carte 1 600/3 275.

✗ ✿ **Casa Quirze,** Laureano Miró 202 🏠 371 10 84 – 🍽 ⓟ. 🖭 ⓞ 🅴 𝖵𝖨𝖲𝖠. 🍴
closed Sunday dinner, Monday and 1 week at Easter – **M** a la carte 1 900/2 850
Spec. Mousseline de rascasse, Higado fresco de oca a la sol, Supremas de lúbina al perfume de ajo.

at the Tibidabo by ⑦ – ⌧ Barcelona 22 – ⓢ 93 :

✗ **La Masía,** 🏠 247 63 50, ≤ Town, sea and mountains – 🖭 ⓞ 🅴 𝖵𝖨𝖲𝖠
M (lunch only) a la carte 1 395/2 440.

on the road to Sant Cugat del Vallés by ⑦ : 11 km – ⌧ 08006 Barcelona – ⓢ 93 :

✗ Can Cortés, urbanización Ciudad Condal Tibidabo 🏠 674 17 04, ≤, ☂, « Old masia,
rustic decor », ⓟ admis. charge – ⓟ. 🖭 ⓞ 🅴 𝖵𝖨𝖲𝖠
closed Sunday dinner.

at the Airport by ⑤ : 12 km – ⌧ Barcelona Airport – ⓢ 93 :

✗✗ Aeropuerto de Barcelona and Salón San Jorge, 🏠 379 02 54 – 🍽.

Argentona Barcelona 🔢 ⑱ and 🔢 ⑳ – pop. 6 515 h. alt. 75 – ⓢ 93.
Barcelona 27.

✗✗ ✿✿ **Racó d'En Binu,** Puig i Cadafalch 14 🏠 797 01 01 – 🍽. 🖭 ⓞ 🅴 𝖵𝖨𝖲𝖠. 🍴
closed Sunday dinner, Monday and 27 May-27 June – **M** a la carte 2 400/4 000
Spec. Pastis de faves a la menta, Lubina en papillote salsa de mariscos, Souffle glace de piñones.

MÁLAGA - MARBELLA

Málaga 29000 🔢 V16 – pop. 503 251 – ⓢ 952 – Sea-side resort - Bullring.

See : Cathedral★ CY – Fine Arts Museum★ (Museo de bellas Artes) DY **M** – Alcazaba★
(museo★) DY – Gibralfaro ≤★★ DY.

Envir. : Finca de la Concepción★ by ④ : 7 km – Road from Málaga to Antequera ≤★★.

🏌 Club de Campo of Málaga by ② : 9 km 🏠 38 11 20 – 🏌 of El Candado by ① : 5 km
🏠 29 46 66.

✈ Málaga by ② : 9 km 🏠 31 19 44 – Iberia : Molina Larios 13, ⌧ 29015, 🏠 31 37 31
and Aviaco : airport 🏠 31 78 58.

🚗 🏠 31 62 49.

⛴ to Melilla : Cia Trasmediterránea, Juan Díaz 4, ⌧ 29015 (CZ), 🏠 22 43 93, Telex
77042.

🅸 Larios 5, ⌧ 29015, 🏠 21 34 45 av. Cervantes, ⌧ 29016 🏠 22 86 00 and Airport 🏠 31 20 44 –
R.A.C.E. (Automóvil Club de Málaga) pl. de las Flores 2, ⌧ 29005, 🏠 21 42 60.

Madrid 546 ④ – Algeciras 133 ② – Córdoba 173 ④ – Sevilla 212 ④ – Valencia 655 ④.

Plan opposite

Centre :

🏨 **Málaga Palacio** without rest, coffee shop only, av. Cortina del Muelle 1, ⌧ 29015, 🏠
21 51 85, Telex 77021, ≤, 🏊, – 🛗 🍽 – 🔔. 🖭 ⓞ 🅴 𝖵𝖨𝖲𝖠. 🍴　　　　　　　　CZ **r**
🛏 400 – **221 rm** 6 100/7 900.

🏨 **Casa Curro** without rest, Sancha de Lara 7, ⌧ 29015, 🏠 22 72 00, Telex 77366 – 🛗 🍽.
🖭 ⓞ 🅴 𝖵𝖨𝖲𝖠. 🍴　　　　　　　　　　　　　　　　　　　　　　　　　　　　　　CZ **e**
🛏 300 – **104 rm** 3 200/4 700.

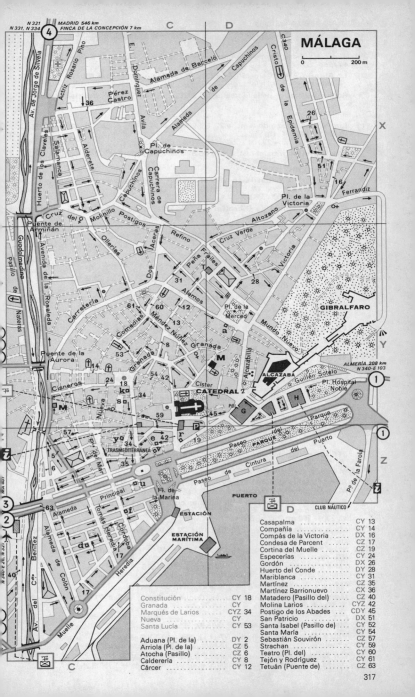

MÁLAGA

0   200 m

317

🏨 **Bahía Málaga**, without rest, Somera 8, ⊠ 29001, 𝒫 22 43 05 – 🗐 🖚wc 🕾   CZ **d**
   44 rm.

🏠 **Venecia**, without rest no ⌿, Alameda Principal 9, ⊠ 29001, 𝒫 21 36 36 – 🗐 🖚wc 🕾
   40 rm.   CZ **u**

XX **La Alegría**, Marín García 10, ⊠ 29005, 𝒫 22 41 43 – 🔳. 𝔸𝔼 ① 𝗘 𝘝𝘐𝘚𝘈   CZ **y**
   closed Saturday – **M** a la carte 1 475/3 350.

X **Cortijo de Pepe**, pl. de la Merced 2, ⊠ 29012, 𝒫 22 40 71, 🛱, Andalusian decor – 🔳
                                                                DY **a**

suburbs :

🏨 **Las Vegas**, paseo de Sancha 22, ⊠ 29016, 𝒫 21 77 12, ≼, 🛱, ⊒, 🖛 – 🗐 🖚wc 🕾
   🅿. 𝔸𝔼 ① 𝘝𝘐𝘚𝘈. 𝒮𝒾 rest   by ①
   M 1 325 – ⌿ 290 – **73 rm** 2 550/4 050 – P 4 525/5 050.

🏨 **Los Naranjos** without rest, paseo de Sancha 35, ⊠ 29016, 𝒫 22 43 19, Telex 77030 – 🗐
   🔳 🖚wc 🕅wc 🕾. 𝔸𝔼 ① 𝘝𝘐𝘚𝘈. 𝒮𝒾   by ①
   ⌿ 400 – **41 rm** 3 500/5 200.

🏨 **Apartogar La Maestranza** without rest, no ⌿, av. Cánovas del Castillo 1, ⊠ 29016,
   𝒫 21 36 18 – 🗐 🖚wc 🕾. 𝔸𝔼 ① 𝗘 𝘝𝘐𝘚𝘈. 𝒮𝒾   by ①
   107 apartments 2 800/3 800.

🏨 **Parador Nacional de Gibralfaro** 📎, ⊠ 29016, 𝒫 22 19 02, 🛱, « Beautiful location
   with ≼ bay and town » – 🖚wc 🕾 🅿. 𝔸𝔼 ① 𝗘 𝘝𝘐𝘚𝘈. 𝒮𝒾   DY
   M 1 600 – ⌿ 500 – **12 rm** 5 200/6 500.

🏨 **Olletas** without rest, Cuba 3, ⊠ 29013, 𝒫 25 20 00 – 🗐 🖚wc 🕾 🅿. 𝒮𝒾
   66 rm 1 800/2 800.   by Cristo de la Epidemia   DX

XX **Calycanto**, av. Pintor Sorolla 51, ⊠ 29016, 𝒫 21 59 14, 🛱 – 🔳   by ①

XX **Antonio Martín**, paseo Marítimo 4, ⊠ 29016, 𝒫 22 21 13, ≼, 🛱 – 🅿   by ①

XX **Café de París**, Vélez Málaga 8, ⊠ 29016, 𝒫 22 50 43 – 🔳. 𝔸𝔼 ① 𝗘 𝘝𝘐𝘚𝘈. 𝒮𝒾   by ①
   M a la carte 1 475/2 620.

X **La Taberna del Pintor**, Maestranza 6, ⊠ 29016, 𝒫 21 53 15, Typical decor – 🔳. 𝔸𝔼 ①
   𝗘 𝘝𝘐𝘚𝘈   by ①
   closed Sunday – **M** a la carte 1 210/2 470.

by the road to Cádiz by ② : 10 km – ⊠ Málaga – ☼ 952 :

🏨 **Guadalmar**, urbanización Guadalmar, ⊠ 29004, 𝒫 31 90 00, Telex 77099, ≼, ⊒, 🖛, 𝒮𝒾
   – 🗐 🔳 🅿 – 🔬 𝔸𝔼 ① 𝗘 𝘝𝘐𝘚𝘈. 𝒮𝒾
   M 1 475 – ⌿ 400 – **195 rm** 4 500/6 500 – P 6 100/7 350.

   Marbella Málaga 𝟜𝟜𝟞 W 15 – pop. 67 882 – ☼ 952 – Beach – Bullring.

   📷 Río Real-Los Monteros by ① : 5 km 𝒫 77 37 76 – 📷 Nueva Andalucía by ② : 5 km
   𝒫 81 22 00 – 📷 Aloha golf, urbanización Aloha by ② : 8 km 𝒫 78 23 88 – 📷 golf Las
   Brisas, Nueva Andalucía by ② 𝒫 78 03 00 – Iberia : paseo Marítimo 𝒫 77 02 84.

   🛈 Miguel Cano 1 𝒫 77 14 42.

   Madrid 602 ① – Algeciras 77 ② – Málaga 56 ①.

Plan opposite

🏨 **El Fuerte**, Castillo San Luis 𝒫 77 15 00, Telex 77523, ≼, 🛱, « Garden with palm-trees »,
   ⊒, 𝒮𝒾 – 🗐 🔳 rest 🅿. 𝔸𝔼 ① 𝘝𝘐𝘚𝘈. 𝒮𝒾 rest   AB **e**
   M 1 750 – ⌿ 500 – **146 rm** 5 500/7 500 – P 6 400/8 150.

🏨 **Skol**, La Fontanilla 𝒫 77 08 00, Telex 78631, ≼, ⊒, 🖛 – 🗐 🔳 rest. 𝔸𝔼 𝗘 𝘝𝘐𝘚𝘈. 𝒮𝒾 rest
   M 1 400 – ⌿ 400 – **200 apartments** 5 700/7 000 – P 6 000/8 200.   A **v**

🏨 **San Cristóbal** without rest, coffee shop only, Ramón y Cajal 18 𝒫 77 12 50, Telex 77712
   – 🗐 🔳 🖚wc 🕅wc 🕾. 𝗘 𝘝𝘐𝘚𝘈. 𝒮𝒾   A **t**
   ⌿ 200 – **100 rm** 2 475/3 950.

🏨 **Lima** without rest, av. Antonio Belón 2 𝒫 77 05 00 – 🗐 🖚wc 🕅wc 🕾. 𝔸𝔼 ① 𝗘 𝘝𝘐𝘚𝘈. 𝒮𝒾
   ⌿ 300 – **64 rm** 2 800/3 950.   A **h**

XXX ☼ **La Fonda**, pl. Santo Cristo 10 𝒫 77 25 12, 🛱, « Pretty Andalusian patio » – 𝔸𝔼 ①
   𝘝𝘐𝘚𝘈. 𝒮𝒾   A **z**
   closed Sunday – **M** (dinner only) a la carte 2 105/4 510
   Spec. Pastel de trucha salsa Ramos, Cazuela de pescados andaluza, Pintada en hojaldre.

XX **Marcuño**, Nuestra Señora de Gracia 26, Seafood – 🔳   A **r**

XX **Gran Marisquería Santiago**, av. Duque de Ahumada 5 𝒫 77 00 78, 🛱, Seafood –
   🔳. 𝔸𝔼 ① 𝗘 𝘝𝘐𝘚𝘈. 𝒮𝒾   A **b**
   M a la carte 1 750/3 750.

X **Mena**, pl. de los Naranjos 10 𝒫 77 15 97, 🛱   A **c**

X **Plaza**, General Chinchilla 2 𝒫 77 11 11, 🛱 – 𝔸𝔼 ① 𝗘 𝘝𝘐𝘚𝘈   AB **s**
   closed Sunday and 15 October-15 February – **M** a la carte 1 850/3 850.

X **Los Naranjos**, pl. de los Naranjos 𝒫 77 18 19, 🛱 – 𝔸𝔼 ① 𝗘 𝘝𝘐𝘚𝘈. 𝒮𝒾   AB **k**
   closed Sunday and 15 November-15 February – **M** a la carte 1 950/3 250.

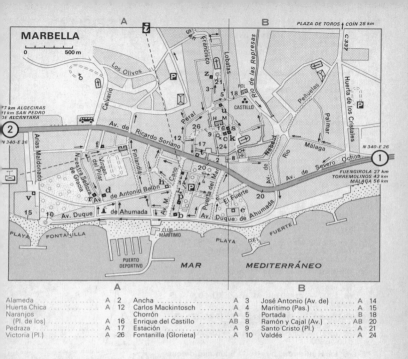

MARBELLA

0   500 m

PLAZA DE TOROS – COÍN 26 km

N 340-E 26

7 km ALGECIRAS
41 km SAN PEDRO
DE ALCÁNTARA

FUENGIROLA 27 km
TORREMOLINOS 43 km
MÁLAGA 56 km

MAR   MEDITERRÁNEO

PUERTO
DEPORTIVO

on the road to Cádiz – ⊠ Marbella – ☎ 952 :

🏨🏨 **Meliá Don Pepe and grill la Farola** ⟨S⟩, by ② : 1 km ℰ 77 03 00, Telex 77055, ≤ sea
and mountains, ⌖, Pianist at dinner, « Subtropical plants », ⊐ heated, ⊠, ⌖, ⌖, ⌖
– 🛗 ▤ 🅟 – 🛆. ᴀᴇ ⑩ ᴇ ᴠɪsᴀ. ⌖
M 3 400 – ⊇ 800 – **218 rm** 11 500/18 000 – P 15 460/17 960.

🏨🏨 **Puente Romano** Ⓜ ⟨S⟩, by ② : 3,5 km ℰ 77 01 00, Telex 77399, ⌖, « Elegant Andalusian
complex in beautiful garden », ⊐ heated, ⌖ – ▤ 🅟 – 🛆. ᴀᴇ ⑩ ᴇ ᴠɪsᴀ. ⌖ rest
M 3 500 – ⊇ 900 – **193 rm** 15 000/22 000 – P 17 700/21 700.

🏨🏨 **Del Golf Nueva Andalucía** ⟨S⟩, urbanización Nueva Andalucía by ② : 7 km and
detour : 4 km, ⊠ apartado 2 Nueva Andalucía, ℰ 78 03 00, Telex 77783, ≤, ⊐ heated,
⊠, ⌖, ⌖ – 🛗 ▤ 🅟 – 🛆. ᴀᴇ ⑩ ᴇ ᴠɪsᴀ. ⌖
M 2 500 – ⊇ 500 – **75 rm** 8 000/16 000 – P 12 500.

🏨🏨 Andalucía Plaza, urbanización Nueva Andalucía by ② : 7,5 km, ⊠ apartado 21 Nueva
Andalucía, ℰ 78 20 00, Telex 77086, ⌖, ⊐ heated, ⌖, ⌖ – 🛗 ▤ 🅟 – 🛆
418 rm.

🏨🏨 **Marbella Club** ⟨S⟩, by ② : 3 km ℰ 77 13 00, Telex 77319, ⌖, « Elegant decor ; garden »,
⊐ heated – ▤ ▤ 🅟. ᴀᴇ ⑩ ᴇ ᴠɪsᴀ
M 3 500 – ⊇ 900 – **71 rm** 14 400/18 000 – P 15 700/21 100.

🏨🏨 **Marbella Dinamar Club 24,** by ② : 6 km, ⊠ Nueva Andalucía, ℰ 78 05 00, Telex
77656, ≤, ⌖, ⊠, ⌖, ⌖ – 🛗 ▤ 🅟 – 🛆. ᴀᴇ ᴠɪsᴀ. ⌖
M 1 950 – ⊇ 650 – **117 rm** 7 500/9 500 – P 8 250/11 000.

🏨🏨 Las Fuentes del Rodeo, by ② : 8 km, ⊠ Nueva Andalucía, ℰ 78 10 00, Telex 77340, ⌖,
« Garden », ⊐, ⌖ – 🅟
90 rm.

🏨🏨 Guadalpín, by ② : 1,5 km ℰ 77 11 00, ⌖, ⊐, ⌖ – 🅟
110 rm.

🏨 **Nagüeles** without rest, by ② : 3,5 km ℰ 77 16 88, ⌖ – 🚽wc 🛁wc. ⌖
15 March-15 October – ⊇ 230 – **17 rm** 1 450/2 500.

🗙🗙🗙 **La Meridiana,** by ② : 3,5 km and detour 1 km - camino de la Cruz - Las Lomas
ℰ 77 61 90, ≤, ⌖, « Terrace-garden » – ▤ 🅟. ᴀᴇ ⑩ ᴇ ᴠɪsᴀ
closed Thursday lunch and 20 November-20 December – **M** (dinner only in summer)
a la carte 2 850/5 250.

XXX **Le Restaurant**, by ② : 8 km and detour to Rodeo Beach Club, ⊠ Nueva Andalucia, ℰ 78 59 00, Telex 77340, ≤, 舒, French rest., « Elegant decor » – **℗**.

X **Orquídea**, urbanización Nueva Andalucía - calle 2 - 21 B by ② : 7,7 km, ⊠ Nueva Andalucía, ℰ 78 16 99, 舒, French rest. – **℗**.
closed Wednesday and 10 January-February – **M** (dinner only) a la carte 1 650/2 575.

on the road to Málaga by ① – ⊠ Marbella – ✿ 952 :

Los Monteros and Grill El Corzo Ⓜ ⚐, by ① : 5,5 km ℰ 77 17 00, Telex 77059, ≤, 舒, Pianist at dinner, « Subtropical garden », ⤴ heated, ⬚, ⅏, ⓕ, – ⬛ ▤ **℗** – ▵ **E** ⚐
M 4 000 – **164 rm** ⌚ 17 400/22 700 – P 19 350/25 400.

Don Carlos Ⓜ ⚐, by ① : 10 km ℰ 83 11 40, Telex 74481, ≤, 舒, Pianist at dinner, « Large garden », ⤴ heated, ⅏ – ⬛ ▤ **℗** – ▵
231 rm.

Estrella del Mar ⚐, by ① : 9 km ℰ 83 12 75, Telex 77086, 舒, ⤴, ⅏ – ⬛ ▤ rest **℗**
season – **98 rm**.

Bellamar (Trade School Hotel), by ① : 1,5 km ℰ 77 23 00, ≤, 舒, ⤴, ⤢, ⅏ – ⬛ ▤ **℗**.
 ⚐
M 1 200 – ⌚ 300 – **51 rm** 2 500/4 000 – P 4 200/4 700.

Belarcos, by ① : 13,5 km ℰ 83 17 44, 舒, ⤴, ⅏ – ⬛ ⌷wc ☎ **℗**. **E**
M 1 200 – ⌚ 375 – **78 rm** 3 400/5 000 – P 5 000/5 900.

XX ✿✿ **La Hacienda**, by ① : 11,5 km and detour 1,5 km ℰ 83 12 67, 舒, « Rustic decor - Patio » – **℗**. **E** ⚐
closed Monday and Tuesday from October to May, Monday dinner in Summer and 15 November-15 December – **M** (dinner only from June to September) a la carte 2 895/5 350
Spec. Crepe de maíz con coquinas y albahaca, Escalope de pato con higos, Souffle helado al vino Málaga.

XX **Chez Charlemagne**, by ① : 8 km ℰ 83 11 05, 舒, French rest. – **℗**.
closed Wednesday and 15 January-15 February – **M** (dinner only) a la carte 1 790/3 720.

SEVILLA 41000 ℗ T 11 12 – pop. 653 833 – alt. 12 – ✿ 954 – Bullring.

See : Cathedral★★★ CV – Giralda★★★ (≤★★) CV – Alcazar★★★ (gardens★★, Admiral's Apartments : Virgin of the Navigators altarpiece★) CX – Maria Luisa Park★★ – Fine Arts Museum★★ AU M1 – Santa Cruz Quarter★ CV – Pilate's House★★ (casa de Pilatos : azulejos★★) DV R – Archeological Museum (Roman department★).

Envir. : Itálica ≤★ 9 km by ⑤.

ⓕ and Racecourse Club Pineda by ③ : 3 km ℰ 61 14 00.

✈ Sevilla - San Pablo by ① : 14 km ℰ 51 65 98 – Iberia : Almirante Lobo 2, ⊠ 41002 ℰ 21 88 00.

🚗 ℰ 22 03 70.

ⓘ av. de la Constitución 21B ⊠ 41004 ℰ 22 14 04 and paseo de Las Delicias ⊠ 41012 ℰ 23 44 65 – R.A.C.E. (R.A.C. de Andalucía) av. Eduardo Dato 22, ⊠ 41002 ℰ 63 13 50.

Madrid 547 ① – La Coruña 959 ⑤ – Lisboa 409 ⑤ – Málaga 215 ② – Valencia 676 ①.

SEVILLA

B · C · D

Torneo
Resolana
PUERTA
MACARENA
a

MURALLAS ALMOHADES
Muñoz

T
la Cruz Roja
Av. de la Ronda Capuchinos

Calatrava
Peral
Feria
San Luis

LA MACARENA

Relator

TORRE DE DON
FADRIQUE

Teodosio
Gran
Poder
Relator
Feria
Feria

Alameda de Hércules

Conde de
Barajas

San Luis

Teodosio
Jesús
Trajano
de
Feria

León

Av. Ronda Capuchinos

PALACIO DE
LAS DUEÑAS

Baños
Pl. de la
Gavidia
POL
19
Pl.
del Duque
Alfonso XII
42

Amor
Laraña
Regina
Doña Mª Coronel
Bustos Tavera
Sol
Matahacas

48

Luna
Jauregui

U

María Auxiliadora

16
Eloy
San
r
45
65
54
54
62

Sierpes

Pl. de la
Encarnación
Pl. Cristo
de Burgos
Pl. S
Leandro

Imagen
34
34

Recaredo

Imperial
12
R
y

San
Pablo
Mendez
Nuñez

Cuesta
del Rosario
Pl. San Francisco
29
13
13
Aguilas
San Esteban

MADRID 545 km
CÓRDOBA 143 km
AEROPUERTO 10 km
N IV

Pl.
Nueva
H

Argote
José
La Florida
L. Montoto

Zaragoza
Castelar
32

a
b
d

GIRALDA
CATEDRAL

a
43

BARRIO DE
STA-CRUZ

59

Pelayo

1

2

N 334
MÁLAGA 209 km
GRANADA 255 km

Ant. Diaz
u
e

Pl.
Sta Cruz
JARDINES DE
MURILLO

25

1

Dos de Mayo

30
63
81

ALCÁZAR

JARDINES
DEL
ALCÁZAR

Av. E. Dato
2

Pd. de Catalina de Ribera

Menéndez

ESTACIÓN
DE CÁDIZ

X

TORRE
DEL ORO

Paseo de Cristóbal Colón

6
36

Av. de
San
Fernanda
Roma
C

Sanjurjo

Pl. Juan
de Austria

PALACIO
DE JUSTICIA

de Cádiz

y
Betis

Puente San
Telmo

PALACIO
DE S. TELMO

Palos de la Frontera

Av. del Cid

Av. del Cid

Av. P
Carlos V

PRADO DE SAN
SEBASTIÁN

1

Pl. de
Cuba
m

Av. de S. Telmo

3
N IV
AUTOPISTA A 4 ❶
CÁDIZ 123 km

3

e

7

Av. de
Portugal

2

B · C · D

Alfonso XIII, San Fernando 2, ⊠ 41004, ℰ 22 28 50, Telex 72725, 🛱, « Magnificent Andalusian building », ⌲, 🛲 – ⊠ ▤ ℗ – 🕍. ⚿ 🚗 🇪 𝘝𝘐𝘚𝘈. ⚘   CX **c**
M 2 300 – ⌲ 520 – **148 rm** 9 000/12 250 – P 10 225/13 100.

Los Lebreros Ⓜ, Luis Morales 2, ⊠ 41005, ℰ 54 91 00, Telex 72772, ⌲ – ⊠ ▤ 🚗 –
🕍. ⚿ ⓞ 🇪 𝘝𝘐𝘚𝘈. ⚘   by Luis Montoto   DV
M 2 500 (see also Rest. La Dehesa below) – ⌲ 550 – **439 rm** 6 000/8 500 – P 8 690/10 690.

Porta Coeli Ⓜ without rest, coffee shop only, av. Eduardo Dato 49, ⊠ 41005, ℰ
57 00 40, Telex 72913 – ⊠ ▤ ℗ – 🕍. ⚿ ⓞ 🇪 𝘝𝘐𝘚𝘈   by E. Dato   DV
⌲ 325 – **246 rm** 6 500/12 000.

Colón, Canalejas 1, ⊠ 41001, ℰ 22 29 00, Telex 72726 – ⊠ ▤ 🚗 ⓞ 🇪 𝘝𝘐𝘚𝘈   AV **m**
M (rest. see El Burladero below) – ⌲ 350 – **262 rm** 6 500/11 000 – P 6 260/7 060.

Macarena, San Juan de Ribera 2, ⊠ 41009, ℰ 37 57 00, Telex 72815, ⌲ – ⊠ ▤ 🚗 –
🕍. ⚿ ⓞ 🇪 𝘝𝘐𝘚𝘈   DT **a**
M 2 500 – ⌲ 550 – **281 rm** 6 000/8 500 – P 8 690/10 690.

Inglaterra, pl. Nueva 7, ⊠ 41001, ℰ 22 49 70, Telex 72244 – ⊠ ▤ 🚗. ⚿ ⓞ 🇪 𝘝𝘐𝘚𝘈. ⚘
M 1 600 – ⌲ 350 – **120 rm** 7 000/10 500 – P 8 250/10 000.   BV **a**

Pasarela Ⓜ without rest, av. de la Borbolla 11, ⊠ 41004, ℰ 41 55 11, Telex 72486 – ⊠
▤ 🚗. ⚿ ⓞ 🇪 𝘝𝘐𝘚𝘈. ⚘   by Av. de Portugal   DX
⌲ 350 – **82 rm** 6 000/8 500.

Resid. and Rest. Fernando III, San José 21, ⊠ 41004, ℰ 21 77 08, Telex 72491, ⌲ –
⊠ ▤ 🚗 – 🕍. ⚿ ⓞ 𝘝𝘐𝘚𝘈. ⚘ rest   CV **z**
M 1 500 – ⌲ 275 – **156 rm** 3 000/4 300.

Bécquer without rest, Reyes Católicos 4, ⊠ 41001, ℰ 22 89 00, Telex 72884 – ⊠ ▤. ⚿
ⓞ 🇪 𝘝𝘐𝘚𝘈. ⚘   AV **s**
⌲ 250 – **126 rm** 2 700/4 000.

América Ⓜ without rest, coffee shop only, Jésus del Gran Poder 2, ⊠ 41002, ℰ
22 09 51, Telex 72709 – ⊠ ▤. ⚿ ⓞ 🇪 𝘝𝘐𝘚𝘈. ⚘   BU **h**
⌲ 250 – **100 rm** 2 445/4 180.

Nuevo Lar, pl. Carmen Benítez 3, ⊠ 41003, ℰ 41 03 61, Telex 72816 – ⊠ ▤ 🚗 – 🕍.
⚿ ⓞ 🇪 𝘝𝘐𝘚𝘈. ⚘   DV **v**
M 1 350 – ⌲ 330 – **137 rm** 5 000/7 000 – P 5 800/7 300.

Alcázar without rest, coffee shop only, Menéndez Pelayo 10, ⊠ 41004, ℰ 41 20 11,
Telex 72360 – ⊠ ▤. ⚿ ⓞ 🇪 𝘝𝘐𝘚𝘈   DX **u**
⌲ 250 – **93 rm** 3 000/4 000.

Fleming, Sierra Nevada 3, Puerta de Carmona, ⊠ 41003, ℰ 41 66 61, Telex 72417 – ⊠
▤ ℗ – 🕍. ⚿ ⓞ 𝘝𝘐𝘚𝘈. ⚘   DV **y**
M 1 300 – ⌲ 330 – **90 rm** 2 800/4 000 – P 4 825/5 625.

Doña María without rest, Don Remondo 19, ⊠ 41004, ℰ 22 49 90, « Elegant classic
decor - terrace with ≤ Giralda », ⌲ – ⊠ ▤. ⚿ ⓞ 𝘝𝘐𝘚𝘈. ⚘   CV **b**
⌲ 350 – **61 rm** 5 500/9 000.

Monte Carmelo without rest, Turia 9, ⊠ 41011, ℰ 27 10 04 – ⊠ ▤ 🚗. ⚿ 🇪 𝘝𝘐𝘚𝘈. ⚘
⌲ 250 – **68 rm** 2 600/4 000.   SW : by pl. de Cuba

La Rábida, Castelar 24, ⊠ 41001, ℰ 22 09 60, 🛱 – ⊠ 🛁wc 🚿wc 🅟. ⚘ rest   BV **d**
M 850 – ⌲ 175 – **90 rm** 1 900/3 200 – P 3 500/6 400.

El Corregidor without rest, Morgado 17, ⊠ 41003, ℰ 38 51 11 – ⊠ ▤ 🛁wc 🅟. ⚿ ⓞ
⌲ 275 – **69 rm** 2 900/5 000.   CT **g**

Venecia without rest, Trajano 31, ⊠ 41002, ℰ 38 11 61 – ⊠ ▤ 🛁wc 🚿wc 🚗. 𝘝𝘐𝘚𝘈
⌲ 250 – **24 rm** 2 400/4 000.   BU **n**

Reyes Católicos without rest, no ⌲, Gravina 57, ⊠ 41001, ℰ 21 12 00 – ⊠ ▤ 🛁wc
🚿wc 🅟. ⚿ ⓞ 🇪 𝘝𝘐𝘚𝘈   AV **n**
26 rm 2 600/3 900.

Murillo and apart. Murillo without rest, Lope de Rueda 9, ⊠ 41004, ℰ 21 60 95 – ⊠
🛁wc 🚿 🅟 – 🕍. ⚿ ⓞ 🇪 𝘝𝘐𝘚𝘈. ⚘   CV **e**
61 rm ⌲ 2 350/3 600 **14 apartments**.

Ducal without rest, pl. Encarnación 19, ⊠ 41003, ℰ 21 51 07 – ⊠ 🛁wc 🚿wc 🅟. ⚿ ⓞ
🇪 𝘝𝘐𝘚𝘈. ⚘   CU **b**
⌲ 190 – **51 rm** 2 600/3 100.

Montecarlo, Gravina 51, ⊠ 41001, ℰ 21 75 02 – ⊠ 🛁wc 🚿wc 🅟. ⚿ ⓞ 🇪 𝘝𝘐𝘚𝘈. ⚘
M 950 – ⌲ 250 – **25 rm** 1 900/3 200 – P 3 400/3 700.   AV **e**

Sevilla without rest, no ⌲, Daoiz 5, ⊠ 41003, ℰ 38 41 61 – ⊠ 🛁wc 🚿wc 🅟. ⚘
29 rm 2 150/2 950.   BU **w**

XXX **Paco Ramos** 1st floor, Reyes Católicos 25, ⊠ 41001, ℰ 21 75 85 – ▤. ⚿ ⓞ 🇪 𝘝𝘐𝘚𝘈
closed Sunday and August – **M** a la carte 1 625/3 000.   AV **c**

XXX **Or-Iza,** Betis 61, ⊠ 41010, ℰ 27 95 85, Basque rest. – ▤. ⚿ ⓞ 🇪 𝘝𝘐𝘚𝘈. ⚘   BX **y**
closed Sunday and August – **M** a la carte 2 025/3 150.

XXX **Maitres,** av. República Argentina 54, ⊠ 41011, ℰ 45 68 80 – ▤. ⚿ ⓞ 🇪 𝘝𝘐𝘚𝘈. ⚘
closed Sunday – **M** a la carte 1 600/3 475.   SW : by pl. de Cuba

XXX **Río Grande,** Betis, ✉ 41010, ☎ 27 39 56, ≤, 🍽, « Large terraces on riverside » – ▤. AE ⓓ E VISA — BX **r**
M a la carte 1 475/2 850.

XXX La Dehesa, Luis Morales 2, ✉ 41005, ☎ 57 62 04, Telex 72772, Typical Andalusian decor - Grills – ▤ — by Luis Montoto DV

XXX El Burladero, José Canalejas 1, ✉ 41003, ☎ 22 29 00, Typical decor – ▤ — AV **m**

XXX **Rincón de Curro,** Virgen de Luján 45, ✉ 41011, ☎ 45 02 38 – ▤. AE ⓓ E VISA. ⛔
closed Sunday dinner – **M** a la carte 1 775/3 275. — SW : by pl. de Cuba

XXX **Figón del Cabildo,** pl. del Cabildo, ✉ 41001, ☎ 22 01 17, 🍽 – ▤. AE ⓓ E VISA. ⛔
M a la carte 1 790/3 275. — BV **e**

XX San Marco, Cuna 6, ✉ 41004, ☎ 21 24 40, « Patio » – ▤ — CU **x**

XX **Jamaica,** Jamaica 16, ✉ 41012, ☎ 61 12 44 – ▤. AE ⓓ VISA. ⛔ — by ③
closed Sunday in Summer and Sunday dinner off season – **M** a la carte 1 750/2 850.

XX **La Raza,** av. Isabel la Católica, ✉ 41013, ☎ 23 20 24, ≤, 🍽 – ▤. AE ⓓ E VISA — CX **e**
M a la carte 1 240/2 700.

XX Bodegón El Riojano, Virgen de la Montaña 12, ✉ 41011, ☎ 45 06 82 – ▤ — SW : by pl. de Cuba

XX **La Albahaca,** pl. Santa Cruz 12, ✉ 41004, ☎ 22 07 14, « Former manor house » – ▤. AE ⓓ E VISA. ⛔ — CV **s**
closed Sunday – **M** a la carte 1 400/2 800.

XX **José Luis Hernandez,** av. República Argentina 13, ✉ 41011, ☎ 27 70 93 – ▤. AE ⓓ E VISA. ⛔ — SW : by pl. de Cuba
closed Saturday and August – **M** a la carte 1 425/2 850.

XX **El Mero,** Betis, ✉ 41010, ☎ 33 42 52, Seafood – ▤. ⓓ E VISA. ⛔ — AX **p**
closed Tuesday in July and August – **M** a la carte 1 550/2 575.

X Cetaria, Luis de Morales - edificio Estadio, ✉ 41005, ☎ 57 87 28, Seafood – ▤ — by av. E. Dato DX

X **La Parra,** Gustavo Gallardo 14, ✉ 41013, ☎ 61 29 59, 🍽, « Patio with pergola » – ▤. VISA. ⛔ — by av. de Portugal DX
closed Saturday, Sunday and 15 August-15 September – **M** a la carte 1 275/2 270.

X San Marco, 1st floor, San Eloy 2, ✉ 41001, ☎ 22 98 27, 🍽, Italian rest. – ▤ — BU **r**

X La Isla, Arfe 25, ✉ 41001, ☎ 21 26 31 – ▤ — BV **u**

X **Los Alcázares,** Miguel de Mañara 10, ✉ 41004, ☎ 21 31 03, Regional decor – ▤. AE E VISA. ⛔ — CX **s**
closed Sunday – **M** a la carte 1 225/3 225.

X **Hostería del Laurel,** pl. de los Venerables 5, ✉ 41004, ☎ 22 02 95, Typical decor – ▤. AE VISA. ⛔ — CV **r**
closed Monday from November to March – **M** a la carte 1 350/2 550.

VALENCIA 46000 445 N 28 29 – pop. 751 734 – alt. 13 – ⚽ 96 – Bullring.

See : Fine Arts Museum★★ (Museo Provincial de Bellas Artes) FX **M3** – Cathedral★ (Miguelete★) EX **A** – Palacio de la Generalidad★ (ceilings★) EX **D** – Lonja★ (silkhall★, Maritime consulate hall : ceiling★) EX **E** – Corpus Christi Collegiate Church★ (Colegio del Patriarca) EY **N** – Ceramics Museum★ (Museo Nacional de Cerámica) EY **M1** – Serranos Towers★ EX **V** – Santo Domingo Monastery (Royal Chapel★) FY **S**.

⛳9 of Manises by ④ : 12 km ☎ 379 08 50 – ⛳18 Club Escorpión NO : 19 km by Liria Road ☎ 160 12 11.

✈ Valencia - Manises Airport by ④ : 9,5 km ☎ 370 34 08 – Iberia : Paz 14, ✉ 46003, ☎ 352 05 00.

🚗 ☎ 351 00 43.

⛴ To the Balearic and Canary Islands : Cía. Trasmediterránea, av. Manuel Soto Ingeniero 15, ✉ 46024, ☎ 367 06 04, Telex 62648.

ℹ Paz 46, ✉ 46003, ☎ 352 24 97 and pl. del País Valenciano 1 ✉ 46016 ☎ 351 04 17 – **R.A.C.E.** (R.A.C. de Valencia) av. Jacinto Benavente 25, ✉ 46005, ☎ 333 94 03.

Madrid 354 ④ – Albacete 184 ③ – Alicante (by coast) 172 ③ – Barcelona 361 ① – Bilbao 610 ① – Castellón de la Plana 75 ① – Málaga 654 ③ – Sevilla 676 ④ – Zaragoza 332 ①.

Plan on following pages

🏨 **Rey Don Jaime** Ⓜ, av. Baleares 2, ✉ 46023, ☎ 360 73 00, Telex 64252, 🏊 – 🛗 ▤ – 🏛. AE ⓓ E VISA. ⛔
M 2 700 – ☕ 550 – **314 rm** 6 500/9 000 – P 9 260/11 260.

🏨 **Astoria Palace,** pl. Rodrigo Botet 5, ✉ 46002, ☎ 352 67 37, Telex 62722 – 🛗 ▤. AE ⓓ E VISA. ⛔ — EY **p**
M 1 850 – ☕ 400 – **207 rm** 5 670/8 715 – P 7 820/9 135.

🏨 **Reina Victoria,** Barcas 4, ✉ 46002, ☎ 352 04 87, Telex 64755 – 🛗 ▤. AE ⓓ E VISA. ⛔ rest — EY **s**
M 1 350 – ☕ 250 – **92 rm** 3 800/6 900 – P 5 950/6 300.

🏨 **Expo H.** without rest, coffee shop only, av. Pío XII-4, ✉ 46009, ☎ 347 09 09, Telex 63212, 🏊 – 🛗 ▤ – 🏛. AE ⓓ E VISA. ⛔
396 rm ☕ 5 420/7 000.

VALENCIA

STREET INDEX

🏤 **Dimar** without rest, coffee shop only, Gran Vía Marqués del Turia 80, ⌧ 46005, ℰ
334 18 07, Telex 62952 – 🛗 ▤ ⟺ – 🔬. 🖭 ⓪ Ⅰ 𝗩𝗜𝗦𝗔. ⚶   FZ **q**
95 rm ⟳ 5 590/7 250.

🏤 **Excelsior** without rest, coffee shop only, Barcelonina 5, ⌧ 46002, ℰ 351 46 12 – 🛗 ▤.
🖭 ⓪ Ⅰ 𝗩𝗜𝗦𝗔. ⚶   EY **e**
⟳ 230 – **65 rm** 2 890/4 500.

🏤 **Oltra** without rest, coffee shop only, pl. del País Valenciano 4, ⌧ 46002, ℰ 352 06 12 –
🛗 ▤, 🖭 ⓪ Ⅰ 𝗩𝗜𝗦𝗔. ⚶   EY **t**
⟳ 275 – **93 rm** 2 825/4 600.

🏛 **Lehos** without rest, coffee shop only, General Urrutia (angle av. de la Plata), ⌧ 46013,
ℰ 334 78 00, 🏊 admis-charge – 🛗 ⌂wc ▥wc ⟺ ⟺ 🅿. 🖭 ⓪ Ⅰ 𝗩𝗜𝗦𝗔. ⚶
⟳ 325 – **104 rm** 2 900/4 550.

🏛 **Renasa** without rest., av. Cataluña 5, ⌧ 46010, ℰ 369 24 50 – 🛗 ▤ ⌂wc ▥wc ⟺. ⓪
𝗩𝗜𝗦𝗔
⟳ 280 – **73 rm** 2700/4600.

🏛 **Inglés,** Marqués de Dos Aguas 6, ⌧ 46002, ℰ 351 64 26 – 🛗 ▤ rest ⌂wc ⟺. 🖭 ⓪ Ⅰ
𝗩𝗜𝗦𝗔   EY **m**
M 1 000 – ⟳ 180 – **55 rm** 3 600/4 500 – P 4 650/5 500.

🏛 **Bristol** without rest., Abadía San Martín 3, ⌧ 46002, ℰ 352 11 76 – 🛗 ⌂wc ▥wc ⟺.
🖭 ⓪ Ⅰ 𝗩𝗜𝗦𝗔   EY **b**
closed December-15 January – ⟳ 200 – **40 rm** 2 430/4 000.

🏛 **Florida** without rest., Padilla 4, ⌧ 46001, ℰ 351 12 84 – 🛗 ⌂wc ▥wc ⟺. 𝗩𝗜𝗦𝗔   DY **e**
⟳ 200 – **45 rm** 2 300/4 000.

XXX **La Hacienda,** Navarro Reverter 12, ⌧ 46004, ℰ 373 18 59 – ▤. 🖭 ⓪ Ⅰ 𝗩𝗜𝗦𝗔. ⚶   FY **y**
closed Saturday lunch and Sunday – **M** a la carte 2 650/4 050.

XXX Los Azahares, Navarro Revester 16, ⌧ 46004, ℰ 334 86 01 – ▤   FY **s**

XXX **El Condestable,** Artes Gráficas 15, ⌧ 46010, ℰ 369 92 50, Castilian decor – ▤. 🖭 ⓪
Ⅰ 𝗩𝗜𝗦𝗔. ⚶
closed Sunday – **M** a la carte 2 025/3 600.

XXX ✿ **Ma Cuina,** Gran Vía Germanías 49, ⌧ 46006, ℰ 341 77 99 – ▤ 🅿. 𝗩𝗜𝗦𝗔   DZ **n**
M a la carte 1 500/3 000
Spec. Hojaldre de verduritas naturales, Pato macerado con salsa de higos, Milhojas.

XXX Les Graelles, pl. Galicia, ⌧ 46010, ℰ 360 47 00 – ▤.

XXX **Mesón del Marisquero,** Félix Pizcueta 7, ⌧ 46004, ℰ 352 97 91 – ▤   EZ **d**
closed Saturday lunch and Sunday except lunch in Winter.

XXX **Lionel,** Pizarro 9, ⌧ 46004, ℰ 351 65 66 – ▤. 🖭 𝗩𝗜𝗦𝗔. ⚶   EZ **b**
closed Sunday – **M** a la carte 1 575/2 520.

XXX **Comodoro,** Transits 3, ⌧ 46002, ℰ 321 38 15 – ▤. 🖭 ⓪ 𝗩𝗜𝗦𝗔. ⚶   EY **r**
closed Sunday and Bank Holidays – **M** a la carte 1 725/3 125.

XX El Cachirulo, Cronista Almela y Vives 3, ⌧ 46010, ℰ 360 10 84, Aragonese rest. – ▤.

XX El Timonel, Felix Pizcueta 13, ⌧ 46004, ℰ 352 63 00 – ▤   EZ **t**

XX **Río Sil,** Mosén Femades 10, ⌧ 46002, ℰ 352 97 64 – ▤. 🖭 ⓪ Ⅰ 𝗩𝗜𝗦𝗔. ⚶   EZ **a**
M a la carte 1 600/2 850.

XX **Mey Mey,** Historiador Diago 19, ⌧ 46007, ℰ 326 07 47, Chinese rest. – ▤. 🖭 𝗩𝗜𝗦𝗔 DZ **e**
M a la carte 1 050/1 920.

X **Marisquería Ismael,** Burriana 40, ⌧ 46005, ℰ 373 57 15 – ▤. 🖭 ⓪ 𝗩𝗜𝗦𝗔. ⚶   FZ **e**
closed Sunday from June to September – **M** a la carte 1 900/3 600.

X **El Plat,** Conde de Altea 41, ⌧ 46005, ℰ 334 96 38, Paella and rice rest. – ▤. 𝗩𝗜𝗦𝗔. ⚶
closed Sunday dinner and Monday – **M** a la carte 1 550/2 650.   FZ **v**

at Playa Puebla de Farnals by ① : 15 km – ⌧ Playa Puebla de Farnals – ✿ 96 :

X **Bergamonte,** ℰ 144 16 12, 🍴, « Typical Valencian "barraca" », 🏊 admis. charge, ⚶
– 🅿. 🖭 𝗩𝗜𝗦𝗔. ⚶
closed Monday – **M** a la carte 1 275/2 050.

on the road to the Airport by ④ : 9,5 km – ⌧ Manises – ✿ 96 :

🏤 **Azafata Sol,** ℰ 154 61 00, Telex 64036 – 🛗 ▤ ⟺ 🅿 – 🔬. 🖭 ⓪ Ⅰ 𝗩𝗜𝗦𝗔. ⚶ rest
M 1 500 – ⟳ 350 – **130 rm** 4 500/6 900 – P 6 130/7 180.

Sweden
Sverige

Stockholm

PRACTICAL INFORMATION

LOCAL CURRENCY

Swedish Kronor : 100 SEK = 11.075 US $ (Jan. 85)

TOURIST INFORMATION

The Tourist Centre is situated in the Sweden House, entrance from Kungsträdgården at Hamngatan. Open Mon-Fri 9am-5pm. Sat. and Sun. 9am-2pm. Telephone weekdays 08/789 20 00, weekends to Excursion Shop 08/789 24 15, to Tourist Centre 08/789 24 18.

FOREIGN EXCHANGE

Banks are open between 9.00am and 3.00pm on weekdays only. Some banks in the centre of the city are usually open weekdays 9am to 5.30pm. Most large hotels have exchange facilities, and Arlanda airport has banking facilities between 7am to 10pm seven days a week.

SHOPPING IN STOCKHOLM

The main shopping streets in the Centre are: Hamngatan, Biblioteksgatan, Drottninggatan.
In the Old Town mainly Västerlånggatan.

THEATRE BOOKINGS

Your hotel porter will be able to make your arrangements or direct you to Theatre Booking Agents.
In addition there is a kiosk at Norrmalmstorg selling tickets for the same day's performances with a reduction of approx. 25 per cent, no booking fee.
In the summer it's open 11am-7.30pm Tues.-Sat. and 11am-5pm Sun. and Mon. During the winter 12 am-7.15pm Tues.-Sat., 12am-4pm Sun., 12am-5pm Mon.

TIPPING

Hotels and restaurants normally include a service charge of 15 per cent. Doormen, baggage porters etc. are generally given a gratuity.
Taxi drivers are customarily tipped about 10 per cent of the amount shown on the meter in addition to the fare.

CAR HIRE

The international car hire companies have branches in Stockholm city and at Arlanda airport. Your hotel porter will be able to give details and help you with your arrangements.

SPEED LIMITS - SEAT BELTS

The maximum permitted speed on motorways and dual carriageways is 110 km/h - 68 mph and 90 km/h - 56 mph on other roads except where a lower speed limit is signposted.
The wearing of seat belts in Sweden is compulsory for drivers and front seat passengers.

STOCKHOLM

STOCKHOLM Sverige ⑨②⓪ MN2 — pop. 649 686 — ✆ 08.
🏌 Svenska Golfförbundet ☎ 753 02 65.
✈ Stockholm-Arlanda N : 41 km ☎ (08) 780 30 30 – SAS : Flygcity, Sveavägen 22 ☎ 780 10 00 – Air Terminal : main railway station.
🚙 Motorail for Southern Europe : SJ Travel Agency, Vasagatan 22 ☎ 762 58 15.
⛴ To Finland and excursions by boat : contact Stockholm Information Service (see below).
🅱 Stockholm Information Service, Tourist Centre, Sverigehuset, Hamngatan 27 ☎ 22 70 00. – Motormännens Riksförbund Kungl. Automobilklubben (Royal Automobile Club) ☎ 67 05 80.
Hamburg 935 – København 630 – Oslo 522.

STOCKHOLM

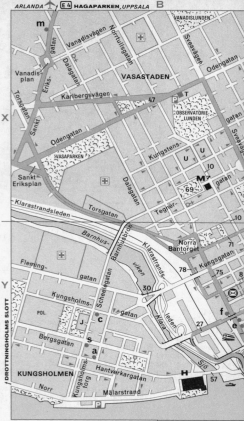

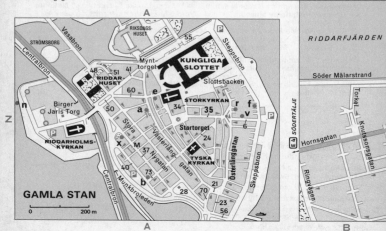

Grand, Södra Blasieholmshamnen 8, S - 103 27, ℰ 22 10 20, Telex 19500, ≤, ⇔ – ⛂ 📺
🖭. ⚲. 🟦 ⓞ E 𝘝𝘪𝘴𝘢   CY   r
M a la carte 160/350 – **350 rm** ⊊ 650/1200.

Sergel Plaza Ⓜ, Brunkebergstorg 9, S-103 27, ℰ 22 66 00, Telex 16711, ⇔, « Tasteful
decor » – ⛂ 🖭 📺 ⇔. ⚲. 🟦 ⓞ E 𝘝𝘪𝘴𝘢   CY   n
M Anna Rella a la carte 105/260 – **Le Café** a la carte 80/160 – **407 rm** ⊊ 650/950.

Sheraton-Stockholm Ⓜ, Tegelbacken 6, S - 101 23, ℰ 14 26 00, Telex 17750, ≤, ⇔ –
⛂ 🖭 📺 🖭 ⚬ ⇔. ⚲. 🟦 ⓞ E 𝘝𝘪𝘴𝘢   CY   a
M a la carte 107/205 – **462 rm** ⊊ 950/1075.

Royal Viking Ⓜ, Vasagatan 1, S - 101 23, ℰ 14 10 00 – ⛂ 🖭 📺 🖭. ⚲.   **400 rm**.   BY   f

Amaranten, Kungsholmsgatan 31, S - 104 20, ℰ 54 10 60, Telex 17498, ⇔ – ⛂ 📺 🖭
&. ⚲. 🟦 ⓞ E 𝘝𝘪𝘴𝘢   BY   c
M (buffet lunch) 200 a la carte 152/240 – **363 rm** ⊊ 510/970.

Anglais, Humlegårdsgatan 23, S - 102 44, ℰ 24 99 00, Telex 19475 – ⛂ 🖭 📺 🖭. ⚲. 🟦
ⓞ E 𝘝𝘪𝘴𝘢   CX   a
M a la carte 130/265 – **211 rm** 450/995.

Strand, Nybrokajen 9, S - 103 27, ℰ 22 29 00, Telex 10504, ≤ – ⛂ 📺 🖭. ⚲.   CDY   x
134 rm.

Stockholm Plaza Ⓜ, Birger Jarlsgatan 29, S-103 95, ℰ 14 51 20, Telex 13982, ⇔ – ⛂
📺 🖭 &. 🟦 ⓞ E 𝘝𝘪𝘴𝘢. ✶   CX   e
M (closed Sunday) a la carte 145/195 – **155 rm** ⊊ 585/685.

Birger Jarl without rest., Tulegatan 8, S - 104 32, ℰ 15 10 20, Telex 11843, ⇔ – ⛂ 🖭 📺
🖭. ⚲. 🟦 ⓞ E 𝘝𝘪𝘴𝘢   CX   z
closed 10 days at Christmas – (unlicensed) – **250 rm** ⊊ 480/650.

Diplomat, Strandvägen 7c, S - 104 40, ℰ 63 58 00, Telex 17119, ≤, ⇔ – ⛂ 📺 🖭. 🟦 ⓞ
E 𝘝𝘪𝘴𝘢   DY   m
M (closed Saturday dinner and Sunday) 95/135 – **130 rm** ⊊ 695/950.

Park, Karlavägen 43, S - 102 45, ℰ 22 96 20, Telex 10666, ⇔ – ⛂ 📺 🖭 ⇔. 🟦 ⓞ E
𝘝𝘪𝘴𝘢   CX   w
closed 20 to 26 December – **M** a la carte 145/320 – **205 rm** ⊊ 740/935.

Reisen, Skeppsbron 12-14, S - 111 30, ℰ 22 32 60, Telex 17494, ≤, ⇔, 🔲 – ⛂ 📺 &.
⚲. 🟦 ⓞ E 𝘝𝘪𝘴𝘢. ✶   AZ   f
closed 22 to 27 December – **M** 105/300 – **125 rm** ⊊ 750/885.

Palace, S : t Eriksgatan 115, S - 100 31, ℰ 24 12 20, Telex 19877, ⇔ – ⛂ 📺 ⇔. ⚲.
212 rm.   BX   m

Continental, Vasagatan, S - 101 21, ℰ 24 40 20, Telex 10100 – ⛂ 🖭 📺 🖭 ⇔. ⚲.
M a la carte 110/201 – **250 rm** ⊊ 600/750.   BY   e

Malmen, Götgatan 49 - 51, S - 102 61, ℰ 22 61 80, Telex 19489, ⇔ – ⛂ 📺 🖭 ⇔. ⚲.
279 rm.   CZ   d

City, Slöjdgatan 7, Hötorget, S - 111 81, ℰ 22 22 40, Telex 12487, ⇔ – ⛂ 📺 🖩wc 🖭
ⓞ E 𝘝𝘪𝘴𝘢. ✶   CY   c
M (closed Sunday lunch) 75/100 (unlicensed) – **300 rm** ⊊ 485/585.

Mornington (Best Western), Nybrogatan 53, S - 114 40, ℰ 63 12 40, Telex 10145, ⇔ –
⛂ 📺 ⇔wc 🖩wc 🖭. ⚲. 🟦 ⓞ E 𝘝𝘪𝘴𝘢   DX   s
M (closed lunch Saturday and Sunday) a la carte 90/195 – **123 rm** ⊊ 470/740.

Wellington without rest., Storgatan 6, S - 114 51, ℰ 67 09 10, Telex 17963, ⇔ – ⛂ 📺
⇔wc ⊛. 🟦 ⓞ E 𝘝𝘪𝘴𝘢   DY   p
50 rm ⊊ 525/720.

Terminus (Best Western), Vasagatan 20, S - 101 23, ℰ 22 26 40, Telex 11749 – ⛂ 📺
⇔wc 🖩wc ⊛. 🟦 ⓞ E 𝘝𝘪𝘴𝘢. ✶   BY   e
closed 21 December-1 January – **M** 58/105 – **135 rm** ⊊ 570/760.

Lady Hamilton without rest., Storkyrkobrinken 5, S-111 28, ℰ 23 46 80, Telex 10434,
⇔, « Swedish rural antiques » – ⛂ 📺 ⇔wc 🖩wc 🖭. 🟦 ⓞ E 𝘝𝘪𝘴𝘢. ✶   AZ   e
34 rm ⊊ 710/920.

Mälardrottningen, Riddarholmen, S - 111 28, ℰ 24 36 00, Telex 15468, ≤, ⇔, « Former
private motor-yacht » – 🖭 📺 🖩wc ⊛. 🟦 ⓞ E 𝘝𝘪𝘴𝘢   AZ   n
M (closed Sunday lunch and Saturday) a la carte 165/280 – **59 rm (cabins)** ⊊ 395/900.

Eden without rest., Sturegatan 10, S - 114 36, ℰ 22 31 60, Telex 10570 – ⛂ 📺 ⇔wc ⊛.
🟦 ⓞ E 𝘝𝘪𝘴𝘢   CX   b
60 rm ⊊ 575/800.

Lord Nelson without rest., Västerlånggatan 22, S-111 29, ℰ 23 23 90, Telex 10434, ⇔,
« Ship style installation, maritime antiques » – ⛂ 📺 🖩wc 🖭. 🟦 ⓞ E 𝘝𝘪𝘴𝘢. ✶   AZ   a
31 rm ⊊ 530/780.

Operakällaren (at Opera House), S-111 86, ℰ 24 27 00, « Opulent classical decor » –
🟦 ⓞ E 𝘝𝘪𝘴𝘢   CY
closed July and 25 December – **M** a la carte 240/500.

Riche, Birger Jarlsgatan 4, S-114 34, ℰ 23 68 40 – ▤. 🟦 ⓞ E 𝘝𝘪𝘴𝘢   CY   e
closed Sunday lunch and Bank Holidays – **M** a la carte 120/295.

Grappe d'Or, Tyska Brinken 36, S - 111 27, ℰ 20 42 50 – 🟦 ⓞ E 𝘝𝘪𝘴𝘢   AZ   b
closed Saturday lunch, Sunday and Bank Holidays – **M** a la carte 130/260.

XXX ✿ **Coq Blanc,** Regeringsgatan 111, S - 111 39, ✆ 11 61 53 – ▣. ⒶⒺ ⓪ Ⲉ 🆅🆂🅰 CX **n**
closed Saturday and Sunday June-August, 6 July-6 August and Bank Holidays – **M**
(buffet lunch) 120 a la carte 205/238
Spec. Marinated tenderloin with herb sauce, Fillets of reindeer à la maison, Strawberry flambé du patron.

XXX **Teatergrillen,** Nybrogatan 3, S-114 34, ✆ 10 70 44, « Theatre atmosphere » – ▣. ⒶⒺ
⓪ Ⲉ 🆅🆂🅰 CY **e**
closed Saturday lunch, Sunday and Bank Holidays – **M** a la carte 120/295.

XX ✿ **L'Escargot,** Scheelegatan 8, S - 112 23, ✆ 53 05 77 – ⒶⒺ ⓪ Ⲉ 🆅🆂🅰 BY **s**
closed Saturday lunch, Sunday and 1 July-19 August – **M** a la carte 166/272
Spec. Escargots au beurre roquefort, Foie gras de canard frais, Poissons et crustacés variés selon la saison.

XX ✿ **Gourmet,** Tegnérgatan 10, S - 113 58, ✆ 31 43 98 – ▣. ⒶⒺ ⓪ Ⲉ 🆅🆂🅰 CX **r**
closed Saturday lunch, Sunday and Bank Holidays – **M** a la carte 160/250
Spec. Flambéed sea-crayfish.

XX **Paul and Norbert,** Strandvägen 9, S - 114 56, ✆ 63 81 83 – ⒶⒺ ⓪ Ⲉ 🆅🆂🅰 DY **m**
*closed Saturday, Sunday, 16 July-4 August, 23 December-6 January, 24 to 31
March and Bank Holidays* – **M** a la carte 150/330.

XX ✿ **Eriks,** Strandvägskajen 17, S - 114 56, ✆ 60 60 60, « Converted barge » – ⒶⒺ ⓪ Ⲉ 🆅🆂🅰
closed Sunday and Christmas-New Year – **M** a la carte 250/320 DY **z**
Spec. Small salmon sausages in three flavours with lobster sauce, Turbot with saffron stuffing, aromatic
vegetables and Noilly Prat sauce, Warm rose-hip soup with vanilla ice-cream.

XX **L'Etage,** Pipersgatan 1, 1st floor, S-112 24, ✆ 52 61 61 – ▣. ⒶⒺ ⓪ Ⲉ 🆅🆂🅰 BY **a**
*closed Saturday lunch, Monday dinner, Sunday, July, 2 weeks at Christmas and Bank
Holidays* – **M** a la carte 125/255.

XX **Coq Roti,** Sturegatan 19, S - 114 36, ✆ 10 25 67 – ▣. ⒶⒺ ⓪ Ⲉ 🆅🆂🅰 CDX **t**
closed Saturday lunch, Sunday and 7 to 28 July – **M** a la carte 130/230.

XX **Källaren Aurora,** Munkbron 11, S-111 28, ✆ 21 93 59, « In the cellars of a 17C house »
– ▣. ⒶⒺ ⓪ Ⲉ 🆅🆂🅰 AZ **x**
closed Sunday – **M** 75/200.

XX **Fem Små Hus,** Nygränd 10, S - 111 30, ✆ 10 87 75, « Cellars, antiques » – ⒶⒺ ⓪ Ⲉ 🆅🆂🅰
M a la carte 120/233. AZ **r**

X **KB,** Smålandsgatan 7, S-111 46, ✆ 11 02 32 – ⒶⒺ ⓪ Ⲉ 🆅🆂🅰 CY **u**
closed lunch Saturday, 15 June-15 August, Bank Holidays and Sunday – **M** a la carte
130/220.

X **Blå Gåsen,** Karlavägen 28, S - 100 41, ✆ 10 02 69 – ⓪ Ⲉ 🆅🆂🅰 CX **f**
closed Saturday, Sunday and Bank Holidays – **M** a la carte 108/204.

X Källaren Diana, Brunnsgränd 2, S - 111 30, ✆ 10 73 10, « 17C cellars » – ▣ AZ **v**

at Arlanda Airport N : by E4 – BX – ✿ 0760 Arlanda :

🏨 **SAS Arlandia,** 190 45, Stockholm - Arlanda ✆ 618 00, Telex 13018, ⇌, 🔲, ⤬ – 🔌 ▣
📺 ☎ 👌 🅿. 🎿. ⒶⒺ ⓪ Ⲉ 🆅🆂🅰
M 140/185 – **210 rm** ⊆ 595/950.

in Djurgården E : 2 km by Strandvägen – DY – ✉ ✿ 08 Stockholm :

XXX **Djurgårdsbrunns Wärdshus,** Djurgårdsbrunnsvägen 68, S - 115 25, ✆ 67 90 95, ≼,
« In Djurgården Park » – ⒶⒺ ⓪ Ⲉ 🆅🆂🅰
closed Sunday dinner – **M** a la carte 118/221.

at Solna NW : 5 km by Sveavägen – BX – and E 4 – ✉ Solna – ✿ 08 Stockholm :

XXX ✿ **Ulriksdals Wärdshus,** 171 71 Solna, N : 3 km in Ulriksdals Slottspark ✆ 85 08 15, ≼,
« Former inn in Royal Park », 🌳 – 🅿. ⒶⒺ ⓪ Ⲉ 🆅🆂🅰
closed 24 to 26 December – **M** (buffet lunch) 140 a la carte 180/265
Spec. Swedish red caviar, Rack of lamb Swedish style, Cloudberry parfait.

XX **Finsmakaren,** Råsundavägen 9, 171 52 Solna, ✆ 27 67 71 – ⒶⒺ ⓪ Ⲉ
closed Saturday, Sunday, 1 July-5 August and 20 December-7 January – **M** a la carte
140/230.

Switzerland
Suisse
Schweiz
Svizzera

Basle
Geneva
Zürich

PRACTICAL INFORMATION

LOCAL CURRENCY

Swiss Franc : 100 F = 38.170 US $ (Jan. 85)

LANGUAGES SPOKEN

German, French and Italian are usually spoken in all administrative departments, shops, hotels and restaurants.

POSTAL SERVICES

In large towns, post offices are open from 7.30am to noon and 1.45pm to 6.30pm, and Saturdays untill 11am. The telephone system is fully automatic.

SHOPPING

Department stores are generally open from 8am to 4pm, except on Saturdays when they close at 4 or 5pm.

In the index of street names, those printed in red are where the principal shops are found.

AIRLINES

A large number of international airlines operate out of the main Swiss airports. For general information ring the number given after the airport symbol and name in the text of each town.

TIPPING

In hotels, restaurants and cafés the service charge is generally included in the prices.

SPEED LIMITS

The speed limit on motorways is 120 km/h - 74 mph, on other roads 80 km/h - 50 mph, and in built up areas 50 km/h - 31 mph.

SEAT BELTS

The wearing of seat belts is compulsory in all Swiss cantons.

BASLE (BASEL) 4000 Switzerland 🔠 ⑩, 🔟 ④ – pop. 180 463 – alt. 273 – ✪ Basle and environs from France 19-41-61, from Switzerland 061.

See : Cathedral (Münster)★★ : ≤★ CY – Zoological Gardens★★★ AZ – The Port (Hafen)※★, Exposition★ CX – Fish Market Fountain★ (Fischmarktbrunnen) BY – Old Streets★ BY – Oberer Rheinweg CY – Museums : Fine Arts★★★ (Kunstmuseum) CY, Historical★ (Historisches Museum) CY, Ethnographic (Museum für Völkerkunde)★ CY M1 – Haus zum Kirschgarten★ CZ, Antiquities (Antikenmuseum)★ CY – ※★ from Bruderholz Water Tower 3,5 km by ⑥.

🏌 private 🖉 68.50.91 (🖉 89) at Hagenthal-le-Bas (68-France) SW : 10 km.

✈ Basle-Mulhouse 🖉 57.31.11 at Basle (Switzerland) by Zollfreie Strasse 8 km and at Saint-Louis (68-France) 🖉 69.00.00 (✪ 🖉 89).

🛈 Blumenrain 2 🖉 22.50.50, Télex 63318 – Automobile Club Suisse, Birsigstr. 4 🖉 23.39.33 – T.C.S., Petrihof, Steinentorstr. 13 🖉 23.19.55.

Paris 551 ⑧ – Bern 95 ⑤ – Freiburg 71 ① – Lyon 387 ⑧ – Mulhouse 35 ⑧ – Strasbourg 145 ①.

Plan on following pages

🏨 **Trois Rois,** Blumenrain 8, ⊠ 4001, 🖉 25.52.52, Telex 62937, ≤, 🌤 – 🛗 🖭 📺 ☎ – 🏠 80. 🖭 ⓪ E VISA. ❄ rest BY **a**
st. : Rôtisserie des Rois **M** 49/69 🍴 – rest Rhy-Deck **M** a la carte approx. 45 🍴 – ☲ 12 – **90 rm** ☲ 145/310, 7 apartments 420/660.

🏨 **Hilton** 🅼 ❀, Aeschengraben 31, ⊠ 4059, 🖉 22.66.22, Telex 62055, 🔲 – 🛗 🖭 📺 ☎ 🕭 – 🏠 50-300. 🖭 ⓪ E VISA. ❄ rest CZ **d**
st. : **M** a la carte 60/80 🍴 – ☲ 9,50 – **217 rm** 115/235, 10 apartments.

🏨 **Hôtel International** 🅼 ❀, Steinentorstrasse 25, ⊠ 4001, 🖉 22.18.70, Telex 962370, 🔲 – 🛗 🖭 📺 ☎ 🕭 – 🏠 25-250. 🖭 ⓪ E VISA. ❄ rest BZ **b**
st. : **Steinenpick M** a la carte 25/60🍴 - **Rôt. Charolaise M** a la carte 60/90 🍴 – **205 rm** ☲ 180/245, 5 apartments 200/500.

🏨 **H. Basel** 🅼 ❀, Münzgasse 12, ⊠ 4001, 🖉 25.24.23, Telex 64199, «Tasteful decor » – 🛗 🖭 rest 📺 🖭 E VISA BY **x**
st. : **M** a la carte 35/65 🍴 – **72 rm** ☲ 89/235.

🏨 **Euler,** Centralbahnplatz 14, ⊠ 4051, 🖉 23.45.00, Telex 62215 – 🛗 🖭 📺 ☎ 🕭 – 🏠 120. 🖭 ⓪ E VISA BZ **a**
st. : **M** a la carte 70/85 🍴 – ☲ 9 – **58 rm** ☲ 106/252, 8 apartments 285/500 – P 149/174.

🏨 **Europe and rest. Quatre Saisons** 🅼, Clarastrasse 43, ⊠ 4058, 🖉 26.80.80, Telex 64103, 🌤 – 🛗 🖭 📺 ☎ 🕭 – 🏠 180. 🖭 E VISA. ❄ rest CX **k**
st. : **M** (closed Sunday) a la carte 70/90 🍴 – **170 rm** ☲ 98/185.

🏨 **Schweizerhof,** Centralbahnplatz 1, ⊠ 4002, 🖉 22.28.33, Telex 62373 – 🛗 🖭 📺 ☎ Ⓟ – 🏠 30-90. 🖭 ⓪ E VISA CZ **n**
st. : **M** a la carte approx. 60 🍴 – **75 rm** ☲ 100/190.

🏨 **Victoria** 🅼, Centralbahnplatz 3, ⊠ 4002, 🖉 22.55.66, Telex 62362 – 🛗 🖭 rest 📺 ☎ – 🏠 25. 🖭 ⓪ E VISA CZ **n**
st. : **M** a la carte approx. 45 🍴 – **115 rm** ☲ 55/160.

🏨 **Métropol** 🅼 without rest, Elisabethenanlage 5 ⊠ 4051 🖉 22.77.21, Telex 62268 – 🛗 📺 ☎ – 🏠 120. 🖭 ⓪ E VISA CZ **a**
closed 16 to 31 December – st. : **46 rm** 🛏 84/129.

🏨 **Alexander** 🅼, Riehenring 85, ⊠ 4058, 🖉 26.70.00, Telex 63325 – 🛗 📺 🚿wc ☎ 🕭. 🖭 ⓪ E VISA. ❄ rest CX **s**
st. : **M** (closed Sunday) a la carte 35/55 🍴 – **64 rm** 🛏 77/176.

🏨 **City,** Henric Petri-Strasse 12, ⊠ 4010, 🖉 23.78.11, Telex 62427 – 🛗 🖭 🛁wc 🕭. 🖭 ⓪ E VISA – st. : **M** a la carte approx. 50 🍴 – **85 rm** ☲ 60/150. CZ **f**

🏨 **Krafft am Rhein,** Rheingasse 12, ⊠ 4058, 🖉 26.88.77, Telex 64360, ≤, 🌤 – 🛗 🛁wc 🚿wc 🕭. 🖭 ⓪ E VISA. ❄ rest CY **z**
st. : **M** a la carte approx. 50 🍴 – **52 rm** ☲ 50/135 – P 92/135.

🏨 **Bernina** without rest, Innere Margarethenstrasse 14, ⊠ 4051, 🖉 23.73.00, Telex 63813 – 🛗 🖭 🛁wc 🚿wc 🕭. 🖭 E VISA BZ **u**
st. : **36 rm** ☲ 50/180 – P 75/100.

🏨 **Drachen,** Aeschenvorstadt 24, ⊠ 4051, 🖉 23.90.90, Telex 62346 – 🛗 🖭 rm 🛁wc 🚿wc 🕭 – 🏠 40. 🖭 ⓪ E VISA CY **w**
st. : **M** (closed Sunday dinner) a la carte 50/65 🍴 – **42 rm** ☲ 78/160 – P 102/132.

🏨 **Muenchnerhof,** Riehenring 75, ⊠ 4058 🖉 26.77.80, Telex 64476 – 🛗 🛁wc 🚿wc 🕭. 🖭 ⓪ VISA – st. : **M** 10/40 🍴 – **40 rm** ☲ 47/170. CX **u**

🏨 **Flügelrad,** Küchengasse 20, ⊠ 4051, 🖉 23.42.41 – 🚿wc BZ **v**
st. : **M** (closed Saturday dinner and Sunday) a la carte approx. 40 🍴 – **30 rm** ☲ 40/120.

🏵🏵 ❀❀ **Stucki,** Bruderholzallee 42, ⊠ 4059, 🖉 35.82.22, « Terrace » – VISA by ⑥
closed 16 July-7 August, Sunday and Monday – st. : **M** 80/135
Spec. Chou farci de ris de veau aux truffes, Canard de Challans rôti, Soufflé au coulis de coings.

🏵 **La Marmite du Beaujolais,** Klybeckstrasse 15, ⊠ 4057, 🖉 33.03.54, Modern decor – 🖭 🖭 ⓪ E VISA CX **e**
closed Sunday and Bank Holidays – st. : **M** a la carte 35/55 🍴.

🏵 **Donati,** St-Johannsvorstadt 48, ⊠ 4056, 🖉 57.09.19, Italian specialities BX **p**
closed July and Monday – st. : **M** 23/27 🍴.

🏵 **Taverne l'Escargot** (basement of SBB Railway Station), Centralbahnstrasse 10, ⊠ 4002, 🖉 22.53.33, Telex 62538 – 🖭 BZ

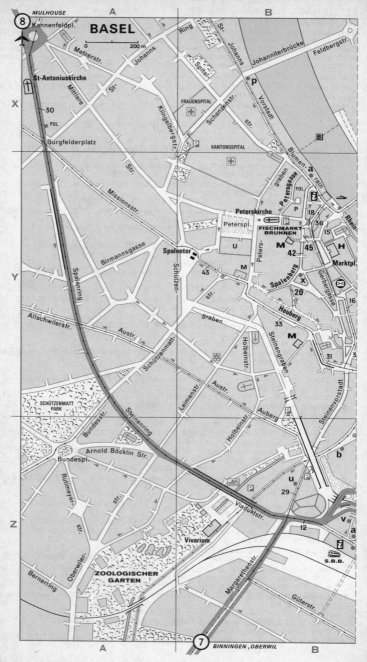

BASEL

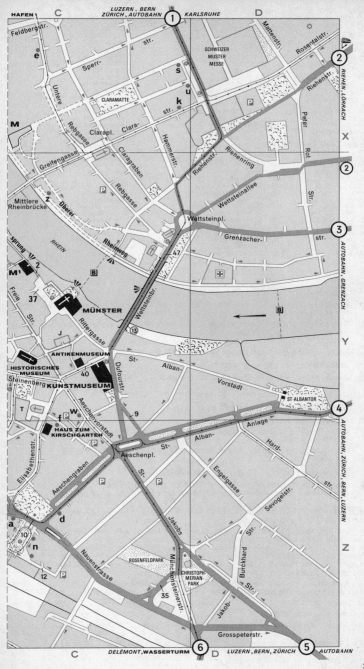

STREET INDEX TO BASEL TOWN PLAN

at Binningen by ⑦ : 2 km – ✉ 4102 Binningen :

🏛 **Schlüssel,** Schlüsselgasse 1 ℰ 47.25.65, 😤, 🌳 – 📶 🛏wc 🖎wc 🚗 🅿. 🆎 ⓪ E 💳
st. : **M** *(closed Sunday)* a la carte approx. 40 ⅃ – **27 rm** ⚂ 45/90.

🎦🎦🎦 **Schloss Binningen,** Schlossgasse 5 ℰ 47.20.55, 😤, « 16C mansion, elegantly decorated, garden » – 🅿. 🆎 ⓪ E 💳
closed 8 to 23 July, 25 February-2 March, Sunday dinner and Monday – **st. : M** 80/110 ⅃.

🎦🎦🎦 Holee-Schloss, Hasenrainstrasse 59 ℰ 47.24.30, ≤ – 🍽.

at Riehen by ② : 5 km – ✉ 4125 Riehen :

🏨 **Ascot** Ⓜ, Baselstrasse 67 ℰ 67.39.51, Telex 62424, « Tasteful decor » – 📶 🍽 rest 📺 🛏wc 🖎wc ☎ 🚗. 🆎 ⓪ E 💳
st. : **M** a la carte approx. 55 ⅃ – **23 rm** ⚂ 84/140 – P 134/168.

at the Basle-Mulhouse airport : by ⑧ : 8 km :

🎦🎦 **Airport rest,** 5th floor in the airport, ≤.

Swiss Side, ✉ 4030 Bâle ℰ 57.32.32 – 🍽. 🆎 ⓪ E 💳
st. : **M** a la carte 45/55 ⅃.

French Side, ✉ 68300 St-Louis ℰ (89) 69.77.48 St-Louis – 🍽. 🆎 ⓪ E 💳
st. : **M** 42/140 FF ⅃.

at Hofstetten by ⑦ : 12,5 km – ✉ 4114 Hofstetten :

🎦 **Landgasthof "Rössli"** with rm, ℰ 75.10.47, 😤 – 🅿. 🆎 ⓪
closed January and Wednesday – **st. : M** a la carte approx. 50 ⅃ – **7 rm** ⚌ 25.

GENEVA Switzerland 🔟🔢 ⑥. 🔢🔢 ⑪ – pop. 157 406 – alt. 375 – Casino – ✿ Geneva and Environs : from France 19-41-22 ; from Switzerland 022.

See : The Shores of the lake ≤★★★ – Parks★★ : Mon Repos, la Perle du Lac and Villa Barton – Botanical Gardens★ : alpine rock-garden★★ – Cathedral★ : 🔆★★ FY F – Reformation Monument★ FYZ D – Palais des Nations★ – Parc de la Grange★ GY – Parc des Eaux-Vives★ – Nave★ of Church of Christ the King – Museums : Art and History★★★ GZ, Ariana★★, Natural History★★ GZ, Petit Palais★ GZ M1, – Baur Collection★ (in a 19C mansion) GZ M2, Old Musical Instruments★ GZ M3.

Exc. : by boat on the lake Rens. Cie Gén. de Nav., Jardin Anglais ℰ 21.25.21 – Mouettes genevoises, 8 quai du Mt-Blanc ℰ 32.29.44 – Swiss Boat, 4 quai du Mont-Blanc ℰ 32.47.47.

🖙 at Cologny ℰ 35.75.40.

✈ Genève-Cointrin ℰ 99.31.11.

🚆 gare Cornavin ℰ 32.53.40 - Automobile Club Suisse, 10 bd Théâtre ℰ 28.07.66 - T.C. Suisse, 9 r. P.-Fatio ℰ 37.12.12.

Paris 513 ⑦ – Bern 154 ② – Bourg-en-B. 118 ⑦ – Lausanne 63 ② – Lyon 159 ⑦ – Torino 252 ⑥.

Plan on following pages

1° - *Rive droite (Cornavin Railway Station - Les Quais - B.I.T.)* – ⊠ **1201** GENEVE

🏨🏨🏨 **Richemond,** Brunswick garden, ⊠ 1211, 𝒫 31.14.00, Telex 22598, ≼, 🏛 – ♨ 🔄 rest
🔳 ☎ – 🛗 50. 🝐 ⓪ Ε 𝘝𝘐𝘚𝘈, ℘ rest   FY **u**
st. : rest **Le Jardin M** a la carte 60/80 ♨ and see also **Le Gentilhomme** – **97 rm** ⊿ 150/400,
21 apartments.

🏨🏨🏨 **Rhône** Ⓜ, quai Turrettini, ⊠ 1201 𝒫 31.98.31, Telex 22213, ≼ – ♨ 🔳 🔄 ☎ ᵫ ⓟ – 🛗
25-150. 🝐 ⓪   EY **r**
st. : **M** 37 ♨ (dinner a la carte) and see also Rôt. **Le Neptune** – **270 rm** ⊿ 150/400, bedrooms
for no smokers, 29 apartments.

🏨🏨🏨 **Noga Hilton** Ⓜ, 19 quai Mt-Blanc ⊠ 1201, 𝒫 31.98.11, Telex 289704, ≼ lake and
Mt-Blanc, 🏛, 🔲 – ♨ 🔳 🔳 ☎ ᵫ – 🛗 450. 🝐 ⓪ Ε 𝘝𝘐𝘚𝘈   GY **y**
st. : see rest. **Le Cygne** below - **La Grignotière M** a la carte approx. 50 ♨ - **Le Bistroquai M**
a la carte approx. 30 ♨ – ⊿ 17 – **300 rm** 220/370, 6 apartments.

🏨🏨🏨 **Président** Ⓜ, 47 quai Wilson, ⊠ 1211, 𝒫 31.10.00, Telex 22780, ≼ lake – ♨ 🔳 🔳 ᵫ
⇔⇔ ⓟ – 🛗 25-80. 🝐 ⓪ Ε 𝘝𝘐𝘚𝘈. ℘ rest   GX **d**
st. : **M** a la carte 75/105 – ⊿ 18 – **160 rm** 180/315, 30 apartments.

🏨🏨🏨 **Les Bergues,** 33 quai Bergues, ⊠ 1201, 𝒫 31.50.50, Telex 23383, ≼ – ♨ 🔳 🔳 ☎ –
350. 🝐 ⓪ Ε 𝘝𝘐𝘚𝘈. ℘ rest   FY **k**
st. : **M Le Pavillon** a la carte approx. 55 ♨ and see also rest. **Amphitryon** – ⊿ 14 – **117 rm**
210/345, 8 apartments.

🏨🏨 **Beau Rivage,** 13 quai Mont-Blanc, ⊠ 1201, 𝒫 31.02.21, Telex 23362, ≼ lake – ♨ 🔳 🔳
☎ ⓟ – 🛗 30-200. 🝐 ⓪ Ε 𝘝𝘐𝘚𝘈   FY **d**
st. : **M** see rest. **Le Chat Botté** below - **Le Quai 13 M** a la carte approx 40 – ⊿ 14 – **120 rm**
140/350, 6 apartments.

🏨🏨 **Ramada Renaissance** Ⓜ, 19 r. Zurich, ⊠ 1201, 𝒫 31.02.41, Telex 289109 – ♨ 🔳 🔳
☎ ⇔ – 🛗 150. 🝐 ⓪ Ε 𝘝𝘐𝘚𝘈. ℘   FX **s**
st. : **La Toquade M** a la carte 55/75 ♨ - **La Cortille M** a la carte approx. 49 - **café Ragueneau**
M a la carte approx. 35 ♨ – ⊿ 17 – **213 rm** 210/260, 7 apartments.

🏨🏨 **Paix,** 11 quai Mont-Blanc, ⊠ 1201, 𝒫 32.61.50, Telex 22552, ≼ – ♨ 🔳 rest 🔳 ☎ – 🛗
80. 🝐 ⓪ Ε 𝘝𝘐𝘚𝘈   FY **s**
st. : **M** a la carte 65/90 ♨ – ⊿ 12 – **106 rm** 140/320, 10 apartments.

🏨🏨 **Bristol** Ⓜ, 10 r. Mont-Blanc, ⊠ 1201, 𝒫 32.44.00, Telex 23739 – ♨ 🔳 rest 🔳 ☎ ᵫ – 🛗
40-120. 🝐 ⓪ Ε 𝘝𝘐𝘚𝘈   FY **w**
st. : **M** a la carte 55/75 ♨ – ⊿ 12 – **100 rm** 190/270, 4 apartments 510.

🏨🏨 **P.L.M. Rotary** Ⓜ, 18 r. Cendrier, ⊠ 1201, 𝒫 31.52.00, Telex 289999 – ♨ 🔳 rest 🔳 ☎.
🝐 ⓪ Ε 𝘝𝘐𝘚𝘈. ℘ rest   FY **t**
st. : **M** 26/45 – **95 rm** ⊿ 150/250.

🏨🏨 **Warwick-Méditerranée** Ⓜ, 14 r. Lausanne, ⊠ 1201, 𝒫 31.62.50, Telex 23630 – ♨ 🔳
🔳 ☎ – 🛗 200. 🝐 ⓪ Ε 𝘝𝘐𝘚𝘈   EY **n**
st. : **M** (closed Saturday) a la carte 60/90 – **168 rm** ⊿ 150/300.

🏨🏨 **Angleterre,** 17 quai Mt-Blanc, ⊠ 1201, 𝒫 32.81.80, Telex 22668, ≼ – ♨ 🔳 rest 🔳 ☎.
🝐 ⓪ Ε 𝘝𝘐𝘚𝘈. ℘ rest   GY **t**
st. : **M** a la carte 50/75 ♨ – **65 rm** ⊿ 140/310, 6 apartments 350/550.

🏨🏨 **Cornavin** without rest, 33 bd James-Fazy, ⊠ 1211, 𝒫 32.21.00, Telex 22853 – ♨ 🔳 ☎.
🝐 ⓪ Ε 𝘝𝘐𝘚𝘈   EY **t**
st. : **125 rm** ⊿ 95/180.

🏨🏨 **Berne,** 26 r. Berne, ⊠ 1201, 𝒫 31.60.00, Telex 22764 – ♨ 🔳 🔳 ☎ – 🛗 30-100. 🝐 ⓪
Ε 𝘝𝘐𝘚𝘈. ℘ rest   FY **x**
st. : **M** 24 – **80 rm** ⊿ 120/160 – P 124/164.

🏨🏨 **Ambassador,** 21 quai Bergues, ⊠ 1201, 𝒫 31.72.00, Telex 23231 – ♨ 🔳 ⓟ – 🛗 40.
🝐 ⓪ Ε 𝘝𝘐𝘚𝘈   FY **p**
st. : **M** 36/46 ♨ – **92 rm** ⊿ 80/200.

🏨🏨 **Amat-Carlton** Ⓜ, 22 r. Amat, ⊠ 1202, 𝒫 31.68.50, Telex 27595 – ♨ kitchenette 🔳 rest
🔳 ☎ ⇔. 🝐 ⓪ Ε 𝘝𝘐𝘚𝘈. ℘ rest   FX **a**
st. : **M** (closed Sunday lunch and Saturday) a la carte 20/40 ♨ – **123 rm** ⊿ 120/200.

🏨 **Alba** without rest, 19 r. Mt-Blanc, ⊠ 1201, 𝒫 32.56.00, Telex 23930 – ♨ 🔳 ⇌wc ☎. 🝐
⓪ Ε 𝘝𝘐𝘚𝘈   FY **a**
st. : **60 rm** ⊿ 125/175.

🏨 **Cristal** Ⓜ 🦶 without rest, 4 r. Pradier ⊠ 1201 𝒫 31.34.00, Telex 289926 – ♨ 🔳 ⇌wc
🔳wc. 🝐 ⓪ Ε 𝘝𝘐𝘚𝘈   FY **e**
st. : **79 rm** ⊿ 110/170.

🏨 **Savoy** Ⓜ, 8 pl. Cornavin ⊠ 1201 𝒫 31.12.55, Telex 27951 – ♨ 🔳 🔳 ⇌wc ☎. 🝐 ⓪ Ε
𝘝𝘐𝘚𝘈. ℘ rest   EY **y**
st. : **M** (closed Saturday dinner and Sunday) a la carte 30/60 ♨ – **50 rm** ⊿ 114/166 – P
136/156.

🏨 **Suisse** Ⓜ without rest, 10 pl. Cornavin, ⊠ 1201, 𝒫 32.66.30, Telex 23868 – ♨ 🔳 ⇌wc
🔳wc ☎   EY **y**
60 rm

🏨 **Astoria** without rest, 6 pl. Cornavin, ⊠ 1211, 𝒫 32.10.25, Telex 22307 – ♨ 🔳 ⇌wc
🔳wc ☎. 🝐 ⓪ Ε 𝘝𝘐𝘚𝘈   EY **y**
st. : **62 rm** ⊿ 72/110.

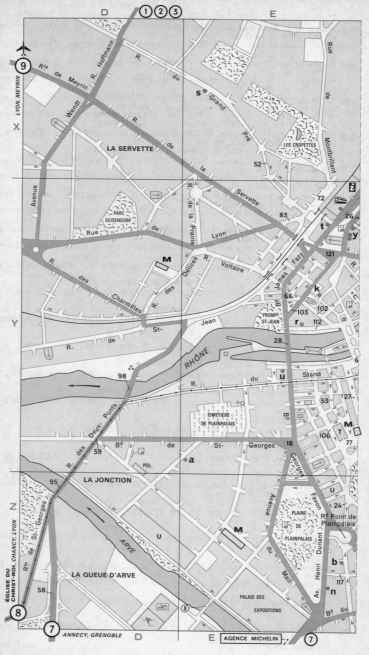

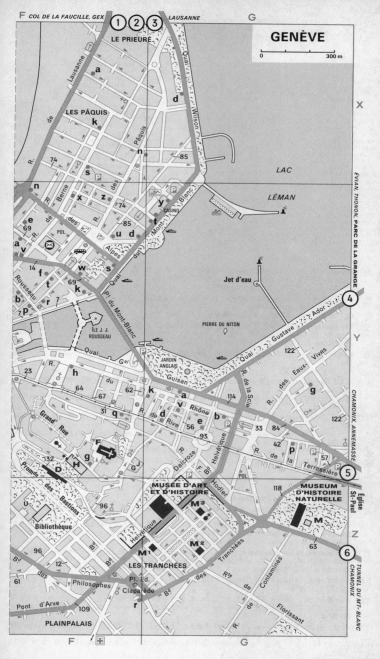

STREET INDEX TO GENEVE TOWN PLAN

🏨 **Balzac** without rest, pl. Navigation, ✉ 1201, 𝒫 31.01.60, Telex 289430 — 📶 📺 🛏wc
📶wc ☎ 📇 🅰🅴 ⑩ 🅴 𝑽𝑰𝑺𝑨
FX **n**
st. : **40 rm** ☲ 60/130, 4 apartments 160.

🏨 **Midi** Ⓜ, pl. Chevelu, ✉ 1201, 𝒫 31.78.00, Telex 23482, 🍴 — 📶 kitchenette 🍽 rest 📺
🛏wc 📶wc ☎. 📇 🅰🅴 ⑩ 🅴 𝑽𝑰𝑺𝑨
FY **r**
st. : **M** a la carte approx. 50 ⅜ — **85 rm** ☲ 100/140.

🏨 **Moderne** without rest, 1 r. Berne, ✉ 1201, 𝒫 32.81.00, Telex 289738 — 📶 📺 🛏wc
📶wc ☎. 📇 🅰🅴 ⑩ 🅴 𝑽𝑰𝑺𝑨
FY **v**
st. : **55 rm** ☲ 48/115.

🏨 **Lido** without rest, 8 r. Chantepoulet, ✉ 1201, 𝒫 31.55.30 — 📶 🛏wc 📶wc ☎. 📇 🅰🅴 ⑩ 🅴
𝑽𝑰𝑺𝑨
FY **v**
st. : **31 rm** ☲ 50/95.

🟏🟏🟏🟏🟏 🟊 **Le Gentilhomme**, Brunswick garden, ✉ 1211, 𝒫 31.14.00 — 📇 📇 🅰🅴 ⑩ 🅴 𝑽𝑰𝑺𝑨 🌫
closed Saturday lunch and Sunday — st. : **M** a la carte 90/120
FY **u**
Spec. Terrine d'artichauts et de langoustines, Ravioli de homard, Aile de volaille aux poireaux. **Wines** Pinot
gris, Muscat.

🟏🟏🟏🟏 🟊 **Le Chat Botté**, 13 quai Mont-Blanc, ✉ 1201, 𝒫 31.65.32, ← — 🍽 📇 🅰🅴 ⑩ 🅴 𝑽𝑰𝑺𝑨
🌫
FY **d**
closed 30 March-14 April, 21 December-5 January, Saturday, Sunday and Bank Holidays —
st. : **M** a la carte 80/90
Spec. Civet de langouste aux deux cépages, Tartare de bar à l'aneth, Gâteau noisette. **Wines** Dezaley, Dôle.

🟏🟏🟏🟏 🟊 **Le Cygne**, 19 Quai Mt-Blanc ✉ 1201 𝒫 31.98.11, ← — 📇 🅰🅴 ⑩ 🅴 𝑽𝑰𝑺𝑨 🌫
GY **y**
st. : **M** a la carte 75/120
Spec. Omble chevalier au fumet d'écrevisses, Bar rôti ou cuit à la fumée de bois, Feuillantine de filet
d'agneau.

🟏🟏🟏🟏 **Amphitryon**, 33 quai Bergues, ✉ 1201, 𝒫 31.50.50
FY **k**

🟏🟏🟏 🟊 **Perle du Lac**, 128 rte de Lausanne ✉ 1202, 𝒫 31.79.35, ←, 🍴 — 📇 🅰🅴 ⑩ 🅴
by ③
closed 22 December-22 January and Monday — st. : **M** a la carte 80/120
Spec. Feuilleté d'asperges vertes et langoustines (February to May), Blanc de turbot aux lentilles et deux
choux, Escalope de truite saumonnée à l'estragon. **Wines** Pinot-gris, Pinot-noir.

🟏🟏🟏 🟊 **Rôtisserie Le Neptune**, quai Turrettini ✉ 1201 𝒫 31.98.31, 🍴 — 📇 📇 🅰🅴 ⑩
closed Saturday, Sunday and Bank Holidays — st. : **M** a la carte 80/105 ⅜
EY **r**
Spec. Tresse de filets de sole et saumon, Fricassée de St-Pierre, Noisettes d'agneau truffées.

🟏🟏🟏 **Tsé Yang**, 19 quai Mont-Blanc ✉ 1201 𝒫 32.50.81, ← — 🍽 📇 🅰🅴 ⑩ 🅴 𝑽𝑰𝑺𝑨 🌫
GY **y**
st. : **M** 65/120 ⅜.

🟏🟏🟏 **Fin Bec**, 55 r. Berne, ✉ 1201, 𝒫 32.29.19, 🍴 — 📇 🅰🅴 ⑩ 🅴 𝑽𝑰𝑺𝑨
FX **k**
closed 1 to 21 August, 25 December-7 January, Saturday and Sunday — st. : **M** a la carte
60/80 ⅜.

🟏🟏🟏 **Aub. Mère Royaume**, 9 r. Corps-Saints, ✉ 1201, 𝒫 32.70.08, « Decorated in the old
Genevan style » — 📇 🅰🅴 ⑩ 🅴 𝑽𝑰𝑺𝑨
EY **k**
closed 15 July-11 August, Saturday, Sunday and Bank Holidays — st. : **M** a la carte 55/75
⅜.

XX **Mövenpick-Cendrier,** 17 r. Cendrier, ⊠ 1201, ℰ 32.50.30 — ▤. ✻ FY **f**
st. : **M** a la carte 38/67 ⅋.

XX **Buffet Cornavin,** 3 pl. Cornavin, ⊠ 1201, ℰ 32.43.06 — 🖭 ⓞ 🗲 𝗩𝗜𝗦𝗔 EY
st. : French rest. **M** a la carte 50/70 ⅋ - Buffet (1st class) **M** a la carte approx. 60.

XX **Locanda Ticinese,** 13 r. Rousseau, ⊠ 1201, ℰ 32.31.70, Italian and Italo Swiss (Ticino)
cuisine — 🖭 ⓞ 🗲 𝗩𝗜𝗦𝗔 FY **b**
closed 15 July-15 August, Saturday dinner and Sunday — st. : **M** a la carte approx. 50 ⅋.

X **Boeuf Rouge,** 17 r. A.-Vincent ⊠ 1201, ℰ 32.75.37, French (Lyons) cuisine FY **z**
closed July, 25 December-2 January, Saturday, Sunday and Bank Holidays — st. : **M** a la
carte approx. 55 ⅋.

2° - to the N (Palais des Nations, Servette) :

🏨 **Intercontinental** Ⓜ ⅖, 7 petit Saconnex, ⊠ 1211, Genève 19 ℰ 34.60.91, Telex 23130,
≤, ☎, 🏊, — 🛗 📺 ☎ ☎ ☎ ② — 🕿 25-270. 🖭 ⓞ 🗲 𝗩𝗜𝗦𝗔. ✻ rest by ①
st. : **Les Continents** (1st floor) (closed Sunday lunch and Saturday) **M** a la carte approx. 80
— ☒ 12 — **320 rm** 180/260, 32 apartments.

🏨 **Grand Pré** without rest, 35 r. Gd-Pré, ⊠ 1202, Genève 16 ℰ 33.91.50, Telex 23284 — 🛗
📺 ➪wc 🛁wc ☎. 🖭 ⓞ 🗲 𝗩𝗜𝗦𝗔 EX **s**
st. : **80 rm** ☒ 95/190.

XXX **Fu Lung,** 30 av. G.-Motta ⊠ 1202 ℰ 34.56.27 — ℗. 🖭 ⓞ 🗲 𝗩𝗜𝗦𝗔 by ①
closed Saturday lunch — st. : **M** 50 ⅋.

3° - Rive gauche (Commercial Centre) :

🏨 **Métropole** Ⓜ, 34 quai Gén.-Guisan ⊠ 1211 ℰ 21.13.44, Telex 421550, ≤, ☎ — 🛗
▤ rest 📺 ⅋ — 🕿 80-200. 🖭 ⓞ 🗲 𝗩𝗜𝗦𝗔. ✻ rest GY **a**
st. : **M** Le Grand Quai **M** 55/90 ⅋ and see rest **L'Arlequin** — **125 rm** ☒ 160/260, 5 apartments 600/750.

🏨 **Armures** Ⓜ ⅖, 1 r. Puits-Saint-Pierre ⊠ 1204 ℰ 28.91.72, Telex 421129 — 🛗 ▤ 📺 ☎
⅋. 🖭 ⓞ 🗲 𝗩𝗜𝗦𝗔 FY **g**
st. : **M** a la carte approx. 45 ⅋ — **24 rm** ☒ 140/250, 4 apartments 280.

🏨 **L'Arbalète,** 3 r. Tour-Maîtresse, ⊠ 1204, ℰ 28.41.55, Telex 427293 — 🛗 ▤ rm 📺 ☎ ⅋
— 🕿 25. 🖭 ⓞ 🗲 𝗩𝗜𝗦𝗔 GY **v**
st. : **M** a la carte approx. 45 ⅋ — **32 rm** ☒ 180/250.

🏨 **Century** without rest, 24 av. Frontenex ⊠ 1207 ℰ 36.80.95, Telex 23223 — 🛗 kitchenette
☎ ℗ — 🕿 35. 🖭 ⓞ 🗲 𝗩𝗜𝗦𝗔 GY **p**
st. : **124 rm** ☒ 108/190, 15 apartments 200/250.

🏨 **Touring Balance,** 13 pl. Longemalle, ⊠ 1204, ℰ 28.71.22, Telex 427634 — 🛗 📺 ➪wc
🛁wc ☎ — 🕿 40. 🖭 ⓞ 🗲 𝗩𝗜𝗦𝗔 GY **k**
st. : **M** (closed Saturday) 34/36 ⅋ — **56 rm** ☒ 60/140 - P 124/168.

🏨 **Lutetia** Ⓜ without rest, 12 r. Carouge, ⊠ 1205, ℰ 20.42.22, Telex 28845 — 🛗 kitchenette
➪wc ☎ EZ **b**
30 rm.

🏨 **Le Grenil,** 7 av. Ste-Clotilde, ⊠ 1205, ℰ 28.30.55, Telex 429307 — 🛗 🛁wc ☎ — 🕿 220.
🖭 ⓞ 🗲 𝗩𝗜𝗦𝗔 EY **a**
st. : **M** a la carte 30/50 ⅋ — **50 rm** ☒ 43/85 - P 67/96.

XXXX ✿ **Parc des Eaux-Vives,** 82 quai Gustave-Ador, ⊠ 1207, ℰ 35.41.40, « Pleasant setting
in extensive park, attractive view », ☎ — ℗. 🖭 ⓞ 🗲 𝗩𝗜𝗦𝗔 by ④
closed 1 January-15 February and Monday — st. : **M** a la carte 75/110
Spec. Gratin de cuisses de grenouilles (September to end May), Ravioli aux morilles, Canard nantais aux
petits oignons. Wines Dardagny, Yvorne.

XXXX ✿ **L'Arlequin,** 34 quai Gén.-Guisan ⊠ 1204 ℰ 21.13.44 — ▤. 🖭 ⓞ 🗲 𝗩𝗜𝗦𝗔. ✻ rm.
✻ rest GY **a**
closed Saturday and Sunday — st. : **M** 55/90
Spec. Terrine de pigeon au foie de canard, Fricassée de langoustines et St-Pierre à l'estragon, Cassolette de
ris de veau aux écrevisses.

XXX **Via Veneto,** 10 r. Tour Maitresse ⊠ 1204 ℰ 21.65.93 — ▤. 🖭 ⓞ 🗲 𝗩𝗜𝗦𝗔 GY **d**
closed July-August, Saturday lunch, Sunday and Bank Holidays — st. : **M** 32/65.

XXX **Mövenpick Fusterie,** 40 r. Rhône ⊠ 1204 ℰ 21.88.55 — ▤. 🖭 ⓞ 🗲 𝗩𝗜𝗦𝗔 FY **h**
closed Sunday — st. : **M Baron de la Mouette** (basement) a la carte 55/75 ⅋.

XXX ✿ **Jardin Rive Gauche,** 116 r. Rhône ⊠ 1204 ℰ 35.65.44 — ▤. 🖭 ⓞ 🗲 𝗩𝗜𝗦𝗔 GY **b**
closed Sunday — st. : **M** a la carte 75/95 ⅋ —
Spec. Ravioli de foie gras, St-Pierre et écrevisses au chablis, Rognon de veau aux échalotes.

XXX **Roberto,** 10 r. P.-Fatio, ⊠ 1204, ℰ 21.80.33, Italian specialities — ▤ GY **e**
closed Saturday dinner and Sunday — st. : **M** a la carte approx. 55 ⅋.

XX ✿ **Béarn** (Goddard), 4 quai Poste, ⊠ 1204, ℰ 21.00.28 — ▤. 🖭 ⓞ 🗲 𝗩𝗜𝗦𝗔 EY **u**
closed mid July-mid August, Saturday lunch and Sunday — st. : **M** 85/110
Spec. Marinade de poularde de Bresse, Soufflé aux truffes fraîches (end of January), Pigeon aux sucs
d'aromates. Wines Dardagny.

XX **Sénat,** 1 r. E.-Yung, ⊠ 1205, ℰ 46.58.10, ☎ — 🖭 ⓞ 🗲 𝗩𝗜𝗦𝗔 FZ **r**
closed Sunday — st. : **M** 30/45 ⅋.

XX **La Pescaille,** 15 av. H.-Dunant, ⊠ 1205, ℰ 29.71.60 — ▤. 🅰🅴 ⓪ 🄴   EZ **n**
closed Saturday lunch and Sunday lunch — **st. : M** a la carte 85/120.

XX **Cavalieri,** 7 r. Cherbuliez, ⊠ 1207, ℰ 35.09.56, Italian cuisine — ▤. 🅰🅴 ⓪ 🄴 *VISA*   GY **g**
closed 1 to 29 July and Monday — **st. : M** a la carte 50/75 ⚬.

XX **Laurent,** 13 r. Madeleine, ⊠ 1204, ℰ 21.24.22 — 🅰🅴 ⓪ 🄴 *VISA*   FY **q**
closed Sunday — **st. : M** 48/72 ⚬.

XX **Parc Bertrand,** 62 rte Florissant, ⊠ 1206, ℰ 47.59.57, 🌳 — 🅰🅴 🄴   GZ **u**
closed 23 December-6 January and Bank Holidays — **st. : M** a la carte 50/80 ⚬.

Environs

by the Lakeside road, Route de Lausanne :

at Bellevue by ③ : 6 km — ⊠ 1293 Bellevue :

🏨 **La Réserve** Ⓜ 🦢, 301 rte de Lausanne ℰ 74.17.41, Telex 23822, ≤, 🌳, « Lakeside and park setting, port with mooring facilities », ⊼, ✗ — ▤ 📺 ☎ & ❶ — 🏛 80. 🅰🅴 ⓪ 🄴 *VISA*. ✗ rest
st. : La Closerie M a la Carte 70/105 — **53 rm** �æ 190/330, 5 apartments 500.

XXX ✿ **Tsé Fung,** 301 rte de Lausanne ℰ 74.17.41, chinese cuisine — ❶. 🅰🅴 ⓪ 🄴 *VISA*. ✗
st. : M 75/95.

at Genthod by ③ : 7 km — ⊠ 1294 Genthod :

XX **Rest. du Château de Genthod,** 1 rte Rennex ℰ 74.19.72, 🌳, 🚲
closed in August, 20 December-10 January, Sunday and Monday — **st. : M** 40/70 ⚬.

Towards Savoy via the Lakeside :

at Cologny by ④ : 3,5 km — ⊠ 1223 Cologny :

XXX ✿ **Aub. du Lion d'or** (Large), au Village ℰ 36.44.32, 🌳, « Overlooking the lake and Geneva, terrace » — ❶. 🅰🅴 ⓪ 🄴 *VISA*
closed 20 December-20 January, Saturday and Sunday — **st. : M** a la carte 80/110
Spec. Filets de loup au gingembre, Bouillabaisse (15 September-May), Aiguillettes de canard. **Wines** Lully, Dézaley.

X **Pavillon de Ruth,** 86 quai Cologny ℰ 52.14.38, ≤, 🌳 — ❶. 🅰🅴 🄴
1 March-20 December and closed Thursday — **st. : M** a la carte approx. 55.

at Vandoeuvres by ④ : 5,5 km — ⊠ 1253 Vandoeuvres :

XX **Cheval Blanc,** ℰ 50.14.01, Italian cuisine — 🅰🅴 🄴 *VISA*. ✗
closed 1 to 21 July, Christmas, 1 January, Sunday and Monday — **st. : M** a la carte 55/75.

at Vésenaz by ④ : 6 km by rte de Thonon — ⊠ 1222 Vésenaz :

🏠 **La Tourelle** without rest, 26 rte Hermance ℰ 52.16.28, park — 🚻wc 🛎 📽 ❶. 🅰🅴 ⓪ 🄴 *VISA*. ✗
closed 15 December-15 January — **st. : 24 rm** �æ 70/120.

XXX **Chez Valentino,** 63 rte Thonon ℰ 52.14.40, 🌳, Italian cuisine, 🚲 — ❶. 🅰🅴 *VISA*. ✗
closed August, 22 December-3 January, Tuesday lunch and Monday — **st. : M** a la carte 55/80 ⚬.

at Collonges by ④ : 8 km — ⊠ 1245 Collonges :

XX **Chambord,** ℰ 52.25.85, 🌳 — 🅰🅴 ⓪ 🄴 *VISA*
closed Monday lunch and Sunday — **st. : M** 65/120.

by route de St-Julien :

at Carouge : 3 km by r. Carouge — ⊠ 1227 Carouge :

XX **Olivier de Provence,** 13 r. J.-Dalphin ℰ 42.04.50, 🌳 — 🅰🅴 ⓪ 🄴 *VISA*
closed Sunday — **st. : M** 55/75.

X **Aub. Communale,** 39 r. Ancienne ℰ 42.22.88, 🌳
closed Monday dinner and Tuesday — **st. : M** a la carte 40/60 ⚬.

at Troinex by ⑦ : 5 km — ⊠ 1256 Troinex :

XXX ✿✿ **Vieux Moulin** (Bouilloux), 89 rte Drize ℰ 42.29.56, 🌳 — ❶. 🅰🅴 🄴 *VISA*
closed 1 to 15 April, 1 to 15 September, Sunday (except lunch from September to June) and Monday — **st. : M** (booking essential) 65/100 and a la carte
Spec. Loup rôti au beurre parfumé, Jarret de veau (January-April). **Wines** Lully, Pinot.

XX **La Chaumière,** r. Fondelle ℰ 84.30.66, 🌳, 🚲 — ❶. 🅰🅴 ⓪ 🄴 *VISA*
closed Sunday dinner and Monday lunch — **st. : M** a la carte 75/95.

at Grand-Lancy by ⑦ : 3 km — ⊠ 1212 Lancy :

XXX ✿ **Marignac** (Pelletier), 32 av. E.-Lance ℰ 94.04.24, park, 🌳 — ▤ ❶. 🅰🅴 ⓪ 🄴 *VISA*
closed 5 to 14 April, 4 to 25 August, Saturday lunch and Sunday — **st. : M** 80/100
Spec. Soupe au foie gras de canard et jus de truffe, Couscous de poissons de mer, Canard de Barbarie aux pêches. **Wines** Dôle blanche, Pinot noir.

at Plan-les-Ouates by ⑦ : 5 km – ✉ **1228** Plan-les-Ouates :

Plan-les-Ouates without rest, 135 rte St-Julien ✆ 94.92.44 – 🛗 ⇔wc ☎. AE ⓓ E VISA
closed 23 December-2 January – **st. : 24 rm** ☐ 42/97.

at Landecy by ⑦ : 7,5 km – ✉ **1257** Landecy :

XX **Au Fer à Cheval,** 37 rte Prieur ✆ 71.10.78, 🏖 – ⓓ E VISA
closed February, Wednesday lunch and Tuesday – **st. : M** 35/90.

by route de Chancy :

at Petit Lancy by ⑧ : 3 km – ✉ **1213** Petit Lancy :

✿ **Host. de la Vendée and rest. Pont Rouge,** 28 chemin Vendée ✆ 92.04.11, Telex 421304, 🏖 – 🛗 TV ☎ Ⓟ – 🏛 80. AE ⓓ E VISA
closed 23 December-6 January – **st. : M** *(closed Saturday lunch and Sunday)* 65/90 🍷 – **30 rm** ☐ 82/155
Spec. Homard au Pineau des Charentes, Coquelet en pie truffé, Pavé de chocolat. **Wines** Lully, Gamay.

X ✿ **Le Curling,** chemin du Fief-de-Chapitre ✆ 93.62.44, ←, 🏖 – E VISA
closed end-July to mid August, 24 December-2 January, Monday lunch and Sunday – **st. : M** 60/80 🍷
Spec. Panaché de mer, Cassolette de homard, Canard poêlé. **Wines** Riesling, Pinot noir.

at Confignon by ⑧ : 6 km – ✉ **1232** Confignon :

XX **Aub. de Confignon,** 6 pl. Église ✆ 57.19.44, 🏖, 🌳
closed Monday – **st. : M** a la carte 40/70.

at Cartigny by ⑧ **:** 12 km – ✉ **1236** Cartigny :

XX **L'Escapade,** 31 r. Trably ✆ 56.12.07, 🏖, 🌳 – Ⓟ. AE ⓓ E VISA
closed, 20 December-end January, Sunday and Monday – **st. : M** 80/100.

Towards the Jura :

at Cointrin by ⑨, route de Meyrin : 4 km – ✉ **1216** Cointrin :

Penta M, 75.77 r. L.-Casaï ✆ 98.47.00, Telex 27044 – 🛗 ▤ TV ☎ 🚗 Ⓟ – 🏛 30-700. AE ⓓ E VISA. ✻ rest AU **v**
st. : M 26/30 🍷 – ☐ 15 – **316 rm** 110/170, bedrooms for non smokers.

Hôtel 33, 82 av. L.-Casai ✆ 98.02.00, 🏖 – 🛗 ⇔wc ☎ Ⓟ. AE ⓓ E VISA
st. : M *(closed Sunday)* a la carte approx. 50 🍷 – **33 rm** ☐ 75/130 – P 91/101.

at the airport of Cointrin by ⑨ : 4 km – ✉ **1215** Genève :

XX **Rôt. Plein Ciel,** ✆ 98.22.88, ← – ▤. AE ⓓ E VISA
st. : M a la carte 60/90.

ZÜRICH 8001 427 ⑥ 21 ⑱ – pop. 367,086 - Alt. 441 m – ☎ 01.

See : The Quays★★ BYZ – Fraumünster cloisters★ (Alter Kreuzgang des Frauenmünsters) BZ **D** – View of the town from the Zürichhorn Gardens★ V – Church of SS. Felix and Regula★ U **E** – Church of Zürich-Altstetten★ U **F** – Zoological Gardens★ (Zoo Dolder) U **K** – Museums : Swiss National Museum★★★ (Schweizerisches Landesmuseum) BY – Fine Arts Museum★★ (Kunsthaus) CZ – Rietberg Museum★★ V **M3.**

✈ Kloten ✆ 812 71 11.

ℹ Offizielles Verkehrsbüro, Bahnhofplatz 15 ✉ 8023 ✆ 211 40 00, Telex 813 744 – A.C.S. Forchstrasse 95 ✉ 8032 ✆ 55 15 00 – T.C.S. Alfred-Escher-Strasse 38 ✉ 8002 ✆ 201 25 36.

Basel 85 ⑦ – Bern 125 ⑦ – Genève 278 ⑦ – Innsbruck 288 ② – Milan 304 ⑤.

Plans on following pages

On the right bank of river Limmat (University, Fine Arts Museum).

✿ **Dolder Grand Hotel and rest. La Rotonde** 🌄, Kurhausstr. 65, ✉ 8032, ✆ 251 62 31, Telex 53449, ← Zurich and lake, 🏖, ⛲, 🏊, 🏌9, park, 🎾 – 🛗 ▤ rest TV ☎ 🚗 Ⓟ. 🏛. AE E VISA. ✻ rest V **f**
M a la carte 40/90 – **194 rm** ☐ 180/360
Spec. Sole du Nord à la fine matelote armoricaine, Langoustines au St.-Saphorin cressonnière.

Eden au Lac, Utoquai 45, ✉ 8023, ✆ 47 94 04, Telex 816339, ←, ⛲, « Tasteful decor » – 🛗 ▤ TV ☎ Ⓟ. 🏛. AE ⓓ E VISA. ✻ rest V **a**
M a la carte 41/87 – **54 rm** ☐ 145/290.

Zurich M, Neumühlequai 42, ✉ 8001, ✆ 363 63 63, Telex 56809, ←, ⛲, 🏊 – 🛗 ▤ TV ☎ 🚗. 🏛. AE ⓓ E VISA U **b**
M a la carte 30/60 – **221 rm** ☐ 140/280.

International M, Am Marktplatz, ✉ 8050, ✆ 311.43.41, Telex 823251, ←, ⛲, 🏊 – 🛗 ▤ TV ☎. 🏛. ✻ rest U **s**
M a la carte 19,50/57,50 – ☐ 8 – **350 rm** 140/190.

Waldhaus Dolder M 🌄, Kurhausstr. 20, ✉ 8030, ✆ 251 93 60, Telex 816460, ← Zürich and lake, 🏖, ⛲, 🏊, 🌳, park, 🎾 – 🛗 ▤ rest TV ☎ 🚗 Ⓟ. 🏛. AE ⓓ E VISA V **r**
M a la carte 29/45 – ☐ 10 – **100 rm** 120/270.

Excelsior, Dufourstr. 24, ⊠ 8008, 𝒫 252 25 00, Telex 59295 – 🛗 🗐 📺 ☎ 🅿 🔬 🆎 ⓪
E 𝘝𝘐𝘚𝘈   CZ f
M a la carte 25,50/58,50 – **40 rm** � 120/220.

Zürich Continental H., Stampfenbachstr. 60, ⊠ 8006, 𝒫 363 33 63, Telex 55393 – 🛗
🗐 📺 ☎ ᕼ 🔬 🆎 ⓪ E 𝘝𝘐𝘚𝘈   U a
M a la carte 30/62 – ⊊ 9 – **134 rm** 113/224.

Bellerive au Lac, Utoquai 47, ⊠ 8008, 𝒫 251 70 10, Telex 816398, ≤, 🏠 – 🛗 📺 ☎.
🔬 🆎 ⓪ E 𝘝𝘐𝘚𝘈   V a
M a la carte 25/59 – **60 rm** ⊊ 130/200.

Europe, Dufourstr. 4, ⊠ 8008, 𝒫 47 10 30, Telex 816461, « Tasteful decor » – 🛗 🗐 📺
🚻wc 🛀wc ☎. 🆎 ⓪ E 𝘝𝘐𝘚𝘈   CZ e
M (coffee shop only) approx. 32 (unlicensed) – **42 rm** ⊊ 95/240.

Zürcherhof, Zähringerstr. 21, ⊠ 8025, 𝒫 47 10 40, Telex 816490, « Tasteful decor » – 🛗 🗐 rest 📺 🚻wc
🛀wc 🐾. 🆎 ⓪ E 𝘝𝘐𝘚𝘈   CY q
M (closed Sunday) a la carte 25/46 – **35 rm** ⊊ 90/150.

Ambassador, Falkenstr. 6, ⊠ 8025, 𝒫 47 76 00, Telex 816508 – 🛗 🗐 📺 🚻wc 🛀wc
☎. 🆎 ⓪ E 𝘝𝘐𝘚𝘈   CZ a
M a la carte 29,50/46 – **45 rm** ⊊ 90/180.

Opéra without rest., Dufourstr. 5, ⊠ 8008, 𝒫 251 90 90, Telex 816480 – 🛗 🗐 📺 🚻wc
🛀wc ☎. 🆎 ⓪ E 𝘝𝘐𝘚𝘈   CZ b
61 rm ⊊ 90/180.

Chesa Rustica, Limmatquai 70, ⊠ 8001, 𝒫 251 92 91, Telex 57380, ≤ – 🛗 📺 🚻wc
🛀wc ☎. 🆎 ⓪ E 𝘝𝘐𝘚𝘈   BY r
M a la carte 35/65 – **23 rm** ⊊ 90/180.

Ammann without rest., Kirchgasse 4, ⊠ 8001, 𝒫 252 72 40, Telex 56208 – 🛗 📺 🚻wc
🛀wc ☎. 🆎 ⓪ E 𝘝𝘐𝘚𝘈   BCZ n
⊊ 13 – **19 rm** 115/170.

Alexander without rest., Niederdorfstr. 40, ⊠ 8001, 𝒫 251 82 03, Telex 57735 – 🛗 🗐
🚻wc 🛀wc 🐾. 🆎 ⓪ E 𝘝𝘐𝘚𝘈   BY x
61 rm ⊊ 60/150.

Théâtre without rest, Seilergraben 69, ⊠ 8023, 𝒫 252 60 62, Telex 56853 – 🛗 📺 🚻wc
🛀wc 🐾. 🆎 ⓪ E 𝘝𝘐𝘚𝘈   CY a
60 rm ⊊ 48/122.

Helmhaus without rest., Schiffländeplatz 30, ⊠ 8001, 𝒫 251 88 10, Telex 816525 – 🛗
🚻wc 🛀wc 🐾. 🆎 ⓪ E 𝘝𝘐𝘚𝘈   BCZ s
25 rm ⊊ 89/143.

XXX ⌘ **Agnès Amberg,** Hottingerstr. 5, ⊠ 8032, 𝒫 251 26 26, tasteful installation – 🆎 ⓪
E 𝘝𝘐𝘚𝘈   CY d
closed Saturday lunch and Sunday – **M** a la carte 55/100
Spec. Ragoût de homard au Sauternes, Gibier (September-December), Soufflé au chocolat.

XX **Haus Zum Rüden,** Limmatquai 42, ⊠ 8001, 𝒫 47 95 90, former guildhall – 🗐. 🆎 ⓪ E
𝘝𝘐𝘚𝘈   BY m
M a la carte 48/86.

XX ⌘ **Riesbächli** (Frau Tschudi), Zollikerstr. 157, ⊠ 8008, 𝒫 55 23 24   V s

XX **Jacky's Stapferstube,** Culmannstr. 45, ⊠ 8006, 𝒫 361 37 48, Meat specialities – 🗐
🅿. 🆎 ⓪ E 𝘝𝘐𝘚𝘈   U r
closed Sunday, Monday and 6 July-6 August – **M** a la carte 38/76.

XX **Bolognese,** Seegartenstr. 14, ⊠ 8008, 𝒫 252 37 37, Telex 58968, Italian rest. – 🆎 ⓪ E
𝘝𝘐𝘚𝘈   V u
closed Saturday and Sunday, 20 December-15 January – **M** a la carte 22/56.

XX **Casa Ferlin,** Stampfenbachstr. 38, ⊠ 8006, 𝒫 362 35 09, Italian rest. – 🆎 ⓪ E 𝘝𝘐𝘚𝘈
closed Saturday lunch, Sunday and mid July-mid August – **M** a la carte 36/66.   BY u

X **Wolfbach,** Wolbachstr. 35, (due to close for renovation, enquire in advance), ⊠ 8032,
𝒫 252 51 80, River Fish rest – 🆎 ⓪ E   V b
M a la carte 38/57,50.

On the left bank of river Limmat (Main railway station, Business centre).

Baur au Lac, Talstr. 1, ⊠ 8022, 𝒫 221 16 50, Telex 813567, « Lakeside setting, park » –
🛗 🗐 📺 ☎ ᕀ 🅿. 🔬 🆎. 🍽 rest   BZ a
M 47/97 – **150 rm** ⊊ 160/360.

Savoy Hotel Baur en Ville Ⓜ, Poststr. 12, ⊠ 8022, 𝒫 211 53 60, Telex 812845 – 🛗 🗐 📺
☎ ᕼ. 🔬   BZ e
112 rm.

Schweizerhof Ⓜ, Bahnhofplatz 7, ⊠ 8023, 𝒫 211 86 40, Telex 813754 – 🛗 🗐 📺 ☎.
🔬 🆎 ⓪ E 𝘝𝘐𝘚𝘈   BY a
M (closed Sunday) a la carte 40/71,50 – **115 rm** ⊊ 145/195.

Zum Storchen, Weinplatz 2, ⊠ 8022, 𝒫 211 55 10, Telex 813354, ≤, « Limmat-side
setting » – 🛗 📺 ☎. 🔬. 🆎 ⓪ E 𝘝𝘐𝘚𝘈 🍽 rest   BY u
M a la carte 35/65 – **77 rm** ⊊ 130/295.

St. Gotthard, Bahnhofstr. 87, ⊠ 8023, 𝒫 211 55 00, Telex 812420 – 🛗 🗐 📺 ☎. 🔬
136 rm.   BY b

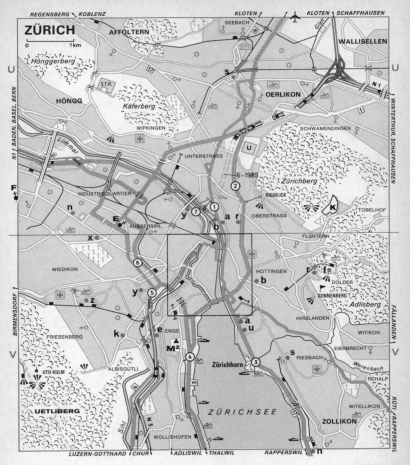

ZÜRICH

0   1km

REGENSBERG – KOBLENZ   AFFOLTERN   KLOTEN   KLOTEN – SCHAFFHAUSEN

SEEBACH   WALLISELLEN

U   *Hönggerberg*   U

N 1 BADEN, BASEL, BERN

HÖNGG   E.T.H.   *Käferberg*   OERLIKON   N 1   WINTERTHUR, SCHAFFHAUSEN

WIPKINGEN   SCHWAMENDINGEN

Limmat

UNTERSTRASS   6 - 1985   *Zürichberg*

F   INDUSTRIEQUARTIER   ②   RIGIBLICK   K   TOBELHOF

n   E   y ⑦ ①   a r   OBERSTRASS

AUSSERSIHL   b   FLUNTERN

x   WIEDIKON   ⑥   HOTTINGEN   r f   DOLDER

BIRMENSDORF   y ⑤   b   SONNENBERG   *Adlisberg*   FALLANDEN

z   k   e ENGE   a   HIRSLANDEN   WITIKON

V   FRIESENBERG   M²   u   EIERBRECHT   RÜTI / RAPPERSWIL   V

ALBISGÜTLI   ④   *Zürichhorn*   s   RIESBACH   *Werenbach*

UTO-KULM   ③   REHALP

UETLIBERG   N 3   WITELLIKON

Sihl   *ZÜRICHSEE*   ZOLLIKON

WOLLISHOFEN

LUZERN-GOTTHARD / CHUR   ADLISWIL / THALWIL   RAPPERSWIL   n

🏨 **Carlton Elite** ⑤ Bahnhofstr. 41, ⊠ 8023, 𝒫 211 65 60, Telex 812781 – 📶 🍽 rest 📺 ☎
    ⅙ 🅿 🕭 🅰🅴 ⓸ 🅴 𝘝𝘐𝘚𝘈   BY **d**
    M *(closed Sunday)* a la carte 29/52 – 🖵 Bb 12 – **72 rm** 120/260.

🏨 **Slpügenschloss,** Splügenstr. 2, ⊠ 8002, 𝒫 201 08 00, Telex 815553 – 📶 📺 ☎ 🅿 🕭
    🅰🅴 ⓸ 🅴 𝘝𝘐𝘚𝘈, ⚘ rest   AZ **e**
    M a la carte 29/56 – **55 rm** 🖵 130/295.

🏨 **Ascot,** Lavaterstr. 15, ⊠ 8027, 𝒫 201 18 00, Telex 815454 – 📶 📶 📺 ☎. 🅰🅴 ⓸ 🅴 𝘝𝘐𝘚𝘈
    M Jockey Club *(closed Saturday lunch)* a la carte 25/62 – **60 rm** 🖵 98/200.   AZ **f**

🏨 **Nova Park** Ⓜ, Badenerstr. 420, ⊠ 8040, 𝒫 491 22 22, Telex 822822, 🕭, 🔭 – 📶 🍽 rest
    📺 ☎ ⅙ 🔄 🅿 🕭 🅰🅴 ⓸ 🅴 𝘝𝘐𝘚𝘈, ⚘ rest   U **n**
    M a la carte 29,50/51,50 – 🖵 9 – **361 rm** 118/175.

🏨 **Atlantis Sheraton** Ⓜ ⑤, Döltschiweg 234, ⊠ 8055, 𝒫 463 00 00, Telex 813338, <, 🔭,
    🔄, 🗙 – 📶 📺 ☎ 🅿 🕭 🅰🅴 ⓸ 🅴 𝘝𝘐𝘚𝘈   V **z**
    M Rotisserie – Döltschi-Stube – **170 rm** 🖵 136/275.

🏨 **Glärnischhof,** Claridenstr. 30, ⊠ 8022, 𝒫 202 47 47, Telex 815366 – 📶 🍽 rest 📺 ☎ 🅿
    🕭 🅰🅴 ⓸ 🅴 𝘝𝘐𝘚𝘈   BZ **k**
    M La Rotisserie a la carte approx. 64 – **70 rm** 🖵 110/200.

🏨 **Glockenhof,** Sihlstr. 31, ⊠ 8001, 𝒫 211 56 50, Telex 812466 – 📶 🍽 rest 📺 ☎ ⅙ 🅰🅴 ⓸
    🅴 𝘝𝘐𝘚𝘈   AY **e**
    M a la carte 25/52 – **106 rm** 🖵 106/156.

ZÜRICH

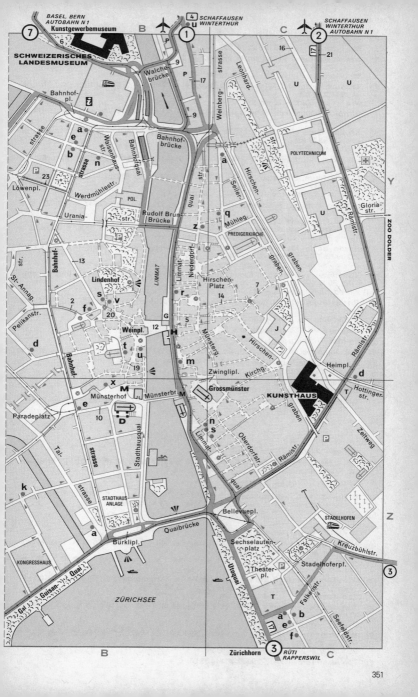

🏨 **Engematthof,** Engimattstr. 14, ⊠ 8002, 𝒫 201 25 04, Telex 56327, 🚗 – 🛗 �️wc 🛁wc
📞 🄿. 🄰🄴 ⓘ 🄴. ⋘   V e
M a la carte 21/52 – **79 rm** ⥥ 74/150.

🏨 **Neues Schloss,** Stockerstr. 17, ⊠ 8022, 𝒫 201 65 60, Telex 815560 – 🛗 📺 �️wc 🛁wc
📞 🈘. 🄰🄴 ⓘ 🄴 🆅🅸🆂🅰   AZ m
M *(closed Sunday)* 22/38 – ⥥ 8 – **58 rm** 140/196.

🏨 **Trümpy,** Sihlquai 9, ⊠ 8005, 𝒫 42 54 00, Telex 822980 – 🛗 ▦ rest 📺 �️wc 🛁wc 📞
🈘. 🄰🄴 ⓘ 🄴 🆅🅸🆂🅰   U v
M a la carte 30/60 – **78 rm** ⥥ 100/160.

🏨 **Simplon** without rest., Schützengasse 16, ⊠ 8023, 𝒫 211 61 11 – 🛗 �️wc 📞. 🄰🄴 ⓘ 🄴
74 rm ⥥ 100/165.   BY e

🏨 **Stoller,** Badenerstr. 357, ⊠ 8040, 𝒫 492 65 00, Telex 822460 – 🛗 📺 �️wc 🛁wc 🐾
⇦. 🄰🄴 ⓘ 🄴 🆅🅸🆂🅰   V x
M a la carte 28/55 – ⥥ 7,50 – **101 rm** 80/135.

🏨 **City,** Lövenstr. 34, ⊠ 8001, 𝒫 211 20 55, Telex 812437 – 🛗 ▦ rest 📺 �️wc 🛁wc 📞
74 rm.   AY h

🏨 **Limmathaus,** Limmatstr. 118, ⊠ 8031, 𝒫 42 52 40, Telex 823161 – 🛗 🛁wc 🐾 🄿. 🈘.
🄰🄴 ⓘ 🄴 🆅🅸🆂🅰   U y
M *(closed Sunday)* approx. 12 – ⥥ 6 – **64 rm** 55/120.

XXX ⚘ **Rebe** (Witschi), Schützengasse 5, ⊠ 8001, 𝒫 221 10 65, Telex 58477 – ▦. 🄰🄴 ⓘ 🄴
🆅🅸🆂🅰 ⋘   BY n
closed Sunday – **M** a la carte 57/110
Spec. Gelée de quatre poissons du lac (15 March-15 June), Fricassée de truite du lac et écrevisses au
Riesling (March-June), Canard sauvage (15 September-15 November).

XXX **Baron de la Mouette** (Mövenpick Dreikönighaus), Beethovenstr. 32, ⊠ 8002, 𝒫
202 09 10, Telex 59956 – ▦. 🄰🄴 ⓘ 🄴 🆅🅸🆂🅰   AZ r
closed 28 June-23 July – **M** a la carte 33/67,50.

XX **Zunfthaus zur Waag,** Münsterhoof 8, ⊠ 8001, 𝒫 211 07 30, Former hatters guildhall
– 🄰🄴 ⓘ 🄴 🆅🅸🆂🅰   BZ x
closed 7 July to 29 July – **M** (booking essential) a la carte 37,50/62.

XX **Rotisserie Lindenhofkeller,** Pfalzgasse 4, ⊠ 8001, 𝒫 211 70 71, 🏮 – 🄰🄴 ⓘ 🄴 🆅🅸🆂🅰
⋘   BY v
closed Saturday, Sunday and 27 July-19 August – **M** a la carte 39/76.

XX Vetliner Keller, Schlüsselgasse 8, ⊠ 8001, 𝒫 221 32 28, « 16C house »   BY t

XX Widder, Widdergasse 6, ⊠ 8001, 𝒫 211 31 50   BY f

XX Accademia Piccoli, Rotwandstr. 48, ⊠ 8004, 𝒫 241 42 02, Italian rest.   AY w

XX **Nouvelle,** Erlachstr. 46, ⊠ 8003, 𝒫 462 63 63 – 🄿. 🄰🄴 ⓘ 🄴 🆅🅸🆂🅰   V y
closed Saturday lunch and Sunday – **M** a la carte 40,50/63.

XX Restaurants im Hauptbahnhof, Bahnhoflatz 15, ⊠ 8023, 𝒫 211 15 10   BY
M Au Prieuré – **Da Capo** Italian rest. – **Alfred-Escher Stribe.**

XX **Osteria da Primo,** Uetlibergstr. 166, ⊠ 8045, 𝒫 463 30 22, Italian rest. – 🄰🄴 ⓘ 🄴 🆅🅸🆂🅰
closed Sunday – **M** a la carte 45/65.   V k

Environs.

by ① to Affoltern :

at Regensdorf : 12 km – ⊠ 8105 Regensdorf :

🏨🏨 Mövenpick Holiday Inn Ⓜ, Watterstr., 𝒫 840 25 20, Telex 53658, 🏊 – 🛗 ▦ 📺 📞 ⚫ ⇦.
🈘 – **M** Grillroom – **149 rm.**

at Dielsdorf : 15,5 km – ⊠ 8157 Dielsdorf :

XX **Bienengarten,** Regensbergerstr. 9, 𝒫 853 12 17, 🏮 – 🄿. 🄰🄴 ⓘ 🄴 🆅🅸🆂🅰
closed 4 October to 27 October, Saturday lunch – **M** a la carte 33/57.

by ② to Schaffhausen :

at Zürich-Kloten (Airport) 10 km :

🏨🏨 **Hilton International Zürich** Ⓜ, Hohenbühlstr. 10, ⊠ 8058, 𝒫 810 31 31, Telex 825428,
🍴, 🏊 – 🛗 ▦ 📺 📞 ⚫ ⇦.
M Sutter's Grill a la carte 42,50/68 – **Taverne** a la carte 29,50/46 – ⥥ 12 – **287 rm**
130/200.

🏨🏨 **Mövenpick Hotel Zürich Airport** Ⓜ, Walter Mitterholzerstr. 8, ⊠ 8152, 𝒫 810 11 11,
Telex 57979, 🍴, 🏊 – 🛗 ▦ 📺 📞 ⚫ 🄿. 🈘. 🄰🄴 ⓘ 🄴 🆅🅸🆂🅰
M a la carte 20/52 – ⥥ 14 – **335 rm** 140/180.

🏨 **Airport,** Oberhauserstr. 30, ⊠ 8152, 𝒫 810 44 44, Telex 825416 – 🛗 ▦ rest 📺 �️wc
🛁wc 📞 ⚫. 🄰🄴 ⓘ 🄴 🆅🅸🆂🅰 ⋘ rest
M 20/68 – **48 rm** ⥥ 110/150.

🏨 **Welcome Inn,** Holbergstr. 1 at Kloten, ⊠ 8302, 𝒫 814 07 27, Telex 825527 – 🛗 🛁wc 📞
⚫. 🄰🄴 ⓘ 🄴 🆅🅸🆂🅰
M a la carte 12/48 – ⥥ 7 – **91 rm** 68/98.

XX Top Air, in Terminal A, ⊠ 8058, 𝒫 814 33 00, ≤.

by ③ North bank :

at Zollikon : 5 km – ✉ **8702** Zollikon :

XXX ❀ **Chez Max** (Kehl), Seestr. 53, ☎ 391 88 77 – 🆎 ⑩ 🇪 *VISA*
closed Sunday and Monday – **M** lunch a la carte 41/88, dinner 110/160
Spec. Tartar de coquille St-Jacques au caviar (October-March), Medaillons de homard, Agneau d'Ecosse
aux pousses de lentilles à la crème.

XX **Wirtschaft zur Höhe,** Höhestr. 73, ☎ 391 59 59, 🏠, 🌳 – ⑫. 🆎 🇪
M *(closed Tuesday, last Monday of the month, 9 to 20 February, 27 July-13 August)* a la
carte 35/67.

at Küsnacht : 6 km – ✉ **8700** Küsnacht :

🏛 **Ermitage,** Seestr. 80, ☎ 910 52 22, Telex 825707, ≤, 🏠, « Attractive lakeside setting,
terrasse and garden » – 🛁wc 🕿 ⑫. 🌿 rest
M 31/65 – 🔄 10 – **25 rm** 120/200.

XXX ❀ **Petermann's Kunststube,** Seestr. 160, ☎ 910 07 15 – ⑫. 🌿
closed Monday, Saturday and Sunday lunch and 22 July-8 August – **M** a la carte 47,50/90
Spec. Rable de lapin aux ravioli de légumes, Blanc de bar cuit à la fumée sur salade de truffes (November-
June), Charlotte au chocolat amer avec sauce aux pistaches.

by ④ to Chur-South bank :

at Rüschlikon : 9 km – ✉ **8803** Rüschlikon :

🏛 **Belvoir** Ⓜ 🏖, Säumerstr. 37, ☎ 724 02 02, Telex 59447, ≤ lake, 🏠 – 🔰 🍴 rest 📺
🛁wc 🚿wc 🕿 ⬅ ⑫. 🏋. 🆎 ⑩ 🇪 *VISA*. 🌿 rest
M a la carte 29/49 – **21 rm** 🔄 70/130.

at Gattikon : 13,5 km – ✉ **8136** Gattikon-Thalwil :

XX ❀ **Sihlhalde,** Sihlhaldenstr. 70, ☎ 720 09 27, 🏠 – ⑩ 🇪 *VISA*
closed Monday, Tuesday and 20 July-15 August – **M** a la carte 34/63
Spec. Filet d'agneau aux deux poivres, Ecrevisses (July-August), Gibier (Sept.-Oct.).

at Wädenswil : 22 km – ✉ **8820** Wädenswil :

XXX ❀ **Eichmühle** (Wannenwetsch), Neugutstr. 933, ☎ 780 34 44 – ⑫. 🆎 ⑩ *VISA*
M a la carte 45/82.

*Town plans of Basle, Geneva and Zürich : with the permission
from Federal directorate for cadastral surveys, 2 January 1985.*

United Kingdom

London
Birmingham
Edinburgh
Glasgow
Leeds
Liverpool
Manchester

PRACTICAL INFORMATION

LOCAL CURRENCY

Pound Sterling : £ 1 = 1.143 US $ (Jan. 85)

TOURIST INFORMATION

Tourist Information offices exist in each city included in the Guide. The telephone number and address is given in each text under ⓘ.

FOREIGN EXCHANGE

Banks are open between 9.30am and 3pm on weekdays only. Most large hotels have exchange facilities, and Heathrow and Gatwick Airports have 24-hour banking facilities.

THEATRE BOOKINGS IN LONDON

Your hotel porter will be able to make your arrangements or direct you to Theatre Booking Agents.

In addition there is a kiosk in Leicester Square selling tickets for the same day's performances at half price plus booking fee. It is open 12-6.30pm.

SHOPPING

In London : Oxford St./Regent St. (department stores, exclusive shops) Bond St. (exclusive shops, antiques)
Knightsbridge area (department stores, exclusive shops, boutiques)

For other towns see the index of street names : those printed in red are where the principal shops are found.

TIPPING

Many hotels and restaurants include a service charge but where this is not the case an amount equivalent to between 10 and 15 per cent of the bill is customary. Additionally doormen, baggage porters and cloakroom attendants are generally given a gratuity.

Taxi drivers are customarily tipped between 10 and 15 per cent of the amount shown on the meter in addition to the fare.

CAR HIRE

The international car hire companies have branches in each major city. Your hotel porter will be able to give details and help you with your arrangements.

SPEED LIMITS

The maximum permitted speed on motorways and dual carriageways is 70 mph (113 km/h.) and 60 mph (97 km/h.) on other roads except where a lower speed limit is signposted.

SEAT BELTS

The wearing of seat belts in the United Kingdom is compulsory for drivers and front seat passengers.

LONDON

LONDON (Greater) 404 folds ④ to ④ — pop. 6 696 008 — ✪ 01.

🛬 Heathrow, ✆ 759 4321, Telex 934892 — **Terminal** : Airbus (A1) from Victoria, Airbus (A2) from Paddington, Airbus (A3) from Euston — Underground (Piccadilly line) frequent service daily — Helicopter service to Gatwick Airport.

🛬 Gatwick, ✆ 0293 (Crawley) 28822 and ✆ 01 (London) 668 4211, by A 23 and M 23 — **Terminal** : Coach service from Victoria Coach Station (Flightline 777) — Railink (Gatwick Express) from Victoria (24 h service) — Helicopter service to Heathrow Airport.

🛬 Stansted, at Bishop's Stortford, ✆ 0279 (Bishop's Stortford) 502380, Telex 81102, NE : 34 m. off M 11 and A 120.

BA Air Terminal : Victoria Station, ✆ 834 2323, p. 16 BX.

British Caledonian Airways, Victoria Air Terminal : Victoria Station, SW1, ✆ 834 9411, p. 16 BX.

🚆 Euston ✆ 387 8541 — King's Cross ✆ 837 4200 ext 4700 — Paddington ✆ 723 7000 ext 3148.

🛈 London Tourist Board, Head Office, 26 Grosvenor Gardens, SW1W 0DU, ✆ 730 3450, Telex 919 041.
National Tourist Information Centre, Victoria Station Forecourt, SW1, ✆ 730 3488.
British Tourist Authority, 64 St. James's St., SW1, ✆ 499 9325.
Telephone Information Service ✆ 730 0791 or Teletourist ✆ 246 8041 (English), 246 8043 (French), 246 8045 (German).

The maps in this section of the Guide are based upon the Ordnance Survey of Great Britain with the permission of the Controller of Her Majesty's Stationery Office. Crown Copyright reserved.

SIGHTS

HISTORIC BUILDINGS AND MONUMENTS

Palace of Westminster★★★ p. 9 NX — Tower of London★★★ p. 10 QU — Banqueting House★★ p. 9 NV — Buckingham Palace★★ p. 16 BV — Kensington Palace★★ p. 8 JV — Lincoln's Inn★★ p. 17 FV — London Bridge★★ p. 10 QV — Royal Hospital Chelsea★★ p. 15 FU — St. Jame's Palace★★ p. 13 EP — South Bank Arts Centre★★ p. 9 NV — The Temple★★ p. 5 NU — Tower Bridge★★ p. 10 QV — Albert Memorial★ p. 14 CQ — Apsley House★ p. 12 BP — George Inn★, Southwark p. 10 QV — Guildhall★ p. 6 PT — Dr Johnson's House★ p. 6 PTU A — Leighton House★ p. 7 GX — The Monument★ (❋★) p. 6 QU G — Royal Opera Arcade★ p. 13 FGN — Staple Inn★ p. 5 NT Y.

CHURCHES

The City Churches

St. Paul's Cathedral★★★ p. 6 PU — St. Bartholomew the Great★★ p. 6 PT K — St. Mary-at-Hill★★ p. 6 QU B — Temple Church★★ p. 5 NU — All Hallows-by-the-Tower (font cover★★, brasses★) p. 6 QU Y — St. Bride★ (steeple★★) p. 6 PU J — St. Giles Cripplegate★ p. 6 PT N — St. Helen Bishopsgate★ (monuments★★) p. 6 QTU R — St. James Garlickhythe (tower and spire★, sword rests★) p. 6 PU R — St. Margaret Lothbury★ p. 6 QT s — St. Margaret Pattens (woodwork★) p. 6 QU N — St. Mary Abchurch★ p. 6 QU X — St. Mary-le-Bow (tower and steeple★★) p. 6 PU G — St. Michael Paternoster Royal (tower and spire★) p. 6 PU D — St. Olave★ p. 6 QU S.

Other Churches

Westminster Abbey★★★ p. 9 MX — Southwark Cathedral★★ p. 10 QV — Queen's Chapel★ p. 13 EP — St. Clement Danes★ p. 17 FV — St. Jame's★ p. 13 EM — St. Margaret's★ p. 9 NX A — St. Martin in-the-Fields★ p. 17 DX — St. Paul's★ (Covent Garden) p. 17 DV — Westminster Roman Catholic Cathedral★ p. 9 MX B.

STREETS — SQUARES — PARKS

The City★★★ p. 6 PU — Regent's Park★★★ (Terraces★★, Zoo★★★) p. 4 KS — Bedford Square★★ p. 5 MT — Belgrave Square★★ p. 16 AV — Burlington Arcade★★ p. 13 DM — Hyde Park★★ p. 8 JU — The Mall★★ p. 13 FP — Picadilly★★ p. 13 EM — St. Jame's Park★★ p. 9 MV — Trafalgar Square★★ p. 17 DX — Whitehall★★ (Horse Guards★) p. 9 MV — Barbican★ p. 6 PT — Bond Street★ pp. 12-13 CK-DM — Charing Cross★ p. 17 DX — Cheyne Walk★ p. 8 JZ — Jermyn Street★ p. 13 EN — Piccadilly Arcade★ p. 13 DEN — Queen Anne's Gate★ p. 9 MX — Regent Street★ p. 13 EM — St. Jame's Square★ p. 13 FN — St. Jame's Street★ p. 13 EN — Shepherd Market★ p. 12 CN — Strand★ p. 17 DX — Victoria Embankment★ p. 17 EX — Waterloo Place★ p. 13 FN.

MUSEUMS

British Museum★★★ p. 5 MT — National Gallery★★★ p. 13 GM — Science Museum★★★ p. 14 CR — Tate Gallery★★★ p. 9 MY — Victoria and Albert Museum★★★ p. 15 DR — Courtauld Institute Galleries★★ p. 5 MT M — Museum of London★★ p. 6 PT M — National Portrait Gallery★★ p. 13 GM — Natural History Museum★★ p. 14 CS — Queen's Gallery★★ p. 16 BV — Wallace Collection★★ p. 12 AH — Imperial War Museum★ p. 10 PX — London Transport Museum★ p. 17 EV — Madame Tussaud's★ p. 4 KT M — Sir John Soane's Museum★ p. 5 NT M — Wellington Museum★ p. 12 BP.

■ ALPHABETICAL LIST OF AREAS INCLUDED

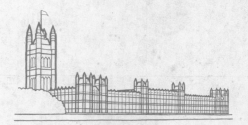

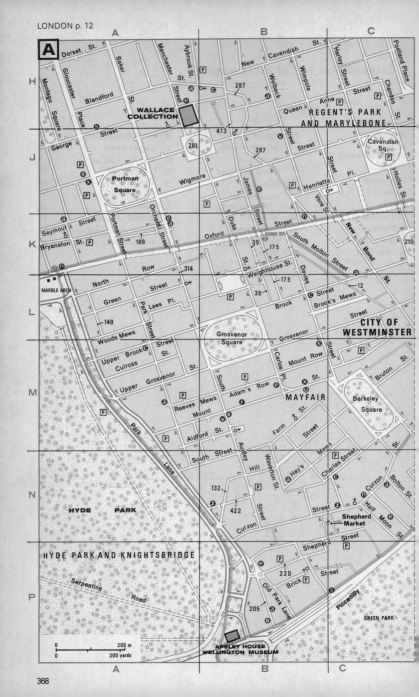

A

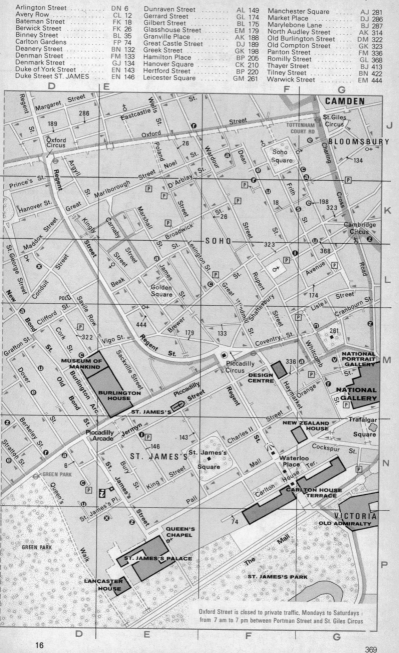

Oxford Street is closed to private traffic, Mondays to Saturdays ; from 7 am to 7 pm between Portman Street and St. Giles Circus

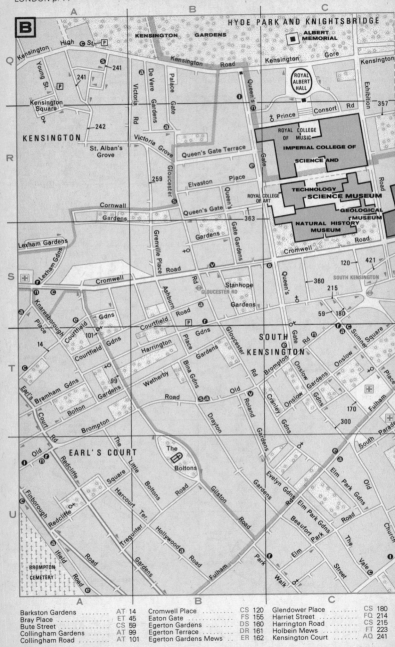

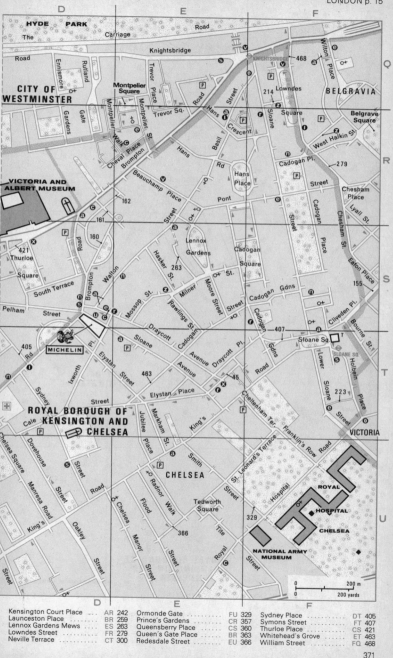

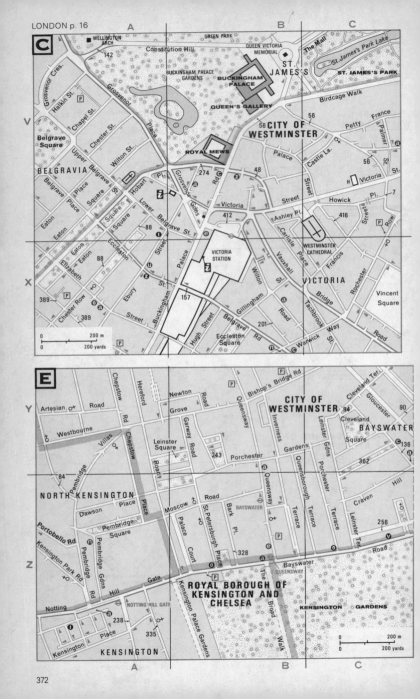

C

WELLINGTON ARCH

142

Constitution Hill

GREEN PARK

QUEEN VICTORIA MEMORIAL

The Mall

St. James's Park Lake

ST. JAMES'S

ST. JAMES'S PARK

Grosvenor Cres.

Halkin St.

Chapel St.

Chester St.

Wilton St.

Upper Belgrave

Grosvenor

Place

BUCKINGHAM PALACE GARDENS

BUCKINGHAM PALACE

QUEEN'S GALLERY

Birdcage Walk

56

CITY OF WESTMINSTER

56

Petty

France

Palmer

St.

Palace

Castle La.

56

V

Belgrave Square

BELGRAVIA

Belgrave Place

Belgrave Place

Eaton Square

Eaton Place

Eaton Place

Elizabeth

88

88

Eccleston

ROYAL MEWS

274

Hobart Pl.

Grosvenor Gdns.

Lower Belgrave St.

Victoria

412

48

Street

Ashley Pl.

Carlisle Place

WESTMINSTER CATHEDRAL

Francis

Street

Victoria

Howick Pl.

416

7

Rochester

Row

X

389

Chester Row

389

Eaton

Street

Ebury

Buckingham

Street

Palace

Road

VICTORIA STATION

157

Wilton St.

Vauxhall

Belgrave Rd

201

Gillingham

Street

Eccleston Square

Warwick St.

Bridge

Tachbrook St.

Road

VICTORIA

Vincent Square

Way

Road

0 ——— 200 m
0 ——— 200 yards

E

Artesian

Road

Chepstow Rd

Hereford Rd

Newton

Road

Grove

Garway

Road

Queensway

Inverness

Bishop's Bridge Rd

CITY OF WESTMINSTER

94

Cleveland Square

Leinster Gdns

Cleveland Terr.

Gloucester

90

BAYSWATER

136

Y

Westbourne

Chepstow Villas

Leinster Square

243

Porchester

Gardens

Queensborough Terrace

Porchester Terrace

362

84

Pembridge

NORTH KENSINGTON

Dawson

Place

Pembridge

Square

Chepstow Road

Moscow Road

St Petersburgh Place

Palace

Court

Bark

Pl.

Road

BAYSWATER

Queensway

Terrace

Leinster Terr.

Craven

Hill

256

Portobello Rd

Kensington Park Rd

Pembridge Gdns

Pembridge Rd

Pembridge

Square

Hill

328

Gate

The Broad Walk

Bayswater

QUEENSWAY

Road

V

Z

Notting

NOTTING HILL GATE

238

335

Kensington

Place

KENSINGTON

Notting Hill Gate

Kensington Palace Gardens

ROYAL BOROUGH OF KENSINGTON AND CHELSEA

KENSINGTON GARDENS

0 ——— 200 m
0 ——— 200 yards

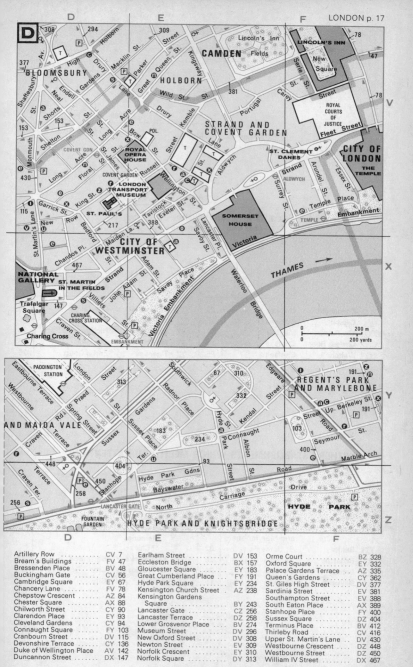

■ **STARRED ESTABLISHMENTS IN LONDON**

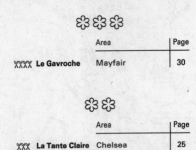

ఘ ఘ ఘ

	Area	Page
XXXX **Le Gavroche**	Mayfair	30

ఘ ఘ

	Area	Page
XXX **La Tante Claire**	Chelsea	25
XX **Chez Nico**	Battersea	28

ఘ

	Area	Page		Area	Page
🏰 **Connaught**	Mayfair	29	XXXX **Le Soufflé**	Mayfair	30
🏛 **Capital**	Chelsea	25	XX **L'Arlequin**	Battersea	28
XXXXX **The Terrace**	Mayfair	30	XX **Lichfield's**	Richmond	28
XXXX **Chelsea Room**	Chelsea	25	XX **Ma Cuisine**	Chelsea	26
XXXX **Waltons**	Chelsea	25	XX **Tiger Lee**	Earl's Court	26

■ **FURTHER ESTABLISHMENTS WHICH MERIT YOUR ATTENTION**

M

XXX **Odins**	Regent's Park and Marylebone	31	XX **Ken Lo's Memories of China**	Victoria	34
XXX **Suntory**	St. James's	32			
XX **Bagatelle**	Chelsea	25	XX **Lampwicks**	Battersea	28
XX **Eatons**	Victoria	34	XX **Le Poulbot**	City	24
XX **Gavvers**	Chelsea	25	X **Bubb's**	City	24

■ RESTAURANTS CLASSIFIED ACCORDING TO TYPE

BISTRO

WESTMINSTER (City of)
Victoria   ✗   **Bumbles**   p. 34

DANCING

WESTMINSTER (City of)
Mayfair   ✗✗✗   **Tiberio**   p. 30

SEAFOOD

CITY OF LONDON
City of London   ✗✗✗   **Wheeler's**   p. 24
—   ✗✗   **Bill Bentley's**   p. 24

KENSINGTON & CHELSEA (Royal Borough of)
Chelsea   ✗✗   **Poissonnerie de l'Avenue**   p. 26
Earl's Court   ✗✗   **Croisette (La)**   p. 26
—   ✗✗   ❀ **Tiger Lee**   p. 26
Kensington   ✗✗   **Quai St. Pierre (Le)**   p. 27

WESTMINSTER (City of)
Mayfair   ✗✗✗✗   **Scott's**   p. 30
—   ✗✗   **Golden Carp**   p. 30
Strand & Covent Garden   ✗✗   **Frère Jacques**   p. 33
—   ✗✗   **Sheekey's**   p. 33
—   ✗   **Grimes**   p. 33

CHINESE

KENSINGTON & CHELSEA (Royal Borough of)
Chelsea   ✗✗✗   **Zen**   p. 25
—   ✗✗   **Good Earth**   p. 26
—   ✗✗   **Good Earth**   p. 26
Earl's Court   ✗✗   ❀ **Tiger Lee**   p. 26
Kensington   ✗✗   **Mama San**   p. 27
South Kensington   ✗✗   **Zen Too**   p. 28

WESTMINSTER (City of)
Hyde Park & Knightsbridge   ✗✗   **Mr. Chow**   p. 29
Mayfair   ✗✗   **Mr Kai**   p. 30
Soho   ✗   **Gallery Rendezvous**   p. 32
Strand & Covent Garden   ✗   **Poons of Covent Garden**   p. 33
Victoria   ✗✗   **Hunan**   p. 34
—   ✗✗   **Ken Lo's Memories of China**   p. 34

ENGLISH

KENSINGTON & CHELSEA (Royal Borough of)
Chelsea   ✗✗   **English Garden**   p. 26
—   ✗✗   **English House**   p. 26

WESTMINSTER (City of)
Strand & Covent Garden   ✗✗✗   **Simpson's-in-the-Strand**   p. 33
Victoria   ✗✗✗   **Lockets**   p. 34
—   ✗   **Tate Gallery Rest.**   p. 34

INDIAN & PAKISTANI (continued)	WESTMINSTER (City of)			
	Bayswater	XXX	**Bombay Palace**	p. 29
	Belgravia	XX	**Salloos**	p. 29
	Hyde Park & Knightsbridge	XXX	**Shezan**	p. 29
	Mayfair	XX	**Gaylord**	p. 30
	Soho	XX	**Red Fort**	p. 32
		X	**Trusha**	p. 32
	Strand & Covent Garden	X	**Taste of India**	p. 33
	Victoria	XXX	**Kundan**	p. 34

ITALIAN	CITY OF LONDON			
	City of London	XXX	**City Tiberio**	p. 24
	—	XX	**Villa Augusta**	p. 24
	KENSINGTON & CHELSEA (Royal Borough of)			
	Chelsea	XX	**Eleven Park Walk**	p. 25
	—	XX	**Mario**	p. 25
	—	XX	**Meridiana**	p. 26
	—	XX	**Ponte Nuovo**	p. 26
	—	XX	**Toto**	p. 26
	—	XX	**Villa Puccini**	p. 26
	Kensington	XX	**Al Gallo d'Oro**	p. 27
	—	XX	**Topo d'Oro**	p. 27
	—	XX	**Trattoo**	p. 27
	WESTMINSTER (City of)			
	Bayswater & Maida Vale	XX	**San Marino**	p. 29
	—	XX	**Trat-West**	p. 29
	Hyde Park & Knightsbridge	XX	**Montpeliano**	p. 29
	Mayfair	XXX	**Cecconi's**	p. 30
	—	XXX	**Tiberio**	p. 30
	—	XX	**Apicella**	p. 30
	—	X	**Trattoria Fiori**	p. 30
	Regent's Park & Marylebone	XX	**Loggia (La)**	p. 31
	Soho	XXX	**Leonis Quo Vadis**	p. 32
	—	XX	**Rugantino**	p. 32
	—	XX	**Terrazza (La)**	p. 32
	—	XX	**Venezia**	p. 32
	—	X	**Romeo e Giulietta**	p. 32
	—	X	**Trattoria Imperia**	p. 32
	Strand & Covent Garden	XX	**Luigi's**	p. 33
	—	X	**Colosseo**	p. 33
	—	X	**Laguna**	p. 33
	Victoria	XX	**Gran Paradiso**	p. 34
	—	X	**Fontana (La)**	p. 34
	—	X	**Mimmo d'Ischia**	p. 34
	—	X	**Villa Medici**	p. 34

JAPANESE	CITY OF LONDON			
	City of London	X	**Ginnan**	p. 24
	WESTMINSTER (City of)			
	Mayfair	XX	**One Two Three**	p. 30
	—	XX	**Miyama**	p. 30
	—	XX	**Shogun**	p. 30
	—	X	**Ikeda**	p. 30
	Regent's Park & Marylebone	XX	**Asuka**	p. 31
	St. James's	XXX	**Suntory**	p. 32
	Soho	XX	**Fuji**	p. 32
	Strand & Covent Garden	XX	**Azami**	p. 33

LONDON AIRPORTS

Heathrow Middx. W : 17 m. by A 4, M 4 – Underground Piccadilly line direct – 404 @ – ✪ 01.

✈ ℘ 759 4321, Telex 934892.

🏨 **Sheraton Skyline,** Bath Rd, Harlington, Hayes, UB3 5BP, ℘ 759 2535, Telex 934254, « Exotic indoor garden with 🎐 » – ☆ 🔟 🍽 🖥 😣 🅿. 🖪. 🔄 🅰🅴 ⓞ 🆅🆂🅰. 🗫
M 14.95 **st.** ⓙ 4.95 – ⌧ 6.10 – **354 rm** 55.00/74.00 **s.**

🏨 **Excelsior** (T.H.F.), Bath Rd, West Drayton, UB7 0DU, ℘ 759 6611, Telex 24525, ⊒ heated – ☆ 🔟 🍽 🖥 😣 🅿. 🖪. 🔄 🅰🅴 ⓞ 🆅🆂🅰
M 8.95 **st.** ⓙ 2.60 – ⌧ 5.50 – **609 rm** 49.50/56.50 **st.**

🏨 **Heathrow Penta,** Bath Rd, Hounslow, TW6 2AQ, ℘ 897 6363, Telex 934660, ≼, 🎐 – ☆ 🔄 🔟 😣 🅿. 🖪. 🔄 🅰🅴 ⓞ 🆅🆂🅰
M 9.50/10.50 **st.** ⓙ 2.50 – ⌧ 5.50 – **670 rm** 58.65/73.60 **st.**

🏨 Holiday Inn, Stockley Rd, West Drayton, UB7 9NA, ℘ 0895 (West Drayton) 445555, Telex 934518, 🎐, 🗫 – ☆ 🔟 😣 🅿. 🖪. 🔄 🅰🅴 ⓞ 🆅🆂🅰
⌧ 4.20 – **400 rm** 48.30/56.75 **st.**

🏨 **Sheraton Heathrow,** Colnbrook by-pass, West Drayton, UB7 0HJ, ℘ 759 2424, Telex 934331, 🎐 – ☆ 🔄 🔟 😣 🅿. 🖪. 🔄 🅰🅴 ⓞ 🆅🆂🅰. 🗫
M a la carte 10.40/14.80 **st.** ⓙ 3.00 – ⌧ 5.25 – **440 rm** 37.00/58.50 **s.**

🏨 **Skyway** (T.H.F.), 140 Bath Rd, Hayes, UB3 5AW, ℘ 759 6311, Telex 23935, ⊒ heated – ☆ 🔄 🔟 😣 🅿. 🖪. 🔄 🅰🅴 ⓞ 🆅🆂🅰
M (closed Saturday lunch) 7.95 **st.** ⓙ 2.60 – ⌧ 5.50 – **440 rm** 40.00/47.00 **st.**

🏨 **Post House** (T.H.F.), Sipson Rd, West Drayton, UB7 0JU, ℘ 759 2323, Telex 934280 – ☆ 🔄 🔟 😣 🅿. 🖪. 🔄 🅰🅴 ⓞ 🆅🆂🅰
M a la carte 11.20/12.95 **st.** ⓙ 3.50 – ⌧ 5.00 – **580 rm** 45.00/52.00 **st.**

🏨 **Crest** (Crest), Bath Rd, Longford, West Drayton, UB7 0EQ, ℘ 759 2400, Telex 934093 – ☆ 🔟 😣 🅿. 🖪. 🔄 🅰🅴 ⓞ 🆅🆂🅰
M approx. 11.00 **st.** – ⌧ 5.25 – **360 rm** 45.00/55.00 **st.**

🏨 **Ariel** (T.H.F.), Bath Rd, Hayes, UB3 5AJ, ℘ 759 2552, Telex 21777 – ☆ 🔟 🚻wc ☎ 🖐 🅿. 🖪. 🔄 🅰🅴 ⓞ 🆅🆂🅰
M 7.95/8.95 **st.** ⓙ 2.75 – ⌧ 5.25 – **178 rm** 42.00/48.00 **st.**

🏨 **Arlington,** Shepiston Lane, Hayes, UB3 1LP, ℘ 573 6162 – 🔟 🚻wc 🚻wc ☎ 🅿. 🖪. 🔄 🅰🅴 ⓞ 🆅🆂🅰
M (closed Saturday lunch) 7.00/17.00 **t.** – ⌧ 3.50 – **80 rm** 32.00/40.00 **st.** – SB (weekends only) 42.00/47.00 **st.**

Gatwick West Sussex S : 28 m. by A 23 and M 23 – Train from Victoria : Gatwick Express 404 T 30 – ✪ 0293 Crawley.

✈ ℘ 28822 and ℘ 01 (London) 668 4211.

🏨 **Gatwick Hilton International,** Gatwick Airport, ✉ West Sussex, RH6 0LL, ℘ 518080, Telex 877021, 🎐 – ☆ 🔄 🔟 😣 🅿. 🖪. 🔄 🅰🅴 ⓞ 🆅🆂🅰. 🗫
M (buffet lunch Saturday) a la carte 9.05/14.85 **st.** ⓙ 4.75 – ⌧ 5.25 – **333 rm** 48.65/74.50 **t.**

🏨 **Gatwick Penta,** Povey Cross Rd, ✉ Surrey, RH6 0BE, ℘ 5533, Telex 87440 – ☆ 🔟 ☎ 🖐 🅿. 🖪. 🔄 🅰🅴 ⓞ 🆅🆂🅰. 🗫
M 7.50/9.95 **st.** ⓙ 3.95 – ⌧ 4.95 – **260 rm** 44.00/62.00 **st.**

🏨 **Post House** (T.H.F.), Povey Cross Rd, ✉ Surrey, RH6 0BA, ℘ 71621, Telex 877351, ⊒ heated – ☆ 🔟 😣 🅿. 🖪. 🔄 🅰🅴 ⓞ 🆅🆂🅰
M (closed Saturday lunch) 7.25/9.75 **st.** ⓙ 2.60 – ⌧ 5.50 – **149 rm** 41.00/52.50 **st.**

🏨 Gatwick Moat House (Q.M.H.), Longbridge Roundabout, ✉ Surrey, RH6 0AB, ℘ 5599, Telex 877138 – ☆ 🔟 🚻wc ☎ 🖐 🅿. 🖪
122 rm.

CAMDEN Except where otherwise stated see pp. 3-6.

Bloomsbury – ✉ NW1/W1/WC1.

🏨 **Russell** (T.H.F.), Russell Sq., WC1B 5BE, ℘ 837 6470, Telex 24615 – ☆ 🔟 ☎. 🖪. 🔄 🅰🅴 ⓞ 🆅🆂🅰   NT o
M (carving rest.) 8.95 **st.** ⓙ 2.60 – ⌧ 6.00 – **318 rm** 44.50/55.00 **st.**

🏨 **Grafton,** 130 Tottenham Court Rd, W1P 9HP, ℘ 388 4131, Telex 297234 – ☆ 🔟 ☎. 🖪. 🔄 🅰🅴 ⓞ 🆅🆂🅰   LT n
M 10.50 **t.** ⓙ 3.00 – ⌧ 6.50 – **171 rm** 55.90/73.90 **st.**

🏨 **Kenilworth,** 97 Great Russell St., WC1B 3LB, ℘ 637 3477 – ☆ 🔟 ☎. 🖪. 🔄 🅰🅴 ⓞ 🆅🆂🅰   MT a
M 10.00 **st.** – ⌧ 5.50 – **182 rm** 44.90/59.90 **st.**

🏨 **Bonnington,** 92 Southampton Row, WC1B 4BH, ℘ 242 2828, Telex 261591 – ☆ 🔟 🚻wc ☎. 🖪. 🔄 🅰🅴 ⓞ 🆅🆂🅰   NT s
M (grill rest. only) (buffet lunch) 8.00 **st.** ⓙ 2.60 – **245 rm** ⌧ 25.50/49.50 **st.**

XXX White Tower, 1 Percy St., W1P 0ET, ℰ 636 8141, Greek rest. – 🔄 AE ⓪ *VISA*   MT u
closed Saturday, Sunday, 3 weeks August, 1 week Christmas and Bank Holidays – **M** a la
carte 12.50/23.00 **t.** 🍷 3.00.

XXX Rue St. Jacques, 5 Charlotte St., ℰ 637 0222 – 🍽 🔄 AE ⓪ *VISA*   MT c
closed Saturday, Sunday, Easter, 3 weeks August, Christmas, New Year and Bank Holidays
– **M** a la carte 13.95/26.30 **t.**

XXX L'Etoile, 30 Charlotte St., W1P 1HJ, ℰ 636 7189, French rest. – AE ⓪ *VISA*   LT e
closed Saturday, Sunday, August and Bank Holidays – **M** a la carte approx. 18.00 **t.**

XX Porte de la Cité, 65 Theobalds Rd, WC1 8TA, ℰ 242 1154, French rest. – 🔄 AE ⓪ *VISA*
closed Saturday, Sunday and Bank Holidays – **M** (lunch only) 14.50 **t.** 🍷 2.85.   NT c

XX Lal Qila, 117 Tottenham Court Rd, W1P 9HL, ℰ 387 4570, Indian rest. – 🔄 AE ⓪ *VISA*
M a la carte 4.45/6.95 **t.**   LT u

XX Les Halles, 57 Theobald's Rd, WC1X 8SP, ℰ 242 6761, French rest. – 🔄 AE ⓪ *VISA*
closed Saturday lunch and Sunday – **M** a la carte 10.10/13.40 **t.** 🍷 3.50.   NT e

X Mon Plaisir, 21 Monmouth St., WC2H 9DD, ℰ 836 7243, French rest.   p. 17 DV a
closed Saturday lunch, Sunday, Easter, Christmas-New Year and Bank Holidays – **M** a la
carte 5.90/11.60 **t.** 🍷 3.50.

Euston – ✉ NW1.

🏨 Kennedy (Mt. Charlotte), 43 Cardington St., NW1 2LP, ℰ 387 4400, Telex 28250 – 📶 📺
⭲wc ☎ 🔄 AE ⓪ *VISA* ⚄   LS r
M 6.75/7.50 **st.** 🍷 2.90 – ⲷ 2.50 – **320 rm** 41.25/52.25 **st.**

Finchley Road – ✉ NW1/NW3.

🏨 Charles Bernard, 5 Frognal, NW3 6AL, ℰ 794 0101, Telex 23560 – 📶 📺 ⭲wc 🅿
🔄 AE ⓪ *VISA*   GR s
M (dinner only) a la carte 6.25/10.00 **st.** 🍷 2.60 – **57 rm** ⲷ 34.50/49.00 **st.**

XX Capability Brown, 351 West End Lane, NW6 1LT, ℰ 794 3234 – 🔄 AE ⓪ *VISA*
closed Saturday lunch, Sunday and Bank Holidays – **M** a la carte 9.00/16.00 **st.** 🍷 2.55.

Hampstead – ✉ NW3.

🏨 Ladbroke Clive (Ladbroke), Primrose Hill Rd, NW3 3NA, ℰ 586 2233, Telex 22759 – 📶
📺 🔄 AE ⚄   KR a
M *(closed lunch Saturday and Bank Holidays)* 9.00 **t.** 🍷 3.25 – ⲷ 5.50 – **84 rm** 42.00/52.00 **t.**

🏨 Swiss Cottage, 4 Adamson Rd, NW3 3HP, ℰ 722 2281, Telex 297232, « Antique furniture collection » – 📶 📺 ⭲wc 📶wc ☎ 🔄 AE ⓪ *VISA* ⚄   JR n
M 5.50/8.00 **t.** 🍷 2.00 – **65 rm** ⲷ 30.00/60.00 **t.**

🏨 Post House (T.H.F.), 215 Haverstock Hill, NW3 4RB, ℰ 794 8121, Telex 262494 – 📶 📺
⭲wc 🅿 🔄 AE ⓪ *VISA*   GR r
M 8.00 **st.** 🍷 2.85 – ⲷ 5.50 – **140 rm** 41.00/48.50 **st.**

XXX Keats, 3-4 Downshire Hill, NW3 1NR, ℰ 435 3544, French rest. – 🔄 AE ⓪ *VISA*   GR i
closed Sunday and 3 weeks August – **M** (dinner only) a la carte 17.50/23.00 **st.** 🍷 8.00.

Holborn – ✉ WC2.

🏨 Drury Lane Moat House (Q.M.H.), 10 Drury Lane, High Holborn, WC2B 5RE, ℰ
836 6666, Telex 8811395 – 📶 📺 🔄 AE ⓪ *VISA* ⚄   p. 17 DV c
M 9.75 **st.** 🍷 3.25 – ⲷ 6.25 – **128 rm** 55.00/73.00 **st.** – SB 67.00/73.00 **st.**

XXX L'Opera, 32 Great Queen St., WC2B 5AA, ℰ 405 9020 – 🔄 AE ⓪ *VISA*   p. 17 EV n
closed Saturday lunch and Sunday – **M** a la carte 11.70/15.60 **t.** 🍷 2.50.

X Last Days of the Raj, 22 Drury Lane, WC2, ℰ 836 1628, Indian rest.   p. 17 DV s

King's Cross – ✉ N1.

🏨 Great Northern, N1 9AN, ℰ 837 5454, Telex 299041 – 📶 📺 ⭲wc 🅿 🔄 AE ⓪
VISA ⚄   MNS s
closed Christmas – **M** (carving rest.) 6.25 **st.** – **79 rm** ⲷ 29.50/59.50 **st.** – SB (weekends only) 49.00/56.00 **st.**

Regent's Park – ✉ NW1.

🏨 White House (Rank), Albany St., NW1 3UP, ℰ 387 1200, Telex 24111 – 📶 📺 ☎ 👍 🔄
🔄 AE ⓪ *VISA*   LS o
M a la carte 7.30/19.25 **t.** 🍷 3.50 – ⲷ 5.75 – **587 rm** 48.00/70.00 **t.**

XX Pratts, Commercial Pl., Camden Lock, NW1 8AF, ℰ 485 9987 – 🔄 AE ⓪ *VISA*   LR a
closed Sunday dinner and 25-26 December – **M** a la carte 11.90/14.90 **t.** 🍷 2.50.

X Chalcot's Bistro, 49 Chalcot Rd, Primrose Hill, NW1 8LS, ℰ 722 1956 – 🔄 ⓪ *VISA*
closed Saturday lunch, Sunday dinner, Monday, Easter, Christmas and Bank Holidays –
M a la carte 8.45/15.75 **t.** 🍷 3.50.   KR u

Swiss Cottage – ✉ NW3.

🏨 **Holiday Inn,** 128 King Henry's Rd, NW3 3ST, ☎ 722 7711, Telex 267396, ⬚ – 🛗 📺 ☎
& 🅿 🔄 🔼 🖭 ⓪ 𝘝𝘐𝘚𝘈   JR a
M 11.75 (wine included)/12.00 **t.** – ☵ 5.75 – **291 rm** 54.00/68.00 **s.**

✕✕ **Peter's,** 65 Fairfax Rd, NW6 4EE, ☎ 624 5804 – 🔼 🖭 ⓪ 𝘝𝘐𝘚𝘈   JR i
closed Saturday lunch and Sunday dinner – **M** a la carte 10.20/13.15 **t.** 🍷 2.35.

CITY OF LONDON Except where otherwise stated see p. 6.

🛈 St. Paul's Churchyard, EC4, ☎ 606 3030 ext 2456.

✕✕✕ **Wheeler's,** 33 Foster Lane, EC2V 6HD, ☎ 606 0896, Seafood   PT o

✕✕✕ **City Tiberio,** 8-11 Lime St., EC3M 7AA, ☎ 623 3616, Italian rest. – 🔼 🖭 ⓪ 𝘝𝘐𝘚𝘈   QU i
closed Saturday, Sunday and Bank Holidays – **M** (lunch only) a la carte 9.50/14.30 **t.**
🍷 2.50.

✕✕ **Le Poulbot** (basement), 45 Cheapside, EC2V 6AR, ☎ 236 4379, French rest. – ▦. 🔼 🖭
⓪ 𝘝𝘐𝘚𝘈   PU i
closed Saturday, Sunday and Bank Holidays – **M** (lunch only) 24.50 **st.**

✕✕ **Bill Bentley's,** Swedeland Court, 202-204 Bishopsgate, EC2M 4NR, ☎ 283 1763, Seafood
– 🔼 ⓪ 𝘝𝘐𝘚𝘈   QT e
closed Saturday, Sunday and Bank Holidays – **M** (lunch only) a la carte 12.70/19.05 **t.**
🍷 2.85.

✕✕ **Shares,** 12-13 Lime St., EC3M 7AA, ☎ 623 1843 – 🔼 🖭 ⓪ 𝘝𝘐𝘚𝘈   QU s
closed Saturday, Sunday and Bank Holidays – **M** (lunch only) 18.50 **t.**

✕✕ **Villa Augusta,** Bucklersbury House, Queen Victoria St., EC4 9XX, ☎ 248 0095, Italian
rest. – 🔼 🖭 ⓪ 𝘝𝘐𝘚𝘈   PQU x
closed Saturday, Sunday and Bank Holidays – **M** (lunch only) a la carte 9.50/14.30 **t.**
🍷 2.50.

✕ **La Bourse Plate,** 78 Leadenhall St., EC3, ☎ 623 5159 – 🔼 🖭 ⓪ 𝘝𝘐𝘚𝘈   QU v
closed Saturday and Sunday – **M** (lunch only) 14.50 **st.** 🍷 2.95.

✕ **Bubb's,** 329 Central Market, Farringdon St., EC1A 9NB, ☎ 236 2435, French rest.   PT a
closed Saturday, Sunday, August and Bank Holidays – **M** (booking essential) a la carte
11.75/13.60 **t.** 🍷 3.50.

✕ **Le Gamin,** 32 Old Bailey, EC4M 7HS, ☎ 236 7931, French rest. – 🔼 🖭 ⓪ 𝘝𝘐𝘚𝘈   PU x
closed Saturday, Sunday and Bank Holidays – **M** (lunch only) 16.75 **st.**

✕ **Ginnan,** 5 Cathedral Pl., St. Paul's, EC4M 7EA, ☎ 236 4120, Japanese rest. – 🔼 🖭 ⓪
𝘝𝘐𝘚𝘈   PT e
closed Saturday dinner, Sunday and Bank Holidays – **M** a la carte 7.50/13.90 **t.** 🍷 3.50.

ISLINGTON pp. 3-6.

Canonbury – ✉ N1.

✕ **Anna's Place,** 90 Mildmay Park, N1, ☎ 249 9379
closed Sunday, Monday, 2 weeks at Easter, August and 2 weeks at Christmas – **M**
(booking essential) (dinner only) a la carte 11.60/15.75 **t.**

Finsbury – ✉ WC1/EC1.

🏨 **Royal Scot Thistle** (Thistle), 100 King's Cross Rd, WC1X 9QT, ☎ 278 2434, Telex 27657
– 🛗 🖨 📺 🚽wc ☎ 🔄 🔼 🖭 ⓪ 𝘝𝘐𝘚𝘈   NS n
M 9.00 **t.** 🍷 3.45 – ☵ 4.95 – **349 rm** 37.50/40.50 **t.** – SB (weekends only) 36.00 **st.**

🏨 London Ryan (Mt. Charlotte), Gwynne Pl., King Cross Rd, WC1X 9QN, ☎ 278 6628, Telex
27728 – 🛗 📺 🚽wc ☎ 🅿 🔼 🖭 ⓪ 𝘝𝘐𝘚𝘈 ⚡   NS a
201 rm ☵ 41.50/52.50.

✕✕ **Café St. Pierre,** 29 Clerkenwell Green (1st floor), EC1, ☎ 251 6606 – 🔼 🖭 ⓪ 𝘝𝘐𝘚𝘈
closed Sunday dinner, 25 December-1 January and Bank Holidays – **M** a la carte
15.40/20.55 **t.** 🍷 4.50.   PT c

Islington – ✉ N1.

✕✕ **Frederick's,** Camden Passage, N1 8EG, ☎ 359 2888, « Conservatory and walled
garden » – 🔼 🖭 ⓪ 𝘝𝘐𝘚𝘈   PR a
closed Sunday, 26 December and 1 January – **M** a la carte 10.95/17.30 **t.** 🍷 3.10.

In this Guide,
a symbol or a character, printed in red or **black**,
does not have the same meaning.
Please read the explanatory pages carefully.

KENSINGTON and CHELSEA (Royal Borough of).

Chelsea – ⊠ SW1/SW3/SW10 – Except where otherwise stated see pp. 14 and 15.

Hyatt Carlton Tower, 2 Cadogan Pl., SW1X 9PY, ℰ 235 5411, Telex 21944, ≤, 凩, ⚒ – ▮ 🖭 ⅣⅤ ☎ 𝐐. ᴀ. ❑ ᴀᴇ ⓞ 𝓥𝓘𝓢𝓐. ⅏   FR **n**
M (see **Chelsea Room** below) – **Rib Room** – ⊆ 7.25 – **228 rm** 110.00/145.00 t.

Sheraton Park Tower, 101 Knightsbridge, SW1X 7RN, ℰ 235 8050, Telex 915899 – ▮
🖭 ⅣⅤ 𝐐 🕭 🛇. ᴀ. ❑ ᴀᴇ 𝓥𝓘𝓢𝓐. ⅏   FQ **v**
M a la carte 15.00/22.00 t. – ⊆ 6.75 – **293 rm** 95.00/116.00 s.

❀ **Capital**, 22-24 Basil St., SW3 1AT, ℰ 589 5171, Telex 919042 – ▮ 🖭 ⅣⅤ ☎. ❑ ᴀᴇ
𝓥𝓘𝓢𝓐.   ER **a**
M 14.50/16.50 st. ⧍ 5.00 – ⊆ 5.95 – **60 rm** 79.35/105.80 st.
Spec. Salade de pigeon rosé aux deux choux, Médaillons de veau à la dariole niçoise, Marquise au chocolat blanc-sauce au café.

Cadogan Thistle (Thistle), 75 Sloane St., SW1X 9SG, ℰ 235 7141, Telex 267893 – ▮ ⅣⅤ
☎ 🛇. ❑ ᴀᴇ ⓞ 𝓥𝓘𝓢𝓐. ⅏   FR **e**
M a la carte 7.50/9.50 t. ⧍ 3.45 – ⊆ 5.25 – **68 rm** 53.00/79.00 t. – SB (weekends only) 62.00 st.

Holiday Inn, 17-25 Sloane St., SW1X 9NU, ℰ 235 4377, Telex 919111, 🔄 – ▮ ⅣⅤ ☎.
ᴀ. ❑ ᴀᴇ ⓞ 𝓥𝓘𝓢𝓐. ⅏   FR **r**
M 11.50/18.50 st. ⧍ 4.00 – ⊆ 6.00 – **206 rm** 81.65/98.90 st.

Basil Street, 8 Basil St., SW3 1AH, ℰ 581 3311, Telex 28379 – ▮ ⅣⅤ ☎. ᴀ. ❑ ᴀᴇ ⓞ
𝓥𝓘𝓢𝓐   FQ **o**
M a la carte 12.50/16.45 st. ⧍ 3.75 – ⊆ 4.85 – **96 rm** 33.00/72.50 st. – SB (weekends only)(winter only) 97.70 st.

Royal Court (Norfolk Cap.), Sloane Sq., SW1W 8EG, ℰ 730 9191, Telex 296818 – ▮ ⅣⅤ
☎ 🛇. ᴀ. ❑ ᴀᴇ ⓞ 𝓥𝓘𝓢𝓐. ⅏   FST **a**
M a la carte 13.85/18.05 st. ⧍ 3.00 – ⊆ 6.40 – **98 rm** 55.00/71.50 t. – SB (May-October) 72.60 st.

L'Hotel without rest., 28 Basil St., SW3 1AT, ℰ 589 6286, Telex 919042 – ▮ ⅣⅤ ⊟wc ☎
𝐐. ᴀᴇ. ⅏   ER **i**
12 rm 60.00 st.

Wilbraham, 1-5 Wilbraham Pl., Sloane St., SW1X 9AE, ℰ 730 8296 – ▮ ⊟wc ☎. ⅏
M (closed Sunday and Bank Holidays) (bar lunch) a la carte 4.50/8.15 t. ⧍ 2.60 – ⊆ 3.00 –
56 rm 22.00/40.00.   FS **n**

Fenja without rest., 69 Cadogan Gdns, SW3 2RB, ℰ 589 1183 – ▮ ⊟wc ☎. ❑ ᴀᴇ ⓞ
𝓥𝓘𝓢𝓐. ⅏   FS **r**
16 rm ⊆ 20.00/60.00 st. – SB (weekends only)(except summer) 53.00 st.

Willett without rest., 32 Sloane Gdns, Sloane Sq., SW1W 8DJ, ℰ 730 0634 – ⅣⅤ ⊟wc.
⅏   FT **s**
17 rm ⊆ 21.00/32.00 t.

XXXX ❀ **Chelsea Room** (at Hyatt Carlton Tower H.), 2 Cadogan Pl., SW1X 9PY, ℰ 235 5411 –
𝐐. ❑ ᴀᴇ ⓞ 𝓥𝓘𝓢𝓐. ⅏   FR **n**
closed Easter Monday and 1 to 3 January – **M** a la carte 19.00/28.00 t. ⧍ 4.70
Spec. Foie gras frais Richelieu, Fricassée de turbot et homard aux concombres, Filet d'agneau au basilic et tomate fraîche.

XXXX ❀ **Waltons**, 121 Walton St., SW3 2HP, ℰ 584 0204 – 🖭 ❑ ᴀᴇ ⓞ 𝓥𝓘𝓢𝓐   DS **a**
closed Christmas, 4 days at Easter and Bank Holidays – **M** a la carte 8.00/22.00 t.
Spec. A cushion of Scotch smoked salmon, Steamed sea bass with lobster-butter sauce, Praline mousse surprise.

XXX ❀❀ **La Tante Claire**, 68 Royal Hospital Rd, SW3 2HP, ℰ 352 6045, French rest. – ᴀᴇ
ⓞ   EU **c**
closed Saturday, Sunday, 10 days at Easter, 10 August-3 September, 24 December-2 January and Bank Holidays – **M** a la carte 22.00/25.20 st.
Spec. La terrine de poireaux et de langoustines, Le pied de cochon aux morilles, La croustade aux pommes.

XXX **Le Français**, 257-259 Fulham Rd, SW3 6HY, ℰ 352 4748, French rest. – ᴀᴇ 𝓥𝓘𝓢𝓐   CU **a**
closed Sunday, Christmas and Bank Holidays – **M** 12.00 s. ⧍ 4.20.

XXX **Zen**, Chelsea Cloisters, Sloane Av., SW3 3DW, ℰ 589 1781, Chinese rest. – ❑ ᴀᴇ ⓞ
𝓥𝓘𝓢𝓐   ET **a**
M a la carte 8.70/16.25 t.

XX **Daphne's**, 112 Draycott Av., SW3 3AE, ℰ 589 4257 – ❑ ᴀᴇ ⓞ 𝓥𝓘𝓢𝓐   DS **e**
closed Sunday and Bank Holidays – **M** (dinner only) a la carte 11.40/17.50 t. ⧍ 3.25.

XX **Eleven Park Walk**, 11 Park Walk, SW10, ℰ 352 3449, Italian rest. – ᴀᴇ   CU **r**
closed Sunday and Bank Holidays – **M** a la carte 10.80/15.10 t. ⧍ 2.50.

XX Mario, 260-262a Brompton Rd, SW3 2AS, ℰ 584 1724, Italian rest.   DS **n**

XX **Gavvers**, 61-63 Lower Sloane St., SW1W 8DH, ℰ 730 5983, French rest. – ⓞ   FT **e**
closed Sunday, July, August, 23 December-2 January and Bank Holidays – **M** (dinner only) 17.75 (wine included) st.

XX **Bagatelle**, 5 Langton St., SW10 0JL, ℰ 351 4185, French rest. – ❑ ᴀᴇ ⓞ 𝓥𝓘𝓢𝓐
closed Sunday and Bank Holidays – **M** a la carte 13.30/17.50 t. ⧍ 2.90.   pp. 7-10   JZ **u**

XX **Bewick's**, 87-89 Walton St., SW3 2HP, ✆ 584 6711 – 🆖 🆎 ⓪ 𝗩𝗜𝗦𝗔   ES n
closed lunch Saturday and Sunday, Easter and 24 December-2 January – **M** a la carte 15.70/20.95 **t.**

XX **Meridiana,** 169 Fulham Rd, SW3 6SP, ✆ 589 8815, Italian rest. – 🆖 🆎 ⓪ 𝗩𝗜𝗦𝗔   DT i
closed 25 December and Bank Holidays – **M** a la carte 12.85/17.50 **t.** ⓵ 3.00.

XX ✿ **Ma Cuisine,** 113 Walton St., SW3 2JY, ✆ 584 7585, French rest. – 🆎 ⓪   DS a
closed Saturday, Sunday, 13 July-12 August and Bank Holidays – **M** a la carte 12.00/16.20 **t.** ⓵ 3.75
Spec. Brouillade de langoustines à la menthe fraîche, Emincé d'agneau aux rognons et celeri, Mousse brûlée.

XX **Toto,** Walton House, Walton St., SW3 2JH, ✆ 589 0075, Italian rest. – 🆖 🆎 𝗩𝗜𝗦𝗔   ES s
closed Christmas – **M** a la carte 14.00/17.50 **t.** ⓵ 2.50.

XX **Good Earth,** 233 Brompton Rd, SW3 2EP, ✆ 584 3658, Chinese rest. – 🆖 🆎 ⓪ 𝗩𝗜𝗦𝗔
M a la carte 7.00/14.35 **t.**   DR c

XX **Good Earth,** 91 King's Rd, SW3, ✆ 352 9231, Chinese rest. – 🆖 🆎 ⓪ 𝗩𝗜𝗦𝗔   EU a
M a la carte 9.00/13.50 **t.** ⓵ 2.30.

XX **Ponte Nuovo,** 126 Fulham Rd, SW3, ✆ 370 6656, Italian rest. – 🆖 🆎 ⓪ 𝗩𝗜𝗦𝗔   CU e
closed Bank Holidays – **M** a la carte 11.50/15.00 **t.** ⓵ 3.20.

XX **Ménage à Trois,** 15 Beauchamp Pl., SW3 1NQ, ✆ 589 4252 – 🆖 🆎 ⓪ 𝗩𝗜𝗦𝗔   ER v
closed Saturday, Sunday and 25-26 December – **M** a la carte 8.65/23.00 **t.** ⓵ 3.00.

XX **English Garden,** 10 Lincoln St., SW3 2TS, ✆ 584 7272, English rest. – 🆖 🆎 ⓪ 𝗩𝗜𝗦𝗔   ET x
closed Christmas Day – **M** a la carte 12.50/17.75 **st.** ⓵ 3.25.

XX **English House,** 3 Milner St., SW3 2QA, ✆ 584 3002, English rest. – 🆖 🆎 ⓪ 𝗩𝗜𝗦𝗔   ES z
closed 25 and 26 December – **M** a la carte 15.25/19.75 **st.** ⓵ 3.50.

XX **Poissonnerie de l'Avenue,** 82 Sloane Av., SW3 3DZ, ✆ 589 2457, Seafood – 🆖 🆎 ⓪ 𝗩𝗜𝗦𝗔   DS u
closed Sunday, 2 weeks Christmas and Bank Holidays – **M** a la carte 10.50/16.30 **t.** ⓵ 3.50.

XX **St. Quentin,** 243 Brompton Rd, SW3 2EP, ✆ 589 8005, Telex 8814322, French rest. – 🆖 🆎 𝗩𝗜𝗦𝗔   DR a
closed 1 week at Christmas – **M** a la carte 10.00/15.30 **t.** ⓵ 4.20.

XX **Villa Puccini,** 5 Draycott Av., SW3, ✆ 584 4003, Italian rest. – 🆖 🆎 ⓪ 𝗩𝗜𝗦𝗔   ET r
M a la carte 7.85/12.35 **t.** ⓵ 2.85.

X **Dan's,** 119 Sydney St., SW3 6NR, ✆ 352 2718 – 🆎 ⓪ 𝗩𝗜𝗦𝗔   DU s
closed Saturday, Sunday and Bank Holidays – **M** a la carte 23.40/30.00 **t.** ⓵ 3.00.

X **Thierry's,** 342 King's Rd, SW3, ✆ 352 3365 – 🆎 ⓪ 𝗩𝗜𝗦𝗔   CU c
closed Sunday, Easter, 19 August-2 September, Christmas and Bank Holidays – **M** (restricted lunch) a la carte 10.75/13.85 **t.** ⓵ 2.75.

X **La Brasserie,** 272 Brompton Rd, SW3 2AW, ✆ 584 1668, French rest. – 🆖 🆎 ⓪ 𝗩𝗜𝗦𝗔   DS s
closed 25-26 December – **M** a la carte 9.10/12.30 **t.** ⓵ 2.70.

▐ **Earl's Court** ▌ – ✉ SW5/SW10 – Except where otherwise stated see pp. 14 and 15.

🏨 **Barkston,** 34-44 Barkston Gdns, SW5 0EW, ✆ 373 7851, Telex 8953154 – 📶 📺 ▭wc
☎ 🔓 🆖 🆎 ⓪ 𝗩𝗜𝗦𝗔   AT c
M (buffet lunch) a la carte 11.15/11.90 **st.** ⓵ 2.85 – ▭ 4.75 – **76 rm** 34.00/40.00 **st.**

🏨 **Hogarth,** 27-35 Hogarth Rd, SW5 0QQ, ✆ 370 6831, Telex 8951994 – 📶 ▭ rest 📺
▭wc ☎ 🅿 🆖 🆎 ⓪ ✖   AS a
closed 24 to 27 December – **M** 6.50/8.00 **st.** ⓵ 3.00 – ▭ 2.60 – **86 rm** 29.00/38.00 **st.**

🏠 **Town House,** 44-48 West Cromwell Rd, SW5 9QL, ✆ 373 4546, Telex 918554, ☞ – 📺
🎞wc ☎ 🆖 🆎 ⓪ 𝗩𝗜𝗦𝗔   HY o
M 6.50 **st.** ⓵ 2.75 – **40 rm** ▭ 24.00/39.00 **st.** – SB 48.00/74.00 **st.**

XXX **Martin's,** 88 Ifield Rd, SW10 9AD, ✆ 352 5641 – 🆖 𝗩𝗜𝗦𝗔   AU e
closed Sunday, last 2 weeks August, 24 to 31 December and Bank Holidays – **M** (dinner only) 17.50 **t.** ⓵ 4.00.

XX ✿ **Tiger Lee,** 251 Old Brompton Rd, SW5 9HP, ✆ 370 2323, Chinese rest., Seafood – ▤. 🆎 ⓪ 𝗩𝗜𝗦𝗔   AU n
closed Christmas Day – **M** (dinner only) a la carte 20.80/27.00 **t.**
Spec. Stuffed baby quail, Homard orientale, Tiger Lee sesame chicken.

XX **La Croisette,** 168 Ifield Rd, SW10 9AF, ✆ 373 3694, French rest., Seafood – 🆎   AU a
closed Tuesday lunch, Monday and 2 weeks at Christmas – **M** 18.00 **t.**

XX **L'Artiste Affamé,** 243 Old Brompton Rd, SW5 9HP, ✆ 373 1659 – 🆖 🆎 ⓪ 𝗩𝗜𝗦𝗔   AU r
closed Sunday and 24 to 26 December – **M** a la carte 9.45/13.25 **t.** ⓵ 2.55.

▐ **Kensington** ▌ – ✉ SW7/W8/W11/W14 – Except where otherwise stated see pp. 7-10.

🏰 **Royal Garden** (Rank), Kensington High St., W8 4PT, ✆ 937 8000, Telex 263151, ≤ – 📶
🔋 📺 ☎ 🔓 🆖 🆎 ⓪ 𝗩𝗜𝗦𝗔 ✖   pp. 14 and 15 AQ c
M Royal Roof *(closed Sunday and Bank Holidays)* (Dancing) a la carte 18.70/24.25 **st.**
⓵ 6.50 – ▭ 6.75 – **411 rm** 69.50/87.50 **st.**

🏰 **Kensington Palace Thistle** (Thistle), De Vere Gdns, W8 5AF, ✆ 937 8121, Telex 262422
– 📶 📺 ☎ 🔓 🆖 🆎 ⓪ 𝗩𝗜𝗦𝗔   pp. 14 and 15 BQ a
M 9.00/10.50 **t.** ⓵ 3.45 – ▭ 5.25 – **316 rm** 49.50/69.50 **t.** – SB (weekends only) 100.00 **st.**

🏨 **Hilton International,** 179-199 Holland Park Av., W11 4UL, ✆ 603 3355, Telex 919763 –
🛗 ▤ 📺 ☎ & 🅿 🔥 🛄 AE ① VISA 🍴
GV **s**
M a la carte 11.90/15.60 t. 🍷 2.80 – �деç 5.55 – **606 rm** 45.00/78.00 t.

🏨 **London Tara** (Best Western), Scarsdale Pl., W8 5SR, ✆ 937 7211, Telex 918834 – 🛗 ▤
📺 ☎ & 🅿 🔥 🛄 AE ① VISA 🍴
HX **u**
M 7.80 t. 🍷 3.30 – ⊇ 5.10 – **840 rm** 43.00/62.00 st. – SB (weekends only) 70.00 st.

🏨 **Kensington Close** (T.H.F.), Wrights Lane, W8 5SP, ✆ 937 8170, Telex 23914, ⃞ – 🛗
📺 ⟷ 🔥 🛄 AE ① VISA
HX **c**
M 5.95/9.45 st. 🍷 2.60 – ⊇ 5.25 – **530 rm** 40.00/49.00 st.

🏠 One-Two-Eight, 128-130 Holland Rd, W14 8BD, ✆ 602 3395, 🌿 – 🛗 🚿wc ☎. 🍴
GX **x**
28 rm

XX **La Pomme d'Amour,** 128 Holland Park Av., W11 4UE, ✆ 229 8532, French rest. – ⃞
AE ① VISA
GV **e**
closed Saturday lunch, Sunday and Bank Holidays – **M** a la carte 9.40/14.60 t. 🍷 2.60.

XX **Al Gallo d'Oro,** 353 Kensington High St., W8 6NW, ✆ 603 6951, Italian rest. – ⃞ ▤
AE ① VISA
GX **a**
closed Saturday lunch and Bank Holidays – **M** a la carte 9.45/13.30 t. 🍷 2.45.

XX **Mama San,** 11 Russell Gdns, W14, ✆ 602 0312, Chinese rest. – ⃞ AE ① VISA
GX **e**
closed Saturday lunch and Bank Holidays – **M** a la carte 9.50/13.80.

XX **Trattoo,** 2 Abingdon Rd, W8 6AF, ✆ 937 4448, Italian rest. – ⃞ AE ① VISA
HX **e**
closed Bank Holidays – **M** a la carte 8.80/11.20 t. 🍷 2.50.

XX **Topo d'oro,** 39 Uxbridge St., W8, ✆ 727 5813, Italian rest. – ⃞ AE ① VISA
closed 25-26 December and Bank Holidays for lunch – **M** a la carte 7.30/13.20 t. 🍷 2.20.
pp. 16 and 17   AZ **a**

XX **Le Quai St. Pierre,** 7 Stratford Rd, W8, ✆ 937 6388, French rest., Seafood
HX **r**
closed Monday lunch, Sunday and 2 weeks at Christmas – **M** a la carte 12.30/17.30 t.

North Kensington – ✉ W2/W10/W11 – Except where otherwise stated see pp. 3-6.

XXX **Leith's,** 92 Kensington Park Rd, W11 2PN, ✆ 229 4481 – ▤. ⃞ AE ① VISA
GU **e**
closed 26-27 August and 4 days at Christmas – **M** (dinner only) 24.00 st.

XX **Chez Moi,** 1 Addison Av., Holland Park, W11 4QS, ✆ 603 8267, French rest. – ⃞ AE ①
VISA
pp. 7-10   GV **n**
closed Sunday, Easter, 2 weeks August and 2 weeks at Christmas – **M** (dinner only) a la
carte 12.00/18.00 t. 🍷 4.00.

XX **Monsieur Thompsons,** 29 Kensington Park Rd, W11, ✆ 727 9957, French rest. – ⃞
AE ① VISA
GU **a**
closed Sunday, Christmas-New Year and Bank Holidays – **M** a la carte 15.80/24.00 t.

X **192,** 192 Kensington Park Rd, W11 2JF, ✆ 229 0482 – ⃞ AE VISA
GU **c**
closed Sunday dinner – **M** a la carte 7.60/13.20 t.

South Kensington – ✉ SW5/SW7/W8 – pp.14 and 15.

🏨 **Gloucester** (Rank), 4-18 Harrington Gdns, SW7 4LH, ✆ 373 6030, Telex 917505 – 🛗 ▤
📺 ☎ & 🅿 🔥 ⃞ AE ① VISA 🍴
BS **r**
M a la carte 14.00/18.45 st. 🍷 3.15 – ⊇ 6.75 – **531 rm** 80.00/90.00 t.

🏨 **John Howard** without rest., 4 Queen's Gate, SW7 5EH, ✆ 581 3011, Telex 8813397 – 🛗
▤ 📺 ☎. ⃞ AE ① VISA 🍴
BQ **i**
⊇ 6.50 – **44 rm** 45.00/82.50 st.

🏨 London International (Swallow), 147c Cromwell Rd, SW5 0TH, ✆ 370 4200, Telex 27260 –
🛗 📺 ☎ 🅿 🔥 – **415 rm**.
AS **c**

🏩 **Vanderbilt,** 76-86 Cromwell Rd, SW7 5BT, ✆ 589 2424, Telex 919867 – 🛗 📺 🚿wc
🚿wc ☎. ⃞ AE ① VISA
BS **v**
M 7.25 t. 🍷 3.00 – ⊇ 5.50 – **230 rm** 39.90/55.90 st.

🏩 **Embassy House** (Embassy), 31-33 Queen's Gate, SW7 5JA, ✆ 584 7222, Telex 8813387
– 🛗 📺 ☎ 🚿wc 🚿wc ☎. ⃞ AE ① VISA 🍴
BR **e**
M (closed lunch Saturday and Sunday) (restricted lunch) 4.75/8.75 st. 🍷 4.50 – **69 rm**
⊇ 38.00/50.00 st.

🏩 **Elizabetta,** 162 Cromwell Rd, SW5 0TT, ✆ 370 4282, Telex 918978 – 🛗 📺 ☎ 🅿. 🍴
AS **a**
84 rm

🏠 **Number Sixteen** without rest., 16 Sumner Pl., SW7 3EG, ✆ 589 5232, Telex 266638, 🌿
– 🚿wc 🚿wc ☎. ⃞ AE ① VISA. 🍴
CT **c**
⊇ 3.00 – **24 rm** 29.00/70.00 st.

🏠 **Alexander** without rest., 9 Sumner Pl., SW7 3EE, ✆ 581 1591, Telex 917133, 🌿 – 🛗 📺
🚿wc 🚿wc ☎
CT **a**
36 rm

XXX **Bombay Brasserie,** Courtfield Close, 140 Gloucester Rd, SW7 4QH, ✆ 370 4040, Indian
rest. – ⃞ AE ① VISA
BS **a**
M a la carte 12.10/15.65 t. 🍷 3.95.

XX **Reads,** 152 Old Brompton Rd, SW5 0BE, ✆ 373 2445 – ⃞ AE ① VISA
BT **a**
closed Sunday dinner, 2 weeks Christmas-New Year and Bank Holidays – **M** a la carte
13.00/16.10 t.

383

XX **Hilaire,** 68 Old Brompton Rd, SW7, ✆ 584 8993 – 🅰 ᴀᴇ ⓞ 𝐕𝐈𝐒𝐀   CT **n**
closed Saturday lunch and Sunday – **M** 9.50/17.50 **t.** ⍩ 3.50.

XX Memories of India, 18 Gloucester Rd, SW7 4RB, ✆ 589 6450, Indian rest.   BR **s**

XX **Zen Too,** 53 Old Brompton Rd, SW7, ✆ 225 1609, Chinese rest. – ▤ 🅰 ᴀᴇ 𝐕𝐈𝐒𝐀
M a la carte 10.10/14.80 **t.** ⍩ 2.75.   CST **r**

X **Chanterelle,** 119 Old Brompton Rd, SW7 3RN, ✆ 373 5522 – 🅰 ᴀᴇ ⓞ 𝐕𝐈𝐒𝐀   BT **v**
closed 24 to 27 December – **M** 7.00/10.00 **t.** ⍩ 2.95.

X **Star of India,** 154 Old Brompton Rd, SW5 0BE, ✆ 373 2901, Indian rest. – 🅰 ᴀᴇ ⓞ 𝐕𝐈𝐒𝐀
closed Bank Holidays – **M** a la carte 7.55/10.40 **t.** ⍩ 3.95.   BT **s**

RICHMOND-UPON-THAMES

Richmond – ⊠ Surrey.

🛆, 🛆 Richmond Park ✆ 876 3205.

🛈 Central Library, Little Green ✆ 940 9125.

XX ❀ **Lichfield's,** 13 Lichfield Terr., Sheen Rd, TW9 1DP, ✆ 940 5236 – 🅰 ᴀᴇ
closed Saturday lunch, Sunday, Monday, 3 weeks August-September and Bank Holidays
– **M** (booking essential) a la carte 15.50/27.00 **t.** ⍩ 3.50
Spec. Nage of lobster and langoustines with ginger butter, Fillets of hare with beetroot and orange, Variations on an apple theme.

WANDSWORTH

Battersea – ⊠ SW8/SW11.

XX ❀❀ **Chez Nico,** 129 Queenstown Rd, SW8 3RH, ✆ 720 6960, French rest. – 🅰 𝐕𝐈𝐒𝐀
closed Monday lunch, Sunday, 1 week Easter, 3 weeks July-August, 1 week Christmas and Bank Holidays – **M** (booking essential) a la carte 22.25/29.00 **st.** ⍩ 5.85
Spec. Parfait fondant de foies de volailles, Suprême de canard au fumet de cèpes, Marquise au chocolat crème anglaise orangée.

XX **Alonso's,** 32 Queenstown Rd, SW8 3RX, ✆ 720 5986 – 🅰 𝐕𝐈𝐒𝐀
closed Saturday lunch, Sunday and Bank Holidays – **M** 7.95/12.50 **t.**

XX **Lampwicks,** 24 Queenstown Rd, SW8 3RX, ✆ 622 7800 – 🅰 ᴀᴇ ⓞ 𝐕𝐈𝐒𝐀
closed Saturday lunch, Sunday, 2 weeks August, 1 week Christmas and Bank Holidays –
M 10.50/16.50 **t.** ⍩ 3.00.

XX ❀ **L'Arlequin,** 123 Queenstown Rd, SW8, ✆ 622 0555, French rest. – 🅰 ⓞ 𝐕𝐈𝐒𝐀
closed Saturday, Sunday, 3 weeks August and Bank Holidays – **M** a la carte 16.20/23.75 **st.**
Spec. Persillé de ris de veau et homard, Papillote de saumon sauvage au gingembre (seasonal), Chaud froid de framboises (seasonal).

WESTMINSTER (City of)

Bayswater and Maida Vale – ⊠ W2/W9 – Except where otherwise stated see pp. 16 and 17.

🏨 **Royal Lancaster** (Rank), Lancaster Terr., W2 2TY, ✆ 262 6737, Telex 24822, ≤ – 🛗 📺
☎ ⅙ 🄿 🏋 🅰 🆁 ⓞ 𝐕𝐈𝐒𝐀 ⌖   DZ **e**
M 11.50/13.95 (wine included) **st.** ⍩ 4.75 – ⌕ 6.50 – **435 rm** 75.00/97.00 **st.** – SB (weekends only) 42.55/45.55 **st.**

🏨 **London Metropole,** Edgware Rd, W2 1JU, ✆ 402 4141, Telex 23711, ≤ – 🛗 ▤ 📺 ☎
🄿 🏋 🅰 ᴀᴇ ⓞ 𝐕𝐈𝐒𝐀 ⌖   pp. 3-6 JT **c**
M a la carte 11.50/18.50 **t.** ⍩ 3.60 – ⌕ 3.50 – **586 rm** 52.50/60.00 **t.** – SB (weekends only) 54.50 **st.**

🏨 Hospitality Inn (Mt. Charlotte), 104 Bayswater Rd, W2 3HL, ✆ 264 4461, Telex 22667, ≤ –
🛗 📺 ☎ 🄿 🅰 ᴀᴇ ⓞ 𝐕𝐈𝐒𝐀   CZ **o**
⌕ 5.50 – **175 rm** 43.45/57.75 **st.**

🏨 **London Embassy** (Embassy), 150 Bayswater Rd, W2 4RT, ✆ 229 1212, Telex 27727 –
🛗 📺 ☎ 🄿 🏋 🅰 𝐕𝐈𝐒𝐀 ⌖   BZ **o**
M (carving lunch) 7.75/8.75 **st.** ⍩ 4.75 – ⌕ 3.50 – **192 rm** 48.00/68.00 **st.** – SB (weekends only) 60.00/66.00 **st.**

🏨 White's (Mt. Charlotte), Bayswater Rd, 90-92 Lancaster Gate, W2 3NR, ✆ 262 2711,
Telex 23922 – 🛗 📺 ⌂wc ☎ 🄿 🏋 🅰 ᴀᴇ ⓞ 𝐕𝐈𝐒𝐀   CZ **v**
61 rm 46.50/58.50 **st.**

🏨 **Coburg** (Best Western), 129 Bayswater Rd, W2 4RJ, ✆ 229 3654, Telex 268235 – 🛗 📺
⌂wc ⊛. 🏋 🅰 ᴀᴇ ⓞ 𝐕𝐈𝐒𝐀   BZ **a**
M 7.50/8.50 **st.** ⍩ 3.50 – **125 rm** ⌕ 25.00/56.00 **st.** – SB (weekends only) 39.00/56.00 **st.**

🏨 **Colonnade,** 2 Warrington Cres., W9 1ER, ✆ 286 1052, Telex 298930 – 🛗 📺 ⌂wc 🚰wc
⊛. 🅰 ᴀᴇ ⓞ   pp. 3-6 JT **e**
M (dinner only) 7.95 **st.** ⍩ 2.50 – **53 rm** ⌕ 25.50/55.00 **t.**

🏨 **Mornington Lancaster** without rest., 12 Lancaster Gate, W2 3LG, ✆ 262 7361, Telex
24281 – 🛗 📺 ⌂wc ⊛. 🅰 ᴀᴇ ⓞ 𝐕𝐈𝐒𝐀   DZ **s**
closed Christmas-New Year – ⌕ 3.00 – **65 rm** 28.00/48.00 **st.**

XXX Bombay Palace, 50 Connaught St., Hyde Park Sq., W2, *?* 723 8855, North Indian   EY **a**

XX **San Marino,** 26 Sussex Pl., W2 2TH, *?* 723 8395, Italian rest. – 🗚 🗚 ⓪ **VISA**   EY **u**
closed Sunday – **M** a la carte 9.40/23.90 **t.** ⱴ 3.50.

XX **Trat West,** 143 Edgware Rd, W2 2HR, *?* 723 8203, Italian rest. – 🗚 🗚 ⓪ **VISA**
closed Bank Holidays – **M** a la carte 8.00/10.60 **t.** ⱴ 2.50.   pp. 3-6 KT **i**

■ **Belgravia** – ✉ SW1 – Except where otherwise stated see pp. 14 and 15.

🏨 Berkeley, Wilton Pl., SW1X 7RL, *?* 235 6000, Telex 919252, 🔲 – 🛗 📺 ☎ & ⇔. ᠘.
🗚 **VISA**   FQ **e**
M Restaurant *(closed Saturday)* a la carte 12.00/27.00 **st.** – **Buttery** *(closed Sunday)* a la
carte 11.75/18.75 **st.** – **153 rm**.

🏨 Lowndes Thistle (Thistle), 21 Lowndes St., SW1X 9ES, *?* 235 6020, Telex 919065 – 🛗
📺 ☎. 🗚 🗚 ⓪ **VISA** 🍴   FR **i**
M 12.50 **t.** ⱴ 3.45 – ⌥ 6.00 – **80 rm** 69.00/95.00 **t.** – SB (weekends only) 83.50 **st.**

XX **Salloos,** 62-64 Kinnerton St., SW1 8ER, *?* 235 4444, Indian and Pakistani rest. – 🗏. 🗚
🗚 ⓪ **VISA**   FQ **a**
closed Sunday and Bank Holidays – **M** a la carte 11.90/15.90 **t.** ⱴ 2.50.

XX **Motcombs,** 26 Motcomb St., SW1X 8JU, *?* 235 6382 – 🗚 🗚 ⓪ **VISA**   FR **z**
closed Saturday lunch, Sunday and Bank Holidays – **M** a la carte 11.35/16.70 **t.** ⱴ 3.50.

■ **Hyde Park and Knightsbridge** – ✉ SW1/SW7 – pp. 14 and 15.

🛗 Fourth Floor, Harrods, Knightsbridge, SW1 *?* 730 0791.

🏨 Hyde Park (T.H.F.), 66 Knightsbridge, SW1Y 7LA, *?* 235 2000, Telex 262057, ⇐ – 🛗 📺.
᠘. 🗚 🗚 ⓪ **VISA**   EQ **v**
M *(closed Saturday lunch)* 12.00/13.50 **st.** ⱴ 4.50 – ⌥ 6.75 – **179 rm** 102.00/115.50 **st.**

XXX Shezan, 16-22 Cheval Pl., Montpelier St., SW7 1ES, *?* 589 7918, Indian and Pakistani
rest.   ER **c**

XX **Mr Chow,** 151 Knightsbridge, SW1X 7PA, *?* 589 7347, Chinese rest. – 🗚 🗚 ⓪ **VISA**
closed Christmas – **M** a la carte 12.40/21.90 **t.** ⱴ 3.00.   EQ **s**

XX Montpeliano, 13 Montpelier St., SW7 1HQ, *?* 589 0032, Italian rest.   ER **e**

■ **Mayfair** – ✉ W1 – pp. 12 and 13.

🏨 Dorchester, Park Lane, W1A 2HJ, *?* 629 8888, Telex 887704 – 🛗 🗏 📺 ☎ & ⇔. ᠘.
🗚 🗚 ⓪ **VISA**. 🍴   BN **z**
M *(see* **The Terrace** *below)* – **Grill** a la carte 16.00/23.20 **st.** ⱴ 3.50 – ⌥ 7.75 – **280 rm**
95.00/135.00 **st.**

🏨 Claridge's, Brook St., W1A 2JQ, *?* 629 8860, Telex 21872 – 🛗 📺 ☎ & 🗚 🗚 **VISA**. 🍴
M a la carte 18.00/28.00 **st.** ⱴ 2.80 – **Causerie** – ⌥ 8.00 – **205 rm** 80.00/135.00 **st.**   BL **c**

🏨 Inn on the Park, Hamilton Pl., Park Lane, W1A 1AZ, *?* 499 0888, Telex 22771 – 🛗 📺
☎ & ⇔. ᠘. 🗚 🗚 ⓪ **VISA**. 🍴   BP **a**
M Four Seasons a la carte 22.50/27.75 **st.** ⱴ 5.25 – **Lanes** a la carte 16.30/18.10 **st.** ⱴ 5.25 –
⌥ 7.25 – **228 rm** 108.00/128.00 **s.**

🏨 Grosvenor House (T.H.F.), Park Lane, W1A 3AA, *?* 499 6363, Telex 24871, 🔲 – 🛗 📺
☎ & ℗. ᠘. 🗚 🗚 ⓪ **VISA**   AM **a**
M *(see* **90 Park Lane** *below)* – ⌥ 6.50 – **470 rm** 92.50/103.00 **st.**

🏨 ⚜ Connaught, 16 Carlos Pl., W1Y 6AL, *?* 499 7070 – 🛗 📺 ☎. 🗚. 🍴   BM **e**
M *(booking essential)* – **90 rm**
Spec. Pâté de turbot froid au homard, sauce pudeur, Rendez-vous du pêcheur, sauce légère au parfum
d'Armorique, Salmis de canard strasbourgeoise en surprise.

🏨 Inter-Continental (Inter-Con.), 1 Hamilton Pl., Hyde Park Corner, W1V 0QY, *?* 409 3131,
Telex 25853 – 🛗 🗏 📺 ☎ & ⇔. ᠘. 🗚 🗚 ⓪ **VISA**. 🍴   BP **o**
M *(see also* **Le Soufflé** *below)* a la carte approx. 14.50 **st.** ⱴ 5.50 – ⌥ 7.50 – **491 rm**
110.00/128.00.

🏨 Athenaeum (Rank), 116 Piccadilly, W1V 0BJ, *?* 499 3464, Telex 261589 – 🛗 📺 ☎. ᠘.
🗚 🗚 ⓪ **VISA**   CP **s**
M a la carte 18.10/24.70 **st.** ⱴ 4.00 – ⌥ 7.00 – **112 rm** 97.00/140.00 **st.** – SB (weekends only) 121.00/146.00 **st.**

🏨 Brown's (T.H.F.), 29-34 Albemarle St., W1A 4SW, *?* 493 6020, Telex 28686 – 🛗 📺 ☎.
᠘. 🗚 🗚 ⓪ **VISA**   DM **e**
M 18.75/20.75 **st.** ⱴ 4.50 – ⌥ 7.00 – **125 rm** 76.50/101.00 **st.**

🏨 May Fair (Inter-Con.), Stratton St., W1A 2AN, *?* 629 7777, Telex 262526 – 🛗 📺 ☎. ᠘.
🗚 🗚 ⓪ **VISA**. 🍴   DN **z**
M 15.00/16.00 **t.** ⱴ 6.00 – ⌥ 7.00 – **327 rm** 77.00/125.00.

🏨 Westbury (T.H.F.), New Bond St., W1A 4UH, *?* 629 7755, Telex 24378 – 🛗 📺 ☎ & ℗.
᠘. 🗚 🗚 ⓪ **VISA**   DM **a**
M 11.25/17.00 **t.** ⱴ 4.25 – ⌥ 7.00 – **242 rm** 75.50/88.00 **st.**

🏨 **Hilton International,** 22 Park Lane, W1A 2HH, 𝄢 493 8000, Telex 24873, ⬅ London –
📶 🔲 📺 🖤 ♿ 🅿️ 🔺 🔼 🔳 ⑩ 𝘝𝘐𝘚𝘈　　　　　　　　　　　　BP e
M a la carte 13.50/34.00 **t.** 🍷 4.00 – ⊐ 6.50 – **501 rm** 95.00/130.00 **t.**

🏨 **Holiday Inn,** 3 Berkeley Sq., W1X 6NE, 𝄢 493 8282, Telex 24561 – 📶 🔲 📺 ☎ 🚗 🔺
🔼 🔳 ⑩ 𝘝𝘐𝘚𝘈 **t.**　　　　　　　　　　　　　　　　　　　　DN r
M a la carte 10.50/20.00 **st.** 🍷 4.00 – ⊐ 7.00 – **186 rm** 78.00/106.00 **st.** – SB (weekends only) 84.00 **st.**

🏨 **Chesterfield (Forum),** 35 Charles St., W1X 8LX, 𝄢 491 2622, Telex 269394 – 📶 📺 ☎ �

87 rm.　　　　　　　　　　　　　　　　　　　　　　　　　　CN c

🏛 **Washington,** 5-7 Curzon St., W1Y 8DT, 𝄢 499 7030, Telex 24540 – 📶 📺 ▭wc ☎ 🔺
🔼 🔳 ⑩ 𝘝𝘐𝘚𝘈 �
　　　　　　　　　　　　　　　　　　　CN n
M 10.00 **st.** 🍷 3.60 – ⊐ 5.50 – **164 rm** 46.50/64.00 **st.**

XXXXX Mirabelle (De Vere), 56 Curzon St., W1Y 8DL, 𝄢 499 4636, 🌿　　　　CN a

XXXXX ❀ **The Terrace** (at Dorchester H.), Park Lane, W1A 2HJ, 𝄢 629 8888, Telex 887704,
French rest. – 🔼 🔳 ⑩ 𝘝𝘐𝘚𝘈　　　　　　　　　　　　　　BN z
closed Sunday – **M** (dinner only) a la carte approx. 28.00 **st.**
Spec. Parfait de foies de volailles aux truffes, Delice de turbot gratiné au basilic-sauce aux poivrons jaunes,
Rosette de bœuf aux échalotes.

XXXXX **90 Park Lane,** (at Grosvenor House H.), Park Lane, W1A 3AA, 𝄢 499 6363 – 🅿️ 🔼 🔳
⑩ 𝘝𝘐𝘚𝘈　　　　　　　　　　　　　　　　　　　　　　AM a
closed Saturday lunch and Sunday – **M** a la carte 19.00/35.25 **st.** 🍷 5.00.

XXXX ❀❀❀ **Le Gavroche,** 43 Upper Brook St., W1P 1PS, 𝄢 408 0881, French rest. – 🔼 🔳
⑩ 𝘝𝘐𝘚𝘈　　　　　　　　　　　　　　　　　　　　　　AM c
closed Saturday, Sunday, 21 December-2 January and Bank Holidays – **M** (booking
essential) a la carte 26.70/37.40 **st.**
Spec. Soufflé suissesse, Assiette du boucher, Sablé aux fraises.

XXXX ❀ **Le Soufflé** (at Inter-Continental H.), 1 Hamilton Pl., Hyde Park Corner, W1V 0QY, 𝄢
409 3131, Telex 25853 – 🅿️ 🔼 🔳 ⑩ 𝘝𝘐𝘚𝘈　　　　　　　　BP o
M 16.80/20.60 **t.** 🍷 5.50
Spec. Les paupiettes de turbot aux langoustines, La caille « comme chez nous », Le magret de canard au
foie gras en cage.

XXXX **Scott's,** 20 Mount St., W1Y 5RB, 𝄢 629 5248, Seafood – 🔼 🔳 ⑩ 𝘝𝘐𝘚𝘈　BM r
closed Sunday lunch and Bank Holidays – **M** a la carte 16.10/24.40 **t.** 🍷 3.00.

XXX **Cecconi's,** 5a Burlington Gdns, W1Y 5DT, 𝄢 434 1500, Italian rest.　　DM c

XXX **Tiberio,** 22 Queen St., W1X 7PJ, 𝄢 629 3561, Italian rest., Dancing – 🔼 🔳 ⑩ 𝘝𝘐𝘚𝘈
closed Saturday lunch, Sunday and Bank Holidays – **M** a la carte 13.25/16.50 **t.** 🍷 2.50.
　　　　　　　　　　　　　　　　　　　　　　　　　　CN z

XX **Greenhouse,** 27a Hay's Mews, W1X 7RJ, 𝄢 499 3331 – 🔼 🔳 ⑩ 𝘝𝘐𝘚𝘈　BN a
closed Saturday lunch, Sunday, 25 December-7 January and Bank Holidays – **M** a la carte
11.80/17.25 **t.** 🍷 2.75.

XX **Langan's Brasserie,** Stratton St., W1X 5FD, 𝄢 493 6437 – 🔼 🔳 ⑩ 𝘝𝘐𝘚𝘈　DN e
closed Saturday lunch, Sunday and Bank Holidays – **M** (booking essential) a la carte
12.40/13.85 **t.** 🍷 3.95.

XX **Miyama,** 38 Clarges St., W1Y 7PJ, 𝄢 499 2443, Japanese rest. – 🔳 🔼 🔳 ⑩ 𝘝𝘐𝘚𝘈
closed Saturday lunch, Sunday, Easter, Christmas-New Year and Bank Holidays – **M** a la
carte 12.50/31.00 **t.** 🍷 3.10.　　　　　　　　　　　　　CN e

XX **Apicella 81,** 4a Mill St., W1R 9TE, 𝄢 499 1308, Italian rest. – 🔼 🔳 ⑩ 𝘝𝘐𝘚𝘈　DL x
closed Saturday lunch, Sunday, Easter, Christmas and Bank Holidays – **M** a la carte
11.00/14.20 **t.** 🍷 2.80.

XX **Shogun** (at Britannia H.), Adams Row, W1, 𝄢 493 1255, Telex 8813271, Japanese rest. –
🔼 🔳 ⑩ 𝘝𝘐𝘚𝘈　　　　　　　　　　　　　　　　　　　BM i
closed Monday – **M** (dinner only) a la carte 11.00/16.50 **s.** 🍷 3.50.

XX **One Two Three,** 27 Davies St., W1, 𝄢 409 0750, Japanese rest. – 🔼 🔳 ⑩ 𝘝𝘐𝘚𝘈　BM s
closed Sunday lunch, Saturday and Bank Holidays – **M** a la carte 8.30/16.40 **t.**

XX **Mr. Kai,** 65 South Audley St., W1, 𝄢 493 8988, Chinese-Peking rest. – 🔼 🔳 ⑩ 𝘝𝘐𝘚𝘈
closed 25-26 December, 1 January and Bank Holidays – **M** a la carte 16.25/22.25 **t.** 🍷 3.95.
　　　　　　　　　　　　　　　　　　　　　　　　　　BM v

XX **Marquis,** 121a Mount St., W1Y 5HB, 𝄢 499 1256 – 🔼 🔳 ⑩ 𝘝𝘐𝘚𝘈　　BM u
closed Sunday and Bank Holidays – **M** a la carte 10.25/14.40 **t.** 🍷 3.00.

XX **Golden Carp,** 8a Mount St., W1Y 5AD, 𝄢 499 3385, Seafood – 🔼 🔳 ⑩ 𝘝𝘐𝘚𝘈　BM x
closed Saturday lunch, Sunday, 3 weeks August and Bank Holidays – **M** a la carte
6.55/13.65 **t.** 🍷 3.50.

XX **Gaylord,** 16 Albemarle St., W1 3HA, 𝄢 629 9802, Indian rest. – 🔼 🔳 ⑩ 𝘝𝘐𝘚𝘈　DM u
M approx. 10.00 **t.** 🍷 3.40.

X **Ikeda,** 30 Brook St., W1Y 1AG, 𝄢 629 2730, Japanese rest. – 🔼 🔳 ⑩ 𝘝𝘐𝘚𝘈　CKL z
closed Sunday lunch, Saturday and Bank Holidays – **M** a la carte 11.20/18.00 **t.** 🍷 2.50.

X **Trattoria Fiori,** 87-88 Mount St., W1Y 5HG, 𝄢 499 1447, Italian rest. – 🔼 🔳 ⑩ 𝘝𝘐𝘚𝘈
closed Sunday and Bank Holidays – **M** a la carte 8.80/11.55 **t.** 🍷 2.50.　　BM o

Regent's Park and Marylebone – ✉ NW1/NW6/NW8/W1 – Except where otherwise stated see pp. 12 and 13.

🅿 Ground Floor, Selfridges, Oxford St., W1 ℰ 730 0791.

Churchill, 30 Portman Sq., W1A 4ZX, ℰ 486 5800, Telex 264831 – 🖾 🗐 📺 ☎ 🕻 🅿 🛆
🔼 🖾 🎫 ✆
M a la carte 12.30/24.70 **st.** 🍷 2.85 – ☲ 7.00 – **489 rm** 84.00/97.00.
AJ **x**

Portman Inter-Continental (Inter-Con.), 22 Portman Sq., W1H 9FL, ℰ 486 5844, Telex
261526 – 🖾 🗐 📺 ☎ 🕻 🅿 🛆 🔼 🖾 🎫 ⓪ 🎫 ✆
M 8.10/14.50 **t.** 🍷 4.60 – ☲ 7.55 – **276 rm** 94.00/105.00.
AJ **o**

Montcalm, Great Cumberland Pl., W1A 2LF, ℰ 402 4288, Telex 28710 – 🖾 🗐 📺 ☎ 🛆
🔼 🖾 🎫 ✆
pp. 16 and 17 FY **x**
M (closed Saturday lunch and Sunday) a la carte 14.20/17.60 **st.** 🍷 2.70 – ☲ 7.00 – **116 rm**
73.00/83.00.

Holiday Inn, 134 George St., W1H 6DN, ℰ 723 1277, Telex 27983, 🔼 – 🖾 🗐 📺 ☎ 🕻
🅿 🛆 🔼 🖾 🎫 ✆
pp. 16 and 17 FY **i**
M 12.50 **t.** 🍷 4.25 – ☲ 7.00 – **241 rm** 85.10/103.50 **st.**

Selfridge Thistle (Thistle), 400 Orchard St., W1H 0JS, ℰ 408 2080, Telex 22361 – 🖾 🗐
📺 ☎ 🕻 🅿 🛆 🔼 ⓪ 🎫 ✆
AK **e**
M 15.00/17.00 **t.** 🍷 3.45 – ☲ 6.00 – **298 rm** 76.00/90.00 **t.** – SB (weekends only) 62.00 **st.**

Ladbroke Westmoreland (Ladbroke), 18 Lodge Rd, NW8 7JT, ℰ 722 7722, Telex 23101
– 🖾 🗐 📺 ☎ 🕻 🅿 🛆 🔼 🖾 🎫 ✆
pp. 3-6 JS **v**
M 18.00 **st.** 🍷 3.15 – ☲ 6.25 – **350 rm** 50.00/68.00 **t.** – SB (weekends only) 53.95/61.95 **st.**

St. George's (T.H.F.), Langham Pl., W1N 8QS, ℰ 580 0111, Telex 27274, ← – 🖾 📺 ☎.
🔼 🖾 🎫 ✆
pp. 3-6 LT **a**
M 11.15/17.75 **ss.** 🍷 4.50 – ☲ 6.00 – **85 rm** 57.50/74.50 **st.**

Cumberland (T.H.F.), Marble Arch, W1A 4RF, ℰ 262 1234, Telex 22215 – 🖾 📺 ☎ 🕻
🛆 🔼 🖾 🎫 ⓪ 🎫
AK **n**
M (carving rest.) 9.25 **t.** 🍷 3.00 – ☲ 6.00 – **910 rm** 55.50/72.00 **st.**

Durrants, 26-32 George St., W1H 6BJ, ℰ 935 8131, Telex 894919 – 🖾 📺 🛏wc ☎. 🛆
🔼 🖾 🎫 ✆
AH **e**
M 15.00/20.00 **st.** 🍷 3.75 – ☲ 4.00 – **103 rm** 28.00/58.00 **st.**

Londoner, 57-59 Welbeck St., W1M 8HS, ℰ 935 4442, Telex 894630 – 🖾 📺 🛏wc ☎.
BJ **v**
M a la carte 7.80/10.10 **t.** 🍷 2.75 – **142 rm** 42.00/55.00 **t.** – SB (weekends only) 55.00 **st.**

Bryanston Court, 56-60 Great Cumberland Pl., W1H 7FD, ℰ 262 3141, Group Telex
262076 – 🖾 📺 🛏wc 🎞wc ☎. 🔼 🖾 ⓪ 🎫
pp. 16 and 17 FY **z**
M (closed Saturday and Sunday) 9.00 **t.** 🍷 2.50 – ☲ 2.50 – **53 rm** 33.00/44.00 **st.**

XXX **Odins**, 27 Devonshire St., W1N 1RS, ℰ 935 7296 – 🎫
pp. 3-6 KT **n**
closed Saturday lunch, Sunday and Bank Holidays – **M** a la carte 13.15/19.40 **t.**

XX **D'Artagnan**, 19 Blandford St., W1H 3AD, ℰ 935 1023, French rest. – 🔼 🎫 ⓪ 🎫
closed Saturday lunch, Sunday, August and Bank Holidays – **M** a la carte 13.55/15.75 **t.**
AH **a**

XX **La Loggia**, 68 Edgware Rd, W2 2EG, ℰ 723 0554, Italian rest. – 🔼 🎫 ⓪ 🎫
closed Sunday and Bank Holidays – **M** a la carte 9.80/17.50 **t.** 🍷 2.65.
pp. 16-17 FY **a**

XX **Asuka**, Berkeley Arcade, 209a Baker St., NW1 6AB, ℰ 486 5026, Japanese rest. – 🔼 🎫
⓪ 🎫
pp. 3-6 KT **u**
closed Saturday lunch, Sunday, 24 December-2 January and Bank Holidays – **M** a la carte
17.60/21.00 **st.**

X **Le Muscadet**, 25 Paddington St., W1, ℰ 935 2883, French rest. – 🔼 🎫
KT **u**
closed Saturday lunch, Sunday, 1 week Easter, 2 weeks August and 23 December-
10 January – **M** a la carte 8.15/13.40 🍷 2.40

X **Au Bois St. Jean**, 122 St. John's Wood High St., NW8 7SG, ℰ 722 0400, French rest.
– 🔼 🎫 ⓪ 🎫
pp. 3-6 JS **e**
closed Saturday lunch and Bank Holidays – **M** 9.00/11.00 **t.** 🍷 2.75.

St. James's – ✉ W1/SW1/WC2 – pp. 12 and 13.

Ritz, Piccadilly, W1V 9DG, ℰ 493 8181, Telex 267200 – 🖾 📺 ☎. 🔼 🖾 🎫 ⓪ 🎫 ✆
M a la carte 25.45/33.65 **st.** 🍷 5.25 – ☲ 7.00 – **139 rm** 80.00/130.00 **st.**
DN **a**

Stafford 🞂, 16-18 St. James's Pl., SW1A 1NJ, ℰ 493 0111, Telex 28602 – 🖾 📺 ☎. 🛆
🎫 ⓪.
DN **u**
M 14.50/16.00 **st.** – ☲ 4.50 – **60 rm** 89.00/120.00 **st.**

Dukes 🞂, 35 St. James's Pl., SW1A 1NY, ℰ 491 4840, Telex 28283 – 🖾 📺 ☎. 🔼 🖾 🎫 ⓪
🎫 ✆
EP **x**
M a la carte 21.00/25.00 **st.** – ☲ 7.50 – **53 rm** 82.00/123.00 **st.**

Cavendish (T.H.F.), Jermyn St., SW1Y 6JF, ℰ 930 2111, Telex 263187 – 🖾 📺 ☎ 🕻 🅿
🛆 🔼 🖾 🎫 ⓪ 🎫
EN **i**
M 10.75/12.75 🍷 3.85 – ☲ 6.00 – **253 rm** 66.50/85.50 **st.**

🏛 **Royal Trafalgar Thistle** (Thistle), Whitcomb St., WC2H 7HG, ☎ 930 4477, Telex 298564
– 🛗 📺 ⇌wc ☎. ⚠ 🅰🅴 ⓞ 𝓥𝓘𝓢𝓐. 🎀 GM r
M 11.00/14.00 ⏶ 3.45 – ⚏ 5.25 – **107 rm** 47.50/59.80 **t.** – SB (weekends only) 67.00 **st.**

🏛 **Pastoria,** 3-6 St. Martin's St., WC2H 7HL, ☎ 930 8641, Telex 25538 – 🛗 📺 ⇌wc ⚐.
⚠ 🅰🅴 ⓞ 𝓥𝓘𝓢𝓐. 🎀 GM v
M *(closed Saturday lunch, Sunday and Bank Holidays)* 10.75 **t.** ⏶ 2.50 – ⚏ 3.25 – **54 rm**
29.90/56.35 **t.** – SB (weekends only) 50.00/60.00 **st.**

XXXXX **Maxim's de Paris,** 32-34 Panton St., SW1, ☎ 839 4809, French rest., Dancing – 🍽. ⚠
🅰🅴 ⓞ 𝓥𝓘𝓢𝓐 GM a
closed Saturday lunch, Sunday and Bank Holidays – **M** a la carte 15.00/25.50 **st.** ⏶ 3.75.

XXX **Suntory,** 72-73 St. James's St., SW1A 1PH, ☎ 409 0201, Japanese rest. – 🍽. ⚠ 🅰🅴 ⓞ
𝓥𝓘𝓢𝓐 EP z
closed Sunday and Bank Holidays – **M** a la carte 12.20/22.50.

XX **Le Caprice,** Arlington House, Arlington St., SW1A 1RT, ☎ 629 2239 – ⚠ 🅰🅴 ⓞ 𝓥𝓘𝓢𝓐
closed Saturday lunch and 24 December-2 January – **M** a la carte 10.00/14.50 **t.** ⏶ 3.25.
DN c

Soho – ⊠ W1/WC2 – pp. 12 and 13.

XXX **Leonis Quo Vadis,** 26-29 Dean St., W1V 6LL, ☎ 437 9585, Italian rest. – ⚠ 🅰🅴 ⓞ 𝓥𝓘𝓢𝓐
closed lunch Saturday, Sunday and Bank Holidays and 25 December – **M** a la carte
10.70/12.85 **t.** ⏶ 2.45. FK u

XX **La Terrazza,** 19 Romilly St., W1V 5TG, ☎ 437 8991, Italian rest. – ⚠ 🅰🅴 ⓞ 𝓥𝓘𝓢𝓐 FL i
closed Christmas Day and Bank Holidays – **M** a la carte 9.85/14.10 **t.** ⏶ 2.50.

XX **L'Escargot,** 48 Greek St., W1V 5LQ, ☎ 437 2679 – ⚠ 🅰🅴 ⓞ 𝓥𝓘𝓢𝓐 GK e
closed Saturday lunch, Sunday and Bank Holidays – **M** a la carte 8.85/15.50 **t.** ⏶ 2.50.

XX **Chesa (Swiss Centre),** 2 New Coventry St., W1V 3HG, ☎ 734 1291 – ⚠ 🅰🅴 ⓞ 𝓥𝓘𝓢𝓐
closed Christmas Day – **M** a la carte 12.40/17.80 **st.** GM n

XX **Gay Hussar,** 2 Greek St., W1V 6NB, ☎ 437 0973, Hungarian rest. GJ c
closed Sunday and Bank Holidays – **M** a la carte 13.50/17.00 **t.** ⏶ 3.00.

XX **Au Jardin des Gourmets,** 5 Greek St., Soho Sq., W1V 5LA, ☎ 437 1816, French rest.
GJ a

XX **Venezia,** 21 Great Chapel St., W1V 3AQ, ☎ 437 6506, Italian rest. – ⚠ 🅰🅴 ⓞ 𝓥𝓘𝓢𝓐
closed Saturday lunch, Sunday and Bank Holidays – **M** a la carte 9.45/14.15 **t.** ⏶ 2.40.
FJ a

XX **Red Fort,** 77 Dean St., W1V 5HA, ☎ 437 2525, Indian rest. – ⚠ 🅰🅴 ⓞ 𝓥𝓘𝓢𝓐 FJK r
M a la carte 8.45/10.80 **t.**

XX **Rugantino,** 26 Romilly St., W1V 5TQ, ☎ 437 5302, Italian rest. – ⚠ 🅰🅴 ⓞ 𝓥𝓘𝓢𝓐 GK u
closed Saturday lunch, Sunday and Bank Holidays – **M** a la carte 8.60/11.10 **t.** ⏶ 2.65.

XX **Fuji,** 36-40 Brewer St., W1R 3HP, ☎ 734 0957, Japanese rest. – ⚠ 🅰🅴 ⓞ 𝓥𝓘𝓢𝓐 FL c
closed lunch Saturday and Sunday and 1 week at Christmas – **M** a la carte 10.10/19.30 **st.**
⏶ 3.80.

X **Frith's,** 14 Frith St., W1, ☎ 439 3370 – ⚠ 🅰🅴 ⓞ 𝓥𝓘𝓢𝓐 FGK s
closed Saturday lunch and Sunday – **M** a la carte 9.80/15.50 **t.** ⏶ 2.50.

X **Romeo e Giulietta,** 11 Sutton Row, W1V 5FE, ☎ 734 4914, Italian rest. – ⚠ 🅰🅴 ⓞ 𝓥𝓘𝓢𝓐
closed Saturday lunch, Sunday and Bank Holidays – **M** a la carte 7.50/12.50 ⏶ 2.20. GJ e

X **Gallery Rendezvous,** 53-55 Beak St., ☎ 734 0445, Chinese-Peking rest. – 🍽. ⚠ 🅰🅴 ⓞ
𝓥𝓘𝓢𝓐 EL a
M a la carte 6.50/11.50 **t.** ⏶ 3.50.

X **Trusha,** 11-12 Dean St., W1V 5AH, ☎ 437 3559, Indian rest. – ⚠ 🅰🅴 ⓞ 𝓥𝓘𝓢𝓐 FJ e
closed Sunday and Bank Holidays – **M** a la carte 4.40/10.65 **t.**

X **Trattoria Imperia,** 19 Charing Cross Rd, WC2H 0ES, ☎ 930 8364, Italian rest. – ⚠ 🅰🅴
ⓞ 𝓥𝓘𝓢𝓐 GM z
closed Saturday lunch, Sunday, 25-26 December and Bank Holidays – **M** a la carte
7.50/12.30 **t.** ⏶ 2.20.

Strand and Covent Garden – ⊠ WC2 – p. 17.

🏛 **Savoy,** Strand, WC2R 0EU, ☎ 836 4343, Telex 24234 – 🛗 📺 ☎ ⇌. 🅖. ⚠ 🅰🅴 ⓞ 𝓥𝓘𝓢𝓐.
🎀 EX a
M Grill *(closed Saturday lunch, Sunday, August and Bank Holidays)* a la carte
17.50/24.50 **st.** ⏶ 5.50 – **River** a la carte 16.70/25.50 **st.** ⏶ 5.50 – ⚏ 6.50 – **200 rm**
90.00/150.00 **st.** – SB (weekends only)(summer only) 148.00 **st.**

🏛 **Waldorf** (T.H.F.), Aldwych, WC2B 4DD, ☎ 836 2400, Telex 24574 – 🛗 📺 ☎. 🅖. ⚠ 🅰🅴
ⓞ 𝓥𝓘𝓢𝓐 EV x
M *(closed lunch Saturday and Sunday)* a la carte 12.95/37.40 **st.** ⏶ 3.20 – ⚏ 6.00 – **310 rm**
57.50/74.50 **st.**

🏛 **Howard,** 12 Temple Pl., WC2R 2FR, ☎ 836 3555, Telex 268047 – 🛗 🍽 📺 ☎ ⅛ ⇌. 🅖.
⚠ 🅰🅴 ⓞ 𝓥𝓘𝓢𝓐. 🎀 FV e
M a la carte 14.20/22.40 **st.** – **136 rm**

🏛 **Charing Cross,** Strand, WC2N 5HX, ☎ 839 7282, Telex 261101 – 🛗 📺 ⇌wc 🚿wc
🅖. ⚠ 🅰🅴 ⓞ 𝓥𝓘𝓢𝓐 DX s
closed Christmas – **M** (carving rest.) 8.75 **st.** – ⚏ 5.75 – **206 rm** 37.00/50.00 **st.**

XXX **Inigo Jones,** 14 Garrick St., WC2E 9BJ, ✆ 836 6456 – 🔲 ⚠ 🅰🅴 ⓪ 𝘝𝘐𝘚𝘈   DV **o**
closed Saturday lunch, Sunday, 1 week Christmas and Bank Holidays – **M** a la carte
23.00/27.00 **t.** ⏷ 3.30.

XXX **Ivy,** 1-5 West St., WC2H 9NE, ✆ 836 4751 – 🔼 🅰🅴 ⓪ 𝘝𝘐𝘚𝘈   DV **e**
closed Saturday lunch, Sunday 25-26 December and Bank Holidays – **M** a la carte
11.00/17.70 **t.** ⏷ 2.75.

XXX **Simpson's-in-the-Strand,** 100 Strand, WC2R 0EW, ✆ 836 9112, English rest. – 🔼
⓪ 𝘝𝘐𝘚𝘈   EV **o**
closed Sunday, Easter, 25-26 December and Bank Holidays – **M** a la carte 7.70/17.30 **st.**
⏷ 2.75.

XX **Thomas de Quincey's,** 36 Tavistock St., WC2E 7PB, ✆ 240 3972 – 🔼 🅰🅴 ⓪ 𝘝𝘐𝘚𝘈
closed Saturday lunch, Sunday, 22 July-12 August and Bank Holidays – **M** a la carte
18.95/21.30 **t.** ⏷ 3.30.   EV **c**

XX **Interlude de Tabaillau,** 7-8 Bow St., WC2, ✆ 379 6473, French rest. – 🔲 🔼 🅰🅴 ⓪
𝘝𝘐𝘚𝘈   DEV **x**
closed Saturday lunch, Sunday, 10 days at Easter, 3 weeks August-September, 10 days at
Christmas and Bank Holidays – **M** 17.50/22.00 **st.**

XX **Grange,** 39 King St., WC2E 8JS, ✆ 240 2939 – 🅰🅴   DV **z**
closed Saturday lunch, Sunday, 5 August-4 September and Bank Holidays – **M** (booking
essential) 13.50 (wine incuded) **t.**

XX **Chez Solange,** 35 Cranbourn St., WC2H 7AD, ✆ 836 5886, French rest. – 🔼 🅰🅴 ⓪ 𝘝𝘐𝘚𝘈
closed Sunday and Bank Holidays – **M** a la carte 9.50/15.10 **t.** ⏷ 3.25.   DV **i**

XX **Sheekey's,** 28-32 St. Martin's Court, WC2N 4AL, ✆ 240 2565, Seafood – 🔼 🅰🅴 ⓪ 𝘝𝘐𝘚𝘈
closed Sunday and Bank Holidays – **M** a la carte 9.30/11.30 **t.**   DV **v**

XX **Luigi's,** 15 Tavistock St., WC2E 7PA, ✆ 240 1795, Italian rest. – 🔼 ⓪ 𝘝𝘐𝘚𝘈   EV **a**
closed Sunday and Bank Holidays – **M** a la carte 12.00/17.40 **t.** ⏷ 2.50.

XX **Azami,** 13-15 West St., WC2H 9BL, ✆ 240 0634, Japanese rest.   pp. 12 and 13   GK **z**

XX **Frère Jacques,** 38 Longacre, WC2, ✆ 836 7823, Seafood – 🔲   DV **n**

X **Taste of India,** 25 Catherine St., WC2B 5JS, ✆ 836 6591, Indian rest. – 🔲 🔼 🅰🅴 ⓪
𝘝𝘐𝘚𝘈   EV **r**
M a la carte 6.95/9.45 **t.**

X **Poons of Covent Garden,** 41 King St., WC2E 8JS, ✆ 240 1743, Chinese rest. – 🅰🅴 ⓪
𝘝𝘐𝘚𝘈   DV **r**
closed Sunday – **M** a la carte 7.75/16.25 **t.** ⏷ 3.50.

X **Magnos Brasserie,** 65a Long Acre, WC2E 9JH, ✆ 836 6077, French rest. – 🔼 🅰🅴 ⓪
𝘝𝘐𝘚𝘈   EV **e**
closed Saturday lunch, Sunday, 24 December-2 January and Bank Holidays – **M** a la carte
10.15/13.15 **t.** ⏷ 3.75.

X **Laguna,** 50 St. Martin's Lane, WC2N 4EA, ✆ 836 0960, Italian rest. – 🔼 🅰🅴 ⓪ 𝘝𝘐𝘚𝘈
M a la carte 9.10/11.20 **t.** ⏷ 3.95.   DV **u**

X **Colosseo,** 12 May's Court, St. Martin's Lane, WC2N 4BS, ✆ 836 6140, Italian rest. – 🔼
🅰🅴 ⓪ 𝘝𝘐𝘚𝘈   DX **e**
closed Saturday lunch, Sunday and Bank Holidays – **M** a la carte 9.65/12.60 **t.** ⏷ 2.10.

X **Grimes,** 6 Garrick St., WC2R 9BH, ✆ 836 7008, Seafood – 🔼 🅰🅴 ⓪ 𝘝𝘐𝘚𝘈   DV **x**
closed Sunday, Christmas and Bank Holidays – **M** a la carte approx. 11.20 **t.** ⏷ 2.40.

Victoria – ✉ SW1 – Except where otherwise stated see p. 16.

🅱 By British Rail Ticket Office, near Platform 15, Victoria Station ✆ 730 0791.

🏨 **Goring,** 15 Beeston Pl., Grosvenor Gdns, SW1W 0JW, ✆ 834 8211, Telex 919166 – 🛗 📺
☎. 🛁. 🔼 🅰🅴 ⓪ 𝘝𝘐𝘚𝘈 ⬝   BV **a**
M 11.50/13.50 **t.** ⏷ 4.50 – **100 rm** 60.00/80.00 **st.**

🏨 **Royal Horseguards Thistle** (Thistle), 2 Whitehall Court, SW1A 2EJ, ✆ 839 3400,
Telex 917096 – 🛗 📺 rest 📺 ☎. 🛁. 🔼 🅰🅴 ⓪ 𝘝𝘐𝘚𝘈   pp. 7-10 NV **a**
M 9.75 **t.** ⏷ 3.45 – ⊑ 5.25 – **280 rm** 49.50/55.00 **t.** – SB (weekends only) 69.50 **st.**

🏨 Stakis St. Ermin's (Stakis), Caxton St., SW1H 0QW, ✆ 222 7888, Telex 917731 – 🛗 📺 ☎.
🛁. ⬝   CV **a**
229 rm

🏨 **Royal Westminster Thistle** (Thistle), Buckingham Palace Rd, SW1W 0QT, ✆ 834 1821,
Telex 916821 – 🛗 📺. 🔼 🅰🅴 ⓪ 𝘝𝘐𝘚𝘈   BV **z**
M 9.25/9.85 **t.** ⏷ 3.45 – ⊑ 5.50 – **135 rm** 49.50/55.00 **t.** – SB (weekends only) 69.70 **st.**

🏨 **Grosvenor,** 101 Buckingham Palace Rd, SW1W 0SJ, ✆ 834 9494, Telex 916006 – 🛗 📺
🛁wc 🛁wc ☎. 🛁. 🔼 🅰🅴 ⓪ 𝘝𝘐𝘚𝘈   BV **e**
closed 1 week at Christmas – **M** 9.50 **t.** ⏷ 3.00 – ⊑ 5.25 – **350 rm** 42.00/50.00 **t.**

🏠 **Ebury Court,** 24-32 Ebury St., SW1W 0LU, ✆ 730 8147 – 🛗 🛁wc ⊞. 🔼 𝘝𝘐𝘚𝘈   AV **i**
M a la carte 6.25/10.45 **t.** ⏷ 2.10 – **39 rm** ⊑ 28.00/52.00 **t.**

🏠 **Hamilton House,** 60-64 Warwick Way, SW1V 1SA, ✆ 821 7113 – 📺 🛁wc ⊞. 🔼 𝘝𝘐𝘚𝘈
M (grill rest. only) (dinner only) a la carte approx. 4.00 **t.** ⏷ 2.10 – **41 rm** ⊑ 19.00/36.00 **t.**
     BX **n**

XXX **Lockets,** Marsham Court, Marsham St., SW1P 4JY, ℰ 834 9552, English rest. – ◪ ◪ AE ⓪ 𝘝𝘐𝘚𝘈   pp. 7-10 MY z
closed Saturday and Sunday – **M** a la carte 11.40/15.65 **t.** ▯ 2.50.

XXX Kundan, 3 Horseferry Rd, SW1P 2AN, ℰ 834 3434, Indian and Pakistani rest. – ◪ AE ⓪ 𝘝𝘐𝘚𝘈   pp. 7-10 NXY a
closed Sunday and Bank Holidays.

XX **Ken Lo's Memories of China,** 67-69 Ebury St., SW1W 0NZ, ℰ 730 7734, Chinese
rest. – ◪ AE ⓪ 𝘝𝘐𝘚𝘈   AX u
M a la carte approx. 15.50 **t.**

XX **The Restaurant,** Dolphin Square, Chichester St., SW1, ℰ 828 3207, French rest., « Art
deco » – ◪ AE ⓪ 𝘝𝘐𝘚𝘈   pp. 7-10 LZ e
closed Sunday, 3 days Christmas, 3 days New Year and Bank Holidays – **M** a la carte
12.00/14.50 **t.** ▯ 3.50.

XX **Pomegranates,** 94 Grosvenor Rd, SW1V 3LG, ℰ 828 6560 – ◪ AE ⓪ 𝘝𝘐𝘚𝘈
closed Saturday lunch, Sunday and Bank Holidays – **M** a la carte 11.75/18.45 **t.** ▯ 3.00.
                                                              pp. 7-10 LMZ a

XX **Eatons,** 49 Elizabeth St., SW1W 9PP, ℰ 730 0074 – ◪ AE ⓪ 𝘝𝘐𝘚𝘈   AX a
closed Saturday, Sunday and Bank Holidays – **M** a la carte 9.50/12.90 **s.** ▯ 2.70.

XX **Ciboure,** 21 Eccleston St., SW1W 9LX, ℰ 730 2505, French rest. – ◪ AE ⓪ 𝘝𝘐𝘚𝘈 AX z
closed Saturday lunch, Sunday and Bank Holidays – **M** a la carte 14.20/16.40 **s.**

XX Hunan, 51 Pimlico Rd, SW1W 8WE, ℰ 730 5712, Chinese rest.   pp. 7-10 KZ a

XX **Gran Paradiso,** 52 Wilton Rd, SW1V 1DE, ℰ 828 5818, Italian rest. – ◪ AE ⓪ 𝘝𝘐𝘚𝘈
closed Saturday lunch, Sunday Easter, Christmas and Bank Holidays – **M** a la carte
9.10/10.30 **t.** ▯ 2.00.   BX a

X **Tapas,** 30 Winchester St., SW1, ℰ 828 3366 – ◪ AE ⓪ 𝘝𝘐𝘚𝘈   pp. 7-10 LZ i
closed Sunday and Bank Holidays – **M** (dinner only) a la carte 8.95/15.85 **t.** ▯ 3.00.

X **La Fontana,** 101 Pimlico Rd, SW1W 8PH, ℰ 730 6630, Italian rest. – AE ⓪ 𝘝𝘐𝘚𝘈
M a la carte 9.15/13.35 **t.** ▯ 2.50.   pp. 14 and 15 FT n

X La Poule au Pot, 231 Ebury St., SW1W 8UT, ℰ 730 7763, French rest.   pp. 7-10 KY n

X **Mimmo d'Ischia,** 61 Elizabeth St., SW1W 9PP, ℰ 730 5406, Italian rest. – ◪ AE ⓪
𝘝𝘐𝘚𝘈   AX o
closed Sunday and Bank Holidays – **M** a la carte 11.00/16.00 **t.** ▯ 3.50.

X **Bumbles,** 16 Buckingham Palace Rd, SW1W 0QP, ℰ 828 2903, Bistro – ◪ AE ⓪ 𝘝𝘐𝘚𝘈
closed Saturday lunch, Sunday and Bank Holidays – **M** a la carte 8.55/10.50 **t.**   BV c

X Tate Gallery Rest., Tate Gallery, Millbank, SW1P 4RG, ℰ 834 6754, English rest., « Rex
Whistler murals »   pp. 7-10 NY c
M (lunch only).

X **Villa Medici,** 35 Belgrave Rd, SW1, ℰ 828 3613, Italian rest. – ◪ AE ⓪ 𝘝𝘐𝘚𝘈   BX c
closed Saturday lunch, Sunday and Bank Holidays – **M** a la carte 7.30/10.40 **t.** ▯ 2.30.

Bray-on-Thames Berks W : 34 m. by M 4 (junction 8-9) and A 308 – 404 R 29 –
pop. 5,818 – ✉ ✆ 0628 Maidenhead

XXXX ✿✿✿ **Waterside Inn,** Ferry Rd, SL6 2AT, ℰ 20691, Telex 8813079, ≼, French rest.,
« Thames-side setting », 🚗 – ℗ ◪ AE ⓪ 𝘝𝘐𝘚𝘈
closed Tuesday lunch, Sunday dinner 20 October-21 April, Monday, 26 December-15
February and Bank Holidays – **M** a la carte 20.40/27.30 **st.**
Spec. Ravioles de homard truffées sauce vierge, Filets de lapereau grillés aux marrons glacés, Panaché de
tarte au citron et délice au cassis.

Great Milton Oxon NW : 49 m. by M 40 (junction 7) and A 329 – 403 404 Q 28 –
pop. 800 – ✉ Oxford – ✆ 084 46.

XXXX ✿✿ **Le Manoir aux Quat'Saisons** 🦢 with rm, OX9 7PD, ℰ 230, ≼, « 15C and 16C
manor house », ⚏ heated, 🚗, park, 🍴 – 📺 🚻wc ✆ ℗ ◪ AE 𝘝𝘐𝘚𝘈 🍴
closed 24 December-21 January – **M** (closed Sunday dinner and Monday) a la carte
27.25/35.30 **st.** ▯ 6.00 – **10 rm** ⊐ 95.00/150.00 **st.** – SB (not weekends)(winter only) 95.00/150.00 **st.**
Spec. Tartare de saumon sauvage à la croque de concombres (May-September), Pigeonneau de Bresse en
croûte de sel au fumet de truffes, Pomme soufflée au coulis d'abricots et glace vanille.

Pleasant hotels and restaurants
are shown in the Guide by a red sign.   🏨 ... 🏠

Please send us the names
of any where you have enjoyed your stay.   XXXXX ... X

Your Michelin Guide will be even better.

BIRMINGHAM West Midlands 🔲🔲🔲 O 26 – pop. 1,014,670 – ECD : Wednesday – ☺ 021.

See : Museum and Art Gallery✶✶ JZ **M1** – Museum of Science and Industry✶ JY **M2** – Cathedral (stained glass windows✶ 19C) KYZ E.

🏌 Cocks Moor Woods, Alcester Rd South, King's Heath 🕿 444 2062, S : 6 ½ m. by A 435 FX –
🏌 Edgbaston, Church Rd 🕿 454 1736, S : 1 m. FX – 🏌 Pype Hayes, Eachelhurst Rd, Walmley 🕿 351 1014, NE : 7 ½ m. – 🏌 Warley, Lightwoods Hill, 🕿 429 2440, W : 5 m.

✈ Birmingham Airport : 🕿 743 6227, E : 6 ½ m. by A 45.

🛈 2 City Arcade, 🕿 643 2514 – National Exhibition Centre 🕿 780 4141.

London 122 – Bristol 91 – Liverpool 102 – Manchester 86 – Nottingham 50.

Plans on following pages

🏨 **Albany** (T.H.F.), Smallbrook, Queensway, B5 4EW, 🕿 643 8171, Telex 337031, ≼, 🔲 –
🛗 📺 🕿 ♿ 🖈 🔲 🄰🄴 ⓪ 𝚅𝙸𝚂𝙰   JKZ **a**
M 6.95/15.00 **st.** ♦ 3.40 – 🖙 5.50 – **254 rm** 43.00/52.50 **st.**

🏨 **Plough and Harrow** (Crest), 135 Hagley Rd, Edgbaston, B16 8LS, W : 1 ½ m. on A 456
🕿 454 4111, Telex 338074, 🚗 – 🛗 📺 🕿 ♿ 🄿 🖈 🔲 🄰🄴 ⓪ 𝚅𝙸𝚂𝙰   EX **a**
M approx. 15.00 **st.** – 🖙 6.00 – **44 rm** 60.50/72.00 **st.**

🏨 **Holiday Inn**, Central Sq., Holiday St., B1 1HH, 🕿 643 2766, Telex 337272, ≼, 🔲 – 🛗 📺
🕿 ♿ 🄿 🖈 🔲 🄰🄴 ⓪ 𝚅𝙸𝚂𝙰   JZ **z**
M 7.45/7.95 **st.** ♦ 2.75 – 🖙 4.25 – **304 rm** 38.00/43.00 **s.**

🏨 **Midland** (Best Western), 128 New St., B2 4JT, 🕿 643 2601, Telex 338419 – 🛗 📺 ♿ 🖈 –
🔲 🄰🄴 ⓪ 𝚅𝙸𝚂𝙰 🎎   KZ **r**
M 10.50/12.50 **st.** – **114 rm** 🖙 21.40/55.00 **st.** – SB (weekends only) 44.00/60.00 **st.**

🏨 **Strathallan Thistle** (Thistle), 225 Hagley Rd, Edgbaston, B16 9RY, W : 2 m. on A 456
🕿 455 9777, Telex 336680 – 🛗 📺 🕿 ♿ 🖈 🔲 🄰🄴 ⓪ 𝚅𝙸𝚂𝙰 🎎
M 9.00/12.00 **t.** ♦ 3.45 – **164 rm** 39.00/48.50 **t.** – SB (weekends only) 52.00 **st.**

🏨 **Grand** (Q.M.H.), Colmore Row, B3 2DA, 🕿 236 7951, Telex 338174 – 🛗 📺 🖈 🔲 🄰🄴 ⓪
𝚅𝙸𝚂𝙰   JKY **c**
closed 4 days at Christmas – **M** 7.95 **st.** ♦ 2.95 – **145 rm** 🖙 42.00/52.00 **st.** – SB (weekends only) 48.00 **st.**

🏨 **Royal Angus Thistle** (Thistle), St. Chad's Queensway, B4 6MY, 🕿 236 4211, Telex
336889 – 🛗 📺 🄿 🖈 🔲 🄰🄴 ⓪ 𝚅𝙸𝚂𝙰 🎎   KY **s**
M 8.75/8.90 **t.** ♦ 3.45 – 🖙 4.75 – **139 rm** 36.00/48.50 **t.** – SB (weekends only) 48.00 **st.**

🏨 **Apollo**, 243-247 Hagley Rd, Edgbaston, B16 9RA, W : 2 ¼ m. on A 456 🕿 455 0271, Telex
336759 – 🛗 🍽 rest 📺 🚾 ♿ 🄿 🖈 🔲 🄰🄴 ⓪ 𝚅𝙸𝚂𝙰   EX **o**
M 9.85/11.25 **st.** ♦ 3.25 – 🖙 4.50 – **130 rm** 30.75/41.00 **s.** – SB (weekends only) 61.70/76.20 **st.**

🏨 **Cobden**, 166-174 Hagley Rd, Edgbaston, B16 9NZ, W : 2 m. on A 456 🕿 454 6621, Group
Telex 339715, 🚗 – 🛗 📺 🚾 ▥🚾 ♿ 🄿 🖈 🔲 🄰🄴 𝚅𝙸𝚂𝙰   EX **n**
closed Christmas – **M** 4.00/7.00 **st.** – **210 rm** 🖙 17.00/38.00 **st.** – SB (weekends only) 41.70/47.70 **st.**

🏨 **Norfolk**, 257-267 Hagley Rd, Edgbaston, B16 9NA, W : 2 ¼ m. on A 456 🕿 454 8071,
Group Telex 339715, 🚗 – 🛗 📺 🚾 ▥🚾 ♿ 🄿 🖈 🔲 🄰🄴 𝚅𝙸𝚂𝙰   EX **u**
closed Christmas – **M** 4.00/7.00 **st.** (unlicensed) – **175 rm** 🖙 16.00/36.00 **st.** – SB (weekends only) 39.70/44.70 **st.**

✕✕ **Sloans**, Chad Sq., off Harborne Rd., Edgbaston, B15 3TQ, 🕿 455 6697, Seafood – 🔲 🄰🄴
⓪ 𝚅𝙸𝚂𝙰   EX **v**
closed Saturday lunch, Sunday and Bank Holidays – **M** a la carte 11.00/23.10 **t.**

✕✕ **Rajdoot**, 12-22 Albert St., B4 7UD, 🕿 643 8805, Indian rest. – 🔲 🄰🄴 ⓪ 𝚅𝙸𝚂𝙰   KZ **c**
closed Sunday lunch and 25-26 December – **M** a la carte 8.80/13.30 **t.** ♦ 2.40.

✕✕ **Jonathans'**, 16-20 Wolverhampton Rd, B68 0LH, W : 4 m. by A 456 🕿 429 3757, English
rest. – 🔲 🄰🄴 ⓪ 𝚅𝙸𝚂𝙰
closed Saturday lunch and 26-27 December – **M** a la carte 11.00/13.00 **st.** ♦ 3.00.

✕✕ **Dynasty**, 93-103 Hurst St., B5 4TE, 🕿 622 1410, Chinese rest.. 🔲 🄰🄴 ⓪ 𝚅𝙸𝚂𝙰   KZ **e**
M 5.00/7.00 **t.** ♦ 2.70.

✕✕ **Lorenzo**, 3 Park St., Digbeth, B5 5JD, 🕿 643 0541, Italian rest. – 🔲 🄰🄴 ⓪ 𝚅𝙸𝚂𝙰   KZ **o**
closed Saturday lunch, Monday dinner, Sunday, 3 weeks July-August and Bank Holidays
– **M** a la carte 7.30/13.20 **t.** ♦ 3.10.

✕ **La Capanna**, 43 Hurst St., B5 4BD, 🕿 622 2287, Italian rest. – 🄿 🔲 🄰🄴 ⓪ 𝚅𝙸𝚂𝙰   KZ **n**
closed Sunday, 25 December and Bank Holidays – **M** a la carte 6.60/10.80 **t.** ♦ 2.40.

✕ **Pinocchio**, 8 Chad Sq., off Harborne Rd, B15 3TQ, W : 2 ¾ m. off A 456 🕿 454 8672,
Italian rest. – 🔲 🄰🄴 ⓪ 𝚅𝙸𝚂𝙰   EX **v**
closed Sunday – **M** a la carte 7.10/11.00 **t.** ♦ 2.50.

at Walmley NE : 6 m. by B 4148 – ✉ Sutton Coldfield – ☺ 021 Birmingham :

🏨 **Penns Hall** (Embassy) 🏊, Penns Lane, B76 8LH, 🕿 351 3111, Telex 335789, 🌿, 🚗 – 🛗
📺 🄿 🖈 🔲 🄰🄴 ⓪ 𝚅𝙸𝚂𝙰 🎎
closed Bank Holidays – **M** (closed Sunday dinner to non-residents) (bar lunch Saturday) a
la carte 11.30/17.50 **st.** ♦ 4.75 – 🖙 4.25 – **115 rm** 30.00/49.00 – SB (weekends only) 45.00/50.00 **st.**

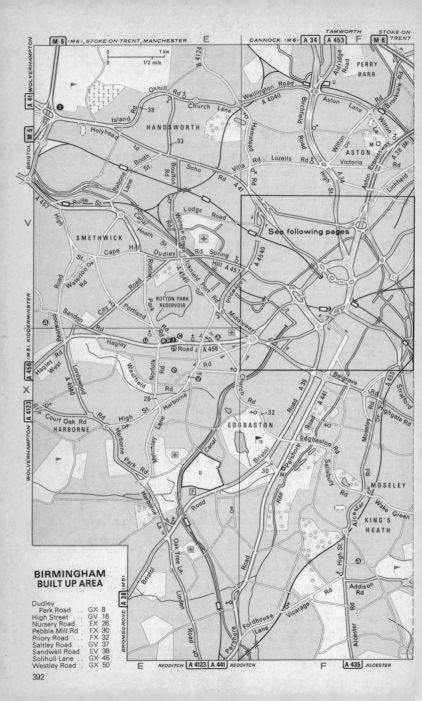

A41 WOLVERHAMPTON

M5

BRISTOL M5

0   1 km
0   1/2 mile

A4124

Oxhill Rd.
Church Lane
Wellington Road
A4040

PERRY BARR

Aldridge Road
Birchfield

Aston Lane

Brookvale Rd.

Island Rd.
38

HANDSWORTH

Holyhead Rd.

33

Hamstead Rd.

Witton Cr.
Witton La.

Wilton Rd.

ASTON

M

Victoria

A38 (M)
Rd.

Lichfield

Booth St.
Boulton Rd.
Soho Rd.

Villa Rd.
A41

Lozells Rd.

High St.

A34

Aston Expressway

A457

Rolfe St.

Canal

Lodge Road

Winson Green Rd.

Spring Hill A457

A4540

See following pages

V

SMETHWICK

Cape Hill

Dudley Road

Heath Rd.

Rotton

Ichfield Port Rd.

Ladywood Middleway

A4540

Waterloo Rd.

City Rd.

Portland Rd.

ROTTON PARK RESERVOIR

Sandon Rd.

Park Road

A38

Belgrave

A435

Stratford Rd.

WOLVERHAMPTON A4123

A456 (M5), KIDDERMINSTER

Hagley Rd.

Hagley Road West

Lordswood Rd.

A4040

Norfolk Rd.

Westfield Rd.

Road A456

Church Rd.

A38

A441

Highgate Rd.

Moseley Rd.

X

26

Harborne

32

Court Oak Rd.
HARBORNE

High St.

Harborne Lane

Metchley Lane

EDGBASTON

18

Bristol Rd.

Edgbaston Rd.

Salisbury Rd.

MOSELEY

Wake Green Rd.

Alcester Rd.

Harborne Park Rd.

Canal

U

P

30

M

Rea

KING'S HEATH

High St.

BROMSGROVE A38 (M5)

Oak Tree La.

Bristol Road

Pershore Road

Fordhouse Lane

Vicarage Road

Alcester Road

Addison Rd.

Linden Road

BIRMINGHAM BUILT UP AREA

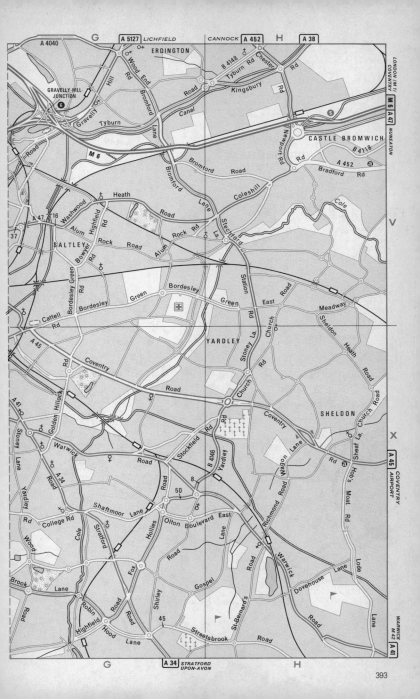

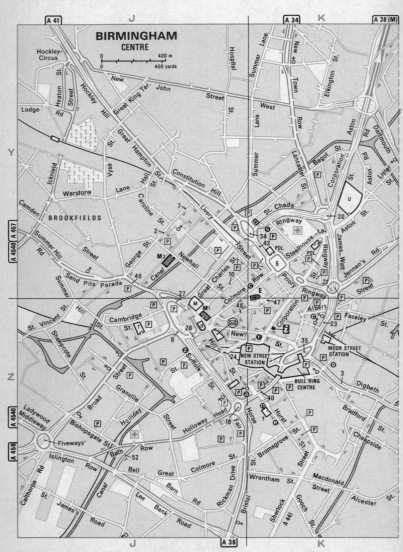

BIRMINGHAM
CENTRE

BIRMINGHAM TOWN PLANS

395

at Castle Bromwich NE : 6 m. by A 47 – ⊠ ✪ Birmingham :

🏨 Bradford Arms, Chester Rd, B36 0AG, ☎ 747 0227 – 📺 ⌁wc ⓒ ⓟ, ◪ 困 ① 𝑉𝐼𝑆𝐴
closed 3 days at Christmas – **M** (grill rest. only) – **30 rm** ⊴ 27.50/32.00 **st.**   HV **a**

at Sutton Coldfield NE : 8 m. by A 38 – ⊠ Sutton Coldfield – ✪ 021 Birmingham :

🏯 **Belfry** (Best Western) ⇘, Lichfield Rd, Wishaw, B76 9PR, E : 3 m. on A 446 ☎
0675 (Curdworth) 70301, Telex 338848, ⩽, ◪, ⬛, ☞, park, ⚒, squash – 📺 ☎ ⓟ, ◪
◪ 困 𝑉𝐼𝑆𝐴
M 8.40/17.35 **st.** 🍷 2.80 – **116 rm** ⊴ 44.50/73.00 **st.** – SB (weekends only) 57.50 **st.**

🏨 **Moor Hall** (Best Western) ⇘, Moor Hall Drive, Four Oaks, B75 6LN, NE : 1 m. by A 453
☎ 308 3751, ☞ – 📺 ⌁wc ☜ ⓟ, ◪, ◪ 困 ① 𝑉𝐼𝑆𝐴, ◪
M 9.95/12.95 **t.** 🍷 3.75 – **50 rm** ⊴ 36.00/43.00 **t.** – SB (weekends only) 42.00/52.00 **st.**

XX La Gondola, Mere Green Precinct, 304 Lichfield Rd, B74 2UW, N : 2 m. on A 5127 ☎
308 6782, Italian rest..

XX **Le Bon Viveur,** 65 Birmingham Rd, B72 1QF, ☎ 355 5836 – ▤, ◪ 困 ① 𝑉𝐼𝑆𝐴
closed Saturday lunch, Sunday, Monday and August – **M** a la carte 9.85/13.45 **t.** 🍷 2.75.

at National Exhibition Centre E : 9 ½ m. on A 45 – ⊠ ✪ 021 Birmingham :

🏯 **Birmingham Metropole,** Blackfirs Lane, Bickenhill, B40 1PP, ☎ 780 4242, Telex 336129,
⩽, squash – 🛗 ▤ 📺 ☎ ⓟ, 𝑉𝐼𝑆𝐴
M a la carte 7.50/17.50 **t.** 🍷 3.00 – ⊴ 3.75 – **501 rm** 45.00/70.00 **t.** – SB (weekends only)(spring only) 48.00/64.90 **st.**

🏨 **Warwick,** Blackfirs Lane, Bickenhill, B40 1PP, ☎ 780 4242, Telex 336129 – 🛗 ▤ 📺
⌁wc ☎ ⓟ, ◪ 困 ① 𝑉𝐼𝑆𝐴
Exhibitions only – **M** a la carte 7.50/17.50 **t.** 🍷 3.00 – ⊴ 3.75 – **200 rm** 41.00/82.00 **t.**

🏨 **Arden,** Coventry Rd, Bickenhill, B92 0EH, S : ½ m. on A 45 ⊠ Solihull ☎
067 55 (Hampton-in-Arden) 3221 – 🛗 📺 ⌁wc ☜ ⓟ, ◪, ◪ 困 ① 𝑉𝐼𝑆𝐴
M 6.95/15.00 **st.** 🍷 1.85 – ⊴ 3.50 – **46 rm** 22.00/36.00 **st.**

at Sheldon SE : 6 m. on A 45 – HX – ⊠ ✪ 021 Birmingham :

🏨 **Wheatsheaf** (Golden Oak), 2225 Coventry Rd, B26 3EH, ☎ 743 6021 – 📺 ▥wc ☜ ⓟ,
◪, ◪ 困 𝑉𝐼𝑆𝐴, ✿
M *(closed Saturday lunch, Sunday and Bank Holidays)* 6.50/8.50 **t.** 🍷 2.70 – **84 rm**   HX **a**
⊴ 31.50/37.00 **t.**

at Birmingham Airport SE : 7 m. on A 45 – ⊠ ✪ 021 Birmingham :

🏯 **Excelsior** (T.H.F.), Coventry Rd, Elmdon, B26 3QW, ☎ 743 8141, Telex 338005 – 📺 ⓟ,
◪, ◪ 困 ① 𝑉𝐼𝑆𝐴
M 6.35/7.95 **st.** 🍷 2.60 – ⊴ 5.50 – **141 rm** 36.00/45.00 **st.**

at West Bromwich NW : 6 m. on A 41 – ⊠ West Bromwich – ✪ 021 Birmingham :

🏨 **West Bromwich Moat House** (Q.M.H.) Birmingham Rd, B70 6RS, S : 1 m. by A 41
☎ 553 6111, Telex 336232 – 🛗 📺 ⌁wc ☜ ⓟ, ◪, ◪ 困 ① 𝑉𝐼𝑆𝐴
M 7.65/7.95 **st.** 🍷 3.40 – **179 rm** ⊴ 36.00/48.00 **st.** – SB (weekends only) 37.00 **st.**

at Great Barr NW : 6 m. on A 34 – ⊠ Great Barr – ✪ 021 Birmingham :

🏨 **Post House** (T.H.F), Chapel Lane, B43 7BG, ☎ 357 7444, Telex 338497, ⤴ heated – 📺
⌁wc ☜ ⓟ, ◪, ◪ 困 ① 𝑉𝐼𝑆𝐴
M a la carte 10.15/15.25 **st.** 🍷 2.60 – ⊴ 5.00 – **204 rm** 34.50/42.00 **st.**

🏨 **Barr,** Pear Tree Drive, Newton Rd, B43 6HS, W : 1 m. by A 4041 ☎ 357 1141, Telex
336406, ☞ – 📺 ⌁wc ☜ ⓟ, ◪, ◪ 困 ① 𝑉𝐼𝑆𝐴, ◪
closed 24 to 26 December – **M** 5.50/6.00 **st.** – **111 rm** ⊴ 33.00/43.00 **st.** – SB (weekends only) 76.00 **st.**

When in Europe never be without :

Michelin **Main Road** Maps (1 inch : 16 miles) ;

Michelin Sectional Maps ;

Michelin Red Guides :

> **Benelux, Deutschland, España Portugal, France,
> Great Britain and Ireland, Italia**

(Hotels and restaurants listed with symbols ; preliminary pages in English)

Michelin Green Guides :

> **Austria, England : The West Country, Germany, Italy, London,
> Portugal, Spain, Switzerland,**

> **Brittany, Châteaux of the Loire, Dordogne, French Riviera,
> Normandy, Paris, Provence**

(Sights and touring programmes described fully in English ; town plans).

See : Castle★ (site★, ≤★★, Regalia★, Scottish United Services Museum★, Scottish National War Memorial) *AC* DZ – National Museum of Antiquities★★ EY **M1** – National Gallery★★ DY **M2** – St. Giles' Cathedral★ EYZ – Charlotte Square★ CY – National Portrait Gallery★ *AC* EY **M1** – Royal Scottish Museum★ EZ **M3** – Old houses and closes near Lawnmarket, Grassmarket★ DEYZ – Abbey of Holyrood★ *AC* – Royal Botanic Gardens★ – Princes Street ≤★★ DY – Palace of Holyrood (State apartments★, historic apartments★★) *AC* – Calton Hill ≤★ EY – Arthur's Seat ≤★ – Drama and Music Festival in summer.

Envir. : Roslyn Chapel★★ (15C) *AC*, S : 6 ½ m. by A 701 – Leith ≤★ of the Firth of Forth, NE : 2 ½ m. – Craigmillar Castle★ (stronghold) 14C, *AC*, SE : 3 m. – Crichton Castle★ (16C) *AC*, SE : 13 m. by A 7.

ᴵ18 Liberton, Kingston Grange, 297 Gilmerton Rd *℘* 664 8580, SE : 3 ½ m. – ᴵ18 Silverknowes, Silverknowes Parkway, *℘* 336 3843, W : 4 m. – ᴵ18 Craigmillar Park, Observatory Rd *℘* 667 2837 – ᴵ18 Carrick Knowe, Glendevon Park *℘* 337 1096, W : 5 m.

✈ *℘* 333 1000, Telex 727615, W : 6 m. by A 8 – **Terminal :** Waverley Bridge.

🚗 *℘* 556 5633.

🛈 5 Waverley Bridge *℘* 226 6591 – Edinburgh Airport *℘* 333 2167 and 344 3125.

Glasgow 46 – Newcastle-upon-Tyne 105.

Plan on next page

🏨 **Caledonian,** Princes St., EH1 2AB, *℘* 225 2433, Telex 72179 – 🛗 📺 ☎ 🅿. 🍸. 🖭 🗚🖲 ⓞ
VISA. ⚓ CY **n**
M (rest. see **Pompadour** below) – � 6.50 – **254 rm** 38.00/85.00 **st.** – SB (weekends only)(winter only) 75.00 **st.**

🏨 **George** (Inter-Con), 19-21 George St., EH2 2PB, *℘* 225 1251, Telex 72570 – 🛗 ▤ rest 📺
☎ & 🅿. 🍸. 🖭 🗚🖲 ⓞ *VISA* DY **z**
M 9.25/9.75 **t.** ♦ 3.00 – ⊇ 6.00 – **196 rm** 38.00/80.00 **t.** – SB (weekends only) 56.50/63.50 **st.**

🏨 **Ladbroke Dragonara** (Ladbroke), Bells Mills, 69 Belford Rd, EH4 3DG, *℘* 332 2545,
Telex 727979 – 🛗 📺 ☎ & 🅿. 🍸. 🖭 🗚🖲 ⓞ *VISA*. ⚓ CY **i**
M 8.95/10.95 **t.** ♦ 3.50 – ⊇ 5.75 – **145 rm** 55.00/85.00 **t.** – SB (weekends only) 58.00/70.00 **st.**

🏨 **Roxburghe** (Best Western), 38 Charlotte Sq., EH2 4HG, *℘* 225 3921, Telex 727054 – 🛗
📺. 🍸. 🖭 🗚🖲 ⓞ DY **o**
M 8.00/11.00 **st.** ♦ 3.00 – ⊇ 5.00 – **72 rm** 40.00/90.00 **st.**

🏨 **Royal Scot** (Swallow), 111 Glasgow Rd, EH12 8NF, W : 4 ½ m. on A 8 *℘* 334 9191, Telex
727197 – 🛗 📺 ☎ & 🅿. 🍸. 🖭 🗚🖲 ⓞ
M (carving rest.) 9.50 **st.** ♦ 3.70 – **252 rm** ⊇ 44.00/56.00 **st.** – SB (weekends only) 50.00 **st.**

🏨 **Post House** (T.H.F.), Corstorphine Rd, EH12 6UA, W : 3 m. on A 8 *℘* 334 8221, Telex
727103, ≤ – 🛗 📺 ⊟wc ⚏ & 🅿. 🍸. 🖭 🗚🖲 ⓞ *VISA*
M a la carte 10.65/16.15 **st.** ♦ 2.45 – ⊇ 5.00 – **208 rm** 39.00/48.00 **st.**

🏨 **Crest** (Crest), Queensferry Rd, EH4 3HL, NW : 2 m. on A 90 *℘* 332 2442, Telex 72541 –
🛗 ▤ rest 📺 ⊟wc ☎ 🅿. 🖭 🗚🖲 ⓞ *VISA*. ⚓
M approx. 12.00 **st.** – ⊇ 5.25 – **120 rm** 43.50/56.00 **st.**

🏨 **King James Thistle** (Thistle), 7 St. James Centre, Leith St., EH1 3SW, *℘* 556 0111,
Telex 727200 – 🛗 📺 ⊟wc ⊪wc ⚏ 🅿. 🍸. 🖭 🗚🖲 ⓞ *VISA*. ⚓ EY **u**
M 9.00/12.50 **t.** ♦ 3.45 – ⊇ 4.75 – **141 rm** 45.00/70.00 **t.** – SB (weekends only) 66.00 **st.**

🏨 **Stakis Grosvenor** (Stakis), Grosvenor St., EH12 5EF, *℘* 226 6001, Telex 72445 – 🛗 📺
⊟wc ⊪wc ☎ & 🍸. CZ **a**
130 rm.

🏨 **Howard,** 32-36 Gt. King St., EH3 6QH, *℘* 557 3500, Telex 727887 – 🛗 📺 ⊟wc ⊪wc ☎
🅿. 🖭 🗚🖲 ⓞ *VISA* DY **s**
closed 24 to 26 December and 31 December-2 January – **M** 6.50/13.50 **t.** ♦ 3.00 – **25 rm**
⊇ 37.50/59.00 **t.**

XXXX **Pompadour** (at Caledonian H.), Princes St., EH1 2AB, *℘* 225 2433, Telex 72179 – 🅿. 🖭
🗚🖲 *VISA* CY **n**
closed lunch Saturday and Sunday – **M** a la carte 9.30/20.50 **st.** ♦ 3.25.

XXX **Prestonfield House** ⚶ with rm, Priestfield Rd, EH16 5UT, SE : 2 ½ m. off A 68
℘ 667 8000, Telex 727396, ≤, « Elegant 17C mansion », 🎋, park – ⊪ ⚛ 🅿. 🖭 🗚🖲 ⓞ
VISA
M a la carte 9.00/14.50 **t.** ♦ 2.50 – **5 rm** ⊇ 40.00/52.50 **t.**

XXX **Howtowdie,** 27a Stafford St., EH3 7BJ, *℘* 225 6291 – 🖭 🗚🖲 ⓞ *VISA* CY **u**
closed Sunday, 25-26 December and 1-2 January – **M** a la carte 19.55/27.85 **t.** ♦ 4.50.

XX **Cosmo,** 58a North Castle St., EH2 3LU, *℘* 226 6743, Italian rest. – 🖭 *VISA* DY **r**
closed Saturday lunch, Sunday and Monday – **M** a la carte 8.85/12.90 **t.** ♦ 2.75.

XX **Raffaelli,** 10-11 Randolph Pl., EH3 7TA, *℘* 225 6060, Italian rest. – 🖭 🗚🖲 ⓞ *VISA* CY **c**
closed Saturday lunch and Sunday – **M** a la carte 7.00/12.05 **t.** ♦ 2.40.

X **L'Auberge,** 56 St. Mary's St., EH1 1SX, *℘* 556 5888, French rest. – 🖭 🗚🖲 *VISA* EYZ **c**
M a la carte 9.20/13.60 **t.** ♦ 3.50.

EDINBURGH

※ **Mermans,** 8-10 Eyre Pl., EH5 5EP, ℰ 556 1177, Seafood – 🆔 🆎 ⓪ 𝘝𝘐𝘚𝘈
closed Sunday, Christmas, New Year and Bank Holidays – **M** (dinner only) a la carte
6.05/13.75 **t.** 🍴 2.60.

※ **Vito's,** 55a Frederick St., EH2 1LH, ℰ 225 5052, Italian rest. – 🆔 🆎 ⓪ 𝘝𝘐𝘚𝘈   DY **i**
closed Sunday and 1 January – **M** a la carte 7.30/14.60 **t.**

at Bonnyrigg S : 8 m. by A 7 on A 6094 – ✉ Bonnyrigg – ✪ 0875 Gorebridge :

🏛 **Dalhousie Castle** 🦢, EH19 3JB, SE : 1 ¼ m. on B 704 ℰ 20153, Telex 72380, ≼,
« Converted 12C castle », 🌳, park – 📺 ℗, 🛎 🆎 ⓪ 𝘝𝘐𝘚𝘈 ✄
M a la carte 12.75/21.95 **t.** – **24 rm** 🖵 53.00/97.50 **t.**

GLASGOW Lanark. (Strathclyde) 🄰🄾🄸 🄰🄾🄸 H 16 – pop. 897,483 – ✪ 041.

See : St. Mungo Cathedral★★★ DYZ – Art Gallery and Museum★★ CY – Provand's Lordship★
DZ **D** – Pollock House★ (Spanish paintings).

🏌 Linn Park, Simshill Rd ℰ 637 5871, S : 4 m. – 🏌 Lethamhill, Cumbernauld Rd ℰ 770 6220
– 🏌 Knightswood, Lincoln Av. ℰ 959 2131, W : 4 m. – 🏌 Ruchill, Brassey St. ℰ 946 9728.

Access to Oban by helicopter.

✈ Glasgow Airport : ℰ 887 1111, Telex 778219, W : 8 m. by M 8 – **Terminal :** Coach service
from Glasgow Central and Queen Street main line Railway Stations and from Anderston Cross
and Buchanan Bus Stations.

✈ see also Prestwick.

🚇 George Sq. ℰ 221 6136/7 or 221 7371/2, Telex 779504.

Edinburgh 46 – Manchester 221.

Plan on following pages

🏨 **Holiday Inn,** Argyle St., Anderston, G3 8RR, ℰ 226 5577, Telex 776355, 🖵 – 📶 🍽 📺
🛎 🕭 🍴 🛝 🆔 🆎 ⓪ 𝘝𝘐𝘚𝘈   CZ **a**
M 11.50/9.95 **st.** – 🖵 5.65 – **296 rm** 46.00/82.00 **s.**

🏨 **Albany** (T.H.F.), Bothwell St., G2 7EN, ℰ 248 2656, Telex 77440, ≼ – 📶 📺 🕭 ℗ 🛝 🛝
🆎 ⓪ 𝘝𝘐𝘚𝘈   CZ **z**
M 9.95 **st.** 🍴 2.85 – 🖵 5.50 – **251 rm** 45.00/57.50 **st.**

🏛 **Glasgow Skean Dhu** (Mt. Charlotte), 36 Cambridge St., G2 3HN, ℰ 332 3311, Telex
777334 – 📶 📺 🕭 ℗ 🛝 🛝 🆔 🆎 ⓪ 𝘝𝘐𝘚𝘈   DY **z**
M 8.50/13.00 **st.** 🍴 2.75 – 🖵 3.95 – **320 rm** 39.50/50.00 **st.** – SB (weekends only) 49.00 **st.**

🏛 **Stakis Grosvenor** (Stakis), Grosvenor Terr., Great Western Rd, G12 0TA, ℰ 339 8811,
Telex 776247 – 📶 📺 🕭 ℗ 🛝 🆔 🆎 ⓪ 𝘝𝘐𝘚𝘈   CY **r**
M 7.00/11.00 **t.** 🍴 3.30 – **95 rm** 🖵 48.50/60.00 **t.** – SB (weekends only) 50.00/54.00 **st.**

🏛 **White House** 🦢 without rest., 11-14 Cleveden Cres., G12 0PA, ℰ 339 9375 – 📺 🛝
🆔 🆎 ⓪ 𝘝𝘐𝘚𝘈 ✄
M (room service only) a la carte approx. 10.75 **t.** – 🖵 4.40 – **32 rm** 30.00/60.00 – SB
(weekends only) 56.70 **st.**

🏛 **Stakis Ingram** (Stakis), 201 Ingram St., G1 1DQ, ℰ 248 4401 – 📶 📺 ⌐wc 🕭 ℗ 🛝
🆔 🆎 ⓪ 𝘝𝘐𝘚𝘈   DZ **c**
M (bar lunch) a la carte 6.95/9.85 **st.** 🍴 3.25 – **90 rm** 🖵 40.00/55.00 **st.** – SB 46.00/64.00 **st.**

🏛 **Bellahouston Swallow** (Swallow), 517 Paisley Rd West, G51 1RW, ℰ 427 3146, Telex
778795 – 📶 📺 ⌐wc 🌡wc 🎛 ℗ 🛝 🆔 🆎 ⓪ 𝘝𝘐𝘚𝘈
M (buffet lunch Saturday) 5.50/7.50 **st.** 🍴 3.25 – **122 rm** 🖵 38.00/46.00 **st.** – SB 40.00 **st.**

🏛 **Crest** (Crest), Argyle St., G2 8LL, ℰ 248 2355, Telex 779652 – 📶 📺 ⌐wc 🕭 🛝 🆔 🆎
⓪ 𝘝𝘐𝘚𝘈 ✄   CZ **x**
M approx. 11.00 **st.** – 🖵 4.95 – **123 rm** 37.50/46.50 **st.**

XXXX **Malmaison** (at Central H.), Gordon St., G1 3SF, ℰ 221 9680, Telex 777771, French rest.
– 🆔 🆎 ⓪ 𝘝𝘐𝘚𝘈   DZ **e**
closed Saturday lunch, Sunday and 2 weeks July – **M** a la carte 15.50/20.50 **t.** 🍴 3.00.

XXX **Ambassador,** 19-20 Blythswood Sq., G2 4AS, ℰ 221 2034, Dancing (Tuesday-Saturday)
– 🆔 🆎 ⓪ 𝘝𝘐𝘚𝘈   CY **u**
closed Sunday and Bank Holidays – **M** (bar lunch Saturday) a la carte 12.20/18.90 **t.**
🍴 3.50.

XX **Colonial,** 25 High St., G1 1LX, ℰ 552 1923 – 🆔 🆎 ⓪ 𝘝𝘐𝘚𝘈   DZ **a**
closed Sunday and Monday – **M** a la carte 7.80/13.30 **t.** 🍴 2.95.

※ **Poacher's,** Ruthven Lane, off Byres Rd, G12 9BG, ℰ 339 0932 – ℗ 🆔 🆎 ⓪ 𝘝𝘐𝘚𝘈
closed Sunday, 25 December and 1-3 January – **M** a la carte 9.00/12.75 **t.** 🍴 2.70.

※ Kensingtons, 164 Darnley St., G41 2LL, ℰ 424 3662.

※ **Ubiquitous Chip,** 12 Ashton Lane, off Byres Rd, G12 8SJ, ℰ 334 5007, Bistro – 🆔 🆎
⓪ 𝘝𝘐𝘚𝘈
closed Sunday, Christmas Day and New Year – **M** a la carte 5.15/15.60 **t.**

at Glasgow Airport Renfrew. (Strathclyde) W : 8 m. by M 8 – ✉ ✪ 041 Glasgow :

🏛 **Excelsior** (T.H.F.), Abbotsinch, PA3 2TR, ℰ 887 1212, Telex 777733 – 📶 📺 🗝 ℗ 🛝 🆔
🆎 ⓪ 𝘝𝘐𝘚𝘈
M 5.25/7.95 **st.** 🍴 2.75 – 🖵 5.50 – **305 rm** 43.00/53.50 **st.**

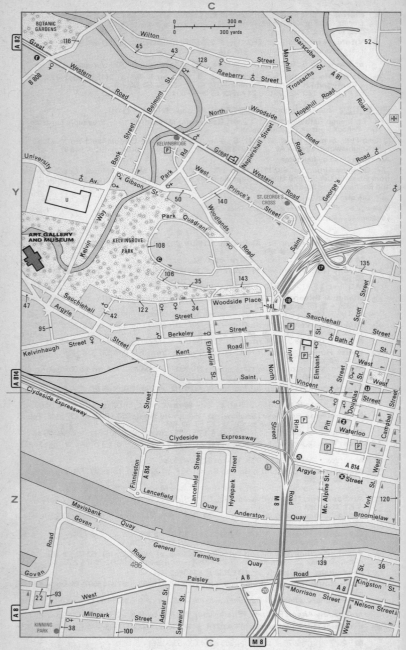

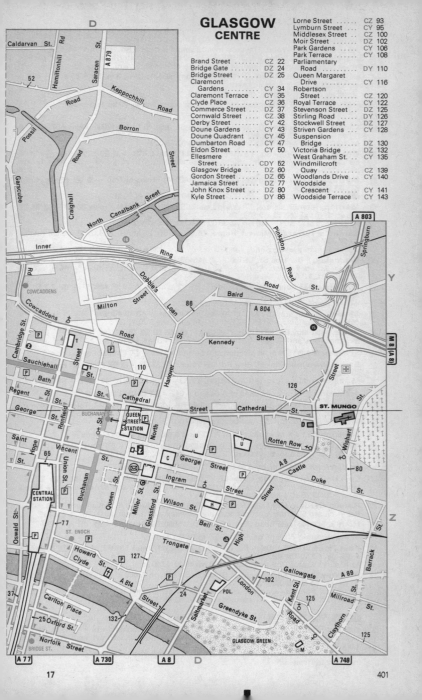

LEEDS West Yorks. 402 P 22 – pop. 496,009 – ECD : Wednesday – ☎ 0532.

See : St. John's Church★ 17C DZ **A** – Envir. : Temple Newsam House★ 17C (interior★★) AC, E : 4 m. – Kirkstall Abbey★ (ruins 12C) AC, NW : 3 m.

ℹ️, ℹ️ The Lady Dorothy Wood, The Lord Irwin, Temple Newsam Rd, Halton ℘ 645624, E : 3 m. – ℹ️ Gotts Park, Armley Ridge Rd, ℘ 638232, W : 2 m. – ℹ️ Horsforth, Layton Rise ℘ 586819, NW : 6 m. – ℹ️ Middleton Park, Town St., Middleton ℘ 700449, S : 3 m.

✈ Leeds and Bradford Airport : ℘ 0532 (Rawdon) 503431, NW : 8 m. by A 65 and A 658 – **Terminal :** Vicar Lane, Bus Station, Leeds.

ℹ️ Central Library, Calverley St. ℘ 462454.

♦London 204 – ♦Liverpool 75 – ♦Manchester 43 – ♦Newcastle-upon-Tyne 95 – ♦Nottingham 74.

Plan on next page

🏨 **Ladbroke Dragonara** (Ladbroke), Neville St., LS1 4BX, ℘ 442000, Telex 557143 – 🛗 📺 ☎ ⚿ 🅿 🔥 🔥 🔼 AE ⑩ VISA — DZ **r**
M 7.25/10.75 **st.** ⓘ 4.45 – ⌷ 5.50 – **234 rm** 44.00/58.00 **st.**

🏨 **Queens** (T.H.F.), City Sq., LS1 1PL, ℘ 431323, Telex 55161 – 🛗 📺 ⌷wc ☎ 🔥 🔼 AE ⑩ VISA – **M** (carving lunch Saturday and Sunday) 4.95/6.50 **st.** ⓘ 3.70 – ⌷ 5.50 – **197 rm** 29.50/52.50 **st.** — DZ **a**

🏨 **Metropole** (T.H.F.), King St., LS1 2HQ, ℘ 450841, Telex 557755 – 🛗 📺 ⌷wc ☎ ⑩ 🔥 🔼 AE ⑩ VISA — CZ **o**
M (carving rest.) 7.95 **st.** ⓘ 2.95 – ⌷ 5.25 – **110 rm** 27.00/41.50 **st.**

🏨 **Merrion,** Merrion Centre, 17 Wade Lane, LS2 8NH, ℘ 439191, Telex 55459 – 🛗 ▤ 📺 ⌷wc ☎ 🅿 🔥 🔼 AE ⑩ VISA 🍴 — DZ **x**
M 5.95/7.75 **st.** ⓘ 3.00 – **120 rm** ⌷ 39.00/55.00 **st.** – SB 46.00 **st.**

🍴🍴🍴 **Gardini's Terrazza,** Minerva House, 16 Greek St., LS1 5RU, ℘ 432880, Italian rest. – 🔼 AE VISA — CDZ **n**
closed Saturday lunch, Sunday and Bank Holidays – **M** a la carte 9.30/12.60 **t.** ⓘ 2.90.

🍴🍴🍴 **Mandalay,** 8 Harrison St., LS1 6PA, ℘ 446453, Indian rest. – 🔼 AE ⑩ VISA — DZ **e**
closed Saturday lunch, Sunday, Easter Monday and 25-26 December – **M** a la carte 9.15/10.00 **t.** ⓘ 3.50.

🍴🍴 **Embassy,** 333 Roundhay Rd, LS8 4HT, NE : 2 ½ m. by A 58 ℘ 490562 – 🅿 🔼 AE ⑩ VISA — BY **v**
closed Sunday – **M** (dinner only) 11.80 **t.** ⓘ 2.50.

🍴🍴 **Shabab,** 2 Eastgate, LS2 7JL, ℘ 468988, Indian rest. – 🔼 AE ⑩ VISA — DZ **v**
closed Sunday lunch and 25 December – **M** a la carte 8.70/12.25 **t.**

🍴 **Rules,** 188 Selby Rd, LS15 0LF, ℘ 604564 – 🅿 🔼 AE ⑩ VISA
M (dinner only and Sunday lunch) a la carte 7.95/11.00 **st.** ⓘ 3.15.

at Seacroft NE : 5 ½ m. at junction of A 64 and A 6120 – ✉ ☎ 0532 Leeds :

🏨 **Stakis Windmill** (Stakis), Ring Rd, LS14 5QP, ℘ 732323 – 🛗 📺 ⌷wc ☎ ⚿ 🅿 🔥 🔼 AE ⑩ VISA
M (grill rest. only) a la carte 5.70/11.25 **st.** ⓘ 2.80 – **40 rm** ⌷ 28.00/44.00 **st.** – SB 46.00 **st.**

at Garforth E : 6 m. at junction of A 64 and A 642 – ✉ ☎ 0532 Leeds :

🏨 **Ladbroke Mercury** (Ladbroke), Wakefield Rd, LS25 1LH, ℘ 866556, Telex 556324 – 📺 ⌷wc ☎ ⚿ 🅿 🔥 🔼 AE ⑩ VISA – **M** (carving rest.) 7.95/9.50 **t.** ⓘ 2.95 – ⌷ 5.50 – **143 rm** 36.00/44.00 **t.** – SB (weekends only) 47.00/49.00 **st.**

at Oulton SE : 6 ¼ m. at junction of A 639 and A 642 – ✉ ☎ 0532 Leeds :

🏨 **Crest** (Crest), The Grove, LS26 8EJ, ℘ 826201, Telex 557646 – 📺 ⌷wc ☎ ⚿ 🅿 🔼 AE ⑩ VISA 🍴 – **M** approx. 11.00 **st.** – ⌷ 5.25 – **40 rm** 42.00/53.00 **st.**

at Horsforth NW : 5 m. by A 65 off A 6120 – ✉ ☎ 0532 Leeds :

🍴🍴🍴 **Low Hall,** Calverley Lane, LS18 4EF, ℘ 588221, « Elizabethan manor », 🌳 – 🅿 🔼 VISA
closed Saturday lunch, Sunday, Monday, 25 to 30 December and Bank Holidays – **M** a la carte 7.70/13.75 **st.** ⓘ 2.50.

🍴🍴 **Roman Garden,** Hall Lane, Hall Park, LS18 5JY, ℘ 587962, ≼, Italian rest. – 🅿 🔼 AE VISA – *closed Saturday lunch, Sunday and Monday* – **M** a la carte 5.00/9.40 **t.** ⓘ 2.75.

🍴🍴 **Morty's,** 141-145 New Road Side, LS18 4QD, ℘ 580293, Seafood – 🅿.

at Bramhope NW : 8 m. on A 660 – ✉ ☎ 0532 Leeds :

🏨 **Post House** (T.H.F.), Otley Rd, LS16 9JJ, ℘ 842911, Telex 556367, ≼ – 🛗 📺 ⌷wc ☎ ⚿ 🅿 🔼 AE ⑩ VISA
M 10.40/13.95 **st.** ⓘ 2.50 – ⌷ 5.00 – **120 rm** 40.00/47.00 **st.**

🏨 **Parkway** (Embassy), Otley Rd, LS16 8AG, S : 2 m. on A 660 ℘ 672551, 🌳 – 📺 ⌷wc ☎ 🅿 🔥 🔼 AE ⑩ VISA 🍴 – **M** *(closed Saturday lunch)* (Sunday dinner residents only) 8.00 **st.** ⓘ 4.75 – ⌷ 4.25 – **39 rm** 30.00/45.00 **st.** – SB (weekends only) 41.00/48.00 **st.**

Ilkley West Yorks NW : 16 m. by A 660 on A 65 – 402 O 22 – pop. 10,930 – ☎ 0943.

🍴🍴🍴 ❀❀ **Box Tree,** 35-37 Church St., LS29 9DR, ℘ 608484, « Ornate decor » – 🔼 AE ⑩ VISA
closed Sunday, Monday, 25 December and 1 January – **M** (dinner only) (booking essential) a la carte 13.00/19.50 **t.**
Spec. Boudin blanc aux girolles, Fricassée de homard au gingembre et sa petite garniture, Timbale de fraises Box Tree (seasonal).

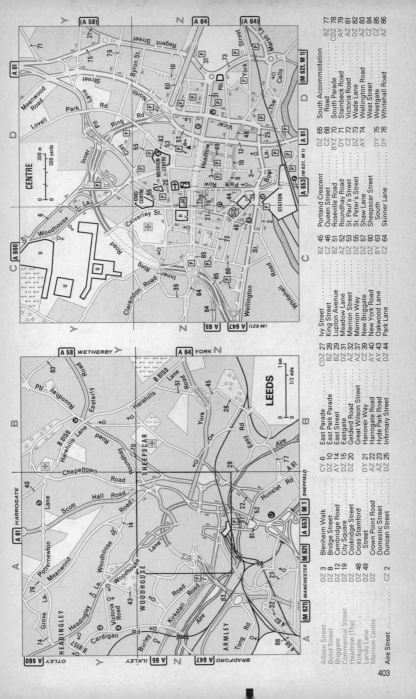

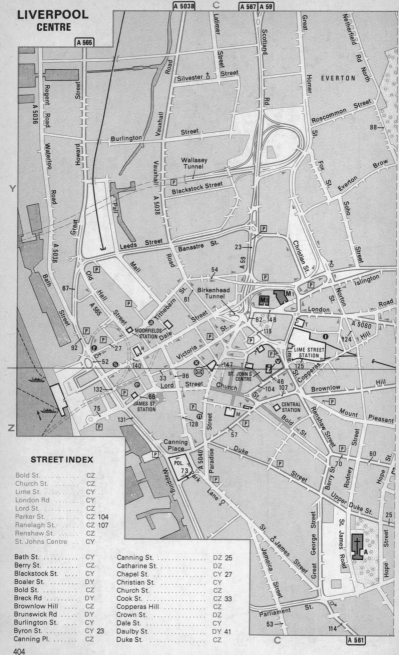

LIVERPOOL
CENTRE

A 5038 C A 567 A 59

A 565

A 5036

A 5036

EVERTON

Y

Silvester

Burlington Street

Wallasey Tunnel

Blackstock Street

Leeds Street

Banastre St.

23

54

Birkenhead Tunnel

62 148

116

67

61

M2 M1

London

A 5080

124

MOORFIELDS STATION

Dale

92

27

LIME STREET STATION

125

52

140

Victoria

33

96

147

Lord Street

Church

St. JOHN'S CENTRE

104 107

46

Copperas

Brownlow Hill

132

66

JAMES ST. STATION

75

CENTRAL STATION

Bold St.

57

131

128

Canning Place

POL 73

Canning Street

Duke

60

70

Paradise

A 5040

53

114

St. James Road

A

A 561

Z

STREET INDEX

404

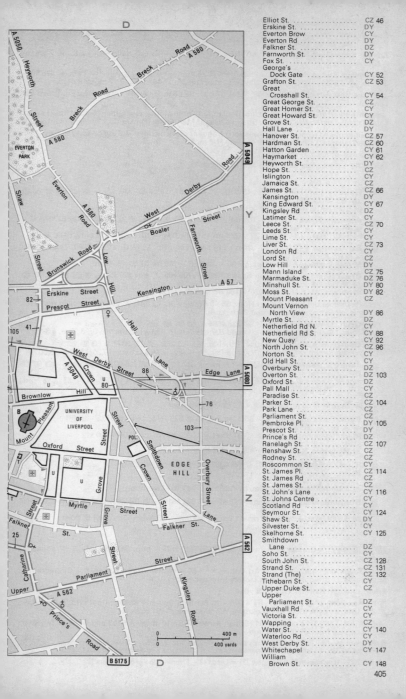

LIVERPOOL Merseyside 402 403 L 23 – pop. 610,113 – ECD : Wednesday – ✆ 051.

See : Walker Art Gallery★★ CY M1 – City of Liverpool Museums★ CY M2 – Anglican Cathedral★ (1904) CZ A – Roman Catholic Cathedral★ (1967) DZ B.

Envir. : Knowsley Safari Park★★ AC, NE : 8 m. by A 57 – Speke Hall★ (16C) AC, SE : 7 m. by A 561.

ᚓ Dunnings Bridge Rd, Bootle ✆ 928 6196, N : 5 m. by A 5036 – ᚓ Allerton Park ✆ 428 1046, S : 5 m. by B 5180 – ᚓ Childwall, Naylor's Rd, Gateacre ✆ 487 9982, E : 7 m. by B 5178.

✈ Liverpool Airport : ✆ 494 0066, Telex 629323, SE : 6 m. by A 561 – **Terminal** : Pier Head and Lime St.

ᚕ to Ireland (Dublin) (B & I Line) 1 nightly (8 h 45 mn) – to Belfast (Belfast Car Ferries) 1 daily (9 h) – to the Isle of Man : Douglas (Isle of Man Steam Packet Co.) 1-5 daily (4 h 15 mn).

ᚕ to Birkenhead (Merseyside Transport) frequent services daily (7-8 mn) – to Wallasey (Merseyside Transport) frequent services daily (7-8 mn).

🛈 29 Lime St. ✆ 709 3631 and 8681.

London 219 – Birmingham 102 – Leeds 75 – Manchester 35.

Plan on preceding pages

🏨 **Holiday Inn,** Paradise St., L1 8JD, ✆ 709 0181, Telex 627270, ▨ – 🛗 ▤ 📺 ☎ ㄅ 🅿.
🏧. 🖃 AE ⓪ VISA   CZ **n**
M 5.00/7.50 t. – **258 rm** � 45.00/60.00 st. – SB (weekends only) 50.00 st.

🏨 **Atlantic Tower Thistle** (Thistle), 30 Chapel St., L3 9RE, ✆ 227 4444, Telex 627070, ← –
🛗 📺 🅿. 🏧. 🖃 AE ⓪ VISA ⋘ –   CY **r**
M 8.00/12.00 ㄅ 3.45 – ⊆ 5.25 – **226 rm** 45.00/66.00 t. – SB (weekends only) 54.00 st.

🏨 **St. George's** (T.H.F.), St. John's Precinct, Lime St., L1 1NQ, ✆ 709 7090, Telex 627630
– 🛗 📺 ㄅ. 🏧. 🖃 AE ⓪ VISA   CY **v**
M (carving rest.) 5.95/7.95 st. ㄅ 2.60 – ⊆ 5.50 – **155 rm** 37.50/48.00 st.

🏨 **Crest** (Crest), Lord Nelson St., L3 5QB, ✆ 709 7050, Telex 627954 – 🛗 📺 ⌷wc ☎ 🅿.
🏧. 🖃 AE ⓪ VISA   CY **i**
M approx. 11.00 st. – ⊆ 5.25 – **160 rm** 40.00/51.00 st.

XXX **Ristorante del Secolo,** First Floor, 36-40 Stanley St., L2 6AL, ✆ 236 4004, Italian rest.
closed Saturday, Sunday and 2 weeks August.   CY **x**

XXX **Oriel,** 16 Water St., L2 8TH, ✆ 236 4664 – 🖃 AE ⓪ VISA   CY **s**
closed Saturday lunch, Sunday and Bank Holidays – **M** a la carte 10.70/26.25 st. ㄅ 3.15.

XXX **Churchill's,** Churchill House, Tithebarn St., L2 2PB, ✆ 227 3877 – 🖃 AE ⓪ VISA   CY **a**
closed Saturday lunch, Sunday and Bank Holidays – **M** a la carte 10.20/14.60 t. ㄅ 2.50.

XX **Jenny's Seafood,** Old Ropery, Fenwick St., L2 7NT, ✆ 236 0332, Seafood – 🖃 AE ⓪
VISA   CZ **e**
closed Saturday lunch, Monday dinner, Sunday and Bank Holidays – **M** a la carte 8.95/13.75 t. ㄅ 2.50.

at Bootle N : 5 m. by A 565 – ✉ ✆ 051 Liverpool :

🏨 **Park,** Park Lane West, L30 3SU, on A 5036 ✆ 525 7555, Telex 629772 – 🛗 📺 ⌷wc ⋔wc
⊛ ㄅ 🅿. 🏧. 🖃 AE ⓪ VISA
M (buffet lunch) a la carte 8.40/11.95 st. ㄅ 3.50 – **60 rm** ⊆ 32.00/40.00 st.

at Waterloo N : 5 ¾ m. by A 565 – ✉ ✆ 051 Liverpool :

🏨 **Royal,** 30 Bath St., L22 5PS, ✆ 928 2332 – 📺 ⌷wc ⋔wc ⊛ 🅿
20 rm.

at Blundellsands N : 6 ½ m. by A 565 – ✉ ✆ 051 Liverpool :

🏨 **Blundellsands,** Serpentine, L23 6TN, ✆ 924 6515 – 🛗 📺 ⌷wc ⊛ 🅿. 🏧. 🖃 AE ⓪
VISA
M 8.50/9.50 st. ㄅ 2.60 – **44 rm** ⊆ 25.00/45.00 st. – SB (weekends only) 55.00 st.

MANCHESTER Greater Manchester 402 403 404 N 23 – pop. 543,650 – ECD : Wednesday
– ✆ 061.

See : Town Hall★ 19C DZ – City Art Gallery★ DZ M – Whitworth Art Gallery★ – Cathedral 15C (chancel★) DZ B – John Ryland's Library (manuscripts★) CZ A.

Envir. : Heaton Hall★ (18C) AC, N : 5 m.

ᚓ Heaton Park, ✆ 773 1085, N : by A 576 – ᚓ Fairfield Golf and Sailing, Booth Rd, Audenshaw, ✆ 370 1641, E : by A 635 – ᚓ Brookdale, Woodhouses ✆ 681 4534, N : 5 m.

✈ ✆ (061) 489 3717 or 489 2404 (British Airways) S : 10 m. by A 5103 and M 56 – **Terminal** : Coach service from Victoria Station.

🛈 Magnum House, Portland St. Piccadilly ✆ 247 3694 and 3712/3 – Town Hall Extension, Lloyd St. ✆ 236 1606/2035 – Manchester International Airport, Concourse and Arrivals Hall ✆ 437 5233.

London 202 – Birmingham 86 – Glasgow 221 – Leeds 43 – Liverpool 35 – ◆Nottingham 72.

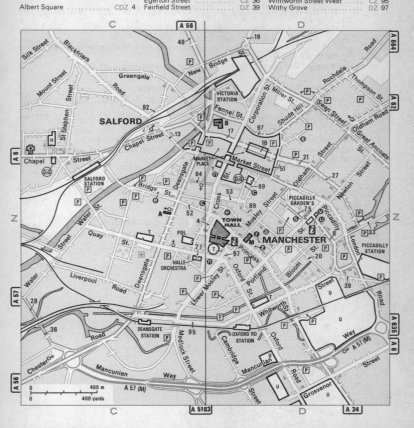

Piccadilly (Embassy), Piccadilly Plaza, M60 1QR, ℰ 236 8414, Telex 668765, ← – 🛗 📺 ☎ Ⓟ. 🅰 🔄 AE ⓪ VISA ❀ DZ **s**
closed 25 to 28 December – **M** a la carte 9.40/14.90 **st.** 🛢 5.05 – ⌕ 5.25 – **250 rm** 49.00/65.00 **st.** – SB (weekends only) 55.00/62.00 **st.**

Midland, Peter St., M60 2DS, ℰ 236 3333, Telex 667797 – 🛗 📺 🅰 🔄 AE ⓪ VISA CDZ **n**
M 17.50 **st.** – ⌕ 5.25 – **296 rm** 28.50/55.00 **st.** – SB (weekends only) 67.50 **st.**

Grand (T.H.F.), Aytoun St., M1 3DR, ℰ 236 9559, Telex 667580 – 🛗 📺 🅰 🔄 AE ⓪ VISA DZ **u**
M (carving rest.) 7.95 **st.** 🛢 2.60 – **146 rm** ⌕ 42.00/50.50 **st.**

Portland Thistle (Thistle), Piccadilly Gdns., M1 6DP, ℰ 228 3400, Telex 669157 – 🛗 📺 ☎ ♿. 🅰 🔄 AE ⓪ VISA ❀ DZ **v**
M 8.50/11.00 🛢 3.45 – ⌕ 5.50 – **221 rm** 45.00/70.00 **t.** – SB (weekends only) 54.00 **st.**

XXX **Terrazza**, 14 Nicholas St., M1 4FE, ℰ 236 4033, Italian rest. – 🔄 AE ⓪ VISA DZ **r**
closed Saturday lunch, Sunday and Bank Holidays – **M** a la carte 10.30/15.30 **t.** 🛢 2.90.

XX **Isola Bella**, 6a Booth St., M2 4AW, ℰ 236 6417, Italian rest. – AE ⓪ VISA DZ **e**
closed Sunday and Bank Holidays – **M** a la carte 9.90/14.40 **st.** 🛢 3.40.

XX **Leen Hong**, 35 George St., ℰ 228 0926, Chinese rest. DZ **z**

XX **Rajdoot,** St. James' House, South King St., M2 6DW, ☏ 834 2176, Indian rest.　　CZ **c**

XX **Gaylord,** Amethyst House, Marriott's Court, Spring Gardens, M2 1EA, ☏ 832 6037, Indian rest. – 🔲 🆎 ⑩ 𝘝𝘐𝘚𝘈　　DZ **c**
M 3.50/10.00 **t.** ⓙ 3.50.

X **Truffles,** 63 Bridge St., M3 6BQ, ☏ 832 9393 – 🔲 🆎 ⑩ 𝘝𝘐𝘚𝘈　　CZ **a**
closed Sunday, Monday, first 2 weeks August and Bank Holidays – **M** a la carte 11.15/14.70 **t.** ⓙ 3.00.

X **Danish Food Centre** (Copenhagen Room), Cross St., M2 7BY, ☏ 832 9924, Smörrebrod – 🔲 🆎 ⑩ 𝘝𝘐𝘚𝘈　　DZ **n**
closed Sunday and Bank Holidays – **M** a la carte 16.00/21.00 **st.**

X **Market,** 30 Edge St., M4 1HN, ☏ 834 3743　　DZ **o**
closed Sunday, Monday, 1 week spring, August and 1 week at Christmas – **M** (dinner only) a la carte 5.00/9.60 **t.** ⓙ 2.75.

X **Yang Sing,** 17 George St., M1 4HE, ☏ 236 2200, Chinese rest. – 🔲 𝘝𝘐𝘚𝘈　　DZ **a**
M a la carte 8.35/11.75 **t.**

　　at Fallowfield S : 3 m. on B 5093 – ✉ ☸ 061 Manchester :

🏨 **Willow Bank,** 340 Wilmslow Rd, M14 6AF, ☏ 224 0461, Telex 668222 – 📺 🛏wc ☎ Ⓟ. 🔲 🆎 ⑩ 𝘝𝘐𝘚𝘈. ⚘
M *(closed lunch Saturday and Sunday)* 3.50/6.00 **st.** ⓙ 3.00 – 🍽 3.75 – **123 rm** 26.00/32.00 **st.** – SB (weekends only) 39.50/51.50 **st.**

　　at Northenden S : 6 ½ m. by A 5103 and M 56 – ✉ ☸ 061 Manchester :

🏨 **Post House** (T.H.F.), Palatine Rd, M22 4FH, ☏ 998 7090, Telex 669248 – 📳 📺 🛏wc ☎ ⅄ Ⓟ. 🏛 🔲 🆎 ⑩ 𝘝𝘐𝘚𝘈
M *(closed Sunday dinner)* 6.95/8.95 **st.** ⓙ 2.60 – 🍽 5.00 – **201 rm** 39.50/46.50 **st.**

　　at Manchester Airport S : 9 m. by A 5103 and M 56 – ✉ ☸ 061 Manchester :

🏩 **Excelsior** (T.H.F.), Ringway Rd, Wythenshawe, M22 5NS, ☏ 437 5811, Telex 668721, ☐ heated – 📳 📺 ☎ ⅄ Ⓟ. 🏛 🔲 🆎 ⑩ 𝘝𝘐𝘚𝘈
M 6.25/8.25 **st.** ⓙ 2.85 – 🍽 5.50 – **304 rm** 46.50/54.00 **st.**

　　at Heald Green S : 10 m. by A 5103 and M 56 – ✉ ☸ 061 Manchester :

XX **La Bonne Auberge,** 224 Finney Lane, SK8 3QA, ☏ 437 5701, French rest. – Ⓟ. 🔲 🆎 ⑩
closed Monday dinner, Sunday and Bank Holidays – **M** a la carte 10.60/13.40 **t.**

MANUFACTURE FRANÇAISE DES PNEUMATIQUES MICHELIN
Société en commandite par actions au capital de 700 000 000 de francs
Place des Carmes-Déchaux - 63 Clermont-Ferrand (France)
R.C.S. Clermont-Fd B 855 200 507

ⓒ **Michelin et Cie, Propriétaires-Éditeurs 1985**
Dépôt légal 4-85 - ISBN 2 06 007 055 - 4

Printed in France 3-85-47
Photocomposition : S.C.I.A. La Chapelle d'Armentières - Impression : Kapp et Lahure n° 4137

AUSTRIA

Salzburg	Salzburg Festival (Festspiele)	30 March to 7 April 27 July to 25 August

BENELUX

Amsterdam	Holland Festival	June
Bruges	Ascension Day Procession	Ascension
Brussels	Guild Procession (Oumegang)	first Thursday of July

FRANCE

Paris	Paris Fair	27 April to 8 May
Cannes	International Film Festival	May
Lyons	Lyons Fair	15 to 24 March 86
Marseilles	Marseilles Fair	20 to 30 Sept

GERMANY

Berlin	Berlin Fair (Grüne Woche)	24 Jan to 2 February 86
Frankfurt	International Fair	23 to 27 February 24 to 28 August
	International Motor Show (IAA)	12 to 22 Sept
	Frankfurt Book Fair	9 to 14 October
Hanover	Hanover Fair	17 to 24 April
Munich	Beer Festival (Oktoberfest)	21 Sept to 6 Oct

IRELAND

Dublin	Dublin Horse Show	6 to 10 August

ITALY

Milan	Milan Fair	14 to 23 April
Palermo	Mediterranean Fair	25 May to 9 June
Turin	Automotor	15 to 19 May

NORWAY

Oslo	NOR-SHIPPING 85	6 to 10 May
	NOR-COM 85	11 to 15 June

PORTUGAL

Lisbon	International Fair	8 to 12 May

SPAIN

Barcelona	International Fair	1 to 9 June
Valencia	International Fair	4 to 12 May

SWEDEN

Stockholm	International Fashion Fair	7 to 10 Sept
	International Computer and Business Efficiency Fair	26 Sept to 2 Oct
	International Technical Fair	17 to 23 October

SWITZERLAND

Geneva	Motor Show	March 86

UNITED KINGDOM

London	London International Boat Show	2 to 12 January 86
	Motor Fair	17 to 27 October
Edinburgh	Arts Festival	11 to 31 August
Leeds	Harrogate International Toy Fair	11 to 16 Jan 86

France
Benelux
Deutschland
España   Portugal
Great Britain and Ireland
Italia